The
Cultural Revolution
in China

Contributors

Richard Baum
William F. Dorrill
Melvin Gurtov
Harry Harding, Jr.
Thomas W. Robinson

The
Cultural Revolution
in China

Edited by Thomas W. Robinson

1971

BERKELEY
LOS ANGELES
LONDON

UNIVERSITY OF CALIFORNIA PRESS

University of California Press
Berkeley and Los Angeles, California

University of California Press, Ltd.
London, England

ISBN: 0-520-01811-7

Library of Congress Catalog Card Number: 77-129609
Printed in the United States of America

Contents

Preface

Shortly after the Red Guard phase of the Great Proletarian Cultural Revolution began in the late summer of 1966, members and consultants of the Social Science Department of The Rand Corporation undertook to make their contribution to understanding those unusual events in China. Of the Rand works studying this era of Chinese Communist history, five are included in this book.*

The subjects chosen for publication in the present volume by no means form a unified whole, although for the most part they concern those Cultural Revolution events thought likely to affect mainland China's relations with the outside world. There is, however, a chronological progression in the presentation that lends coherence to the book. Thus, for instance, William Dorrill's study traces the background to the events of 1966 and beyond, Thomas Robinson's work takes up the story where Dorrill leaves off and brings it down to the latter half of 1967, and Richard Baum relates events in the agricultural sphere to the central politics of the Cul-

---

* Other Rand works on the Cultural Revolution include the following. Harry Harding, Jr.: "Modernization and Mao: The Logic of the Cultural Revolution and the 1970s," P-4442, August 1970. Thomas W. Robinson: "The Sino-Soviet Border Dispute: Background, Development and the March 1969 Clashes," RM-6171-PR, August 1970; "Chou En-lai: A Statement of his Political Style—With Comparisons with Mao Tse-tung and Lin Piao," P-4474, October 1970; "Lin Piao, 1907–1949," R-526-PR, November 1970; and "Lin Piao, 1950–1970," [forthcoming 1971]. Melvin Gurtov, *Southeast Asia Tomorrow: Problems and Prospects for U.S. Policy*, Baltimore, 1970; "The Style of Politics and Foreign Policy in Communist China," in Joseph M. Kitagawa, ed., *Understanding Modern China*, Chicago, 1969; and "The Purge of Lo Jui-ch'ing: The Politics of Chinese Strategic Planning" (with Harry Harding, Jr.), R-548-PR, December 1970.

tural Revolution through 1968. Moreover, the remaining two studies can be regarded as complementing in detail some of the generalities advanced by the other three authors. Harry Harding's discourse on ideology, for instance, analyzes some of the points raised by Dorrill, while Melvin Gurtov's inquiry into the turmoil in the Foreign Ministry spells out some of the matters raised in outline by Robinson.

All of these studies, however, were worked out by the authors independently and, while they did attempt to take advantage of the data, analysis, and conclusions presented by their colleagues, no attempt was made, either in their writings or in the preparation of this book, to reconcile differences of opinion. Thus, the reader will find a series of works each of which can be considered on its own merits but which, taken together, will lead hopefully to an enhanced understanding of the Cultural Revolution period of Chinese Communist history.

Two omissions should be noted. First, none of the components of this book analyze events beyond early 1968; most of the authors' attention is devoted, in fact, to the events of the years 1966 and 1967. Thus, chronologically, about half of the Cultural Revolution is not covered, if one considers its effective termination to be the Ninth Congress of the Chinese Communist Party in April 1969. No justification can be given for this, aside from the proclivities and schedules of the authors, and that the events of 1968 and 1969 were largely the playing out of conflicts and developments which had their origins in the previous two years. Study of the former period thus is prerequisite to understanding the latter.

The second omissions is perhaps more serious. There is no study in this volume directly concerned with the role of the People's Liberation Army in the Cultural Revolution. Yet the Army was a prime actor in this period, its present head is Mao's chosen successor, and it is the chief beneficiary of the social and political changes wrought by Mao and his followers. A number of studies of the military component in the Cultural Revolution are underway, however, and perhaps they can comprise part of a successor volume to the present book.

It will be some time before the data on Chinese Communist history since 1949 presented by the Cultural Revolution is sorted out and integrated sufficiently with what is already known to produce a definitive work on recent Chinese political history. Similarly, much preliminary work will have to be done before the Cultural Revolution itself can be correctly perceived. One way to such knowledge lies through a series of well-chosen case studies of particular events and developments critical to an understanding of the larger whole. The authors hope their work will be comprehended in this light, as well as be evaluated for their contribution to the particular subjects dealt with below.*

* Note should be made of the date of completion of the various manuscripts. Dorrill: August 1968; Harding: September 1969; Robinson: July 1969; Gurtov: March 1969; Baum: February 1970.

Acknowledgments

The authors wish to register a debt of gratitude to their colleagues and to the following individuals who assisted in one way or another in preparing and improving the manuscripts for this book: Christine D'Arc, Anna Sun Ford, Alexander George, John Hogan, Alice Hsieh, Donald Klein, Nathan Leites, John Lewis, Michael Oksenberg, Betsy Schmidt, John Service, William Stewart, Raymond Tang, Alan Whiting, and K. C. Yeh.

Additionally, acknowledgment is made of the sponsorship of the United States Air Force which, under its Project Rand contract, made possible the writing of the chapters below. Finally, production of this book would have been impossible without the encouragement and cooperation of many individuals and offices at The Rand Corporation.

Contributors

THOMAS W. ROBINSON is a staff member of the Social Science Department, The Rand Corporation, specializing in Chinese and Soviet domestic politics and foreign policy. His Ph.D. dissertation, "Hans J. Morgenthau's Theory of International Relations," was recently accepted at Columbia University. He has written several Rand monographs, including "The Sino-Soviet Border Conflicts," and "Lin Piao," and has published articles and reviews in *International Studies Quarterly, The Annals,* the *Journal of Asian Studies, The China Quarterly, The American Political Science Review, Asian Survey, Slavic Review* and *Studies in Soviet Thought.* He has taught political science, international relations, and Soviet and Chinese government at Dartmouth College, Columbia University, the University of California, Los Angeles, and the University of Southern California.

RICHARD BAUM is currently Assistant Professor of Political Science, U.C.L.A. He received his Ph.D. from Berkeley this year. He is the author of "Red and Expert: The Politico-Ideological Foundations of China's Great Leap Forward," *Asian Survey,* September 1964; "Ideology Redivivus," *Problems of Communism,* May–June 1967; "Apples, Oranges, and the Comparative Study of Poiltical Parties," *The Western Political Quarterly,* March 1967; "Liu Shao-ch'i and the Cadre Question," *Asian Survey,* April 1968 (co-author, Frederick C. Teiwes); *Ssu-Ch'ing: The Socialist Education Movement of 1962–1966* (Berkeley: Center for Chinese Studies, 1968) (co-author, Frederick C. Teiwes); *Bibliographic Guide to Kwangtung Communes, 1959–1967* (Hong Kong: Union Research Institute, 1968); "China: Year of the Mangoes," *Asian Survey,* January 1969; and

"Revolution and Reaction in the Chinese Countryside: The Socialist Education Movement in Cultural Revolutionary Perspective," *The China Quarterly*, April–June 1969.

WILLIAM F. DORRILL is presently Associate Professor of Political Science at the University of Pittsburgh, Director of the University Center for International Studies, and Chairman of the Asian Studies Program. His previous positions include Project Chairman for China Studies at the Research Analysis Corporation, staff member of the Social Science Department at The Rand Corporation, and a foreign affairs analyst for the United States government. His Ph.D. dissertation at Harvard University dealt with the history of the Kiangsi period of the Chinese Communist movement.

MELVIN GURTOV is a staff member of the Social Science Department, The Rand Corporation, specializing in the politics and foreign policies of China and Southeast Asia. He recently published *Southeast Asia Tomorrow: Problems and Prospects for U.S. Policy of United States Policy in Southeast Asia* (Baltimore, 1970) and previously published *The First Vietnam Crisis: Chinese Communist Strategy and United States Involvement, 1953–1954* (New York, 1967). In addition, he has written several Rand monographs on Asian affairs and contributed articles to such journals as *The China Quarterly, Asian Survey,* and *Current History*. Finally, he is contributing author of three books: *The Communist Revolution in Asia,* edited by R. A. Scalapino (Englewood Cliffs, N.J., 1969); *Understanding Modern China,* edited by J. Kitagawa (Chicago, 1969); and *Vietnam and American Foreign Policy,* edited by J. Boettiger (Boston, 1968). He recently obtained his Ph.D. degree in Political Science at U.C.L.A.

HARRY HARDING, JR., is Instructor of Political Science at Swarthmore College and a Consultant to The Rand Corporation. His Ph.D. dissertation, in progress at Stanford University, deals with the policymaking process in Communist China.

1

Introduction

THOMAS W. ROBINSON

The Great Proletarian Cultural Revolution in China is by general consent one of the most important events in the twentieth-century history of that country, rivaling the fall of the Ch'ing Dynasty in 1911 and the Communist conquest of 1945–1949. Not only were many of the principles by which the Communist Party of China had ruled the Mainland since 1949 thrown over—from above by Mao Tse-tung and his ruling group and from below by the Red Guards and similar mass organizations—but what began as a cultural and then a political purge of a few leaders just below the top quickly and surprisingly broadened into a mass movement having many of the aspects of revolution. At one point, the very fabric of the country and the future of Maoist rule was in doubt. Moreover, the Cultural Revolution has profound ideological implications: here was a relatively successful Communist state and Party systematically destroying most of its ruling element and preventing, through manipulations of the politico-cultural superstructure, what Mao feared would become irreversible, deleterious changes in the economic base. Hence, both Lenin and Marx were stood on their heads. Finally, the influence of the Cultural Revolution was felt in other countries, directly as China's foreign policy became dependent upon the twists and turns of the domestic conflict and indirectly as groups of young people, perceiving superficial parallels between the situation in China and that in their own countries, sought to carry out their own cultural revolutions.

For scholars and analysts, the Cultural Revolution provides a unique opportunity to examine the innards of China's political process, as well as the role of such factors as personality, family, and bureaucracy, and such institutions as the Party, the military, the student organizations, and the government ministries. Although it is difficult to draw firm and lasting conclusions about a society in such a high degree of flux, the unprecedented range and type of information imparted by Cultural Revolutionary sources—especially Red Guard posters and newspapers—provide a rare glimpse not possible before and one which will probably not be equalled for some time. Of equal importance is that many of the internal workings of Chinese institutions, as well as information on decisions and rivalries as far back as the beginnings of the Communist movement in China, are discernible with a new clarity. This will surely force the rewriting of much of Chinese Communist history as well as give insight into the possible future roles of individual actors. Thus, it is clear that the information provided in Cultural Revolution documents will require the study of mainland China, and our attitudes toward it, to undergo a significant reorientation.

Years will probably pass, however, before a definitive history of the Cultural Revolution can be written. Before that, the data must be organized and bits of the puzzle fitted into place little by little. In the interim, however, it is possible to write a number of detailed case studies on central aspects of the period, taking advantage in particular of the rich documentation provided by the Red Guards. If subjects are carefully chosen and properly interrelated, such studies can provide critical building blocks for constructing a definitive analysis. The present volume seeks to contribute to that task. An equally important goal is to enable the reader to trace the history of the Cultural Revolution from its origins at least down to the point where its direction seems clearly evident. Thus, one contribution, William F. Dorrill's, analyzes the background and early development of the Cultural Revolution; another, Harry Harding, Jr.'s, considers some of the major points of ideological disagreement; two others, Richard Baum's and Thomas W. Robinson's, trace the political history of the era; while Melvin Gurtov's and Robinson's subject the foreign policy sphere to analysis. Thus, while making no claims to completeness, the studies included below are representative of problems and developments of the period as a whole.

Much of what happened during the course of the Cultural Revolution after the Eleventh Plenum of the Party's Eighth Central Committee in August 1966 depended greatly on events which occurred as much as a decade earlier. William F. Dorrill's study attempts to organize and analyze the background of the Cultural Revolution, both chronologically and conceptually, and sets the stage for work on the Cultural Revolution period itself. His work is a detailed survey of domestic political events in China from the failure of the Great Leap Forward in 1959 to the onset of the active phase of the Cultural Revolution in 1966.

Various theories have been advanced to explain the Cultural Revolution. Some Western critics have seen it as essentially a power struggle for the succession to Mao, some as a clash over domestic and foreign policy, still others as mainly an ideological dispute. Professor Dorrill sees it not as a master plan of Mao's but as a logical series of spontaneous eruptions. Although he is aware that the various interpretations are not mutually exclusive—that indeed there is likely to be a close interaction of power struggle, policy debate, and ideological conflict—he tries to clarify their separate roles, their sequential and causal relationships, and their relative importance.

As early as 1956, there were signs of strain and frustration within the Peking leadership arising from an apparent division over methods of speeding up the pace of industrialization and modernization and increasing agricultural production, and from a growing disenchantment with the Soviet model. The leadership seemed to have weathered these early disagreements; although in March 1957 Mao called for a protracted struggle to defeat erroneous ideas and "revisionism," there is no proof that a serious rift then existed between Mao and some of his lieutenants (especially Liu Shao-ch'i and Teng Hsiao-p'ing), as recently alleged in the Red Guard press. While the momentous program of the Great Leap Forward and the communes, launched in 1958, suggested a general shift leftward, it also implied a consensus of the leadership, and was enthusiastically endorsed by Liu, Teng, and Minister of Defense P'eng Teh-huai. Later in 1958, as the Great Leap Forward took an economically disastrous turn and the Sino-Soviet rift grew, Mao gave up (voluntarily, Professor Dorrill believes) his control over the daily affairs of state, without, however, relinquishing supreme authority.

Not until August 1959, when the Eighth Plenum of the Grand Committee met at Lushan and initiated an official retreat from the economic program of 1958, did a major leadership crisis become apparent. Many of the charges subsequently raised by the Red Guards have turned on an alleged "rightist" anti-Mao conspiracy antedating the Lushan meeting and said to explain the criticism there, expressed particularly by P'eng Teh-huai. The few available records, including P'eng's "Letter of Opinion," suggest that P'eng may well have been openly outspoken in his attack on economic and commercial policies, but that his criticism was compatible with the shift in policy decided upon at Lushan. Moreover, charges of an earlier conspiracy with Khrushchev for the overthrow of Mao are almost certainly unfounded.

In the aftermath of the Lushan debate, P'eng was censured and removed from office, Party dominance was reaffirmed, and the remaining leaders closed ranks and proceeded to mitigate the rigid and unworkable features of the economic system. This relaxation was accompanied by greater intellectual tolerance, which in the early 1960s resulted in a markedly freer expression of ideas in literature and the press.

The Tenth Plenum, in September 1962, marked the end of that liberal period. Mao resumed his active leadership role, condemned "bourgeois" trends in art, literature, and the economy, and called for a nationwide campaign of "socialist education" and "class struggle" to maintain the purity of the Revolution. Though it brought about no radical shift in policy, the Tenth Plenum ushered in a period of renewed emphasis on ideology and on the thought and personality of Mao. Lin Piao as the new Minister of Defense plunged into highly successful efforts to strengthen political and ideological work in the People's Liberation Army (PLA), setting a trend away from military professionalism. But the Party and government were less than enthusiastically responsive, and this may have suggested to Mao and his coterie the danger of another secular trend. That response may thus have caused them to launch, in 1963-1964, a further ideological purification campaign, which brought tightened intellectual and cultural controls and denunciations of prominent philosophers, writers, and artists. Disappointed by the lack of fervor that the campaign was able to arouse and by China's inability to regain the momentum of the 1950s, the Maoist leadership shifted still further leftward in mid-1964, with a violent attack on those with allegedly "capitalist" and "revisionist" leanings. The tones of this attack clearly anticipated the Cultural Revolution. "Work teams" were dispatched from the center to "clean up" deficiencies in the rural situation, to indoctrinate local people, and to institute reforms. In the economic agencies, a network of political departments modeled on the PLA supplemented the propaganda apparatus.

But in 1965, as external and internal problems mounted, there was a perceptible decline in ideological pressures. This new orientation possibly reflected a prudent disposition in some quarters to meet the country's need for greater productivity and, in view of the threatening involvement in Vietnam, national unity. Nothing in the measures taken by exponents of this conciliatory, pragmatic approach, however, suggested the "bourgeois reactionary," counterrevolutionary, "Soviet revisionist" tendencies of which Liu, Teng, and others have since been accused.

Toward the end of 1965, Mao appealed for renewal of the ideological struggle (his reaction, perhaps, to an internal debate and criticism of his person or leadership), and singled out for public pillory a famous playwright. With this, the relative power of top leaders seemed to shift, and Lin Piao emerged more and more as a major theoretician and Liu Shao-ch'i lost ground. But the differences in the fall and winter of 1965–1966 over aspects of economic and military policy apparently did not result in simple alignments of opposing opinions and personalities, and division occurred within, rather than between, the various institutions. As time went on, however, dissension came to revolve less around such substantive issues than around the person and thought of Mao. In 1967, revolutionary wallposters were to make the sensational charge that several of the top leaders had planned a military coup for February 1966 to oust Mao. While apparently some behind-the-scenes efforts took place in early 1966 to keep the growing campaign of socialist education within the limits of academic discussion, there is no indication that those who feared the excesses of Maoist purification were aiming for more than protection of the status quo. Yet the growing factional antagonisms were to erupt into open conflict that spring, when the Party, in a Central Committee circular of May 16, endorsed Mao's attack on P'eng Chen, the Mayor of Peking, and other "counterrevolutionaries," dissolved and replaced the group theretofore in charge of the Cultural Revolution, and threatened to remove or transfer all disloyal "bourgeois" elements in Party, government, army, and cultural life. With this, the Cultural Revolution began in earnest.

Changes in the Party's leadership and a purge of its central propaganda apparatus reflected the new Maoist militancy, as did the tone of the Party organ *Jen-min Jih-pao*. In May, June, and July of 1966, the Cultural Revolution spread from Peking to the provinces, directed against educators, writers, and artists as well as their supervisors in the propaganda organs. Initially, the Party's main instruments of enforcement at the local level were the "work teams"; though violence and terror were used, they apparently were applied selectively, as the Party sought to maintain some order and discipline. Ultimately, however, Party authority clashed with the impatient revolutionary left over the unauthorized publication of a wallposter by a Peking University instructor: Mao himself ordered it distributed throughout China, a portent of the future direction of the Cultural Revolution and testimony to Mao's power and his determination to go "to the masses."

In July 1966 Mao returned to active leadership, the Party recalled the controversial work teams, and it convened a Central Work Conference. In August, under Mao's personal direction, the Eleventh Plenum of the Central Committee adopted a program of historic importance, and in the most far-reaching reorganization since 1949, it changed the order of the top leadership, putting Lin in second and Chou En-lai in third place after Mao. The Plenum's final communiqué (August 12, 1966) dealt with the whole range of China's foreign and domestic problems and stressed the central place of Mao's thought in the development of Marxism-Leninism.

Mao's increasingly utopian aspirations and fundamentalist concepts of the revolutionary mission were further spelled out as the new leadership was chosen. In the months following, however, these leaders and groups of the Cultural Revolution—backed, somewhat uncertainly, by the PLA and served by the destructive Red Guards—were to prove as unsuccessful as their predecessors in resolving political crises and effecting the ideological transformation so insistently and unrealistically demanded by Mao.

Professor Dorrill thus looks to the details of the political history of China from 1959 to 1965 to explain the outbreak of the Cultural Revolution. Professor Harding, on the other hand, takes the analysis of ideological ideas as his approach, by examining the Cultural Revolution as a struggle between two different conceptions of policy-making procedure, organization behavior, and Party structure. Such an approach also helps revise earlier Western analyses of Chinese Communist policy-making and organization, most of which have now been outdated by the innovations and modifications imposed by Mao Tse-tung and his followers.

Professor Harding's purpose is twofold. First, he attempts to explain the differences between the "Maoist" and the "Liuist" conceptions of policy-making and organization, thereby indicating important elements in the ideological and political struggle between Mao and his opponents. He then describes the changes in Chinese Communist theories of policy-making and organization produced by the Cultural Revolution, and assesses their probable effects on the Chinese political system.

Taking as one dimension of policy-making the relative use of dogmatic and pragmatic criteria in decision-making and, as the other, the degree of institutionalized, direct mass participation in the policy-making process, he identifies four modes of policy-making: dogmatic mass-line, pragmatic mass-line, dogmatic elitist, and pragmatic elitist. The Cultural Revolution was informed by the disagreement between Maoists and Liuists over the applicability of these policy-making modes to different issues, which may be summarized as follows:

Issue-Area	Maoist Position	Liuist Position
Ideological and doctrinal questions	Dogmatic mass-line	Dogmatic mass-line
Political, social, and macro-economic questions	Dogmatic mass-line	Dogmatic mass-line
Technical and managerial (micro-economic) questions	Pragmatic mass-line	Pragmatic elitist

Several important points emerge from this breakdown. First, policy-making under the mass-line can be either pragmatic or dogmatic. The dogmatic mass-line, advocated by the Maoists for political, social, and macro-economic questions, is based on the assumption that every problem has a single correct solution and that the solution is contained exclusively in the thought of Mao Tse-tung. Because decision-making is thus a process of identifying the option that most closely corresponds to dogma, correctness is more important than consensus in the formulation of policy. To the same questions, the Liuists apply the pragmatic mass-line, which is essentially a minimax mode of analysis. If disagreements arise, the Liuists, unlike the Maoists, emphasize compromise as a tactic for creating consensus.

Second, the disagreement between the Maoists and the Liuists is not total, but depends upon the issue. To resolve ideological questions, for example, both factions advocate the dogmatic mass-line. On technical questions, both recognize the need for pragmatic criteria, while disagreeing on the desirability of mass participation. And on political issues, both seek mass participation in policy-making but differ over the suitability of dogmatic decision criteria.

Third, the Cultural Revolution is not a clear-cut struggle between pragmatism and dogmatism. The Liuists accept the need for dogmatic decision criteria on some issues, and the Maoists admit the necessity for pragmatism on others. Still, the Maoists advocate the use of dogmatic criteria for more issues than do the Liuists. Fourth, the Cultural Revolution can be interpreted as a debate over the question of elitism. Unlike the Liuists, the Maoists do not accept any form of elitism for any domestic questions.

Policy-making in China will, in Harding's view, be carried on by a Communist Party largely restructured during the past few years. On the eve of the Cultural Revolution, he argues in congruence with Dorrill, Mao Tse-tung had serious reservations about the way in which the Party was performing each of its four major activities. First of all, Mao felt that the Party's *definition of purpose* had become perverted: the Party was concerned more with its own self-preservation and its members' social status and political power than with carrying on the revolution in China. It had, in short, become institutionalized. As to *task performance,* Mao saw that the Party had become bogged down in bureaucratic procedures, had been fractured into policy factions and personal cliques, and was formulating incorrect, revisionist policies—all largely because elitism had gradually replaced the mass-line. These errors had persisted, Mao believed, because the Party's *control mechanisms* were ineffective. Party leaders who identified deeply with the Party machine— men such as Teng Hsiao-p'ing and Liu Shao-ch'i—relied too strongly on internal disciplinary procedures such as self-criticism and mild rectification campaigns. They were not willing, as Mao came to feel was necessary, to employ mass criticism and severe struggle to eradicate the "revisionist" and "bourgeois" tendencies in the Party. Finally, prevailing Party *recruitment policies* favored technical and managerial skills and slighted ideological qualifications. This led Mao to fear that Chinese society would be irreparably damaged by bureaucratism and revisionism unless the Party underwent drastic change, "cleansed the class ranks," and took in "fresh blood."

Mao attempted to remedy these problems by two major reforms: he promulgated a new Party constitution and he created revolutionary committees. Professor Harding's analysis leads to the conclusion that Maoist normative organizational theory minimizes formal and specialized bureaucratic structure, combines Party and state functions into one organization, recruits along social class lines, uses the "masses" to supervise and discipline Party members, and decentralizes administrative power. The Party leader remains above Party discipline so that he can set goals, define dogma, and check tendencies toward decay, ossification, and revisionism.

Implementation of these organizational revisions will, Harding believes, probably produce stress in the Chinese political system. While the mass-line can be an effective mode of both decision-making and social integration, its dogmatic variant may lead not only to impractical decisions but also to factionalism and fragmentation. In a purely Maoist society, the only permissible form of conflict resolution is compliance with dogma. Compromise, logical analysis, and even submission to authority are all illegitimate. In the prevailing politicized atmosphere in China, this can only have one of the following effects: first, compliance will become a matter of covert negotiation between superiors and subordinates, with subordinates refusing (supposedly on ideological grounds) to obey unpopular directives until modifications or side-payments are made; or second, refusing to compromise, the two sides will resort to force, each attempting to impose its will on the other and each justifying its actions in the name of class struggle; or third, the two sides will appeal to high authority (ultimately to Mao, Lin, and the Politburo) for arbitration of their dispute, a right guaranteed in the new Party constitution. Demands for intervention and appeals for arbitration will flood the Party Center, contributing to "input overload" there. The disputants may resist even the Center's resolution of the disagreement, compelling the Center either to compromise or to employ force itself.

Both direct mass representation on the revolutionary committees and decentralization of administrative power promise to increase the responsiveness of policy-making bodies to local demands and conditions. But the institutionalization of the revolutionary committee system may produce five parallel and competing bureaucracies: the mass organizations, the Party, the army, the revolutionary committee, and the remnants of the state ministries. Such administrative decentralization—designed to prevent a new bureaucratization of Chinese society—is likely to lead to fragmentation and stagnation unless the Center can effectively veto unacceptable local decisions and unless the Center's ideological guidelines are generally compatible with the interests of China's localities and the desires of China's people.

Many of the political problems of organization and bureaucracy alluded to in Professor Harding's work are described and analyzed by Thomas Robinson's study of Chou En-lai's behavior during the Cultural Revolution. His study attempts to integrate the political history of the important first year of the Cultural Revolution with an analysis of the "political style" of Chou En-lai, the Premier of the State Council in Communist

China and possible successor to Mao Tse-tung. Chou has long been regarded as one of modern China's outstanding politicians and statesmen
and as a fascinating political figure in his own right, a man whose remarkable talent for political survival during four stormy decades of Chinese Communist Party history has long been noted.

Before the Eleventh Plenum, in 1966, Chou appears to have voted with
the winning side in every Cultural Revolution debate, regardless of the
probable policy consequences of the issue under discussion. Thus his
reputed "pragmatism" seemed to have surfaced first in the *political* dimension, and it was only after his political position was secured that he
allowed himself to appraise an issue on its merits. At the outset of the
Eleventh Plenum, however, it was by no means clear that the Mao-Lin
faction would emerge the winner; this put Chou in a quandary. Circumstantial evidence suggests that Chou may have solved the problem by
bartering his vote to the Mao-Lin group in exchange for their pledge to
protect the governmental apparatus—Chou's own sphere—from Cultural
Revolution attack.

These promises were broken one by one during the succeeding months,
and the success of Chou's political activity came more and more to depend on his personal rather than his institutional power base. Beginning
with the January Revolution, however, his involvement in domestic politics sharply increased, reaching a peak in May and June of 1967. Correspondingly, Chou's foreign policy activities declined as he sought to
advance and defend his private goals (maintenance of personal power
and preservation of China's industrial and managerial capital) as well
as to carry out the tasks assigned him by Mao (trouble-shooting, directing
Red Guard activities, negotiating agreements between revolutionary
groups).

The vital first year of the Cultural Revolution may be divided into
four successive periods, and Chou's role in each phase may be taken both
as an indicator of the intensity and direction of Cultural Revolutionary
activities and as the framework for understanding Chou's own style.

During the Red Guard heyday in August and December of 1966, Chou
attempted to control and discipline the young revolutionaries while at
the same time encouraging them to fulfill Peking's directives. This contradictory goal required a dual tactic: Chou first spoke a strong revolutionary line, then suggested practical policies which would, if effected,
restrain the violent excesses and factionalism of the Red Guards. While

his basic and unwavering proposition was that revolution must not be allowed to endanger production, Chou's dilatory tactics succeeded only so long as he dealt personally with relatively small groups. Ultimately, the massive size and momentum of the Red Guard movement over-whelmed his persuasive abilities. Thus, when personal attacks on his policies and "unhealthy" class background were made, Chou felt the necessity to shift to the left. It was this flexibility, in addition to the en-hanced value of Chou's administrative talent in a chaotic China, which helped to preserve his number three position in the Party hierarchy. It appears, in fact, that his influence over the Red Guards actually increased during December and early January. In a few cases, his forsenic style alone prevented certain acts of violence threatened by the young fanatics.

Chou's political difficulties by no means ended with this triumph over the Red Guard extremists, for the January Revolution period expanded the range of Cultural Revolution targets. New "Revolutionary Rebels" appeared first in Shanghai and attempted to "seize power" from estab-lished Party, government, and industrial leaders. This Maoist policy backfired when the local leadership resisted the takeovers and the rebel groups themselves split. The resultant violence could only be halted by the reluctant intervention of the People's Liberation Army, beginning in early February.

Once again Chou urged the rebels to "carry out revolution *and* pro-mote production," but as before, he realized that the second half of this, his favorite slogan, would have to suffer. To maintain his influence, Chou established his revolutionary credentials through speeches and directives favoring the rebels. Next, he took cautious steps toward resolving real grievances(for example, wage policies, the apprentice system, and infla-tion) which had contributed to the economic dislocations in Shanghai and elsewhere. This pattern of activity in fact characterized Chou's be-havior throughout the Cultural Revolution period; first, he enhanced his personal authority through speeches, meetings, and references to Mao; then he drew on the store of influence thus created to limit the damage by the revolutionaries. In many cases, he redefined policies while "clari-fying" them, or coined interpretive formulas that would, in effect, curb the disruptions.

In order to protect his closest associates on the State Council, Chou supplied token victims from the lower echelons of the central state appa-ratus. This trick appeased the Red Guards and revolutionary rebels, at

least temporarily, for none of the six state offices (the most important
bureaus in the State Council) experienced Red Guard power seizures.
Chou further attempted to immunize the State Council (and hence his
own position) by stressing its and his own close association with the
Military Affairs Committee (Lin Piao, Mao's chosen successor) and the
Cultural Revolution Small Group (Chiang Ch'ing, Mao's wife).

Beginning with the "February adverse current," Chou faced a new
series of challenges. First, he failed in his attempt to "revive the reputation" of an important lieutenant, T'an Ch'en-lin. Thereafter, Red Guard
wall posters seriously attacked Chou's position, until Chiang Ch'ing had
to remind the rebels of Chou's proximity to Mao. The episode served to
underline the decline in his political standing; it also emphasized, however, that in the end it was Mao himself who stood behind Chou. At the
same time, in May of 1967, certain post hoc evidence suggests that Chou
may have encountered high-level opposition from some members of the
Small Group. With Mao's support, however, he had no trouble in overcoming this challenge.

Not surprisingly, Chou established a harmonious working relationship
with the army leadership during this period of military ascendancy. With
Mao's blessing, and possibly at his instigation, Chou took the initiative in
defending the new "leading role" of the People's Liberation Army. As
always, he refined and redefined central policy directives for his rebel
audiences with the hope of redirecting and dampening their subsequent
behavior. Unfortunately, his detailed advice on the methods for correct
power seizures was often ignored, with the deleterious effects on production that he had predicted. On the other hand, Chou was able to prevent
the formation of dysfunctional "revolutionary committees" inside State
Council organs, a significant victory which measurably aided in preserving his political status.

The Wuhan Incident of late July 1967 capped a series of violent clashes
in Hupeh Province and symbolized the seriousness of the disorder which
the Cultural Revolution had forced upon China. The Wuhan Incident
had to be dealt with frontally because it was a case of actual military
insubordination of province against center. Chou's role again demonstrated his value to Mao, as he dramatically negotiated the release of two
kidnapped Central Committee members (narrowly escaping capture himself), and directed the mass Peking celebrations welcoming home the
freed officials. He presided over the trial of the commander of the Wuhan

Military District (who was castigated and dismissed, along with other top local leaders). Loyalist troops, apparently under Lin Piao's personal direction, entered Wuhan to quell the strife, and by the end of the month a negotiated settlement appealed to both sides.

For personal, political, and practical reasons, Chou En-lai's foreign policy duties declined sharply during this first frantic year of the Cultural Revolution. Just when he was totally preoccupied with the Wuhan Incident and other domestic crises, the Red Guards attacked Foreign Minister Ch'en Yi and even seized power in the Ministry itself. Once again, Chou failed to "revive the reputation" of this close colleague, although by extending his personal influence to the limit he did succeed in rescuing Ch'en from outright dismissal and purge. In late August 1967, Chou took the offensive, put on his own "seize power" movement, and successfully freed the Foreign Ministry from Red Guard control. From this point forward, he was able to devote more attention to foreign affairs without fear of Red Guard attack.

Chou had little opportunity to participate in the new phase of deteriorating Sino-Soviet relations which began with the Cultural Revolution. However, an analysis of his speeches on this subject leads to the conclusion that, while still anti-Soviet, he was less rabid than the official policy line. This was matched by similar moderation in Soviet references to Chou, suggesting that he tried, successfully, to prevent a formal diplomatic break between the two Communist giants.

The period from August 1967 to the end of the Cultural Revolution, in April 1969, serves as a means of determining whether the political style Chou exhibited before then was in fact representative. A survey of the nature and direction of Chou's involvement in domestic politics and foreign policy formulation reveals that there was no essential difference in the manner in which he carried out his duties, in the way in which he played the political game in China, in his institutional and personal relationships, and in the structure of his personal or public goals. One major change did occur, however: Chou more and more shifted the intensity of his involvement from domestic matters to foreign policy concern. The probable reason was Mao's desire to use Chou in the most efficient manner. After August 1967 most domestic problems were under control, and foreign affairs, which had been relatively neglected, demanded an ever-increasing share of Peking's attention. By the end of 1968, therefore, Chou was devoting almost all of his time to the foreign sphere. Once again, a shift in the mix of Chou's policy concerns signified a change in priorities which the Peking regime felt was necessary.

It is possible, on the basis of this study's investigation of Chou's political "style," on the foundation of work previously published on Mao Tse-tung's style, and on the basis of Robinson's concurrent work on Lin Piao, to draw comparisons between these three top Chinese Communist leaders. Chou differs in many respects from both Mao and Lin, but the character of the differences is such that he fills in the weak points of the styles of the other two men. Thus, it seems reasonable to conclude that Chou has worked well under Mao because Mao has needed him in the personal as well as the institutional sense (and increasingly so in recent years), and that should Lin Piao succeed in keeping the mantle of the Maoist succession, he will depend on Chou in the same ways for his continued rule. It does not seem, on the other hand, that Chou himself is qualified personally to succeed Mao (and thus oust Lin) or that he would even wish to occupy the post of Party Chairman. Finally, it seems that while Chou possesses some of the qualities traditionally associated with charisma, a necessary quality for political leaders, he does not have all or even the most important of them. Hence, Chou has wisely filled the post of number two or number three man in the Party hierarchy, a situation that will probably continue into the future.

A more detailed study of the Cultural Revolution interaction between the Red Guard movement and the conduct of one of Chou's Ministries is provided by Melvin Gurtov. He focuses on the confrontation that developed in 1967 between Red Guard groups within the Foreign Ministry and the foreign affairs bureaucracy under Minister Ch'en Yi, explaining not only the consequences of that conflict for the Ministry and Ch'en but also its impact on China's foreign relations. Foreign Minister Ch'en Yi appears to have opposed from the beginning any intrusion of the Cultural Revolution mass movement into his bureaucratic domain. He first revealed his opposition by sending "work teams" to institutions linked to the Foreign Ministry in order to protect long-time professionals and party officials against Red Guard harassment. Ch'en's adamant resistance to a "revolution" within the Ministry evidently led the Cultural Revolution group under Chiang Ch'ing to sanction an "investigation" of the Foreign Minister, to demand a self-criticism from him, and to permit the establishment of internal Red Guard "liaison stations" to oversee its work. The ebb and flow of the Cultural Revolution gave Ch'en Yi opportunities, however, to maintain senior personnel in office by seeking to mediate between "conservative" and "rebel" elements in the Ministry and its embassies abroad.

The radicals reached the peak of their power in August 1967, when for about two weeks they apparently gained control of the Foreign Ministry. Thereafter, they rapidly lost the regime's favor and Ch'en Yi emerged from the prolonged encounter with his position intact. Although the Maoist leadership had consistently opposed the extremists' aim of seizing power in the Foreign Ministry and overthrowing the Foreign Minister, their support of the criticism of Ch'en and their intrusions on the Ministry's work may have greatly weakened Ch'en's authority, prestige, and health.

Although Ch'en Yi functioned as Foreign Minister throughout the confrontation with the Red Guards, China's foreign relations yielded to the radical influence of the Cultural Revolution in several places. The two most dramatic instances of Chinese efforts to propagandize the Maoist cult abroad were in Burma and Cambodia. In Burma, the timing and phasing of Peking's response to the anti-China riots there beginning in June 1967 suggest that it was the action of local Chinese and Burmese officials which caused it to come out openly in support of the Communist White Flag's aim of overthrowing the Ne Win government. Peking seems to have been forced into a position in which it considered diplomatic confrontation with Burma preferable to a humiliating compromise. The standoff with Cambodia was precipitated by the propaganda activities of the Chinese embassy and the New China News Agency. But not only did this fail to produce violence, as in Burma, but it also peaked just when the Cultural Revolution had moved to a stage of consolidation and retreat. Resolution of the Sino-Cambodian crisis was hence more easily accomplished, probably due in part to the excellent personal relations between Chou En-lai and Sihanouk and to Peking's appreciation of the importance of Cambodian friendship to its foreign policy.

Mr. Gurtov concludes that analysts of China's foreign affairs should distinguish between foreign relations and foreign policy. In terms of foreign relations, the crude propaganda activities of Chinese missions abroad seeking to demonstrate their loyalty to Mao's "thoughts" doubtless undercut Peking's diplomatic posture. Countries that experienced Chinese cultural intervention were thus likely to keep up their guard when hosting Chinese missions. Moreover, the recall of nearly every Chinese ambassador and many lower ranking officers to Peking, beginning about December 1966, raised questions about the morale and effectiveness of the foreign service. Many, perhaps most, of the ambassadors were not returned to their posts.

In terms of foreign policy, on the other hand, the Cultural Revolution is better judged as an aberration rather than a permanent new strand in Peking's policy orientation. The conflicts involving Ch'en Yi and the Foreign Ministry did not seem to have concerned substantive policy issues. Moreover, events since the fall of 1967 indicate a return to relative moderation in China's diplomacy. These include efforts by Peking to ease tensions with those countries that were directly affected by the overflow of the Cultural Revolution.

The Cultural Revolution has generally—and rightfully—been regarded primarily as an urban phenomenon. Nevertheless, the tumultuous events that took place in China's cities did have their direct counterparts in at least some rural villages in the vast Chinese hinterland. Red Guard uprisings, power seizures, "adverse currents," factionalism, and military intervention were also very much a part of the rural scene.

In the final essay in this volume, Richard Baum describes and analyzes the rural impact of the Cultural Revolution. Starting with the initial mobilization and nationwide dispersal of the Red Guards in August 1966, Professor Baum traces the sources and manifestations of political conflict in the countryside through successive stages of the Cultural Revolution. Basing his narrative on Party and Red Guard sources as well as reports of a number of refugees from (and foreign visitors to) mainland China, he concludes that early Red Guard and "Revolutionary Rebel" activities were confined to a limited number of rural communes and villages in the suburbs immediately surrounding China's 125 large and medium-sized cities. By the January Revolution of 1967, however, the scope of the conflict had enlarged to encompass a significant number of more remote communes and villages. The Cultural Revolution became a truly universal movement in the countryside only in the autumn of 1968, well after the most radical and destructive phases of the Revolution in the cities had been concluded.

Two factors explain the relative tardiness with which the Cultural Revolution came to the countryside. First, certain top-level policy-makers in Peking were apparently unwilling to see critical agricultural production processes delayed or disrupted by revolutionary agitation and "great debates" in the villages. Second, the very remoteness of many of China's rural communes and villages effectively insulated them from much urban-centered turmoil. These factors notwithstanding, by the spring of 1967 the phenomenon of political conflict between "rebels" and "power-holders" had become quite pronounced in the countryside.

The main axis of conflict around which "rebel" and "powerholder" factions polarized in rural China was the participants' orientation toward the local political establishment. On the powerholders' side were those groups and individuals having a vested interest in maintaining the status quo or selected components of it. Among these "conservative" forces were the majority of "principal" rural cadres, such as commune and production brigade-level Party secretaries and chief administrative officers; those lower-ranking officials whose primary loyalties lay with their superiors; ordinary peasants who had ties of kindship or other ties with village leaders; and those more affluent or tradition-bound peasants who possessed an economic stake in the status quo or had been alienated by the provocative (and often destructive) actions of the militant young Red Guards.

At the other end of the rural political spectrum stood a variety of individuals and social groups whose only common characteristic was their alienation from, and consequent opposition to, the local political status quo. These "rebel" forces included retribution-minded former cadres and other elements who had been purged or otherwise subjected to discipline during earlier rectification campaigns; ambitious or opportunistic subaltern officials or would-be officials cherishing hopes of upward political mobility by riding the winds of revolutionary change; those temporary or rural contract laborers wishing to repeal the highly discriminatory "worker-peasant system"; intellectual youths who, having been sent to the countryside, had a profound distaste for agricultural labor; and those ordinary peasants harboring various personal or familial grudges against local powerholders.

Thus, under conditions of personal and political insecurity fostered by the Maoist call to "bombard the headquarters" and "seize power," rural rebels and powerholders alike were often more strongly motivated by considerations of self-preservation and self-aggrandizement than by abstract considerations of moral or ideological principle. It is within the context of such basic motivations that Professor Baum examines the manifold obstacles that prevented the Maoists from realizing the imperative to "fight self-interest, establish the public interest." When the call for rebels to "seize power" from bourgeois powerholders was issued in January 1967, pro- and anti-status quo forces in many rural areas became locked in a bitter struggle for survival. What had earlier been a situation of pluralistic "interest group" politics, involving conflicting demands and pressures for the dispensation of political and economic benefits, now became an all-out confrontation between the organized supporters and opponents of the local rural establishment. In the somewhat oversimplified vocabulary of game theory, a non-zero-sum game was thus converted into a zero-sum game. In this situation of "pure conflict," the burning question was no longer *La revolution pour quoi?*, but rather *Le pouvoir pour qui?* And in many instances, this latter question was resolved only with the active intervention of the PLA.

In a study of factional conflict in the famous "pauper's co-op" in Hopei province, Professor Baum examines the role of the People's Liberation Army in "supporting the left" in local rural power struggles in the aftermath of the January Revolution. He concludes that the army frequently play a "conservative" role—supporting incumbent powerholders—in the process of resolving local factional disputes in the countryside. Military conservatism can be traced to two main factors: the natural reluctance of professional soldiers to underwrite radical anti-authoritarian mass movements; and the personal and professional bonds of solidarity which link local and regional Army commanders to veteran Party cadres in the provinces.

Despite the increasing frequency and intensity of political conflict in the countryside during and after the January Revolution, Professor Baum finds that the Cultural Revolution did not exert an overwhelmingly negative impact upon the quantity of agricultural goods produced in China. Although productive enterprises were disrupted in some rural areas, total agricultural output at the end of the Cultural Revolution remained roughly at pre-1966 levels.

In the autumn and winter of 1968–1969, as the Cultural Revolution drew to a close, a number of major rural organizational and administrative reforms were introduced. Following the convocation of the Central Committee's Twelfth Plenum in October 1968, the Maoists initiated a movement to merge and consolidate rural communes and production brigades in several provinces. In addition, a new system of rural labor remuneration—the so-called "Tachai system" of work point evaluation—was widely introduced to restrict individual material incentives in agriculture. Finally, in an effort to enhance local rural self-reliance, the Maoists launched a concerted drive to decentralize rural industrial, educational, medical, and supply and marketing services. The anticipated effect of these reforms was to lay economic and administrative foundations for a new "leap forward" in Chinese agriculture.

On the basis of these five case studies, together with the post-1968 history of the Cultural Revolution, what sorts of generalizations can be advanced? First, the evidence is persuasive that the Cultural Revolution did possess several aspects of a genuine revolution. The situation did in fact get out of hand at several points in time and in a number of provinces and institutions. And many of the developments—the January Revolution, the February adverse currents, the military intervention, the Wuhan events, seizure of the Foreign Ministry, and the Tachai experience—were not planned for by the Maoist group. These and similar events often seem to have taken on a life of their own, and at times were more reacted to than managed by Mao and his followers. Second, politics in China—at least during the Cultural Revolution—appeared startlingly similar in characterization and process to the political process in those countries where we normally have more highly developed data bases. In this writer's opinion, Chinese Communist politics *does* bear a close relationship to the political game played in other—even non-Communist, Western—states. The unusual data provided by Cultural Revolution sources does (and will continue) to demonstrate this. Thus the Cultural Revolution must be viewed more as a period during which the Chinese political scene was opened clearly to view rather than merely as a departure from the established norm. This viewpoint seems to be supported by the studies' detailed look at specific developments. The closer one gets to the scenes of action, the more such familiar elements as personal rivalry, institutional conflict, and disputes over proposed policies and administration come to the fore and the more purely ideological matters fade into the background.

The important question of the role of ideology is faced directly by most of the five studies. Ideological matters seemed to occupy the center of attention in the pre- and early Cultural Revolutionary periods. Personal Motivations continued to have a strong ideological component throughout the Cultural Revolution, particularly as expressed by the Red Guards, Revolutionary Rebels, and other groups aiming to "seize power" from the "small group" of presumed ideological deviates within the Party. But the more the Cultural Revolution progressed, and as more detailed knowledge comes forth, the more ideology as dogma seemed to disintegrate into ideology as a surrogate for conflict over issues and as a cover for politics. In fact, the Cultural Revolution and its documentation seem to point to the conclusion that much of the post-1949 history of mainland China must be interpreted quite differently: far from a history of the working out of Mao's ideological precepts or of the imposition of a centralized, totalitarian administrative system on several hundred million unwilling subjects, recent Chinese history seems more a continuation of traditional themes. Court politics are played in Peking, the center vies with the provincial peripheries for authority, and high military figures dispute with politicians over policies toward the foreigner. These subjects are familiar to every student of Chinese history. This is not to say that recent Chinese history does not have its unique elements. But it is now possible for the continuities with the Chinese past to again receive their proper weight.

Two final points are addressed by the studies. First, while the political situation sometimes does appear to be critical, at no time did the viability of Communist rule on the mainland or the ability of Mao and his group to survive seem to be in question. The various hierarchies—the Party, the government, and the army in particular—were indeed assaulted. But none succumbed completely and each managed to rise again from the ashes. Perhaps the demonstrable viability of the institutions which Mao created, even in the face of Mao's own attacks, is the best proof of the difficulty of carrying out a social revolution from above in such a vast and variegated country as China. Finally, the foreign policy variable appears to be more important than the Chinese leaders seem to have presumed. It is true that China attempted with considerable success to insulate herself from the outside world while dealing with internal problems. But the very process of the Cultural Revolution influenced the outside, not only in the case of the Foreign Ministry episode, and the "outside" adopted policies that affected the Cultural Revolution in turn. It is significant, for instance, that the end of the Cultural Revolution is foreshadowed (if not actually dated) by the Sino-Soviet border incidents in March 1969: those incidents themselves were partly the result of Soviet fears and precautions taken as a result of perceived excesses inside China. Thus, even in China it proved impossible to forget the essential unity of the world in the modern era, the fact that what happens in one place affects events elsewhere, and that the web of domestic, foreign, and international politics is essentially seamless. One result of the Cultural Revolution, paradoxically, may be a much greater degree of Chinese involvement with the rest of the world.

2

Power, Policy, and Ideology in the Making of the Chinese Cultural Revolution

WILLIAM F. DORRILL

For over three years, mainland China was caught in the grip of an internal struggle which must rank as one of the world's most far-reaching political developments in this decade. Its official appellation, "the Great Proletarian Cultural Revolution," fails to convey adequately either the totality of the struggle or the intense passion and violence that characterized it. It was a watershed in the history of the Chinese Communist revolution. The leadership and the policies which emerged from the chaos will determine China's power, direction, and pace of development for many years to come. In so doing, they will exercise a profound influence on the course of world history.

Despite its manifest importance, our knowledge of China's Cultural Revolution remains remarkably superficial. To be sure, the gross features and the more dramatic manifestations, such as the purge of government leaders and the rampages of the Red Guards, are well known. However, they do not tell us much about the underlying causes and the essential nature of the issues and contending forces. Without a clear understanding of these it is difficult to proceed to any confident—let alone definitive—assessment of either the current trends and future prospects of the upheaval or its implications for Chinese policy.

In part, the persisting confusion and obscurity stem from the paucity of verifiable data. While much can be learned from critical examination and exegesis of published Chinese sources such as official statements and press and radio comment, these rarely are intended to reveal or even to hint at sensitive "inside" information; far more often, their purpose is to mislead or distort.[1] In consequence, some of the more zealous prac-

[1] For example, in February 1967, the spokesman of a provincial radio station

titioners of "Aesopian" translation have come to diametrically opposed but equally plausible conclusions as to the principal protagonists, viewpoints, and issues in the Cultural Revolution.

The problem is further complicated by the fact that much of our information on internal political developments is in the form of unsubstantiated indictments, which often appear first in *ta-tzu-pao,* the unofficial "large-character posters" that virtually any "revolutionary" individual or group can put up. Thus, the sensational charge that a "black gang" in the Peking Municipal Committee of the Chinese Communist Party (CCP) was conspiring to restore capitalism, and the shocking allegation that for years Mao Tse-tung had been betrayed by many of his trusted lieutenants, do not in themselves constitute credible evidence but must be verified or modified in the light of other sources.

Reports from foreign observers in China, as well as from the trickle of refugees and defectors who come out of China, could do much to clarify the situation. However, these sources have thus far been very restricted in their geographic coverage. Sometimes, as in the case of some Soviet commentaries, they are tainted by political bias and exaggeration. Or, they may be severely limited in substance—doing little more than repeat the unconfirmed, conflicting *ta-tzu-pao* and Red Guard newspapers. These remarks are not meant, of course, to gainsay the very real value of information that can be gleaned from official statements, *ta-tzu-pao,* foreign press reports, and similar sources. The intent, rather, is to suggest the extraordinary need for caution and critical scrutiny in interpreting them.

Apart from the problem of evidence, our understanding of the meaning of the Cultural Revolution and of the forces underlying it is hampered by the complexity of the struggle itself. There have been indications that, at least in its early stages, some of Peking's highest Party, governmental, and military leaders—men presumably "on the inside"—were thoroughly confused about what was happening. Conceivably, the uncertainties and surprises that accompanied the struggle were part of a devious master plan drawn up by Mao in advance and calculated to entrap his unsuspecting enemies. If so, its full genius has yet to be revealed, for the

---

candidly told local critics (perhaps the previous management, recently ousted by "revolutionary rebels") who thought the broadcasts too one-sided: "The one-sided reporting is correct. Our fighting force will grow and the one-sided reporting will grow stronger. There will always be only one-sided reporting, the voice of the revolutionaries." (Anhwei People's Broadcasting Station, February 14, 1967, as quoted in *China News Analysis,* No. 649 [February 24, 1967] p. 1.)

strategy, even after the end of the Cultural Revolution, has not yet delivered a decisive victory. Moreover, much of what has happened has appeared to have been unplanned and unanticipated—a series of spontaneous eruptions and a capricious interaction of forces as the struggle unfolded.

Many hypotheses and interpretations have now been advanced, with varying degrees of confidence, to explain the upheaval in China. They have tended to focus on one or a combination of three elements: power, policy, and ideology. Thus, the Great Proletarian Cultural Revolution has been viewed variously as essentially a power struggle, a clash over domestic and foreign policies, and a conflict over ideology. For example, a well-known academic specialist has emphasized the factional struggle within the Peking regime;[2] a high U.S. official described it as primarily "a debate on policy between revolutionary romantics and pragmatists";[3] and a prominent Hong Kong-based journalist has defined the main issue as "whether the approach to China's problems shall be spiritual or material."[4] A former Chinese Communist trade official who sought political asylum in the United States in 1966 has described the Cultural Revolution as a power struggle of ambitious men competing for the succession to Mao, and, at the same time, a policy conflict between moderates and extremists, with heavy ideological overtones.[5]

Interpretations of actual events will vary, then, according to the interpreter's emphasis on one or another of the three basic elements. Furthermore, these diverse analyses of the nature of the struggle can lead to even wider and more significant differences when it comes to assessing the implications of the Cultural Revolution for the future of China. Some analysts, stressing the primacy of the succession problem, view it as having precipitated a polarization of the leadership along policy lines and heightened the inevitable tension between revolutionary aspirations and practical limitations. Others maintain that it was deep-rooted policy differences in the first instance which triggered the power struggle.

[2] Chalmers Johnson, "Communist China's Political Turmoil," SAIS Review, Winter 1968, pp. 5–24.
[3] Walt W. Rostow, Assistant to the President for National Security Affairs, speaking at the University of Leeds, as quoted in The New York Times, February 24, 1967.
[4] Stanley Karnow, The Washington Post, December 20, 1966.
[5] Miao Chen-pai, as quoted in The Washington Post, September 4, 1966, and U.S. News and World Report, November 7, 1966. As a member of the Chinese Communist Party, Miao was privy to internal Party directives and explanations of the Cultural Revolution until the time of his defection, in July 1966.

Still others trace the origin to a widespread loss of ideological commitment. And, as will be suggested in this study, it is possible to see in it
an attempt by Mao to push China toward new and unprecedented
heights of faith and fervor.

These hypotheses need not, of course, be mutually exclusive. Indeed,
any rigidly monocausal explanation would, on the face of it, be suspect.
There was unquestionably a close interconnection and interaction between the power struggle, the policy debate, and the ideological conflict.
For an understanding of the Cultural Revolution, however, it would
seem useful and perhaps even necessary to try to clarify their separate
roles, their sequential and causal relationships, and their relative importance.

Thus, one properly takes note of Peking's official claim that the "main
aim" of the Cultural Revolution was "to overthrow the handful of
Party people in authority taking the capitalist road, especially the handful of top Party persons" doing so.[6] But to understand what this really
means one must inquire more specifically into the "who" and "why."
Was what happened primarily the rivalry of ambitious or embittered
leaders bent on reordering the succession, avenging old wrongs, or satisfying personal drives for prestige and influence? Or, if the struggle was
a dispute over principles, what issues of policy or ideology divided the
contending forces?

The present study seeks to arrive at more complete and discriminating
answers to these questions through an analysis of the origins and early
development of the Cultural Revolution. In the attempt to identify major
trends and to elucidate the role of underlying factors, the treatment of
events will be selective rather than exhaustive. Though its main focus is
on the background and the beginnings of the Cultural Revolution, the
study will also consider and evaluate relevant evidence from later phases
of the struggle. It will draw attention to available analyses of the subject[7] in order both to avoid duplication and to indicate significant simi-
larities or differences of interpretation.

[6] From the commentary entitled "Take Hold of the Principal Contradiction, Keep
to the General Orientation of the Struggle," *Hung Ch'i,* No. 7 (May 1967).
[7] For example, Harry Gelman, "Mao and the Permanent Purge," *Problems of
Communism,* Vol. 15, No. 6 (November–December 1966) pp. 2–14; Philip Bridgham, "Mao's 'Cultural Revolution': Origin and Development," *The China Quarterly,*
No. 29 (January–March 1967) pp. 1–35; Gene T. Hsiao, "The Background and
Development of 'The Proletarian Cultural Revolution'," *Asian Survey,* Vol. 8, No.

THE SEEDS OF CONFLICT:
HISTORICAL BACKGROUND

The origins of the Cultural Revolution can be traced back
at least a decade. It is possible, in retrospect, to detect ominous strains
within the Peking leadership as early as 1956. By that time, the unifying
revolutionary vision and program, shared so long and so successfully by
Mao and his lieutenants—from the Long March, through the fighting
against Japan and the Kuomintang, and during the establishment and
early years of the Communist regime—had begun to face new and unprecedentedly serious challenges.

In response to a combination of disappointments and persistent difficulties associated with modernization, economic development, and the
administering of a huge and complex government, the Chinese leaders
now began to grope for a new path, with all the uncertainty and potential disagreement that this entailed. Surging nationalist pride and
rising expectations informed their mood, in tandem with a darkening,
doctrinaire suspicion of incipient "revisionist" trends in the U.S.S.R. Despite their continued self-confidence and basic unity of outlook and goals,
members of the inner circle in Peking felt frustrated by their inability
to accelerate the pace of modernization and were divided over methods
for increasing agricultural production and speeding industrialization.
Many resented Moscow's parsimonious and patronizing attitude, and
particularly Khrushchev's denunciation of Stalin and its potential meaning for Mao. Looking abroad, they were bewildered by the Hungarian
revolt; at home, they were shocked by the outpouring of criticism from
intellectuals during the "Hundred Flowers" campaign. Under the impact
of these pressures and emotions, Peking began to modify and even to
abandon major elements of the Soviet model that had shaped the organization and policies of the government, the economy, and the army of
mainland China during the early 1950s.

Despite the inner tensions that accompanied the search for new solutions and the move toward greater independence, it is important to note
that the Chinese leaders remained essentially united in outlook. Their
general orientation led them to temper revolutionary aspirations and
doctrinal demands with consideration for the practical requirements of

6 (June 1967) pp. 389–404; L. La Dany, "Mao's China: The Decline of a Dynasty,"
Foreign Affairs, Vol. 45, No. 4 (July 1967) pp. 610–623.

modernization. Thus, official policies reflected their tolerance of a modicum of personal incentives, the acceptance (under careful supervision) of economic, scientific, and managerial participation in society by "bourgeois" elements, and the encouragement of specialized education and professional development along with rigorous political indoctrination. This balanced orientation allowed the new regime to make rapid progress toward both modernization and socialization. Moreover, it enabled the leadership to weather, first, an apparent power struggle, which culminated in the purge of Kao Kang and Jao Shu-shih in 1954, and, in 1955–1956, a sharp debate over the speed of agricultural collectivization.

In the next two years, a series of important policy decisions reflected a significant weakening—though no more than that—in the balance that had characterized the regime's orientation. The "anti-rightist" campaign of 1957 resulted in the purge of thousands of "counterrevolutionary" dissidents, especially intellectuals, and marked a general tightening of Party control over society. Prior to it, Mao had delivered his celebrated speech "On the Correct Handling of Contradictions Among the People," in which he declared that most conflicts in Communist-ruled societies were "nonantagonistic" differences among "the people" and, hence, could be resolved by discussion and persuasion, However, in this speech, as in an address delivered to a National Conference on Propaganda Work in March 1957, Mao stressed the necessity of a protracted ideological struggle to uproot "all erroneous ideas, all poisonous weeds, all ghosts and monsters" and to combat "revisionism," which he branded as more dangerous than dogmatism.[8]

It is possible in retrospect, to construe these and other statements of that period as indicating that Mao was more deeply concerned than were other top leaders over the threat posed to the regime by ideological impurities and, concomitantly, appreciated more keenly the need for ideo-

---

[8] It is worth noting, however, that in the concluding section of his speech on contradictions Mao still urged solidarity with the U.S.S.R. and declared: "we should learn from the good experience of all countries, socialist or capitalist, but the main thing is still to learn from the Soviet Union"—albeit in a selective manner. In the Cultural Revolution these exhortations were ignored, although the incongruous passages still appear in republications of the speech (for example, the revised Foreign Languages Press version published by *China Pictorial* in 1967, p. 31).

Mao's address to the National Conference on Propaganda Work was one of his four works published for the first time in *Selected Readings of Mao Tse-tung's Writings* (Mao Tse-tung Chu-tso Hsüan-tu), 1964. Salient extracts were quoted in the "circular" of the CCP's Central Committee dated May 16, 1966, and published by the *New China News Agency* (*NCNA*) exactly one year later, on May 16, 1967.

logical and class struggle.[9] Yet such a conclusion as to differences in degree of solicitude would still be far from establishing the existence of the kind of basic cleavage between Mao and his chief lieutenants, notably Liu Shao-ch'i and Teng Hsiao-p'ing, that has recently been described in the unofficial Red Guard press.[10]

The launching of the Great Leap Forward and the communes, in 1958, gave positive content to the leaders' shared determination to follow a new and uniquely Chinese path to socialism. While it reflected a general shift leftward in the regime's orientation and involved a commitment to rapid development through mass mobilization and ideological motivation, the move was made with such remarkable facility and such widespread, unstinting enthusiasm as to suggest a broad consensus among the top leadership. To be sure, given the magnitude of the change, it is reasonable to suppose that some elements harbored silent doubts or reservations.[11] But the important thing to note here is that these were not

[9] This was a recurrent propaganda theme in the Cultural Revolution, particularly in 1967. In a letter dated October 16, 1954, but released by *NCNA* only as recently as May 26, 1967, Mao appears to have taken a remarkably keen interest at that early date in supporting two youthful critics who had accused a "bourgeois" literary figure of "poisoning" the minds of young people with his studies of classical works such as *The Dream of the Red Chamber*. Mao evidently thought their efforts (and initial difficulty in getting a hearing), as well as his own criticism of two then current films, worthy of a letter to his colleagues on the Politburo.

[10] Red Guard newspapers have quoted alleged statements by Liu before local Party meetings in 1957 which, among other things, denied the possibility of contradictions in a socialist society and advanced a whole series of "rightist" economic views such as the advocacy of limited free markets and material incentives. It should be noted, however, that these statements cannot be authenticated on the basis of available credible evidence; even if they proved to be literally true, their truncated appearance, out of context, could easily distort the original meaning. Certainly, the Red Guard accusations and innuendoes to the effect that Liu and Teng were taking a rightist and anti-Party tack, besides implying that the two men were indulging an unlikely political death wish, are not substantiated either by their published statements at the time or by the line taken in official publications for which they would have had responsibility during the Hundred Flowers and Anti-Rightist campaigns.

[11] Thus, articles by Ch'en Po-ta and "Commentator" in *Hung Ch'i* (Nos. 4 and 11 [1958] respectively) attacked dissident views on economic policy. Although they did not accuse any top leaders by name or clearly indicate the level to which the alleged dissent had reached, it was at about this time that Ch'en Yün, one of the regime's foremost economic leaders—he was first vice-premier of the State Council as well as a member of the Politburo Standing Committee—went into political eclipse. It remains difficult to document the precise reasons for Ch'en Yün's disappearance, but they probably were related to his prominent identification with the First Five-Year Plan and the relatively balanced, gradual Soviet model of economic development. (See relevant discussions in Franz Schurmann, *Ideology and Organ-*

serious enough to impel public expression, or to polarize opinion within the leadership. In launching the Great Leap at the Second Session of the Eighth CCP Congress, in May 1958, Liu Shao-ch'i enthusiastically endorsed the leftward course and the economic speedup, lavishing praise on its author, Mao Tse-tung.[12] Although adjustments were made in subsequent months, as aspects of the radical new scheme proved functionally unsound (particularly in the commune system), Liu grandly portrayed it in the *World Marxist Review* as a model for the entire Communist world as late as October 1959, seven months after Khrushchev's stinging, if implicit, criticism of the commune idea at the Twenty-First Congress of the CPSU.

While the foregoing tends to focus on domestic factors in Peking's decision to shift to the utopian policy of the Leap Forward, it is not intended to minimize the influence of the growing Sino-Soviet tension and rivalry. Already generally disenchanted with the Soviet model for China, the Chinese were becoming increasingly disappointed as the Soviet Union failed to fulfill their expectations of large military and economic aid. In pushing arrogantly ahead with the communes and radical economic measures of the Leap Forward in the face of Soviet warnings, they were not only giving vent to an overweening nationalism but apparently claiming the role of Moscow's rival for leadership of the world Communist movement, touting their own as an alternate and more rapid path to Communism that threatened to shorten the lead of the Soviets.[13]

As in the matter of economic policy, there may well have been marginal differences of opinion within the Peking leadership over the tactics to be used or the severity of the challenge that should be hurled at

---

ization in Communist China [Berkeley, 1966] pp. 76, 204–205, 208; Werner Klatt [ed.], *The Chinese Model* [Hong Kong, 1965] pp. 181, 202; and Howard Boorman [ed.], *Biographical Dictionary of Republican China* [New York, 1967] p. 266.) One of the ironies of the first phase of the Cultural Revolution was the reappearance—albeit with questionable powers—of this "rightist" economic planner in the most unlikely company of Mao and the Red Guard ralliers in the fall of 1966.

[12] Indeed, Liu's statements and actions were so positive as to prompt at least one scholar to advance the thesis that it was "Liu rather than Mao who must be regarded as the main sponsor of the Great Leap Forward." (Harold Hinton, "Intra-Party Politics and Economic Policy in Communist China," *World Politics*, Vol. 12, No. 4 [July 1960] p. 515.) The decision to launch the commune system was made in August 1958 at an enlarged Politburo meeting held at Peitaiho; it was announced in *Jen-min Jih-pao* on September 1, 1958. Pilot "people's communes," notably the Weihsing (Sputnik) commune in Honan, had begun to appear the previous April.

[13] Franz Michael, "Who Is Ahead on the Way to Communism?" *Communist Affairs*, Vol. 4, No. 6 (November–December 1965).

Moscow. But the fact to be noted here is that all leaders—including those later denounced as the "Chinese Khrushchev" (Liu Shao-ch'i), his "chief accomplice" (Teng Hsiao-p'ing), and the Peking "black gang" chieftain (P'eng Chen)—displayed a strongly nationalist and anti-Soviet bias. Despite later Red Guard accusations and innuendoes to the contrary, there simply is no credible evidence that any one of the top leaders of the regime was less genuinely patriotic or significantly more pro-Soviet than Mao Tse-tung. Nor is there any reason why the subsequent collapse of the Leap Forward—and, concomitantly, the failure of Peking's bid for world Communist leadership—should necessarily have undermined Mao's position more than that of Liu, Teng, P'eng, or others who were in the top echelon in 1958–1959. All of them had firmly espoused the policies that failed (except perhaps P'eng Teh-huai, who, however, voiced his dissent only in mid-1959); though the boat might be sinking, they were all in it together. The writer cannot agree with the contention of Professor Franz Michael that the two disasters—failure of the Leap Forward and the Sino-Soviet rift—thoroughly and singularly discredited Mao and resulted in his removal from power, while leaving Liu Shao-ch'i politically unscathed and determined "to dismantle Mao's radical program" in favor of "a more rational economic development" plan.[14] Without belittling the impact of the Sino-Soviet dispute on the Peking regime as a whole, this author believes that one must look elsewhere for the decisive factors that gave rise to the Cultural Revolution and the split among the Chinese leaders.

Perhaps a word should be said here about Mao's alleged complaint, as reported in Red Guard sources, that he was pushed aside and "pigeonholed" in 1958 by the ambitious and erring Liu and his chief accomplice, Teng Hsiao-p'ing.[15] Unquestionably, Mao did relinquish his post as Chairman of the Republic—but not his more powerful position as Chairman of the Party—at the time of the Sixth Plenum of the CCP Central Committee, in December 1958. His proposal not to stand for reelection as

[14] Franz Michael, "Moscow and the Current Chinese Crisis," *Current History,* Vol. 53, No. 313 (September 1967) p. 142.

[15] These charges were contained in accounts of an angry speech said to have been delivered by Mao to a work conference of the CCP Central Committee on October 26, 1966. Purported texts of the speech were published in Red Guard newspapers— one, an eight-page pamphlet entitled "Criticism by the Central Chairman Against Liu Shao-ch'i and Teng Hsiao-p'ing"—which were posted on walls in Peking on January 4 and 6, 1967, and subsequently reported by correspondents of *Mainichi Shimbun* and *Yomiuri Shimbun.*

state Chairman seemed plausible and amicable at the time, and Liu Shao-ch'i's subsequent election to that office was entirely logical.[16] Overt preparations for the succession had been under way for at least two years, and Liu had been the heir apparent since 1945. Even the Red Guard posters quoted Mao as having himself decided in 1956 to divide the Politburo Standing Committee into a "first" and a "second line" in order to prepare for an orderly succession and avoid problems such as had arisen after Stalin's death. According to the posters, however, Mao withdrew to the less active "second line" (following the Eighth CCP Congress, presumably) and then alleged that serious "decentralism" and other errors had occurred under the "front-line" leadership of Liu Shao-ch'i, who had been given important policy powers as first Vice-Chairman of the Central Committee, and Teng Hsiao-p'ing, who managed the Party's daily work in the newly created post of General Secretary.

The Eighth Party Congress (September 1956) also created the post of Honorary Chairman of the CCP, presumably as a niche for Mao after his retirement. Moreover, it adopted a new Party Constitution, the preamble of which, in contrast to the preamble of the Constitution of 1945 that it replaced, failed to include "the thought of Mao Tse-tung" among basic guidelines for action. These measures were in accord with the CCP's then accepted opposition to the "cult of the individual," in limited deference to the policy initiated by the Soviets in February 1956 at the Twentieth Congress of the CPSU. Thus, it is not surprising that Teng Hsiao-p'ing, in his report to the Eighth CCP Congress, lent general support to criticism of the "cult of the individual" (but not specifically to the de-Stalinization campaign), or that Liu Shao-ch'i, without actually raising that theme, failed to voice explicit praise of Mao's thought—an omission that his Red Guard accusers were to recall a decade later.

It is possible to view these developments in 1956 as a deliberate deroga-

---

[16] Commenting on the significance of Liu's elevation, Howard Boorman later observed: "Mao thus made his closest 'comrade in arms' in Party leadership his successor as chief of state during his lifetime, a probable attempt to raise Liu above all possible rivals and thus to insure his later succession to the truly decisive position of chairman of the Party." ("Liu Shao-c'hi: A Political Profile," *The China Quarterly*, No. 10 [April–June 1962] p. 17.) This view was not untypical of those expressed by Western observers before the onset of the Cultural Revolution. However, the veteran Yugoslav journalist Branku Bogunovic recently recalled that there was considerable uncertainty among foreign correspondents in Peking in 1959 as to whether the man chosen to succeed Mao as President of the Republic would be Liu Shao-ch'i or Chou En-lai. (See Bogunovic's analysis, as translated from the Belgrade newspaper *Borba*, in *Atlas*, December 1967, p. 17.)

tion of Mao's stature and power by others in the top leadership, and even, with Gene T. Hsiao, as the "seed" of the Cultural Revolution,[17] but the evidence thus far available does not warrant such conclusions. For example, Ch'en Yi, replying to Liu Shao-ch'i's accusers (and his own), has stoutly maintained that Mao himself and the Politburo approved Liu's report to the Eighth Congress.[18] Presumably, this was the case with Teng Hsiao-p'ing's report as well. Moreover, a high-ranking Japanese Communist Party official, long resident in China, has pointed out that the 1956 revision of the CCP Constitution, which was intended among other things to prevent the growth of any "cult of the individual," was written with Party Chairman Mao Tse-tung's "guidance and approval."[19] Although the preamble of the revised Constitution failed to mention Mao's thought, Franz Schurmann has observed that in practice, "since the latter part of the 1950's, the dualism originally stated in the 1945 Party Rules has been revised" in even stronger form: "Marxism-Leninism and the thought of Mao Tse-tung."[20] Finally, in assessing the impact of events in 1956 on Mao's position, one should bear in mind that even the Red Guard poster accounts of Mao's remarks indicated that Mao was not coerced or overpowered; he voluntarily stood aside in 1956 to groom his chief lieutenants for the succession. Whether or not they later misused their power, it had been Mao's decision to delegate it to them.

Two years after Mao had taken the step that he apparently came to regret, the mistake was compounded, according to the reports, when he was forced to step down as Chairman of the Republic. From then on, Liu and Teng are said to have treated him like "their dead parent at a funeral." After 1959, according to one Red Guard account, Teng went so far as to refuse to brief him on the work of the Secretariat. Yet the charge that Mao was forced aside by Liu and Teng around 1958 and thereafter suffered a decisive loss of power to these disloyal lieutenants must be regarded as greatly exaggerated if not completely untrue.[21] Al-

[17] *Asian Survey*, Vol. 8, No. 6 (June 1967) p. 392.

[18] "I was there all the time," Ch'en averred. Quoted in the Red Guard newspaper, *Hung Wi Chün Pao*, of April 8, 1967.

[19] Ichiro Sunama, "Return from Peking," Part 2, *Akahata*, November 4, 1967.

[20] *Ideology and Organization in Communist China*, p. 21.

[21] Indeed, upon consulting the text of Mao's October 1966 speech, in which the allegations reportedly were made, the impression is strong that Mao preferred to be in the "second front," as he termed it, and others to man the "first front," which concerned immediate and routine matters. Mao's reason is that, by so dividing responsibility, "when I went to see God, the State would not be thrown into great convulsions." See text, contained in a Red Guard pamphlet, "Long Live Mao Tse-

though Mao voluntarily and temporarily relinquished control over many day-to-day decisions, this does not prove that he was forced to give up the supreme leadership or even that his position was seriously jeopardized. If Liu and Teng had usurped power in the way that Red Guard sources have suggested, how could Mao have retained the Party chairmanship, leaving conspicuously open the post of Honorary Chairman that had been created in 1956 in evident anticipation of his retirement? As Party Chairman he could hardly have been denied briefings on the work of the Secretariat, if he had insisted upon them. Moreover, it would seem rash to discount entirely the explanation proffered by the Central Committee in 1958 that it was Mao himself who had proposed not seeking reelection as state Chairman (though with the proviso that he could be nominated for another term if "special circumstances" arose) in order to be free to do theoretical work, an activity whose effects were subsequently demonstrated in Peking's posture and polemics vis-à-vis Moscow.[22]

A possible explanation of developments after 1958 is that an aging and somewhat embittered Mao, perplexed at the failure of his Great Leap and commune schemes to usher in the millennium, voluntarily withdrew into the background and, for the next few years, concentrated largely on finding theoretical formulas that would justify his practical failures and meet the threat of Soviet "revisionism." He may have left to his chief lieutenants the more unpleasant and difficult decisions aimed at China's "recovery" and even, on occasion, have yielded on some matters of policy to those in opposition, be it as a result of his own uncertainty or as a way of effecting a tactical accommodation. Whatever may have been his active role or true feelings during the disastrous years 1959–1961, a time of economic collapse and the alienation of Peking's erstwhile Soviet allies, Mao continued to enjoy a position of unrivaled stature and ultimate

---

tung Thought" (n.d., n.p.) as translated in *Current Background*, No. 891 (October 8, 1969) pp. 75–77.

[22] The Sixth Plenum (November–December 1958), while calling for modifications in the commune system, categorically declared it to be the form of organization best designed to speed socialist construction and effect the transition from collective to "whole-people's ownership," that is, from socialist to Communist society. There is no evidence that Mao opposed either the modifications called for or the general approval of the concept reiterated by the plenary session. He may have been disappointed later over the compromises on economic policy adopted by the Seventh Plenum (April 1959) and popularized in the phrases "walking on two legs" and "taking the whole country as a coordinated chess game." But the trend toward moderation discernible in those compromises was soon reversed, as the Ninth Plenum, in August 1959, launched its attack against "rightist-inclined conservatism."

authority in China.[23] This was reflected in the military establishment, where his faithful comrade-in-arms Lin Piao rapidly rose to unchallenged control, maintaining discipline and morale when hard times threatened disorder and greatly raising the army's place in society, all the while emphasizing the primacy of politics and the thought of Mao Tse-tung.[24] Mao's continuing power and his ability to preserve unity of outlook and orientation among the top leadership despite the buffeting storms of economic setbacks were graphically demonstrated in the late summer of 1959, although his prestige did not emerge from that process unscathed.

Details of the Eighth Plenum of the Central Committee, convened by

[23] Thus, in the winter of 1959–1960, at the height of the crisis precipitated by the collapse of the Leap Forward, Li Fu-ch'un felt it necessary—and, presumably, conclusive—to declare that the new policy of "agriculture as the foundation" was based on Mao's own instructions (*Hung Ch'i*, No. 1 [January 1960]). The fact that Mao retained ultimate authority during this period has more recently been underscored in the confession of Liu Shao-ch'i, alleged to have been made at a Party conference in October 1966 (perhaps the same meeting at which Mao delivered the accusations noted above), in which Liu admitted (if we may trust the *ta-tzu-pao* text) having had his "rightist deviations" overruled by Mao in both 1962 and 1964. On at least one occasion, possibly in 1962, he had found it necessary to make a special trip to report to Mao, who was temporarily not in Peking. (The text of Liu's purported self-criticism was published in *Mainichi Shimbun*, January 28 and 29, 1967.)

[24] In May 1958, Lin Piao was elevated to the Politburo Standing Committee (as one of five newly appointed vice-chairmen of the Central Committee), thereby coming to outrank the Minister of Defense, P'eng Teh-huai, who was also a Politburo member. Almost immediately thereafter, in his other capacity of vice-chairman of the CCP's Military Affairs Committee, Lin led a *cheng feng* rectification movement in the top echelon of the People's Liberation Army (PLA). This campaign, which lasted from May 27 to July 22, in effect put an end to the influence of the Russian military model in the PLA. It apparently capped one of the Communist regime's three major internal struggles alluded to in an Army Day editorial that appeared on August 1, 1966, in *Chieh-fang Chün Pao* (*Liberation Army Daily*). It also prepared the way for issuance of a revised set of basic principles on Party-army relations, which emphasized the CCP's control over the PLA and "politics in command." These developments, incidentally, grew out of Moscow's agreement, in October 1957, to provide China with technical and other assistance needed toward the acquisition of a Chinese nuclear capability. According to Peking's later polemics on the subject, the Soviets failed to deliver on schedule, and finally abrogated the agreement unilaterally in June 1959. (See "Statement by the Spokesman of the Chinese Government," August 15, 1963, in *Peking Review*, No. 33 [August 16, 1963] p. 14.) Soviet sources have confirmed that the Chinese never forgave the U.S.S.R. for failing to provide China with "samples of atomic weapons." (See a 1963 study by A. I. Iorysh and M. I. Lazarev, as quoted in *Soviet Space Programs, 1962–1965*. Staff Report, Committee on Aeronautical and Space Science, U.S. Senate, 89th Congress, 2nd Session, December 30, 1966 [Government Printing Office, Washington, D.C., 1966] p. 522.)

Mao at Lushan in August 1959, remain obscure,[25] but there is little doubt
that it witnessed a major crisis within the leadership. The final communiqué condemned the "emergence of right opportunists" who criticized
the Leap Forward, and it enjoined Party committees at all levels to overcome such tendencies. Subsequently, Minister of Defense P'eng Teh-huai
and other important military and political figures disappeared from
public life.[26]

Notwithstanding this circumstantial evidence, the tendentious explanations that followed (mainly in the form of indictments), and even the
fuller documentation published more recently, our knowledge of the
issues debated at Lushan and of the alignments of protagonists in the
debates remains sketchy and one-sided. What, actually, happened? Did
P'eng, as some analysts contend, attack "the whole range of Mao's
radical domestic and foreign policies," thereby establishing the preconditions for a "crisis of confidence in Mao's leadership" when these policies
continued to fail in later years? [27] Or does the evidence indicate that "the
main dispute was over military policies," as others have suggested? [28]
Can we "assert with confidence that P'eng was the leader of an 'anti-
Party' group in the Politburo," which had made clandestine contact with
Soviet leaders in an effort to secure their support for an attack on the
Maoist leadership at Lushan? [29] These interpretations would seem to
bear careful reexamination.

[25] According to Red Guard sources, Chairman Mao "personally convened" the
Lushan Plenum, another indication of his continued hold on the top leadership. See
Chiao-yu Ko-ming (Educational Revolution), a booklet published by the Peking
Educational Revolution Liaison Committee on May 6, 1967, as translated in *Joint
Publications Research Service (JPRS)* 41, 932, July 21, 1967 (*Translations on Com-
munist China: Political and Sociological,* No. 411) p. 32.

[26] Among those who left were Huang K'o-ch'eng (PLA Chief of Staff), T'an
Cheng (Director of the General Political Department of the PLA), Hung Hsueh-
chih (Rear Services Director), and, on the civilian side, Vice-Minister of Foreign
Affairs Chang Wen-t'ien (a former ambassador to the U.S.S.R.) and Hunan First
Party Secretary Chou Hsiao-chou. Earlier opponents of the leftward course in eco-
nomic policy, such as Ch'en Yün, remained in political oblivion.

[27] This interpretation has been advanced by Philip Bridgham (*The China Quarterly,* No. 29 [January–March 1967] p. 2), who also suggests that P'eng proposed
policies rivaling Mao's and "featuring Soviet military, economic, and technical assistance." More recently, an almost identical interpretation has been offered by the
British scholar Brian Hook in "China's Cultural Revolution: The Preconditions in
Historical Perspective," *The World Today,* Vol. 23, No. 11 (November 1967) p. 463.

[28] John Gittings, *The Role of the Chinese Army* (London, 1967) p. 226.

[29] David A. Charles (pseud.), "The Dismissal of Marshal P'eng Teh-huai," *The
China Quarterly,* No. 8 (October–December 1961) p. 64 and *passim.*

Recently published documents charge that P'eng Teh-huai, in a letter to Mao on July 14, 1959, and in subsequent speeches at the Eighth Plenum, painted a maliciously black picture of economic conditions, disparaging the "victory" of the Leap Forward, exaggerating the current "transient and partial shortcomings," and opposing the people's communes and the policy of high-speed development, as well as the mass movements for economic construction, high yields in agriculture, and "backyard furnace" production of iron and steel. These charges against P'eng appear in excerpts of the purported text of a censure resolution passed at the conclusion of the Eighth Plenum, on August 16, 1959, but published only eight years later.[30] Secondary sources available during the Cultural Revolution, which may tend to embellish the allegations contained in the censure resolution, depict P'eng as an outspoken critic of economic policy, who caustically referred to the Leap Forward as "a rush of blood to the brain," regarded the mass movements (as for "backyard" steel) as so much "petty-bourgeois fanaticism," and thought the people's communes "a mess" for having been "set up too early."[31] A purportedly accurate version of the 1959 "letter of opinion" (i-chien-shu) from P'eng to Mao quote P'eng as bluntly complaining about "leftist" tendencies ("always wanting to enter Communism at one bound," obsession with being "the first"), and "failure to seek truth from facts," all of which had led to "hasty and excessive plans" in 1958 and resulted in failure to readjust imbalances in production and to "slow down a bit" so as to bring the frenzied, disorganized economy under control.[32]

Not only, as suggested above, may recent secondary sources exaggerate the extent of P'eng's guilt as accepted at the time, but the literal authenticity of newly published texts of P'eng's "letter of opinion" and even of the Central Committee's resolution of censure is not beyond question. Given the eight-year delay in publication and the heavy bias of the sources, it would seem entirely possible that the primary documents have

[30] *Hung Ch'i*, No. 13 (August 17, 1967) pp. 18–20.

[31] See "From the Defeat of P'eng Teh-huai to the Bankruptcy of China's Khrushchev," *ibid.*, pp. 21–24.

[32] "P'eng Teh-huai's so-called 'Letter of Opinion' to Chairman Mao at the 1959 Lushan Conference," *Ko-ming Ch'uan-lien (Exchange of Revolutionary Experience)*, Peking, August 24, 1967. In *SCMP (Survey of China Mainland Press)* 4032 (October 2, 1967) pp. 1–5. Also translated in *Current Background*, No. 851 (April 26, 1968) pp. 19–23. A Chinese text is in *Tsu Kuo* (Kowloon, Hong Kong), No. 48 (March 1, 1968) pp. 42–44. Mao's comments on P'eng at Lushan, including his emotional July 23, 1959, speech, are translated in *Chinese Law and Government*, Vol. 1, No. 4 (Winter 1968–1969) pp. 25–46.

been altered or distorted to add support to more recent, Maoist interpretations.[33]

Actually, P'eng's criticisms may have been more restrained and balanced than the later charges against him would indicate. In the July 14 "letter of opinion" to Mao, for example (if we assume the authenticity of available texts), P'eng called for greater accuracy and realism in production figures—a sentiment seemingly shared by the majority of his colleagues, to judge by the decision passed at Lushan to improve statistical reporting. While advocating changes in the communes to bring distribution more closely in line with labor, P'eng praised the commune system as having lifted the peasantry out of poverty and speeded the advance from socialism to Communism. His warnings against "leftist" fanaticism were coupled with appeals to uphold the "mass line" and avoid rightist tendencies. Similarly, his criticisms of economic defects—some of which he attributed simply to lack of experience—were matched by expressions of confidence in the Leap Forward, as in the statement that "conditions for continued Leap Forward are present." He agreed with Mao that "the achievements are tremendous, the problems are numerous, the experience is rich, and the future is bright." Indeed, he averred that, if present defects could be overcome—by furthering the corrective action already taken in conferences at Wuchang, Chengchow, and Shanghai—it would be possible to overtake the British level of production in only four years' time instead of the target of fifteen years originally set in the Leap Forward.

Subsequent commentaries by Cultural Revolutionaries have ripped P'eng's colorful phrases out of context and greatly distorted the position actually taken in his letter. For example, his advocacy of "balance" and "simultaneous attention" to both economic measures and "putting politics in command" (as well as his warning not to disregard scientific and economic laws) was now attacked as "eclecticism," denial of the primacy of politics, and a bourgeois effort to "put money in command"; his

[33] Thus, the author shares M. La Dany's suspicions as to the literal accuracy of the Eighth Plenum censure resolution (*China News Analysis*, No. 685 [November 17, 1967]). He is not, however, persuaded by La Dany's argument that the reference in the resolution (as now published) to the dismissal of P'eng and others from various posts is contradicted by more credible evidence that those men actually were removed only after the Lushan Plenum—at a meeting of the CCP Military Affairs Committee. The resolution as published in *Hung Ch'i* in August 1967 merely says that it is "essential to transfer P'eng" and the others from their responsible positions (except for membership in the Central Committee and Politburo), leaving the act of dismissal to other organs.

proposal to alter economic policies was described as a dark plot to completely abandon the communes and the Leap Forward.[34]

P'eng's remarks, however, were not entirely at odds with the prevailing orientation at Lushan. It is sometimes forgotten that the most notable actions taken by the plenary session, aside from the censure of P'eng, were a drastic revision downward of production claims for 1958 and goals for 1959, and a further retreat from the communes, as collective ownership and accounting were shifted downward to the production brigades at the next-lower level.[35]

Since even his attackers admit that P'eng made "outward pretensions of support" for Mao and the Party's general line, we are left to ponder why the Eighth Plenum felt it necessary, not merely to overrule him, but to condemn his criticisms as constituting a "right opportunist line" that challenged "Party leadership in socialist construction," and to accuse him of leading an "anti-Party clique"—where "viewpoint" might have been the more accurate term—a continuation of the 1954 Kao Kang and Jao Shu-shih plot. If P'eng had been seriously implicated in the "Kao and Jao anti-Party alliance," as is charged, it is difficult to understand why he should have been rewarded with an appointment as Minister of Defense in November 1954—just after the wholesale purge of Kao and Jao subordinates in the Northeast and East China regional administrations in

[34] See "From the Defeat of P'eng Teh-huai," *Hung Ch'i*, No. 13 (August 17, 1967); see also "Principal Crimes of P'eng Teh-huai, Big Ambitionist and Schemer," from the Canton Red Guard tabloids *Chingkangshan* and *Kuang-tung Wen-i Chan-pao*, translated in *SCMP* 4047 (October 25, 1967). "Down with Big Conspirator, Big Ambitionist, Big Warlord P'eng Teh-huai—Collected Materials Against P'eng Teh-huai," Tsinghua University Chingkang Mountain Corps, Peking, November 1967 (in *Current Background*, No. 851 [April 26, 1968] pp. 1–31); *Union Research Service* (Kowloon, Hong Kong), "The 'Criminal Record' of P'eng Teh-huai," Vol. 50, Nos. 15 and 16 (February 20 and 23, 1967); and *Union Research Service*, "Supporting Documents to P'eng Teh-huai's Reactionary History," Vol. 50, No. 17 (February 27, 1968).

[35] As Harold C. Hinton has pointed out, the revised production claims for 1958—while still not necessarily accurate—reflected "an admitted overestimate of 50 per cent" in agriculture and represented a complete "writing-off of the output of the 'native' [backyard] furnaces as unusable in modern industry." ("Intra-Party Politics and Economic Policy in Communist China," *World Politics*, July 1960, p. 522; see also Schurmann, *Ideology and Organization in Communist China*, p. 491.) Although there was a brief, partial return to the earlier mass mobilization policies in the fall of 1959—in the wake of the "anti-rightist" campaign—the general retreat from the communes and from the manic economic policies of the Leap Forward continued after mid-1960. Unfortunately, from November 1959 on, the regime's ban on the export of local and regional newspapers hindered the flow of information on economic trends.

June, and after Liu Shao-ch'i had given intimations of the coming intra-Party purge at the CCP Fourth Plenum (of the Seventh Congress) in February. If P'eng actually made a self-criticism during the struggle against Kao and Jao in 1954, as is claimed in the newly published Lushan Plenum resolution, it would more likely have been the result of his association with Kao in 1953 as a member of the State Planning Commission (chaired by Kao, with Jao a member) than any serious charge that P'eng had participated in or led an anti-Party clique. In retrospect, P'eng's greater crime—and the one implicating him in the 1954 factional struggle—may have been his alleged deletion of a passage paying homage to the guidance of Mao's thoughts from a 1953 draft of regulations for PLA Party committees.[36]

Even allowing for a high degree of exaggeration in the charges raised against him (especially his implication with the Kao and Jao plot)—an exaggeration probably thought necessary to help shake P'eng's blameless reputation and wide following—it is possible to discern several reasons why his colleagues in the Central Committee decided on the drastic action of censure and dismissal. P'eng's candid exposure of "defects" in the regime's Leap Forward and commune policies reflected on most of the Party leaders; and, accordingly, not only Mao but also Liu Shao-ch'i and Teng Hsiao-p'ing would seem to have had an interest in silencing if not discrediting him. But P'eng would not be silenced. His arguments apparently struck a responsive chord among other leaders at Lushan—not to mention their potential appeal to the Chinese masses straining under the burden of frenetic Leap Forward campaigns and economic setbacks.

In his "letter of opinion" of July 14, according to some accounts, P'eng pointedly rebuked those responsible for domestic programs when he charged, "We have not handled the problems of economic construction

---

[36] See "Settle Accounts with P'eng Teh-huai," *Jen-min Jih-pao*, August 17, 1967. A translation of P'eng's reputed self-examination after Lushan, delivered at the 8th Plenum of the 8th Central Committee, is in *Current Background*, No. 851 (April 26, 1928) pp. 27–31. This is also translated in *Union Research Service*, Vol. 50, No. 17 (February 27, 1968) as "P'eng Teh-huai's Statement of Confession," extracted while in custody during December 28, 1966–January 5, 1967. Both of these were originally published in *Collected Materials on P'eng Teh-huai*, Tsing-hua University Chingkangshan Corps, Peking. In these documents, as well as those referenced in note 32 above, most of the charges against P'eng concerned his alleged military shortcomings. Very little space is devoted to P'eng's reputed association with Kao and Jao and then only in a general accusatory manner.

as successfully as we dealt with the problem of shelling Quemoy and quelling the revolt in Tibet." Moreover, he called attention to the worsening shortages of food and clothing with the warning that "the people urgently demand a change of the present conditions." The Eighth Plenum censure resolution of August 16 complained that P'eng had, time and again, asserted: "If the Chinese workers and peasants were not as good as they are, a Hungarian incident would have occurred in China and it would have been necessary to invite Soviet troops in."

The effect of these arguments apparently had begun to tell. The resolution declared that because of his influential position in the Party and the military establishment and his pretention of candor and frugality, P'eng "could and did mislead a number of people" at Lushan. In addition to his "handful" of accomplices (the resolution named Huang K'o-ch'eng, Chang Wen-t'ien, and Chou Hsiao-chou) and perhaps also to the rightists, there were presumed to have been "political speculators and alien class elements" and those with a personal grudge who had "sneaked into the Party," all of whom rose up at Lushan to launch a "fierce onslaught" against the Maoist leadership and general line.

Worst perhaps in the eyes of his colleagues was the fact that P'eng was as stubborn and uncompromising as he was outspoken. Not only did he refuse to recant when overruled, but he apparently declined even to meet halfway those willing to restore to the regime's policies a limited measure of realism. In his letter of July 14, for example, while noting that the greatly exaggerated reports of increased agricultural output had been revised downward (from the original claim of a twofold increase to one of 35 percent), P'eng refused to accept even the new figures and complained that they still contained inaccuracies. Though he probably was right, this statement may well have alienated potential allies who were leaning toward piecemeal reform. In the end, P'eng's die-hard style of aggressive, unyielding dissent—which may have culminated in a direct, heated confrontation with Mao—probably contributed as much to his undoing as the substance of his complaint.

According to the account of David Charles,[37] based upon reports of tendentious, confidential briefings given to CCP members soon after P'eng's dismissal, the Party leaders at Lushan were taken aback by his bold initiative and—either from surprise or in an attempt to smoke out

[37] "The Dismissal of Marshal P'eng Teh-huai," *The China Quarterly*, October–December 1961, pp. 67–68.

the opposition—allowed a protracted debate to proceed. In it P'eng was supported by Huang K'o-ch'eng, Chang Wen-t'ien, and others, including the venerable Lin Po-ch'ü (who died in May 1960). Ultimately, however, all wavering and dissent were smothered, as the leadership united behind a resolution (presumably that of August 16) which reaffirmed the absolute correctness of the Party line, rejected P'eng's criticisms without compromise, and condemned him for factional activity—specifically, for going beyond permissible expression of dissent in the Politburo to lobby within the Central Committee. (This last distinction, mentioned by Charles, does not appear in later documentation.) At one point in the debate it was suggested that any attempt to disgrace P'eng might trigger a revolt in the PLA, whereupon Mao "declared with tears in his eyes that, if this happened, he would go back to the villages and recruit another army. The generals present then got up in turn and pledged their loyalty to Mao and to the Central Committee." [38]

Although the evidence now available indicates that the main theme of P'eng Teh-huai's dissent at Lushan was opposition to certain aspects of the Leap Forward and commune policies,[39] the military implications of his criticism very likely were also a significant issue in the dispute, whether or not they figured prominently in the debate. The fact that serious dissent of any kind should have come from high in the military establishment must have been extremely disturbing to most Party leaders; and P'eng's insistent stress on restoring economic realism carried obvious implications for the allocation of military resources and for political-military relations. Given the nature of P'eng's criticisms at Lushan, the subsequent removal of top military officers—and the fact that their removal was not paralleled by a purge of civilian planners and administrators—makes it appear that the conflict was less a dispute between exponents of contending general economic policies than a dissent by the military (with scattered civilian support) over certain aspects of the prevailing policy, notably the adverse impact of Leap Forward measures

[38] *Ibid.,* p. 68.

[39] This, essentially, is also the conclusion reached earlier by David Charles on the basis of the reported briefings to Party members soon after P'eng's dismissal in 1959. "The shortcomings of the Great Leap Forward," says Charles, were the "main theme" of P'eng's memorandum (or "letter of opinion") presented at the Eighth Plenum. In general, he "preferred to concentrate his attack on the political and economic policies of the Party rather than air his professional [military] grievances. Throughout, P'eng acted as a senior member of the Politburo rather than as a dissatisfied Minister of Defense." (*Ibid.,* pp. 65, 67.)

on military capabilities and the Party's growing domination over all facets of army life.

Although the Cultural Revolution has provided much new information as to the chief culprits at Lushan and their crimes, the result has not been to lighten the onus of guilt or to shift it from the military officers associated with P'eng Teh-huai. The "economists," who were so roundly criticized during the Cultural Revolution, have never been identified as the enemies who launched the "fierce onslaught on the Party's general line, the Great Leap Forward, and the people's communes" at Lushan.

While David Charles' article may have been lacking in documentary support, the charges against P'eng Teh-huai made public during the Cultural Revolution tend to confirm those portions of Charles' account which were based on reports of the first round of confidential briefings to CCP members after P'eng's dismissal. In other words, the newly published documentation indicates that, in general, these were indeed the charges that constituted the grounds for the dismissal. (Whether or not the indictment accurately described P'eng's behavior and the debate at Lushan is another matter.) As we shall see, however, a second category of reports used by Charles, which told of later briefings to "selected cadres" beginning in the summer of 1960—after a revival of interest in the P'eng Teh-huai affair coinciding with a dramatic worsening of Sino-Soviet relations—provides a much less credible basis of evidence as to the charges (true or not) which brought P'eng's removal.[40]

Whether at Lushan or earlier, P'eng and his fellow dissidents evidently opposed the Party's assignment of ever-heavier economic and other non-military tasks to the army and resisted further political encroachments that threatened to undermine military training and organization.[41] How-

---

[40] For a discussion of the two categories of reports used by Charles, see his bibliographic note, *ibid.*, p. 65.

[41] On August 1, 1966, *Chieh-fang Chün Pao* printed a description of the second major struggle in the PLA after the establishment of the People's Republic, which reported that in 1959 an "anti-Party clique" took advantage of important posts it had acquired in the army to attempt to abolish political work and Party leadership, as well as the army's assigned tasks in socialist construction, mass work, and militia organization. While no minutes of the Lushan discussions are available, the speeches of P'eng Teh-huai and T'an Cheng at the Eighth Party Congress two years earlier revealed the two men's concern that Party control not be allowed to impair "individual responsibility" in command and that "guerrilla habits" not undermine discipline and impede modernization. However, they also warned against uncritical borrowing of "foreign military experience" and urged a uniquely Chinese approach to military development. See *Eighth National Congress of the Communist Party of*

ever, this opposition is not to be equated with the recent, sweeping charge that P'eng was all along a "careerist" who had "usurped" his position in the army to advance a full-fledged revisionist and "bourgeois military line," calling for "modernization at the expense of revolution-ization," regarding the role of man in modern warfare as secondary to that of "technique, steel, and machines," and "nullifying political work in the army." [42] Although there may be an element of truth in some of these charges (for example, that P'eng sought to maintain a balance be-tween political and military requirements, that he wished to modernize PLA organization and capabilities, that he valued Soviet assistance), it is only by gross distortion of the evidence that P'eng is made to appear, in retrospect, a thoroughly deceitful and disloyal lieutenant, bent on abandoning the PLA's revolutionary traditions, Party leadership, and Maoist doctrines and on turning the army into "a tool for bringing about the restoration of capitalism."

Perhaps the best evidence of P'eng's dissent in the area of military affairs is to be found in issues of the secret army periodical *Kung-tso T'ung-hsün* (Work Bulletin) covering the first half of 1961.[43] Individual numbers of this journal, which was published by the PLA's General Political Department, charge that P'eng Teh-huai, Huang K'o-ch'eng, Hung Hsueh-chih, and other, unnamed officers (notably, "XX") ad-vocated a "bourgeois military line" (nowhere fully defined), violated Mao's principles of army-building and combat, took a "simple military viewpoint," instituted "warlordism" (maltreating troops and straining relations between officers and men), and practiced "dogmatism" (in particular, by fostering "superstitious belief in everything foreign and free transplantation of raw foreign things"). More specifically, one or another of them was accused of neglecting the study of Mao's thoughts (the General Political Department, for example, was said to have failed to give adequate support to the army's Political Academy), delaying the compilation of native Chinese military manuals for two years after Mao

---

China, Vol. 2, *Speeches,* Foreign Languages Press (Peking, 1956) pp. 32–37, 41–43, and 259–278.

[42] See, for example, the following articles: "Let Us Go Forward Triumphantly Along Chairman Mao's Proletarian Line of Army Building," *Hung Ch'i,* No. 12 (August 1, 1967); "Principal Crimes of P'eng Teh-huai," *ibid.* (August 17, 1967); and "Settle Accounts with P'eng Teh-huai," *Jen-min Jih-pao,* August 17, 1967.

[43] Translated and edited in J. Chester Cheng, *The Politics of the Chinese Red Army* (Stanford, 1966).

(at an enlarged meeting of the Military Affairs Committee in 1958) had ordered them, and slighting Party organization in the army (especially at the company level), thereby creating a "general atmosphere of perfunctory service and indifference." [44]

It is extremely difficult to evaluate the accuracy of these accusations as they applied to P'eng and others who were dismissed after Lushan. For the most part, the charges in the 1961 periodical appear as fragmentary and tendentious remarks without specificity and concreteness. They may well exaggerate the degree of guilt, deliberately using P'eng and the other dissidents as scapegoats for the PLA's manifest defects and weaknesses—particularly in political organization, training, and discipline— in the wake of the disastrous Leap Forward. Still, they present a much less sweeping indictment than has appeared in commentaries published subsequently during the Cultural Revolution.

It is hard to believe, however, that P'eng should have been an exponent of a thorough-going bourgeois "military professionalism" and at the same time have adopted—in opposition to Mao, allegedly—a "completely passive attitude" towards military planning and preparedness (the negation of the Maoist "active defense"), paid little or no attention to the building of air, naval, and even ground forces, and neglected both the manufacture of conventional arms and the advancement of science and technology.

Conceivably, one so desirous of "regularization and modernization" could have become overly dependent on Soviet techniques and arms assistance. But it is at least questionable that a person of P'eng's nationalist pride and professional judgment would, as was charged, have opposed the creation of "an independent and complete network of modern national defense industries" and refused to endorse the development of a Chinese advanced weapons program (including atomic and hydrogen bombs and intercontinental missiles), particularly as Sino-Soviet relations worsened after 1958. (He may, however, have objected to the excessive pace of the efforts to develop these indigenous capabilities.) Still more improbable is it that P'eng and his supporters were engaged in a plot with Khrushchev to overthrow CCP leadership and set up a "revisionist" regime in China. This charge, based on inferences that go far beyond the facts adduced, is incompatible with P'eng's long record of loyal service to Mao and the Party.

[44] See *Kung-tso T'ung-hsün*, Nos. 2, 3, 8, 24, 26, and 29, *ibid.*

Recent attacks against P'eng have made vague and unsubstantiated references to his "illicit relations with foreign countries."[45] This allegation, however, did not appear in the indictment—a remarkably detailed one—of the censure resolution passed by the Eighth Plenum on August 16, 1959 (as published eight years later). Indeed, the closest the resolution came to identifying P'eng's attitude toward the U.S.S.R. was to quote his aforementioned observation that, considering the economic consequences of the Leap Forward "if the Chinese workers and peasants were not as good as they are, a Hungarian incident would have occurred in China, and it would have been necessary to invite Soviet troops in." The statement, if authentic, would seem to reveal P'eng as delivering a warning to prevent Soviet intervention rather than suggesting that he was secretly conspiring to foster such intervention. Moreover, available issues of the secret military journal *Kung-tso T'ung hsün,* though critical of the PLA's excessive imitation of "foreign countries" (presumably the U.S.S.R.) during P'eng's leadership,[46] nowhere suggest that he or any of the other condemned generals conspired with Khrushchev or had improper contacts with Soviet officials. Nor have similar innuendoes of conspiracy been substantiated by Peking's quotation, in anti-Soviet polemics of 1963 and 1964, of statements attributed to Khrushchev which expressed friendship and sympathy for unnamed dissident Chinese leaders ("anti-Party elements," in Peking's terminology) who had courageously criticized the Leap Forward policies.

Probably the most important source of evidence remaining to support the notion of P'eng's culpability in his contacts with Soviet officials is the celebrated article by David Charles that appeared in *The China Quarterly* of October–December 1961. As has been pointed out, Charles' account is based largely on reports of two rounds of confidential briefings given to CCP members and "selected cadres" after P'eng's dismissal. Subsequent evidence has tended to support the authenticity of charges contained in the first round. Yet Charles admits that it was only in the later briefings, "which coincided with the exacerbation of Sino-Soviet relations in the summer of 1960," that "selected cadres were told about P'eng Teh-huai's contacts with the Soviet leadership—an aspect of the case which had been concealed [if it existed] in the earlier general briefing."[47] The coincidence between the dramatically widening Sino-Soviet rift in mid-

---

[45] See, for example, "From the Defeat of P'eng Teh-huai," *ibid.*
[46] See Nos. 26 and 29 (July 13 and August 1, 1961, respectively).
[47] "The Dismissal of Marshal P'ing Teh-huai," p. 65.

1961 and the sudden revelation of P'eng's "illicit relations," seen against the fact that no such allegation was raised in either the Lushan censure resolution (even in its present form) or *Kung-tso T'ung-hsün,* suggests the possibility that this charge was invented ex post facto, or greatly exaggerated on the basis of very tenuous evidence, to bolster Peking's case against Moscow and ensure a firm base of cadre support for it in China.

The hypothesis that P'eng conspired with Khrushchev to overthrow Mao has also been argued from a rather strained interpretation of some of his public statements prior to 1959 and from circumstantial evidence of contacts with Soviet officials in the course of official journeys abroad. Thus, P'eng's praise of the Soviet armed forces in 1957 as a model for the modernization of the PLA is sometimes cited as evidence of his anti-Maoist bias (his objection, for instance, to Mao's stress on the importance of men over weapons). However, P'eng's words seem perfectly appropriate and anything but disloyal when one recalls that they were uttered in the context of the Sino-Soviet agreement on assistance in nuclear and military technology, concluded in 1957, which Mao presumably also favored at the time. Besides, as pointed out earlier, Mao was still willing to sing the praises of the Soviet Union as late as 1957.

P'eng Teh-huai's seven-week "military goodwill mission" to the Warsaw Pact nations in the spring of 1959 inevitably put him in contact with Soviet leaders, but no evidence has been adduced that he conspired with them against Mao. In the absence of hard evidence one can, of course, speculate endlessly about the possibility of "illicit relations." Such charges, however, have often been grossly exaggerated by the Chinese Communists, as in the case of spy charges against American missionaries and, more recently, Indian diplomats. Moreover, not only would treasonable activity have been out of character for P'eng, but he also was probably realistic enough to calculate accurately the limitations and dangers of disloyal connivance with Soviet officials. Without wishing to rule out once and for all the *possibility* of P'eng Teh-huai's involvement with the Soviets, this writer believes that until we have better evidence to support such a hypothesis, there are good reasons for preferring a less sweeping interpretation of the affair.

Whatever may have been the true nature of P'eng Teh-huai's dissent at Lushan, and whatever the cause of the subsequent purge, the incident created a severe test of the regime's cohesion and resiliency. It was as much in the spirit of prophecy as of admonition, as it turns out, that a contemporary *Jen-min Jih-pao* editorial, drawing upon the lessons of great heresies of the past (notably those of Kautsky, Plekanov, and Ch'en Tu-hsiu), warned that proletarian revolutionaries could always "degenerate" into bourgeois revolutionaries.[48] The top leaders, though profoundly shaken, quickly closed ranks and retained their essential unity; affirming the correctness of the regime's general policy orientation, they continued to alter its more radical and unworkable features.

During 1960 and 1961, as economic conditions worsened, the regime was forced to retreat further from the Leap Forward program and to relax controls over society. Successive years of bad harvests and inept management had wiped out earlier agricultural surpluses earmarked for investment and left severe food shortages and the threat of widespread famine. Plans for rapid industrialization were shattered in mid-1960 as Soviet technical assistance was precipitously withdrawn and scarce hard currency went into wheat imports for food-deficit areas.

In the first half of the year, there had been a momentary resurgence of the Leap Forward, with the renewal of mass labor campaigns and, in some areas, the recollectivization of private plots and the reopening of communal mess halls. In March 1960—according to charges aired in the Cultural Revolution—Mao Tse-tung drafted a document known as the "Anshan Steel Constitution" (*An-kang Hsien-fa*). It laid down "five fundamental principles for socialist industry," stressing such things as political leadership, reinforcement of Party guidance, and the promotion of mass movements in the operation of factories and mines. By the fall of 1960, however, this revival of the Leap Forward had again proved extremely disappointing, the early harvests having been even poorer than those of 1959.

In January 1961, the Ninth Plenum of the Central Committee, while continuing to mouth the empty clichés of a vanished utopian confidence, adopted a sober and realistic policy aimed at recovery and consolidation. Agriculture was given priority over industry; primary responsibility for management was shifted downward from the commune to the production

---

[48] *Jen-min Jih-pao,* September 1, 1959. This theme may have been a reflection of Mao's thinking at Lushan. Recent accounts of the session quote him as saying: "This struggle at Lushan is a class struggle, a continuation of the life-and-death struggle between the two major antagonistic classes—the bourgeoisie and the proletariat." Observing that it had raged throughout the last decade of "socialist revolution," he predicted that it would continue in Party and nation for another twenty to fifty years. "In short," he concluded, "the struggle will cease only when classes die out completely." ("From the Defeat of P'eng Teh-huai," *Hung Ch'i,* No. 13 [August 17, 1967].)

brigade and finally to the production team; and material incentives such as private plots and free markets were increasingly employed to stimulate output.

In September 1961, according to recent accusations, "the handful of top capitalist authorities in the Party" illegally published erroneous new directives for industry known as the "Seventy Articles of Industry" (literally, the draft of a "Work Regulation for State-Operated Industrial Enterprises"). The new draft allegedly ignored the thought of Mao, contravened the principles of his "Anshan Steel Constitution," and de-emphasized the class struggle, treating industrial enterprises as primarily "economic organizations," and advocating such concepts as "production first," technology, material incentives, worker safety, and "plant management by experts" (excluding ordinary workers).

This condemnation, like other criticisms of its kind, entirely ignored the policy changes wrought by the Ninth Plenum, to whose decisions Mao and even members of his present coterie have not specifically taken exception; it judged guilt or innocence by Party criteria that were valid (and accepted by the "top capitalist-roaders") in earlier or later periods. The "Seventy Articles" (to which only fragmentary and probably distorted references appear in the recent indictments) would seem to have been squarely in line with the orientation announced by the Ninth Plenum, just as Mao's "Anshan Steel Constitution" was consonant with the Party line prevailing in March 1960. The same kind of rebuttal can be applied to the more familiar charge that, after 1961, Liu Shao-ch'i and others advocated the "three-self, one guarantee" system (*san tzu i pao*), favoring the extension of private plots and free markets as well as an increase in the number of small enterprises exercising sole responsibility for their own profit and loss, and fixing or guaranteeing the fulfillment of production quotas based on the individual household. Not only does this charge distort Liu's position to make it appear that he favored an out-and-out "restoration of capitalism" (rather than a few limited and temporary tactical concessions to stave off imminent economic disaster), but it completely ignores two facts: that at the time of the Ninth Plenum Mao was, after all, Chairman of the Central Committee and that even subsequently he never condemned that session or its actions.[49]

---

[49] The above-mentioned charges in regard to Mao's "Anshan Steel Constitution" and the "Seventy Articles of Industry" appeared in a series of articles published in *Pei-ching Jih-pao* (Peking Daily) of July 15 and 16, 1967. The *san tzu i pao* charge against Liu was developed, among other places, in an article in *Hung Ch'i*, No. 13

Despite the economic reverses of 1960–1961, there was no discernible disposition in the top leadership to seek salvation through a return to the Soviet model or a rapprochement with Moscow. As in the mid-1950's, China would find her own way, building anew through dogged self-reliance.

Relaxation of economic controls was accompanied by a more tolerant attitude toward intellectuals. In August 1961, Ch'en Yi told graduates of Peking's institutes of higher learning that in ordinary schools (as opposed to political academies) demands for indoctrination and manual labor should not be allowed to interfere unduly with specialized studies, needed for their contribution to socialist construction. If one wanted to ride in an airplane, the skill of the pilot would count for more than his political purity.[50] (One wonders what Ch'en's fate might have been today had he used the metaphor of the helmsman, so closely identified with Mao—"our Great Helmsman"—in the Cultural Revolution.) Not surprisingly, many intellectuals took advantage of this atmosphere of greater freedom to engage in subtle, sophisticated sniping at the leaders and policies they held responsible for China's economic catastrophe and international isolation. It is difficult even now to be completely sure about the extent of this criticism, for most of the incriminating evidence has been furnished, belatedly, by the prosecution in the Cultural Revolution and consists only in incomplete quotations alleged to contain offensive double meanings, many of these hidden in historical allegory.[51]

(August 17, 1967) and in the fourth instalment of a series attacking Liu that was published by *Chieh-fang Chün Pao* and excerpted by *NCNA* October 25, 1967. For a discussion of the brief resurgence of the Leap Forward in 1960 and the retreat from it in 1961, see Marion Larsen, "China's Agriculture Under Communism," in *An Economic Profile of Mainland China,* Studies Prepared for the Joint Economic Committee, U.S. Congress, Vol. 1 (Government Printing Office, Washington, D.C., 1967) pp. 220–221.

[50] *Chung-kuo Ch'ing-nien (China Youth)*, No. 17 (September 1, 1961). Another, related theme that began to be sounded at that time was the importance of restoring some balance between demands for physical and mental labor, on the one hand, and the human body's need for rest, on the other—an idea largely ignored during the frenetic activity of the Leap Forward, to the detriment of health and productivity. As Fu Lien-chang (once Mao's trusted personal physician) pointed out in an article to youth, "the alternation of studying and work with recreation and rest is the necessary law governing human life." (*Chung-kuo Ch'ing-nien,* No. 19–20 [October 1961].)

[51] In the present atmosphere of paranoid reexamination of former writings and statements, it is sometimes forgotten that, on the key issue of attitudes toward the position and thought of Mao, the "liberal" period of 1959–1962 exhibited a rising tide of public adulation. Thus, the Hong Kong correspondent of *The Economist,*

The criticism appears to have been most acute in Peking, where prominent writers, like the historian Wu Han (who was also deputy mayor), and Party propaganda officials such as Teng T'o, Liao Mo-sha, and Li Chi employed periodicals and newspapers controlled by the Municipal Party Committee to launch their veiled attacks. Thus, Wu Han's series of essays and plays published between 1959 and 1962 on the heroic but much-abused Ming dynasty officials Hai Jui and Yu Chien were later interpreted by the arbiters of the Cultural Revolution as a defense of P'eng Teh-huai, an attack on Mao, and a demand that unfairly dismissed officials be reinstated.[52]

---

writing in the fall of 1960, noted a dramatic rise in "the cult of Mao" that had begun early the preceding year: "As the ideological dispute with Moscow waxed," he observed, "so did the deification of the omiscient Mao gather weight and momentum. And so presumably will it continue to do." (October 1, 1960, p. 53.)

[52] In mid-August 1967, during a renewed Maoist attack on Liu Shao-ch'i, the charge was raised that in 1962 "the Khrushchev of China" had encouraged P'eng Teh-huai to write an 80,000-word statement aimed at effecting a reversal of his Lushan censure and dismissal. According to an article in *Hung Ch'i*, No. 13 (August 17, 1967), Liu "openly tried to reverse the verdict" at an enlarged work conference of the Central Committee held in January 1962, at which he defended P'eng's dissent, observing that much of it was in accord with the facts, and deplored the struggle against P'eng and his associates as one that had overstepped its limits. Still more recent Maoist sources maintain that, in the course of the "vigorous struggle," Liu launched a "frantic attack" against Mao, declaring that "to oppose Chairman Mao is only to oppose one individual" and advocating the principle of open opposition within the Party as well as among the people. He allegedly was immediately supported by Lu Ting-i, who recalled that even the ancient emperors had tolerated opposition, as was shown by the case of Wei Cheng, a dissident statesman of the T'ang dynasty whose biography Liu had recently ordered to be published. Afterward Liu was said to have mobilized his supporters and intensified his schemes to usurp Party and state leadership, assisted in this effort by P'eng Chen, who spread the suggestion that Chairman Mao be asked "to make his exit." (*Jen-min Jih-pao*, November 9, 1967.)

If these charges are true, and if Liu's motive in urging P'eng Teh-huai's reinstatement was actually to challenge Mao's authority—as opposed to honoring the Lushan censure resolution by heeding its admonition to manifest "an attitude of great sincerity and warmth" toward P'eng to "help him recognize and rectify his mistake," which would have been good Maoist doctrine—there might have been good cause for Mao's alarm. The plays and operas on the theme of Hai Jui's unjust dismissal from office, for example, could then be seen as part of a deliberate plot to prepare public opinion for P'eng Teh-huai's restoration. Similarly, the Central Committee's relaxation of economic controls in the early 1960s—permitting free rural markets, private garden plots, and other incentives through which to raise production—could be construed as evidence of a conspiracy to restore capitalism.

The accusations also indicate, however, that Liu did not succeed in promoting P'eng Teh-huai's exoneration and restoration of power. If Mao and his followers

Similarly, essays and newspaper columns authored or co-authored by Teng T'o during this period were viewed in 1966 as having slyly satirized the Leap Forward for its boasts and illusions, praised the unyielding spirit of righteous officials unjustly dismissed, deprecated before all the world the "empty talk" of "East Wind prevailing over West," and, worst of all, parodied Mao as a victim of "amnesia," a man who monopolized decisions, rejected good advice, and needed a "complete rest," or cure, by a blow to the head from "a specially made club." [53]

From the viewpoint of those whose suspicions were aroused, the covert, esoteric criticisms of the intellectuals may well have seemed less serious than the toleration—even protection—of those critics by the Peking CCP's first secretary, P'eng Chen, and the Party's central propaganda apparatus under Lu Ting-i and his deputy, Chou Yang. Although these men remained unexceptionably hard-line and pro-Mao in their public statements and behavior, they were ultimately accountable for the misdeeds of those over whom they held authority. Indeed, Chou Yang, for one, was accused during the Cultural Revolution of having acted hypocritically, in remaining publicly upright while privately condemning the "subjective idealism" of the Great Leap, defending "revisionist" writers, and damping down the rising adulation of Mao.[54]

---

were thus strong enough to thwart Liu's alleged bid, one wonders why they did not at the time make any move to expose the conspiracy and curb Liu's power. Instead, Liu enjoyed a role of increasing prominence and responsibility with Mao's acquiescence if not his blessing. If Liu did attempt in some way (perhaps now exaggerated) to rehabilitate P'eng Teh-huai or to encourage greater freedom of opposition (but not "excessive struggle") within the Party in 1962, his actions evidently were not regarded by Mao and his supporters as so seriously offensive or threatening to their authority as to require any overt response.

[53] Excerpts from Teng T'o's writings singled out for condemnation may be found in Yao Wen-yüan, "On the 'Three-Family Village'," and in Lin Chieh et al. (comp.), "Teng T'o's 'Evening Chats at Yenshan' Is Anti-Party and Anti-Socialist Double-Talk," originally published in May 1966 and reprinted in *The Great Socialist Cultural Revolution in China*, Vols. 1 and 2 (Peking, 1966). Many of the materials concerning the Wu Han episode have been collected and translated as "The Case of Wu Han in the Cultural Revolution," *Chinese Studies in History and Philosophy*, Vol. 2, No. 1 (Fall 1968), No. 3 (Spring 1969); Vol. 3, No. 1 (Fall 1969), and No. 2 (Winter 1968–1970).

[54] K. S. Karol, who had had a lengthy interview with him in the spring of 1965, believes that this indictment against Chou Yang contains "puzzling polemical falsifications." He reports that in their interview Chou had "sharply attacked" many of the very ideas that are now being imputed to him: "He is accused, for example," writes Karol, "of having considered the 'bourgeois realism of the nineteenth century' as the summit of the arts, while in fact he told [Karol] exactly the opposite. It is

As regards the liberal phase of the early 1960s, it should be noted that the accused critics have stoutly protested their innocence of deliberate wrongdoing. Innocent or guilty, the subtle criticisms for which they were blamed were not likely at that time to find a very wide audience, since considerable sophistication would have been required to translate their hidden meanings. Though much is made of them now, they did not then provoke either acknowledgment or rebuttal from those supposedly attacked. More important, they had no perceptible effect on the orientation or policies of the regime, whatever may have been their influence on individuals.

Nevertheless, it is entirely possible that Mao—alerted perhaps by his censorious political secretary, Ch'en Po-ta, and his termagant wife, Chiang Ch'ing—suspected the critics and, grievously wounded by their personal barbs, became obsessed with what he believed to be their potential threat to his own power and place in history and to the orientation of the regime itself. Such an obsession would have coincided with the conviction of other leaders, around mid-1962, that a general collapse had been averted and some progress was being made toward recovery—a prospect which presented an opening for the gradual reimposition of tight social controls. Many of the top leaders besides Mao probably thought such a move desirable, alarmed as they were by the "spontaneous tendencies to capitalism" they detected among the peasantry in the course of the decentralization of collective farming and the acquisition of private plots and sideline production, and found reflected also in a rash of articles by urban economists advocating price and profit mechanisms as a basis for industrial planning and management.[55]

claimed that he was in agreement with Ting Ling during the Yenan controversies of 1942 and that he was her protector during the Hundred Flowers crisis of 1957, although in fact he was her main opponent. He is presented to the world as an admirer of Khrushchev, although in fact he talked to [Karol] about the former Soviet premier with complete contempt." Indeed, Chou, in talking with Karol, seemed to anticipate themes of the Cultural Revolution when he condemned the rigidity of the Soviet regime for having stifled the growth of proletarian culture in Russia. He criticized the CPSU, much as Mao might have, for entertaining the "absurd theory" that the class struggle and contradictions had ended with nationalization of the means of production. Such an analysis, he contended, had led the Soviets to an art that was "neither realistic nor socialistic—[but] simply a version of bourgeois art." K. S. Karol, *China: The Other Communism* (New York, 1966) pp. 276–277, 284–285.

[55] Probably the most notable of these articles was entitled "A Tentative Discussion on Economic Accounting of Industrial Enterprises," and signed by two obscure

A lamentable paucity of reliable data makes it impossible to determine the extent of sympathy, if any, among individual leaders for the relatively liberal economic views aired in the first part of 1962. The noticeable cessation thereafter of any free discussion of this kind, however, and the firm action taken by the Tenth Plenum in September to tighten controls and restrict "capitalist tendencies," suggest the absence of any serious deviation within the top leadership from the basic goals and principles of Communist economic management. Although most of the limited economic freedoms of the earlier period were to be retained, the leadership appeared determined to curb any further relaxation of controls over collectivized agriculture or small-scale industry and commerce. True, one of the charges heard during the Cultural Revolution was that Liu Shao-ch'i, Teng Hsiao-p'ing (referred to as "the other top capitalist-roader"), and others were doing everything in their power in 1962 to restore capitalist agricultural and industrial policies; indeed, Teng Hsiao-p'ing, speaking in July 1962 at a meeting of the Communist Youth League's Central Committee that was also attended by P'eng Chen, Lu Ting-i, and Yang Shang-k'un, was said to have advocated a return to an individual peasant economy, declaring that "black or white, if cats can catch mice, they are all right." But when Mao criticized these views (which may actually have gone little beyond a reiteration of certain "compromise" features of the economic policy then in effect), Teng reportedly was "scared out of his wits," ordered the offending remarks deleted from the minutes of the meeting, urged his hearers not to spread false information, and confessed: "I forgot to stress the question of collective economy. I did not mean to invent some theory to reject collective economy." [56]

At the Tenth Plenum of the Central Committee, in September 1962, Mao, who is said to have convened that meeting, resumed a more active leadership role. He condemned "bourgeois" trends not only in literature and art but also in the economy, speaking out especially against the restoration of limited private ownership and incentives in agriculture, and he urged more intensive political education for youth to maintain the purity of the Revolution. To counter the objectionable trends and ensure the desired influence among the masses, Mao called for a nationwide campaign of "class struggle" and "socialist education," and he subse-

---

economists, Yang Jun-jui and Li Hsun. Published in *Jen-min Jih-pao*, July 19, 1962, and translated in *SCMP* 2817, September 12, 1962.

[56] Radio Peking (Domestic Service) December 3, 1967; *Jen-min Jih-pao*, February 10, 1968.

quently gave instructions for the launching of a mass movement for socialist education in the rural areas.[57]

According to sources associated with the Cultural Revolution—though these may border on the apocryphal—Mao also used the Tenth Plenum to let it be known (privately, at least) that he considered himself the target of subtle literary attacks. He allegedly said that "The use of fiction for carrying out anti-Party activities is a great invention" and intimated that P'eng Teh-huai—or whoever was writing in his behalf—was one of the great "inventors." [58] Mao must have been gratified by the session's final communiqué, which acknowledged the need to continue the class struggle throughout the long period of transition to Communism, decried such persistent bourgeois influences in society as the force of old habits and spontaneous tendencies toward capitalism, and urged vigilance against attempts by reactionary elements to restore capitalism.

In addition to the communiqué, the Central Committee promulgated a resolution in September 1962 designed to strengthen the collective economy through the communes and to further agricultural production, and to these ends issued a revision of the "Sixty Regulations" governing rural work, which had been adopted in the more liberal atmosphere of 1961. A text of the revised draft was published in Taiwan in May 1965 by the National Security Bureau, Republic of China.[59]

Although the Tenth Plenum marked the end of the liberal period brought on by the failure of the Leap Forward, the tightening of controls in the years following was not accompanied by radical shifts in the regime's policies. From 1963 onward, the most remarkable change, at a more basic level, was the rapidly rising emphasis on ideology, particularly as personified in Mao and crystallized in his thought. Ideology was used both as an instrument of social rectification and as a way of stimulating the masses to greater efforts toward the attainment of revolutionary goals. Beyond this, in the face of continuing intractable problems in the objective situation, and in the absence of any new and promising solutions, the great ideological revival came more and more to serve as a kind of cosmic panacea. If carried to its logical conclusion, such an approach became a threat to the tenuous balance between ideal and practical

[57] "Struggle Between the Two Roads in China's Countryside," *Hung Ch'i*, No. 16 (November 23, 1967).

[58] See Wen Hung-chun *et al.*, "Pao-wei Yenan," *Jen-min Jih-pao*, November 12, 1967.

[59] "Nung-ts'un Jen-min Kung-she Kung-tso T'iao-li Hsin-cheng Ts'ao-an" (Revised Draft of Work Regulations for Rural People's Communes).

components in the regime's orientation—a balance that had been restored in the early 1960s after it had been affected by the disastrous course
of the manic Leap Forward.[60] Leaders who had been able to unite in
approving the unprecedented shift leftward in 1958 did not necessarily
feel disposed, after their brush with disaster, to seek national salvation
through a new campaign aimed at reviving the class struggle and getting
the masses to give their hearts to Chairman Mao. Even the more chastened
and realistic among them, however, probably were willing to support
the revival in its early stages, be it because of their abiding faith in
indoctrination and an inability to suggest anything better, or be it,
simply, because Mao demanded it and because concessions in the "cultural" area appeared to them as a way of limiting interference elsewhere.

Moreover, Lin Piao, upon assuming P'eng Teh-huai's position as Minister of Defense, had plunged immediately into efforts to strengthen political and ideological work in the PLA, advancing slogans such as the
"Four Firsts," which emphasized the human element, politics, ideology,
and the living of ideology. Although intensive work toward the achievement of a nuclear capability continued, it was a distinctly separate effort
with little, if any, impact on the general trend away from military professionalism. Lin repeatedly called on members of the armed forces to
study and live by the thoughts of Mao. In 1961 he had a small volume
of the Chairman's sayings compiled and printed for use in the army—
the precursor of the little red-covered book later waved by millions of
chanting Red Guards.[61] In the controlled military environment, the

---

[60] An indication of the attempt to restore the balance during the liberal "recovery"
period was the action of the Ninth Plenum, which moderated the radical economic
policies of the Leap Forward and at the same time called for a major rectification
campaign. (See *Jen-min Jih-pao,* January 21, 1961.) This campaign, however, which
in somewhat vague terms was ordered to proceed "stage by stage and area by area"
throughout the nation, did not prove to have the impact of the later "socialist education movement."

[61] Ironically, the later volume included a statement in which Mao spoke favorably
of Liu Shao-ch'i, a passage that was deleted only in the second, revised edition of
the book, in May 1967, over a year after the Cultural Revolution had publicly
erupted. In looking back to the origins of the Cultural Revolution, it is also interesting to note that a call for the posting of *ta-tzu-pao* and for a course of "unity-
criticism-unity" was issued in the PLA at the same time that Lin Piao launched the
army's campaign to "study the thought of Mao Tse-tung." That campaign was based
on a resolution of October 20, 1960 (for the "Strengthening of Political and Ideological Work in the Army"), which Lin had guided through an enlarged meeting
of the Military Affairs Committee. (See *Kung-tso T'ung-hsün,* No. 3 [January 7,
1966] in Cheng, *The Politics of the Chinese Red Army,* pp. 66, 74, 77.)

emphasis on Maoist faith and works was rapidly intensified, although it is fair to assume that skepticism, even if suppressed, continued to be felt in some quarters of so vast and varied an institution as the military. After a brief relaxation of controls during the darkest period of the economic slump, the army rapidly put "politics in command" and, beginning in December 1963, was held up as a model for the entire nation to emulate. Soon afterward, a program was launched to create PLA-style political departments in all industrial, financial, and commercial units of the government, from the national ministries down to local enterprises, and to have a parallel structure of departments for economic affairs at all levels of the Party.[62] The army under Lin Piao thus became the most powerful institutional convert to the new, revivalist ideological approach.

Party and government were less positive in their response. Besides enjoying more freedom of expression than did soldiers under military discipline, the civilian personnel represented a higher level of educational attainment and, by and large, a greater degree of spiritual independence. While reiterating dutifully the outworn slogans of the Great Leap, administrative spokesmen began to hint that "policy" errors, as well as bad weather and the perfidious Soviets, had contributed to its failure.[63] In the countryside the "class struggle" campaign lagged, and, despite sporadic and sometimes intensive rectification drives—directed particularly against the hapless rural cadres who were charged with corruption and inefficiency—there seemed little disposition to abolish the earlier concessions to private incentives. In some areas, the ambitious attempt to politicize the nation's economic and commercial organs apparently ran into difficulties, as ministers and managers refused to accept the new cadres (often soldiers) sent out to create the PLA-type political departments and, instead, installed their own trusted personnel in these posts.[64] It is conceivable that Mao and some of his most devoted disciples (for example, Lin Piao and Chiang Ch'ing) may also have been disturbed— and personally resentful—over another "secular" trend, represented by

[62] See discussion in Chalmers Johnson, "Lin Piao's Army and Its Role in Chinese Society," Part II, Current Scene, Vol. 4, No. 14 (July 15, 1966) pp. 4-6.

[63] This admission appeared publicly in a Jen-min Jih-pao editorial of December 4, 1963. Individual exhaustion, disillusionment, and self-interest were added to an already growing process of bureaucratization and routinization in the civilian organs, rendering them less keenly responsive to Maoist revolutionary goals.

[64] Red Guard sources have leveled this charge at, among others, the venerable T'an Chen-lin (Minister of Agriculture) and the conspicuously successful Yü Ch'iu-li (Minister of Petroleum).

the rising prestige of Liu Shao-ch'i, his upgrading of the chairmanship of the Republic, and the more prominent role assumed by his wife, Wang Kuang-mei, as "first lady." [65]

In the winter of 1963–1964, the regime, spurred by an insistent Mao, responded to all the frustrations and pressures that had arisen in the objective situation with a marked renewal of emphasis on ideological education and purification. A nationwide "socialist education" campaign was aimed at reeducating the entire population in socialist ideology, which, in addition to stressing the "class struggle," was increasingly identified with the thought of Mao Tse-tung. The masses were exhorted

[65] Liu's position as heir apparent to Mao was greatly enhanced by the republication, in 1962, of "How To Be a Good Communist" (perhaps better translated "On the Cultivation of Communist Party Members"), which Liu had originally written at Yenan in 1939. The unprecedented prominence and wide dissemination accorded this work in 1962 suggested an attempt to put Liu almost on a par with Mao as a leading theoretician of the Chinese revolution, with Liu the architect of victory in the cities, and Mao the guiding genius in the countryside. While criticisms of Liu in the Cultural Revolution have since charged that the republication of this book (especially in the light of certain revisions incorporated in it) was deliberately designed to denigrate Mao, this is an extremely arbitrary interpretation and the very opposite of the impression left by Peking's official media at the time. To be sure, aspects of the work—such as the relatively moderate tone of the 1962 version, the soft-pedaling of "struggle," the condemnation of "dogmatism," and the exhortation to "self"-cultivation—can now be faulted on the basis of changed criteria. However, Liu's continuing veneration of Mao seems unquestionable, as two American specialists pointed out at the time, when they wrote that the revised work "showed signs of increased deference to Mao, suggesting a deliberate intent on the author's part to profess his personal subordination to Mao's authority. Thus, Liu inserted many quotations from Mao—some of them in poor context—which had not been in the original Yenan lectures, and he also left out a statement he had made in the earlier text to the effect that in the CCP 'we . . . do not idolize anybody.'" (A. A. Cohen and C. F. Steffins, "Disillusionment Within the Ranks," *Problems of Communism*, Vol. 12, No. 3 [May–June 1963] pp. 12–13.)

In a recently published self-criticism, Liu himself allegedly said that the 1962 reprint of his revised treatise was undertaken "because some people had it carried forward and because a certain person had revised the book on [Liu's] behalf." The text of Liu's confession was contained in a Peking *ta-tzu-pao* of August 2, a résumé of which was published in *Mainichi Shimbun*, August 3, 1967. Still later, Red Guard sources declared that Liu had falsely identified the "certain person" responsible for the second edition of his book as K'ang Sheng. They pronounced this a malicious lie because in January 1962, K'ang allegedly dissolved a special "compilation committee" which the Party's Central Secretariat (at Teng Hsiao-p'ing's instigation) had established a year earlier specifically to edit the "Selected Works of Liu Shao-ch'i." This last charge, which cannot be verified, appeared in the Canton *Wen-ko T'ung-hsün (Cultural Revolution Bulletin)* of December 11, 1967 translated in *SCMP* 4097, January 11, 1968, pp. 5–7.

to study and apply Mao's thought in the manner of the PLA's "ordinary extraordinary" hero, Lei Feng.[66] The lessons learned were to be applied in "three great revolutionary movements"—the class struggle and the struggles for production and scientific experimentation.[67] Mao had warned that only through these struggles could China guard against the evils of bureaucratism, revisionism, and dogmatism.[68] In his view, there was a very real danger of a counterrevolutionary restoration that would ultimately lead to China's "changing color." [69]

The renewed emphasis on indoctrination was accompanied by a severe tightening of controls in the intellectual and cultural sphere. In the autumn of 1963, Chou Yang, deputy head of the CCP Propaganda Department, called upon intellectuals to struggle relentlessly against all expressions of dialectical unity, revisionism, and humanism. Under such admonitions a campaign of surprising intensity was unleashed against prominent philosophers, writers, and artists. In mid-1964, what had started as an apparent philosophical debate over differing interpretations of the concept of "contradictions" resulted in the furious condemnation of Yang Hsien-chen, a well-known Party theoretician, member of the Central

[66] For example, see the editorial "Endeavor to Learn Well the Thought of Mao Tse-tung," *Jen-min Jih-pao,* March 26, 1964. During the next two years a nationwide campaign unfolded for the study of Mao's thought, which came to be presented as a panacea for all human problems. In the course of the Cultural Revolution it was charged, however, that Liu Shao-ch'i and others were critical of the resumption of Mao study. Liu was said to have declared in 1964 that "formalism" and "oversimplification" were infecting the program. (See the third of seven articles in *Chieh-fang Chün Pao* attacking Liu, as excerpted by NCNA, Peking, October 12, 1967.) If authentic, these "slanderous" remarks of Liu's—undocumented phrases taken out of context—did not appreciably affect the rising adulation of Mao.

[67] *Jen-min Jih-pao,* January 1, 1964.

[68] See his draft of a "Resolution of the Central Committee of the Chinese Communist Party on Some Problems in Current Rural Work," May 20, 1963, as published in *Issues and Studies* (Taiwan), Vol. 2, No. 8 (May 1966) pp. 58–59. The passage containing that warning also was quoted in an article by Jen Li-hsin in *Jen-min Jih-pao,* May 21, 1967. It is interesting to observe that, although the above draft resolution—also known as the "ten-point decision"—was primarily designed to deal with concrete economic and cadre problems, it stressed the importance of ideological regeneration, containing this statement by Mao: "The correct thinking that is representative of the ideologically advanced class will develop into a material force to reform the society as well as the world once it comes into the grasp of the masses."

[69] See excerpt from Mao's "The Seven Well-written Documents of Chekiang Province Concerning the Cadres' Participation in Physical Labor," as quoted in "Khrushchev's Phoney Communism and Its Historical Lessons for the World," *Peking Review,* No. 29 (July 17, 1964) p. 26.

Committee, and former head of the Higher Party School. Yang was censured for his notion that "two combine into one" (instead of "one divides into two"), a concept said to neglect the proper Maoist emphasis on struggle and to leave the way open for reconciliation with class enemies and revisionists. The attack on Yang served at once to help define the philosophical basis for the new revolutionary struggle to ensure China's eternal "redness," and to underline the serious importance of the new drive—from which not even members of the Central Committee were to be immune. Subsequent campaigns cut down such prominent thinkers and essayists as Chou Ku-ch'eng, who had argued that art should transcend classes and reflect the entire "spirit of the age," and Feng Ting, who had deprecated the "cult of personality" and stressed the values of human happiness and tranquility, and they attacked among other celebrated literary figures Ouyang Shan, Hsia Yen, Shao Chuan-lin, Fan Hsing, and, ultimately, even the Minister of Culture, Shen Yen-ping (Mao Tun), who was not reappointed in 1965.

At the same time, measures were being taken to "reform" the substance of literature, art, and music. Although these efforts were not always well publicized at the time, we were informed in 1967: "In 1963, under the guidance of Chairman Mao himself, the revolution in literature and art was launched in China, marked mainly by the reform of the dramatic arts; *that was, in fact, the beginning of the Great Proletarian Cultural Revolution.*" [70] (Emphasis added.) Western music was banned outright. At the urging of Mao's wife, Chiang Ch'ing, a former Shanghai movie actress, the traditional Peking opera was rewritten in an effort to cut out "feudal" vestiges and highlight revolutionary mores and themes, an attempt that was later termed "a clarion call" of the Cultural Revolution and even "the great beginning" of it.[71] Ironically, one of the most vigorous and outspoken champions of the Chinese opera "reform" in 1964 was P'eng Chen, head of the CCP's Peking Municipal Committee. His political star rose rapidly thereafter, and in September he received the supreme accolade, official recognition as a "close comrade in arms" of Chairman Mao.

Progress in implementing the new Maoist ideology was evident in many areas. On June 30, 1964, *Hung Ch'i* spoke of "a big revolution on the

[70] *Jen-min Jih-pao,* January 1, 1967.
[71] See article in *Hung Ch'i,* No. 6 (February 1967), which also printed the text of a speech delivered the previous July by Chiang Ch'ing before a forum of artists and officials who were connected with a festival of the new opera in Peking.

cultural front." At the same time, there was talk of eliminating entirely the traditional intellectual, whose specialized knowledge was a product of book learning and who was divorced from physical labor. In August the Central Committee issued a directive on "Two Educational Systems and Two Systems of Labor," which called for the resumption of the work-study schools that had thrived early during the Leap Forward but had disappeared in 1959. In September a booklet entitled "A Great Revolution on the Cultural Front" went on sale throughout the country.[72]

Mao nevertheless remained dissatisfied with the pace of change and the less-than-universal fervor inspired by his revivalist approach to China's problems. He was troubled by reports of flagging enthusiasm, capitalist tendencies, and corruption among the rural population and cadres. He was particularly concerned about the revolutionary commitment and the stamina of the younger generation, inexperienced and untested in combat, to whom the present aging leadership would soon have to entrust the regime.[73] Indeed, he had begun to have doubts about the effectiveness, if not the reliability, of some elements within the Party and governmental leadership, especially in the propaganda apparatus.[74]

[72] Radio Peking (Domestic Service), September 5, 1964. In addition to editorials from *Hung Ch'i* and *Jen-min Jih-pao,* the booklet contained speeches by Ko Ch'ing-shih, P'eng Chen, and Lu Ting-i regarding cultural reforms in drama and the Peking opera.

[73] Interestingly, the swelling tide of concern over "revolutionary successors" in 1964 followed an important statement by U.S. Assistant Secretary of State Roger Hilsman, on December 13, 1963, which forecast a profound erosion of ideology in "the more sophisticated second echelon of leadership" in China. (*Department of State Bulletin,* January 6, 1964.) In January 1965, Mao frankly voiced his doubts and anxiety about the younger generation in an interview with the American journalist Edgar Snow. (See *The New Republic,* February 27, 1965, p. 23.) Recent comment in the Cultural Revolution has reiterated Peking's extreme sensitivity to U.S. expressions of hope, at about the time of Hilsman's speech, that "new elements" would emerge in China to "promote liberalization from inside the regime." (See, for example, an article attacking Lu Ting-i in *Jen-min Jih-pao,* November 9, 1967.)

[74] In September 1963, on the basis of four months' experience in the new phase of the "socialist education movement" inaugurated by Mao's "ten-point decision" of May 20 (see note 68 above), the Party's Central Committee issued a revised draft of that resolution, entitled "Some Concrete Policy Decisions on the Rural Socialist Education Movement." (For the text see *Issues and Studies,* Vol. 2, No. 9, June 1966.) The new draft referred to the May 20 resolution as a "great document" which still possessed "guiding authority"; it praised Mao's "analyses and instructions" on the continuing class struggle in socialist society, and explained the present revision as motivated solely by the desire to deal with concrete problems of policy that had been revealed by the experience of the intervening months. Accounts published in the Cultural Revolution, however, have since charged that the new draft was con-

As early as December 1963, if we may believe newly published sources, Mao had warned that a "handful" in the CCP were continuing to promote feudal art forms. Six months later he told the Chinese Federation of Literary and Art Circles that, ever since 1949, literary workers, in their associations and in "most of their publications," had failed to carry out the policies of the Party, had "acted as high and mighty bureaucrats," and had been divorced from the people and from the revolution; he added that "in recent years" they had even "slid to the verge of revisionism," threatening, in the absence of thorough reform, "at some future date to become groups like the Hungarian Petofi Club." [75] Mao's emphasis on deviations and threats in the cultural area—which, in view of the other pressing issues then confronting the regime, would seem to have been an inordinate preoccupation with a secondary problem—provides an important clue to his assessment of China's real ills and his ordering of priorities in prescribing the remedies. Just as the Petofi Club provided the ideological spark for the Hungarian revolution in

---

cocted by "the other top capitalist-roader" (Teng Hsiao-p'ing) in direct opposition to Mao's "ten-point decision." By employing "counterrevolutionary two-faced tactics" (as in adopting the approved slogans), Teng allegedly "negated the essential content" of Mao's concept of the class struggle, protecting capitalist elements while obstructing or attacking the masses, especially the poor and lower-middle-class peasants. He was accused of thus promoting a "bourgeois reactionary line which was 'left' in form but 'right' in essence" in order to "stamp out the flames of the socialist education movement" previously lit by Mao. (See "Struggle Between the Two Roads in China's Countryside," *Hung Ch'i,* No. 16 [November 23, 1967].) Presumably, the same or similar charges would apply to a second revised draft of the "ten-point decision," bearing the same title as the first, which was adopted by the Central Committee in September 1964. (Text in *Issues and Studies,* Vol. 1, No. 10, July 1965.)

Although a full evaluation of these charges will require further study and more information, these preliminary observations are possible: A comparison of the three drafts (May 1963, September 1963, and September 1964) does not in itself reveal any basic contradictions; it is possible to account for the differences in emphasis as well as for additions and changes in the later texts without accepting the present Maoist allegation that they were intended to scuttle the "socialist education movement" and promote the restoration of capitalism. Since even the latter-day Maoist critics admit that Teng and his associates employed a line which, though "right" in essence, was "left" in form, any confident judgment of the issue probably must await more and better evidence. In the meantime, it is worth noting that, whatever actual differences existed between Mao and other top leaders at the time as regards the rural socialist education movement, they concerned matters of cadre policy and ideology rather than economic issues.

[75] Excerpts quoted in "Fight To Safeguard the Dictatorship of the Proletariat," *Hung Ch'i,* No. 8 (May 1967).

1956, Mao feared that the existing ideological superstructure in China ("ideological" here connoting "political," "cultural," and "psychological"), unless brought into line with the revolutionary base of the socialist economy and society, would become the means for a restoration of capitalism. These thoughts were reflected in the important anti-Soviet polemic "On Khrushchev's Phoney Communism and Its Historical Lessons for the World," published in July 1964. This treatise, believed to have been penned by Mao himself, pointed to the alleged embourgeoisement of Soviet society in recent years as the path of degeneration into which China would also be drawn unless the people, profiting by the "negative example" of "Khrushchevite revisionism," prepared for a long and bitter struggle between socialism and capitalism and trained millions of successors to carry the revolution forward "from our highest organizations down to the grass roots." [76]

Although these doubts and anxieties were felt most acutely perhaps by Mao and his immediate circle, they probably were shared by those in the top leadership who were deeply disturbed by China's drifting and her inability to regain the rapid momentum of the 1950s. The result was a further shift toward the one-sided Maoist emphasis on indoctrination and purification. At the same time, despite the resistance noted above, the establishment of PLA-style political departments in the nation's economic and commercial offices continued and increasingly assumed the nature of a supplementary network paralleling the existing propaganda apparatus.

From mid-1964 onward, the regime carried on an intensive campaign to "cultivate revolutionary successors," focusing on the criteria for selecting worthy heirs and on their training and tempering through struggle and hardship. One of the most authoritative statements on the nature of this campaign came from An Tzu-wen, then the Director of the Central Committee's Organization Department. In language anticipating

[76] *Peking Review*, No. 29 (July 17, 1964) p. 26. ("On Khrushchev's Phoney Communism," originally appeared in *Hung Ch'i*, No. 13, and *Jen-min Jih-pao* of July 14, 1964—the two periodicals' ninth and final editorial comment on an open letter published by the CPSU a year earlier.) In addition to the prevailing general emphasis on purity of doctrine and the primacy of politics, the issue of political reliability and effectiveness within the leadership—as distinct from the masses—was becoming an increasingly prominent theme, as in this statement from a *Jen-min Jih-pao* editorial of August 3: "It is the nucleus of leadership that decides the direction for the advance of the revolutionary cause. Whether the nucleus of leadership of our Party and state at all levels consists of real proletarian revolutionaries or not is a decisive matter for the success and failure of our entire revolutionary cause."

that of the Cultural Revolution (which, ironically, he did not politically survive to see), An charged that even in the Party there were individuals who pretended to serve Marxism-Leninism but in reality opposed it, tolerating the notion of class compromise, undermining socialist literature, and hindering the socialization of agriculture. He concluded that the real test of a worthy successor was a person's attitude toward the proletariat and toward socialism in the struggle between two classes and two lines; it determined whether he was devoted to socialism or was in effect working for the "restoration of capitalism." [77]

In the summer of 1964, a decision apparently was reached to transform the "socialist education campaign" into a movement of unprecedented force that would permeate society. During the spring, several high Party officials had conducted personal inspection tours in the countryside, and had discovered in many communes alarming evidence of gross inefficiency and corrupt "capitalist" and "revisionist" practices among the local cadres in charge of "socialist education." To rectify the situation, a greatly intensified "Four Clearances" (*Ssu-ch'ing*) campaign was launched to screen and reindoctrinate lower-level cadres, tighten rural Party organizations, and clean up the financial operations and management of the communes.

The focus of the attack was the basic level of cadres in charge of the rural production brigades and teams. They were accused of failing to check the growth of "spontaneous capitalist tendencies" among the peasantry, by permitting, for example, the expansion of private, sideline production at the expense of collective work, and of engaging in personal extravagance, bribery, and the misappropriation of funds (for example, a team's awarding itself excessive subsidies when calculating work points). In accordance with a CCP Central Committee directive of September 1964, the masses of poor and middle peasants were mobilized and urged to probe into such abuses, and to speak out boldly against any wrongdoing of the cadres, particularly in the four "unclean" areas of account

---

[77] An Tzu-wen, "Cultivating Successors to the Revolutionary Cause—A Strategic Task for Our Party," *Hung Ch'i*, No. 17–18 (September 1964). The suspicions and fears of Mao and other leaders concerned about ideological trends must have been further aroused by the discovery in December 1964 of a scandalous hoax: A celebrated painting of young commune laborers harvesting grain, which was reproduced in full color on the back cover of the Communist Youth League monthly, was found to contain several cleverly hidden ideographs and symbols ridiculing Mao and his Great Leap and repudiating Communism. (See Charles Taylor, *Reporter in Red China* [New York, 1966] pp. 15–16.)

books, warehouses, state properties, and work points of communes and production brigades. An important organizational feature of the *Ssu-ch'ing* campaign was the use of special "work teams," composed of outsiders (often urban university students) and led by higher-level officials, which were dispatched to investigate conditions and carry out indoctrination and reform measures.

As a result, a storm of criticism and abuse broke over the rural cadres at the basic level toward the end of 1964, reducing their effectiveness and severely undermining their prestige and authority. As Chou En-lai described it in December 1964, the "historic" movement was to achieve a thorough "cleaning up and 'capital construction' in the political, economic, ideological, and organizational fields . . . so as to promote proletarian ideology and eradicate bourgeois ideology." [78]

THE APPEARANCE OF CONFLICT:
PRECIPITATING FACTORS

At Mao's impatient urging the regime continued on course after 1964 toward a more militant, heavily ideological orientation. As be-

[78] See his "Report on the Work of the Government" (Summary), December 21–22, 1964, in *Main Documents of the First Session of the Third National People's Congress* (Peking, 1965) p. 28.

While the *Ssu-ch'ing* campaign undoubtedly involved severe and demoralizing attacks against basic-level rural cadres in the latter part of 1964, there is no persuasive evidence to support the charge later raised in the Cultural Revolution that these attacks were the product of a "bourgeois reactionary" cadre policy—"'Left' in form but 'Right' in essence"—which was allegedly authored by Liu Shao-ch'i and designed to "hit hard at the many in order to protect the few." Even assuming that Liu did write the September 1964 draft of the CCP Central Committee's "Some Concrete Policy Decisions in Regard to the Rural Socialist Education Movement" (the second revised draft of the "ten-point decision" mentioned in note 74), it should be noted that this document, though more hard-hitting and harsh than the earlier drafts, was not directed solely against the basic-level rural cadres; it called also for an exposure and criticism of "certain cadres of higher-level organizations" who had "instigated, supported, and protected" the erring basic-level cadres. Thus, it would not seem to have been designed to "hit hard at the many in order to protect the few." In the opinion of Richard Baum and Frederick C. Teiwes; "if Liu committed mistakes in 1964, these mistakes were probably confined to encouraging widespread investigation and criticism of basic level cadres; they were unlikely to have been conceived as part of a systematic effort to protect higher level 'powerholders'". Baum and Teiwes also point out that Liu did not become politically culpable of such mistakes until after the outbreak of the Cultural Revolution, with its radically altered political criteria and reordered power structure. ("Liu Shao-ch'i and the Cadre Question," *Asian Survey*, Vol. 8, No. 4 [April 1968]; for a contemporary view, see Harald Munthe-Kaas, "China's 'Four Cleanups'," *Far Eastern Economic Review*, June 9, 1966, p. 480.)

fore, this appeared to enjoy the united support of the nation's leaders—whether from unquestioning deference to Mao's wishes or from an inability to suggest more attractive alternatives. In practical terms, moreover, the general trend seemed to be not so much toward radical policy changes as toward an intensified application of "more of the same" in the ideological and cultural sphere. During 1965, however, with China's mounting internal and external problems, which included her own failure to gain economic momentum and the United States' growing military involvement in Vietnam, there were indications in some quarters of a disposition to pull back and not to pin all hopes of salvation on Maoist ideology.

Yet this reluctance was clearly a matter of elementary prudence; it was not dictated by any desire to break with the cardinal policies of the past and go into active opposition. Contrary to later allegations, it was not tantamount to embracing a renascent "capitalist line" or "Soviet revisionism." How far removed the advocates of a modified course were from a "Soviet revisionist" policy was dramatically demonstrated, for example, by the behavior of Liu Shao-ch'i, Teng Hsiao-p'ing, and P'eng Chen—the three men who were later condemned as the top "capitalist-roaders"—at the Soviet Embassy's National Day celebrations in Peking on November 7, 1964. Far from relaxing in the satisfaction of Khrushchev's recent downfall or the pride of China's first nuclear detonation, P'eng Chen went out of his way to deliver a scathing attack on the entire Soviet "revisionist leadership," implying that Khrushchev's fate awaited them all (including his host, Ambassador Chervonenko) and suggesting that the class enemy of the Chinese revolution was to be found right there, in the Soviet Embassy. After witnessing the incident, Yugoslav correspondent Branku Bogunovic made the following entry in his diary: "Liu Shao-ch'i, Teng Hsiao-p'ing, and P'eng Chen . . . came tonight to the Soviet Embassy, firmly determined to humiliate the enemy and bring him to his knees. I think they left the embassy believing they had succeeded. While Ambassador Chervonenko . . . tried to maintain a polite attitude . . . , they answered him with provocation and insults. . . . What happened this evening in the Soviet Embassy in Peking demonstrated the highest triumph of dogmatic forces in the C.C.P." [79]

Although Chou En-lai, in his major report to the Third National People's Congress at the end of 1964, emphasized the necessity of the

---

[79] See Bogunovic's account, as translated from the Belgrade newspaper *Borba*, in *Atlas*, December 1967, p. 16.

class struggle and warned against complacency,[80] there was a perceptible decline in the militancy of the struggle during the first half of 1965. That summer, in contrast to the earlier stress on frugal living and personal sacrifice for the revolution, the regime's propaganda media carried a spate of demands for greater attention to the health and material welfare of the people and published directives designed to effect a better balance between work (including political training) and rest.[81] Such conciliatory and pragmatic measures, which constituted no more than a minimal tactical response to the immediate need to spur production and cement national unity in preparation for possible warfare in Vietnam, did not contravene the regime's general trend toward a Mao-centered, spiritual-revivalist orientation. In retrospect, however, it appears that the aging, suspicious Mao and his most intimate, supersensitive followers placed just the opposite interpretation on them.

By the end of 1964, differences of serious potential import had apparently begun to arise among some of the leadership over the implementation of the "Four Cleanups" movement. If we may believe the

[80] See *Main Documents of the First Session,* especially pp. 25–39. Many of the observations made by Chou in this report were to be repeated—phrase by phrase—in the Cultural Revolution. However, the "top capitalist-roaders," who in 1964 were very much in authority, gave no hint of dissent at that time from such notions as the following: "From 1959 to 1962, when China's economy experienced temporary difficulties . . . the class enemies at home launched renewed attacks on socialism. . . . In the domestic field, quite a few people actively advocated the extension of plots for private use and of free markets . . . 'reversing previous correct decisions.' . . . in the international field they advocated the liquidation of struggle in our relations with imperialism, the reactionaries and modern revisionism, and reduction of assistance and support to the revolutionary struggle of other peoples." It is highly unlikely that Liu Shao-ch'i (who was reelected Chairman of the Republic at the 1964 NPC session), Teng Hsiao-p'ing, P'eng Chen, or other leaders later condemned in the Cultural Revolution could have taken those charges as relating to themselves at the time. Even if others had entertained such suspicions they would have been reassured by Chou's confident assertion that "the nucleus of leadership of our Party and state is guided by Mao Tse-tung's thinking." (*Ibid.,* pp. 26–27.) It is also worth noting that Chou was joined in his class-struggle appeal by Lo Jui-ch'ing, who, moreover, went out of his way to praise Lin Piao for applying the thought of Mao Tse-tung and to attack P'eng Teh-huai. Both Lo and the venerable Ho Lung used the NPC platform not only to laud Mao's military thought but to denounce "the bourgeois military line" and "the revisionist military line"—the very positions which they were later accused of having espoused and for which they were purged in the Cultural Revolution. (For reports of their speeches at the National People's Congress see *Peking Review,* No. 2 [January 8, 1965] pp. 10, 12.)

[81] See articles and editorials in *Jen-min Jih-pao,* June 21 and August 10, 1965; *Ta Kung Pao,* November 10, 1965; *Chung-kuo Ch'ing-nien,* August 14, 1965.

charges belatedly raised against prominent Party leaders such as Liu
Shao-ch'i, Teng Hsiao-p'ing, and P'eng Chen, they and others were
guilty of withholding support from the effort and even of sabotaging it.
Thus, Liu and his wife, Wang Kuang-mei, who personally took charge
of the campaign in a rural Hopei production brigade (the T'aoyuan
Brigade), were later accused of carrying out a "bourgeois reactionary
line" there and of attempting to have their experience emulated throughout the nation.[82] Similarly, P'eng Chen was charged with having tried
(unsuccessfully) to overturn verdicts against several "class enemies" identified in a village struggle near Peking.[83] There were also deprecating
references to a "false rectification campaign" said to have taken place in
the cultural departments under the Party's Peking Municipal Committee in 1964.[84] Early the following year, according to Red Guard newspapers and posters, P'eng Chen and Teng Hsiao-p'ing intervened at
Peking University to suppress revolutionary activists who were criticizing
President Lu P'ing, and to promote counterrevolutionary elements to the
"work team" charged with investigating the situation.

Unfortunately, the only available evidence for these accusations is ex
post facto and comes exclusively from the side of the prosecution. In the
absence of information that can be authenticated, it is impossible to determine either the truth of the charges or the degree to which Mao and his
present associates actually distrusted P'eng Chen and other leaders at the
time.

There is little doubt, however, that Mao was dissatisfied with the progress that was being made in the "Four Cleanups" movement. From a
sifting of information and misinformation presented in the Cultural Revolution it would appear that, by the latter part of 1964, he had become
seriously disappointed with the "spiritless" prosecution of the campaign
and its inability to achieve any deep or dramatic results. Attributing this
to failure to unleash the class struggle fully in the countryside, he is said
to have blamed those in charge of the movement for being overly concerned with purging the corrupt and ineffectual low-level cadres instead
of giving full rein to the poor and lower-middle peasants' struggle against
the last vestiges of capitalist influence. In January 1965 he apparently gave

[82] See, for example, "Sham Four Clearances, Real Restoration," *Jen-min Jih-pao*,
September 6, 1967.
[83] *Jen-min Jih-pao*, April 25, 1967, p. 4.
[84] See article criticizing T'ien Han in *Jen-min Jih-pao*, December 6, 1966.

vent to this dissatisfaction at a Politburo-sponsored National Work Conference, where he proposed a new draft of guidelines for the "socialist education movement," the now-famous "Twenty-Three Articles." [85]

The new document, without renouncing the previous guidelines of the campaign (incorporated in the September 1963 and September 1964 revisions of Mao's "Ten-Point Decision"), stressed the necessity of unfettered mass mobilization and "struggle." Also, perhaps to ensure the requisite local leadership for this intensified effort, it shifted the focus of attack away from the hapless basic-level cadres, suggesting that the vast majority were essentially good, and that their mistakes could be corrected through persuasion and education. Accordingly, the extremist measures of the investigating "work teams" of outsiders were to be curbed, and the teams reduced in size. Although the "Twenty-three Articles" did not shrink from recommending harsh measures against the few incorrigible cadres, their thrust was to encourage greater solidarity between the cadres and the masses. At the same time, the new document set as a basic objective of the campaign the rectification of "those authorities within the Party who are taking the capitalist road."

On the basis of these changes in emphasis, Cultural Revolutionary sources have recently claimed that as early as January 1965 Mao had used the "Twenty-Three Articles" to launch a severe criticism against Liu Shao-ch'i, Teng Hsiao-p'ing, and other Party figures for their leadership of the "Four Cleanups" movement. Red Guard sources have even quoted Chou En-lai as recalling that Mao by then had "nearly lost all hope in Liu Shao-ch'i." [86] Available evidence, however, does not bear this out. Already the aforementioned Party directive of September 1964, which has been attributed to Liu, had suggested that cadre errors should be traced to their roots in the higher organs of the Party. Although the "Twenty-Three Articles" did mark an easing of the struggle against local cadres,

[85] The "Twenty-Three Articles" were set down in a summary of the conference discussion (dated January 14, 1965) entitled "Some Problems Currently Raised in the Rural Socialist Education Movement" (Nung-ts'un She-hui Chu-i Chaio-yü Yün-tung Chung Mu-ch'ien T'i-ch'u Ti I-hsieh Wen-t'i). A text, printed by the CCP's Fukien Provincial Committee on January 18, was made available in Taiwan by the Intelligence Bureau of the Ministry of National Defense (Republic of China) the following year, on February 2, 1966.

[86] See text of an address attributed to Chou that was published in the Canton Revolutionary Rebel newspaper *Hung Chan Pao*, No. 15 (November 29, 1967) and translated in *JPRS*, 44,574, March 4, 1968 (*Translations on Communist China*, No. 1) p. 31.

they did not cause a major shift in the "Four Cleanups" campaign toward a high-level Party purge.[87] A comparison with the Party directives of September 1963 and 1964—themselves revisions of Mao's original "Ten-Point Decision"—fails to show that the Articles constituted a basic political attack on the Party directives or that they laid down entirely new "proletarian revolutionary" guidelines for the "Four Cleanups" designed to help the campaign strengthen socialism in the rural communes. Moreover, the textual differences between the various documents do not point to a dispute within the leadership over substantive economic policies; rather, they suggest variations in emphasis as to methods for carrying out the socialist education movement.

Nevertheless, the efforts of Party authorities to keep the campaign in bounds—which in some cases may have involved condemning as "counterrevolutionary" some particularly vengeful and unruly poor-peasant elements—were later construed by the more militant Maoists as proof of a deliberate attempt to suppress the class struggle. (Indeed, some may have felt so at the time.) More and more, the ultra-suspicious came to regard the whole emphasis on reeducation and reform as a way of turning "socialist education" into an exercise in formal learning and of relying, like the Kuomintang, on "tutelage." Similarly, the widespread purge of local cadres in 1964 came to be viewed by some, in retrospect, as an unfair and indiscriminate attack on "the many good and comparatively good" lower-level functionaries, designed to shield their superiors from blame in the rural situation. In Mao's increasingly distorted perspective, the stress placed on cleansing the "Four Uncleans" eventually appeared as only a means of avoiding genuine socialist revolution in the countryside and as ignoring the basic contradiction of the ideological struggle between socialism and capitalism.[88]

Thus, by mid-1965 if not earlier, Mao and his closest disciples were obsessed with the idea of national salvation through ideological struggle. In the atmosphere of rising tension and utopian expectation, any action that tended to slow or divert the process was interpreted as a deliberate counterrevolutionary threat. Any person who showed less than single-minded devotion to Mao and enthusiasm for his increasingly one-sided

[87] See the excellent analysis on this point by Richard Baum and Frederick C. Teiwes in *Asian Survey*, Vol. 8, No. 4 (April 1968) pp. 336–338.

[88] For a résumé of the Maoist interpretation—at least, as it has been revealed in the hindsight of the Cultural Revolution—see "Struggle Between the Two Roads in China's Countryside," *Hung Ch'i*, No. 16 (November 23, 1967).

ideological approach to China's problems was suspected of disloyalty. More and more, objective difficulties were attributed to willful opposition to Mao and his thought. Not only were present differences magnified in efforts to substantiate a given charge, but the root causes were sought in the alleged dissident's past criticisms and slights, real or imagined, particularly as these were discovered through the often highly arbitrary reexamination of his writings.

Things came to a head in September and October of 1965, after Mao, either during a Central Committee work conference or at one of the related meetings held in Peking at about the same time, called for a general renewal of the struggle against "reactionary bourgeois ideology" and, in particular, for criticism of Wu Han and his play *Hai Jui Dismissed from Office*.[89] Unfortunately, no text of Mao's speeches or instructions is available, and we can only guess at their content and tone from a few bits of indirect evidence. Judging from subsequent claims that the Great Proletarian Cultural Revolution began here and was "initiated and led" by Mao from this time forward, one can speculate that he used the conference in the fall of 1965 as a forum in which to voice his deepening dissatisfaction with the pace of the ideological revival, to reiterate and perhaps elaborate his increasingly utopian and self-centered vision of national salvation, and to demand an all-out effort to propagate the faith and wipe out all traces of "bourgeois" or "revisionist" sentiment.[90]

Mao was evidently determined now to force the issue, and to compel his colleagues to make a clear choice between his new vision and the orientation of the past, which, though increasingly "red," still contained important balancing elements of flexibility, "expertness," tolerance of imperfection, and a general willingness to make concessions to reality while pursuing Communist revolutionary goals. It was not a case of Liu Shao-ch'i, Teng Hsiao-p'ing, P'eng Chen, or others' proposing to launch the regime on a rightist course toward the restoration of capitalism; it was,

[89] According to evidence presented in 1967, Mao made these demands at an enlarged session of the Politburo Standing Committee that included "leading comrades of all the regional bureaus" of the CCP. This meeting ran from September on into October 1965. (See "Central Committee Circular" of May 16, 1967.) Although this would seem to point to a series of discussions, or debates, lasting days or possibly even weeks, a Peking wall poster speaking of Mao's participation in the conference gave the date of September 10. (*Mainichi Shim-bun*, April 27, 1967.)

[90] Some Red Guard sources had quoted Mao as asking his colleagues point-blank what they would do if revisionism appeared in the Central Committee, and then suggesting that there was great danger that this would happen.

rather, a case of Mao's insisting on a radical departure from the status quo with its more moderate leftward momentum.

In all probability, the meetings of top Party leaders in the early autumn of 1965 were the occasion of searching discussions and even perhaps of sharp debates. Resistance to Mao's demands and to his leadership apparently did not approach the point of outright opposition reached by P'eng Teh-huai at Lushan six years earlier. According to secret Party documents, however, P'eng Chen did go so far as to suggest, at a national conference of propaganda officials in September, that, since everyone had a right to speak and all were equal before the truth, even Mao should submit to criticism if he were wrong. And, at the same meeting, Lu Ting-i reportedly made a speech attacking Stalin which Mao interpreted as a challenge to his own position.[91]

Ironically, however, P'eng Chen was named one of the "group of five" (perhaps the principal member) that was created in the wake of the autumn meetings to lead the first stage of the cultural purification—the investigation and criticism of Wu Han. K'ang Sheng, a stalwart Mao supporter and veteran intelligence specialist, was also named to the group. This mixed composition suggests that the selection was made by a shaky consensus of disturbed and divided leaders. Thus, P'eng Chen's prominent assignment may have been sought by the more moderate elements to balance the likes of K'ang Sheng—or vice versa—and to avoid a completely one-sided investigation. It is also possible that Mao insisted on placing P'eng in the forefront so as to be able to test his loyalty and, indirectly, that of other powerful Party leaders, such as Liu Shao-ch'i and Teng Hsiao-p'ing, whose position might be adversely affected by the conviction of Wu Han and his defenders.[92]

[91] Reports of the criticisms by P'eng and Lu were contained in secret Party documents seen by a former Chinese trade official, Miao Chen-pai, who defected to the United States in July 1966. (*The Washington Star,* August 31, 1966.) The phrase "everyone is equal before the truth" was publicly condemned as a "bourgeois slogan" in an article by Ch'in Chung-ssu in *Chung-kuo Ch'ing-nien,* June 16, 1966.

[92] According to Miao Chen-pai, P'eng Chen was specifically designated by Mao to lead the Cultural Revolution. (*The Washington Post,* September 4, 1966.) A Russian commentary names Lu Ting-i, Chou Yang, and Wu Leng-hsi as members of the group besides K'ang Sheng, suggesting thereby that the group was weighted heavily against Mao, to judge by the subsequent fate of those men. (See Yakovlev Ivanovich, "The Tragedy of China," *Za Rubezhom [Abroad],* Moscow, No. 40 [September–October 1967] as translated in *JPRS* 43,132, October 27, 1967 [*Translations on Communist China: Political and Sociological,* No. 427] p. 10.) It should be noted, however, that Lu Ting-i and Chou Yang were likely candidates for such a group simply by virtue of their official positions in cultural and propaganda affairs.

Although the situation harbored potential threats to Wu Han's friends and superiors, notably in the Peking Municipal CCP Committee (a potential that may seem even greater in hindsight), there was as yet no necessary indicator that Mao was bent on a major high-level purge of the Party. Campaigns had been launched before against prominent literary figures—some of whom had connections in the hierarchy of the regime—without touching off a major power struggle. Even if the Cultural Revolution was indeed essentially a power struggle at this point, there was still time for those whom Mao had not directly condemned to prove their loyalty and salvage their positions—assuming they did not aspire to challenge him.[93] To be sure, hints of shifts in the relative power of a few of the top leaders were perceptible in August and September 1965—most notably in the fizzling of an attempt to build up the stature of Liu Shao-ch'i and in the sudden emergence of Lin Piao as an eminent theoretician (with the publication of his "Long Live the Victory of the People's War"). Nevertheless, no major change seemed to be in prospect that threatened to upset the existing power rankings or to reorder the succession to Mao, all of which had apparently been settled for several years.

Perhaps it would be well to consider at this point the theory, sometimes advanced, that the conflict which arose in the fall of 1965 and precipitated the subsequent Cultural Revolution was basically a dispute over economic or military policies. It would seem reasonable to suppose that the Chinese leaders were discouraged by continuing economic difficulties, shocked by conspicuous reverses in foreign policy (in Indonesia, Africa, and elsewhere), and anxious over the growing risks of a military confrontation with the United States in Vietnam. In the absence of hard evidence, we may hypothesize further that opinions in the leadership differed on how to respond to these problems. Indeed, such differences may have reflected two distinct policy positions: the relatively practical-minded, conservative, pragmatic, and "secular" outlook presumably found most often among administrators, economists, and professional soldiers, and the more revolutionary, radical, utopian, and doctrinaire position

[93] It has been said that leaders such as P'eng Chen, Lu Ting-i, and Chou Yang were already too compromised by the similarity of some of their previous statements to those of the condemned to avoid prosecution by the wrathful Mao. This interpretation seems to overlook the characteristic ambiguity of the statements in question, which would provide considerable latitude for those not directly implicated to dissociate themselves from the condemned in forthright contrition, and it fails to take account also of the familiar Maoist exhortation to redeem the offender rather than seek retribution.

loosely associated with the Party apparatchiks and political commissars.

It has been theorized that the leadership, in trying to decide on the major goals and allocations for the Third Five-Year Plan (scheduled to begin in 1966), became seriously split over whether to continue the previous line of moderate economic advance, which meant tolerating certain small concessions to private incentive, or to launch another Great Leap Forward.[94] In the course of the Cultural Revolution numerous accusations were raised against the "handful" in authority in the Party who were following the "capitalist road"; they included charges of economic policy deviations before the Tenth Plenum (1962) and of errors in cadre policy thereafter. There is no direct evidence, however, that any high-level debate on basic economic strategy took place in the fall of 1965. A few professional economists, such as Sun Yeh-fang, were criticized for sniping at the Leap Forward or advocating (especially in the "liberal" early 1960s) "revisionist" price and profit theories at variance with the Party line—albeit ideas which did not result in any important shift in the regime's economic policies.[95] In addition, the "handful" of accused Party leaders were censured for either espousing or implementing policies that, although sanctioned at the time by the Central Committee (including, presumably, Chairman Mao), have since been modified or abandoned in accordance with the central leadership's changes in the economic line.

While one can challenge the fairness of these indictments and question whether the ideas so condemned were influential enough to cause major policy changes, it is nevertheless reasonable to suppose that differences existed within the leadership that were related at least indirectly to economic issues. No doubt, Mao's demands for heavy emphasis on political indoctrination and mass mobilization were deeply disturbing to the economic realists, who foresaw another huge diversion of physical and mental energy from both current production and future scientific and technological development. But the available evidence does not show that these general grounds for disagreement actually precipitated a clash over economic policy in the fall of 1965. It neither identifies protagonists and

[94] See Chu-yuan Cheng, "The Cultural Revolution and China's Economy," *Current History*, Vol. 53, No. 313 (September 1967) p. 150. Unfortunately, Dr. Cheng offers no documentation for this hypothesis, but argues mainly from circumstantial inference and intuition that "debates on the line of economic development" toward the end of 1965 helped lead to a "titanic power struggle."

[95] See Meng Kuei and Hsiao Lin, "On Sun Yeh-fang's Reactionary Political Stand and Economic Programme," *Peking Review*, Nos. 43 and 44 (October 2 and 28, 1966) an article originally published in *Hung Ch'i*, No. 10 (August 10, 1966).

factions nor reveals conflicting positions on concrete questions of economic policy. Whatever economic debate may have taken place on the eve of the Cultural Revolution, it was not so profound as to account for the later Maoist condemnation or for major changes in economic policy designed to rectify previous "errors." [96]

Some have argued that the internal dispute which came to a head in the fall of 1965 sprang from a deep disagreement over military strategy and doctrine. As to strategy, the large-scale intervention of U.S. combat forces in Vietnam that year undoubtedly heightened Peking's anxieties and internal tensions. There certainly would appear to have been much room for disagreement, whether in the course of assessing the American "threat" to Vietnam and ultimately to China, or of redefining China's goals and priorities (such as the "fraternal" commitment to the Vietnamese "war of national liberation" as against the requirements for defense of the Chinese homeland). On the likely premise of increased tension and disagreement in Peking one can hypothesize that a bitter debate over policy was splitting the leadership into two or more factions —"hawks," "doves," and possibly intermediate groupings.[97] Unfortunately, evidence for divergent positions on strategy must be marshaled almost entirely from interpretations of the public statements of various leaders, especially from the debatable kind of inference based on the belief that departures from standard phraseology and differences in nuance reveal hidden meanings.

[96] In the fall of 1965 the most notable change bearing on economic policy occurred in the socialist education campaign, where the main focus shifted from basic-level cadres to their *hsien*-level superiors. The latter were forced to confess to "bureaucratism," "commandism," "revisionism," and other sins. In a new emulation campaign that began in February 1966, they were exhorted to follow the example of Chiao Yü-lu, a selfless, courageous rural Party secretary who had dedicated himself to the service of the masses. At the same time, the Party leadership continued, as it had done since 1963 or earlier, to emphasize the goal of collectivized agriculture, calling for the reduction of "excessive" private cultivation and forbidding the division of land among individual peasant households. Neither before nor after the onset of the Cultural Revolution, however, was there any major move to eliminate all private incentive measures, to reverse the rising investment in the production of chemical fertilizer for agriculture, or to return precipitously to a system in which the commune was the basic unit of agricultural management.

[97] The well-known analyst of Communist affairs Victor Zorza wrote in November 1966: "It was the dissatisfaction of the professional military leaders with the policy which the ruling group was trying to impose on them that brought the struggle to a head. . . . The real struggle began a year ago [in the fall of 1965], with Lin Piao's attempt to suppress the military opposition in the person of Lo Jui-ch'ing, the Chief of Staff." *The Manchester Guardian*, November 3, 1966.

Extrapolating from such evidence, one can argue that Chief of Staff Lo Jui-ch'ing, in an address he gave on the anniversary of V-E Day in May 1965, forecast the danger of an early confrontation with the United States, emphasized the need for intensive conventional military preparations to meet this threat, and even urged "united action" with the U.S.S.R. in order to facilitate this preparation, regain the protection of the Soviet nuclear deterrent, and make possible the "active defense" of Vietnam (including, perhaps, an armed invasion), thus ensuring a favorable outcome there. One may go on to say that this strategic line of the "professionals" was emphatically rejected by Lin Piao (representing Mao and, some believe, P'eng Chen) in his V-J Day anniversary article on "people's wars," which seemed to stress the efficacy of China's involvement in Vietnam and the low risk it entailed, the unacceptability of even a partial reconciliation with the Soviet "revisionists," and the desirability of defending China against possible invasion by having the masses withdraw to the interior and mobilize for guerrilla warfare.[98] Between these two posi-

---

[98] In an article entitled "China's Cautious American Policy" (Current History, Vol. 53, No. 313 [September 1967]) Ishwer C. Ojha, an exponent of this general line of interpretation, maintains that the U.S. intervention in Vietnam after February 1965 led to a polarization of strategic views within the Chinese leadership and the formation of "two well-defined factions." The "interventionists," led by Lo Jui-ch'ing and P'eng Chen (who were joined by Liu Shao-ch'i in early 1966), expected U.S. operations in Vietnam to lead to war with China and were determined to render "unconditional help" to the Vietnamese Communists even though this might necessitate cooperation with the U.S.S.R. The "noninterventionists," led by Lin Piao and supported by Mao—and, with lesser emphasis, Chou En-lai—did not believe the war would spill over into North Vietnam and China and "offered only conditional assistance to Vietnam." By August 1966, Ojha says, the debate was resolved in favor of the noninterventionists.

Unfortunately, Ojha's case is built almost entirely on very debatable interpretations of selected published statements of the Chinese leaders. One wonders, for example, whether Lo Jui-ch'ing's fear that U.S. escalation would lead to war with China was not shared by many Maoists at the time. (Certainly, Wang Jen-chung, a power in Peking for several months after August 1966, had candidly expressed his fear of an inevitable war from his base in Hankow in the autumn of 1965.) According to Ojha, Lo Jui-ch'ing favored a strategy of "active defense." Yet it was precisely for not accepting the "active defense" strategy that his successor as Acting Chief of Staff, Yang Ch'eng-wu, was to condemn him in 1967. (Peking Review, No. 46 [November 10, 1967].) Actually, the one credited with having devised the concept of "active defense" is Mao, whereas P'eng Teh-huai and Lo have been faulted—perhaps unjustly—for failing to subscribe to it. Ojha contends that Lo Jui-ch'ing's strategy, which presupposed "some form of Soviet cooperation," was supported by P'eng Chen. Yet the Russians regarded P'eng Chen as perhaps the most rabidly anti-Soviet leader in Peking at the time. At times, Ojha's use of evidence is questionable, as when he cites as representative of Mao's and Lin's position an article of July 1965 by Ho Lung

tions some analysts hypothesize, on rather less evidence, the existence of a third faction, led by Liu Shao-ch'i and Teng Hsiao-p'ing, which was mainly interested in China's internal development but aligned itself with the "hawks" on the issue of more active Chinese intervention in Vietnam in order to justify a rapprochement with the U.S.S.R., its true purpose being the restoration of Soviet economic and technical assistance.[99]

For several reasons, this line of argument is difficult to accept. First, it lacks adequate foundation in evidence, for it relies almost exclusively on esoteric messages in the public statements of certain leaders, rather than on any clear and unequivocal expression—in word or deed—of dissent or deviation. The interpretations derived from this "Aesopian translation" are strained if not downright arbitrary. Thus, respected analysts viewing the same evidence and relying on much the same method of textual exegesis have reached very different conclusions as to the nature of the dispute and the alignments of personalities.[100] More important, exegetical interpretations that find in the strategic debates the chief source of the Cultural Revolution often fail to acknowledge that these debates or similar sources also afford evidence to the contrary. Thus, they do not take account of Lo Jui-ch'ing's enthusiastic endorsement of Lin Piao's famous article following its publication in September, of the consistently "hardline" anti-Soviet stance adopted by Liu Shao-ch'i and Teng Hsiao-

---

—the man who is now in disgrace for allegedly having undermined that very position at the time.

[99] An interpretation along these lines, but positing a subsequent split of the Mao-Lin faction with P'eng Chen, has been advanced by Uri Ra'anan. ("Rooting for Mao," *The New Leader,* March 13, 1967.) See also Ra'anan's longer study, "Peking's Foreign Policy Debate, 1965–1966," in Tang Tsou (ed.), *China in Crisis,* Vol. 2 (Chicago: University of Chicago Press, 1968) pp. 23–72. For a different opinion, see Harry Harding, Jr. and Melvin Gurtov, "The Purge of Lo Jui-ch'ing: The Politics of Chinese Strategic Planning" (Santa Monica, California: The Rand Corporation, 1970).

[100] For example, compare Ra'anan ("Rooting for Mao") with the following: (1) Franz Schurmann ("What Is Happening in China?" *The New York Review of Books,* October 20, 1966), emphasizes Lo Jui-ch'ing's uncompromising hostility to the Soviet "revisionists." He aligns P'eng Chen with Lo among the "hardliners" on national liberation strategy, and locates Liu Shao-ch'i "to the 'left' of Mao," whom he describes as "the man of the middle course, avoiding both the extremes of the right and the left." (2) Morton Halperin and John Lewis ("New Tensions in Army-Party Relations in China, 1965–66," *The China Quarterly,* No. 26 [April–June 1966]) recall the "Party position" taken by Lo Jui-ch'ing in December 1964, which contrasted with that of such military "professionals" as Yang Yung (who, ironically, survived the purges of the Cultural Revolution until 1967—longer, that is, than "Party" men like Wang Jen-chung).

p'ing, and of P'eng Chen's violent condemnation of "revisionist" coward-
ice and his militant call for revolutionary warfare during a visit to Indonesia in May 1965, as seen against the puzzling allegations by Hsieh
Fu-chih and K'ang Sheng, later on, that P'eng had glorified Soviet "revisionism" and advocated capitulation with imperialism. Such contrary
evidence may, of course, demonstrate only that Communist spokesmen
reserve their disagreements for private debate, but to say this would be
to cast doubt on any interpretation arrived at largely by textual exegesis.
The fact that Peking's strategy and commitments with respect to the
war in Vietnam appear to have remained unchanged and to have suffered no criticism from either the Maoists or their adversaries (although
the latter have been accused of opposition on many other points) strongly
suggests that whatever disagreements may have developed on that issue
in the fall of 1965 were not divisive enough to have precipitated the Cultural Revolution.

The difficulty of substantiating the existence of a regime-splitting debate
over Vietnam strategy should not, however, obscure the likelihood that
the military establishment was divided on other issues. We know that
sometime in late 1965 or early 1966 Lo Jui-ch'ing was removed as Chief
of Staff, to be replaced by the "acting" Yang Ch'eng-wu. Moreover, on
August 1, 1966, an important editorial in the PLA newspaper *Chieh-fang
Chün Pao* revealed that a "big struggle" had taken place in the armed
forces not long ago, the third major internal conflict since 1949. According to the editorial, it had been a struggle against important officers who
"had given first consideration to military affairs, techniques, and specialized work."

This suggests—and subsequent indictments have made clear—that Lo
Jui-ch'ing and others associated with him in the military establishment
were believed to have sought by various means to lessen the disruption
of military training, professional specialization, and combat preparedness
that Mao's increasingly unbalanced, utopian vision of the PLA threatened
to bring about.[101] This is not to say that they wished to reverse the trend

---

[101] Lo's sins were catalogued in a surge of vitriolic articles published in the late
summer and fall of 1967 and culminating in a sweeping condemnation of Lo by his
successor, Yang Ch'eng-wu. (See *Peking Review,* No. 46 [November 10, 1967].) In
addition to the familiar pattern by which his deviations were traced back to Wang
Ming in World War II and Lo was accused of complicity in the Kao-Jao and P'eng
Teh-huai "anti-Party intrigue"—a remarkable allegation in view of his promotion
to Chief of Staff after Lushan and the high commendation for loyal service he

entirely and to impose a "bourgeois military line," as has been charged.[102] Had they not, while continuing modest efforts to modernize the armed forces in preceding years, led in implementing a steady stream of measures to abandon the Soviet military model, "put politics in command," emphasize the importance of men over weapons, and "democratize" the armed forces through measures that included the abolition of ranks? To Mao in his radical and utopian mood, however, any admonitions to "go slow," and even feeble resistance to the growing demands for political indoctrination, as well as any questioning of the use of troops for non-military economic and mass mobilization tasks or the ultimate goal of

received from Mao and Lin Piao (*Kung-tso T'ung hsün* of March 2, 1961)—the most serious charges against Lo were centered on his resistance to the excessive pursuit of Mao study in the army and on his modest interest in developing military skills. Lo, apparently in an effort to maintain a balance in the PLA's training activities, had supported army-wide tournaments for competition in military skills during 1964, and the Maoists interpreted this as a diversion from political activities and opposition to Mao's thoughts on army-building. (*Jen-min Jih-pao*, August 28, 1967.) Also, Lo's attempt to promote the study of Marxism-Leninism-Stalinism was later branded a denigration of Mao study, and his entirely natural conduct in transmitting the reports of Liu Shao-ch'i (his superior as Chief of State) and publicizing Liu's second edition of "Self-Cultivation" was construed as having been designed to vitiate Mao's position of absolute authority in the army. When an exasperated Lo condemned ritual Mao study as "dogmatism," this was duly noted, especially by Lin Piao, who seems increasingly to have regarded Lo as a rival to be watched. When Lo allegedly questioned the appropriateness of Mao's thought as guidance in state affairs and challenged Lin Piao's claim that it was the acme of Marxism-Leninism, the trap was effectively baited.

[102] See "Basic Differences Between the Proletarian and Bourgeois Military Lines," *Peking Review*, No. 48 (November 24, 1967). Aside from the charge that its exponents (Lo Jui-ch'ing, P'eng Teh-huai, and others) overvalued weapons and technique and undervalued politics and Mao study, the authors of this article—"proletarian revolutionaries" in offices of the PLA General Staff headquarters—seem to have defined the most serious manifestations of the "bourgeois military line" as opposition to the buildup of militia and regional forces (as distinguished from main forces) and resistance to the Maoist policy of "active defense." The latter concept is far from clear, but, as contrasted with the alleged "passive defense" of Mao's adversaries (which would build up widespread defensive works and deploy main forces around the country to man them), it would appear to emphasize the mobilization of local forces and the old guerrilla strategy of "luring the enemy to penetrate deep" into Chinese territory, followed at propitious times by a concentration of superior defending forces for battles of annihilation against the invader. If this is, in fact, what the Maoists mean by "active defense, it has not resulted in any major shifts in recruitment, organization, or deployment since the purge of the opposition in the Cultural Revolution. The PLA shows no signs of reverting to a conglomeration of guerrilla armies that would fall back to "lure" an invading force into the interior.

78   WILLIAM F. DORRILL

a worker-peasant army of nonspecialists, were indications of flagging enthusiasm that aroused serious doubts of reliability and furnished grounds for dismissal.

This is not to discount the likelihood that Mao's increasingly immoderate emphasis and the priority he accorded to "army building" gave rise to real and substantial opposition in many quarters. But it is entirely possible that the hapless Lo Jui-ch'ing was purged not so much for his particularly advanced "professional" viewpoint or for any "bourgeois" inclinations (after all, his background was in Party and secret-police work and he would hardly have been selected to replace P'eng Teh-huai had he not been considered politically oriented and reliable) as because of his vacillating and ineffective leadership. Mao may have wished to make an example of him before the powerful regional commanders—who were not to be so easily displaced. The removal of Lo also served to strengthen Lin Piao's control over the military establishment.

In sum, though differences over aspects of economic and military policy undoubtedly existed in the fall and winter of 1965–1966, they were extremely complex, and their precise nature is difficult to establish.[103] Springing from a variety of viewpoints, interests, and motivations that were not always clear or consistent, they did not result in a simple alignment of opposing opinions and personalities over the whole range of issues. Thus, it is difficult even now to categorize the disputants. Presumed "hard-liners" have since been among those most severely criticized, while "soft-liners" have survived (some of them having actually been

[103] Some of those who maintain that the Cultural Revolution sprang primarily from substantive policy differences have cited as evidence ta-tzu-pao allegations that certain "anti-Party" leaders following a "bourgeois" line had seized upon the difficulties of China's "three hard years" (after the failure of the Great Leap) to advance a policy of san-ho i-shao (literally, "three reconciliations and one less": reconciliation with reaction, imperialism, and modern revisionism, and less support to revolutionary struggles abroad). A recent self-criticism attributed to Liu Shao-ch'i tends to cast serious doubt on the validity of this sweeping and inadequately documented accusation—at least, insofar as any such tendencies influenced the top leadership. In his alleged self-criticism, which was contained in a Peking wall poster of August 2, 1967, Liu declared that, while the san-ho i-shao might have been advocated by individual comrades, it was never brought up at any meeting of the Central Committee, and that he "did not even know of the existence of such an opinion." Liu also denied that he had ever during that period attacked the "three red flags" (the policies of the Leap Forward, the people's communes, and the general line)—and all his published statements and actions at the time certainly would seem to bear this out. (A résumé of this self-criticism was published in Mainichi Shimbun, August 3, 1967.)

restored from previous disgrace). Nor were the divisions along institutional lines, as, for example, between the Party and the army; they occurred instead *within* the major institutions. All of this suggests that the growing division among the leaders was not primarily the result of a split between proponents and opponents of certain domestic or foreign policy measures. It was a disagreement not so much over the particular methods, direction, and speed to be employed in order to attain commonly agreed-upon national objectives—such as "modernization" or "great power status"—as over the nature of those basic goals themselves and the general approach to them.

The previous discussion indicates that more was at issue by the end of 1965 than the economic or military policies espoused by the different leaders. To be sure, the mounting problems Peking encountered in both domestic and foreign policies, and the failures already sustained in those fields, probably intensified existing disagreements, but they did not radically alter the terms of these debates. The factor that now intruded to place the entire range of policy disputes in a different perspective was the Maoist drive for ideological revolution. As attitudes toward the thought and personality of Chairman Mao became the primary issue, substantive differences over specific policies lost some of their importance and urgency, for their solution would be determined by the outcome of that primary struggle.

For Mao and his closest followers, national policy goals such as economic development or enhancement of national power (at least, as measured by the usual indices) were decidedly subordinate to the attainment of an ideologically pure, revolutionary environment. Their increasingly one-sided stress on indoctrination and spiritual revival as the key to all of China's problems and aspirations sprang from a growing fear, after the Leap Forward debacle, that revisionism, as in the U.S.S.R. was threatening to take over the minds of the Chinese people and their leaders. They contended that even after a Communist regime has come to power through revolution, there is a continuing danger that this power may be wrested again from the proletariat—perhaps for a prolonged period of time—by the wiles and treachery of the remaining bourgeois elements. It was to prevent such a "capitalist restoration" in China that the Maoists sought to change the outlook of society by establishing the absolute authority of the thought of Mao Tse-tung. The "great mental force generated by Mao's thought" would then be transformed into a "great material force" able to maintain the dictatorship of the proletariat and to "establish the ideological foundations for the consolidation of the socialist system and insure the gradual transition to Communism." [104]

Other leaders, probably including the vast majority of the CCP Central Committee, evidently saw in the existing environment—already highly politicized and oriented toward the left—no menacing conflict between the requirements of ideology and those of national power, and no need to embark on a more radically leftist, ideology-obsessed course in order to subordinate the latter interest to the former. This was not because they had been greatly corrupted by latent capitalist influences, as the Maoists were later to charge. Nor did it necessarily imply (as some Western observers have suggested) that the dissenting high-level leaders had become unduly mellowed by the natural processes of bureaucratization and routinization resulting from their long tenure in power—although such trends had become painfully manifest among lower-echelon cadres in the Socialist Education and "Four Cleanups" movements. Indeed, the overt attitudes of the top dissenters must have been almost unexceptionable (their behavior certainly was unorganized and ineffectual), for their Maoist adversaries could do little more than condemn them for having espoused positions which, though sanctioned even by Mao at the time, were later altered by the Central Committee; for the rest, their opponents have been largely reduced to allegations of dissident thoughts and motives and to the lame indictment that they had "waved the red flag to oppose the red flag."

The immediate issue in the fall of 1965 that was to divide the leadership and precipitate the Cultural Revolution arose over Mao's seemingly insignificant demand for criticism of Wu Han and his "bourgeois" literary

---

[104] This statement of the Maoist position appeared later in the Cultural Revolution in the course of a seven-article attack on "China's Khrushchev" (Liu Shao-ch'i) published in *Chieh-fang Chün Pao* between September 17 and December 4, 1967. The passages quoted above were from the third article, released by *NCNA* on October 12. In the first article of the series (*NCNA*, Sepetmber 17, 1967) Lin Piao was quoted as having stressed the primacy of ideological regeneration: "It is possible to overthrow the political power of the bourgeoisie and other exploiting classes within a comparatively short period of time. It is also possible to overthrow their systems of ownership within a short time. But it is in no way a simple and easy matter to sweep them out of their positions on the ideological front. That will take a very long time. And if victory is not won on this front, then the victories gained in the political and economic spheres might all be lost." In a later article of the series (*NCNA*, October 25, 1967) Mao himself was quoted as having taught: "ideological education is the key link to be grasped in uniting the whole Party for great political struggles. Unless this is done, the Party cannot accomplish any of its political tasks."

productions. Dissatisfied with the progress of the campaign to defame Wu, Mao directed an obscure journalist, Yao Wen-yüan, to write a critique of Wu's famous play, *Hai Jui Dismissed from Office*. This critique, now said to have been written "under the direct guidance" of Mao's wife,[105] labeled the play a "big poisonous weed" that served the interests of unnamed anti-Party elements and class enemies. Publication of the article in the Shanghai *Wen Hui Pao* on November 10, 1965, apparently came as a surprise to P'eng Chen and the Peking Municipal CCP Committee, one of whose representatives immediately telephoned the Shanghai Party Committee for an explanation of the article and of the reason that Peking had not been told of it in advance of publication.[106] Reproduction of the article in the Shanghai Party organ *Chieh-fang Jih-pao* and, more significant still, in the army newspaper *Chieh-fang Chün Pao* at the end of November indicated Mao's determination to press the attack and undoubtedly heightened the anxiety in Peking.

Yet there was no immediate sign of a general eagerness to join in the assault. The predominant mood was one of uncertainty and confusion, with hints of resistance in some quarters. Although the national Party daily, *Jen-min Jih-pao*, as well as the Peking Committee's *Peking Jih-pao*, finally reprinted Yao Wen-yüan's article, their accompanying editorials avoided taking sides—in striking contrast to the comments of the army editors—and called for open debate of the case. For several weeks there was indeed a relatively free discussion, in which some of Wu Han's Peking associates, most notably Teng T'o, attempted to conduct an active defense. In addition, several powerful Party leaders—including, according to later indictments, P'eng Chen and deputy propaganda chief Chou Yang—worked intensively behind the scenes. Despite these efforts, however, Wu Han's cause was lost, and on December 30, 1965, *Jen-min Jih-pao* printed his self-criticism. In it, Wu admitted that he had "forgotten class struggle" and made other "serious" mistakes in his writings, but he continued to defend the purity of his intentions and stopped short of a summary confession of political guilt. Similarly, his vulnerable defenders began anxiously—and, as time would prove, vainly—to try to make the most of the distinction between "academic error" and political culpability.

After the attack on Wu, Mao disappeared from the public eye, perhaps to plan "cultural" attacks on others with the help of Ch'en Po-ta and Chiang Ch'ing. He later intimated that he had left Peking because of

[105] On Chiang Ch'ing's role, see *NCNA* dispatch of May 29, 1967.
[106] See article by Ch'i Pen-yü in *Hung Ch'i*, No. 7 (May 1966).

the lack of support there for his campaign against Wu Han.[107] If so, one may speculate on the significance of the rising prominence of P'eng Chen and Liu Shao-ch'i in the capital at about that time.[108] On the other hand, Chou Yang, who was more immediately vulnerable than either P'eng or Liu, delivered a widely publicized address, on November 29, which strongly endorsed Mao's demand for renewed class struggle in literature and art. Besides warning against the danger of a Hungarian-style Petofi Club's emerging in China, Chou censured the bourgeois-feudalist tendencies in culture during 1961–1962, praised the reform of the Peking opera (spurred by Chiang Ch'ing), and explicitly praised Lin Piao and the PLA as models of cultural orthodoxy.[109]

Despite its universally acclaimed example and its leadership in the criticism of Wu Han, the PLA apparently was not without internal differences and difficulties. In late November, about the time of Mao's disappearance, Lo Jui-ch'ing vanished from public view. It was not to become clear until mid-1966 that Lo had actually been removed as Chief of Staff of the Armed Forces, and both the exact time and the reasons for his dismissal remain obscure. One may conjecture that a growing anxiety over China's unpreparedness for war had lessened his enthusiasm for Mao's unbalanced notions of "army-building" and the guerrilla mystique, and that disenchantment had resulted in uninspired leadership over subordinate military commanders and eventually perhaps had led to a break with Lin Piao. The occasion for such a split (which Mao and Lin might have forced to permit them to tighten control over the PLA) could have come around November, when Lin proclaimed a five-point directive for the work of the army in 1966, an order that established the "living study and application of the thought of Mao Tse-tung" as the highest directive for all army work, the criterion for testing loyalty and efficiency, and the basis for a more vigorous policy of promotions.[110] (The

[107] In a speech of October 26, 1966 (published in a Red Guard newspaper in December), Mao reportedly declared that, a year earlier, he had felt that his ideas could not be carried out in Peking, and that this was the reason the criticism of Wu Han had begun in Shanghai.

[108] P'eng was the featured speaker at the October 1 National Day celebrations; Liu was named chairman of the Preparatory Committee for the Sun Yat-sen Centennial (to be observed in 1966) and, in December 1965 he was lionized as the hero of the "December 9" Student Movement on its thirtieth anniversary.

[109] The text of Chou Yang's speech, which was originally delivered at a national conference of "spare-time" writers, appeared in *Hung Ch'i*, No. 1 (January 1966).

[110] *Jen-min Jih-pao*, November 27, 1965. The order also reiterated the leading role of "politics" over military concerns. Later, Red Guard sources were to charge that

abolition of ranks in the PLA, which had been ordered several months earlier, had already greatly reduced the independence, mobility, and prerogatives of professional officers.)

Whatever the precise timing of his deposition, Lo evidently was not present at an important twenty-day conference of the PLA's General Political Department in January 1966. The meeting was presided over by Director of the Political Department Hsiao Hua, who in his main report suggested the existence of dissension within the armed forces over the role politics should play, warned that from then on promotions would be closely related to one's ideological rectitude, and pointedly praised Lin Piao for "creatively applying" the military thought of Mao Tse-tung.[111] Other prominent leaders identified as addressing the PLA meeting were Chou En-lai, Teng Hsiao-p'ing, P'eng Chen, Yeh Chien-ying, and Yang Ch'eng-wu, then Deputy Chief of Staff. (Yang later replaced Lo Jui-ch'ing as Acting Chief of Staff, but was himself purged in the spring of 1968.) The presence of Teng and P'eng, which seems somewhat ironic in retrospect, indicates that both were still among the top leaders carrying out the ideological rectification, and it suggests that the issues which led to their downfall were distinct from those immediately responsible for the purge of Lo Jui-ch'ing.

The new year had begun with another call for a sharpening of the class struggle and greater emphasis on the study of Mao's thoughts.[112] Succeeding weeks saw the unfolding of a campaign of unprecedented

---

Lo Jui-ch'ing had "opposed" and "distorted" Lin's five-point directive, stressing only its principle of "training hard in difficult skills and in fighting at close quarters and at night" (while relegating Mao study to a secondary position) and emphasizing— "with ulterior motives"—that if "the problem of methods" were not solved, even the best "guideline" would be of no avail. This contention appeared in an article entitled "Lo Jui-ch'ing Desires To Die Ten Thousand Times for His Crimes," published in a joint issue of the Canton Red Guard newspapers *Chinghangshan* and *Kwang-tung Wei-i Chan-pao*, Nos. 7–8 (September 5, 1967).

[111] News reports of the conference were published on January 25, and the text of Hsiao Hua's speech appeared in *Jen-min Jih-pao* that same day. The main themes of the speech were reiterated on February 6 in an article in *Jeu-min Jih-pao*, which put senior PLA cadres on notice that military achievements in the first half of life did not necessarily assure the correctness of political views in the second half. Other articles and statements about this time criticized the stress that allegedly was being placed on military technique to the neglect of "politics," and called for greater emphasis on political indoctrination.

[112] A nationwide movement for the study of Mao's thoughts had been gradually gaining force for about two years, particularly since the publication of an editorial in *Jen-min Jih-pao*, on March 26, 1964, summoning the masses to "learn earnestly the thought of Mao Tse-tung."

zeal to glorify Mao and his works, a swelling chorus of adulation bordering on deification. By the end of January the relatively restrained *Jen-min Jih-pao* was enthusiastically expounding on the "worldwide significance" of Mao's thoughts and noting with approval that army recruits were presented a copy of Mao's writings before anything else. Propaganda sources found an ever-widening range of problems that could be successfully solved through Mao study—from the treatment of burn victims to improvement of the PLA's combat effectiveness. Regional bureaus of the CCP joined loudly in the praise, the Central-South Bureau resolving on January 16 that the thought of Mao Tse-tung was "the apex of contemporary Marxism and the highest and most lively form of Marxism" (a paean that may help account for First Secretary T'ao Chu's subsequent meteoric, if short-lived, rise in power).[113] Commentators spoke openly of Mao as the successor to Marx, Lenin, and Stalin, and some declared that, in consequence, the center of world Communism had moved from the U.S.S.R. to China.

Although February and March saw something of a lull in public attacks against Wu Han, we now know that intensive ideological discussions and political maneuvering went on behind the scenes. From January 25 to March 5, a national conference of political workers in industry and communications met in Peking, following which Lin Piao, exceeding his authority as PLA commander, addressed a letter of commendation to the civilian participants, praising them for placing Mao study first and doubtless raising suspicions in some quarters that he was trying to move into control of the labor movement.[114] Within the army, Lin glowingly introduced Mao's wife, Chiang Ch'ing, as she came to preside over a PLA forum on literature and art. The forum itself, held February 2–20, 1966, arrived at the sweeping conclusion that China's litera-

---

[113] T'ao had probably already ingratiated himself with the Maoists by taking a strong position of support for reform of the traditional Chinese opera (for example, in a statement of February 20, 1965, recalled in a *Jen-min Jih-pao* article of July 29 that year) and by continuing to exalt the Leap Forward and denounce critics of the commune system (as in an article written for *Hung Ch'i*, No. 8 [July 1965]).

[114] Although dated March 11, 1966, Lin's letter was not published for some three months, by which time the purge of the CCP's central propaganda organs was openly under way. (See *Jen-min Jih-pao*, June 19, 1966.) If this delay in publication was actually part of a deliberate attempt by some Party leaders to throttle Lin's growing power or to obstruct the swelling Maoist ideological tide, it would help explain the subsequent sweeping purge of CCP propaganda organs. On the basis of the unverified or circumstantial evidence now at hand, however, this possibility can only be suggested.

ture, drama, cinema, opera, and art all had been politically misguided—
an echo of Mao's bitter complaint of 1964 that his ideas on culture had
been ignored for years.[115]

The widening differences within the leadership over the nature and
role of ideology, which precipitated an increasingly open, if subtle, debate
in the fall and winter of 1965 and early 1966, gradually and almost inexo-
rably took on the character of a power struggle, as the chief protagonists
were unable either to resolve or to live with their differences within the
existing power structure. For the Maoists, who had initiated the dispute
and continued on the offensive, the clash of ideas was no academic matter, although it could be argued in philosophical terms. While they regarded the persistence of "reactionary ideas" and wily bourgeois influences as the basic cause of the feared "capitalist restoration," they saw
the ideological struggle as involving the ultimate question of state power.
This was clearly expressed after the Cultural Revolution had entered
openly upon the struggle for power: "Forgetting about state power means
forgetting about politics, forgetting about the basic theses of Marxism
and switching to economism, anarchism and utopianism and becoming
muddle-headed. In the last analysis, the class struggle in the ideological
field between the proletariat and the bourgeoisie is a struggle for leadership." [116]

In the early part of 1966, however, the relationship between the ideological struggle and the regime's power structure was only gradually
becoming clear to those in the leadership who were not fully committed
to a militant Maoist position. In Peking, anxious and bewildered Party
leaders, while echoing the praise of Mao, calling for emulation of a loyal
rural Party secretary, Chiao Yu-lu, and joining campaigns of invective
against such prominent literary figures as T'ien Han and Chien Po-
tsan, made desperate behind-the-scenes efforts to prevent the criticism
of Wu Han and others from leading to a high-level purge of the regime.

On February 12, according to recent Maoist sources, P'eng Chen released to the CCP, in the name of the Central Committee, an "Outline
Report on the Current Academic Discussion" purportedly made by the
"group of five" in charge of the Cultural Revolution. This report, which
evidently tried to channel the criticism of Wu Han into a politically in-

---

[115] A summary of the forum's work and conclusions was printed in *Hung Ch'i*,
No. 9 (May 1967). (See also *NCNA,* May 28, 1967.)

[116] From an editoral entitled "Sweep Away All Monsters," *Jen-min Jih-pao,* June
1, 1966.

nocous "academic" dispute, allegedly was released with the backing of
Liu Shao-ch'i but without the approval of K'ang Sheng.[117] Mao counterattacked on March 17 with a stinging, categorical condemnation of
Wu Han, charging that he and his ilk were no better than followers of
Chiang Kai-shek's Kuomintang and that the Peking Municipal Committee would have to be dissolved if it shielded him further.[118] Three
days later he is said to have raged: "The Central Propaganda Ministry
is the palace of the king of Hades [that is, Chou Yang] and so we must
overthrow the king and liberate the small devils." [119] These outbursts
(if we may accept their authenticity) were not even hinted at in published sources at the time; they probably were confined either to a small
circle in the top leadership or only to Mao's immediate coterie. It is interesting to note, moreover, that Mao was not yet ready to single out P'eng
Chen for direct attack even in private—either because he still hoped to
win P'eng over or, possibly, because he wanted to bait a bigger trap.

The conflict over ideology and general orientation, which thus far
had been the primary force in the Cultural Revolution, was now becoming entwined with a struggle for power. Available evidence does not,
however, bear out the subsequent allegations and innuendoes that ambitious Party figures such as P'eng Chen cynically moved to seize power
for themselves. It suggests, rather, that successive leaders who came
under Maoist attack (either directly, or indirectly through their pro-
tégés and subordinates) attempted in desperation to preserve the status
quo—the existing balance of power within the regime, including the
well-defined order of succession. While considerations of power thus
came to play a role, the conflict was still far from being, at its heart, a
classic power struggle. It was not fundamentally an unprincipled strife

[117] See the May 16, 1966, Circular of the Central Committee. According to this
source, P'eng Chen held no discussions within the "group of five" and exploited his
position as chairman of the group to rush through a draft of the "outline report"
and submit it to the Party in the name of the Central Committee. Among other
errors, the report was said to have diverted argument from the central political
issues in the Wu Han case, to have raised the slogan "everyone is equal before the
truth," and to have stressed "again and again that the struggle must be conducted
'under direction,' 'with prudence,' 'with caution,' and 'with the approval of the leading bodies concerned.' "

[118] This information, which cannot be verified, is from a ta-tzu-pao posted in
Peking on April 25, 1967, and quoted in Mainichi Shimbun two days later.

[119] This quotation appears in an article entitled "Chronology of the Two-Road
Struggle on the Educational Front in the Past 17 Years," which was included in
Chiao-yu Ko-ming (Educational Revolution). See JPRS 41,932, July 21, 1967 (Trans-
lations on Communist China: Political and Sociological, No. 411) p. 50.

arising out of conflicting personal ambitions and loyalties. Even if we hypothesize that internal tensions and disagreements within the leadership led to the emergence of informal alignments and interest groups, there is still no evidence that these coalesced into power factions operating with a distinct and relatively consistent membership and dedicated primarily to the seizure of power.

To be sure, unofficial wall posters put up by "revolutionary rebels" in 1967 were to make the sensational charge that several top Party leaders (including Liu Shao-ch'i, P'eng Chen, and Lo Jui-ch'ing) had plotted to oust Mao and seize power in a military coup d'état scheduled for February 1966.[120] If such a coup had been planned, it seems curious that its discovery and prevention should not have been revealed for a year, and stranger still that in the interim (even after Mao and Lin Piao consolidated their control at the Eleventh Plenum) the chief conspirators could have been entrusted with the highest responsibilities in state and Party, including the prosecution of the Cultural Revolution. Indeed, later ta-tzu-pao quote Chou En-lai as denying the alleged February plot, but officially sanctioned newspapers have continued to speak vaguely of an attempted coup, though perhaps more in reference to a suspected general threat over the years than to any concrete, specifically documented conspiracy.[121]

[120] A ta-tzu-pao posted in Peking on April 17, 1967, and signed by "revolutionary employees of the Peking CCP Committee" declared that information compiled from records of the Committee showed P'eng Chen and Liu Shao-ch'i to have plotted for several years to stockpile food, arms, medicine, and gasoline, independent of central control, in Peking suburbs in preparation for the February 1966 coup. This and other posters named Lo Jui-ch'ing, Lu Ting-i, and Yang Shang-k'un among the leaders of the plot and identified Teng Hsiao-p'ing (along with Liu Shao-ch'i) as an "arch-conspirator." Other posters have emphasized Ho Lung's alleged role in the coup, suggesting that Ho later attempted to use his military connections around the country (particularly in Szechuan) to prepare for a seizure of power. Thus far, these charges have not been specifically documented in official sources and cannot be verified on the basis of available evidence.

[121] Thus, a Jen-min Jih-pao editorial of April 17, 1967, in the course of an attack on Liu Shao-ch'i, referred in vague generalities to an attempt by P'eng Chen in the past to engineer a coup in behalf of Liu; it did not specify when that attempt took place. On April 28, according to Peking wallposters of May 7, Chou En-lai explicitly denied the existence of the rumored plot for a February 1966 coup. Admitting that P'eng Chen had ordered food to be stored in Peking suburbs to guard against any future crisis, Chou nevertheless argued that this action had subsequently been misinterpreted by the ultra-suspicious "Revolutionary Rebels." Chou's denial was indirectly supported by K'ang Sheng, who, although loath to criticize the suspicions of the rumormongers, suggested that P'eng Chen's stationing of troops near Peking

While there is no evidence that the leaders who had run afoul of Mao's intensifying drive to purify the regime were aiming for anything more than preserving the status quo, their position became untenable in late March, when Liu Shao-ch'i, perhaps now the strongest force for order and cohesion in the Politburo, left Peking with his wife on a state visit to Pakistan and Afghanistan and later to Burma. It is interesting, in retrospect, to note that their departure, on March 26, in company with Ch'en I and his wife, came just before the last public appearance of P'eng Chen,[122] and that Lu Ting-i also disappeared from the scene about this time.

Early in April, newspaper attacks against Wu Han resumed after a lull of several weeks. For the first time, the Party organ *Jen-min Jih-pao* joined in condemning *Hai Jui Dismissed from Office,* calling it a "poisonous weed," and the critics freely alleged that Wu Han had actually intended to exonerate P'eng Teh-huai. Meanwhile, the army's *Chieh-fang Chün Pao* stressed the responsibility of those in positions of leadership—including, rather pointedly, secretaries of Party committees—for the errors of their subordinates, and called for a renewal of self-criticism even among veteran and highly-placed cadres. On April 14 Kuo Mo-jo,

University and the People's University in February 1966 might have been misunderstood by the revolutionary students. (Extracts of the quoted statement by Chou and K'ang appeared in *Yomiuri Shimbun,* May 8, 1967.)

[122] On the afternoon of March 26 P'eng Chen welcomed to Peking a delegation of the Japanese Communist Party led by its General Secretary, Kenji Miyamoto. The subsequent disagreement of Japanese and Chinese leaders over the issue of damping down the Sino-Soviet dispute in order to provide "united assistance" in Vietnam has led some analysts to connect P'eng's words of friendship and praise for the Japanese with his subsequent downfall. However, it should be remembered that Moscow has specifically identified P'eng as one of the foremost enemies of Sino-Soviet cooperation, and many of his statements over the years did indeed reflect a decidedly anti-Soviet bias. Moreover, the proliferating Maoist charges against P'eng have not included allegations of improper connivance with the Miyamoto delegation. More recently, Japanese Communist Party (JCP) sources have claimed that a joint CCP-JCP communiqué was actually prepared (some say it was also signed) after discussions at Peking in which trusted supporters of Mao—including Chou En-lai and K'ang Sheng—participated though Liu Shao-ch'i and Teng Hsiao-p'ing did not. While the contents of this draft communiqué have not been revealed—and it may well have been an innocuous document—both Japanese and Chinese sources agree that it was subsequently scrapped on Mao's personal orders when the Miyamoto delegation visited him in Shanghai. If so, it would indicate that Mao wielded supreme power in the regime well before the purges of the Cultural Revolution. Japanese accounts of the affair were published in the JCP organ *Akahata* on November 4 and 7, 1967, in articles by Ichiro Sunama and Junichi Konno, respectively.

president of the Academy of Sciences and perhaps the best-known intellectual in the regime, made a groveling and extravagant confession of error, condemning all that he had ever written as "worthless" in the light of Mao's pristine standards and suitable only for burning. Two days later, the newspapers of the Peking Municipal Party Committee, *Peking Jih-pao* and *Ch'ien-hsien,* published abject self-criticisms in which they reproached themselves for having printed not only the objectionable works of Wu Han but also articles by Teng T'o and Liao Mo-sha, who had not been previously condemned.

THE FIRST PHASE OF THE CULTURAL REVOLUTION

On April 18, 1966, an editorial in *Chieh-fang Chün Pao* in effect publicly ushered in the first phase of the Great Proletarian Cultural Revolution, although it made no formal announcement of a new campaign and even spoke of a "socialist cultural revolution" as having developed over the preceding three years.[123] Tracing the "struggle of two roads" in Party history from Mao's 1942 criticism of Wang Ming forward, the editorial noted the intensification of that struggle which began after the Tenth Plenum (September 1962) and was subsequently manifested in the reform of the Peking opera. The article then called for a new upsurge of Maoist ideological study and mass criticism that would foster a proletarian outlook and eliminate the bourgeois vestiges in Chinese culture (notably, the "superstitious reverence" for the liberal literature and art of the 1930s).[124] The leading role and authoritative manner assumed by *Chieh-fang Chün Pao* in this and other editorials, in May

[123] Periodization always tends to be arbitrary, but it can be a useful device for organizing historical phenomena. Thus, the author is not disposed to quarrel with an editorial of the Shanghai *Wen Hui Pao* (September 30, 1967) which has dated the "first stage" of the Cultural Revolution as beginning with the Maoist attack on Wu Han in November 1965 (possibly to call attention to the significance of *Wen Hui Pao*'s role in the attack). His position in the present analysis, however, is that, even though dissension and conflict first came to the surface in the fall of 1965, the concerted and publicized drive to launch an unprecedentedly sweeping and profound "cultural revolution" came only in April of the following year.

[124] "Hold High the Great Red Banner of Mao Tse-tung's Thought and Actively Participate in the Great Socialist Cultural Revolution," *Chieh-fang Chün Pao,* April 18, 1966. Subsequently, Chou Yang and other figures active in the "national defense literature" of the 1930s were to be linked to Wang Ming, as rightists who opposed the "proletarian" line of Mao and Lu Hsün.

and June of 1966, made it apparent that Mao looked to the PLA (or, at least, its General Political Department) and Lin Piao to carry out the Cultural Revolution, although it was admitted that some elements in the army had opposed this assignment. The militant tone of these articles, as reflected in such titles as "Never Forget the Class Struggle" (May 4) and "Open Fire on the Black Anti-Party and Anti-Socialist Line!" (May 8), portended a violent and thorough purge, which would go beyond literary and art circles to strike at "bourgeois" elements in the Party and army and thereby to achieve a basic ideological "rectification" touching all of society.

Meanwhile, there was intense political maneuvering behind the scenes as the Peking Party Committee tried desperately to withstand the Maoist assault. The April 16 self-criticism of the Peking newspapers under the Committee's control was rejected by the Maoists as a fraud, though this was not revealed until the publication of a withering editorial in *Chieh-fang Chün Pao* on May 8. During most of the critical period of March 26 to April 19, Liu Shao-ch'i was traveling abroad (except for a brief return to Sinkiang in the first days of April) on a trip that turned out to be much more extensive than originally announced. On April 21, two days after Liu's unceremonious return to China, Mao, who was vacationing with Lin Piao in Hangchow, is reported to have sent a blunt letter criticizing P'eng Chen to a meeting of the Politburo Standing Committee chaired by Liu. According to the same source, a "central conference" of the leaders in Hangchow had already "fatally" censured P'eng.[125] When he thereupon attempted to evade responsibility by shifting the blame for errors of the Peking Committee to Teng T'o, Mao again denounced him. A Red Guard account of the backstage maneuvering in late April stresses the role of Liu Jen (Second Secretary of the Peking Committee and Political Commissar of the Peking garrison), who allegedly spread the story that P'eng Chen's only mistake was in regard to the aforementioned "Outline Report" of the "group of five," released in February 1966.[126]

---

[125]This information is from a Peking wall poster put up on April 25, 1967, and summarized in *Mainichi Shimbun* on April 27, 1967. Earlier, the Red Guard newspaper *Chan Pao* (February 24, 1967) had referred to "documents" criticizing P'eng Chen and the Peking CCP Committee which were sent to it by Mao on April 21, 1966.

[126] *Chan Pao,* February 24, 1967. Liu Jen was also accused of conspiring secretly with other members of the Peking Party Committee (notably, Cheng T'ien-hsiang) to thwart Mao's criticism, and of later burning compromising documents of the Committee to evade censure.

These and other defensive maneuvers were interpreted by the Maoists as exposing the "revisionist nature" of P'eng and his associates, who were described as having crawled out of their holes like "poisonous snakes" under the increasingly rigorous tests of ideological loyalty.[127] Apparently, some of Mao's followers still did not fully grasp the extent of Mao's suspicions and the depth of his determination to purge the Party leadership.[128] These became clearer in early May, as *Chieh-fang Chün Pao* and the Shanghai Party newspapers launched a series of increasingly violent attacks against the Peking CCP press, Teng T'o, and finally the "black gang" in the Municipal Party Committee. P'eng Chen's days were numbered.

The axe fell at an enlarged conference of the Politburo that was convened by Mao some time in May, probably around the middle of the month. It is entirely possible that the meeting did not take place in Peking. At least, Mao appears to have entertained a visiting Albanian delegation elsewhere early that month (perhaps at Shanghai on May 5, three days before *Chieh-fang Chün Pao* had publicly rejected the self-criticism of the Peking Party press).[129] Whatever the precise date and

[127] See, for example, the sensational exposé entitled "Thoroughly Criticize and Repudiate the Revisionist Line of Some of the Principal Leading Members of the Former Peking Municipal Party Committee" in *Hung Ch'i*, No. 9 (July 1966).

[128] Thus, in a speech on April 30, 1967, Ch'i Pen-yü recalled that when Mao, on April 30, 1966, had exclaimed that Khrushchevites were all around "being raised as our successors" while the people slept, "we could not understand what he meant." At that time, Ch'i continued, traitorous elements still had a strong hold on the Party Central Committee and its propaganda and organization departments as well as on government offices. (A résumé of Ch'i's speech was published in *Mainichi Shimbun*, May 12, 1967.) It may be significant that Mao's unpublicized remarks of April 1966 came two days after Liu Shao-ch'i had addressed a visiting Albanian delegation in a major speech in which, though he delivered a scathing attack on Soviet "revisionism," he neglected to mention Mao, to praise his thought, and to refer to the Cultural Revolution.

[129] On May 10 Radio Peking announced that Mao had met earlier with the visiting Albanians led by Mehmet Shehu and had hosted a banquet in their honor (date and place unspecified). It was his first public appearance in nearly six months. On May 11 *Jen-min Jih-pao* and other newspapers gave prominent coverage to the event, featuring a banquet photograph that showed Mao with most of his top lieutenants and the Albanian guests. Interestingly enough, Teng Hsiao-p'ing was seen seated immediately on Mao's right, flanked by Chou en-lai and, in third place, Lin Piao (who had also been out of the public eye for several months). Liu Shao-ch'i, who was not present—although he entertained the Albanians during both their earlier and later visits to Peking—had presumably remained in the capital. While we cannot be absolutely sure from present evidence just when or where the banquet occurred, the best guess would be that it was held at Shanghai on the afternoon and

site of the fateful Politburo conference, we are now told that Mao used the session to launch an open attack directly against P'eng Chen and others of "the counterrevolutionary clique." [130]

Mao's indictment received the official endorsement of the Party in a Central Committee Circular of May 16, 1966, which dissolved the "group of five" and its offices, revoked the controversial "Outline Report" which P'eng Chen had rashly circulated on February 12, and established a new group, directly under the Standing Committee of the Politburo, to carry out the Cultural Revolution.[131] Besides calling upon the CCP to "criticize and repudiate" what were termed the anti-Party, antisocialist "so-called academic authorities," the Circular warned that "representatives of the bourgeoisie" had sneaked into Party, government, army, and cultural spheres and that they must be either removed or transferred to other positions: "Some of them we have already seen through, others we have not. Some we still trust and are training as our successors. There are, for example, people of the Khrushchev brand still nestling in our midst." "Above all," said the Circular, such people must not be entrusted with leading the Cultural Revolution. However, it assumed that "many" were still as-

___

evening of May 5, since we know that Teng, Chou, and others listed as present were there with the Albanians on that day, and since the visitors' announced schedule would have permitted a lengthy talk and evening banquet then—but not so easily on other days of their itinerary. Had the banquet been held in Peking, it seems unlikely that Liu Shao-ch'i would have been absent from it.

[130] This information, which comes from a recent Red Guard Booklet (*Chiao-yu Ko-ming*, translation in *JPRS* 41,932, July 21, 1967 [*Translations on Communist China: Political and Sociological*, No. 411]), identified other members of the "clique" as Lu Ting-i, Lo Jui-ch'ing, and Yang Shang-k'un. This may exaggerate the scope of Mao's concept of "the counterrevolutionary clique" at that time, although the four men have been linked in subsequent Red Guard accusations. The focus of Mao's attack probably was P'eng Chen and the Peking Party Committee. The relatively less powerful leaders Lu, Lo, and Yang managed to elude public humiliation for a month or more after P'eng's downfall—although Lo, at least, had probably been secretly suspended some months before the May conference.

[131] The May 16 circular, which was not published for a year (*NCNA*, May 16, 1967), was originally sent to all CCP regional bureaus, all committees of provincial and equivalent level, all departments and commissions under the Central Committee, all leading Party members and groups in state and mass organizations, and the PLA's General Political Department. Moreover, it directed that these recipients send copies of both the circular and the erroneous "outline" of February 12 down to Party committees at the *hsien* level in the civil administration and at the regimental level in the PLA. Radio Peking, in commenting on the significance of the May 16 circular a year later, declared that it had "for the first time . . . systematically presented the theory, line, principles, and policy of the Great Proletarian Cultural Revolution" (*NCNA*, May 17, 1967).

signed to such tasks, thereby creating an "extremely dangerous" situation. The dismissal of P'eng Chen was belatedly revealed in an announcement, on June 3, 1966, that the Peking Party Committee had been reorganized some time before under a new first secretary, Li Hsüeh-feng.[132] In all likelihood the purge of the CCP's central propaganda apparatus began at about the same time, although the replacement of Lu Ting-i and Chou Yang was not publicly announced until July. Significantly, the central Party organ, *Jen-min Jih-pao,* rather abruptly assumed an extreme Maoist tone in a series of editorials published in the first week of June. Afterward, the army's *Chieh-fang Chün Pao*—until then the leading voice of the press in the Cultural Revolution—went to some lengths of deference to affirm the authoritative nature of these statements.

Meanwhile, Mao and other top leaders were publicly and privately explaining the nature and objectives of the "great revolution that touches people to their very souls." On May 1, 1966, Chou En-lai told a Sino-Albanian friendship meeting in Peking: "A socialist cultural revolution of great historic significance is being launched in our country. This is a fierce and protracted struggle of 'who will win,' the proletariat or the bourgeoisie, in the ideological field. We must vigorously promote proletarian ideology and eradicate bourgeois ideology in the academic, educational and journalistic fields, in art, literature, and in all other fields of culture. This is a key question in the development in depth of our socialist revolution at the present stage, a question concerning the situation as a whole and a matter of the first magnitude affecting the destiny and the future of our Party and country."[133]

A few days later, on May 7, Mao issued an unpublicized directive pointing toward the ultimate goal of this ideological revolution—the new Communist man, imbued with proletarian consciousness and able to act in all social roles. He declared that persons in all walks of life—soldiers, laborers, peasants, intellectuals, Party cadres, and others—should be trained in politics, culture, and military affairs so as to become useful in industry, agriculture, and warfare, or wherever else needed.[134] Other au-

---

[132] In keeping with the regime's usual practice of refraining from public attacks on disgraced Politburo members, P'eng Chen's name was not mentioned in the official press (as opposed to unofficial sources such as Red Guard posters) until the publication of the May 16, 1966, resolution in May 1967.

[133] *NCNA,* May 1, 1966.

[134] The content of Mao's May 7 directive was publicized a year later in articles celebrating the anniversary of its drafting. (See, in particular, *Jen-min Jih-pao,* May 8, 1967.) In education, Mao foresaw an end to the traditional domination of

thoritative statements pointed out, however, that before these objectives could be realized it was necessary to uproot all "bourgeois" elements standing in opposition to socialism and the thought of Mao Tse-tung: "Without destruction, there will be no construction." [135]

Thus, as the Cultural Revolution unfolded, during late May, June, and July of 1966, spreading out from Peking into the provinces, its main fire was directed against the presumed agents of "bourgeois" ideology on the cultural front—educators, writers, and artists as well as their official supervisors in the CCP propaganda apparatus. Concentrating initially on institutions of higher learning—notably the universities in Peking, Nanking, Shanghai, and Wuhan—the humiliation and purging of academic officials extended downward through the entire educational system; the attack culminated in an announcement, on June 13, of a six-month suspension of all regular schooling to permit the formulation of new and ideologically purer criteria for student admission.

At the time, the main instruments for implementing the purge at the local level were "work teams" that the Party committees sent out to the schools and universities under their jurisdiction. Ultimate control evidently was vested in an ad hoc group within the regular central Party apparatus dominated by Liu Shao-ch'i and Teng Hsiao-p'ing.[136] The phenomenon of the work teams, which effectively put local Party officials in charge of directing and supervising the Cultural Revolution, was not a new organizational device, having been employed earlier in the "socialist education campaign." In the absence of new, specific directives on how to carry out the Cultural Revolution, the teams used the techniques developed in previous rectification drives, which included the selective application of violence and terror, always carefully limited and kept under tight Party control. Such concern for order and discipline was, of course, diametrically opposed to the prevailing atmosphere of militancy, intoler-

---

"bourgeois intellectuals" (specialists or professionals) by such means as reduced curricula and a broadened, albeit more superficial, scope of studies.

[135] *Jen-min Jih-pao*, June 4, 1966.

[136] It will be recalled that the May 16, 1966, circular of the Central Committee called for the establishment of a new group, directly under the Politburo Standing Committee, to take charge of the Cultural Revolution—replacing P'eng Chen's "group of five." We may infer that Mao, as Chairman of the Standing Committee, approved this arrangement, which, until he himself chose to play a more active and direct role in Peking, gave overall responsibility for guiding the Cultural Revolution to Liu and Teng. Presumably this would have been the case even though, as we shall see below, on July 9 Ch'en Po-ta was revealed to be the "leader of the group in charge of the Cultural Revolution."

ance, and suspicion engendered by the Maoist ideological revival and the consequent denigration of formerly venerated teachers and officials.

The inevitable clash between Party authority and the revolutionary "left" occurred toward the end of May, when Nieh Yüan-tzu, a philosophy instructor at Peking University, and six of her students, purportedly on their own initiative, posted a *ta-tzu-pao* directly criticizing the university's president and CCP Committee. The newly reorganized Peking Municipal Party Committee, apparently sensing the potential danger in such unauthorized attacks, ordered the poster taken down. At this point the matter was brought to the attention of Mao (perhaps by Chiang Ch'ing), who on June 1 personally ordered that the poster be published throughout China.[137] It appeared in *Jen-min Jih-pao* the following day, a portent of the future direction of the Cultural Revolution and testimony to Mao's ultimate power. In approving this "first Marxist-Leninist poster," as it is now called, Mao emphasized his determination to "go to the masses." His action, according to later assessments, "kindled the flames of the Great Proletarian Cultural Revolution and set in motion the mass movement." [138] Moreover, Mao's curious reference to the poster as the "declaration of the Peking People's Commune in the 1960s" is now cited as evidence that he foresaw the emergence of a "new form" of state organization—one which, elaborating on the model of the Paris Commune of 1871, would mobilize China's huge population to smash the old order, seize power from "the handful" of Party authorities "taking the capitalist road," and create an entirely new revolutionary situation and a proletarian dictatorship.[139]

Although Mao evidently overruled the new Peking CCP Committee on the unauthorized posting of *ta-tzu-pao,* he gave no open hint of a general or profound dissatisfaction with the leadership of the Cultural Revolution at the time, and left the regular Party apparatus in charge of it through June and July. It was subsequently charged, however, that during this period "one, two, or even several responsible persons in the

[137] See speech by K'ang Sheng on September 8, 1966, in *Current Background,* U.S. Consulate General, Hong Kong, No. 819 (March 10, 1967).

[138] See New Year's editorial entitled "Carry the Great Proletarian Cultural Revolution Through to the End" in *Jen-min Jih-pao,* January 1, 1967. Chou En-lai later referred to Mao's order for publication of the poster as "the first signal" of the Cultural Revolution. (See his speech to a Congress of Red Guards of Peking Universities released by *NCNA* on March 2, 1967.)

[139] These claims of Mao's foresight were made in an editorial entitled "On the Struggle of the Proletarian Revolutionaries to Seize Power," published in *Hung Ch'i,* No. 3 (February 3, 1967).

Central Committee" seized upon Mao's absence from Peking to attempt to sabotage the Cultural Revolution. They allegedly tried to impose a "bourgeois dictatorship" on all sectors under their control, advancing a "bourgeois reactionary line," "clamping down on different views," and carrying out a "white terror" to suppress the revolutionary activists.[140] More specifically, according to the later indictments, the CCP apparatus under Liu Shao-ch'i and Teng Hsiao-p'ing hurriedly dispatched work teams throughout the country without consulting Mao, who "as early as June" had urged that the teams "not be sent out hastily." [141] It might be more accurate to say that Liu and Teng sent the teams in response to a rising number of calls from organizations and schools for investigation and purge of their leaders, and that the moderateness of this response was in keeping with the practice employed in the earlier "Four Cleanups" campaign. An alternative, the critics later pointed out, would have been for the Party apparatus to give the left activists in local organizations free rein to promote spontaneous and uncontrolled "revolution." [142]

Whatever may have been the intent behind their dispatch, the work

[140] *Jen-min Jih-pao,* January 1, 1967.

[141] See November 28, 1966, speech of Chiang Ch'ing at Peking rally of literature and art workers, excerpts of which appeared in *Hung Ch'i,* No. 15 (December 13, 1966). In a speech by T'ao Chu in December, publicized in a Peking *ta-tzu-pao* posted on December 14, 1966, Liu and Teng were publicly named as leaders of the plot to sabotage the Cultural Revolution (during Mao's absence from Peking in June and July). (*The Washington Post,* December 15, 1966.) According to one Red Guard source, Liu dispatched the work teams despite the fact that, during a conference held at Hangchow on June 9, 1966, Mao had warned against sending them out. (*Ching-kang-shan,* February 1 and 8, 1967.)

[142] On August 22, in an address at Tsinghua University, Chou En-lai declared that when local organs requested that work teams be sent to them ("according to the requirement of the Four Clearances [Cleanups] campaign"), the Party Center and Peking Municipal CCP Committee could have employed either of two measures: "One was to send the work team which would seize the power of the black gang, or suspected black gang, or the capitalist authoritarian elements. . . . The alternative was to let the people of the particular unit promote the revolution themselves and throw everything into confusion for a period." In the latter case, he took it for granted that "the people would rise up themselves to promote the revolution under the call of the Great Proletarian Cultural Revolution and follow the revolutionary path," an assumption that Liu, Teng, and other Party regulars apparently were unwilling to make. Chou complained that the Party authorities failed to "experiment" with both courses of action, electing only to send out the work teams. Moreover, the teams were not clearly instructed as to "policy and tasks" and inevitably made mistakes. (See the text of Chou's speech, as translated from a collection of materials on the Cultural Revolution published in Canton on October 28, 1966, in *JPRS* 41,313, June 8, 1967 [*Translations on Communist China: Political and Sociological,* No. 398].)

teams seem to have acted with less than all-out enthusiasm on encountering the raging mass criticism and the purging of prominent intellectuals and Party officials. Faced in many places with a situation rapidly approaching anarchy, they tried to maintain some semblance of order and Party control. As a militant young kindergarten teacher later complained: "The work team was the fire-extinguishing team. Upon its arrival [at the school], it immediately urged us to "calm down, and not be excessive." It, in fact, encouraged the bourgeois authoritarians and discouraged the revolutionary masses." [143]

As the struggle deepened, pitting individuals and groups against each other all of whom claimed to be for Mao and revolution, distinctions between "true" and "false" revolutionaries became increasingly subjective and debatable. As the work teams had not been given clear criteria for judgment, they tended to procrastinate and to damp down student extremism. For example, the team that Mme Liu Shao-ch'i (Wang Kuang-mei) led to Tsinghua University on June 21 began, as she later allegedly confessed, by demanding "adequate preparation" before anyone could level accusations at individuals. Terming its critics "false leftists" and "troublesome schemers" (a charge not without some foundation), the team maneuvered to prolong the debate, thereby "leading to a situation in which students struggled against students, and the battlefield was enlarged." Ultimately, according to Mme Liu, "We could no longer control the situation and therefore resorted to strong political repression." [144] Thus, what may have begun as a normal, if not perfectly legitimate, concern of the CCP's "organization men" for discipline and stability ended in alienation of the "revolutionary leftists," who—even in the absence of any coercion—would likely have viewed the "work teams" as part of a plot to sabotage the Cultural Revolution.[145]

[143] See article by Hsü Chien-hua in the Red Guard periodical *Hung-se Chih-kung* (*Red Staff Members and Workers*), No. 3, January 29, 1967. (Translation in *JPRS* 41,107, May 22, 1967 [*Translations on Communist China: Political and Sociological,* No. 396].) Hsü had posted *ta-tzu-pao* attacking her kindergarten principal in early June, and this apparently had resulted in the dispatch of a work team to the school. She was speechless with anger when the team overrode her criticism and suggested that those resisting its decision were "counterrevolutionary." However, her protest to the newly reorganized Peking Muncipal CCP Committee was ignored, and, because of her persistent efforts to purge the principal, she was subsequently branded an "ambitious individual" (which may not have been far from the truth).

[144] An account of Mme Liu's confession, said to have been written in October 1966, was published in *The Washington Post,* December 28, 1966.

[145] It would, of course, be difficult, if not impossible, to identify and weigh pre-

All this is not to say, of course, that Liu and the Party apparatus were totally blameless. Their support for Mao's increasingly radical campaign of indoctrination and purge was at best lukewarm, and they evidently were bending every effort to bring it under firm Party control. While Liu continued to play a very prominent political role after his return from the extended spring trip to South and Southeast Asia—he presided at the May Day fete at Tien-an-men, entertained State visitors, and, as late as July 22, 1966, was keynote speaker at a massive Vietnam war rally —he remained strangely quiet on the burning topics of Mao's thought and Cultural Revolution, in contrast even to such "moderates" as Chou En-lai. *Jen-min Jih-pao* on July 1 quoted approving references to Mao's thought by Liu and Teng Hsiao-p'ing, as well as by Chou and Lin Piao, but it did not substantially increase the public commitment of the Party apparatus to the increasingly fanatical leftward course prescribed by Mao.[146]

Some of the most damaging evidence against Liu Shao-ch'i for his role in this period has been supplied in his own alleged confessions (none of which, however, has been accepted by the Maoists to date). According to these, Liu presided over the CCP Center in Mao's absence from Peking and was in charge of the Cultural Revolution for approximately fifty days after June 1, 1966. During this period he acknowledged having made mistakes of policy, notably in the dispatch of work teams which suppressed the revolutionary masses, instituted local news blackouts, and forbade street demonstrations or the posting of *ta-tzu-pao*. This, according to Liu's reported admission, led to a situation, beginning in Peking, in which students were set against students, true "revolutionaries" (a small minority in most cases) were accused of being counterrevolutionary,

---

cisely all the varied motives driving the "revolutionary leftists." Their opposition almost certainly sprang from a range of mixed motives, personal and psychological as well as ideological. Some probably were congenital radicals and malcontents; at least a few nourished real or imagined grievances against the established authorities; some may have acted primarily from considerations of personal ambition, while others were sincerely driven by an uncompromising idealism or rigid, puritanical zeal. In any event, it would seem reasonable to suppose that in the prevailing unstable, iconoclastic atmosphere, and given an ill-defined—almost open-ended—mandate to criticize, many students were likely to be disposed toward extremism.

[146] Among other things, this editorial (celebrating the CCP's 45th anniversary) attempted to establish a criterion for separating "true" from "false" revolutionaries. It declared: "One's attitude toward Mao Tse-tung's thought is the yardstick distinguishing the genuine revolutionary from the sham revolutionary and the counterrevolutionary, the Marxist-Leninist from the revisionist."

student clashes erupted, and an "atmosphere of terror" prevailed in many schools.[147]

Other sources have indirectly confirmed Liu's efforts at this time to retain some measure of discipline and Party control over the rapidly spreading conditions of chaotic, violent struggle in the universities and other institutions. For example, at Liu's suggestion a "Socialist Institute" was established outside Peking, where some five-hundred prominent artists, writers, teachers, and cultural officials who had been attacked were sent for criticisms and reform under protective custody, thus saved for a time from bodily injury by uncontrolled and increasingly hysterical mobs of student activists.[148] Similarly, Liu Shao-ch'i and T'ao Chu are now

[147] In his first self-criticism (delivered at a Party meeting in October 1966 but reported only on December 26, 1966, in a Red Guard poster), Liu maintained that the work teams were initially dispatched to schools and organizations in the capital *through* the reorganized Peking CCP committee, in response to "very active" requests by important officials of departments under the Central Committee and by the central headquarters of the Communist Youth League. This would help explain the subsequent violent criticism against the new Peking Party committee (under Li Hsüeh-feng). Liu went on to explain that, after news of the dispatch of work teams to Peking institutions was published, requests flooded in for the sending of such teams to many other parts of the country. The content of Liu's first confession was reported in *Asahi,* December 27, 1966, and *Mainichi Shimbun,* January 28 and 29, 1967. Lengthy extracts later appeared in *Current Scene,* Vol. 5, No. 9 (May 31, 1967). A full translation is in *Issues and Studies,* Vol. 6, No. 9 (June 1970) pp. 90–98.

In a second self-criticism (said to have been written for a group of Peking Red Guards on July 9, 1967, and reported in *Mainichi Shimbun* on July 31), Liu repeated that in June and July of 1966 he had made errors in "policy line and direction" when he sent out work teams which then proceeded to suppress the "revolutionary teachers and students." He added that this mistake was compounded in early August, when for three days he went to the Peking Architectural College to direct the activities of the Cultural Revolution, in company with Li Hsüeh-feng, Liu Lan-t'ao, Ku Mu, and Ch'i Pen-yü. In this position Liu restricted the posting of *ta-tzu-pao* and punished as "counterrevolutionaries" students who tried to distribute bulletins from Peking University—actions that were admittedly in "violation" of the May 16 Central Committee circular (and, as we shall presently see, of Mao's proposal of July 24 that work teams be recalled). A full text of this "confession" has now been published. See *SCMP* 4037, October 1967. A third "confession" has recently come to light. Apparently written some time before its appearance in July–August 1967 on a Red Guard wall poster, it appears to be more a rebuttal than a self-criticism and adds nothing new to the story. See *Chinese Law and Government,* Vol. 1, No. 1 (Spring 1968) pp. 75–80.

[148] The celebrated violinist Ma Ts'e-ts'ung, who was President of the Central Music Academy in Peking before he fled the mainland, later recounted his fifty-day incarceration at the Socialist Institute. The program of criticism and thought reform was far from mild, but it was conducted under the disciplined supervision of army

said to have mitigated the proposals for reform of the educational system in July, which called, among other things, for the reconvening of primary and middle schools in the fall. The proposals later were attacked as part of a dark plot to "strangle" the development of the Cultural Revolution in the schools.[149]

Such evidence of moderation and reticence in the face of a runaway Cultural Revolution should not obscure the very substantial "reforms" that were being carried out under the over-all leadership of Liu and the Party apparatus. As early as June 9, 1966, the All-China Federation of Trade Unions called upon its constituent organs to place the Cultural Revolution "in the topmost position of all work" and regard it as "the center of current trade union work" (although emphasizing that it was to be carried out under firm CCP guidance).[150] Simultaneously with these intensified efforts to mobilize mass support for the Cultural Revolution, the purge of high-level Party and government officials was stepped up. In early July, after a barrage of public attacks against Chou Yang and Lin Mo-han, important changes were revealed in the leadership of several key Party organs: T'ao Chu was named head of the Central Committee's Propaganda Department, a post previously held by Lu Ting-i; he and Yeh Chien-ying were appointed to the Secretariat (Yeh

men. However, the inmates were subjected to much greater abuse and personal danger when, occasionally, they were sent back to their respective schools for mass criticism. When Ma and his companions arrived at the Socialist Institute in mid-June of 1966, they were told that they would be there from eight to twelve months, depending on their progress in reforming. On August 9, however, they were suddenly returned to the hostile environment of Peking, perhaps an indication of Liu Shao-ch'i's loss of power at that time. (See Ma Ts'e-ts'ung's story in *Life,* June 2, 1967.)

    [149] "Chronology of the Two-Road Struggle," translation in *JPRS* 41,932, July 21, 1967 (*Translations on Communist China: Political and Sociological*, No. 411) p. 52.

    [150] *Kung-jen Jih-pao,* June 10, 1966. The June 9 notice instructed trade union organizations to act "under the leadership of Party committees at all levels" and to strive to be "competent assistants to the Party." It viewed the Cultural Revolution primarily in ideological terms, as "a struggle between Marxism-Leninism and Mao Tse-tung's thought, on the one side, and capitalist and revisionist ideology, on the other." It summoned trade unionists to develop "a high degree of revolutionary fervor," unite with the masses, take an active part in criticizing bourgeois intellectual "authorities," unmask the anti-Party "black gang" (destroying the "three-family villages" and sweeping away all "monsters"), wipe out the influence of "black lines" in the trade unions, and eradicate the "four olds" (old ideology, culture, habits, and customs). Regarding Mao's thought as "the supreme directive for all work" and "never forgetting the class struggle," the trade unions were to become "schools for creatively studying and applying Chairman Mao's works."

presumably replacing Lo Jui-ch'ing in that body); and Ch'en Po-ta, Mao's trusted political secretary, was referred to as "leader of the group in charge of the Cultural Revolution."[151] It has been estimated that, by the end of July, at least one hundred and sixty-five prominent literary figures, professors, and officials responsible for cultural and propaganda work had been purged.[152]

Despite these accomplishments, Mao appeared to be dissatisfied. In part, his displeasure may have resulted from unrealistically high expectations for the Cultural Revolution following the purge of P'eng Chen and the inauguration of a new leadership for the Revolution in mid-May.[153] By any standard, however, there were grounds for disappointment, as the local work teams, unclear as to their mission, stirred up a storm of resistance among "revolutionary leftists." At Peking University the team was itself purged by radical activists. At Tsinghua University, where Mme Liu's team successfully stemmed the opposition for a time, a minority of students in the affiliated middle school organized into a militant combat group—precursor of the Red Guards—dedicated to rebellion against the "revisionist leadership." Moreover, there is evidence that in some places PLA political cadres assigned to the work teams worked at cross purposes with the Party leadership, actively encouraging the rebellious elements. (However, this alone would not justify the inference of

[151] See *NCNA* dispatches of July 7, 9, and 10, 1966. Possible factors in T'ao Chu's sudden elevation from regional to national leadership were suggested on p. 84 above. The puzzling story of his equally precipitous fall from power in late December 1966 lies beyond the scope of the present study. Despite the subsequent Maoist attempts to link him with the alleged crimes of Liu Shao-ch'i, in June and July 1966, it would seem more likely that T'ao was not regarded as having erred until some time after August, when his political star reached its zenith.

[152] See Chün-tu Hsüeh, "The Cultural Revolution and Leadership Crisis in Communist China," *Political Science Quarterly*, Vol. 82, No. 2 (June 1967) p. 178. While the vast majority of Hsüeh's total were purged in the public phase of the Cultural Revolution after mid-April 1966, he apparently also included among the 165 the handful of prominent officials dismissed during the earlier stages of the "socialist education campaign." On the other hand, the Hong Kong-based American journalist Robert Elegant has estimated that, during the two months of June and July alone, "more than 300 senior propagandists and educators were purged." (*The Los Angeles Times*, April 9, 1967.)

[153] The following October, in his speech to a Party work conference, Mao recalled his profound dissatisfaction at the lack of attention paid to articles and Central Committee announcements publicizing the Cultural Revolution in the period from January to May. Presumably, he expected much more from the new leadership prescribed in the Central Committee circular of May 16. This speech is translated in *Current Background*, No. 89 (October 8, 1969) pp. 75–77.

some analysts that Mao was conspiring with Lin Piao to sabotage the efforts of the teams so as to discredit and entrap top CCP leaders like Liu and Teng.)[154]

On July 18, 1966, two days after his celebrated swim in the Yangtze,[155] Mao returned to Peking, where from then on he was to play a more active role in the leadership of the Cultural Revolution. His influence was dramatically manifested only six days later, on July 24, when the Party decided to recall the controversial "work teams" and to convene a Central Work Conference.[156] Shortly thereafter, on August 1, the Elev-

[154] An article in *Hung Ch'i,* No. 5 (March 30, 1967), tells of the participation of three PLA political cadres on the work team sent to carry out the Cultural Revolution at Nanking University. Beginning in late June, they covertly played an independent role, disagreeing with and then opposing the provincial CCP Committee's orders and encouraging student attacks on high university officials. These activities were all the more serious as one of the three men was deputy political commissar of the Kiangsu Provincial Military district.

In assessing the significance of this story it should be noted that such reports of PLA sabotage of the Party-led work teams have not been widespread. Even in this single case, moreover, there is no indication that the PLA trio acted on higher orders from the military establishment (that is, Lin Piao). Indeed, the deputy commissar might have been acting in direct opposition to the wishes of his superior (whose position on the matter was not revealed). The history of the PLA in the Cultural Revolution is replete with examples of bold deputy commissars who were promoted for daring to "rebel." Thus, the *Hung Ch'i* article, far from substantiating a Mao-Lin plot to sabotage the work teams (much less to entrap Liu and Teng), may be no more than the account of a single case of three especially zealous—or unscrupulously ambitious—PLA cadres who sought to spark student unrest and refused to abide by the provincial CCP committee's order to cool things down (an order that may have been supported by the commissar of the Military District).

[155] According to official accounts released nine days after the event, Mao swam a distance of almost 15 kilometers in the Yangtze (downstream, presumably) in the incredible time of one hour and five minutes. He was accompanied by Wang Jen-chung, Second Secretary of the CCP Central South Bureau, First Secretary T'ao Chu having previously departed for Peking. For an account of the controversial swim see Michael Freeberne, "The Great Splash Forward," *Problems of Communism,* Vol. 15, No. 6 (November–December 1966). More recently, Red Guard sources have suggested that not all Chinese leaders appreciated Mao's marathon feat, an attitude which later got some into difficulties. Teng Hsiao-p'ing is quoted as having expressed the rash view, doubtless in private, that "Everyone suffers from subjectivism, Mao Tse-tung also. Thus, many people did not want him to go for a swim, but he completely ignored them." (Quoted from *Hsin Pei-ta,* January 30, 1967, in *The New York Times,* January 31, 1967.)

[156] See Liu Shao-ch'i's self-criticisms of October 1966 and July 1967, *Mainichi Shimbun,* January 28 and 29, and July 13, 1967. In his second confession, as noted earlier, Liu admitted having continued to support the work team at the Peking Architectural College as late as the beginning of August 1966.

enth Plenum of the CCP Central Committee convened in Peking, the
first such meeting in nearly four years.[157]

Even before its work had been concluded, pushing the Cultural Revolution to a new stage of development, Mao had further revealed his objectives and his determination to induce sweeping changes. On August 1,
Chieh-fang Chün Pao in its Army Day editorial quoted excerpts from
Mao's previously unpublicized directive of May 7, in which he exhorted
the PLA to become a "Great School" where soldiers mastered politics and
culture as well as the military arts.[158] The new Maoist vision revealed in
this statement was of a pure, utopian Communist society, in which all

---

[157] According to a sensational press report from Peking, first published in the
Yugoslav journal *Politica* and later reprinted in other periodicals, Liu Shao-ch'i and
his adherents had attempted earlier to call a plenary session of the Central Committee, on July 21, to impeach Mao during his absence from Peking. This was said
to be in retaliation for Mao's PLA-backed seizure of mass media in early June and
for the purge of P'eng Chen—who was now busily traveling in the northwest and
southwest lobbying for the support of Central Committee members. By mid-July,
with half of those members in Peking and anti-Mao troops on the way from Shensi,
the chances of impeachment looked good. However, says the report, on July 17 and
18 Lin Piao moved forces into strategic points around Peking and Tientsin and
proceeded to take over the capital garrison, arrest Lo Jui-ch'ing (allegedly Liu's
ally), and restore Mao's position. In these circumstances Teng Hsiao-p'ing, the CCP
Secretary General, changed his mind and refused to call the plenary session of the
Central Committee that Liu had requested. With the situation firmly under control,
Mao returned to Peking in triumph on July 28.

As Gene T. Hsiao has pointed out (*Asian Survey*, Vol. 8, No. 6 [June 1967] pp.
389–404) this account is of doubtful validity, for the overwhelming weight of evidence indicates that Mao returned to Peking on July 18 and that Lo Jui-ch'ing was
not arrested until December 1966 (although he had been dismissed from office
months earlier). While it can be argued that these facts do not necessarily contradict
the essential elements of the "impeachment theory," other aspects of the situation
would tend to do so. For example, Liu was the most prominent leader in evidence
at a massive Vietnam war rally in Peking on July 22, the day after the planned impeachment plenum was to have taken place. Indeed, Liu seems to have retained
his power until the August plenum convened. Moreover, it seems doubtful that
Liu and his friends desired to restore P'eng Chen—much less had any realistic hope
of doing so—after the general condemnation of the Peking "black gang" in May,
June, and early July. One could also question whether the alleged troop movements
around Peking (which have not been corroborated elsewhere) would have been
necessary, inasmuch as Mao had apparently censured P'eng Chen effectively from
Hangchow, or that they would have intimidated dissident Central Committeemen,
dissuading them from assembling. Until more persuasive evidence can be adduced,
the "impeachment theory" remains interesting but improbable.

[158] As indicated above, the date and context of the quoted statements by Mao
were not made public until May 1967.

individual interests and occupational differences (such as those between industry and agriculture, mental and manual work, and urban and rural concerns) would have been eliminated and the ideal of a completely selfless and interchangeable man realized. Mao evidently viewed this goal as attainable only through complete commitment to the regenerative process of all-out ideological struggle, and, by implication, to the total social mobilization needed to carry out such fundamentally transforming criticism and political study (with primary emphasis on the thought and example of Mao himself). Those previously entrusted with the leadership of this enterprise—initially, P'eng Chen, and later the regular Party apparatus under Liu and Teng—had failed to demonstrate their unreserved faith in or commitment to this goal by not pursuing it with the enthusiasm, speed, and efficiency demanded by an increasingly impatient and inflexible Mao.

In word and action, therefore, Mao now began to reveal that he intended to withdraw the mandate for directing the Cultural Revolution from the Party officialdom and to confer it directly on the "masses," which meant, ultimately, on the activating "left revolutionaries" among them. He hinted at this in a letter to the nascent Red Guards at Tsinghua commending their steadfast revolutionary orientation and promising support for all who shared it elsewhere in the country. On August 4, Mao reportedly sent Chou En-lai to Tsinghua so that he might personally reverse the censure and end the disciplinary measures taken against rebellious students by the work team under Mme Liu Shao-ch'i.[159] That the busy Chou and other top leaders should have been compelled to occupy themselves seriously with the sophomoric antics and feuds of local uni-

[159] An indication of the immature and often petty and personal nature of the student rebellion may be seen in the later testimony of Chu Teh-i, one of its leaders at Tsinghua. On April 10, 1967, Chu spoke at a mass Red Guard rally of how he had attempted suicide (and sustained a permanently disabling foot injury in leaping onto railroad tracks) after Mme Liu's work team had confined him to a dormitory and ordered him to write a self-criticism. This punishment, hardly grounds for attempting suicide to any normal personality, does not seem to have been excessive in view of Chu's own account of his behavior. Was he being condemned for some lofty defense of Maoist principles? He made no such claim. Rather, in the din of "democratic" discussion he apparently had played the petty role of troublemaker, raising accusations against fellow students who came from the families of high officials (they included a daughter of Liu Shao-ch'i and a son of Ho Lung), charging that they were "sitting on the same bench as the work team," and even suggesting that Liu had sent his wife to conspire with the team. (See David Oancia's dispatch in *The New York Times*, April 14, 1967.)

versity students is indicative of the bizarre revolution in priorities that Mao and his supporters sought for the regime.

Although by then the Eleventh Plenary Session of the Central Committee was well under way, Mao was not content to confine his views to its precincts—perhaps because, initially, he was unable to win decisive support for them there. He continued his extracurricular activities by personally writing a *ta-tzu-pao*, on August 5, entitled "Bombard the Headquarters, My First Big Character Poster." It began by reiterating the importance of the May 25 Peking University wallposter by Nieh Yüan-tzu and her group of students, and then called upon all comrades to reread it along with the accompanying commentary that Mao had ordered printed in *Jen-min Jih-pao* on June 2. Despite the publication of these "well-written" messages, he complained, "in the last fifty days or more, certain leading comrades from the Central Committee to local districts have taken the opposite road, have adopted a reactionary, bourgeois standpoint, have implemented a dictatorship of the bourgeoisie, have struck down the great stirring Cultural Revolution movement, have confused right and wrong, mixed up black and white, attempted to exterminate the revolutionaries, suppressed divergent views, implemented a White Terror, have spread the power of the bourgeoisie with an air of self-satisfaction and destroyed the spirit of the proletariat." [160] He went on to imply that these mistakes were related to unspecified rightist tendencies in 1962 (before the Tenth Plenum?) and to "left-in-form-but-actually-rightist" deviations in 1964 (perhaps a reference to the intensified "Four Cleanups" campaign). Once again, Mao, frustrated by the failure of the ideological revolution to keep up with his rising expectations, sought an explanation, or rationalization, in the hidden motives of those he had entrusted with its leadership—motives to be gleaned from a tortuous, arbitrary, and at times paranoid reinvestigation of their previously accepted statements and actions. Thus the lines were drawn for the Eleventh Session.

The Central Committee's meeting in the first twelve days of August 1966 was billed as a "plenary session," but attendance evidently was spotty, and the participants were a very mixed lot. Although no complete list of those present was announced, important provincial leaders are known to have been absent. Moreover, the later sessions appear to have

---

[160] Text taken from the Tsinghua Red Guard paper *Ching-kang-shan* of April 6, 1967, as it appeared in *Current Scene,* Vol. 5, No. 9 (May 31, 1967).

been packed with "revolutionary" students and teachers from Peking institutions. The resistance to the decisions of the meeting that subsequently became widespread within the Party apparatus, and the open Maoist attacks against the vast majority of Central Committeemen (by deed, if not always by name) suggest either that the Eleventh Plenum did not have a quorum when the critical resolutions were passed or that those voting misunderstood the nature and implications of Mao's proposals.[161] It is also possible, of course, that the participants were temporarily mesmerized by Mao's pretensions of authority or were intimidated —within the limits of legality—by the kibitzing "revolutionary" masses. In any event, under Mao's personal direction the Eleventh Plenum proceeded to adopt a program of historic import for the Chinese revolution and to make the most far-reaching changes in the Party's top leadership since its rise to power in 1949.

The sixteen-point "Decision Concerning the Great Proletarian Cultural Revolution," adopted on August 8, termed the campaign in progress "a great revolution that touches people to their very souls" and a new, broader, and deeper stage of China's "socialist revolution." [162] It charged that, although the bourgeoisie had been overthrown in the earlier stages, representatives of that class were "still trying to use old ideas, culture, customs, and habits of the exploiting classes [the "four olds"] to corrupt the masses, capture their minds, and endeavor to stage a comeback." To counter this "ideological" challenge, the document declared, the proletariat must do the exact opposite, employing new imperatives—styled as the "four news"—in order to "change the mental outlook of the whole of society." The present objective was "to struggle against and overthrow those persons in authority who are taking the capitalist road, to criticize and repudiate the reactionary bourgeois academic 'authorities' and the ideology of the bourgeoisie and all other exploiting classes and to transform education, literature and art and all other parts of the superstructure not in correspondence with the socialist economic base." In pursuing this goal, the Decision averred, "the only method" was for "the masses to

[161] This may have been hinted at later in Chiang Ch'ing's speech of November 28, where she insisted that concern for the legal niceties of "minority" and "majority" were less important than one's class viewpoint and true espousal of Marxism-Leninism and the "correct" Maoist line. (See excerpts of the speech in *Hung Ch'i*, No. 15 [December 1966].)

[162] "Decision of the Central Committee of the Chinese Communist Party Concerning the Great Proletarian Cultural Revolution," Foreign Languages Press (Peking, 1966).

liberate themselves." This meant that the Party leadership "at all levels" (presumably, however, only the levels below the Mao-dominated Central Committee) must dare boldly to "arouse the masses"—making the "fullest use" of *ta-tzu-pao* and great debates "to argue matters out"—to "distinguish right from wrong," "criticize the wrong views, and expose all the ghosts and monsters."[163]

To give practical leadership to the struggle (which, because of the ingrained "four olds," would take "a very, very long time"), the Decision of August 8 specified that "cultural revolutionary groups, committees, and congresses," already emerging, be permanently established in educational institutions, governmental organs, "factories, mines, other enterprises, urban districts, and villages." These leading groups, themselves subject to higher Party authority, were to be elected in "a system of general elections like that of the Paris Commune," their members chosen from lists of nominees submitted by the "revolutionary masses," who could also criticize and recall them.

Despite the militant general exhortation to carry out "daring" mass criticism and ideological struggle, the document of August 8 exhibited a certain moderation and balance less evident in subsequent Maoist statements and behavior. It assumed that "the great majority of cadres" were "good or comparatively good" and ordered that "strictest care" be taken to distinguish errant comrades (who should be exposed and persuaded to reform) from "the handful" of anti-Party rightists in power. The latter, after being repudiated and overthrown, were still to "be given a chance to turn over a new leaf." In the contention of views inevitable in mass debates, in which nonantagonistic contradictions "among the people" would find expression, reason and persuasion should be emphasized, rather than coercion and force; the minority was to be allowed to argue its case and reserve its views, and care was to be exercised to prevent a situation of the masses' struggling among themselves rather than against

[163] In pointed reference to the work teams previously dispatched to universities and other institutions by the Party apparatus, the August 8 Decision (Article 7) warned against unnamed persons who had organized "counterattacks" against the masses of those who put up *ta-tzu-pao,* and had advanced such slogans as "opposition to the leaders of a unit or a work team means opposition to the Central Committee of the Party . . . means counterrevolution." It deplored the fact that "a number of persons who suffer from serious ideological errors" (especially some of the anti-Party rightists) were taking advantage of inevitable mistakes and shortcomings in the mass movement to "spread rumors," agitate, and brand some of the masses as "counterrevolutionaries."

erring or counterrevolutionary elements. The Party leadership was urged to discover, strengthen, and rely on the "revolutionary left," isolate the "reactionary rightists," and strive to "win over the middle and unite with the great majority." But, even so, it was expected that unity with 95 percent of the cadres and masses would only be achieved "by the end of the movement." [164]

Other evidence of moderation included the stipulations that press criticism of individuals be cleared with higher Party organs; that "patriotic" and productive scientific and technical personnel be helped "gradually" to transform their ideological viewpoint and work style; that the armed forces be allowed to carry out the Cultural Revolution independently (under the CCP's Military Affairs Commission); and that the campaign "to revolutionize people's ideology" not stand in the way of developing economic production ("take hold of the revolution and stimulate production"). These concessions to reality may have been exacted by the more pragmatic Party leaders as a price for their acquiescence in the broader decisions. They may have been the bait with which the Maoists sought to trap suspected opponents. Or they may have been deliberately inserted by a militant but still rational Mao as a means either of ensuring the ultimate success of the Cultural Revolution or of facilitating a "fallback" position in times of tactical retreat (the "zigzags" of the "revolutionary road").

The final "communiqué" of the Eleventh Plenum, adopted on August 12, 1966, was in some ways a more radical document, reflecting the decisive triumph that Mao and his supporters scored at the session.[165] One

[164] It is interesting to recall that regime spokesmen had previously used the figure of 95 percent as descriptive of that proportion of the population *already* united in loyalty and devotion to the socialist revolution. See, for example, Chou En-lai's speech to the National People's Congress in December 1964, which appeared in *Peking Review*, No. 1 (January 1, 1965).

[165] It is possible that Mao succeeded only in the last few days of the plenum in securing a complete victory and crushing all effective resistance within the Central Committee to his radical cultural revolutionary program, with its stress on the Mao cult. Such a hypothesis would help explain an otherwise mysterious incident involving Mao which occurred on August 10-11, shortly after approval of the sixteen-point Decision with its minimal concessions to moderation. On the evening of August 10, Mao made his first public appearance in Peking in nearly nine months, reportedly greeting a crowd of devotees at "the place of the Party Central." The first edition of *Jen-min Jih-pao* on the following day carried news of the event, recording a few innocuous words by Mao (such as "Comrades, how are you?") but emphasizing the god-like effect of his presence on the people ("Come quickly

conspicuous feature was its emphatic praise of Mao, which suggested ever stronger efforts to foster unquestioning belief in his omniscient leadership: "Comrade Mao Tse-tung is the greatest Marxist-Leninist of our era. Comrade Mao Tse-tung has inherited, defended, and developed Marxism-Leninism with genius, creatively and in an all-round way, and has raised it to a completely new stage. Mao Tse-tung's thought is Marxism-Leninism of the era in which imperialism is heading for total collapse and socialism is advancing to worldwide victory. It is the guiding principle for all the work of our Party and country." [166] The communiqué stressed that the intensive study of Mao's works by all Party members and the entire nation in the Cultural Revolution was an event of "historic significance." A year later, an official reassessment of the Eleventh Plenum would conclude that its greatest historical contribution was to be found in the "scientific exposition" of the place of Mao's thought in the development of Marxism-Leninism, and the resulting consolidation of his "absolute authority." [167]

The Eleventh Plenum resulted in extensive changes in the top Party leadership. As later information (such as order of appearance at mass rallies) was to confirm, Lin Piao replaced Liu Shao-ch'i as second in command under Mao. Lin's was the only name other than Mao's to appear in the published documentation of the Plenum, and recent accounts have revealed that he was accorded the title of "deputy supreme commander" of the Party and called Mao's "closest comrade-in-arms." [168]

---

and touch the hand that has just been shaken by Chairman Mao"). Almost as soon as the edition made its appearance, it was suddenly and inexplicably withdrawn from circulation. The second edition, which was published that afternoon, did not contain the worshipful account of Mao's public appearance. The story did, however, appear in the August 12 *Jen-min Jih-pao*. One may speculate—and no more—that, in the interval, dissident Central Committeemen had objected to the story (or certain aspects of it), perhaps from a broader basis of opposition to further Mao-ization of the Cultural Revolution, and had then been crushed by the Maoist juggernaut, which made the most of his mass appeal, demonstrated once again, and of his personal prestige among the "revolutionary" Peking students and teachers who now packed the plenary session.

[166] "Communiqué of the Eleventh Plenary Session of the Eighth Central Committee of the Communist Party of China," Foreign Languages Press (Peking, 1966).

[167] See editorial entitled "A Great Milestone" in *Jen-min Jih-pao*, August 8, 1967.

[168] *Ibid*. Red Guard *ta-tzu-pao* posted in Peking in the late fall of 1966 purported to give the text of a terse speech by Lin Piao at the Eleventh Plenum. The full text is translated in *SCMP Supplement*, No. 159 (December 16, 1966) pp. 38–41. In it Lin bluntly declared that Mao had chosen him to be his chief lieutenant and to

According to Liu Shao-ch'i, who fell from second to eighth place in the (unofficial) rankings, the meeting elected a new Politburo Standing Committee.[169] Subsequent evidence suggests that the membership of the committee was enlarged from seven to ten or, possibly, eleven. After Chou En-lai, who retained third place in the leadership, T'ao Chu was spectacularly catapulted into the fourth position, followed by Ch'en Po-ta, Teng Hsiao-p'ing, K'ang Sheng, Liu Shao-ch'i, Chu Teh, Li Fu-ch'un, and, possibly, Ch'en Yün.

Available evidence, however, does not point to a classic power struggle as the main cause of these developments. The changes in the order of power and succession, significant as they were in the historical context of a therefore extraordinary continuity, do not suggest the clash of organized factions or drastic purge of losers characteristic of the classic power struggle, in which considerations of policy and ideology are ruthlessly subordinated to the prime goal of seizing or protecting personal power. This is not to say, of course, that such concerns were absent, but they were not the dominant factor.[170]

Nor did the August 12 communiqué, which (in contrast with the earlier sixteen-point Decision) dealt with the whole range of China's domestic and foreign policy problems, give any hint that the Eleventh Plenum had been called primarily to rectify past policy errors. Indeed, on two issues that some analysts have considered the root causes of the Cultural

---

implement his orders without compromise. However, Lin also indicated that he would retain some discretion in the implementation, saying that he would neither interfere with Mao on major matters nor bother him about minor ones.

[169] See his self-criticism of October 1966 (*Mainichi Shimbun*, January 29, 1967). In an undated wall poster purporting to give Mao's speech to the closing session of the plenum (on the afternoon of August 12), he noted that there had been a "readjustment" among the memberships of the Politburo, its Standing Committee, and the Secretariat.

[170] It will be recalled that the August 8 Decision had called for the complete discrediting and overthrow of "those within the Party who are in authority and are taking the capitalist road," and at one point had termed this "the main target of the present movement." Moreover, Lin Piao, in his major speech, reportedly promised that the plenum would "dismiss erring leaders." Liu, in his October confession, revealed that during the second half of the plenary session his errors had been discussed and he had submitted to discipline.

It should also be noted, however, that the Eleventh Plenum placed emphasis on ideological reformation ("treat the illness in order to save the patient," "unity, criticism, unity") and that the critical leaders were not actually dismissed, although some were in effect demoted and the inner circle of top officials was enlarged to include more militant Maoists.

Revolution—economic policy and Vietnam strategy—the Mao-dominated Plenum voiced specific approval of past decisions, promised no sweeping changes, and gave no indication of having had to overcome disagreement. Thus, the communiqué went beyond perfunctory general approval to applaud specifically the successful implementation of "the policy of re-adjustment, consolidation, filling out, and raising of standards" adopted after the collapse of the Leap Forward, and it also put the plenary session on record as agreeing "fully" with "all the measures already taken and all actions to be taken" in support of the Communist effort in Vietnam. It would seem, therefore, that the division within the leadership which had led to the calling of the Eleventh Plenum was due to something much more profound and immediate than substantive policy differences. Though such differences no doubt existed, they were not the primary force that precipitated and accelerated the crisis.

Rather, at the heart of the crisis which the Eleventh Plenum had been called to resolve was the conflict over ideology and basic orientation—or, as it had come to be more narrowly focused, over the scope, implemen-tation, and leadership of the Great Proletarian Cultural Revolution. From the Maoist point of view, until these issues were resolved—thereby per-mitting the total indoctrination, purification, and mobilization of Chinese society—questions of foreign and domestic policy would remain of sec-ondary importance, if not largely irrelevant. So, too, the issue of who should rule and succeed Mao was, in the first instance, a problem of ideological attitudes and behavioral orientation. This was borne out by the statements of Lin Piao, the new heir apparent (whose elevation may be ascribed primarily to his diligent and effective espousal of the Maoist vision), at the plenary session of August 1966: In calling for organiza-tional changes in the Party leadership, Lin defined the criteria for dis-missal or promotion as one's attitude toward the thought of Mao, one's cooperation with ideological work and, in particular, the Cultural Revo-lution, and one's possession or lack of "revolutionary zeal."

In the first phase of the Cultural Revolution, the regular Party appa-ratus under Liu Shao-ch'i and Teng Hsiao-p'ing had failed the test of leadership. At the Eleventh Plenum the increasingly utopian aspirations and fundamentalist requirements of the mission, as defined by Mao, were further clarified and the task of accomplishing it was transferred to other hands. In the months following, however, the new leadership of Mao, Lin, Chou, and the "cultural revolutionary groups"—backed (somewhat

uncertainly) by the PLA, prodded by Chiang Ch'ing, and served by the
rambunctious and destructive Red Guards—was to prove no more successful than its predecessors at coping with the inner ambiguities and contradictions, resolving the deepening political crisis, and effecting the ideological transformation of China so insistently and unrealistically demanded by Mao.

3
Maoist Theories
of Policy-Making and
Organization

HARRY HARDING, JR.

During the early and middle 1960s, there emerged in Communist China serious discrepancies between two conceptions of policy-making, organizational behavior, and organizational structure: that held by Communist Party chairman Mao Tse-tung and his followers, and that held by a loose coalition of Party and government officials, bureaucrats, and technicians led by chief of state Liu Shao-ch'i. Long-standing but muted differences became more severe and more salient as the two sets of prescriptions evolved in different directions. The Great Proletarian Cultural Revolution, climaxed in April 1969 by the Ninth National Congress of the Chinese Communist Party (CCP), represents in large part a struggle between these two opposing viewpoints. And the apparent victory of the Maoist faction in that struggle has wrought major changes in Chinese Communist theories of policy-making and organization.[1] First, it produced major innovations in organizational structure and policy-making procedure, most notably a new form of administrative organ, the revolutionary committee, and a new constitution for the CCP. Second, in denouncing and then finally purging Liu Shao-ch'i, the Cultural Revolution led to the total rejection or the significant modification of each of his major contributions to Chinese Communist organizational theory: his understanding of the definition and applicability of the "mass-line," his view of the nature and purpose of the Party, his guidelines for political struggle and conflict resolution within the Party, and his recruitment criteria for Party membership and Party office.

Because of these changes, Western analyses of Chinese Communist policy-making and organizational behavior made before the Cultural

[1] Such theories are, of course, normative rather than empirical.

Revolution are now partially out of date.[2] It is therefore necessary to revise those analyses to include the theoretical innovations and modifications occasioned by the Cultural Revolution. Such an undertaking will simultaneously indicate important elements in the ideological and political struggle between Mao Tse-tung and his opponents.

This chapter, then, is a study of two competing Chinese Communist theories of policy-making and organization as of the close of the Ninth Party Congress. It is a study in three parts: (1) a discussion of modes of policy-making, (2) an analysis of Cultural Revolution prescriptions for organizational structure and task performance, and (3) an estimate of the effects of the implementation of these theories on stress and tension in the Chinese political system.

Some preliminary caveats are required. First, much of this essay is an attempt to abstract what might be called, in accordance with current Chinese practice, the "two lines"—Maoist and Liuist—on policy-making and organization. This approach may have tempted the writer to force dichotomies where none exist. Throughout the paper an effort is made to avoid the tendency to see total divergence between Mao and his opponents and to indicate points of congruence as well as of conflict.

Second, adopting the concept of the "two lines" may encourage the assumption that both Mao's supporters and his opponents form coherent factions, each with a clear and consistent ideology. This is not the case. The labels "Maoist" and "Liuist" are used as a convenient shorthand to refer to two complex coalitions. The relationships between the components of each coalition and the variations in their respective conceptions of policy-making and organization are major questions which deserve further study. This essay, however, is written in the belief that the juxtaposition of the two coalitions, while obscuring some of the rich fabric of the Cultural Revolution, can also provide useful insights to its origins and meaning.

Third, virtually any research on contemporary China encounters severe data problems. Information is available in considerable quantity, but its reliability and implications are often uncertain. In an attempt to cope with these difficulties, the following procedures were followed in the

[2] The most prominent studies are John Wilson Lewis, *Leadership in Communist China* (Ithaca, N.Y., 1963); Franz Schurmann, *Ideology and Organization in Communist China* (Berkeley, 1966); and A. Doak Barnett, *Cadres, Bureaucracy, and Political Power in Communist China* (New York, 1968).

preparation of this study. To infer the Maoist positions on organizational questions, several types of materials were used:

1. The 1969 Constitution of the CCP.
2. The pre-Cultural Revolution writings of Mao Tse-tung.
3. Official Cultural Revolution statements: statements by major central leaders (including Mao) and directives from central organs of power (State Council, Central Committee, Cultural Revolution Group, Military Affairs Committee, etc.).
4. Semi-official Cultural Revolution documents: editorials and articles appearing in official periodicals (*Jen-min Jih-pao, Hung-ch'i, Chieh-fang-chün Pao,* and *Peking Review*), provincial newspapers, radio stations, etc.
5. Non-official Cultural Revolution documents: pamphlets and wall posters (*ta-tze-pao*) of Red Guard and other "revolutionary rebel" groups. These documents are the most voluminous (and often the most interesting) but the least reliable. Frequently, however, they do provide ideas and information that are later reflected in semi-official documents and in official statements. A filtered flow of information passes from non-official through semi-official to official sources. Thus, for example, one may see a wide range of charges against a given Party leader in Red Guard sources one month, and then see selections from these criticisms in semi-official or official sources several months later. One may also see a variety of proposals for organizational reform in non-official and semi-official sources, a few of which are later endorsed by official statements.

Unfortunately, the infrequency, brevity, and ambiguity of Mao's own public statements during the Cultural Revolution make it difficult to infer his positions directly. But if one relies on semi-official or non-official exegeses, a serious problem arises: the positions attributed to Mao during the Cultural Revolution are not always consistent with his own earlier writings.[3] The explanation offered here is that the Cultural Revolution documents accurately reflect the changing views of a changing Mao, and that the Cultural Revolution represents in part Mao's attempt to restruc-

---

[3] These inconsistencies will be identified as they appear in the paper, but they might conveniently be summarized here. The Cultural Revolution documents differ from Mao's earlier writings as to (1) the applicability of "collective leadership and individual responsibility," (2) the claims made for the Thought of Mao Tse-tung as a body of knowledge, (3) the number of options that will emerge during discussion of questions of principle, (4) the necessity for developing strategies to cope with risk, (5) the proper policy toward intellectuals and experts, and (6) the applicability of the mass-line for technical and administrative decisions.

ture Chinese institutions to correspond with his revised theories of policy-making and organization. But it is also possible that the Cultural Revolution documents reflect the views of Mao's "followers" rather than those of the Chairman himself. This study will not attempt to explore this fascinating hypothesis. Rather, reference will be made only to "Maoist" positions, employing a deliberately ambiguous term to postpone the major (and perhaps unanswerable) question of the extent of agreement between Mao and his followers and the degree of disagreement among the various Maoist factions.[4]

In contrast to the vast quantity of Cultural Revolution materials issued by Mao's supporters, his opponents have had virtually no public opportunity to put forward their views or to refute the charges made against them. To infer their positions, then, we must rely to a dismaying degree on two sources: pre-Cultural Revolution speeches and essays by Mao's opponents, and Maoist polemics published during the Cultural Revolution. While speeches and essays prepared in the 1940s and 1950s provide an inadequate basis for analysis of events in the 1960s, and while the Maoist polemics are laden with vituperative and distorted characterizations of their opponents, both sources are valuable if used with care. As guidelines to the analysis of the Cultural Revolution documents, we may postulate the following assumptions:

First, Maoists quote their opponents accurately, even though these quotations may be taken out of context and their implications distorted. Such quotations may provide useful insights if compared with contemporaneous Maoist statements, or if judiciously re-analyzed in their historical and rhetorical context.

Second, the theoretical and operational deviations ascribed to Liu Shao-ch'i were in fact committed, but not necessarily by Liu himself. Rather, Liu is used by the Maoists as a symbol of a divided opposition group. In

[4] We know that at least two factions were so radical that they were suppressed. One was the Sheng-wu-lien of Hunan Province, apparently a student group, which opposed the establishment of revolutionary committees, criticized the lenient treatment afforded most bureaucrats, and proposed a purge of the PLA. See *Union Research Service*, Vol. 51, No. 19–20 (June 7, 1968), and Vol. 51, No. 5–6 (April 19, 1968); and Klaus Mehnert, *Peking and the New Left: At Home and Abroad* (China Research Monograph No. 4, Center for Chinese Studies, University of California at Berkeley, 1969). The other was the "leftist" component of the central Cultural Revolution Group (Wang Li, Ch'i Pen-yü, Kuan Feng, and Mu Hsin), purged in late 1967. The views of this virulently radical clique may have influenced some of the documents used in this study, but most of the materials analyzed here were published well after their purge.

fact, three distinct components of the opposition to Mao are discussed in this paper: the central Party leaders purged in the Cultural Revolution, notably Liu Shao-ch'i, Teng Hsiao-p'ing, and P'eng Chen; major regional and provincial Party officials, such as T'ao Chu (Central-South Region), Wang En-mao (Sinkiang), and Li Ching-ch'üan (Southwest Region); and the technicians and "experts" in lower levels of both Party and government. Again, while it is not the purpose of this study to analyze fully the relationships among these three groups, it is important to realize that their conceptions of policy-making and organization may differ.

A final problem concerns the linkages between theory and practice. The concepts discussed in this study are, as already indicated, largely normative prescriptions. Although serious efforts are under way to put Maoist theories of organization and policy-making into operation, the success of these efforts is as yet uncertain. There is a need for studies of Maoist organizational structures and policy-making procedures in practice, as well as in theory.[5] It is possible to speculate, for example, that the prescriptions are not meant to be implemented in toto, but rather, sufficiently to combat opposing forces in the system. Just as a pilot must oversteer his airplane when it is flying in a crosswind, so Mao may be trying to keep China on course by pushing it to the left of the true target.[6] Because of this gap between theory and reality—and because of the inadequacies of available data—the propositions and conclusions presented in this paper should be considered tentative and speculative.

POLICY-MAKING

Analysts of the policy-making process frequently adopt the convenient assumption that policy-making groups and organizations are homogeneous units, acting like single individuals, which gather and process information from the political environment.[7] If this assumption

[5] Such studies are currently being prepared by two analysts who were instrumental in sparking and sustaining this writer's interest in these questions, Michel Oksenberg and Thomas Robinson.

[6] Some evidence for this speculation will be provided in the discussion of the fate of "experts" in the Cultural Revolution, in the following section on policy-making.

[7] Of value in the preparation of this section were the following descriptions and analyses of the policy-making process: Myres S. McDougall and Harold D. Lasswell, "The Identification and Appraisal of Diverse Systems of Public Order," *American Journal of International Law*, Vol. 53, No. 1 (January 1959) pp. 1–29; Charles E. Lindblom, *The Policy-Making Process* (Englewood Cliffs, N.J., 1968); Zbigniew

is made, policy-making can be conceptualized as a set of five tasks:[8]

1. Problem selection. Since attention spans are limited, no decision-making unit can cope simultaneously with all unsolved problems and unresolved issues. Some selection process is necessary to draw up a manageable agenda of problems for decision-makers to tackle. At times, problem selection involves no choice—the issue is forced upon the policy-makers by external crises or internal political pressures. But at other times, policy-makers can select the problem whose solution they believe would be most beneficial to the system or most advantageous to their own political positions.

2. Proposal formulation. After the problem has been selected, possible solutions are collected from both inside and outside the policy-making unit.

3. Policy selection (decision). A proposal is selected as policy. This process is usually assumed to be rational (that is, selection of the option that combines maximum probable gains with minimum probable costs), but it need not be. Irrational elements may be introduced by stress, crisis, time constraints, previous commitments, contingency plans, or operating procedures. A major portion of the policy-selection stage may involve establishing the criteria for decision: the values to be maximized, the goals to be sought, and the levels of cost and risk to be accepted.

4. Policy implementation.

5. Policy appraisal. After the policy is implemented, its actual effects are compared against the criteria established in the policy selection stage. This appraisal may lead to the ratification and extension of the policy, to its modification, or to its complete termination. It is during this stage that feedback reaches the policy-making unit.

A more sophisticated approach to policy-making analysis is to drop the assumption that the policy-making group is an integrated, homogeneous

---

Brzezinski and Samuel Huntington, *Political Power, USA/USSR* (New York, 1965) Chap. 4; Jan F. Triska and David D. Finley, *Soviet Foreign Policy* (New York, 1968); Glenn D. Paige, *The Korean Decision* (New York, 1968), Chap. 1; Joseph Frankel, *The Making of Foreign Policy: An Analysis of Decision-Making* (London, 1963), Chaps. 13–15; and Graham T. Allison, *Conceptual Models and the Cuban Missile Crisis: Rational Policy, Organization Process, and Bureaucratic Outcomes* (Santa Monica, Calif.: The Rand Corporation, P-3919, August 1968).

[8] Note that (1) policy implementation and policy appraisal are, in the following model, considered to be integral components of the overall policy-making process rather than parts of a separate, subsequent process, and (2) both problem selection and policy appraisal may involve extensive decision processes themselves, since an element of choice is inherent in each.

unit and to recognize the possibility of disagreement and conflict within it. To the tasks outlined above a sixth is added: resolving the differences of opinion that arise among the policy-makers in the course of the other five tasks. Disagreements over which issues to tackle, disputes over the goals and values to be pursued, divergent predictions concerning the outcomes of various options, resistance within the organization to implementing the policy finally selected, different appraisals of the policy's effects—all these represent additional elements that complicate group policy-making.

There is no single method for carrying out all these six tasks. Different individuals, groups, and organizations may employ different policy-making *modes,* each acting in the belief that its chosen mode will produce the most satisfactory results if correctly applied. Furthermore, the same policy-maker may employ different modes for different issues. And debates may arise among policy-makers as to the best mode for solving a certain kind of problem. It is a major theme of this study that such procedural disputes—disagreements over the definition and applicability of policy-making modes—were a major characteristic of the Chinese Cultural Revolution.

These disputes suggest the relevance of two dimensions along which policy-making modes may differ: (1) the degree of mass participation[9] in the process, particularly in the stages of proposal formation and policy appraisal; and (2) the relative use of pragmatic and dogmatic criteria for making decisions.[10] These two dimensions combine to generate four possible policy-making modes:

[9] "Mass participation" refers to direct, institutionalized consultation between policy-makers and their constituents. Excluded from this concept are indirect forms of participation in policy-making such as elections (in which only policy-makers, not policy itself, are selected) and uninstitutionalized forms of participation such as protest demonstrations.

[10] As used here, "pragmatic" means that the options under consideration are compared with each other and are evaluated in terms of their outcomes; "dogmatic" means that the options are compared with established doctrine and are evaluated in terms of their conformity to its tenets. A Maoist would, of course, deny the validity of this distinction. He would argue that, since doctrine is derived from practice and is tested in practice, dogmatic criteria are simultaneously pragmatic. This claim should be considered seriously; certainly "dogmatic" is not employed here in a pejorative sense. Indeed, the two sets of criteria often suggest the same policy choice. On the other hand, the degree of correspondence between doctrine and practice may vary considerably. In fact, the reliance of theoreticians on a large bureaucracy for reports on concrete situations and the resistance of doctrine itself to modification (see below, note 46) both pose obstacles to the realization of "pragmatic doctrine."

	Pragmatic Criteria	*Dogmatic Criteria*
High mass participation	Pragmatic mass-line	Dogmatic mass-line
Low mass participation	Pragmatic elitist	Dogmatic elitist

This section will further describe the pragmatic mass-line, the dogmatic mass-line, and the pragmatic elitist modes,[11] will identify their respective proponents, and will attempt to analyze the fate of each mode in the Cultural Revolution.

The "mass-line" is advocated by both Mao Tse-tung and Liu Shao-ch'i[12] as a mode of policy-making; it includes procedures for information gathering, problem selection, proposal formulation, policy selection, policy implementation, and policy appraisal. Mao's essay, "Some Questions Concerning Methods of Leadership," written in 1943, remains the most basic and most important description of the mass-line: "In all the practical work of our Party, all correct leadership is necessarily from the masses, to the masses. This means: take the ideas of the masses (scattered and unsystematic ideas) and concentrate them (through study turn them into concentrated and systematic ideas), then go to the masses and propagate and explain these ideas until the masses embrace them as their own, hold fast to them and translate them into action, and test the correctness of the ideas in such action." [13]

In this passage Mao is, in effect, assuming that policy-making is to be performed by the hypothetical "homogeneous" unit mentioned above, or by a single individual. How, according to this view, should each of the first five policy-making tasks be performed?

1. Problem selection. The policy-maker (hereafter, "cadre") gathers information on social, political, and economic conditions in the system. According to Mao's theory of contradictions, each social problem is the manifestation of one of the unresolved contradictions inherent in all social situations. One of these unresolved contradictions "is necessarily the principal contradiction whose existence and development determine and influence the existence and development of the other contradic-

[11] One can speculate that in a Maoist regime foreign policy decisions would be made by a mode using dogmatic criteria but low mass participation. As foreign policy is outside the scope of this study, this "dogmatic elitist" policy-making mode will not be discussed further.

[12] *On the Party* [1945] (Peking, 1950).

[13] "Some Questions Concerning Methods of Leadership" [1943], in *Selected Readings from the Works of Mao Tse-tung* (Peking, 1967), p. 236. This volume will hereafter be cited as *SR*.

tions."[14] Therefore, the cadre's research should analyze the principal unresolved contradiction in the social situation under study; in so doing, he is identifying the problem whose solution is most urgent.

2. Proposal formulation. The cadre "takes the ideas of the masses" on how to solve the problem.

3. Policy selection (decision). The cadre "concentrates" (Mao also uses the phrase "sums up"[15]) these ideas, and authorizes the result as Party policy. What these two expressions (in Chinese, *chi-chung* and *tsung-chieh,* respectively) mean in practice is, as we shall see, not at all clear. In fact, their ambiguity provides a crucial component of a major dispute between Mao and his opponents over policy-making procedure.

4. Policy implementation. The cadre is to "go to the masses" and, preferably by persuasion, enlist them in implementing the policy; the masses are to "hold fast" to the policy and "translate [it] into action."

5. Policy appraisal. The "correctness" of the policy is determined in the course of implementation.

Thus, the basic form of the mass-line is a series of interactions between an individual cadre (the "leader") and the masses (the "led"). Two major derivatives of the mass-line acknowledge that most policy-making is performed not by individuals but by groups (committees) within organizations. The derivative applicable to committees is known as "collective leadership with individual responsibility," and that applicable to the organization as a whole is called "democratic centralism." The same process of investigation of conditions, summarization of proposals, authorization of policy, and implementation of the decision[16] applies in each, with the analogous roles filled as follows:

Principle	Leader	Led
Mass-line	Cadre	Masses
Collective leadership with individual responsibility	Committee chairman	Committee members
Democratic centralism	Higher organ	Lower organs

Mao Tse-tung and the Party opposition would undoubtedly agree on this general outline of the mass-line and its derivatives as a mode for

[14] Mao, "On Contradiction [1937]," *SR,* p. 89.
[15] "Some Questions Concerning Methods of Leadership," p. 237.
[16] The terms are from Lewis, *Leadership in Communist China,* p. 72.

making doctrinal, political, social, and economic decisions.[17] But, as the
following pages will try to indicate, they disagree on (1) the criteria to
be used in making decisions and resolving disputes; (2) the best procedures for coping with risks; and (3) the range of the applicability of
the mass-line as a problem-solving strategy.

In *On Inner-Party Struggle,* Liu Shao-ch'i divides political and social
problems into two types, "questions of principle" and "practical and concrete problems," whose solution requires two different forms of the mass-
line.[18] For "questions of principle," Liu advocates using the dogmatic
mass-line, a policy-making mode that combines high mass participation
with dogmatic decisional criteria.[19] But for "practical and concrete problems," Liu proposes a variant of the mass-line that is considerably more
pragmatic, retaining high mass participation but employing different
criteria for decision. The two forms of the mass-line, which are in effect
two separate methods of "summarization," reflect different conceptions
of policy alternatives and lead to different criteria for choosing among
them.

In contrast to Liu, Maoist statements during the Cultural Revolution
have argued that no distinction can be made between questions of principle and practical problems, that *all* issues are questions of principle, that
to insist otherwise is to "negate the class struggle" and to ignore the

[17] One caveat should be made, however. Although Mao himself laid the basis for
the theory of collective leadership and individual responsibility (CL/IR) in his
directive "On Strengthening the Party Committee System" (*SR,* pp. 293–294), and
although major portions of that directive are cited in *Quotations from Chairman
Mao Tse-tung* (Peking, 1966), Section X, "Leadership of Party Committees," CL/IR
is not mentioned as an organizational principle of the Party in the 1969 constitution
as it was in Article 19(5) of the 1956 constitution. And while during the Cultural
Revolution literature frequently called for the implementation of the mass-line and
the improvement of democratic centralism in the Party, this writer has seen none
that advocated collective leadership and individual responsibility. A likely reason for
this omission is that the Maoists consider the political situation still so fluid that recourse to purely individual (dictatorial) leadership at various levels must be retained
as a legitimate option. There is no point in giving the opposition ammunition with
which to attack the obvious cases of non-collective leadership. It should be pointed
out, however, that CL/IR has not been *condemned,* nor has it been associated with
Liu or Teng. This suggests the possibility of its reintroduction in the future, when
the political situation has stabilized.

[18] *On Inner-Party Struggle* [1941] (Peking, n.d.) pp. 50ff.

[19] This is not to say that Mao and Liu have identical models for the operation of
the dogmatic mass-line. Mao and his followers make greater claims for the power of
Maoist doctrine than does Liu; see second assumption, p. 123.

"class basis of truth," and that therefore only the dogmatic mass-line is a legitimate policy-making mode.

Thus, Liuists and Maoists disagree on the correct policy-making mode to be applied to political, social, and macro-economic issues. Both factions advocate the use of the mass-line; both approve of high levels of mass participation in the policy-making process. But where the Maoists insist that dogmatic criteria be used to evaluate the proposals generated through consultation with the masses, the Liuists suggest that pragmatic criteria be employed. The discussion below compares these two viewpoints and the two variants of the mass-line.

The Maoist dogmatic mass-line is based on the following assumptions:

1. Every problem has a single correct solution; there is a one-to-one correspondence between problem and solution. Problem-solving is, therefore, less a matter of *choice* among options than a *diagnostic process,* the accumulation of sufficient information so that the nature of the problem and the single correct solution become apparent.

2. The Thought of Mao Tse-tung, as supplemented by the Chairman's "latest directives," already contains all social laws and theories necessary to make such a diagnosis. This assumption is crucial and represents a major addition to the claims made for Maoism. Previously, Maoist models of problem-solving and policy-making were based on the premise that all the laws governing social behavior are discoverable and that the procedures set forth in "On Practice"[20] and "On Contradiction" provided the *means* for discovering them. Now, however, Mao's thought has become dogmatized: social laws are not only "knowable" but already "known"; Maoism does not merely help men *find* solutions but already *contains* them. Many of Mao's opponents were criticized in Cultural Revolution documents for refusing to accept this refinement. P'eng Chen, for example, was quoted as saying in 1966 that Maoism can "open the way" for solving social problems. To the Maoists, he was thereby erroneously implying that "Mao Tse-tung's Thought has *not yet* opened the way for us [to solve problems] and that the way has to be opened anew."[21]

[20] Mao, "On Practice," *SR,* pp. 64–65.

[21] "Circular of Central Committee of Chinese Communist Party (May 16, 1966)," in *Peking Review,* No. 21 (May 19, 1967) Section 10. Italics added. Both Lyman Van Slyke and Michel Oksenberg have suggested to the writer that, to use Franz Schurmann's terms, the Cultural Revolution represents the elevation of "Maoism" from the realm of "thought" or "practical ideology" (a set of ideas that provides

3. *All* differences of opinion—even within the Party—are based on *class* differences.[22] Conversely, those Party members with the same class standpoint and employing the same information will inevitably arrive at the same conclusions.[23] Thus disagreements may arise during policy discussions for two reasons: (1) incomplete or incorrect information, or miscalculation, or (2) different class standpoints. If a disagreement is caused by miscalculation or by incomplete information, it can quickly be resolved. But if the disagreement persists, it must reflect differences in class standpoint.

4. Policy choice occurs only between two contradictory options: the proletarian (0) and the bourgeois, revisionist, feudal, or imperialist (not-0). In the course of discussion, a polarization will occur between 0 and not-0; possibilities that seem, at first glance, to be additional alternatives will, upon more careful scrutiny, fall into one of the two opposing categories. This assumption seems to represent a change in Mao's thinking. In the past, he assumed that a trichotomization would occur between the left, the middle, and the right. Now, these three categories are to be read as "left in form but right in essence," "left," and "right"—that is, a dichotomy. A recent *Hung-ch'i* editorial quoted Mao as saying, "There are basically only two schools, the proletarian and the bourgeois. It is one or the other, either the proletarian or the bourgeois world outlook." [24]

5. Given such a dichotomization, one option is necessarily correct, and the other incorrect. Mao has explicitly declared that *all* contradictions—both those "between ourselves and the enemy" (antagonistic) and those "among the people" (non-antagonistic)—are "a matter of drawing a

---

methods of action) to that of "theory" or "pure ideology" (a set of ideas that provides a unified and conscious world-view). (See Schurmann, *Ideology and Organization*, pp. 22ff.) As Mao once applied Marxism-Leninism to China, the Chairman's disciples (notably Lin Piao) are now to apply Maoism to the current situation. While this argument is persuasive, it should be noted that the CCP still refers to Mao's works as "thought" (*szu-hsiang*), not "theory" (*chu-yi*).

[22] As Mao wrote in "On Contradiction," p. 76, "Every difference in men's concepts should be regarded as reflecting an *objective* contradiction. . . . Opposition and struggle between ideas . . . is a reflection within the Party of contradictions *between classes* and between the old and the new in society." Italics added.

[23] See Lewis, *Leadership in Communist China*, p. 161.

[24] "Make a Class Analysis of Factionalism," *Hung-ch'i* editorial, in *Peking Review*, No. 19 (May 10, 1968) p. 3. The quotation is taken from Mao's "Speech at Chinese Communist Party's National Conference on Propaganda Work," in *SR*, p. 393.

clear distinction *between right and wrong*." [25] The Thought of Mao Tse-tung provides the relevant criteria for identifying the "correct" proposal; the cadre's task is to assign the proper labels to the two options at hand.

On the basis of these assumptions, we can abstract the Maoist mode for dogmatic mass-line policy-making. Investigation and study of a problem will yield information and proposals, each of which is incomplete, but which fit together—like pieces of a jigsaw puzzle—into the correct remedy. The remedy will be in accordance with the Thought of Mao Tse-tung, which is the highest and most complete systematization of the ideas of the working classes.

Thus, in the Maoist mode, summarization is a process of accumulation, addition, and synthesis that can be virtually automatic. The policy-maker is very similar to a high school student solving a physics problem or constructing a geometric proof. The student's textbook contains not only all the relevant axioms, postulates, and formulae, but also (in the back) the correct solution itself. The Chinese Communist cadre's text is the "little red book," [26] which concisely sets forth all necessary social knowledge and the solution to all social problems. Like the student, the cadre —after summarizing the ideas of the masses—checks his answer against those contained in his copy of the *Quotations*. Or, unable to arrive at his own solution, he summarizes the available information, identifies the problem, and obtains the solution directly from dogma. In short, every problem is assumed to have one correct solution; the cadre's task is to find it.

An obvious question arises. What if the proposals do not fit together so neatly? Suppose they are contradictory rather than partial and complementary? What has "gone wrong," and what should be done about it?

For Maoists, the crucial dimension of disagreement and conflict in the decision-making process is its persistence. Perhaps the conflict is illusory, based merely on miscalculation, different sources of data, incomplete information, and the like. If so, discussion will quickly clarify the dispute and the correct solution will readily be recognized. But if the disagreement persists despite discussion, sufficient evidence exists that a class contradiction is at work. If so, continued discussion alone will not resolve

[25] Mao, "On the Correct Handling of Contradictions Among the People," *SR*, p. 352. Italics added.
[26] There are now other little red books, such as *Chairman Mao Tse-tung on People's War*, but *Quotations* remains *the* little red book.

the contradiction, but it will collapse the various proposals into two contradictory options. The selection of the "correct" option is then made by comparing each option with the Thought of Mao Tse-tung. No other criterion (such as how many people support which option or what their reasons are) is necessary; correctness means correspondence with the Thought of Mao.[27] As a recent editorial enjoined: "Use Mao Tse-tung Thought to analyze and resolve contradictions . . . [and] to distinguish right and wrong." [28]

As an example of Maoist problem analysis as just described, we might cite the case of the Revolutionary Committee of Wenhsien, a county in Honan Province. Soon after its establishment, a problem arose: in employing the mass-line, could the cadres make extensive use of the Poor and Lower Middle Peasants Association, or must they bypass the representatives of the peasantry and deal directly with the masses? In the investigatory report of the Revolutionary Committee's activities, this issue was posed in the following terms: "After the county revolutionary committee was established in the storms of class struggle, its leading members still had differences in their understanding of whom to rely on. The overwhelming majority of committee members held that it was necessary to rely firmly on the *broad masses* of the poor and lower-middle peasants. However, certain members of its standing committee felt that it was only necessary to rely on a former poor and lower-middle *peasant organization.* Heated arguments took place." [29]

Debate and discussion continued, but—according to the report—"no one would give in." The persistence of dissent clearly indicated that class forces were at work. The dispute was finally settled by checking the two different "answers" against the little red book, which revealed that: "The task of struggle-criticism-transformation cannot be carried out well by merely relying on a section of the poor and lower-middle peasants and it can be accomplished well only by relying firmly on the masses of poor and lower-middle peasants." [30] The article concluded by stressing that

[27] See, for example, "Place Mao Tse-tung's Thought in Command of Everything," *Jen-min Jih-pao, Hung-ch'i,* and *Chieh-fang-chün Pao* joint editorial, January 1, 1969; "Whose Opinion Should Prevail?" *Hung-ch'i,* No. 2 (1969); and "Make a Class Analysis of Factionalism," pp. 3–4.

[28] "Three Strands of Rope Tightly Twisted Into One," *Hung-ch'i,* Nos. 6–7 (1969) in *Peking Review,* No. 6 (July 18, 1969) pp. 11–14.

[29] "A County Revolutionary Committee Having Close Ties with the Masses," *Peking Review,* No. 6 (February 7, 1969) pp. 6–7. Italics added.

[30] *Ibid.*

this dispute represented "the dividing line between Chairman Mao's revolutionary line and the bourgeois reactionary line."

Thus two options were discovered. By checking them against the writings of Chairman Mao, one option was labeled "bourgeois," and the other "revolutionary." No other criteria were employed to analyze the two options. In this example, the majority opinion prevailed, but (in theory, at least) this was mere coincidence.[31]

As both the general analysis and the specific example indicate, correctness is more important than consensus. Disputes should be sharpened, not glossed over; the very persistence of a dispute despite discussion provides a necessary reason not to compromise. Nonetheless, there are two mechanisms built into the dogmatic mode that tend to force compliance with the decision taken. First, there is the threat of being labeled a class enemy. Those who continue overt opposition to the "correct" policy run the risk of being told that the contradiction between themselves and the rest of the group has become antagonistic.[32] Second, even if they decide that the risk of continued opposition is still worthwhile—perhaps given their conviction that the policy chosen would have disastrous consequences—they will nonetheless find that their continued opposition has made adherence to the policy even more tenacious. Objections raised by class enemies only make Maoists more convinced that their policy is correct: "Vigorous attacks by the capitulationists and diehards testify to its revolutionary and progressive nature and add to its lustre."[33] Opposition to revealed "truth," in short, is both fruitless and dangerous, no matter how well-founded it may be.[34]

The pragmatic mode of the mass-line combines reliance on mass participation in the proposal-formulation and policy-appraisal stages with the use of pragmatic criteria in the decision stage. It probably originated with Liu Shao-ch'i's realization that not all issues could best be resolved on the basis of dogmatic criteria.

Liu agrees with Mao that "questions of principle" are class-based and

[31] For an article stressing that the majority view should prevail *only if* it conforms to the "basic interests" of the masses (that is, to the Thought of Mao), see "Whose Opinion Should Prevail?", n. 27 above.

[32] For an explicit warning that continued opposition to established policy would lead to being so labeled, see "Realize Unified Leadership," *Chekiang Jih-pao,* March 30, 1969.

[33] Mao, "To Be Attacked by the Enemy is Not a Bad Thing But a Good Thing," *SR,* p. 130.

[34] One is reminded of Don Quixote's response to the attempts of his friends to "prove" that his quest was merely a delusion: "Facts are the enemy of truth."

must be handled uncompromisingly according to the dogmatic mass-line. But Liu believes that there are also "practical and concrete" problems, which must be handled differently.[35] For each such problem there are several feasible solutions. These options do not represent a simple dichotomy between right and wrong (0 and not-0), but rather "various ways and roads" (0_1, 0_2, 0_3, and so on), each with a degree of merit and a degree of risk. There is no expectation that the information collected by policy-makers will converge into a single option, or even into two contradictory options.

The mode presented by Liu for the solution of such "practical and concrete" problems is the "rational choice" model familiar to organization theorists everywhere, posing a choice, under conditions of uncertainty, among several possible options, the relative merits of which may be obscured because of inadequate information regarding their costs and risks. Selection among these alternatives is made by calculating the expected utility of each option (by subtracting the probable costs from the probable gains) and choosing the option with the highest expected utility. If such procedures are followed, the policy-maker may well reject the option that *might* bring the highest gain in favor of an option which, although less desirable, has a *better* chance of being successfully effected. No analyst has expressed this "minimax" strategy of choice under conditions of uncertainty any more succinctly than Liu Shao-ch'i himself: "There are often several solutions for concrete and practical problems. . . . These ways and roads have their respective merits and demerits so far as the situations confronting us at the time are concerned. Some ways and roads are the most advantageous to us but they are risky so, to play safe, we had better take the less advantageous ways and roads." [36]

It may occur that for each of the known options the expected cost is greater than the expected gain, or that uncertainty and risk are too great to permit a decision. If so, *none* of the options will be chosen as policy,

---

[35] A major theme in both *On Inner-Party Struggle* and *How To Be a Good Communist* (Peking, 1964) is the insistence that the two kinds of problems not be confused. One of Liu's major fears is that all differences in the Party will be magnified into matters of principle, and that the resulting continuous and bitter struggles will tear the Party apart: "The principle of inner-Party struggle does not mean that when there are no differences of principle . . . in the Party, we should deliberately magnify into 'differences of principle' divergences of opinion among comrades on questions of a purely practical nature." (*How To Be a Good Communist*, p. 88.)

[36] *On Inner-Party Struggle*, p. 50.

even if this entails vetoing the "unanimous" voice of the masses.[37] The problem will remain unsolved pending the invention of new alternatives or the acquisition of new information that favorably alters cost, gain, or risk calculations. There is thus no assumption that a "correct" solution exists for every problem.

The criteria used in such calculations are not necessarily political or ideological. For example, Teng Hsiao-p'ing, in his 1956 report on the revision of the Party constitution, called for "classification, analysis, critical judgment, and synthesis" of the information and opinions obtained by cadres during their investigations, but did not mention the necessity of using political criteria.[38] Such a view has been condemned by the Maoists; to them, since all proposals are class-based, even the suggestion that decisions can be made on apolitical criteria is to hide the "class basis of truth" and thus to "negate class struggle."

The procedures of the pragmatic mass-line for dealing with disagreements among policy-makers are markedly different from those of the dogmatic mass-line. To Liu Shao-ch'i, disagreement over the correct solution to "concrete and practical problems" is not necessarily class-based; honest disagreements over cost, risk, and utility estimates may arise even among men with similar goals and values. In such cases Liu would argue that "two can be merged into one":[39] compromise and consensus are major values to be promoted within the Party. Persistence of a dispute despite discussion is a good reason to compromise: "[On practical matters] we should not always persist in our views, always ask others to give up their views, to acquiesce, and to deal with matters in accordance with our views. If so, we would only delay the settlement of issues, sharpen the disputes, and strengthen the tendency to idle talk in the Party, and obstruct unity among the comrades. That is why *we should make all possible compromises* with Party members holding different views concerning questions of a purely practical character."[40] There can even be

---

[37] For an example of such a veto—vehemently condemned by the Maoists—see "Today's 'Foolish Old Man' Nurtured by Mao Tse-tung Thought," *Peking Review*, No. 29 (July 18, 1969) pp. 14-17. This particular case will be discussed in some detail below.

[38] Teng Hsiao-p'ing, *Report on the Revision of the Constitution* (Peking, 1956) p. 61.

[39] The phrase is not from Liu but from the philosopher Yang Hsien-chen. It is suggested, however, that Liu would agree with its implications.

[40] Liu, *On Inner-Party Struggle*, p. 50. Italics added.

temporary compromises with those in the Party "who hold divergent views regarding certain questions of principle which are relatively not so important or urgent." [41] In short, incorporated in the pragmatic mass-line are such consensus-building tactics as logrolling and bargaining, which are anathema to those who advocate a dogmatic approach to policy-making.[42]

To cope with the problem of uncertainty inherent in policy planning, all policy-makers must evolve strategies of risk-taking and risk control. The strategies developed by Mao Tse-tung[43] and Liu Shao-ch'i are by no means totally dissimilar: they share a common reliance on models and experimentation. But there are significant differences between their approaches toward risk calculations prior to a policy decision, toward experimentation, and toward the use of models to reduce the risk of inaccurate policy implementation.

Unlike Mao, Liu has advocated the incorporation of risk considerations into the policy-maker's pre-decision calculations. As noted above, he has written that risk calculations before a decision is made may induce a policy-maker to choose "less advantageous ways and roads" over options that are more advantageous but more risky. Mao Tse-tung apparently believes that attempting to determine the risk or viability of an option before it is actually implemented is futile: "Only through the practice of the people . . . can we verify whether a policy is correct or wrong and determine to what extent it is correct or wrong." [44] Thus, instead of

---

[41] *Ibid.*, p. 52.

[42] For the sources of differences between Mao's and Liu's policy-making styles, see Tang Tsou, "The Cultural Revolution and the Chinese Political System," *China Quarterly*, No. 38 (April–June 1969) pp. 63–91. Tsou argues that the source can be traced to the differing roles of the two men both before and after 1949, with Liu as "co-ordinator" and "executor" and Mao as "initiator" and "promoter." See also John Wilson Lewis, "Leader, Commissar, and Bureaucrat: The Chinese Political System in the Last Days of the Revolution," in Ping-ti Ho and Tang Tsou (eds.), *China in Crisis* (Chicago, 1968) Vol. 1, pp. 449–481.

[43] Mao's strategy for dealing with risk is superfluous if one assumes that the use of his ideology makes policy formulation infallible. This contradiction may be resolved in one of several ways: (1) the two elements of Mao's policy-making program are simply inconsistent; (2) the use of his ideology makes general policy prescriptions infallible, but the details of implementation must be worked out by trial and error; or (3) Mao's risk-taking strategy was worked out before the dogmatization of his ideology, at a time when his writings contained only the methods for finding answers, not the answers themselves.

[44] *Quotations*, p. 6.

calculating the probability of failure in advance, Mao seems to assume that policy initially *will* fail: "Generally speaking, whether in the course of changing nature or of changing society, men's original ideas, theories, plans, or programmes are seldom realized without any alteration. This is because . . . [they] fail to correspond with reality in whole or in part and are wholly or partially incorrect.[45] To correct the errors, investigation is made, during policy implementation, of the effects of the policy, and policy is revised accordingly.[46] Risk is controlled, not by calculating it in advance but by keeping policy flexible.[47]

[45] Mao, "On Practice," pp. 64–65.

[46] A more recent quotation from Mao suggests that policy can be revised only if the revision is in conformity with doctrine: "Knowledge . . . is applied in social practice to ascertain whether the theories, policies, plans or measures meet with the anticipated success. *Generally speaking,* those that succeed are correct and those that fail are incorrect." (Mao, "Where Do Correct Ideas Come From?" [1963], *SR,* p. 405. Italics added.) The qualification "generally speaking" explicitly admits the possibility that policy that is doctrinally correct can nonetheless fail. Mao goes on to say that failure in such a case is due to the temporary "balance of forces," and that policy should *not* be altered because it will "triumph sooner or later." Mao believes in flexibility, but only if dogma is not compromised.

[47] Readers of an earlier draft of this essay pointed out that this section might be interpreted as a suggestion that Mao is "reckless" or "irrational," particularly in foreign policy. Such an inference would be totally unwarranted. The type of risk control strategy described here is as respectable, reasonable, and "rational" as are attempts to calculate risks in advance. One can predict, not that Mao will embark on reckless foreign policy initiatives, but that he will select policy options that (1) facilitate the maintenance of strict central control over their execution, (2) are reversible and thus preserve flexibility, and (3) provide opportunities to assess the outcome before irrevocably committing China to their pursuit. Evidence for these propositions is already available. In the intervention in the Korean War in 1950, the Quemoy crises of 1954–55 and 1958, and the invasion of India in 1962, the initial Chinese actions were either tentative (Korea and India) or reversible (Quemoy). As to the maintenance of central control, apparently reliable Red Guard sources have accused Lo Jui-ch'ing (former chief of staff) of delegating to the Foochow military district the authority to "take the initiative to attack the enemy [in the Taiwan Strait] . . . so as not to miss the chance of battle." Lo acted, according to the Red Guard sources, in defiance of the Military Affairs Committee, which had ordered that all combat actions in the Straits be approved in advance by the Central Committee. Lo was described as "rash" and "reckless," not so much for advocating risky actions, but for delegating responsibility for decisions away from the center. See Liaison Center for Repudiating Liu, Teng, and T'ao, Chinese Science and Technology University's Tungfanghung Commune, Red Guard Congress, "Down with Lo Jui-ch'ing, Usurper of the Army Power," July 1967. Translation in *Selections from China Mainland Magazines,* No. 641 (January 20, 1969) pp. 1–12. This is virtually identical to a text purported to be the report of a Central Committee

As a further means of reducing risk, Liu Shao-ch'i has relied largely on small-scale, controlled experiments. "Key points," experimental units, and pilot projects are used to develop and test techniques that can later be employed on a larger scale. For example, Liu was quoted in a Red Guard document as saying: "We must not set up too many [communes] at one stroke and go too fast. We should first conduct experiments to create the models and then gradually set them up in a well-prepared, methodical and orderly manner, by separate stages and groups. . . . The practice of daring to think, speak, and act should not be followed on a nationwide scale but should be carried out in a small scope with typical experiments conducted first." [48]

Both this statement by Liu (very likely a criticism of Mao's communization strategy) and Mao's own writings indicate that Mao has a different understanding of the role of experimentation and models in risk control. Mao does not rely on small-scale experimentation in pre-selected units before reaching a decision.[49] Rather, he relies on the iterative features of the mass-line: large-scale experimentation is to be conducted after a tentative decision has been made, and policy is to be modified in accordance with the feedback received. As Mao declared: "Put [policies] to the test in *many* different units . . . , then concentrate the new experience (sum it up) and draw up new directives for the guidance of the masses generally." [50]

Such testing and revising of the tentative policy decision may have to be done "many times" before the "anticipated results can be achieved in practice." [51] But each failure is acceptable, for losses are relatively small, and valuable lessons are learned from each mistake. A characteristic application of this strategy is to rely on competition among various units

---

Work Group formed to investigate Lo. See "Report on the Question of the Errors Committed by Lo Jui-ch'ing," April 20, 1966, in *Issues and Studies* (Taipei) Vol. 5, No. 11 (August 1969) pp. 87–101.

[48] Quoted in "Selected Edition of Liu Shao-ch'i's Counterrevolutionary Revisionist Crimes," by Nank'ai University, August 18 Red Rebel Regiment, Liaison Station (under the banner, "Pledging to Fight a Bloody Battle with Liu-Teng-T'ao to the End"), April 1967, in *Selections from China Mainland Magazines*, No. 652 (April 28, 1969) pp. 27–29.

[49] In fact, the experimental farms developed in the late 1950s and early 1960s were criticized during the Cultural Revolution as being unrepresentative of local conditions, isolated from the masses, and divorced from political study. Radio Chengtu (Szechwan), February 13, 1968.

[50] Mao, "Some Questions Concerning Methods of Leadership," p. 237. Italics added.

[51] Mao, "On Practice," p. 65.

—each employing whatever methods and techniques it thinks will work best—in order to identify the best means of implementing predetermined policy.[52] The most successful unit is then held up for emulation. The essential difference between Mao and Liu here is that they identify their models at different points in time. Liu *pre*-selects the model as the locus of planned experimentation; Mao *post*-selects the model after the results of the competition are in.

So far, we have discussed the functions of models as devices for policy appraisal, risk reduction, and proposal formation. Another major role of models is to aid in securing policy implementation: once the model is identified, its "case-history" is disseminated for emulation. This role is particularly prominent in China, for emulation of models is a major element in Chinese cultural learning patterns. As John H. Weakland has put it, for Chinese, "Imaginative preparation . . . may largely be a process of discovering the models to which a present or potential situation conforms and considering the permutations which they may undergo." [53] But Mao's excessive reliance on the use of models has produced "blindness," as Liu has reportedly said. To Liu, learning from models is more effective than trying to implement vague directives, but relying on models runs the risk of mechanically copying the experiences of other units, without analyzing the special conditions and characteristics that contributed to their success: "It appears that promotion at the present time of the method of comparing with, learning from, catching up with the advanced and helping the backward [a model-emulation campaign in the early '60s] is better than the past method of abstractedly calling for exertion of efforts and aiming high. But if the method is overly promoted, blindness may also be produced." [54]

Mao's major shortcoming is his reliance on a *single* model for the implementation of *national* policy. Because of China's diversity, this model has merely exhortatory value and little practical use. The success of the model convinced Mao that "it can be done," but this does not aid other units throughout the country. Their attempt to copy the model can "produce blindness"; Mao's enthusiasm over a single success may lead him to authorize policy that is infeasible on a national scale. Indeed, one ex-

---

[52] See Isabel and David Crook, *The First Years of Yangyi Commune* (London, 1966) Chap. 18.

[53] "The Organization of Action in Chinese Culture," *Psychiatry,* Vol. 13, No. 3 (August, 1950) pp. 361–370.

[54] Quoted in "Selected Edition of Liu Shao-ch'i's Counterrevolutionary Revisionist Crimes," *op. cit.,* p. 23.

planation of the failure of the commune movement is that Mao was unduly impressed by successful prototypes in the neighboring provinces of Hopei and Honan, established those atypical cases as models for national policy, and thus insisted on communization in areas with widely divergent political, economic, and social conditions.[55]

A graphic illustration of the operational differences between the two policy-making modes is the construction of an aqueduct between two rivers in Chiyuan County of Honan Province.[56] The basic problem was simple. The county lies in a rugged, mountainous region, between the Chinho and Mangho Rivers. Because of the contour of the land, water for irrigation was inadequate, drought was a constant and serious threat, and grain yields were consistently low. Given the proximity of the two rivers, the peasants naturally would "dream and spin tales that someday the Chinho would flow to the mountain districts and become a boon to the land." A relatively small-scale irrigation project in 1957 had diverted some of the water of the Mangho to Chiyuan County, but had since proved inadequate. The Mangho was a small stream with an insufficient flow of water. For a satisfactory irrigation system, it would be necessary to supplement water from the Mangho with water from the larger Chinho.

The basic-level cadres discovered that the masses hoped that an aqueduct would be dug connecting the two rivers. Water could flow from the Chinho into the Mangho, and then through the 1957 project to the fields of Chiyuan. As the construction of an aqueduct was the "unanimous desire of the masses," a proposal was drawn up and presented to the Chiyuan Party Committee in 1959. But the county cadres, employing the pragmatic variant of the mass-line, critically analyzed the proposal in terms of its costs, gains, and risks. The county cadres admitted that the gains achieved from constructing an aqueduct would be considerable. But they concluded that the successful completion of the project would, because of the mountainous character of the land, require technical and financial resources that were unavailable at the time. Accordingly, they vetoed the project on the grounds that "the masses are short of reserves having been through several years of natural calamities, so we can't take

[55] See Schurmann, *Ideology and Organization*, pp. 474ff. for the location of the prototypical communes.

[56] The following section is based on "Today's 'Foolish Old Man' Nurtured by Mao Tse-tung Thought," pp. 14–17. This case study is not necessarily accurate in every detail. It is based upon a retrospective rewriting of history by the Maoists, intended to clarify the differences between two styles of decision-making, rather than to present an objective historical account.

on this engineering job. As there is no state investment, we can't start this work."

But continued demands for more adequate irrigation led the county Party officials to invent a compromise: they proposed that a pumping station be constructed instead of the aqueduct. The costs and risks of such a project were considerably lower, and the gains would still be substantial, although not as great as those of the aqueduct. Of the three options—doing nothing, constructing the aqueduct, or installing the pumping station—the latter seemed the most feasible. Doing nothing was still seen as preferable to embarking on the costly and risky aqueduct construction project.

The Maoists, writing about this decision in 1969, presented a retrospective critique that points out several differences between the dogmatic and pragmatic mass-lines:

1. According to the *pragmatists,* the original proposal was vetoed because its probable costs outweighed its probable gains and because outside resources necessary to reduce the risks were not available.

2. According to the *Maoists,* the original proposal to build the aqueduct represented the unanimous view of the masses, did not conflict with doctrine, and therefore should not have been vetoed. The criteria used by the pragmatists were not contained in the Thought of Mao, and thus were illegitimate.

3. According to the *pragmatists,* the grounds for the veto were economic and technical.

4. According to the *Maoists,* the grounds for the veto were political and were class-based: the county Party cadres were "capitalist-roaders" singing a "worn-out Right opportunist tune," and their cost calculations violated Maoist maxims that "the masses can perform miracles."

5. According to the *pragmatists,* a compromise (the pumping station) could be devised that could substantially meet the demands of the peasants and the basic-level cadres at more acceptable levels of cost and risk.

6. According to the *Maoists,* such a compromise was a "deceptive" and illegitimate way of settling a class-based dispute. The disagreement could properly be resolved only when the county cadres accepted the fact that constructing the aqueduct was the only "correct" option. The pumping station was seen not as a third option, but merely as a deceptive variant of doing nothing.

The differences between the dogmatic and pragmatic mass-lines may be summarized as follows:

Characteristic	Dogmatic Mass-line	Pragmatic Mass-line
Basic model of "summarization"	Diagnostic: identification of the "correct" option	Rational choice: selection of most feasible option, with highest expected utility
Basis of factions	Class standpoint	Different information, analyses, predictions
Number of options	Two	Several
Criteria for decision	Dogmatic: options compared with doctrine	Pragmatic: options compared with each other in the context of the concrete situation
Basis for resolution of factional disputes	"Correctness"	Agreement on cost and risk calculations, or compromise
Risk control	Post-decision risk control through feedback and policy modification	Pre-decision risk control through prediction, calculation and experimentation

Mao Tse-tung's attitudes toward Chinese intellectuals and experts[57] have always been somewhat ambivalent. On the one hand, he has recognized that "China needs the services of as many intellectuals as possible for the colossal tasks of socialist construction." [58] But on the other hand, he has feared that intellectuals and experts tend to be divorced from the masses, hold undesirable attitudes and values because of their predominantly bourgeois backgrounds, and even make serious and costly errors because of their lack of practical experience and their unwillingness to engage in physical labor.

[57] The term "expert" here refers to those Party and government bureaucrats and industrial and scientific technicians who employ the pragmatic elitist mode of decision-making, characterized by a reliance on expertise and rational decisional criteria. The term "intellectual" is used interchangeably with "expert" in the sense that all experts are simultaneously intellectuals. Chinese Communists define "intellectuals" in several ways: (1) as a *class* ("mental workers"), (2) by *educational achievement* ("all those who have had middle school or higher education"), and (3) by *occupation* ("university and middle school teachers and staff members, university and middle school students, primary school teachers, engineers and technicians"). See Mao, "Rectify the Party's Style of Work," *SR*, p. 186, n. 2.

[58] Mao, "On the Correct Handling of Contradictions Among the People," p. 370.

Until the Cultural Revolution, Mao's policy towards China's experts and intellectuals was (1) to *contain* their influence within technical and micro-economic spheres, relying on mass-line policy-making modes for social and political decisions; and (2) periodically to attempt to *reform* the attitudes and values of which he disapproved.[59] But in the 1960s Mao apparently arrived at a new perception of Chinese intellectuals and experts that made these two strategies seem inadequate. He came to realize that experts are by nature an elite, a minority that can exercise influence disproportionate to its numbers because of its possession of special resources. Increasingly, Mao found, experts had formed an independent power center espousing attitudes and values which he opposed.

They thought they had "the 'capital' to bargain with the Party and the people"[60] for political power, high income, and prestige; they strove to justify their influence by making their activities seem "mysterious" and beyond the ken of the masses; and they attempted to perpetuate their existence as an elite by molding "revisionist successors" in an educational system which they controlled and which favored youth of bourgeois background. On the basis of these new perceptions, Mao changed his strategy from containment and reform to an attempt to destroy intellectuals and experts as a social class.

A major element of Mao's attack on experts during the Cultural Revolution was an unprecedented effort to *deny* the desirability of employing experts for policy-making and decision-making and to *affirm* the feasibility of the dogmatic mass-line as a mode for solving even technical problems. The dogmatic mass-line, Mao's spokesmen claimed, is applicable to all issues; would automatically produce correct results, thereby surpassing pragmatic elitist decision-making; and would not require special training to employ. "Expert" knowledge can be derived simply from a thorough investigation and study of the opinions of the masses: "To investigate a problem is to solve it. Just get moving on your two legs, go the rounds of every section placed under your charge and 'inquire

[59] Morton White makes the point that political leaders can adopt any of three strategies in dealing with intellectuals who espouse "undesirable" attitudes and values: they can grant them a degree of autonomy but attempt to *contain* their influence within prescribed areas; they can admit their value to society but attempt to *reform* their undesirable attitudes and values; or they can deny altogether their value to society and attempt to *destroy* them as a class. See his "Reflections on Anti-Intellectualism," *Daedalus*, Vol. 91, No. 3 (Summer 1962) pp. 457–468.

[60] "Letter of Fourth Class of Senior Third Grade, Peking No. 1 Girls' Middle School," *China Reconstructs*, Vol. 15, No. 10 (October 1966) pp. 52–53.

into everything' . . . and then you will be able to solve the problems, *however little your ability."* [61]

In short, at the beginning of the Cultural Revolution Mao and his followers no longer merely said that experts and intellectuals posed a problem because, despite their valuable and necessary skills, they were politically and ideologically deficient. Instead, they claimed that the skills and expertise acquired in higher education and technical training are a sham, that "the lowly are most intelligent—the elite are most ignorant," and that the functions of the experts could be filled by ordinary workers and peasants perfectly satisfactorily. "Workers armed with Mao Tse-tung's Thought can perform miracles."

The Cultural Revolution ideal was to create a society in which every man would be an intellectual, every citizen an expert. China as a society with an intellectual class would be replaced by a society in which everyone would be a "peasant-intellectual" or a "worker-intellectual." Mao's ideal semi-intellectual would be ideologically correct, constantly purging himself of bourgeois and revisionist elements. He would be taught the necessary theory and skills to make important contributions to production, where his task would be to help solve practical problems as they arose. He would be available for leadership positions but would neither demand nor expect them; he would spring to the fore when needed, but would selflessly return to the ranks when the job was done; he would be a leader, yet would not act like an official.

Thus, the replacement of the pragmatic elitist mode of decision-making —with its reliance on experts—by the dogmatic mass-line was seen to have two advantages. First, it would prevent the waste and errors of the pragmatic elitist mode by assuring that decision-makers maintained close ties with the masses and workers. Second, the dogmatic mass-line—which did not require that the decision-maker possess expertise or advanced training—could justify the elimination of experts and intellectuals as a social class in China.

This hyper-romantic vision could not, of course, be realized. From the beginning of the Cultural Revolution the ideal was qualified and compromised. Scientists and technicians engaged in national defense work were exempted by the August 16 Directive from participation in the Cultural Revolution. And one of Mao's "latest directives," issued in autumn 1968, declared: "The majority or the vast majority of the students trained in the old schools and colleges can integrate themselves with the

[61] Mao, "Oppose Book Worship," *SR*, p. 34. Italics added.

workers, peasants, and soldiers, and some have made inventions or innovations; they must, however, be re-educated by the workers, peasants, and soldiers under the guidance of the correct line, and thoroughly change their old ideology. Such intellectuals will be welcomed by the workers, peasants, and soldiers." With this directive, Mao retreated from a strategy of destruction to one of reform.

But the emphasis on the mass-line for technical decisions continues. It is now institutionalized in at least one factory by the creation of the "three-in-one organization of scientific research." [62] The tasks of the experts are now to be performed in tandem with the workers and "revolutionary cadres." The implication is that the workers and cadres will represent the opinions and ideas of the masses, and the technicians and experts will analyze and choose among them. The new system, in short, seems very much like the *pragmatic* mass-line described above, with high mass participation institutionalized in the decision-making process, but with continued reliance upon rational critera for decisions. The experts will be retained, but they will be subject to ideological reform campaigns and supervision by ordinary workers. In addition, continued emphasis will likely be placed on the recruitment and training of technical personnel from worker-peasant backgrounds.

Summary

Experienced politicians in China and elsewhere realize that the character of the policy-making process has a significant impact on the content of policy. The way in which a society formulates policies—the breadth of participation in the policy-making process and the criteria employed in reaching decisions—strongly influences what its politics will be. But even though they agree that procedures are important, Chinese leaders have differed as to which specific policy-making procedures are most conducive to the formation of effective policy. In this section we have identified four such policy-making procedures or "modes": the dogmatic mass-line, the pragmatic mass-line, dogmatic elitism, and pragmatic elitism. And we have argued that a crucial component of the Chinese Cultural Revolution was a debate over the relative applicability of these four policy-making modes to the solution of political and social problems.

[62] "Loyang Tractor Plant Advances Along the Road of Self-Reliance," *Peking Review*, No. 25 (June 20, 1969) pp. 3–4, 11. This institutionalization of the mass-line is modelled after the revolutionary committees described below. See also "Achievements in Mass Technical Innovations," *Peking Review*, No. 30 (July 25, 1969) pp. 30–31.

A common interpretation of the Cultural Revolution is that the struggle between the Maoists and the Liuists represents a struggle between dogmatism and pragmatism and between the mass-line and elitism. This dichotomization, however, is an oversimplification. The differences between the Maoists and the Liuists are more subtle. One way of sharpening our understanding of this aspect of the Cultural Revolution is through the concept of "issue-area." [63] Neither Maoists nor Liuists seek to apply a single set of policy-making procedures to all problems. Rather, their choice of policy-making mode is dependent upon the kind of question under consideration; Chinese decision-makers understand that policy-making procedures suitable for one kind of problem may produce inadequate decisions if applied to a different issue. A valid comparison of the Maoist and Liuist positions therefore requires that we consider each issue-area separately.

The notion of "issue-area" has been implicit throughout the preceding discussion. The "questions of principle" referred to by Liu Shao-ch'i are ideological and doctrinal issues; his "practical and concrete problems" appear to comprise political, social, and macro-economic questions. And the debates during the Cultural Revolution over the role of experts and intellectuals in Chinese society have largely been discussions of the proper personnel and procedures for solving technical and managerial (micro-economic) questions. In tackling these three sets of domestic issues, the Maoists and the Liuists employ competing sets of policy-making modes. The positions of the two factions may be summarized as follows:

Issue-Area	Maoist Position	Liuist Position
Ideological and doctrinal questions	Dogmatic mass-line	Dogmatic mass-line
Political, social, and macro-economic questions	Dogmatic mass-line	Pragmatic mass-line
Technical and managerial (micro-economic) questions	Pragmatic mass-line	Pragmatic elitist

[63] For an introduction to the concept of "issue-area," particularly in foreign policy analysis, see James N. Rosenau, "Pre-Theories and Theories of Foreign Policy," in R. Barry Farrell (ed.), *Approaches to Comparative and International Politics* (Evanston, Ill., 1966) pp. 27–92; and Rosenau, "Foreign Policy as an Issue-Area,"

When the Cultural Revolution is viewed in these terms, some important conclusions emerge. First, the procedural disagreement between the Maoists and the Liuists is not total, but is dependent upon the issue. To resolve ideological questions, for example, both factions advocate the dogmatic mass-line. On technical questions, both recognize the need for pragmatic criteria, while disagreeing on the desirability of mass participation. And on political issues, both seek mass participation in policy-making but differ over the suitabilty of dogmatic decision criteria. Second, the Cultural Revolution is not a clear-cut struggle between pragmatism and dogmatism. The Liuists accept the need for dogmatic decision criteria on some issues, and the Maoists admit the necessity for pragmatism on others. Still, the Maoists advocate the use of dogmatic criteria for *more* issues than do the Liuists. Finally, the Cultural Revolution can be interpreted as a dispute over the acceptability of elitism in that Mao—unlike Liu Shao-ch'i—does not apply elitist modes of policy-making to any domestic issue-area.

The struggle between pragmatism and dogmatism can be seen quite clearly in political, social, and macro-economic issues. Here, both factions advocate the mass-line and approve of high levels of mass participation in the decision-making process; but they differ over the criteria that should be used to analyze policy proposals and resolve disputes among policy-makers. The crux of the dispute is the Maoist assumption that in discussions of public policy, as in discussions of dogma and ideology, divergent policy proposals stem from different class standpoints, and that policy-making is therefore a form of class struggle. This assumption the Liuists reject. While the Liuists accept the necessity for minimax analysis, compromise, and bargaining, the Maoists insist that conformity with dogma is the only criterion for decisions about public policy.

The struggle between elitism and the mass-line is clearest in the technical-managerial issue-area. As previously indicated, the Maoists initially advocated the dogmatic mass-line for the solution of these problems as a way of justifying the elimination of experts and intellectuals as a social class in China. When it became obvious that the "miracles" performed by "workers armed with Mao Tse-tung's Thought" were not sufficient for continued technological innovation and managerial efficiency, the Maoists retreated a bit: while they still insist that the mass-line be applied to these problems, they now seem willing to accept its pragmatic

in James N. Rosenau (ed.), *Domestic Sources of Foreign Policy* (New York, 1967) pp. 11–50.

variant, as institutionalized in the "three-in-one" organizations for research and management. The knowledge and skills of technicians and managers will be used in the policy-making process, but the participation of mass representatives in all domestic decisions will restrict the power and influence of China's ideologically unreliable intellectuals and experts.

PARTY ORGANIZATION

A principal aim of the Cultural Revolution has been the rectification and reform of the Chinese Communist Party. According to a major *Hung-ch'i* editorial of Autumn 1968: "The great proletarian cultural revolution is an open Party consolidation movement carried out on an unprecedented scale by revolutionary methods. In scope and depth, in profundity of ideological criticism and repudiation and in thoroughness of organizational consolidation, it far surpasses any previous Party consolidation movement since liberation." [64]

A distinguishing feature of such "organizational consolidation" has been its sweeping reform of Party structures, which has supplemented the customary rectification of individual Party members. In the early 1960s, the Maoists seem to have finally discovered for themselves one of the major tenets of organization theory: people's behavior is determined not only by their own values and attitudes but also by the goals and structure of the organization in which they work. Consequently, no thoroughgoing program of Party reform can rely solely on the re-education of Party members; it must also involve the restructuring of organizational activities. In short, the reform of role occupants must be accompanied by the reform of role structures.

This section examines the two major examples of organizational restructuring that occurred during the Cultural Revolution—the adoption of a new constitution and the creation of revolutionary committees—in an effort to infer some of the components of Maoist normative organizational theory. A fruitful way of ordering such an analysis is to consider, in turn, three major organizational activities: (1) the organization's definition of purpose and its relationship with other major societal actors, (2) discipline and control, and (3) recruitment. Finally, we will discuss

[64] "Absorb Fresh Blood from the Proletariat—An Important Question in Party Consolidation," editorial in *Hung-ch'i*, No. 4 (October 14, 1968), in *Peking Review*, No. 43 (October 25, 1968) p. 4.

the structural characteristics of the organization: its levels of centralization, specialization, and formalization.[65]

The Cultural Revolution has revealed that the primary goal of a Maoist CCP is less the creation of a utopian society than constant struggle against a virtually immortal and persistently powerful enemy. Maoists have severely criticized Liu Shao-ch'i for his vision of an idyllic future Communist society in which "there will be no exploiters and oppressors, no landlords and capitalists, no imperialists and fascists, nor will there be any oppressed and exploited people, or any of the darkness, ignorance, and backwardness resulting from the system of exploitation. . . . By then all humanity will consist of unselfish, intelligent, highly cultured and skilled Communist workers; mutual assistance and affection will prevail among men and there will be no such irrationalities as mutual suspicion and deception, mutual injury, mutual slaughter and war." [66]

According to the Maoists, Liu described the Communist society as "a bed of roses, without darkness or contradiction," thereby neglecting the need for continual struggle against the class enemy.[67] These charges are unfair to Liu. Immediately after the passage just cited, Liu went on to warn that victory for the Communist cause "can only be won through long and arduous struggle." And he admitted that, even after the Communist Party seizes power, the struggle against the influence of the exploiting classes would have to continue "for a long time." But the Maoists seem to feel that even holding out the promise of a future utopia is an invitation to complacency and relaxation.

The primary goal of a Maoist party, then, is to steel itself, to keep itself pure, and to continue the struggle. This middle-range goal is an idealized *process* rather than an idealized *final state*. Accordingly, the Cultural Revolution is not a millenarian rebellion seeking a utopia. Rather, it is

---

[65] These dimensions for analyzing organizations are drawn from Parsons' functional needs of social systems, as described in Chalmers Johnson, *Revolutionary Change* (Boston, 1966) pp. 57ff; from D. S. Pugh *et al.*, "A Conceptual Scheme for Organizational Analysis," *Administrative Science Quarterly*, Vol. 8, No. 3 (December 1963) pp. 289–315; and from R. H. Hall *et al.*, "An Examination of the Blau-Scott and Etzioni Typologies," *Administrative Science Quarterly*, Vol. 12, No. 1 (June 1967) pp. 118–139. A fourth organizational activity is, naturally, goal attainment, which has already been discussed in the preceding section.

[66] Liu, *How To Be a Good Communist*, p. 36.

[67] "Betrayal of Proletarian Dictatorship is Essential Element in the Book of 'Self-Cultivation,' " *Jen-min Jih-pao* and *Hung-ch'i* joint editoral, in *Peking Review*, No. 20 (May 12, 1967) p. 9.

both a jacquerie and a "nostalgic" rebellion, seeking both to purge those who usurped Mao's power in the Party and to restore the Party to the lean instrument of revolution that it had been in the Yenan days.[68]

The CCP serves as a link between the leader and society. The Cultural Revolution saw a redefinition of the Party's relationships with both society and the leader. As to the former, the Maoists altered the way in which the Party is to provide society with political guidance. Before the Cultural Revolution, the administration of the state was characterized by dual rule:[69] the supervision of any government organ was to be shared by its own superiors in the state machinery (who would supervise the technical details of the work), and its Party branch (which would supervise ideological and political affairs). This division of supervisory powers was based on Section 7 of Mao's essay, "Some Questions Concerning Methods of Leadership," a section written specifically to increase the Party's control over governmental operations during the Yenan period.[70] And the concept of dual rule was written into Article 51 of the old constitution: "Since special conditions obtain in public institutions and organizations, the primary Party organizations therein are in no position to guide and supervise their work, but they should supervise ideologically and politically all Party members in the said institutions and organizations."

But, interestingly enough, Section 7 of Mao's essay is not quoted at all in the little red book, and no section comparable to Article 51 appears in the new constitution. The objection to dual rule seems to be twofold: (1) that it gave the Party insufficient control over state operations, and (2) that it gave rise to two complete bureaucracies—one Party, one state

---

[68] According to Chalmers Johnson, jacqueries are rebellions "motivated by a belief that the system had been betrayed by its elite" and that "one or more of their authority statuses is occupied by a usurper." "Nostalgic rebellions" is my own term for what Johnson described as rebellions "which espouse the revival or reintroduction of an idealized society that allegedly existed in the society's own past." See Johnson, op. cit., pp. 136–137. On the Cultural Revolution's deposing of usurpers, see Lin Piao, "Report to the Ninth National Congress of the Communist Party of China," Peking Review, No. 18 (April 28, 1969) p. 16: "Liu Shao-ch'i gathered together a gang of renegades, enemy agents, and capitalist-roaders . . . [and] usurped important Party and government posts." Italics added.

[69] For a discussion of the distinction between dual rule and vertical rule, see Schurmann, Ideology and Organization, pp. 188–194.

[70] Mao, "Some Questions Concerning Methods of Leadership," pp. 237–238. For the background of the inclusion of the dual rule section in this essay, see Mark Selden, "The Yenan Legacy: The Mass Line," in A. Doak Barnett (ed.), Chinese Communist Politics in Action (Seattle, 1969) pp. 99–151.

—parallel to each other. In his political report to the Ninth Party Congress, Lin Piao criticized the "organs of state power" as a "duplicative administrative structure divorced from the masses." [71] In accordance with an early 1968 directive of Mao Tse-tung, Lin declared, this duplication in administrative structure is to be eliminated; revolutionary committees will combine both Party and governmental functions in one unit under the principle of "unified leadership." [72] The doctrine of unified leadership is written into the new constitution as one of the organizational principles of the Party (Article 7), replacing the concept of dual rule.

As to the relationship between the Party and the leader, Mao's ideal CCP is a smoothly running transmission belt between him and the masses, a static-free communications network for gathering and disseminating information and directives, and a frictionless organizational machine for implementing his policy decisions. Mao does not want the Party to become an institution with goals and purposes of its own. The Party is to have no goals other than the ones he authorizes; it is not even to value its own self-preservation, for it is to be discarded, remolded, or bypassed at the will of the leader. Mao wants to play neither the role of "honorary chairman," stripped of influence and divorced from Party operations, nor that of chief executive officer, bound by institutional norms and enveloped by the Party. Rather, he wants to remain in constant contact but slightly aloof, so that he can both set the Party's goals and actively supervise their pursuit. Too close to the Party, he would be restricted. Too remote from the Party, he would be unable to control it.

This conception of the relation between leader and Party is diametrically opposed to that held by Liu Shao-ch'i and Teng Hsiao-p'ing, the chief stewards of the Party apparatus. Teng publicly declared in 1956: "Unlike the leaders of the exploiting classes in the past, the leaders of the working class party stand not above the masses, but in their midst, *not above the Party, but within it.* Precisely because of this, they must set an example in . . . obeying the Party organization and observing Party discipline. Love for the leader is essentially an expression of love for the interests of

---

[71] Lin, "Report to the Ninth National Congress," p. 20.

[72] Mao's directive is quoted in *ibid.* In one model factory, for example, the Party's leading group concurrently served as the revolution committee's standing committee; the separation was in name only—"Using Chairman Mao's Line on Party Building to Consolidate the Party Organization," *Peking Review,* No. 15 (April 11, 1969) p. 36. Overlapping membership in Party and state organs, which had existed particularly at lower levels, was to be vastly increased.

the Party, the class, and the people, and not the deification of the individual." [73] And as Liu reportedly wrote more recently (1962): "Unless in the name of the organization, no one is allowed to lead. Comrade Mao Tse-tung is the leader of the whole Party, but he too submits to Party leadership." [74] For Teng and Liu, then, love for the leader is love for the Party; for Mao, however, love for the Party is love for the leader. In a Maoist society, only the position of the leader is a social institution, valued for itself. The Party remains an organization, valued only for its service to the leader. [75]

How do Party leaders assure that their policy decisions are effectively and accurately implemented by lower levels in the organization? The new Party constitution and other Cultural Revolution documents have established new procedures for maintaining discipline and control in the Party, based upon considerable innovation, experimentation, and debate during the Cultural Revolution. In order fully to understand the new control structures, we must first discover the strains in the Party that led Mao and his followers to discard the old control system, and then discuss their theories of Party discipline and their prescriptions for organizational control.

A major source of strain and tension in the CCP—and indeed in any organization—is the complex and conflicting set of demands and expectations placed on cadres at all levels. [76] Demands from above for production in greater quantity and quality at lower cost conflict with demands from below for more central assistance and lower quotas. Demands from above for uniform compliance conflict with demands from below for waivers and dispensations to meet local conditions. These conflicting role pressures are compounded by psychocultural factors, for, according to Richard H. Solomon, vertical communication is extremely difficult for Chinese be-

[73] Teng, *Report on the Revision of the Constitution*, p. 82. Italics added.

[74] Liu, "Organizational and Disciplinary Cultivation," quoted in "Selected Edition of Liu Shao-ch'i's Counterrevolutionary Revisionist Crimes," by Nank'ai University, August 18 Red Rebel Regiment, Liaison Station (under the banner, "Pledging to Fight a Bloody Battle with Liu-Teng-T'ao to the End"), April 1967, in *Selections from China Mainland Magazines*, No. 651 (April 22, 1969) p. 21.

[75] This distinction between "institution" and "organization" is based on Philip Selznick, *Leadership in Administration* (Berkeley, 1957). To Selznick, organizations are "expendable tools," designed to perform a task; institutions are organizations or roles that are infused with value for members of the organization or members of society.

[76] For a valuable study of these "role pressures" and their impact on both organization and individual, see Robert L. Kahn *et al.*, *Organizational Stress: Studies in Role Conflict and Ambiguity* (New York, 1964).

cause of their ambivalent feelings toward authority.[77] As a result, the stress and tension for each cadre are quite severe. And their attempts— out of self-defense—to balance the incompatible demands on them may lead to serious violations of organizational norms and discipline.

Lower-level cadres,[78] for example, may attempt to minimize responsibility, avoid making decisions, flatter their superiors, file false reports, and engage in corruption—all of which are potentially damaging to the system's decision-making ability and to the regime's ability to secure compliance from the basic levels.[79] At the middle levels, these organizational tensions contributed to the creation of "independent kingdoms"—intraorganizational cliques whose members were more committed to their bailiwicks, their colleagues, and themselves than to the center. These independent kingdoms produced serious disruption of Party communications and distortion of Party staffing policy. Downward communication was disrupted by distorting or pigeonholing unpopular central directives, by quoting them out of context, and even by forging them. Upward communication was disrupted by filing false reports, overly optimistic reports, or no reports at all. As the PLA *Bulletin of Activities* summarized the problem, middle-level cadres had "created a communication block by failing to relay in time instructions of the Party and their superiors on the one hand and failing to submit reports to their superiors on the other." [80] In addition, middle-level cadres were accused of placing their friends in key posts, of unjustly attacking and dismissing rivals, and thus of creating "watertight" Party organs and committees virtually impervious to outside pressure.

These strains in the Party became particularly intense in the "three hard years" following the Great Leap Forward. The ranks of cadres throughout China were plagued by corruption, extortion, squandering of state resources, speculation in state funds and state property, and a

[77] See, for example, "Communications Patterns and the Chinese Revolution," *China Quarterly*, No. 32 (October–December 1967) pp. 88–110.

[78] Throughout this paper, "center" refers to the Central Committee and organs attached to it; "lower" and "basic" levels refer to levels below the *hsien* (county); and "middle" level refers to *hsien*, provincial, and regional organs.

[79] On these tactics, see Michel Oksenberg, "China: A Quiet Crisis in Revolution," *Asian Survey*, Vol. 6, No. 1 (January 1966) pp. 3–11; and *idem* "The Institutionalization of the Chinese Communist Revolution: The Ladder of Success on the Eve of the Cultural Revolution," *China Quarterly*, No. 36 (October–December 1968) pp. 61–92.

[80] Quoted in Philip Bridgham, "Mao's Cultural Revolution: Origin and Development," *China Quarterly*, No. 29 (January–March 1967) pp. 1–35.

high rate of turnover. And the established Party control structures seemed unable to cope with the problem to Mao's satisfaction.

The theories of discipline of Mao and Liu are closely related to their views on factions in policy-making. A theory of discipline, in effect, represents the answer to the question, "What happens if factions persist after a policy decision has been made?"

As indicated above, Liu Shao-ch'i believes that factions within the Party usually represent honest disagreements over the best solutions to problems, and that differences of opinion among such factions—even on minor questions of principle—should be compromised in the formulation of policy. Once the decision has been made, however, it must be carried out. Party members who disagree may appeal the decision to a higher level, but they must obey the directive if the appeal is denied. The obedience of the Party member, in short, is not contingent on his perception of the correctness of the directive; it is, rather, unconditional. Insistence on absolute obedience and discipline is necessary, Liu has written, because of the heterogeneous composition of the Party; if everyone were allowed to go his own way, the Party would become irreparably fragmented.[81]

The Maoist critique of Liu's views reveals the perennial Chinese Communist concern over the proper relationship between democracy and centralism. Mao paradoxically rejects the concept of unconditional obedience but accepts the necessity for much harsher disciplinary measures than does Liu. Mao's position is based on the premise that factions are class-based and that disciplinary questions in the Party are therefore forms of class struggle. Obedience is to be based on the political correctness of the directive; policy directives that are not correct (not in accordance with the Thought of Mao) are not to be implemented. Liu is accordingly accused of advocating a "one-man dictatorship," of insisting on absolute obedience in an attempt to turn Party members into "docile tools" so that they would "obey and follow his anti-Party, anti-Socialist instructions."[82]

But if a lower level decides that a directive is incorrect, what is to be

---

[81] Liu, *On the Party,* pp. 17, 100.

[82] "Resolutely Defend the Party Principle of Democratic Centralism," *Peking Review,* No. 16 (April 19, 1968) pp. 20–22. Indeed, in the original draft of the new constitution, obedience to superiors was not mentioned as a duty of a Party member. Even in the final version, lower organs are merely placed "subordinate to" higher organs, rather than specifically ordered (as they were in the old constitution) to "obey" their superiors.

done?[83] According to Mao's solution, lower levels may address a criticism of the directive to any higher organ, including the Central Committee.[84] The higher organ must carefully examine the criticism to see whether or not it corresponds with Maoist ideology. If the criticism is found to be correct, the policy must be reversed.[85] But if the higher organ believes that the original instruction is correct, it is to discuss the question with members of the lower organ and patiently persuade them that the policy is correct. In short, criticism should be handled in such a way that both levels "learn from each other" until agreement is reached.

Once again, Maoists fall back on two assumptions: first, that their ideology provides a clear set of answers and criteria for all policy questions, and second, that based on those criteria, agreement can always be reached between those who truly possess the proletarian standpoint.

The latter assumption leads to the conclusion that if agreement still cannot be reached after patient discussion, there must exist class enemies who must be ferreted out. Because the opposition has now been clearly identified as a class enemy, the relationship is one of antagonistic contradiction, and the most severe kinds of struggle tactics are to be employed. Obedience to *correct* orders (as opposed to *any* orders) is not an expression of the "slave mentality" advocated by Liu Shao-ch'i, but rather an expression of "proletarian party spirit."

The persistence of corruption and speculation, of "commandism" and "tailism," and of "independent kingdoms" and "watertight" fiefdoms made Mao increasingly dissatisfied with the established procedures for Party control and Party reform. The Party stewards—relying on the regular Party control commissions, on routinized self-criticism and self-cultivation, and on the dispatch of work teams to supervise the basic-level cadres—seemed unable or unwilling to solve the Party's disciplinary problems.[86] Mao's suspicions were by no means unjustified. In many

[83] For a Maoist attempt to sort out these problems see T'ang Hsiao-tao, "Submission or Boycott?" *Jen-min Jih-pao*, December 17, 1967, in *Current Background*, No. 849 (March 11, 1968) pp. 14-15.

[84] Under the old constitution (Article 26), such an appeal could be addressed only to the organ issuing the directive.

[85] On revision of policy by a higher organ to comply with "correct" criticism, see "A County Revolutionary Committee Having Close Ties With the Masses," pp. 6-7.

[86] Two such rectification campaigns—allegedly administered by Liu Shao-ch'i, Teng Hsiao-p'ing, and P'eng Chen—were the Socialist Education Movement (1962-66) and the socialist (as opposed to proletarian) cultural revolution (November 1965-July 1966). On the former, see Richard Baum and Frederick Teiwes, *Ssu-ch'ing:*

cases, the middle-level cadres gave only lip service to the rectification programs, and the lower-level cadres knew it. As one put it, "The higher-ups always talk about morality but they have something different in their hearts. Their words and actions never coincide." [87]

Mao's approach was to bypass the formal Party machinery and to create extra-organizational methods for Party reform. It was to this end that he oversaw the formation of Poor and Lower Middle Peasant Associations (PLMPA's), in the belief that if the PLMPA's could control the cadres, then he could control the PLMPA's. Similarly, he welcomed the emergence of the Red Guards, for they too seemed at first to be an organization that could easily be appropriated as an instrument for Party reform. And Mao's faith in extra-organizational control is also reflected in the new Party constitution. The old intra-organizational control structure—the system of control commissions—does not appear in the new constitution. Rather, it provides for direct supervision by the masses: "Leading bodies of the Party at all levels shall constantly listen to the opinions of the masses both inside and outside the Party and accept their supervision" (Article 5).

Other Cultural Revolution documents have indicated that this supervision is to take four forms. First, there is increased emphasis on direct, face-to-face contact between cadres and masses during the investigation stage of the mass-line; cadres are told to rely on personal inspection and research rather than on written reports and staff briefings. As Mao directed in late 1967: "From now on, cadres should go to the grass-roots

---

The Socialist Education Movement of 1962–66 (China Research Monograph No. 2, Center for Chinese Studies, University of California at Berkeley, 1968); and Baum and Teiwes, "Liu Shao-ch'i and the Cadre Question," *Asian Survey*, Vol. 8, No. 4 (April 1968), pp. 323–345. On the latter, see "Circular of Central Committee of Chinese Communist Party (May 16, 1966)," and " 'Hit Hard at Many in Order to Protect a Handful' is a Component Part of the Bourgeois Reactionary Line," *Hung-ch'i*, No. 5 (March 30, 1967), in *Peking Review*, No. 15 (April 7, 1967) pp. 18–20. These campaigns, conducted primarily by means of work teams led by middle- (and often central-) level cadres, have been condemned by the Maoists for exaggerating the number of errant cadres, for placing restrictions on participation by the masses, for limiting the scope of the rectification, and for protecting the truly "revisionist power-holders" while transferring or dismissing vast numbers of merely "mistaken" or "benighted" cadres. The criticisms deal largely with the content of the campaigns, but the attacks on the work teams and on "closed door reform" (self-criticism and study) indicate Maoist rethinking of rectification procedures as well.

[87] Quoted in Charles Neuhauser, "The Chinese Communist Party in the 1960s: Prelude to the Cultural Revolution," *China Quarterly*, No. 32 (October–December 1967) p. 10.

level and make investigations; they should persist in the mass-line, consult the masses on matters that have come up, and be their pupils." [88] A second form is mass criticism during the policy-implementation stage of the mass-line.[89] Third, the masses are to be represented on all revolutionary committees. Such representation, it is affirmed, "provides the revolutionary committees at [various] levels with a broad mass foundation. Direct participation by the revolutionary masses in the running of the country and the enforcement of revolutionary supervision from below over the organs of political power at various levels play a very important role in ensuring that our leading groups at all levels always adhere to the mass-line, maintain the closest relations with the masses, represent their interests at all times and serve the people heart and soul." [90]

Finally, the masses are to be permitted to attend Party branch meetings. Under the principle of "unified leadership," representation of the masses on revolutionary committees contributes to supervision over the Party, since revolutionary committee standing committees are simultaneously Party leading groups. But to provide even closer control, Mao has directed (probably at the First Plenum of the Ninth Central Committee) that "the masses outside the Party attend the [Party "reconsolidation"] meetings and give comments." [91] Party reform is no longer to be conducted behind closed doors.

The maintenance of organizational unity and discipline depends not only on control structures but also on recruitment policies. A third organizational issue in the Cultural Revolution has been the standards to be used in the recruitment of new Party members.

As an indication of the importance of the recruitment issue, all but one of Liu Shao-ch'i's "six theories of party-building" (each roundly condemned by the Maoists)[92] have immediate application to recruitment

[88] Quoted in "Cadres Should Go Among the Masses," *Jen-min Jih-pao* editorial, November 19, 1967, in *Peking Review*, No. 48 (November 24, 1967) pp. 6–8.

[89] For example, see "A County Revolutionary Committee Having Close Ties with the Masses," pp. 6–7.

[90] "Revolutionary Committees Are Fine," *Jen-min Jih-pao, Hung-ch'i*, and *Chieh-fang-chün Pao* joint editorial, in *Peking Review*, No. 14 (April 5, 1968) pp. 6–7.

[91] *Peking Review*, No. 27 (July 4, 1969) p. 1.

[92] The six theories are (1) the theory of "the dying out of the class struggle," (2) the theory of "docile tools," (3) the theory of "entering the Party in order to become an official," (4) the theory that "the masses are backward," (5) the theory of "inner-Party peace," and (6) the theory of "merging public and private interests." See "Thoroughly Repudiate Liu Shao-ch'i's Counter-Revolutionary Revisionist Line on Party Building," *Peking Review*, No. 51 (December 20, 1968) pp. 10–15.

policy. According to the Maoist critiques, Liu neglected class background in recruitment in favor of technical expertise and management skills, and was willing to offer the possibility of promotion and personal gain as incentives to potential Party members. These policies "opened the door" for all kinds of bourgeois, revisionist, and self-serving elements to enter the Party.

To correct this situation, the new constitution drastically altered Party admission criteria, so that Party membership is now based much more stringently on *class*. The old constitution stipulated: "Membership in the Party is open to any Chinese citizen who works and does not exploit the labor of others, accepts the program and Constitution of the Party, joins and works in one of the Party organizations, carries out the Party's decisions, and pays membership dues as required" (Article 1).

The new constitution states: "Any Chinese worker, poor peasant, lower-middle peasant, revolutionary armyman or any other revolutionary element who has reached the age of 18, who accepts the Constitution of the Party, joins a Party organization and works actively in it, carries out the Party's decisions, observes Party discipline and pays membership dues may become a member of the Communist Party of China" (Article 1).

Thus the Maoist approach to recruitment is highly selective, an attempt to keep the "class ranks" of the Party pure by admitting only those of "revolutionary" background. Liu Shao-ch'i's approach, as set forth in *How To Be a Good Communist,* was quite different. Liu recognized the practical impossibility of restricting membership to those with "demonstrated proletarian standpoint," especially when the Party needed new members to supervise the administration of its rapidly expanding territory. He was therefore willing to accept lower—but more realistic— admission criteria, while putting faith in the Party's disciplinary and educational measures to keep its heterogeneous membership in line:

It is not a bad thing that [those lacking a firm proletarian standpoint] turn to the Communist Party. . . . We welcome them—everyone except for enemy agents, traitors, careerists, and ambitious climbers. Provided they accept and are ready to abide by the Party's Programme and Constitution, work in one of the Party organizations and pay membership dues, they may be admitted into the Communist Party. As for deepening their study and understanding of Communism and the Party's Programme and Constitution, they can do so after joining the Party. . . . Indeed, for most people it is impossible to have a profound understanding of Communism and the Party's Programme and Constitution before joining the Party. That is why we only prescribe acceptance, *and not a thorough understanding,* of the Party's Programme and Constitution as a condition for admission.[93]

Mao, who came to distrust both the disciplinary and educational systems of the Party by the mid-1960s, obviously found this approach unsatisfactory. To him, it was this recruitment policy that had facilitated the "usurpation" of Party and governmental power by his opponents at all levels.

The new Party constitution, Maoist polemics, and the course of the Cultural Revolution all indicate that the new Party and the new revolutionary committees will be less specialized, less formalized, and will have elements of both greater centralization and greater decentralization than the old Party and governmental structures.

The revolutionary vision of Mao Tse-tung has little room for specialization of either men or structures. To Mao, specialization merely creates shortness of vision, unnecessary social cleavages, and barriers to communication. In his Directive of May 7, 1966, Mao in effect called for interchangeability of roles in all segments of society. Specialization of function would no longer exist: Workers would become peasants, peasants would become soldiers, and soldiers would become workers. Coordination and communication would be promoted not by building linkages between specialized roles, but by enabling men to transfer from one role to another.

Translated into organizational terms, Mao's attack on specialization appears as a call for "simple and efficient structure." Emphasized throughout the Cultural Revolution, this slogan has been made an organizational principle in the new Party constitution (Article 7). A good summary of the Maoist position appeared in a *Wen-hui-pao* editorial criticizing "pluralism": "Pluralism is an old trick with many demerits. You take charge of politics and I production, so that there are many systems, many different groups of men, many organs with a big staff at many different levels; meetings are held excessively, contradictions are numerous and troubles are frequent. . . . The plural form of organization impedes the bringing of proletarian politics to the fore, bars the leaders from going among the masses, and hinders the organization of a revolutionized leading group that keeps in contact with the masses."[94] To Maoists,

---

[93] Liu, *How To Be a Good Communist,* pp. 56–57. Italics added.
[94] "It Is Necessary to Exercise Unified Leadership," *Wen-hui-pao* editorial, April 21, 1968, in *Survey of the China Mainland Press,* No. 4178 (May 15, 1968) pp. 1–2.

excessive division of labor and excessive specialization lead to delay, departmentalism, and lack of coordination.

The major model in the application of the principle of "simple and efficient structure" is the Revolutionary Committee of Lingpao County, Honan Province.[95] *Jen-min Jih-pao* commended the report of the committee's experience to all revolutionary committees and governmental departments. The Lingpao reforms proceeded in two phases. In Phase I (January 1968) the old government and Party organs were replaced by a revolutionary committee of 10 sections. (While information on government and Party structure in Lingpao before the Cultural Revolution is not available, a typical county studied by A. Doak Barnett contained 35 major government and party units in 1962.)[96] That was, however, insufficient. According to the report, "The administrative structure was still unwieldy. . . . Many problems could not be solved in good time, thus adversely affecting both revolution and production." As a result, in Phase II (probably June or July 1968), the revolutionary committee was trimmed once again, both in the number of staff (from 100 to 30) and in the number of sections (from 10 to 4). The administrations of Barnett's "County X" and the two Lingpao reforms are compared in the accompanying table.

An indication of the lack of formalization in the new Party structure may be derived from comparison of the Party constitutions of 1956 and 1969. In the old constitution, specification of the functions and powers of Party congresses, committees, and secretariats above the primary level required 16 articles (Articles 31–46). In the new constitution, discussion of the same organs constitutes three very brief articles, which deal not at all with powers, only with structure. For example, in the old constitution the National Party Congress is given the power (1) to elect the Central Committee, (2) to hear and examine reports from the Central Committee and other central organs, (3) to determine the Party's line and policy, and (4) to revise the Party constitution (Article 32). In the new constitution, the National Party Congress is formally empowered only to elect the Central Committee, although the Ninth Party Congress (which adopted the new constitution) did in fact perform the other three functions as well.

[95] "A County Revolutionary Committee Takes the Road of Having 'Better Troops and Simpler Administration,'" *Peking Review*, No. 32 (August 9, 1968) pp. 17–19.
[96] Barnett, *Cadres, Bureaucracy, and Political Power in Communist China*, Part II.

Disciplinary procedures are also left unformalized in the new constitution. The 1956 constitution devoted six articles (Articles 13–18) to discipline of Party members. It provided that disciplinary measures must be approved by either a higher Party committee or a higher Party control commission; that the accused had the right to defend himself; and that the convicted could appeal disciplinary measures to higher Party committees and control commissions up to and including the Central Committee. The 1969 constitution, in contrast, devotes only one article to disciplinary proceedings: there is no provision that disciplinary measures need be approved by higher Party organs or that Party members have the right of defense and appeal. Instead, the constitution provides a virtual blank check for a Party purge: "Proven renegades, enemy agents, absolutely unrepentant persons in power taking the capitalist road, degenerates, and alien class elements must be cleared out of the Party and not be re-admitted" (Article 4).

Still another set of procedures left unformalized are those of elections. The provision in the old constitution that "the leading bodies of the Party at all levels are elected" (Article 19(1)), has now been replaced by "the leading bodies of the Party at all levels are elected *through democratic consultation*" (Article 5, italics added). What this means is uncertain; election through democratic consultation, according to one source, refers to selection "as a result of repeated arguments, deliberations, consultations, and examinations. The cadres are discussed and examined by the revolutionary masses and approved of by the leadership, and besides there are always partial replacements and adjustments." [97]

Whether the lack of formalization represents a deliberate decision to keep structures flexible or simply reflects uncertainty as to the most desirable procedures remains to be seen. Given Mao's past predilection to rely on formalized procedures (such as the mass-line) as insurance for correct performance, one suspects the latter explanation to be the more plausible.

The degree of local initiative in policy-making has been a major issue throughout the Cultural Revolution. At the beginning of 1967, cadres frightened by the excesses of the Red Guards and by the potential consequences of making mistakes tended to pass problems upward rather than attempt to make decisions themselves. This apparently caused considerable confusion at the top, and Chou En-lai warned of a "big plot to pass

[97] "Absorb Fresh Blood from the Proletariat," p. 7.

ADMINISTRATIVE STRUCTURE IN TWO CHINESE COUNTIES: "COUNTY X" (1962), AND LINGPAO COUNTY UNDERGOING REFORM (1968)

Function	Administrative Organ			
	"County X"		Lingpao County	
	Party	Government	First Reform January 1968	Second Reform June–July 1968
Organization and personnel (Administration)[a]	Organization department	Personnel section	Personnel section	Administration
	Party committee staff	People's council staff office	Secretariat	
Political and legal	Political and legal department	Political and legal staff office; public security bureau	County affairs section	Security
Armed forces work	Seacoast department	Military service bureau	—	—
United front work	United front department	Overseas Chinese affairs section	—	—
Culture and education	Propaganda and education department	Education bureau; culture bureau; health bureau	Culture and health section; political and propaganda work section; cultural revolution group	Political work

				Production
Rural work	Rural work department	Agriculture, forestry, and water conservancy staff office; agriculture bureau; water conservancy bureau; agriculture and land reclamation bureau	Rural work section	
Finance and trade	Finance and trade department	Finance and trade staff office; finance and tax bureau; communications bureau; grain bureau	Finance and trade section	
Industry and commerce	Industry and commerce department	Industry bureau; construction bureau; communications bureau	Industry and communications section	
(Statistics)[a]	—	Planning and statistics committee	Statistics section	—
(Control)[a]	Control commission	Civil affairs section; labor bureau; market management committee	—	—
(Miscellaneous)[a]	—	—	—	—
TOTAL NUMBER OF ADMINISTRATIVE UNITS	10	24	10	4

SOURCE: For 1962: A. Doak Barnett, *Cadres, Bureaucracy and Political Power in Communist China* (New York, 1968), pp. 458–459. For 1968: "A County Revolutionary Committee Takes the Road of Having 'Better Troops and Simpler Administration,'" *Peking Review*, August 9, 1968, pp. 17–19.

[a] Not included in Barnett's functional systems.

the burden of all kinds of contradictions [problems] up to us." [98] This abdication of decision-making power by lower levels was coupled with an increase in the total number of problems actually being processed by the system, as the power struggle between the two sides increased in both scope and violence.

In August 1967, however, following the Wuhan Incident, Lin Piao reversed Chou's call for decentralization in an effort to preserve control for the leaders in Peking. Local decision-making initiative was severely curtailed: "One must report to and ask instructions from Chairman Mao, the Central Committee, and the Cultural Revolution Group. You must not think that you have yourself understood and need not report to the center; you must not think that it is clear and that you can deal with it yourself. . . . You need not fear that you are causing trouble to the center. No matter whether it is a big or small affair, *everything* must be reported and instructions sought for. The Premier and Cultural Revolution Group comrades are working day and night. You can send telegrams or [make] trunk calls." [99]

Now that the situation is less chaotic, local initiative in decision-making has once again been increased. To use Franz Schurmann's terms, the final outcome of the Cultural Revolution seems to be a combination of "centralization" and "decentralization I," that is, power to the center and the bottom at the expense of the middle.

Legislation—the general, strategic direction of the Party—is to remain centralized. The Party center retains control over supreme directives and ideological pronouncements, the convening of all Party congresses, and the election of Party committee members at all levels. Such an arrangement suggests that the center will exercise its power primarily through general statements of policy and specific vetoes, rather than through the supervision of detail. Administration—the specific, tactical direction of the Party—is to be decentralized. Ideally, problems will be solved at the grass-roots level; the basic-level Party and administrative organs are told, "we cannot consistently wait for the leadership at higher levels to map out all the work details for us." [100]

---

[98] Quoted in Philip Bridgham, "Mao's Cultural Revolution in 1967: The Struggle to Seize Power," *China Quarterly,* No. 34 (April–June 1968) p. 10.

[99] Quoted in Quarterly Chronicle and Documentation," *China Quarterly,* No. 32 (October–December 1967) p. 200. Italics added.

[100] "To Be Good at Translating the Party's Policy into Action by the Masses," *Jenmin Jih-pao* editorial, February 17, 1969.

This decentralization may be a rationalization of Peking's current inability to provide central direction. But more important, it is also due to a reluctance by the Maoists to reconstruct the large, middle-level bureaucracy that would be required to transmit and administer detailed central directives. The Maoists have apparently concluded that it was the middle-level bureaucracy that was primarily responsible for distorting central directives in the past. By maintaining general direction at the very top and by delegating most specific decisions to the very bottom, the Maoists can reduce the functions and power of the middle levels. As in the case of the experts, an effort is under way to minimize the need for—and thus the center's reliance on—Party members who have proven unreliable. In the meantime, it seems that the middle level's transmission and control functions are being performed by the army.[101]

Summary

On the eve of the Cultural Revolution, Mao Tse-tung had serious reservations about the way in which the CCP was performing its four major activities. First of all, Mao felt that the Party's definition of purpose had become perverted: the Party was concerned more with its own self-preservation and its members' social status and political prestige than with carrying on the revolution in China. It had, in short, become institutionalized. It was no longer the instrument for revolution that Mao had created. Indeed, it was more the master of the leader than the leader was the master of the Party; the creation had supplanted and subordinated its creator.

As to task performance, Mao felt that the Party had become bogged down in bureaucratic procedures, had lost (or had deliberately broken) contact with the masses, and had fractured into a myriad policy factions and personal cliques. As a result, the Party was no longer a transmission belt between Mao (the leader) and the masses (his followers). It had instead become a block to communications, formulating incorrect, revisionist policies of its own or else perverting the correct, proletarian policies which Mao had entrusted to it.

These errors of task performance had persisted, Mao believed, because the Party's control mechanisms were ineffective. Party leaders who identi-

---

[101] Michel Oksenberg, in a private communication, has pointed out that as the middle level of the Party has been weakened, the middle level of the army (particularly the provincial commands) has been strengthened correspondingly.

fied deeply with the Party machine—men such as Teng Hsiao-p'ing and Liu Shao-ch'i—relied too strongly on internal disciplinary procedures such as self-criticism and mild rectification campaigns; they were not willing, as Mao came to feel was necessary, to employ mass criticism and severe struggle in an attempt to eradicate the "revisionist" and "bourgeois" tendencies in the Party.

Finally, the prevailing Party recruitment polices, which favored technical and managerial skills and slighted ideological qualifications, produced in Mao a fear that Chinese society would be irreparably damaged by bureaucratism and revisionism unless the Party underwent drastic change.

To remedy these problems, the following concepts and structures have been adopted:

1. Dual rule, in which the governing of China was shared by Party and state, is to be replaced by unified leadership, in which the revolutionary committees will assume both Party and state functions.

2. The leader of the Party is to remain above Party discipline, so that he can set the Party's goals and check tendencies toward decay, ossification, and revisionism.

3. The disciplinary system based on inner-Party mechanisms (the control commissions, self-criticism, Party discussion meetings, and so on) is to be replaced by supervision by the masses. This will take three forms: re-emphasis of the mass-line as a mode of policy-making, representation of the masses on revolutionary committees, and mass attendance at Party meetings.

4. Recruitment criteria, although still somewhat vague, are to be based much more stringently on social class.

5. Specialization of structure is to be reduced.

6. Party structure is to remain unformalized pending the formulation and codification of desirable procedures.

7. Legislation—the general, strategic direction of the Party—is to be centralized. Administration—the specific, tactical direction of the Party—is to be decentralized. Power is granted to the center and the bottom at the expense of the middle, which the Maoists feel was the primary obstacle to the implementation of their policies during the early and middle 1960s.

CONCLUSION

In *A Systems Analysis of Political Life,* David Easton suggests stress as the organizing concept for the study of political systems.[102] To Easton, stress is any threat to the effective performance of either of a system's two "essential functions": making decisions and gaining compliance. Easton's work provides a useful framework for estimating and evaluating the effects that Maoist theories of policy-making and organization, if implemented, will have on the Chinese political system. How adequate are Maoist organizational theories as models for making decisions and securing compliance? How well do they provide for the reduction or control of threats to the performance of these two "essential functions"? [103]

Setting aside for the moment the question of decision criteria, the mass-line appears in many respects to provide an effective program for both decision-making and social integration:

1. It places considerable emphasis on thorough investigation and research by policy-makers.

2. It provides an effective means of restricting and regulating the flow of demands to policy-makers[104] by giving legitimacy to demands only when articulated under the guidance of cadres. That is, the masses can legitimately present their views only when asked to do so. At the same time, the emphasis on constant investigation reduces the possibility that a backlog of unheard and unsatisfied demands will threaten the level of support for the regime.

3. As Easton points out, a high level of "input volume"—the multitude of problems facing decision-makers—can threaten effective task-perform-

---

[102] New York, John Wiley & Sons, Inc., 1965. For a summary, see Oran Young, *Systems of Political Science* (Englewood Cliffs, N.J., 1968) pp. 37–44.

[103] It should not be assumed that stress is always dysfunctional for a political system (or, for that matter, for an individual). Indeed, a moderate degree of stress may be more conducive to efficient and effective task performance than either low stress or high stress. On the relation between level of stress and task performance in individuals, see I. L. Janis and H. Leventhal, "Human Reaction to Stress," in E. F. Borgetta and W. W. Lambert (eds.), *Handbook of Personality Theory and Research* (Chicago, 1968) pp. 1041–1085. On the relation between level of stress and performance for organizations, see Lewis A. Coser, *Continuities in the Study of Social Conflict* (New York, 1967) Chap. 1. As the work of Richard H. Solomon and Robert J. Lifton has indicated, the "operational code" of Mao Tse-tung includes several techniques deliberately to induce psychological and systemic stress in order to attain the regime's objectives.

[104] Easton calls this process "gate-keeping" (*op. cit.,* Chap. 6).

ance if not properly regulated.[105] The mass-line aids in the assignment of task priorities by prescribing that cadres concentrate on the principal contradiction at each point. (It additionally assumes that the successful resolution of the principal contradiction will greatly facilitate the solution of secondary problems.)[106]

4. The mass-line provides a strategy for risk-taking based on the repeated testing and modification of policy. Experimentation and trial and error prevent inflexible commitment to infeasible policies. (On the other hand, the Chinese fascination with models also carries the danger that decision-makers will, on the basis of success in a few prototypical units, overconfidently authorize policy on a broader scale than is objectively warranted.)

The use of dogmatic decision criteria, however, adds some potentially stress-creating aspects to the mass-line model. Granted, a dogmatic approach to policy-making offers assurance that every problem can be correctly diagnosed if the proper procedures are followed. Granted, by using dogmatic criteria all "legitimate" demands can be aggregated into a single policy option, and conflict and disagreement are therefore "illegitimate." But these assumptions may create self-confidence and unity at the expense of wisdom and creativity. The assumption that dogma holds the answers to all problems may blind decision-makers to more realistic and feasible solutions; the assumption that opposition is illegitimate may deprive leaders of discerning criticisms of their policies.

Most important, systems of organizational discipline and programs for policy-making based on dogma alone can function only if dogma is specific, and if complete compilations of doctrine are available to everyone. But Maoist dogma in its most familiar form is a slim volume of general and ambiguous aphorisms, supplemented occasionally by "supreme directives" of comparable vagueness. Such a body of dogma doubtless creates as many disputes as it resolves.

Yet no other method of conflict resolution is permitted. To compromise is to "neglect class struggle." To reason is to "ignore the class basis of truth." To submit to authority is to become a "docile tool." But if dogma is to be the arbiter of all disagreements, who then is to be the arbiter of dogma? In the politicized atmosphere now pervading China, continued reliance on dogma can only have the following effects:

1. Compliance will become a matter of covert negotiation between su-

[105] Ibid., Chap. 4.
[106] Mao, "On Contradiction," p. 89.

periors and subordinates, with subordinates refusing (supposedly on ideological grounds) to obey unpopular directives until modifications or side-payments are made. Or:

2. Refusing to compromise, the two sides will resort to force, each attempting to impose its will on the other and each justifying its actions in the name of "class struggle." Or:

3. The two sides will appeal to higher authority (ultimately Mao, Lin, and the Politburo) for arbitration of their dispute, as is guaranteed in the new Party constitution. Demands for intervention and appeals for decision will flood the Party center, contributing to "input overload" there. Even the center's definitive resolution of the disagreement may be resisted, compelling the center either to compromise or to employ force itself.

As Teng Hsiao-p'ing once commented, the possibilities for chaos, fragmentation, and factionalism in such a situation are endless: "Since *this* group of people can rise up to overthrow *that* group of people, why can't *that* group of people rise up to overthrow *this* group of people?" [107]

Three significant features of post-Cultural Revolution organization are direct mass participation in policy-making, the replacement of "dual rule" by "unified leadership," and the increasing power of the center and the basic level at the expense of the middle.

Mass representation on revolutionary committees seems to be an effective way of increasing the responsiveness of policy-making bodies to local demands and conditions. The "three-in-one combination" for policy-making and technical innovation is quite similar in both form and function to direct community participation in poverty agencies in the United States. But one wonders what will happen as this "three-in-one" system becomes routinized. One possible effect is that the mass organizations will become increasingly powerful, selecting "mass" representatives to serve on revolutionary committees at all levels. If this occurs, a second possible effect is the nightmarish growth of five parallel bureaucracies in China. Each component of the revolutionary committees would possess its own hierarchy: the Party, the mass organizations, and the army. The system of revolutionary committees—extending from the provinces down to the basic levels—would form a bureaucracy of its own. And the ministries of the State Council might well retain their own nationwide organizations, although this state machinery would probably be considerably weaker

---

[107] Quoted in "Take the Initiative and Launch a Sustained Attack on the Class Enemy," *Peking Review*, No. 19 (May 10, 1968) pp. 11–14. Italics added.

than it was before the Cultural Revolution. In short, "dual rule" would be replaced not by "unified leadership" but by "quintuple rule."

The reemergence of such bureaucracies will, in theory, be prevented by increasing decentralization. Vast middle-level organizations will not develop because they will not be needed: most decisions will be made at the basic levels. Such a plan seems viable. But will the center be able to provide—and enforce—the general guidance and the specific vetoes necessary to prevent the fragmentation and stagnation of the system? Increased decentralization will alleviate stress on cadres by reducing the flow of central directives. Nevertheless, role stress will continue to be a major problem as long as central Party policy remains less a response to the desires of the Chinese people than a reflection of what dogma decrees those desires should be.[108] As in the past, inactivity, corruption, disobedience, and high resignation rates at the basic levels may plague the Party in the future.

Despite their shortcomings, however, Maoist theories of policy-making and organization represent serious attempts to tackle some serious problems—the implications of bureaucratization, routinization, and specialization in a modernizing society. They should neither be dismissed as the fantasies of a senile peasant, nor be embraced as the insights of a visionary sage. Instead, they deserve careful and critical attention, and their success or failure in the China of the 1970s will provide valuable lessons for us all.

[108] For a study of this trend and its effects on policy implementation, see Chalmers Johnson, "Chinese Communist Leadership and Mass Response: The Yenan Period and the Socialist Education Campaign," in Ho and Tsou (eds.), *China in Crisis*, pp. 397–437.

4
Chou En-lai and
the Cultural Revolution
in China

THOMAS W. ROBINSON

Of the three great institutional hierarchies in China during the "Great Proletarian Cultural Revolution"—the Party, the army, and the government—it may be said with certainty that the third of these, the government, has been a far weaker force than the Party or the army.[1] The goverment has, in fact, been a dependent variable, its position at nearly every stage being the result of more active interplay between the other two institutions and constrained by the activities of their mass-organizational off-shoots, the Red Guards and the Revolutionary Rebels. Furthermore, as time went on, the government not only found that at most levels of administration it was shorn of its personnel through purge, but also discovered its very functions and authority usurped by newer, extra-legal bodies—"great alliances," "three-way alliances," "preparatory committees," and "revolutionary committees," in addition to out-and-out military administration. Thus, to determine what really happened during the Cultural Revolution years 1966 and 1967, one probably should look outside the government for answers. This has, in fact, been the propensity of most observers since 1949.

Nonetheless, it may be appropriate and revealing to investigate certain aspects of the governmental response to those pressures for several reasons. First, the government has not always been so passive. This was surely true, for instance, in the so-called January Revolution period in Shanghai in 1967, when industrial managers and local ministerial repre-

[1] We adopt a narrow definition of the term "government" in this chapter. We mean only the State Council at the center—its ministries, departments, and personnel. We exclude the provincial levels of governmental administration, and also such economic administrators as factory managers.

sentatives strongly resisted the Red Guards and their Revolutionary Rebel allies. Second, if we are to take seriously the accusations of the Mao-Lin "mainstream" party faction against the Liu-Teng "power" faction (although there are good reasons not to accept the Mao-Lin line in its entirety), we may gain insights into the modes of governmental operation in China, especially in the post-Great Leap Forward period of 1960–65 and even during the Cultural Revolution itself. Third, since the government and the Party have historically been intermixed to a high degree, and since, in recent stages of the Cultural Revolution the military has directly taken over many governmental duties—at least at the local and provincial levels—we may, by studying the role of the government, hope to uncover relationships between the army and the Party (as well as intra-Party and intra-army connections) which might not otherwise emerge. We may also seek to understand how the Cultural Revolution has influenced China's foreign relations, since the Foreign Ministry was one of the governmental institutions seriously affected by the activities of the newly created mass organizations. Finally, by devoting attention to the government, we would hope to analyze the operational "style" of certain key personalities, in particular that of Premier Chou En-lai.

Although good reasons thus exist why the government's role during the Cultural Revolution should be thoroughly investigated, other reasons point to the difficulty of such a task. Foremost is the enormity of the matter. Any definitive study of the government would have, in effect, to be a history of the Cultural Revolution as a whole. Given the richness—both qualitative and quantitative—of the data for this period, such a work would probably take years to complete. Although the general outlines of the Cultural Revolution are well understood, a number of intermediate level studies need first to be produced to provide the basis for a general historical analysis of the government's part in the Cultural Revolution. Further, while the documentary materials produced during the Cultural Revolution are the most detailed that are likely to come into our hands for some time, they are still in a primitive state of organization. Lists, indices, and chronologies will have to precede major writing efforts. Finally, the present writer's own survey of large numbers of Cultural Revolution documents leads him to suspect that in the case of the government, if not of the Party or the army, essential pieces in the historical picture are still missing. Information seems to be lacking, for instance, as to what extent the ministries of the State Council actually stopped operations, how extensive the purge was within the central departments, or how far down it extended.

These limitations place severe constraints upon the prospects for understanding, in any definitive manner, the government's place during the period 1965-69. Nonetheless, it does seem possible to begin by considering in detail a critical input: the role of the Premier of the State Council (and thus the single most important person in the government), Chou En-lai. Several reasons favor our undertaking this task. First, a great deal of material exists on Chou's activities: speeches, reports of his movements, and records of a large number of political movements and decisions in which he played a central part. Second, Chou is important beyond his governmental position. As number three in the Chinese Communist hierarchy behind Mao Tse-tung and Lin Piao, Chou was at the center of almost every important Cultural Revolution decision. The record of his activities thus affords us insight into the parts played by each of the personal and institutional actors at the center in Peking and, at times, at lower levels as well. Third, while Chou's titular authority stemmed from his position on the State Council, in reality he wore several hats, some simultaneously, some in turn. Thus, for several months he was the organizer of and chief consultant to the Red Guards. Occasionally he played a role in the military. He centered in himself China's foreign policy. At times he evidently ran several ministries when their heads were under criticism or purged. Chou thus stood *between* the government bureaucrat, the Party ideologue, the youthful revolutionary, and the military activist turned governor. Finally, Chou is both fascinating to study in his own right and important as concerns his role in the post-Cultural Revolution (and possibly post-Maoist) periods. Both his political "style" and his ability to survive every twist and turn of policy mark him as one of the outstanding Chinese political figures of the twentieth century. By studying Chou, then, we are in essence learning about Communist China as a whole.

Space does not permit us to analyze and relate Chou's role from the August 1966 Eleventh Plenum of the Chinese Communist Party, which formally initiated the Cultural Revolution, to its apparent end at the Party's Ninth Congress in April 1969. We shall be concerned only with the twelve-month period from early August 1966 to the end of July 1967; this was the most decisive period of the Cultural Revolution as a whole. Primary documentation will be speeches by Chou and reports concerning his activity and movements. We will not, however, focus on aspects of Chou's personality except where his personal attributes relate to Cultural Revolution developments. But we do include these questions: What are Chou's chances for political survival in the long run? And will the policies associated with his name stand a chance of gaining final acceptance?

Our format will be as follows. First, we briefly trace the background to the active phase of the Cultural Revolution and outline what we know of Chou's own political "style." Next, we look, in a general way, at the number and type of his activities during this period to indicate critical times for Chou, when he exercised some influence and when he was pushed aside. We want to learn, too, when Chou was forced to swing his attention from external affairs to internal politics. These considerations serve to introduce our two major sections. The first deals with Chou's handling of Cultural Revolution developments, focusing primarily on the January Revolution and the Wuhan incident of July 1967. The second covers Chou's views on a series of controversial problems, both internal and external to China. We wish to know how, and to what extent, Chou's views differed from the officially held line of the Mao-Lin faction. Having answered these questions—to the extent that limited data permits us to draw conclusions—we finish by analyzing Chou's personal position during the Cultural Revolution with regard to the Mao-Lin "mainstream," the Liu-Teng "power" faction, and such leaders as Chiang Ch'ing and Chen Po-ta.[2]

Although a number of findings will be set forth, two major conclusions emerge. First, Chou took as his goals keeping the bureaucratic, economic, and scientific establishments in operation and preventing as much slippage as possible in China's foreign relations. Second, Chou's standing in the Cultural Revolution has been the result of two opposing factors. On the one hand, during the purges and disorders attendant upon the Cultural Revolution, the factor of his experience—in administration, in bureaucratic politics, and in diplomacy—tended to make his value to the Mao-Lin faction rise even higher than its level in previous periods. Experience served him well, as Chou performed impressively in almost every instance where he was given authority to make an important decision. On the other hand, there is the very bigness of China. In the Cultural Revolution most of the violence and rapid change occurred at the pro-

[2] "Mainstream" and "power" factions are the Japanese terms for the Maoist group and its opposition, presumably led by Liu Shao-ch'i. It is not clear that such factions existed, but we retain the terms for their shorthand value.

vincial and city levels, away from Peking (although Peking itself was by no means quiescent). Chou's authority in this period lay in his personal ability to reason with and convince the contending parties either to compromise or, in the case of attempted criticisms and draggings out, to meliorate their present and planned activities. His authority also derived from his ability to speak in the name of the central authorities. On a number of occasions he used this institutional backing to issue directives and instructions not only in the name of the State Council but also under the aegis of the Central Committee, the Military Affairs Committee, and the Cultural Revolution Small Group. In less stormy times, personal and institutional authority would have carried him a long way, at least to the point of ensuring the national stability and productivity which seem historically to have been his goals. In the Cultural Revolution period, however, groups on all sides were taking affairs into their own hands, with the result that directives were ignored or flaunted, and that often local events moved too quickly for the center to keep up. The upshot was that Chou had to fall back upon the remnants of his personal authority, buttressed upon occasion by Mao and Lin themselves. But China and the Cultural Revolution proved too much for one man to handle: Chou increasingly rushed from one crisis to the next, discovering that several fires would break out elsewhere during the time it took him to extinguish one of them. Thus, Chou was swept along by the rush of events, at certain times, as much as anyone else, and it is only toward the end of the period under consideration that we find him able to overcome some of the adverse currents.

CHOU'S POLITICAL STYLE AND THE
BACKGROUND OF THE CULTURAL REVOLUTION

Before turning to Chou's role in the Cultural Revolution, we must set the stage by considering both the manner in which he has dealt with political conflict (his "political style") and those developments in the Cultural Revolution before August 1966 which bear upon his subsequent activities. Despite the voluminous literature describing Chou's career and personality, comparatively little attention has been devoted to the specific of his political style.[3] Judgments are often made about Chou.

[3] This description draws upon the records of several observers set down at various stages of Chou's career. Among them are: Edgar Snow, *Red Star Over China* (New York, 1938) pp. 44–49 and his *The Other Side of the River* (London, 1963) pp.

He is said to have a talent for either coming up on the correct side of every political struggle or, if he chooses wrongly, of convincing the winning side to readmit him to the fold, usually in his former position. He has been described as the *pu-tao-weng* (the weighted doll which always bobs up again when pushed over) of the Chinese Communist Party. His talent as a successful negotiator is known in many countries. He knows how to compromise but can also be entirely unyielding if the situation and his superiors require it. He is obviously an accomplished and experienced administrator, resisting the temptation to turn his administrative office into an independent policy-making center. Instead, he is a trustworthy agent of his party superiors. He is no doubt a faithful Marxist and Maoist, but he has shown even less originality in the ideological sphere than the current heir-apparent, Lin Piao. Adjectives which have been used to describe him include: elastic, flexible, and resilient; agile, but cool, logical, empirical, and realistic; self-confident, and urbane. He is of singular purpose despite the tendentious paths he sometimes finds necessary to take to reach his goals. He exhibits a type of charisma, but unlike Mao's, it apparently extends no further than his physical presence.[4] Chou's authority thus seems to be limited both by his lack of an autonomous political base and by his inability to influence those outside of his immediate range. He has compensated for these limitations with sheer energy, by packing as much activity and physical movement into as short a time as possible. These qualities of Chou's political style stood out during the Cultural Revolution and partially explain his ability to survive and his inability to master the stream of events which constantly threatened to engulf him.

While we do not undertake here to review the full background of the Cultural Revolution, it will be helpful to cite those developments which affected Chou's political fortunes during the twelve-month period we are considering.[5] Three sets of such developments seem important for our

---

86–100; Robert Elegant, *China's Red Masters* (New York, 1951); Richard Hughes, "Peking's 'Indispensable' Front Man," *New York Times Magazine,* October 4, 1964, pp. 16, 113, 114; Howard L. Boorman (ed.), *Biographic Dictionary of Republican China, Vol. 1: Ai-Ch'ü* (New York, 1967) pp. 391–405; Kai-Yu Hsu, *Chou En-lai* (Garden City, N.Y., 1968); *Fei-ch'ing Yen-chiu,* Vol. 1, No. 4 (April 30, 1967) pp. 96–113; and Günther Stein, *The Challenge of Red China* (New York, 1945).

[4] More will be said about Chou and charisma in the conclusion to this chapter.

[5] Although the pre-August 1966 period is still (and probably will remain) imperfectly understood, the following provide well-researched analyses: P. W. Bridgham, "Mao's Cultural Revolution: Origin and Development," *The China Quarterly,* No.

purposes. First, by August 1966 most of the important issues which had been under debate for the prior year had largely been resolved. Ideologically, the question of how to treat the intellectual and political deviations of certain literary men, such as Wu Han, had been answered with apparent success for over half a year. The two pressing international questions, Sino-Soviet relations in the post-Khrushchev era and the proper Chinese response to the American intervention in Vietnam, had apparently been resolved early in 1966. The concomitant differences over military strategy, training policy, and equipment to be procured for the People's Liberation Army were also temporarily overcome, albeit not without struggle. With regard to the economy, a new Five-Year Plan was already in operation, and although neither goals nor results have been announced, presumably it was the agreed basis for China's industrial and agricultural production plans for 1966. Relative priorities of investment were thus unlikely to have been prime topics for debate at the Eleventh Central Committee Plenum in August.[6] And the purge of top Party and military figures was either completed—as in the case of P'eng Chen and Lo Jui-ch'ing—or it was clear that others were in grave danger of being purged, and hence were to be avoided—as with Liu Shao-ch'i and Teng Hsiao-p'ing.[7] It is surely possible that all the above questions could have been reopened at the Eleventh Plenum, once it became apparent that a face-off between the opposing sides was inevitable. But the point we wish to present here is that the Eleventh Plenum was probably not called to consider these specific issues alone, nor was it likely that the lines of division were unknown at the beginning of the meeting. Chou En-lai surely knew who was on what side and had probably made up his mind at the outset. The interesting point is that on all the above issues, if Chou is really the realistic empiricist he is supposed to be, he should have opted for the *revisionist* side of all these issues. That he apparently did not do so demonstrates that Chou applies these same qualities to the political

---

29 (January–March 1967) pp. 1–35; Gene T. Hsiao, "The Background and Development of 'The Proletarian Cultural Revolution,'" *Asian Survey*, Vol. 7, No. 6 (June 1967) pp. 389–404; Michel Oksenberg, "China: Forcing the Revolution to a New Stage," *Asian Survey*, Vol. 7, No. 1 (January 1967) pp. 1–15; and Charles Neuhauser, "The Impact of the Cultural Revolution on the Party Machine: Some Observations on a Revolution in Progress," *Asian Survey*, Vol. 7, No. 6 (June 1968) pp. 465–487; and the chapter by William Dorrill, above.

[6] Related questions, such as the level of monetary incentives for workers, may have been discussed.

[7] On this point, see Bridgham, *op. cit.*, pp. 23ff.

sphere first and only then considers the issues on their merits. Although undoubtedly he is less "ideologically" motivated than either Mao or Lin, questions of political power would seem to come out strongly ahead, in his order of priorities, of practical issues. Only when he is convinced that his position is firm will he allow himself to deal with the issues on their merits.

The Eleventh Plenum was convoked to deal with two unresolved questions. First, how to assure the revolutionary vitality of succeeding generations through reform of the education system? More important, how should the Cultural Revolution itself be implemented? Mao's confidence in the ability and loyalty of Liu and Teng must have been broken as a result of their handling of the investigative work teams in the sixty-day period following P'eng Chen's downfall.[8] Sensing that P'eng's fate might befall them too, Liu and Teng apparently had tried to suppress the Cultural Revolution by limiting it to the academic-intellectual sphere. They also tried to work from "above" (through the Central Committee work teams) and not from "below" (through the emergent mass organizations). These were evidently the last straws as far as Mao was concerned, and he moved against them in August. There is little doubt that Chou En-lai was involved in the undercurrent of events from June to August which led to the outburst at the Plenum. Although there is scant evidence for it, we may hypothesize that very early Chou decided to hedge his bets and withdrew, for the most part, from the Cultural Revolution debates leading up to the Eleventh Plenum. Once the predominance of the Mao-Lin faction was obvious, he came off the fence to join their side. The question then becomes: at what point and in what manner was that predominance made manifest?

It is equally impossible to determine whether or not Chou exacted a price from Mao and Lin for his support. It seems apparent now that the Maoist faction needed all the support it could get at the Plenum. But it would not be in accordance with Chou's personality to stay on the fence just to raise his value to the competing sides.[9] True, he would tend to be

[8] More recent evidence—the multitude of charges against Liu that he had differed with Mao on many different issues, and Lin Piao's Ninth Party Congress speech—point to the conclusion that the dispute had been going on for some years.

[9] Still, there do exist theories of coalition politics which dictate just such a course of action for those who are able to put off joining a coalition until the last. They can then maximize their value to the winning coalition by making it a minimum winning coalition. See William F. Riker, *The Theory of Political Coalitions* (New Haven, 1962). It is interesting to note that, in our evaluation, the Standing Com-

as noncommittal as possible for as long as possible, but in order to protect his own future and not to raise the rewards he might obtain from the winning side.[10] The result, however, might well be the same, namely, an appeal by either faction to Chou to join their side, sweetened by whatever concessions they could credibly offer. This, in fact, is the kind of position which negotiators and mediators like to find themselves, for only then are they able to get their way on substantive issues. And Chou's reputation as negotiator and mediator was well-known. Also, as head of the governmental apparatus, he desired to see a successful Five-Year Plan and hoped that the Cultural Revolution would not weaken China's foreign policy position. The only evidence, admittedly circumstantial, that some concessions were made to Chou is the Sixteen Point Declaration itself, issued on August 8, 1966.[11] We notice that at least ten of the sixteen points promised relatively easy treatment of the government.[12] Thus, for instance, points two, three, and five promised that the coming purge would be directed against the Party and not the government. Further, the character of the Cultural Revolution was to be "nonviolent" (points four and six), while the new forms of authority—cultural revolution groups, committees, and congresses (point nine)—would pose no imminent threat to the government. Educational reform was also to be nonviolent, despite

---

mittee division shows a 6-5 split in favor of the Mao-Lin faction. In that case, such a coalition was indeed a minimum winning coalition and Chou's adherence to the Mao-Lin side would make the win possible. It would then remain to be shown whether Chou committed himself at the last moment or whether he sided with Mao at the outset.

[10] Chou's long Party career demonstrates that his role has not been that of fence-sitter but of go-between. Constantly at the center of the political process, he naturally found it difficult to detach himself from one coalition, latch onto another, and then switch back to the first (or to a third). Further, since the middle thirties Chou had always adhered to the Maoist "side" and had, therefore, Mao's trust. It would have been extraordinary if, after over thirty-five years of such a relationship, Chou had explicitly gone over to a neutral position. More likely is the possibility that for some time he had been used as a messenger and conciliator between the Maoist "side" and the Liuist "side." But this does not necessarily cast doubt upon the possibility that his very go-between status itself maximized his value to Mao and that Mao felt constrained to "pay" Chou for his services and for not defecting to the other side. And if a bargaining situation thus emerged between Chou and Mao, it would not necessarily have been explicit.

[11] An English translation is in *Peking Review*, No. 33 (August 12, 1966) pp. 6-11. The original was published in *Jen-min Jih-pao*, August 9, 1966, pp. 1 and 2.

[12] This does not "prove," of course, that specific concessions were made to Chou. But, if they were carried out to the fullest extent (they were not), Chou's task would have been much easier.

closure of the schools (point ten). Some dilution of Cultural Revolution radicalism was implicit in the promise (point thirteen) to integrate the Cultural Revolution movement with the older Socialist Education Movement. Finally, two promises were made, in points twelve and fourteen, which seemed designed explicitly to placate Chou: certain classes (scientists and technicians) were to be specifically exempted from participation in the Cultural Revolution; and an explicit connection was made between the Cultural Revolution and the necessity to stimulate production. Almost all of these "pledges" (if that is what they were) would be broken in the succeeding months, and perhaps Mao had no intention of adhering to them. But in August, the wording of the sixteen points may have won Chou's adherence to Mao's side.

THE TYPE AND RANGE OF CHOU'S APPEARANCES AS AN INDEX OF HIS ACTIVITIES

As a first approximation to Chou's role during the active phase of the Cultural Revolution, we might total up his activities and appearances then. Surveying reports of his activities,[13] and grouping them into appropriate categories, we can produce the accompanying tabulation. We also display this data in a graph, which puts it in a form convenient for analysis. Here we have registered three trends: Chou's total appearances by month; those concerning internal affairs; and those dealing with external affairs.[14] We may draw a number of conclusions from this graph if we assume that Chou's appearances roughly indicate the type and, to a lesser extent, the intensity[15] of his involvement in the political process.[16]

First of all, it may be hypothesized that the general trend of Chou's ap-

[13] References are cited further on in the chapter.

[14] We have combined categories one and two for external affairs, minus one concert appearance in May and three in June, which involved no foreign dignitaries. All the rest were connected with Chou's activities on the domestic front.

[15] The number of appearances is, of course, no sure indicator of the quality of appearance. Mao Tse-tung rarely appears but his involvement in the political process is intense. In Chou's case, number and intensity of involvement are more closely related since the average number of appearances per unit time is high.

[16] This brings up a question of the reliability and completeness of the data. Obviously, the data is incomplete, inasmuch as we do not have (nor can we ever, under present circumstances, have) a complete record of his activities. However, in the active phase of the Cultural Revolution reported here, the phenomenon of Red Guard wall posters (ta-tzu-pao) helped a great deal to fill in the gap.

CHOU EN-LAI'S APPEARANCES AND ACTIVITIES FROM AUGUST 1966 THROUGH JULY 1967

Activity

Month	Total number of appearances	Receives delegates from abroad	Attends receptions, banquets, concerts	Talks to, receives Red Guards	Mass talks	Rallies attended	Meets workers, Rev'y. Rebels	Miscl. visits: memorials, hospitals	Greets returning CCP delegates	Issues instructions, criticizes, defends, denies	Attends official meetings
1966											
Aug.	33	16	4	9	2	1	0	0	0	0	1
Sept.	21	9	3	6	1	0	1	0	0	1	0
Oct.	15	8	2	2	0(?)	2	0	1	0	0	0
Nov.	12	4	0	0	3	3	0	0	1	1	0
Dec.	12	2	3	0	2	2	0	0	0	3	0
1967											
Jan.	35	1	1	2	1	3	14	0	0	13	0
Feb.	28	5	1	1	2	0	7	1	0	10	1
Mar.	14	4	1	1	0	0	4	0	0	3	1
Apr.	18	4	1	2	1	0	3	0	1	4	2
May	25	7	3	0	1	5	2	0	1	4	2
June	23	9	7	1	0	1	0	2	0	3	0
July	12	4	1	0	0	2	0	0	4	0	1
Totals	248	73	27	24	13	19	31	4	7	42	8

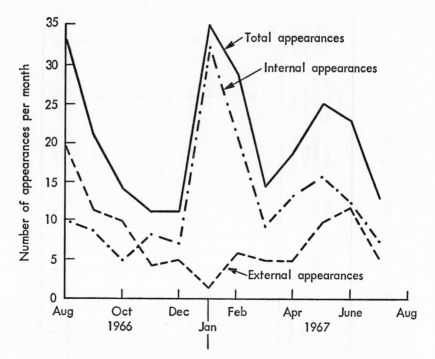

pearances reflects in some measure the *change* in his importance during the period. If this is so, his relative importance actually declined from the beginning of the Red Guard phase of the Cultural Revolution in August 1966 and continued to drop until the year's end. It rebounded considerably in January 1967, however, as he played a central role in the January Revolution. From then his involvement and importance, in general, grew, and attained a peak in May and June (with some decline in February and March). After June we cannot assess these due to the disappearance of most Red Guard posters. (There is no doubt, however, that in July he again played a central role, as evidenced by the "Wuhan incident.")

Second, it is instructive to compare Chou's foreign relations activities with his involvement in domestic politics. In normal times we would expect Chou to sustain a fairly high level of diplomatic activity—meeting with visiting foreign dignitaries, giving banquets, and the like—and a lower level of publically announced activities on the domestic scene. This was the case in August 1966. From then on, however, his involvement in foreign affairs dropped steadily, reaching a nadir in January of 1967, perhaps reflecting his preoccupation with the Red Guard phase of the Cultural Revolution and China's overall constriction of foreign affairs involvement. In January, his time was almost entirely taken up with the January Revolution in Shanghai. From February to mid-April his duties were distributed in about constant proportion: a fairly high level in domestic affairs (but below that of January) and a low level in foreign relations. In late April, May, and June, both factors rose, indicating that Chou was taking on more domestic duties and had taken over, temporarily, some of Ch'en Yi's duties in the Foreign Ministry, while the latter was undergoing criticism. After June, however, activity declined in both spheres (the change in domestic appearances had begun after May), reflecting perhaps not only the impasse in China's foreign relation but also the army's growing authority over provincial and city administration. Chou's influence had, concomitantly, suffered a relative decline.

Third, looking more closely at each type of appearance, we note that: first, foreign-relations appearances declined as a proportion of total activities; second, his involvement with the Red Guards and his talks at mass gatherings continued at a constant but fairly low level; and third, there were variations in his attendance at mass rallies, meetings with Revolutionary Rebels, and his propensity to issue instructions and directives. These variations indicate that, for Chou, crucial periods, respectively, were the fall of 1966 and the early summer of 1967, the late spring of 1967, and the January Revolution days. They indicate not only the general trend of Cultural Revolution events, but also Chou's tendency to become involved rather heavily in each of them.

CHOU EN-LAI'S ACTIVITIES AND POSITION IN THE CULTURAL REVOLUTION, 1966–1967

We turn now to an accounting and analysis of Chou's involvement in the first year of the Cultural Revolution. Four chronological divisions categorize the period. The Red Guard period extends from the Eleventh Plenum in August 1966 to the latter part of December. This was succeeded by the January Revolution period, comprising January 1967 and the first part of February, and was followed by the "seize power" period of spring and early summer.[17] The final period which we consider

---

[17] The latter was actually an extension of the former, in the sense that many of the principles and procedures worked out in Shanghai and Peking in January were thereafter in part extended to the whole country. The two periods combined to form a longer period during which the army more and more assumed authority for administration on the provincial and city levels.

encompasses the events around the "Wuhan Incident" of late July and early August 1967.

The Red Guard Period

This period extended from the formation of Red Guard units in the early summer to the initial period of violence in August and September, and to the attempts in October and November to sidetrack the Red Guards through mass rallies and "long marches" in the countryside; it ended when the Red Guard monopoly of revolutionary violence was broken by the Revolutionary Rebel "seize power" movement in December and January.[18] During the entirety of this period, Chou En-lai pursued two somewhat divergent policies. On the one hand, he followed, and tried to anticipate and help shape, the Mao-Lin line of the moment; he also took part in the numerous public occasions and rallies which made up the façade of the movement. On the other hand, he tried at almost every stage to inject notes of unity and sanity, both to constrain the more violent outbursts and to control the direction of the revolution. He was only partially successful in these attempts, for the personal persuasiveness which had served him so well in the past was less useful in the new situation. Now Red Guard disorders were simultaneously created at widely separated localities, and the sheer number of Red Guards flooding first Peking and then every major urban center overtaxed both his great energy and his personal charisma. Speeches before tens of thousands and even millions of massed Red Guards were no substitute, as he probably well knew, for bureaucratic order or small-group negotiations, the two devices he had previously used so successfully to enforce his policy. But whenever Chou was able to place himself in a position of personal contact with a relatively small number of Red Guards, he was usually able to convince them to tone down their criticism, to cease their violent activities, to stop their infighting, and to strive for organizational unity.

How did Chou attempt to carry out the Mao-Lin policy toward the Red Guards? He functioned chiefly during the late summer and early fall of 1966 in the dual role of interpreter to the Red Guards of the vague and generalized directives from above and organizer-general of Red Guard detachments. Fortunately, we have possession of a number of his formal and informal speeches before Red Guard bodies which tell us a

[18] For a definitive study of the genesis and expansion of the Red Guard movement in this period, see John Israel, "The Red Guards in Historical Perspective," *The China Quarterly*, No. 30 (April–June 1967) pp. 1–32.

great deal about Red Guard activities, Chou's own policies, and his operating style. Looking at these documents as a group,[19] four themes emerge: one, the organization of the Red Guards, including the problems of factionalism, revolutionary qualifications, and relations between Peking-based and local Red Guards; two, the proper and improper techniques of revolutionary struggle, especially the questions of the kinds of struggle to use, who is and who is not the enemy, determining revolutionary qualifications of party cadres, Red Guard freedoms and their limitations, and the necessity to control Red Guard demonstrations; three, the work team question; and four, whether the Cultural Revolution should be extended to industry and agriculture, symbolized by Chou's slogan of "revolution and production." In all these cases, Chou's purpose was to discipline and control the Red Guards while at the same time stimulating them to carry out their revolutionary assignments to the maximum. This goal was reflected in the forensic style which Chou exhibited in these talks: in one section he would agree with what his audience was doing, while in the

[19] This analysis is based upon the following sources: "Premier Chou En-lai's Speech at Tsing Hua University on 22 August," in *Wu-ch'an-chieh-chi Wen-hua Ta-ko-ming Yu-kuan Ts'ai-liao Hui-pien* (*Collection of Materials Pertaining to the Great Proletarian Cultural Revolution*), Canton, October 28, 1966, Vol. 1, pp. 42–46 (translation in *JPRS* 41,313, *Translations on Communist China: Political and Sociological*, No. 398, June 1967, pp. 14–21); "Premier Chou's Speech at the Capitol Red Guard Delegates' Conference," *ibid.*, pp. 22–23; "Prairie Fire" Fighting Detachment of the Tsinan University History Department, "Chou En-lai's August 30 Speech," reprinted in a *JPRS* publication of August 1, 1967, *Samples of Red Guard Publications*; "Speech Delivered at Red Guard Commanding Headquarters on 9 September," *Wu-ch'an-chieh-chi Wen-hua Ta-ko-ming Ts'ai-liao Hui-pien* (*Collection of Materials Pertaining to the Great Proletarian Cultural Revolution*), Canton, October 28, 1966, Vol. 2, p. 8 (translation in *JPRS* 40,974, *Translations on Communist China: Political and Sociological*, No. 394, 10 May 1967, p. 1); and the following Speeches translated in American Consulate General, Hong Kong, *Current Background*, No. 819, March 10, 1967 (pages noted in parentheses): "Premier Chou's Speech (of September 1) to Representatives of Peking's 'Red Guards'" (pp. 16–21); "Speech by Premier Chou En-lai on September 10 at Oath-Taking Rally of Those Going Out to Establish Revolutionary Ties" (pp. 28–39); "Speech by Premier Chou at Altar of Agriculture Park on September 13, 1966" (pp. 40–48); "Speech by Premier Chou at Reception of Red Guard Representatives at Chung Nan Hai on October 3 (5?)" (pp. 49–59); and "Premier Chou's October 18 Speech at the Workers' Stadium" (pp. 65–67). Additionally there is the important "Speech of Premier Chou of September 25, 1966," published in the *Collection of the Leaders' Speeches*, IV, November 1966, and distributed "for internal distribution only" by the Tsing Hua University Defend-the-East Corps. I am indebted to Melvin Gurtov for obtaining this document for me. The speeches of August 22 and September 25 are of central importance for the study of Chou's informal style. Because the latter speech has not yet been translated, Appendix B presents an English version.

following section he would plead or suggest that they do something else, often the opposite of what they had just done. With this in mind, let us look at each of these topics in turn.

As to questions of organization, while Chou stated that it was natural and even desirable that Red Guard groups with different views and with disparate leadership coexist temporarily, he went on to say that organization should be stricter and more compact. The way to accomplish this, he said, was to set up liaison centers and gradually to amalgamate units, first within a given school, then among various schools in a given area, and finally among different areas. Only then, he said, would the Red Guards become an "organized, disciplined, reliable, and powerful reserve of the People's Liberation Army." It was also important to develop the proper relationships between Peking and local Red Guards. The major point again was that such ties should be planned and organized in advance. The role of the Peking Red Guards was to organize Red Guard detachments in other parts of the country. Care must be taken, however, not to offend the sensibilities of local students: support and approval of local Red Guards should be obtained prior to any revolutionary action, and Peking students sent to local areas should avoid imposing themselves on local units or acting in a conceited and absolutist manner. Peking Red Guards should also abjure from organizing links between third cities: only links between Peking and outlying centers of population should be forged. In this manner, Chou and the Party center could hope to exercise some degree of control over the movement.

Closely allied to the question of organization was the problem of internecine struggle and factionalism.[20] Chou was of course vitally interested

[20] Red Guard factionalism was grounded not only in personal and inter-unit competition for power and influence within the movement, but equally in the inability of Red Guards to decide who among the ranks of students should be allowed to join. The root of the problem lay in the contradiction between the social composition of the college and middle-school student population (which disproportionately represented city dwellers and children of Party members), and the call to accept only "Five Red Category" students into the ranks of the Red Guards (the Five Red Categories included children whose class origins were defined as worker, poor and lower middle peasants, revolutionary cadres, revolutionary army men, and descendants of revolutionary martyrs). Chou admitted that of the more than ten million Red Guards organized by early September only a minority were of this approved class background. This minority apparently had been more aggressive than its numbers warranted, however, for Chou berated his audiences with the fact that non-Five Red Category Red Guards were afraid to go out into the streets to participate in revolutionary activities for they were prohibited from wearing their Red Guard armbands. That sort of thing must stop, said Chou, and Red Guards must continue

in preventing the already rampant factionalism from worsening and tearing apart the Red Guard movement (as in fact later happened). On the other hand, he had to support verbally *all* factions in order to retain personal credibility and to reinforce their motivation to carry out their revolutionary tasks. Thus, Chou sought to minimize ideological, personal, and organizational differences between minority and majority factions within the movement. He expressed his faith that the various factions would at some point find it possible to merge, and he tried to mollify each side with the constantly reiterated statement that all factions were revolutionary (which was patently untrue, as Chou later admitted). The important thing was for the factions to stop fighting among themselves. In particular, there must be no oppression of minority factions and no forced mergers. Red Guards should realize, said Chou, that while all were revolutionary, some often were conceited, disobedient, disruptive, and generally "did as they wished."

A stop must be put to this misbehavior, he said. Red Guards must recognize that their youthfulness impaired their complete understanding of the situation. Red Guards must therefore exercise more patience and self-restraint, must "work, learn, and study." If you study, said Chou, small deviations will not matter. In studying, however, care must be taken not to become mere quotation-mongers of Mao's works: one must go beyond Mao to consider the practical details of each situation.[21] One good way to integrate Mao's theories with practical reality was to follow the "3–8" style of the People's Liberation Army.[22]

---

to admit into the ranks children of non-Five Red Categories, as long as they had repudiated their class background. Since the boundaries between these categories were ill-defined and not easily subject to historical verification, and since it was impossible to judge sincerely what constituted rejection of class background, the seeds were firmly planted for the growth of widespread class struggle over this issue.

[21] Interestingly, in his September 9 talks, Chou took the students to task for reading Mao's works too literally: it was not enough to try again after repeated failures, as urged by Mao; one should in addition make sure he is correct in the first place. Remarks such as this provide clues to Chou's real attitude to "the thought of Mao Tse-tung" and the difficulty of having to live with it.

[22] Thus, Chou bowed in the direction of Mao and Lin Piao (who had for many years stressed the relevance of the "3–8" working style in the country at large as well as in the army) while at the same time calling for action based on somewhat more practical grounds. The "3–8" working style consists of governing one's activities in accordance with three phrases: "firm, correct political orientation"; "a plain, hard-working style"; and "flexibility in strategy and tactics"—and eight Chinese characters, translated as "unity, alertness, earnestness, and liveliness."

Chou was also very concerned with the methods of struggle and their abuse by the Red Guards. He advocated, of course, the use of reason, not force, in revolutionary struggle. Although force was always easier physically, hurting the body does not convince. Only by penetrating the soul could the "four olds" be replaced by the "four news." [23] The Cultural Revolution was to be an ideological revolution, Chou claimed, and as such the principles of class struggle must be adopted. These included such standards as "relying on the left, educating and winning over the middle, and isolating the right"; "uniting with the working class, and also with the peasantry and the Army"; and learning from the people and going to the masses. It was important to debate and consult with the masses and "when opinions differ, wait." One has to be careful to make distinctions, said Chou, between "struggle by reasoning and struggle by force, between today and tomorrow, between the new kinds of contradictions, inside and outside the schools, local areas and outside areas, and China and foreign countries." It was true that at times overt physical struggle would be necessary, but on such occasions Red Guards should let the public Security Department and the Army take over. Particular care should be taken in nationality areas so as not to inflame local sensibilities, and in Shanghai foreigners should in no case be subject to any more than verbal harassment. Finally, such tactics as unauthorized search, confiscation, and destruction of public property must at all costs cease.

Chou was most forthright concerning Red Guard excesses in determining who belonged to the side of the revolutionaries and who was to be regarded as the enemy. Since early August, Red Guards had been attacking "power-holders" as a group without any attempt to distinguish between revolutionary and "reactionary" elements within that category. The process, if it continued unchecked, threatened to bring down not only the top reaches of the Party (which was the "proper" area of struggle) but also the administrative apparatus at the center and in the provinces, and thus promised to affect adversely production in industry and agriculture. Therefore, Chou, as Mao's top administrative official, moved as decisively as possible to brake the Red Guards' expansion of the Cultural Revolution to every corner of the country. At the same time, he could not afford to shut off revolutionary pressures entirely, lest he himself come under attack from below and suspicion from above as covertly siding with the "capitalist-roaders" and "black elements" who were thought to lurk everywhere in the Party. Chou thus had to walk a tightrope between

[23] Old (new) culture, habits, customs, and ideas.

two extremes. He solved the dilemma here, as in other areas, by appearing to be on the revolutionary side; but at the same time he made certain practical suggestions which, if carried out, would have slowed the pace or reversed the direction of Red Guard activities. For example, he sought to distinguish between good and bad elements: reformed landlords, for instance, should not be struggled against, while "escapee" landlords hiding in the cities should be exposed. There were also two kinds of rightists: those who had succeeded in ridding themselves of their rightist titles and therefore no longer contemplated evil acts, and those who persisted in capitalist activities despite pledges to reform. "It is necessary to see," said Chou, "whether they are engaged in current counterrevolutionary activity. If they have proved themselves more or less honest, we shall have to give them a chance." "If former rightists have honestly submitted to reform and accept surveillance, there is no reason to prosecute them." The bourgeoisie must indeed be criticized but they should not be "pulled down" nor should their property or bank accounts be confiscated. Red Guards must also learn to exempt members of the democratic (non-Communist) parties because of their advanced age, and they must not search the houses of people "of high standing" nor destroy monuments. To counterbalance this, Chou recommended hitting hard at "hooligans," whose numbers had apparently multiplied since the school closure and because of the Red Guard propensity to reject many available and willing students, and at the "reactionary minority."

Although the Cultural Revolution at that stage was directed against Party "power-holders" in the larger cities and in Party and governmental units, Chou cautioned that not all power-holders had taken the capitalist road. The extremist opinion that all power-holders are reactionaries was absurd, said Chou, for at some point the leadership must be trusted. In the last analysis whether one were revolutionary or reactionary must be determined in the course of the revolution; deeds and present revolutionary attitude were to be weighed as heavily as revolutionary heritage. And that heritage itself was not entirely reducible to class origin: if one had been termed a revolutionary by the Kuomintang, then that would be a good indication of one's enduring revolutionary loyalty.[24] In Chou's

[24] This was, of course, rank heresy, for such reasoning could well be applied to Liu Shao-ch'i and Teng Hsiao-p'ing, the alleged leaders of the "bourgeois" reactionary line, both of whom had Kuomintang prices on their heads during the pre-1949 civil war era. Evidently, remarks such as this later got Chou into trouble with the Red Guards. As we shall show, a major reason why Chou sought to dilute the class origin argument was that his own social background was far from pure, ac-

opinion, class origin as the sole criterion in judging revolutionary qualifications was ridiculous: "class determinism," he said, "is fatalism."

Blame for carrying out decisions now judged to be counterrevolutionary could not be placed on lower bodies. They had merely carried out orders from above, and thus responsibility should rest only on the shoulders of the higher units. Even in the those higher units, blame should not be placed on those who made honest mistakes in carrying out decisions, revolutionary or not. "Making mistakes is one thing," said Chou, "but it cannot be said that the [mistake maker] is thereby nonrevolutionary, still less counterrevolutionary. This is different from the formation of an independent kingdom, splitting the Party, and setting up another party. A distinction must be made." Mistakes must be examined before conclusions can be drawn, even when those mistakes "have become a contradiction between the enemy and ourselves." In fact, Chou regarded the whole question of contradictions as a difficult one, for to him there did not seem to be a clear-cut boundary between the two kinds of contradictions. The dividing line between contradictions "among the people" and those between "the people and its enemies" was to Chou a variable boundary, dependent in part on the *actions* of these two classes. Thus, what was at a given time a nonantagonistic contradiction among sectors of the "people" could through mishandling become an antagonistic contradiction with the "enemy." The wrong kind of Red Guard activity, in other words, could cause such a division of Chinese society as to threaten its very existence. Avoidance of such a crisis depended, however, on Red Guard moderation in deciding who was an enemy and adjusting their methods accordingly.

Chou also attempted to advise the Red Guards on their organizational freedoms, particularly in regard to the question of demonstrations. Here again Chou's style was first to line up solidly with the Red Guards and then to modify details which, if adhered to, would have significantly limited their activities. Chou praised the Red Guards' "freedoms" as not only exceeding those of Western students but going even beyond those six freedoms guaranteed by the Chinese Constitution.[25] For instance, Red Guards had the "right" to leave the classrooms to conduct revolution and

cording to the Marxist-Maoist criteria. Perhaps one reason that Mao let this sort of remark pass was that his own class origin was also impure.

[25] Article 87 of the 1954 Constitution grants six freedoms: speech, press, assembly, association, possession, and demonstration.

the "right" to print their own newspapers without Party censorship.[26] The Maoist leadership, according to Chou, "helped" the students to establish and maintain those rights by the very fact that the leadership was not restricting them.[27] The students therefore had a duty to listen to Chou's suggestions and to "trust in and be amenable to" directives issued by the Party center. In particular the students should moderate the extremist character of their mass demonstrations. It was all right, said Chou, to demonstrate in front of the Soviet Embassy in Peking, but they should stay out of the Embassy compound and refrain from putting up posters on Embassy walls.[28] Chou warned that demonstrations which got out of hand would be suppressed, because the external world would otherwise conclude mistakenly that Chairman Mao was trying to exterminate his enemies physically.

Chou found the work team question at least as difficult to manage as problems of organization and tactics. During their operative period (June and July of 1966), the teams sent to universities and schools by Liu Shaoch'i and Teng Hsiao-p'ing created havoc among the students. According to the Maoist prosecution, one of the purposes of the work teams was apparently to purge students judged disloyal to Mao (and Liu). Many students were branded (unjustly in their opinions) as anti-Party, anti-socialist elements; long name lists were drawn up; and detailed investigatory materials were collected. By August, the student movement was divided into work team supporters, a majority by Chou's own admission, and a persecuted minority. After the Eleventh Plenum, the work teams were declared to have acted incorrectly and the formerly persecuted minority now found itself courted by Mao as the true carrier of the Communist virtues. The upshot, as the ensuing situation showed, was that many students and work team members were now subject to attack for their past behavior. Chou's task was therefore to try to prevent internecine strife among the students from pulverizing of the ranks of high school and college-age youths (both the non-Red Guard majority and the Red Guard minority having points of vulnerability), and to safeguard former work team personnel. Adopting his standard tactic, Chou first told the Red

[26] But not the right to print their own pictures. These, Chou said, had to be obtained from the official New China News Agency.

[27] Chou's logic in this regard is rather extraordinary.

[28] On the other hand, he said it was all right to paste posters on Soviet trains passing through Chinese territory.

Guards what they wanted to hear. The work teams must be repudiated, since they "maintained the old order." Their work must therefore be undone; their blacklists and investigatory material must be burned and their charges annulled. On the other hand, Chou drew a distinction between team members as individuals and their political work. Teams should be absolved, for the most part, since real responsibility lay with those who sent out the teams in the first place—the Peking Party "clique." Furthermore, Chou drew his (by now familiar) distinction between mistakes in orientation (for example, "left in form, right in essence,") and mistakes in line (carrying out policy formulated from above). Thus did Chou attempt to save the work team members while retaining his own ideological credentials.

Finally, Chou addressed himself to the problem of the geographic and institutional limits of the Cultural Revolution and to the related issue of the comparative emphasis to be laid on revolution and production. His basic proposition, from which he never deviated, was that revolution and production should be equally stressed. Chou visualized a Cultural Revolution based on a division of labor: the students would handle ideological struggle in the large and middle-sized cities, and in schools, government, and Party organs. The physical means for this struggle would be provided by the workers and peasants who, incidentally, were also contributing to the Cultural Revolution by carrying out the Socialist Education Movement. Unlike students who could lay aside their books, workers could not lay down their tools to promote revolution; "otherwise," said Chou, "what shall we eat?" Famine would threaten and war preparations would cease. It was indeed permissible for Red Guards to go to factories, but they should first get permission from local revolutionary committees. In any case, they should stay out of the shops. Just to guarantee that revolution would not disrupt production, Red Guard units within the factories were ordered disbanded.[29] Isolating the student Red Guards from the workers would also reduce strife between them.[30] The Cultural Rev-

[29] All of these policies were flouted more and more in the Red Guard period. This reality would be ratified as official policy, as we shall see, in the January Revolution Period. As Chou no doubt predicted, the Cultural Revolution would lead to a decline in production as well as to the purge of his Ministerial colleagues in the State Council. Chou could only play for time, hoping that when the inevitable intervention in industry came, it would be less severe and shorter in duration than if he himself had hastened the process.

[30] Incidents had already occurred in which students had forced their way into shops and workers had resisted or, even worse, the leaders of some units (not specified) had actually incited workers to beat up students.

olution must also not extend to several categories (Lenin's phrase, the "commanding heights," would not be inappropriate) of state institutions. These included not only the news agencies, radio and television stations, and archives, but also important ministries, State Council departments, and the courts.[31]

It soon became apparent, however, that events were overtaking Chou. In the process of destroying the "four olds," the Red Guards did invade ministries and factories, did interrupt production, did destroy monuments and attack and kill their opponents, and did divide themselves into mutually contending factions. Chou was fighting a losing game in all these areas, as he probably knew. More serious, for the first (but not the last) time he came under personal attack from some Red Guards both for his policies and his "poor" class background.[32] Finally, it was clear that there were major differences of emphasis between himself and Lin Piao. At one huge Red Guard rally in Peking, Lin Piao and Chou both gave speeches, and it is instructive to compare them. Chou devoted almost two-thirds of his talk to the necessity to keep production rising and reiterated that one of the basic purposes of the Cultural Revolution was greater productivity. Lin, on the other hand, did not emphasize production at all; instead, he spoke in apocalyptic terms of the need to bombard the Party headquarters, overthrow the small handful of "capitalist-road-ers," and get rid of "monsters and demons." Although it is true that Lin did caution the Red Guards against disunity with the workers and the error of ultra-leftism, these were mere footnotes to an otherwise bombastic speech. Red Guards, listening to the two speeches for guidance, knowing that Lin stood closest to Mao himself in authority, and possessing a propensity for mischief in any case, could hardly be blamed if they went on to further destruction rather than to the type of nonviolent, rational criticism-while-maintaining-production advocated by Chou.[33] The two speeches thus hinted that Lin and Chou, despite their being the two top leaders (aside from Mao himself) in the Cultural Revolution, held

[31] All these would be prime targets in the January Revolution.

[32] Chou alluded to those attacks in his speeches of September 10 and 25, and October 3. In the September 25 speech he chose to spend a great deal of time on the insufficiency of class background as the sole criterion for revolutionary acceptability, and he invoked Mao's own authority to discredit the accusation that his previous speeches had been "big poison."

[33] The two speeches can be found in *Jen-min Jih-pao*, September 15, 1967; *New China News Agency* of the same date; *Hung Ch'i* (*Red Flag*) No. 12 (September 17, 1967); and *JPRS* 39,235, December 22, 1967 (*Communist China Digest*, No. 177) pp. 90–91.

seriously divergent views at an early stage of the Cultural Revolution concerning its purposes and priorities.

Comparisons of such speeches as these and the course of events in the early autumn of 1966 show that Chou was on the defensive. In order to protect his political position and yet do what he could to prevent further deterioration, Chou had no choice but to move leftward. That he did so is evident in both his activities in the succeeding two months and in one rather remarkable statement. In a conversation with some visiting Japanese Liberal Democratic Party Diet members, Chou stated that one's personal opinions should "advance or beat a retreat" according to the decision of the majority. In other words, one should shift with the "wind" (that is, Mao's opinion). The one danger, said Chou, is a tendency to turn conservative.[34] Chou put this philosophy into practice by moving leftward to catch up with Red Guard radicalism and to deal with them on terms equal to what such radical leaders of the Cultural Revolution as Lin, Chiang Ch'ing, and Ch'en Po-ta could offer. Thus, his speech on September 30, the eve of the National Day celebrations,[35] his speech at the "National Rally of Teachers and Students to Pledge Fierce Attack on the Bourgeois Reactionary Line" of October 6,[36] his speech before a mass rally of Red Guards of November 3,[37] his speech to Red Guard "long march detachments" on November 15,[38] and his speech on November 28 to a rally (20,000 strong) of Peking literary and art workers,[39] were all standard Cultural Revolution fare: praisings of Mao and Lin (and, to consolidate his position, praise of Chiang Ch'ing, whose power was rising rapidly), of the Red Guards, the masses, proletarian art and literature, and the like. By the end of November when the Red Guard move-

[34] Tokyo, *Yomiuri Shimbun*, September 26, 1966; translated in U.S. Embassy, Tokyo, *Daily Summary of the Japanese Press (DSJP)*, September 23–26, 1966, p. 31.

[35] *Jen-min Jih-pao*, September 30, 1966; *New China News Agency*, September 30; translation in *JPRS* 39,790, December 28, 1966 (*Communist China Digest*, No. 178) pp. 32–34.

[36] *Wu-ch'an-chieh-chi Wen-hua Ta-ko-ming Yu-kuan Ts'ai-liao Hui-pien* (*Collection of Articles Pertaining to the Great Proletarian Cultural Revolution*), Canton, October 28, 1966, Vol. 4, pp. 10–11; translated in *JPRS* 40,391, 24 March 1967 (*Translations on Communist China: Political and Sociological*, No. 387) pp. 11–13.

[37] *Hung Ch'i*, No. 15 (December 13, 1966) pp. 12–13; translated in *JPRS* 39,532, 16 January 1967 (*Translations from "Hung Ch'i,"* No. 41) pp. 17–20.

[38] *New China News Agency*, broadcast in English, November 15, 1966.

[39] *New China News Agency*, Peking, December 3, 1966; reproduced in American Consulate General, Hong Kong, *Survey of the China Mainland Press (SCMP) 3836*, December 8, 1966, pp. 10–12.

ment had reached a climax (the eighth and last mass rally of Red Guards was held on November 24 and 25) and Mao was already beginning to plan new revolutionary initiatives and new groups to revolutionize, Chou had reestablished himself as a faithful spokesman of the Mao-Lin line. Having thus provided himself with sufficient ideological leverage, Chou was ready to try again to gain control of developments.[40]

By the beginning of December, then, Chou had succeeded in his campaign among the Red Guards to protect his waning authority. If our argument is accepted, three factors were responsible: (1) Chou's leftward ideological shift made when he felt threatened, to an uncertain extent, by Chiang Ch'ing and Ch'en Po-ta; (2) still further deterioration of the situation in the country due to Red Guard activity, which enhanced the value of Chou's administrative and negotiatory skills; and (3) his seeming ability to resolve his differences with Mao and Lin, despite his apparent "revisionist" inclinations, as noted above. Evidently the two top leaders were not willing to jeopardize domestic safety[41] to the extent of putting Chou aside.

Another set of factors, however, may have caused Chou to radicalize his opinions in October and November. These stemmed from the decision of the Politburo, reported to have met in October, to begin a new, even more violent phase of the Cultural Revolution by enlisting the workers and peasants—whose organized detachments were to be called Revolutionary Rebels—in the struggle to overthrow established authority. If this were implemented, it would logically require attacks upon government ministries themselves. It was still unclear whether attacks would cease at the external bounds of the Party. Moreover, everyone knew that the governmental apparatus was manned, at every decision-making level, by Party cadres. That the ministries were indeed to be attacked is seen from Lin Piao's talk at the November 3 Red Guard rally in Peking. On that occasion, Lin called for criticism not only of the Party but of the govern-

[40] On or about October 25 Chou was reported to have issued two oral "emergency instructions" dealing with sending non-Peking Red Guards back to their native places and keeping Peking Red Guards in the city. There is no doubt that these instructions, if the report is correct, marked the beginning of the reassertion of practical influence by Chou. It apparently took another month, however, for Chou to reassert the right to issue instructions to mass organizations and to have ratified his position as number three behind Mao and Lin and ahead of Chiang Ch'ing, Ch'en Po-ta, and K'ang Sheng.

[41] And China's international standing, which was to many symbolized by Chou. We postpone consideration of this topic until later.

ment as well [42] and called for "extensive democracy" in every aspect of life. These phrases could only be interpreted (and probably were so taken) by the Red Guards and their worker allies as an open invitation to invade every enterprise and ministry in the government. Interestingly, Chou remained silent at this rally, in contrast to previous occasions. Although most of November passed in comparative tranquillity, as the last of the Red Guards were shuttled before Mao in Tien An Men and then sent back home or on "long marches," the speech by Chiang Ch'ing on November 28 seemed to signal a new upturn in revolutionary militancy. It is perhaps from this occasion that we can date the train of events leading to the January Revolution. Chou's speech on that occasion was a mixture of panderings to Chiang Ch'ing (demonstrating just how far he had to go to retain influence) and a restatement—in much more subdued tones—of the themes informing Chiang's speech. One does not get the impression that Chou had his heart in that talk.

During December and climaxing in Chou's Red Guard meeting of January 8, 1967, Chou's influence over the Red Guards seemed to increase steadily. His purpose at this juncture seems to have been threefold. On the one hand, he repeatedly urged the Red Guards, in stark contrast with his policy in early August, to unite their disparate groups into a single body. Obviously, unity would facilitate control from above (which Chou then lacked) and the emerging Red Guard alliance with the workers. Thus, at a meeting with Red Guard representatives on December 23, Chou, Chiang Ch'ing, and Ch'en Po-ta all reportedly demanded Red Guard unification.[43] On the other hand, Chou wished to complete the job of clearing the Red Guards out of Peking and of returning them to their localities before the disorders expected during the "seize power" phase. He also wished to shave off the "rough edges," as he put it, of the movement. What this meant was that the seemingly infinite series of splits, which had developed in the movement during previous months over who was ideologically correct and over the contest for prestige among the various units, should now be healed in preparation for the January events.[44] And in the third place, Chou wished to increase his influence

[42] *New China News Agency*, November 4, 1966; translated in *Peking Review*, No. 46 (November 11, 1966) pp. 10–11.

[43] Tokyo, *Mainichi Shimbun*, 28 December 1966, translated in *DSJP*, December 28, 1966, p, 9.

[44] See, respectively, *New China News Agency*, December 29, 1968, and *Hung-Wei-Ping Pao* (*Red Guard Bulletin*), Peking, No. 15 (December 22, 1966) p. 4; trans-

over the direction and extent of denunciation of those government officials who were now, for the first time, coming under heavy Red Guard fire. Thus, at a Red Guard meeting in Peking on December 9, Chou agreed that struggle rallies could now be held against Liao Cheng-chih (who had angered the Red Guards by planning a reception for the "Japanese-Chinese Youth Great Exchange"),[45] Lu Ting-i, Lo Jui-ch'ing, and Yang Shang-k'un. At a rally of seven thousand Red Guards in Peking on December 30 to denounce Jung Kao-t'ang, Vice-Chairman of the Physical Culture and Sports Commission and Assistant Secretary of the Party Commission on Physical Culture, Chou showed how he would attempt to handle such occasions. On the one hand (having failed or not wishing to save the official in question), Chou read out a long fact-filled speech detailing the "crimes" of Jung. This may have had the effect (and perhaps, therefore, it was Chou's purpose) of short-circuiting possible violent acts being directed against Jung. On the other hand, his speech went on to "encourage the revolutionary leftist . . . to educate and help the conservative" and to direct his attacks (in Lin Piao's phrase) against their souls and not their skins.[46] Thus there was a dual strategy in Chou's attempt to do what he could to shield his lieutenants from violence, once it became evident that rallies against them must be held, while simultaneously participating in the purge process.

The climax of Chou's involvement with the Red Guards—and, for that matter, the peak of his influence over them—came on January 8, 1967, at a Red Guard conference in Peking. This time the targets of criticism (although they were evidently not there in person) were Liu Shao-ch'i and Teng Hsiao-p'ing themselves. Here, Chou sought, in a rather spectacular

---

lated in *JPRS* 40234, March 13, 1967 (*Translations on Communist China: Political and Sociological*, No. 383) pp. 7–9.

[45] Apparently Liao—possibly acting under Chou's orders—tried to make union of the disparate Red Guard units in Peking a precondition of forming a reception committee, with the result that "scuffles" broke out among some of the youths attending the restaurant planning meeting and the meeting had to be stopped. General resentment was focused against Liao, so that Chou, seeing that Liao's usefulness was gone but yet not willing to see his own plans for Red Guard unity permanently wrecked, gave his permission for Liao to be thrown to the Red Guard lions. It was only two weeks later, on December 23, that Chou, as we have noted, was able to line up the big guns—Chiang Ch'ing and Ch'en Po-ta—to demand Red Guard reorganization. See Tokyo, *Yomiuri Shimbun*, December 15, 1966, and *Sankei*, December 16, 1966 (translated in *DSJP*, December 17, 1966).

[46] *JPRS* 40,284, 15 May 1967 (*Translations on Communist China: Political and Sociological*, No. 384) pp. 29–30.

manner, amidst the tumult of combined Red Guard and emergent Revolutionary Rebel struggle rallies, to draw a clear distinction between the
kinds of thoughts and actions which the forces of the Cultural Revolution
opposed—the "bourgeois reactionary line"—and the physical persons who
had (or were still) carrying out that line:

How should we point the spearhead of our struggles? When we criticize the bourgeoisie reactionary line, the line will be defined first, and
then persons will become objects of criticism. This means, in other words,
the bourgeois reactionary line represented by Liu and Teng. [At this
moment, some people shouted: Down with Liu Shao-ch'i and Teng
Hsiao-p'ing! Premier Chou *instantly turned his back on them*. The masses
shouted "Down with the bourgeois reactionary line!" Then the Premier,
at last, turned to the masses.] (Emphasis added.)
There is some difference in the slogans which you shouted just now.
We should thoroughly criticize the bourgeois reactionary line represented
by Lin and Teng, and we should smash it. However, the other slogan is
open to question. Under the decision made by the Eleventh Central Committee Plenum, these two men are still Party Central Committee Standing Committee members. I am speaking to you, representing the Party.
Your shouting that slogan in my face drives me in a hard position.[47]

In other words, Chou insisted on the "legal" point that an individual's
office to some degree immunized him from criticism. He distinguished
both between the person versus his error (the person could be reeducated,
the error must be exposed and corrected) and the physical person versus
the mental-spiritual person. Those were to be the lines of defense which
Chou would stake out in the period of the "January Revolution."
One further point might be noted in our accounting of Chou's domestic political activity during the Red Guard period: his position in the
leadership hierarchy. At no time was Chou's place anything less than
third, just below Mao and Lin.[48] Where comparisons can be made between Lin and Chou, the former was always accorded full prominence.
Lin and Mao were always placed together on a pedestal several notches
above the rest. Nevertheless, it was equally true that Chou was always
regarded as *primus inter pares* among all the others. Although Chiang

[47] *Tokyo Shimbun*, January 11, 1967 (translated in *DSJP*, January 13, 1967). The
information was taken from a wall poster dated January 10 which, in turn, was
said to have been the tape recorded record of Chou's statement.
[48] As evidenced by his place in listings of leaders on official and nonofficial occasions and by the space accorded him in the media.

Ch'ing pressured him in October and November (causing Chou to move leftward, as we have noted above), she at no time supplanted him and by mid-December even showed signs of having receded. Thus, at the outset of the January Revolution, Chou retained at least as strong a position vis-à-vis the various groups active in the Cultural Revolution as he had had at the beginning of the Red Guard period six months earlier.

The January Revolution Period

In order to understand Chou's role in the January Revolution, it is necessary first to describe briefly the course of this violent outburst and to list its major developments. The beginnings of the January Revolution can be traced to internal party decisions in late October 1966, and to speeches by Ch'en Po-ta and Chiang Ch'ing in November and December.[49] In essence, it represented an attempt by Mao and his followers to extend the Cultural Revolution to the entirety of Chinese society. Hitherto, it had been confined largely to the major cities, upper levels of the Party, students, and intellectuals. Now the intention was to extend the Cultural Revolution to all lower reaches of the Party, into governmental administration at every level, and into the economy, both industrial and agricultural sectors. The "seize power" movement, which developed in mid-January out of the January Revolution experience in Shanghai, was differentially applied. The government seemed to suffer comparatively less than the Party in that the State Council and the ministries were allowed to continue operating and that the purge of government offices in the capital did not extend too far below some of the top personnel. The Party, on the other hand, was all but officially abrogated at several levels: at regional, provincial, and possibly the *hsien* levels, the responsible party committees seemed, whether officially acknowledged or not, to cease functioning.[50] The proposed vehicle for this movement would be the Red Guards writ large, that is, the creation at every level, ministry, and enterprise, of "Revolutionary Rebel" groups of loyal Maoists who would physically wrest power from the local ruling bodies. These groups made their first appearance in December 1966, and by January of 1967 they were strong enough in Shanghai to attempt to throw out the "small group of

[49] See Philip Bridgham, "Mao's Cultural Revolution in 1967: The Struggle to Seize Power," *The China Quarterly*, No. 34 (April–June 1968) pp. 7–8, and the references cited therein.

[50] Charles Neuhauser, "The Impact of the Cultural Revolution on the Party Machine: Some Observations on a Revolution in Progress," *Asian Survey*, Vol. 8, No. 6 (June 1968) pp. 465–488.

capitalist power-holders" in that city and to replace them with a new ruling group consisting of the Red Guards, Revolutionary Rebels, and other mass revolutionary organizations. The model for the new kind of government and party administration was nothing less than the Paris Commune itself, and the attempt to set up that type of political authority in Shanghai was originally cited as the example to be followed by revolutionary elements throughout China.

The January Revolution in Shanghai, much to the Maoists' dismay, ran aground almost as soon as it began. Although opposition and turmoil were no doubt expected, the scale of both was surprising. The local Party secretaries, administrators, and plant managers did not passively accept the supervision of their erstwhile subordinates or usurpation of offices, which in many cases they had occupied for many years. They possessed a number of devices useful in resisting the Maoist onslaught, all of which they employed in the ensuing fray. These included paying year-end bonuses and travel allowances to workers to go to Peking and present grievances, thus creating worker allegiance to local leaders; allowing and encouraging strikes and shutdowns to occur in protest and retaliation against the violence of the Maoists; and creating revolutionary groups under their own control to preempt the Maoist drive by conducting "fake" power seizures. For their part, the Maoists, acting from below (but with official sanction) also conducted strikes, seized key facilities, and attempted to monopolize the information media. The result was a series of escalating demands and refusals, work stoppages, and clashes which rapidly grew in intensity during late December and early January. Furthermore, the rebels themselves split into as many groups as there were institutions to be seized, and they soon fell to struggling for power among themselves. Chaos and anarchy quickly mounted, principally in Shanghai, but also in a number of other industrial centers; and it seemed for a time that the central authorities in Peking had lost control of the direction and scale of events. Just as serious, in the eyes of the Maoist leadership, the revolutionaries were stymied in their attempt to extend the revolution to other areas; if they remained unassisted, the balance of forces threatened to move in favor of those resisting attack.[51] When added to the problem of

---

[51] We do not mean to imply that those resisting attack were ideologically anti-Maoist, although some may well have been so. There is no record during the January Revolution of any public utterance which could be construed as a direct attack on Mao or his policies. Often resistance to Red Guard and Revolutionary Rebel attack was explicitly justified in Mao's name.

what to do with the large numbers of workers in Peking who had come to press their grievances,[52] the mounting series of bloody clashes in cities throughout China, signs that groups hitherto tied to particular localities —such as peasants and former student-turned-peasant—were now taking advantage of the breakdown of authority to move into the cities, and indications that the economy was feeling the effects of the turmoil, it was clear that the Maoist authorities would have to change their policy, at least temporarily, to avoid total anarchy.

The Party center quickly attempted to restore order. In late January, it was decreed that the Shanghai example should not be followed elsewhere, especially in Peking. Now, not Shanghai but Heilungkiang, and not the Paris Commune but the "Three-Way Alliance" (of revolutionaries, the People's Liberation Army, and revolutionary cadres) were to act as models for emulation. Revolutionary committees were to substitute for the now-displaced Party committees and, in some cases, state administrative offices. The Maoists also revised their policy on cadres, declaring that their skills should be utilized and that they should not be summarily removed from their jobs. Further, the disunity apparent among the revolutionaries was denounced and efforts were begun to restore it. Finally, and most importantly, the People's Liberation Army (PLA) was called in both to halt the most extreme disorders and to throw its influence behind the revolutionary left in its bid to take power.[53]

[52] For another interpretation of the events in Shanghai, see Evelyn Anderson, "Shanghai: The Masses Unleashed," *Problems of Communism*, Vol. 17, No. 1 (January–February 1968) pp. 12–21. Mrs. Anderson sees the January events as the effects of a minority of workers, organizing themselves into Revolutionary Rebel organizations, to restore city services, break the strikes, and temporarily fill the power vacuum left in December by the removal of local Party administrators. In her interpretation, the Revolutionary Rebels moved against their fellow workers in an effort to restore order, rather than to create more disorder so as to seize power themselves. This interpretation is not fully accepted here. Although it may be true that one of their goals was to break the strikes, the Revolutionary Rebels also seem to have been bent on overthrowing what was left of the local administration and permanently setting themselves up in office. In this, they had more than tacit support from the Mao-Lin group in Peking. See also Neale Hunter, *Shanghai Journal* (New York, 1969).

[53] The official Eight-Point Directive to this end was issued on January 28, but wall posters reported that Mao had instructed Lin on January 21 to command the PLA to intervene. See "Order of the Military Commission of the Central Committee," January 28, 1967 (included in *Collection of Documents Concerning the Great Proletarian Cultural Revolution*, May 1967, issued by the "Propagandists of Mao Tse-tung's Thought, Peking College of Chemical Engineering," and translated in *Current Background*, No. 852 [May 6, 1968] pp. 54–55); and Sofia BTA Interna-

The army had always been an element of support for the Red Guards but had kept in the background since the beginning of the Red Guard phase in August 1966. That it was at last being brought in actively was evidenced not only by its participation in and leadership of "seize power" activities and the new "Three-Way Alliance" but also by its presence in almost all organs of the economy, administration, and communications. Military control commissions were established in all those provinces and cities—the great majority—where revolutionary committees had not yet been established. Thus the PLA constituted, in the absence of a Party and governmental apparatus, the locus of power throughout the country.

The army was, understandably, somewhat confused and not a little reluctant to undertake its new task. It had a tradition of noninvolvement in politics (although the Party and the army had been closely intermixed during the revolutionary takeover era) and a professional interest in national defense, from which domestic political strife could only detract. It also found that its terms of reference for intervention were either insufficient to cope with the complexities of the situation or were composed of mutually contradictory directives.[54] The upshot of these conflicting pressures was that the army moved cautiously in its initial involvement and, left to itself to establish priorities among contradictory goals, tended to stress restoration of order, at whatever the cost in violence, over support of leftist forces. Also, for about a month after late January, it was necessary to tone down the leftward impetus of the revolutionaries until military control commissions had established themselves and to convince all concerned (including some units of the army itself) that the army was now to be the leading element in the Cultural Revolution.[55]

---

tional Service, January 23, 1967, reporting on a Revolutionary Rebel poster of January 22. The poster repeated a conversation reportedly taking place between Mao and Lin on the night of January 21. The poster was reputed to have been put up by the "Revolutionary Rebel Red Flag Regiment 1226," presumably the detachment inside NCNA (Radio Tokyo, January 23, 1967) and is included in the *Collection of Documents*, pp. 49–50. The Chinese rendition can be viewed in *Hsing-Huo Liao-yüan* (*A Single Spark Can Start a Prairie Fire*), January 27, 1967, p. 4 (copy on deposit at Center for Chinese Studies, University of Michigan, Ann Arbor).

[54] This is true, for instance, of the aforementioned Eight-Point Directive: the army was enjoined from using violence and yet was told to remove anti-Maoists from power at all costs. It was to side with the leftists, who were creating the disorders, but at the same time it was supposed to restore order.

[55] For further analysis and exposition of the January Revolution period, see Bridgham, *op. cit.*, pp. 7–15; Neuhauser, *op. cit.*; Chalmers Johnson, "China: The Cultural Revolution in Structural Perspective," *Asian Survey*, Vol. 8, No. 1 (Janu-

Chou En-lai's role in the revolutionary storm from January through February seems as complex as the period itself. His problems were, if anything, magnified compared with those of the Red Guard period. Having just achieved what he probably considered to be a victory over the Red Guards, he was now faced with a vast expansion in the number of revolutionaries as the Revolutionary Rebel units came into existence. In essence, he would be faced with the same problems vis-à-vis the Revolutionary Rebels that he had hitherto encountered from the Red Guards and, as we shall see, he used similar tactics in attempting to bring them under his control. Another, perhaps more crucial problem was how to keep the economy and administration from suffering too much from disruptive revolutionary forays. He had probably given up the idea of working for actual economic gains or keeping the governmental apparatus totally immune to attack. He clearly chose to swim against the tide during the short period before "seize power" became the officially sanctioned slogan,[56] but after mid-January he apparently decided to try to redirect the "seize power" movement into less destructive channels. He agreed to allow certain high officials to be criticized or removed only after drawn-out negotiations, and he did what he could to minimize economic dislocations. In these regards, too, parallels are evident between his operational "style" in this period and in the earlier Red Guard period.

A third set of problems concerned his relations with other powerful political personalities and groups. His problems with the Cultural Revolution Group and especially Chiang Ch'ing remained serious after January, for the group was still quite active. These difficulties were compounded after late January by the political activity of the People's Liberation Army. In this period, we shall see that Chou not only managed to deal effectively with the Cultural Revolution Group but also increased his power in the military area to the point where he actually issued orders to military units.[57]

---

ary 1968) pp. 5–8; John Gittings, "The Chinese Army's Role in the Cultural Revolution," *Pacific Affairs*, Vol. 39, No. 4 (Fall 1967) pp. 269–289; and Neale Hunter, *Shanghai Journal, op. cit.*

[56] *Hung Ch'i*, No. 2 (January 16, 1967) seems to be the first official (non-Red Guard) central organ to carry the slogan. See the editorial "Proletarian Revolutionary Elements Unite" on pp. 22–24.

[57] We do not mean to imply in this and in statements immediately preceding that Chou's power was entirely personal. He, as everyone else in China, served at the pleasure of Mao and his power increased in the January Revolution period because

Finally, Chou strove to preserve a minimal working structure at the highest level of the governmental apparatus. He attempted to preserve the position and authority of State Council ministers as well as the continued existence of the Council. He was differentially successful at both of these tasks: in the long run only some of his ministers politically survived the new onslaught, while the State Council more and more became a euphemism for Chou himself.

Chou was very anxious, first, that the disorders evident in Shanghai and elsewhere not spread to Peking and the rest of the country and, second, that the situation be kept under control through central directives issued *before* the scale of disorder reached unmanageable proportions. On the other hand, if Mao's wish was now that the revolutionary forces be allowed to "seize power," Chou would have to go along if he wished to retain his influence.[58] Previous to the "seize power" order, Chou must have been fairly well satisfied with the equilibrating nature of the phrase "carry out revolution and promote production" which had been his central Cultural Revolution slogan for some time. During the early January events in Shanghai, however, it was quite evident that revolutionary strife was rapidly destroying this equality and that the sanctity of production was being threatened. Chou's dilemma was how to restore the equilibrium and still support the inevitably destructive power seizures.

Chou's dilemma is reflected in two related activities in the January 8–15 period, when the effects of the Shanghai events were acutely felt in Peking and other large centers of population. Thousands of workers clogged the railways attempting to get into the city to press their economic grievances to the central authorities and, once in Peking, they apparently created security hazards and contributed to economic dislocations. Under these circumstances, Chou characteristically made parallel moves stressing alternate sides of the "carry out revolution, promote production" formula. On the one hand, at a mass meeting of railway workers on January 10,[59]

Mao felt that Chou could most effectively preserve important political and economic remnants from total disintegration. Nonetheless, within this constraint Chou's "political style" seems worthy of investigation, as do his efforts to expand the acceptable limits (to Mao) of his power.

[58] It is also true that Chou was himself more positively and personally motivated to see recalcitrant local authorities removed after it was clear that they were resisting Revolutionary Rebels acting under orders from the Party center. To condone such local disobedience would endanger the very integrity of Peking's domestic authority as well as precipitate the country into a new series of centrifugal battles which China could ill afford.

[59] *Asahi,* January 12, 1967, carries the fullest account, which is drawn from a Red

he urged the railwaymen to help redress the imbalance between the two sides of the equation by transporting released workers back to their original areas and by working harder and cooperating with Chou's suggestions to unclog the system. Chou blamed the Liu-Teng faction for the contemporary disruption, accusing them of "ignoring production and destroying the revolution." The purpose of the Cultural Revolution was not economic, he said, as the power-faction would have it; rather, it was political and ideological. The economy must not be allowed to deteriorate, lest the very foundation for promoting revolution be destroyed. Conduct the Cultural Revolution at the local level, he suggested; then both production and ouster of the "small group of capitalist-roaders" could be assured. But if the Liu-Teng power-faction was indeed responsible for disrupting the "carry out revolution, promote production" equation, then it would have to be dealt with severely. And this would mean unleasing revolutionary forces to struggle against them. Thus, on the other hand, in order to restore that equilibrium, Chou would have to favor its temporary destruction through some sort of movement to wrest power away from the Liu-Teng group.[60] The trick would be to do the job of overthrowing that group without at the same time allowing the revolutionaries so much freedom of action that they too might threaten the economic order.

The tightrope which Chou thereby had to walk can be seen clearly even before the official beginning of the "seize power" stage. A reading of a Six-Point Directive issued jointly with Hsieh Fu-chih,[61] the Minister for Public Security, makes clear that the law and the security police would operate in favor of the revolutionaries: revolutionary crowds and organizations were to be defended; it was made illegal to attack or confine revolutionary groups; exchange of experience for members of antirevolutionary groups would not be permitted nor could such persons join revolutionary organizations; reactionary language would not be allowed, and those who put up posters against Mao or Lin Piao or who inveighed

---

Guard wall poster put up in Peking by the Peking Railway Academy. Other accounts are in *Nihon Keizai*, *Yomiuri Shimbun*, and *Tokyo Shimbun* of January 12. All can be found translated in *DSJP*, January 12, 1967.

[60] That is, if the Liu-Teng was indeed a group in the sense of being both organized and in control of large sectors of the economy and polity throughout the country. There is still no indication that such a group existed.

[61] "Some Provisions Concerning the Strengthening of Public Security Work in the Great Proletarian Cultural Revolution" (issued January 13, 1967), *Chung Fa*, No. 19(66); included in *Collection of Documents, Current Background*, No. 852, pp. 44-45.

against revolutionary policies or organizations would be punished; and "antirevolutionary flagrant offenses"—murder, arson, pillage, espionage, and theft of state secrets—would also be punished. By implication, revolutionary violations of this same sort, with the obvious exception of espionage, would not be punished as severely if at all.

It is interesting not only that the operation of this "law" would be one-sided but also that the revolutionary organizations would be empowered to "exercise supervision" over the public security organs charged with carrying out arrests in accordance with the Six Points. Furthermore, revolutionary bodies were to be allowed to watch over the Party, the government, and the army itself to make sure that these bodies would not "distort these rules, invent facts, and suppress the revolutionary masses." [62] All of these measures were designed to ease the tasks of the revolutionary organizations. The fact that they were issued over Chou's signature probably indicates his approval. If the "power-faction" had indeed disrupted the revolutionary and productive processes through various "economism" measures, Chou would then have had little choice but to restore the legitimacy of revolution. Not only was the purpose of the Cultural Revolution itself being questioned by the Liu-Teng faction (their authority would have to be broken on this ground alone) but their resistance to extension of the Cultural Revolution activities to factories and mines destroyed the revolution-production equation. Thus, paradoxically, in order to restore the balance in emphasis, Chou found himself forced to approve a change in the revolutionary process which could in the short run only lead to further decline in production. For Mao the central question was: will the revolutionizing of Chinese society continue? For Chou the question was additionally: will the administrative directions of the central government continue to be accepted at local levels, or will a new era unfold when the Cultural Revolution would not only fail to achieve its Maoist goals but when the power of local authorities vis-à-vis the center would also increase immeasurably? Since neither Mao nor Chou could afford the latter series of events to come to pass, one can speculate that they were probably more united in their determination to overcome the Liu-Teng opposition than would have been the case were Chou's motivations merely his loyalty to Mao or his desire to retain personal power.

Having made known his policy toward the Revolutionary Rebels (in

[62] From the wording and implication of this document one might therefore infer that the decision to allow nationwide power seizures had been made at least by January 9, the date of issue of the Six Point Directive.

his railway worker speech of January 10) and toward the opposition (in the Six Point Directive of January 9), Chou moved to deal with the causes of the economic dislocations in Shanghai and elsewhere. This primarily concerned the wage policy in Chinese industry toward regular workers, temporary and contract workers, part-work part-study workers, and apprentices. As we noted, many regular workers had apparently received abnormally large wage increases, year-end bonuses, and allowances for traveling to Peking to present grievances. Many such workers, accordingly, had extra money in their pockets, with the promise of more, and were thus probably converted into supporters of the local authorities. Economically, such serious short-term dislocations as inflation and runs on consumer outlets could easily arise, while politically there was the obvious risk that the Revolutionary Rebels would encounter open hostility among workers in those plants which they were ordered to revolutionize.

Temporary and contract workers were an even greater problem.[63] Apparently they had for years worked under oppressive economic and social conditions without any prospect of improvement in their situation. With the industrial dislocations in Shanghai in December and January, sizable numbers of temporary and contract workers were discharged, and they apparently demonstrated in large numbers against the system. Some attempt was made in early January to gain this group's support for the Cultural Revolution forces by blaming Liu Shao-ch'i and his "capitalist-roaders" for the existence of the system and by promising back wages for those discharged from work. However, by January 10 it was probably clear to Chou that the threat to the economic system posed by assenting to the workers' demands and by their political activity was more serious than the risks either of attempting to restore the status quo ante or of tergiversation. Since both the widespread disorders and the incipient onslaught of the "seize power" movement made the success of a policy of status quo ante highly problematic, Chou opted for a policy which combined caution, personal appeal, and repression. Many of the elements of this policy are evident in his "Emergency Instructions Concerning Wages" [64] issued

[63] For an account of the plight of this group and its role in the January events, see "Source of Labor Discontent in China: The Worker-Peasant System," *Current Scene*, Vol. 6, No. 5, 1968, and the references cited therein. We have drawn on that account although we have departed from some of the interpretations presented there.

[64] *Yomiuri Shimbun*, January 19, 1967. Translated in *DSJP*, January 19, 1967, p. 34. The instructions were issued jointly by Chou and by Liu Ning-i, Chairman of the All-China Federation of Trade Unions.

on January 13. Caution was displayed in points one and three: there was to be no quick change for temporary and contract workers from contract wage rates to piece rates, lest the economic dislocations and consequent inflationary pressures be too great, nor should there be any attempt to force local authorities to take back en masse those contract and temporary workers discharged from their work. Rather, in both cases, small but initial steps should be taken to begin the process of replacing the contract system over the long term.[65] Equivocation is evident in point three, which promised the replacement of the apprentice system[66] with the part-work part-study system, but which then stated that the system "will not be revised for the time being." Tergiversation is also shown in point five, in which Chou promised that wage increases not already in effect should go through, but added the qualification that in every case "senior officials" (Chou and those of his Ministers on the Maoist side of the fence) must first ratify the increases. Finally, a threat of repression of the opposition is clear in point four, which declares that it is for the Central Committee and not the "power-faction" to prescribe changes in the wage system and that violations will have to be struggled against.

Thus, Chou had quickly set forth two official decrees in his two-pronged attempt to overcome the January disorders and to enable the Cultural Revolution to press forward toward its Maoist goals. Chou now moved to assure that the positions thus outlined in theory would be attained in practice. Two tactics were used. One was an intensive round of personal consultations, appeals, speeches, and meetings with workers and revolutionary groups. The other was a series of practical initiatives in disparate areas whose purpose was to put back together, as much as possible, the economic pieces left over from the Shanghai events; to forestall those events from occurring in Peking and elsewhere; and to minimize the economic and administrative dislocations in the "seize power" period which officially began after January 15.

Considering the latter objective first, Chou set forth his composite solution to those problems in the "business supervision" formula. One major

[65] This conclusion is not actually stated in points one and three of the instructions but is strongly implied.

[66] The apprentice system, like the worker-peasant contract system, contained a number of explosive issues. Apprentices served over long periods (2–3 years) for very low wages; promotion came very slowly with no assurance that they would remain workers (they could very well be sent to the countryside); and the senior workers themselves faced transfer to the countryside once the apprentices had learned their skills.

question in the "seize power" movement was just how far to go in seizing power. Did the term mean physical seizure and operation by the revolutionaries of some or all political, economic, and communications centers, or did it mean that the Revolutionary Rebels should act only as a veto group to assure compliance from local authorities and managers? In other words, was the seizure of power to be direct or indirect? Characteristically, Chou advocated a mixed policy: while encouraging direct seizure of political and communications organs, at the same time he spoke in favor of Revolutionary Rebel-Red Guard supervision of the economic and management activities of local authorities, who would thus remain in office. "It is not necessary for us to seize and control everything as was done in Shanghai . . . we must form organs to supervise the functions, and have the responsible persons work earnestly so that they will not stand in the background." [67] He verbally attempted to show to the revolutionaries that the business supervision formula (instead of the Shanghai-evolved "requisition control" formula) was quite distinct from the "bourgeois authorities' " trick of standing back and allowing the rebels to make a mess of things. It is probable that Chou preferred the former policy because he feared explosive disorganization as a result of inept worker-student attempts to run the economy directly. It is possible that Chou also hoped to see the business supervision formula applied to seizure of Peking *political* organs. However, it is more probable that he approved of the mass-based requisition control treatment of Party organs in return for application of the business supervision formula to economic enterprises. In fact, the Revolutionary Rebels seized the headquarters of the Peking City Party Committee and the local Public Security Bureau on January 17 and 18, respectively, while they did generally apply the business-supervision formula to economic and commercial institutions. [68] It was true that, beginning on January 18, some of the ministries of the State Council experienced "power seizures" in the sense that Revolutionary Rebel take-

[67] Speech at a "Grand Rally to Push the Revolution, Promote Production, and Destroy Thoroughly the New Counterattack by the Bourgeois Reactionary Line," reported on a wall poster January 16, and published in the *Tokyo Shimbun,* January 17, 1967. Translated in part in *DSJP,* January 19, 1967, p. 11. Interestingly, Ch'en Po-ta, who also was reported to have spoken at the rally, took the same attitude. See *Nihon Keizai,* January 18, 1967 (evening edition), translated in *DSJP,* January 19, 1967, p. 36.

[68] The question of power seizure techniques for State Council ministries had still to be faced. Ministries were both political and economic organs, and their treatment directly concerned Chou, as head of the State Council. As we shall see, he attempted to separate this question from the other two.

over committees occupied the premises. In on case at least the takeover committee announced that the minister himself was removed (Tuan Chun-yi, of the First Machine Building Ministry). But it appears, first, that the takeover did not then extend to all ministries; second, that the brunt of the revolutionary effort was directed against Party and communications institutions and not against government ministries and state committees; and third (and most importantly from our point of view), that the takeovers in selected ministries followed the business-supervision model. For instance, ministry personnel were ordered to remain at work or return to work within the day. From all indications, disruption of ministerial activity at this time (as compared with other occasions later on in the year) was minimal.[69]

In addition to specifying the appropriate kind of power seizure and minimalizing disruption of State Council activities, Chou also was assigned the task of calming those workers who had come to Peking to press their grievances (some reports spoke of numbers as high as a million). He had to convince them to return to their homes and employment. Two tactics were used: one personal and positive, and the other institutional and negative. In the latter case, Chou curtailed incentives for remaining in Peking by closing stores and banks, rationing daily necessities, and forbidding the sale of nonessential consumer goods. An "Emergency Notification" was issued to this end on January 17.[70] Furthermore, to put teeth into the declaration, the People's Liberation Army and the security police were called out to protect the banks from the apparently large crowds attempting to withdraw their money.[71] Finally, on January 29,

[69] *Nihon Keizai*, January 21, 1967 (evening edition), summary in *DSJP*, January 24, 1967, p. 9. Sofia BTA International Service on January 21 reported Chou as stating that by then "over 30 Central bodies and a part of the industrial enterprises" were in Rebel hands in Peking. He went on to say that the Central Committee supported power seizures of the requisition control variant in Party organs but this source did not report his giving any such approval in the case of economic enterprises. This report is corroborated by a Red Guard newspaper report of Chou's January 19 speech before a group of Peking working-class Revolutionary Rebels. See *Tung-fang-hung Pao* (*The East Is Red*), February 3, 1967, p. 3 (copy on deposit at Center for Chinese Studies, University of California, Berkeley).

[70] *Sankei*, January 18, 1967, reporting a wall poster put up by the Red Guards of the Metropolitan Third Headquarters of the Geological School, the Industrial School, the Machine School, and the Aviation School. Translated in *DSJP*, January 19, 1967, p. 39.

[71] *Tokyo Shimbun*, January 20, 1967; translation in *DSJP*, January 20, 1967, p. 33. This decision appears to be independent of the policy pressed from January 21 to use the PLA directly as an instrument to control power seizures.

Chou announced through the State Council that there would be no Spring Festival in 1967 because of the disruptions already inflicted upon the transportation and financial systems of the country.[72]

From the personal perspective, Chou initiated a whirlwind round of meetings, speeches, discussions, and private exchanges with workers.[73] At these meetings, he invariably pointed out the reasons for the "seize power" movement, the right and the wrong ways to carry it out, exceptions to the power-seizure impetus, and principles by which Revolutionary Rebels should organize themselves.[74] The rebels must seize power,

[72] *Jen-min Jih-pao*, January 30, 1967, p. 1.

[73] One Japanese correspondent in Peking reported that Chou was "staying up until three or even five in the morning every day," that "he is taking overall charge of looking after the Red Guards . . . attending conferences . . . listening to their complaints, preparing places for them to stay and arranging the means of transportation for them." See *Asahi*, January 13, 1967 (translation in *DSJP*, January 13, 1967, pp. 27–28).

[74] Material from which the following analysis is drawn includes, in chronological order: "Speeches of State Council Premier Comrade Chou En-lai and Cultural Revolution member Comrade Wang Li," *Yu-tien Pao-lei* (*Postal Telegraph Thunderstorm*), January 12, 1967, p. 2 (Berkeley collection); "Interview with Representatives of the Red Guards of the Peking Aviation Institute" (and other groups), January 12, 1967, reported in *Sankei*, January 13, 1967 (translated in *DSJP*, January 13, 1967, pp. 30–31); "Chou En-lai's Speech on the Afternoon of the 13th (Summary)," *T'ieh-tao Hung-ch'i* (*Railroad Red Flag*), January 20, 1967, p. 3 (California and Michigan Collections; partial translation in *DSJP*, January 14, 1967, p. 7, reporting on a *Nihon Keizai* article of January 16); "Speech at a Rally for the Rollback by the Bourgeoise Reactionary Line," January 15, 1967, as reported in *Sankei* and *Tokyo Shimbun*, January 17, 1967; "Summary of Comrade Chou En-lai's Speech," January 17, 1967, *T'ieh-tao Hung Ch'i*, January 20, 1967, p. 3 (California and Michigan Collections); report of Chou's speech at an "Oath-taking Rally of the United Committee of the Finance-System Revolutionary Rebels," in *Shou-Tu Hung Wei-ping* (*Capital Red Guard*), January 21, 1968, p. 3 (California Collection); Speech (apparently delivered sometime before January 18, 1968) to the Railway University Workers, *Hung Wei Pao* (*Red Guard Newspaper*), January 18, 1968, pp. 2, 4 (California Collection); Speech by Comrade Chou En-lai and Responsible Comrades of the Central Cultural Revolution [Small Group] Welcoming Representatives of Peking Worker Revolutionary Rebels," January 19, 1967, *Tung-fang-hung Pao* (*The East Is Red Newspaper*), February 3, 1967, p. 2 (California Collection); "Premier Chou's Speech" (of January 21, approximate date, from internal evidence), *Tung-fang-hung* (*The East Is Red*), January 22, 1967, p. 4 (Michigan Collection); "Chou En-lai Represents Chairman Mao, Vice-Chairman Lin, The Central Committee, The State Council, The Military Affairs Committee, [and] The Central Cultural Revolution [Small Group]," a speech of January 22, 1968, *Tung-fang Chan-Pao* (*East Wind Combat Paper*), February 16, 1967, p. 5 (California Collection; partial translations occur in "Chou En-lai's Directive to the Proletarian Revolutionary Rebels," *Translations on Communist China: Political and Sociological*, No. 396, May 22, 1967 (*JPRS* 41,107), pp. 4–5; *Mainichi Shimbun*, January 23, 1967,

according to Chou, because of the increasingly corrosive influence of "economism." Economism had to be opposed because it unbalanced the equation between revolution and production in favor of the latter. Although normally Chou would have tended to stress production over revolution or at least to modify revolutionary activity to preserve production (hence his adherence to the "business supervision" formula), now he found that the Mao-Lin decision to carry revolutionary upheavals into industry and agriculture jeopardized his own political position. Furthermore, the "economists" own activities allegedly promoted a breakdown of production: they encouraged the workers to strike and to stop essential services; they approved referring to Peking for decision even questions of the most local significance; they encouraged workers and staff to go to Peking to press their grievances personally and provided them with money and free tickets for the purpose; and they engaged in outright bribes in order to gain worker allegiance. Thus, in this new period Chou had nothing to lose and everything to gain from direct moves against many of the factory managers.

There was a right and wrong way to seize local power, according to Chou. In the first place, it was essential to unify revolutionary ranks. If splits developed, not force but persuasion should be used to heal them. In fact, said Chou, to bring together the revolutionary ranks by force constituted the bourgeois reactionary line. In organizing the revolutionaries, the best method was by profession and by industry, depending on the local situation; revolutionaries organized along such lines could well substitute for the now defunct trade-union organizations. Only when there was unity of the revolutionary forces and when those forces had organized themselves properly could a power seizure take place.[75]

In the second place, said Chou, power seizure must be carried out primarily by members of the unit in question. While there could occasionally be outside support (either Red Guard, other Revolutionary Rebel, or military), such support should be regarded as only supplementary to the

---

and *Nihon Keizai,* January 23, 1967, translated in *DSJP,* January 25, 1968, pp. 21–22. Chinese summaries can be found in *Hsing-Huo Liao-Yuan* (*A Single Spark Can Ignite a Prairie Fire*), January 27, 1967, p. 4 (Michigan Collection), and *Chin Chun Pao* (*Advance Forward Newspaper*), February 28, 1968, p. 3 (Michigan Collection); and "Summary of Premier Chou's Speech Welcoming a Conference of Revolutionary Rebel Organizations in the Railway System," given January 27–28, 1967, in *Huo Ch'e T'o* (*Locomotive*), February 2, 1967, p. 1 (California Collection).
[75] Despite Chou's advocacy of this go-slow approach in the January Revolution, succeeding events show that this advice was little heeded.

local forces within the unit.[76] Chou also advocated carrying out the seize power initiative before the Revolutionary Rebel organizations had had a chance to amalgamate into a national organization. This is interesting, for Chou would thereby allow potential power to slip into local, possibly more extreme hands. He could well have expected to have a major say in the control over and the policy of an all-China mass Revolutionary Rebel organization, but in the short run he could look forward only to disorganization and near-anarchy (which is in fact what took place) stemming from decentralized decision-making. The probable reasons why he advocated decentralization of revolutionary authority are that, politically, he had little choice in the matter (since Mao and Lin had given the signal and the movement was already well-advanced), and that he had little to lose in the removal of the more recalcitrant factory managers. Still, he risked, and in the end lost, a great deal by agreeing to allow criticism and possible removal of major elements of management expertise—from factory manager to State Council minister—in the Chinese administrative structure. He probably felt that he could successfully defend his more important subordinates whenever necessary. In any case, Mao's and Lin's willingness to retain a modicum of expert guidance, the application of the business supervision formula, and Chou's own personal authority would combine to save his indispensable lieutenants. This logic was justified in the short run (that is, in the succeeding few months); later the purge of administrative and management chiefs took a heavy toll at every level.[77]

In the third place, the revolutionaries should seize power for the very purpose of restoring the production-revolution equation. That is, production should not be disrupted by the power seizure but should in fact be enhanced by it. Chou several times cautioned Revolutionary Rebel assemblies not to direct their power seizures "at society itself," that is, not to adopt the requisition-control formula. There was no need, Chou said, seventeen years after the Communist takeover and under conditions of proletarian dictatorship, to overthrow the entire power structure in industry, in government, and in the Party, and set up a completely new

[76] One implication of this principle, which Chou quickly put forward, was that since the local revolutionary organizations needed all the support they could get, it was the duty of those who had come to Peking to return immediately to their home units.

[77] Chou probably also reassured himself that he could successfully argue for different and preferential treatment of the central ministries and State Council offices. He did in fact so argue, as we shall see.

structure in its place. It would be better to perform a surgical operation by removing the really bad elements, exercise proletarian dictatorship over the wavering few, and adopt the business supervision formula in connection with unwilling factory management personnel. For good reason, as events turned out, Chou obviously worried that mass power seizure from below would get out of hand, causing intrarevolutionary strife, social anarchy, and decline in industrial output. He therefore coined and consistently put forth the slogan that "power should be seized from below but according to Mao's direction from above." In the specific context, of course, "Mao's direction from above" meant Chou's own authority, and it was by this means that Chou hoped to retain and to maximize his own power. As long as he could communicate with the rebels, Chou probably reasoned, he could control events and channel developments in the directions he wished.

Chou also made clear his attitude toward power seizures in the central Party and government apparatus. First, as in other organs, when it was necessary to seize power, it must be done from within. As Chou stated, power seizure must proceed according to "established hierarchies, links, systems, and organs." Second, it was not necessary to throw out all leading elements. In the central agencies it was particularly necessary to tread lightly, to treat leaders as individual cases, and to exercise supervision over them but not to throw them out without cause. Under no circumstances were they to be dismissed out of hand. Finally, according to Chou, no power seizures could be carried out against the Central Committee, the State Council (Chou's own office), the Cultural Revolution Small Group, and the People's Liberation Army. Chou reasoned, again, that under China's proletarian dictatorship, these highest organs of that dictatorship must be "trusted" in their tasks of carrying out that dictatorship.[78] Adopting one of Lin Piao's military analogies, Chou stated that

[78] The implications of such a doctrine for Marxist-Leninist political theory are interesting. Apparently, under conditions of proletarian dictatorship and in consonance with the "mass line," the rank and file political activist has the right—and the duty—to oversee the operations of all levels of policy and administration above him except for the very top-most organs of policy. Evidently, the sins of revisionism and dogmatism can penetrate throughout the Party and the government except to the very top levels, where some sanitizing barrier presumably exists. The doctrine is especially interesting since it directly contradicts the Maoist line on the reactionary nature of a number of people—Liu Shao-ch'i, Teng Hsiao-p'ing, and others—who stood at the very apex of Party authority. It is not known whether this reasoning was accepted by the Revolutionary Rebels, although Chou made the same declaration on two separate occasions in the pre-January 22 period. It is known, of course,

the "Cultural Revolution Group is the General Staff, the Military Affairs Committee is the General Headquarters, and the State Council is the Executive organ of the Great Proletarian Cultural Revolution." Chou thereby hoped to immunize himself and his associates from attack.

Chou's efforts to avoid dismissal, if not attack, for himself and his ministers in the State Council brings up two related questions. First, how did he respond to direct attacks upon himself and his colleagues? Second, how successful was he in defending himself and his associates against those attacks? We have very little information during the January Revolution period on the first question. What we do have (almost exclusively the reports filed by Japanese correspondents in Peking) points to the following conclusions. First, Chou was quick to defend against attacks against his closest associates. In the speech of January 8 to Red Guards,[79] Chou sought to safeguard the positions and persons of five State Council vice-Premiers—Li Hsien-nien, Li Fu-ch'un, T'an Chen-lin, Ch'en Yi, and Hsieh Fu-chih. He also made clear that they were on the Mao-Lin side as opposed to the Liu-Teng faction, and were doing a creditable job of administration. While it was true that they might have committed mistakes in the past, Chou said, and therefore were susceptible to criticism, they should not be ousted from office. Nor should they be disturbed in their work, he said, much less physically dragged out and humiliated. As we shall see, Chou was not as successful on later occasions in defending some of these same associates. Although Hsieh Fu-chih, Li Hsien-nien, and Li Fu-ch'un survived the coming months without a further increase in the scale or kind of attacks against them (and thus remained relatively secure in their positions), Ch'en Yi and T'an Chen-lin were not so lucky. The former was increasingly subjected to severe and direct attack (so much so that in the summer of 1967 he lost his ministry temporarily to invading Red Guards) while the latter was removed from office altogether.[80]

In his January defense of the five vice-Premiers, we can see the outline of Chou's strategy for keeping a semblance of order in State Council activities during the "seize power" and subsequent periods. Those vice-Premiers, ministers, vice-Ministers, state committee Chairmen, and their

---

that the rebels were successful in pressing their attacks against a number of people at this presumably sacrosanct level.

[79] Cited above, note 47.

[80] For a detailed study of Ch'en Yi's problems in the Ministry of Foreign Affairs, see Melvin Gurtov's essay, Chapter 5 of this volume.

deputies who were most important to him, and who were also ideologically defensible,[81] Chou went out of his way to protect. This was the
case with Hsieh Fu-chih and the two Li's. Those who were important to him but had committed some acts of heresy he would allow to
be criticized, even severely. That was Ch'en Yi's case. But those who
were relatively unimportant in State Council work and who had trans-
gressed ideologically, Chou would not seek to prevent from being dragged
out, struggled against, arrested, and purged from their posts. T'an Chen-
lin fit this description.[82] Chou's trick was to supply candidates in the
latter two categories to satisfy Red Guards and Revolutionary Rebels,
while at the same time assuring a modicum of administrative efficiency
in the work of the Council. In the long run, of course, more and more
of the available officials might be cast into the latter two categories and
"eaten up" by the revolutionary forces. That is what actually happened,
probably much to Chou's private chagrin, although in January and
February he hoped for a fairly short "seize power" period. And if the
"seize power" period stretched out (which it did), Chou probably calculated that he could "feed" officials to the revolutionaries at a slow enough
rate that disruptions would be minimized. This strategy, together with
insistence upon the "business supervision" formula and an occasional
timely assist from Mao or Lin, kept the higher administrative structure
from complete collapse.[83]

[81] Meaning that they had no direct connection with the Liu-Teng group; had
accepted the principles, sincerely or not, of the "seize power" movement; and were
able to accept criticism and engage in self-criticism in an acceptable manner.

[82] T'an, who was both a vice-Premier and Director of the Staff Office for Agriculture and Forestry, came under increasing criticism in March 1967 and was apparently dismissed from his post sometime thereafter. He did not appear at the October
1, 1967, National Day celebrations, which is the traditional way to determine a
person's status. Additionally, in November 1968, he came under renewed attack for
his alleged role in the "February (1967) adverse current." We shall discuss the
"February adverse current" in more detail later.

[83] That Chou was "successful" in applying this strategy of slow retreat is demonstrated by the percentage of ministers and vice-ministers who were relieved (as
judged by their final public appearance) in various time periods. For the half-year
periods from January 1965 through the close of 1967, these percentages were as
follows: 14 percent, 16 percent, 16 percent, 25 percent, 10 percent, and 20 percent.
See Donald W. Klein, "The State Council in the Cultural Revolution," *The China
Quarterly*, No. 35 (July–September 1968), Table IV, p. 83. Two articles in *Tsu Kuo*
(*China Monthly*, Hong Kong, Union Research Institute)—by T'ai T'i, "Chinese
Communist Political Structure in 1967," No. 50 (May 1968) pp. 2–6, and Yu Heng,
"Changes in Chinese Communist Leadership During the Cultural Revolution," No.
46 (January 1968) pp. 14–23—tend to bear out these figures, as does Fang Chun-

Chou's second effort in response to attacks was to call for reinstatement of those leaders who were "subjected to kangaroo court, purged, or oppressed by mistake." This so-called "revival of reputation" would grant such officials the opportunity to give genuine self-criticism and hopefully convince "the masses" to accept it. Apparently Red Guard and Revolutionary Rebel criticism had caused the officials to withdraw and isolate themselves within their respective institutions. Although much of the earlier criticism and procedures had unfairly branded those officials, nevertheless the very separation of leader and mass caused the revolutionary elements to suspect that the officials were in fact followers of the Liu-Teng "black line." Chou attempted, through his "revival of reputations" instructions (issued January 12), to break this vicious circle.[84] However, he was not particularly successful in this venture. Little more was heard of "revival of reputations" after mid-January, probably because the very momentum of the "seize power" movement militated against reinstatement of officials.[85] In the short run, some officials may have been able, through timely self-criticism, to thus avert danger of removal from office (at least one such case was the Minister of Railways, Lü Cheng-ts'ao). In the longer run, it seems that almost none of the high-ranking State Council officials escaped either severe criticism or actual ouster.[86]

kuei, "Analysis of the Situation of the Chinese Communist Leadership Group As Seen from the Bandit 'October 1' [1967] Celebrations," *Fei-ch'ing Yen-chiu (Studies on Chinese Communism)*, Vol. 1, No. 10 (October 1967) pp. 1–14, and the same author's "The New Communist Hierarchy as Seen from the 'October 11' [1968] Celebrations," *Fei-ch'ing Yen-chiu*, Vol. 2, No. 11 (November 1968) pp. 5–12.

[84] *Mainichi Shimbun*, January 20, 1967, reporting on a Red Guard wall poster reputedly posted on January 19 and containing Chou's instructions of the 12th. Translation in *DSJP*, January 21–23, 1967, p. 6.

[85] There does exist a document, "CCP Peking Municipal Committee's View Concerning Rehabilitation," which spells out in some detail who must and who must not be rehabilitated after attacks, and gives some procedures for effectuating rehabilitation. See *Current Background*, No. 852 (May 6, 1968) containing the *Collection of Documents Concerning the Great Proletarian Cultural Revolution*, Vol. 1 from which the document just cited is drawn, pp. 36–37. Although the document is undated, its order in the *Collection* indicates that it probably was published sometime between December 31, 1966, and January 11, 1967, that is, just before Chou gave his "revival of reputatons" talk.

[86] There is a superficial resemblance between Chou's phrase "revival of reputations" and the later slogan attributed to the Liu-Teng faction "reversal of verdicts." It is probably no more than that, however, for there is a substantive difference between the two terms. "Revival of reputation" refers to rectification of errors committed by Red Guards and others during the excessive zeal of the Cultural Revolution. Chou often spoke of Red Guard excesses, as well as honest errors of omission or commission by officials attempting to carry out the Maoist Party line.

Finally, how did Chou handle attacks against himself? Chou had been the target of some oblique attacks during the early stages of the Red Guard period.[87] However, the situation seemed to change when it became clear that Chou's person and position were being personally guaranteed by Mao and Lin themselves. Anti-Chou posters were first seen by reporters on January 6, 1967. According to Japanese correspondents, "huge banners were put up before the reviewing stands in Tienanmen Square" in Peking demanding that Chou "be buried alive." Apparently Red Guards criticized Chou for his defense of the five vice-Premiers previously mentioned, for one such poster reportedly asked: "Why is Comrade Chou En-lai preventing [Li Hsien-nien] from being exposed to public criticism?" [88] These attacks evidently continued until January 9 or 10, for the Red Guards of the Foreign Trade Academy reportedly posted this demand: "Burn Chou En-lai's right-wing opportunism at the stake." Two reactions to these activities are recorded. First, Japanese correspondents reported that the Party center put out a policy statement warning that Chou was not to be criticized at all.[89] Second, a somewhat amusing conversation is reported to have occurred in Peking between K'ang Sheng, a leading member of the Cultural Revolution Small Group, and some Red Guard representatives:

K'ang Sheng: There are Red Guards who posted a wall poster criticizing Prime Minister Chou En-lai in front of the Tienanmen Gate. What is the meaning of all this?
Red Guard: It's a counterrevolutionary act.
K'ang Sheng: Then, what are you going to do?

"Reversal of verdicts," on the other hand, referred to an alleged attempt on the part of Liu Shao-ch'i and others to rescind several of the policy directives of the Party, particularly those promulgated after the Cultural Revolution officially began in August 1966 and those aimed specifically at Liu and his policies. "Revival of reputations" dealt with people; "reversal of verdicts" concerned policies. It was, of course, somewhat natural for Red Guards to confuse the two: it takes people to carry out policies, and the Red Guards were ordered to attack people for carrying out certain policies and failing to put others into practice.

[87] These included a massing of Red Guards on November 8 before the State Council building, displaying banners asking to speak to Chou. Even earlier, Chou's own speech of September 25, 1966 (translated in Appendix B), indicates he had been subjected to verbal and wall poster attacks.

[88] Tokyo General Overseas Service in English, January 7, 1967.

[89] *Mainichi Shimbun*, January 19, 1967. Translation in *DSJP*, January 20, 1967, p. 35. The present writer has not found confirmation of this statement in other sources.

Red Guard: Catch them.
K'ang Sheng: Right! [90]

That seemed to end, for some time, Red Guard efforts, such as they were, to unseat Chou.

We can now assess briefly Chou's overall success in defending his associates in the State Council during the January Revolution period and beyond.[91] We mentioned above that, whereas Chou found the upper reaches of the governmental establishment continually under attack throughout the Cultural Revolution, he was nevertheless able to "feed" his ministers to the hungry revolutionaries at a constant but slow rate. The result apparently was that at no time was Chou faced with the imminent collapse of the administrative machine, at least at the central level. We also found that Chou regarded certain of his more important ministers as at least temporarily indispensable, for occasionally he placed his own political power and reputation on the line in their defense. It remains to be seen, however, what happened to the central government apparatus as a whole during the "seize power" phase beginning in mid-January (when for the first time the ministries of the State Council were explicitly attacked), and what the situation was in the long run in regard to the total turnover of ministers and others in the central government establishment. The following points can be made.[92]

Only three of nine state committees, thirty of forty ministries, six of the twenty-four bureaus and commissions, and none of the six Staff offices experienced officially or unofficially sanctioned power seizures by Revo-

[90] See Takada's dispatch in *Mainichi Shimbun,* January 19, 1967 (translation in *DSJP,* January 20, 1967, p. 35). Another, more serious episode of Red Guard criticism of Chou occurred in June, as we shall see below.

[91] Consideration of Chou's policy toward "power seizures" is continued below.

[92] This section depends on the following sources: Ch'in Ti, "Chinese Communist Political Institutions in 1967," *Tsu Kuo,* No. 5 (May 1968) pp. 2–6; Fang Chun-kuei, "An Analysis of the Situation of the Chinese Communist Leading Group as of the 'October 1' Celebration," *Fei-ch'ing Yen-chiu (Studies on Chinese Communism),* Vol. 1, No. 10 (October 1967) pp. 1–14; Yu Hsing, "Changes in the Chinese Communist Elite During the Cultural Revolution," *Tsu Kuo,* No. 46 (January 1968) pp. 14–23; Fang Chun-kuei, "The Current Situation of the Chinese Communist Leadership Group as Viewed from the May 1st Rally at Peking," *Fei-ch'ing Yen-chiu (Studies on Chinese Communism),* Vol. 2, No. 5 (May 1968) pp. 6–8; S. K. Chin and S. K. Ho, "Internal Changes, Party and Administrative Structure and Personnel," *The China Mainland Review,* Vol. 2, No. 4 (March 1967) and Vol. 2, Supplement (June 1967) pp. 262–332 and 390–445 respectively; "A Shocking Situation," *Tung-fang-hung (The East Is Red),* circa early June 1968 (translation in *JPRS* 47,297, *Translations on Communist China,* No. 39, January 22, 1968, p. 38).

lutionary Rebels or Red Guards. Furthermore, of the forty-nine commissions and ministries comprising the core of the State Council, only the Scientific and Technical Commission had an official Revolutionary Committee. A year after power seizure first began, many of the original ministers and vice-ministers (or their equivalents in the other State Council organs) still appeared in public and had not therefore been removed from office. This tally must be counted as a relative victory for Chou.

Second, military administration was the order of the day in many ministries. For instance, the Military Affairs Committee and the State Council issued a joint order on January 26, 1967, prohibiting power seizure from below (that is, by Revolutionary Rebels), and imposing a form of military rule over the Civil Aviation Organization.[93] The Military Affairs Committee (as well as, at times, the Party center and the Cultural Revolution Small Group) often joined with the State Council in sending out notifications and orders which normally would have been issued by the State Council alone. Superficially, these developments indicate a weakened position of the State Council as a result of power seizures and military takeover. But although this was possibly the case, the fact remains that the State Council was at no time in danger of losing its official status.

Furthermore, with the military's backing, State Council orders carried the threat of military force and set definite limits beyond which the revolutionary forces could not transgress in their attacks on the Council and on Chou himself. That this was the case is shown by occasional orders sent out to curtail Revolutionary Rebel activities. Thus, for instance, on February 4, the State Council and the Military Affairs Committee issued a joint order forbidding power seizures in defense-related areas and ministries. In a number of other important ministries and committees, outside (but not always internal) takeover was prohibited, and where extramural Revolutionary Rebels had already taken over, they were ordered to retire.[94] Meanwhile, Chou continued his active defense of certain important

---

[93] "Order of the State Council and the Military [Affairs] Commission of the Central Committee Concerning the Taking Over of the Civil Aviation System by the Army," January 26, 1967. In Propagandists of Mao Tse-tung's Thought, Peking College of Chemical Engineering (eds.), Collection of Documents (Current Background, No. 852) p. 53.

[94] "Notification by the State Council and the Military Commission of the Central Committee Forbidding Exchange of Revolutionary Experience in Industrial and Mining Units, Scientific Research Organs, Designing Units and Capital Construction Units Under the Industrial System for National Defense," Collection of Documents (Current Background, No. 852, p. 61).

ministers (the Ministers of Finance, Security, and Foreign Affairs are the best examples) and saw to it that the criticism directed against many of the others was not so severe as to lead to their downfall.[95]

Despite these measures, taken by both the military under Lin Piao and by Chou himself to preserve the State Council, the turnover in the ministries and committees was high. As of National Day, October 1, 1967, this is how the situation appeared. At the top of the State Council, the premier (Chou) and seven out of the fifteen vice-premiers were still active, if appearance in Tienanmen Square indicates continuation in office; just below this level, in the six staff officers, three chairmen and five vice-chairmen were still active, three chairmen and twelve vice-chairmen had been attacked and removed, and thirteen other vice-chairmen had been attacked but not necessarily (or not yet) removed; of the 49 ministries and state commissions, 15 ministers, 27 vice-ministers, 4 commission chairmen, and 15 commission vice-chairmen apparently continued in office, while 17 ministers, 60 vice-ministers, 5 commission chairmen, and 31 vice-chairmen were evidently removed from office.[96] Apparently most of these changes were made with a minimum of overt violence.

This did not mean, however, that there was very little or no disruption. Apparently all State Council ministries and committees had their own Revolutionary Rebel faction (or factions); and where more than one group existed, power struggles usually ensued. This, together with experienced cadres either being shunted or stepping aside and the PLA's inability to fill these shoes completely, meant that there was bound to be a general decline in efficiency. At the height of the "seize power" movement, for instance, Chou complained that only a handful of high-ranking State Council cadres were left to administer state affairs, and at times even clerical workers were pressed into service to fill the posts of those permanently or temporarily under attack.[97]

[95] There are even cases in which Chou had arrested ministerial subordinates who attempted to carry out internal power seizures against their superiors. This was the situation in the Ministry of Finance.

[96] Numbers vary, depending on source, time of count, and criteria used to decide a person's status. In Appendix C we have listed the State Council persons concerned, their positions and ministries, their date of first criticism, and (to the extent that it is available) their last public appearance in 1967. In the list just presented, the numbers for each group sometimes do not add up to the total number of offices known to exist. The gap represents those persons whose status is uncertain.

[97] "Meeting Between Premier Chou and Representatives of Revolutionary Organizations of the Industry and Communications System," February 1, 1967, in *Hung T'ieh-tao* (*Red Railway*), February 11, 1967 (Berkeley Collection).

The Period of Military Takeover

Once the "seize power" movement moved into high gear, after January 15, and the army had emerged after January 22 as the leading force in efforts to overthrow representatives of the "small handful" at every level of the Party, the situation for Chou took on a vastly different complexion. Demands presented by the new situation suddenly eclipsed such problems as the "business supervision" versus the "requisition control" formula, and how to convince the tens of thousands of visiting workers in Peking to return home.

To approach an understanding of Chou En-lai's role in this new period, we shall first sketch the major political developments from the beginning of military intervention in late January to the Wuhan Incident of late July and its aftermath.[98] The dominant feature of this period, of course, was the vastly increased political influence of the People's Liberation Army, which became involved or prevailed in almost every aspect of life. Initially the army was not the radicalizing agent it later became. It was first assigned the task of restoring a semblance of order to many of the large cities which had been ravaged during the January Revolution. Disorders by now had spread to some of the ministries, to certain sectors of industry and mines, and to areas of the countryside. Army intervention was effected through the "Three-Way Alliance" between the revolutionary mass organizations, the army itself, and the "revolutionary leading cadres." The army was to serve as the leading element of this alliance which in turn provided the basis for the provincial revolutionary committees. The cadres presented a problem, however: they had been vehemently attacked during the January Revolution and were not, as a rule, holding office. Their inability to do their jobs was one of the main causes of the January disorders. The cadres would have to be rehabilitated, if only partially, before the "Three-Way Alliance" could function. A "mild cadres policy" was thus instituted.

[98] Aside from the documentation presented below, we rely on the following general references. Philip Bridgham, "Mao's Cultural Revolution in 1967," *China Quarterly,* No. 34 (April–June 1967) pp. 1–37; Chalmers Johnson, "China: The Cultural Revolution in Structural Perspective," *Asian Survey,* Vol. 8, No. 1 (January 1968) pp. 1–15; Charles Neuhauser, "The Impact of the Cultural Revolution," *op. cit.; Far Eastern Economic Review Yearbook,* 1968; Thomas J. Weiss, "Communist China," *Yearbook of International Communist Affairs, 1967* (Stanford, 1968); and Wang Hsiao-tang *et al.,* "Special Issue Summarizing the Year [1967]," *Fei-ch'ing Yen-chiu,* (*Studies on Chinese Communism*), Vol. 1, No. 12 (December 1967) pp. 1–97.

But what political categories would be reinstated and how far up and down the administrative hierarchy should rehabilitation extend? Evidently no firm rules in this regard were promulgated, because some ministries (particularly those associated with the Staff Office for Agriculture and Forestry, headed by T'an Chen-lin) restored to power almost all of the cadres previously fired, and instituted "false power seizures," manned by cadres who had not yet been dismissed, to preempt the revolutionary initiative. While we may doubt the subsequent charge that such rehabilitation was intended to extend even to Liu Shao-ch'i and Teng Hsiao-p'ing, it nonetheless appears that the "February adverse current" of "reversing verdicts" encompassed many provinces and implicated through collusion many army officers at or below the level of military districts.

The Maoists reacted with a renewed tightening up and leftward movement, beginning in early April.[99] In order to accomplish the goal of more and genuine power seizures, however, the political safety of the revolutionary forces would have to be guaranteed by the army, which up to then had evidently cooperated with those already in power to suppress the rebel elements. Thus, the army would have to be prohibited from interfering in power seizures. On April 6, the Military Affairs Committee issued such an order prohibiting the army from opening fire on the mass organizations, from calling them counterrevolutionary, from arresting them, or taking any action at all toward them without prior instructions from Peking.[100] The Party center hoped to weld together the mass organizations and the army in the "seize power" task, and to this end the army was ordered to establish provisional military control commissions until genuine revolutionary committees (embodying the "Three-Way Alliance") could be established. But the assumption of a natural harmony of interests between the army and the Revolutionary Rebels was in fact not justified, for the army continued to be charged with the task of political and economical administration, a naturally conservative function. The upshot was both military paralysis and renewed leftist violence. The revolutionary forces continued their attacks against the "small handful" (a task which the Mao-Lin leadership had now facilitated by beginning

[99] Party work conferences were reported to have been held on March 14–18 to discuss the "adverse current" and on March 27–28 to consider the new movement to denounce Liu and Teng. See *Nihon Keizai*, April 6, 1967, and *Yomiuri Shimbun*, April 10, 1967, as translated in *DSJP*, April 8–10, 1967, p. 11, and April 11, 1967, p. 13.

[100] "Order of the Military Commission of the CCP Central Committee," April 6, 1967; in *Collection of Documents* (*Current Background*, No. 852) pp. 115–116.

the massive campaign to criticize "China's Khrushchev" (Liu Shao-ch'i), but they split into violently contending factions. Initiated in part to oust the "small number of capitalist-roaders" from power at the center, the Cultural Revolution now became an ever-widening struggle for the spoils of power at all levels of the state. Furthermore, the revolutionary forces now began to attack the army, both verbally and violently, for carrying out their administrative and economic duties, while the army was forbidden to strike back. Thus in May and beyond, the level and extent of violence throughout China quickly escalated.[101]

It appears (following Bridgham's argument) that the Central Committee was divided on how to cope with the situation, which was fast approaching the crisis stage. As in other situations in which a division in the country at large causes a division (although not necessarily along the same lines) within Party leadership, the method chosen for dealing with the problem was to dispatch investigative teams to ascertain the real situation and to mediate between the contending groups. By late June and early July two such teams (in Yunnan and Anhwei provinces) had managed to negotiate cooling-off agreements among the parties concerned and, had they been successful throughout the country, a new phase of relative moderation might have begun. At this point, in mid-July, however, the so-called Wuhan Incident occurred. The Wuhan military authorities not only sided with the "conservative" Revolutionary Rebel faction (in violation of a reported Central Committee directive of early July to strive for unity among revolution forces and between those forces and the army), but also threw down a direct, regionally based challenge to the Party center in Peking. This had some of the markings of warlord politics, and Peking chose to regard it most seriously.[102] The Central Committee, through Lin Piao himself, elected to chastise not merely the "conservative" Revolutionary Rebels but also elements in the army, like Ch'en Tsai-tao, the Commander of the Wuhan Military Region. It called him both counterrevolutionary (siding with the wrong revolutionary fac-

---

[101] The Party center on June 6 issued an obviously unenforceable order prohibiting "armed struggle, assaults, destruction, pillage, house raids, and unauthorized arrest" (*Yomiuri Shimbun,* June 8, 1967, translation in *DSJP,* June 8, 1967, p. 29). Although reports of bloody struggles mounted in every province, and although industrial (if not agricultural) production reportedly began to show significant declines, the army continued to be enjoined from using force to restore order (*Chieh-fang-chün Pao* editorial of June 27, 1967).

[102] We shall attempt to reconstruct the background and some of the details of the Wuhan Incident below.

tion) and disobedient (responding to local problems with local, not Peking-ordered solutions). The upshot, in August, was further violence and disorder, leading to anarchy in some places. Peking responded by moving even further leftward in the decisions to arm certain Red Guard units and to extend the "power seizure" to the military itself. The revolution- ary forces were given a hunting license to drag out not only the "hand- ful" in the Party, but now also the "handful in the army." Only when the level of bloodshed, disorganization, and factionalism threatened the army itself did the Mao-Lin faction decide that it was time to pull back and institute another period of relative moderation. This began in Sep- tember and lasted, for the most part, until the end of the year.

Our task is to try to understand the role of Chou En-lai in this panoply of events. We will divide our analysis into the following five topics: the relationship of Chou to the "February adverse current" and particularly to the activities of T'an Chen-lin; Chou's defense of his associates, as well as himself, from attacks; relations between Chou and the Cultural Revo- lution Small Group; Chou's role in the People's Liberation Army and its problems; and his relations with the revolutionary forces of the left and the furtherance of the "seize power" movement.

As for the "February adverse current of reversal of verdicts," the prob- lem was whether, and to what degree, to rehabilitate selected cadres for inclusion in the new revolutionary committees. As we have noted, no clear instructions seem to have been issued covering criteria for rehabili- tation. Normally, such instructions should have come from Chou himself (or at least have been issued jointly by the Party and the State Council), but it is easy to understand why he was reluctant to commit himself. On the one hand, he probably wished to see as much rehabilitation as possi- ble to restore the State Council ministries' pre-January level of efficiency. On the other hand, he knew that the political criteria for purging the cadres precluded such wholesale rehabilitation. Further, he had already been denounced for shielding certain ministers from attack and was on record as favoring the "revival of reputations,"[103] a phrase very similar, if not synonymous with the "reversal of verdicts" allegedly advocated by T'an and by Liu Shao-ch'i and Teng Hsiao-p'ing.[104] In considering how

[103] See note 86.
[104] Not much hard information is available on the "adverse current." Apparently, the central issue was the propriety of the activities of T'an (Head of the Staff Office for Agriculture and Forestry, and also a member of the Party Secretariat and Politburo), who allegedly tried to rehabilitate *all* cadres previously criticized and removed *and* to prevent any further seizures of power. The vehicle for the second

to treat the T'an Chen-lin affair, Chou had two choices. First, he could admit that T'an was in fact carrying out Chou's own dictates and attempt to defend him; this is essentially what he had done early in January. Or Chou could claim that T'an had gone beyond the limits of his orders and had used the relative security provided by Chou's political umbrella to move all the way back on the cadres issue. In that case, Chou would then have to agree to criticism of, and self-criticism by, T'an and defend him by persuading the revolutionaries to accept such criticisms. If unsuccessful, Chou would be forced to protect himself by allowing T'an to be removed from his post.

Chou chose the latter alternative, in contrast to his action in January, apparently because of the post-April connection between the February "adverse current" and the emerging campaign against Liu and Teng. Once it became clear that political fortunes turned almost uniquely on one's attitude toward Liu and Teng, Chou probably realized that at some

of these activities were so-called "false power seizures," perpetrated by cadres already in power, and organizing—and then disbanding—Revolutionary Rebel sections in the ministries and departments under his command. *Ching Kang Shan Pao* (*Ching Kang Mountain News*), March 15, 1967 (as reprinted in *Tsu Kuo*, No. 53 [August 1968] p. 21) stated that there were three levels to the February adverse current. (1) T'an himself, at the State Council level, attempted to "reverse the correct verdict on the representatives of the bourgeois" by taking advantage of the "shortcomings" of the seize power movement and by usurping power; (2) the middle level, said to be represented by Chiang Nan-hsiang, then Minister of Education and President of Tsinghua University; (3) the lowest level (apparently among students at Tsinghua opposed to the local Red Guard units), said to have been led by T'an Li-fu (the latter may have been T'an Chen-lin's son). One of the documents vilifying the February adverse current published more than a year later spoke of T'an sending his own son on private missions back and forth from Peking to Chekiang. (See *Chekiang Daily*, as reported on the Chekiang Provincial Radio, June 28, 1968.) Once the campaign to denigrate the characters of Liu Shao-ch'i and Teng Hsiao-p'ing got under way (officially after April 1), attempts were made to link the February adverse current and T'an himself to the "bourgeois reactionary line" (see, for instance, the *Ching Kang Shan Pao* article quoted above, the collection of documents on the February adverse current contained in *Union Research Service*, "Further Criticize and Repudiate the 'Adverse February Current'," Vol. 53, No. 24 (December 20, 1968) and the report of K'ang Sheng's speech at a Peking rally, March 27, 1968, published in *Tsu Kuo*, No. 53 [August 1968] p. 21). While we may harbor doubts as to the veracity of the charge of connections between T'an and Liu, it remains true that Chou had to take those accusations into account when considering his own political fortunes. See also "T'an Chen-lin in the February Adverse Current," *Chungshan University Red Flag*, No. 63, Canton, April 4, 1968 (translated in *SCMP* 4169, May 2, 1969, pp. 7–10), and *China News Analysis*, Hong Kong, issues No. 728, 733, 736, 739, and 747.

point he would have to abandon his support of T'an.[105] His previous strategy, however, would be retained: if Chou could no longer protect T'an through forbidding Red Guard criticism, then he could first delay comment (in the hopes that the matter would blow over); second, he could allow controlled public criticism sessions as a lightning rod to prevent T'an from being removed; and finally, if these failed to stem the tide, he would agree to T'an's dismissal.[106] Thus, after admitting on April 28 that the policy of rehabilitating all cadres regardless of past mistakes was an "extremely grave" mistake,[107] only on May 23 did Chou associate himself with Revolutionary Rebel attempts to overthrow T'an. Even then he told a Peking rally that he would not allow T'an to be dragged out to a mass criticism rally but would permit only a smaller criticism meeting to be held. And it was only on June 15 (after a further considerable delay), that Chou acceded to the rebel plan to criticize T'an. Finally, it was not clear that T'an had actually been removed until his nonappearance at the October 1 National Day celebrations (which is to say, Chou had successfully engineered a quiet, efficient removal).[108] Nonetheless, the very fact that T'an was finally removed indicates Chou's first failure to protect his associates.[109]

[105] He also realized that he would have to criticize Liu Shao-ch'i and Teng Hsiao-p'ing. This he did, reportedly for the first time (according to *Tokyo Domestic Radio Service*, April 13, 1967, reporting a Peking wall poster) in early April.

[106] Chou used the same technique in connection with the contemporaneous criticism of Ch'en Yi. In that case, however, he was successful, having been pushed only to the controlled criticism stage. See Gurtov, Chapter 5 of this volume.

[107] Prague *CTK International Service*, April 28, 1967.

[108] *Yomiuri Shimbun*, May 26, 1967 (translated in *DSJP*, May 26, 1967, p. 6), and *Mainichi Shimbun*, June 15, 1967 (translated in *DSJP*, June 15, 1967, p. 5).

[109] To say nothing of the difficulty which Chou was then experiencing in keeping Ch'en Yi in office. On the other hand, Chou did not seem to have had any particular difficulty in preserving the political integrity of some other high State Council officials. Thus, in late March, Chou again successfully defended Li Hsien-nien and Yü Ch'iu-li against Red Guard attacks. With regard to Yü, Chou is reported to have asked: "Can't you realize yet which headquarters Yü Ch'iu-li is siding with? How could I be with him receiving you if he were not on the side of Chairman Mao?" See *Asahi*, March 27, 1967, as translated in *DSJP*, March 28, 1967, p. 35. This is a classic example of Chou's use of double appeal to authority (his own and Mao's) as a subterfuge for discussion of the facts. And in early May, Chou again came to Li Hsien-nien's aid, this time by using his now familiar tactic of allowing a criticism session and then declaring that no further such occasions would be permitted. Something of a twist is present in Chou's tactics on this occasion: "The rebels said they did not agree with his proposal and that they would continue their criticism of Li Hsien-nien. According to the poster, Chou En-lai became angry upon hearing this

Given this, we might alert ourselves to the possibility that his political position was indeed deteriorating. In fact, we have two supporting indications (although they are far from conclusive) that this may have been the case. One of these was the resurgence of wall poster attacks against Chou by various revolutionary groups in March, April, and May. In each case, they were put down either by wall poster counter-campaigns or by declarations of support from high-ranking members of the Maoist leadership. Thus, on March 17, apparently in response to revolutionary criticism of Chou for supporting Li Hsien-nien, posters were put up all over Peking stating: "Premier Chou is Chairman Mao's close comrade in arms" and "Premier Chou is a member of Chairman Mao's headquarters." The next day Japanese correspondents reported that a Peking congress of Red Guards had warned its affiliated organizations that no one was allowed to criticize Chou on pain of being terms counterrevolutionary.[110] Despite these appeals and strictures, Red Guard criticism of Chou apparently went on as before, for on April 18, a month later, the same Red Guard congress had to issue another instruction, saying that "Premier Chou En-lai is Chairman Mao Tse-tung's close comrade-in-arms, and you should not harbor any doubts about him. To post a wall newspaper attacking Premier Chou will be considered a counterrevolutionary act." [111] Finally, in May, in connection with Chou's shielding from criticism of Ch'en Yi, Ch'en Po-ta, head of the Central Committee Cultural Revolution Group, was forced to issue a statement: "Premier Chou is respected abroad, as well as at home. He is a representative Chinese. He is in a responsible position of carrying out the policies of Chairman Mao and Vice-Chairman Lin Piao. No one is allowed to find fault with Premier Chou En-lai under any circumstances." [112] We suspect, therefore, that Chou was finding it increasingly difficult to maintain his own

---

reply and told the rebels to do what they would." (Sofia *BTA International Service,* May 16, 1967, reporting on a poster describing a speech by Chou of May 4.) Although it is difficult to say whether the Red Guards persisted in their efforts, it nonetheless appears that Li Hsien-nien did not suffer unduly from their activities. He continued his regular round of appearances during the rest of the year. If this is so, then Chou's reported "anger" probably served its deterrent purpose.

[110] *Tokyo Shimbun,* March 18, 1967 (translated in *DSJP,* March 18, 1967, p. 13), and *Tokyo Shimbun,* March 30, 1967 (translated in *DSJP,* April 30, 1967, p. 24).

[111] *Mainichi Shimbun,* April 26, 1967 (translated in *DSJP,* April 27, 1967, p. 7).

[112] *Asahi,* June 1, 1967 (translated in *DSJP,* June 2, 1967, p. 27). It would be difficult to find a more cogent statement of the Maoist leadership's rationale for guaranteeing Chou's position and person.

political position, particularly when one of the Maoist leaders had to step in to call a halt to attacks against Chou.[113]

The other indication, admittedly poorly documented and based largely on rumor, is that there may have existed a high-level organization within the Maoist camp, the so-called "May 16 Group." [114] If we are to believe the accusations later leveled against the May 16 Group, one of its basic purposes was to overthrow Chou, or, failing that, to set Chou and the Cultural Revolution Group (Chiang Ch'ing, Ch'en Po-ta, K'ang Sheng, and others) at odds.[115] The May 16 Group is said to have been composed largely of students, concentrated for the most part in Peking (but allegedly with at least one branch in Canton) and to have originated as far back as the beginning of the Cultural Revolution. Although it reportedly held its first "congress" only on July 1, 1967, and was "formally inaugurated" on August 3 (and was forcibly disbanded in a bloody clash on September 6), it was supposed to have operated since September 1966, at that time directed principally at Ch'en Po-ta and Chiang Ch'ing, and

[113] Although it appears that Ch'en Po-ta's statement ended, at least until the fall, direct and overt criticism of Chou, attacks from Red Guard quarters began again after the Wuhan Incident and became severe enough to warrant further leadership declarations of support for him. This culminated in a speech by Hsieh Fu-chih and Ch'en Po-ta (published in *Wen-ko T'ung-hsin*, Canton, October 9, 1967, and translated in *JPRS* 43903, *Communist China Digest*, No. 193 [January 8, 1968]) giving perhaps the most complete defense for Chou's guaranteed position yet issued. Hsieh said, in part, that "the Premier acts under the leadership of Chairman Mao and the Central Committee. The Premier handles important affairs of State. . . . at home and abroad the Premier enjoys a high prestige, and you cannot oppose him. . . . the Premier is the chief staff officer to Chairman Mao and Vice-Chairman Lin. . . . the Premier cannot be beaten down. The Premier is the representative of our state . . . the Premier has a fine political style. Your opposition to the Premier will bring joy to Liu and Teng and to the imperialists and revisionists. The imperialists and revisionists are afraid of the Premier."

[114] Documentation concerning the May 16 Group includes: "The May 16 Military Group in Kwangtung," *Tsu Kuo* (*China Monthly*), No. 49 (May 1968) pp. 49–51; "Red Flag" of Tach'ing Commune of Peking Petroleum Institute, "Drag Out Counter-Revolutionary Double-Dealer Ch'i Pen-yü," February 26, 1968 (translated in *SCMP*, 4137, March 13, 1968, pp. 1–3); and the important "The May 16 Red Guard Corps of Peking," a collection of documents originally published in Peking in September 1967, by the Revolutionary Rebel Commune of the Peking College of Iron and Steel Industry of the Red Guard Congress of the Capitol and translated in *Collection of Documents, Current Background*, No. 844. See also Hsuan Mu, "The Yang Ch'eng-wu Case," *Fei-ch'ing Yen-chiu* (*Studies on Chinese Communism*), Vol. 2, No. 8 (August 1968) especially pp. 54–56.

[115] It also was said to work for the overthrow of the "small handful" of reactionaries within the Army.

more actively since the turn of the year, when they began to attack Chou himself. It took its name from the "May 16 Notification," which "signifies the new crest of the second great cultural revolution" and which attacked Chou as a "double dealer playing with counterrevolution" in order to support the conservatives and to safeguard his position. It allegedly began in the Department of Philosophy and Social Sciences of the Chinese Academy of Sciences (headed by such Party members as Wu Ch'uan-ch'i, Lin Chieh, Mu Hsin, P'an Tzu-nien, Chao I-ya, Hung T'ao, Lo Feng, Hsiao Ch'ien, Ch'en Ta-lun, Lu Cheng-i, and Ch'in Hua-lung). Apparently after February, leadership passed to the June 16 Group in the Peking Foreign Languages Institute (headed by Liu Ling-k'ai). The May 16 Group called itself the "Fourth Headquarters," alleging that the "First Headquarters" (the proletarian headquarters) was headed by Mao Tse-tung, the "Second Headquarters" (the bourgeois headquarters) by Liu Shao-ch'i and Teng Hsiao-p'ing, and the "Third Headquarters" by Chou En-lai.

There seems to be a close correspondence between the alleged anti-Chou activities of the May 16 Group and the reports of wall posters pasted up against him, as we have recorded earlier.[116] It does not necessarily follow, however, that a single conspiratorial group initiated all anti-Chou activities. Perhaps the propensity of the Mao-Lin leadership to lump together disparate opposition and to see conspiracies where in fact none existed was at work here, too. In any case, Chou himself seems to

[116] Thus, the June 16 Group reportedly first wanted to attack Chou in September 1966, but could not do so openly. The May 16 Group began in early January 1967 to "compile blacklist information against Premier Chou," and decided to get at Chou also through attacking five of his vice-Premiers. They openly attacked Chou from this point forward. In February, March, and April, they moved to expose Li Fu-ch'un, Ch'en Yi, and Yü Ch'iu-li as a further means of undermining Chou. Beginning in March, they also attempted to create discord between Chou and the Cultural Revolution Small Group, while at the same time engaging in a stepped-up poster campaign against Chou. This culminated in a May 16 Notification. Finally, in June and July, they became bold enough to address Chou directly (albeit through posters) in such statements as: "Ten Questions Put to Chou XX"; "The Spokesman for Which Class?"; "Declaration of Bombardment"; "Twenty-Three Whys"; "Expose a Big Conspiracy of Li XX and his Ilk"; "Twenty Whys"; "Letter to the Revolutionary Comrades-in-Arms of the Agriculture Sector"; "Stern Statement"; "T'an Chen-lin is the Key of Keys to the Agricultural Sector"; and "Never Forget Class Struggle." Unfortunately, these documents do not seem to be available outside China, and our only manner of reconstituting their contents is through analysis of accusatory material. See Collection of Documents (Current Background, No. 844) op. cit.

have taken the matter in stride, reportedly declaring that "I do not want to emphasize the 'May 16' counterrevolutionary group; there are only several people involved and it is nothing to get excited about." [117] Although Chou thus publicly belittled the May 16 Group, it appears that its membership was broad enough to include not only numerous Red Guard factions in two major cities, but more seriously, members of the Cultural Revolution Group (Kuan Feng, Wang Li, Mu Hsin, and later Ch'i Pen-yu). [118] If, then, we are to believe the "facts" about the May 16 Group presented by the Maoist leadership, Chou must actually have been very concerned about their activities. Kuan, Wang, Mu, and Ch'i were later removed from the Cultural Revolution Group for "counterrevolutionary double dealing," thus easing pressure from the left on Chou. However, the very fact of their removal, when placed alongside the Maoist "evidence" against the May 16 Group, bolsters at least the suspicion that there may have been some high-level moves against Chou. But the evidence does not allow us to proceed beyond this.

On the other hand, down to August 1967 Chou's relations with other important members of the Cultural Revolution Group seem to have been formerly correct at least. We have no evidence (at least in the period under consideration) of discord between Chou and Chiang Ch'ing, K'ang Sheng, and Ch'en Po-ta. In fact, Chou increasingly depended on the Cultural Revolution Group for support, as attacks grew against his vice-Premiers. Thus, we find a fair number of speeches by Cultural Revolution Group members in favor of Chou after the Wuhan Incident. [119] The relationship between Chou and the three most important members of the Cultural Revolution Group were in fact mutually supporting during difcult times. Thus, while it is certainly possible that the basis for the dispute between Chou and Chiang Ch'ing, which was to emerge progressively after September, [120] was laid in the late spring and summer of 1967, there

[117] *Tsu Kuo (China Monthly)* No. 49, *op. cit.*, p. 49.
[118] Putting aside, for the moment, Lin Chieh, the Editor of *Red Flag*, who was added to the Cultural Revolution Small Group only in the late spring of 1967.
[119] See notes 111–113 above and "Leaders of the Central Committee Severely Denounce the 'May 16 Corps,'" in *Collection of Documents* (*Current Background*, No. 844), pp. 1–2. The latter contains excerpts from alleged speeches by Ch'en Po-ta (August 11), K'ang Sheng (August 28 and September 1), and Chiang Ch'ing (August 11, September 1, and September 5).
[120] This is based largely on Chou's tongue-in-cheek remark sometime around the beginning of November that "arduous struggle has impaired Chiang Ch'ing's health but spiritual consolation and inspiration will certainly make up for the loss" (see *SCMP* 4076, November 8, 1967, p. 3, quoting the Canton *Wen-ko T'ung-hsun*).

seems to be little or no overt evidence in the period before August 1967 that there was competition between Chou and Chiang Ch'ing.[121] The dispute quickened after the purge of Ch'i Pen-yü in January 1968 and the Yang Ch'eng-wu incident of March. On the other hand, it is difficult to

---

Facts and Features, Vol. 1, No. 16 (May 29, 1968) p. 7, a publication of the Institute of International Relations, Republic of China, issued a different version of this remark: "The intense struggle of the Cultural Revolution has influenced the health of Comrade Chiang Ch'ing and it is better to ask her to rest for some time." *Ming Pao,* Hong Kong, December 15, 1967, p. 4, printed what purports to be the original Chinese: "In the past few months she [Chiang Ch'ing] has worked hard . . . so we asked her to take good rest." There is the speculation that the leaders of the May 16 Group were supported behind the scenes by Chiang Ch'ing, who jettisoned them when their cause appeared to be lost. There is also evidence after the turn of the year that Chiang Ch'ing, as head of an "ultra-leftist" faction within the Maoist leadership, was competing for influence with Chou, cast as the leader of the "rightist" forces within the Maoist faction. Thus, for instance, Chou's warnings against leftism, issued in a speech of April 7 (instead of a balanced diatribe against leftism and rightism equally); the demotion of Li Fu-ch'ün (Chou's longtime supporter and confidant) from the Standing Committee of the Politburo to a mere member of the Politburo; and the obvious downgrading of Yü Ch'iu-li, whom Chou had strenuously defended previously, all are taken as evidence of a weakening of Chou's position and a strengthening of Chiang Ch'ing's. Chiang Ch'ing was supposed to have continued her reassertion of power in the late spring in 1968. Thereafter, however, Chiang Ch'ing was said to have received a setback, revealed in parallel speeches by herself and Chou on September 7, 1968, on the occasion of "celebrating" the formation of the last provincial revolutionary committee. It was clear on this occasion that Chou was completely in command of the proceedings and that Chiang Ch'ing was either brought in at the last moment to utter a few carefully chosen words or that she was deliberately kept in the dark concerning the details of the meeting. (See, in these regards, *China News Summary,* Nos. 215, 218, 219, 225, 237, and 249, and the references cited therein. I am indebted to Professor Richard Baum for calling these references to my attention. On Chiang Ch'ing, see also *Current Scene,* Vol. 7, No. 1 [January 6, 1969] and the references cited there.)

[121] A rather strange perturbation occurred in late January of 1967. On January 19, Ch'en Po-ta and Chiang Ch'ing were alleged (in wall posters read by Japanese correspondents) to have criticized Hsiao Hua, Director of the General Political Department of the People's Liberation Army and long-time member of Lin Piao's entourage within the Army. Among other charges, Chiang Ch'ing was reported to have stated that "He [Hsiao Hua] looked down on the Party Central Cultural Revolution Small Group, and when he was requested to attend its conference, he did not come on the pretext that he had to meet Premier Chou for some arrangements." Ch'en Po-ta said: "Hsiao Hua seems to be a gentleman, but he is not a good soldier. Especially he possesses a strong sense of the elite. He tried to change the military led by Chairman Mao into bourgeois forces." On January 21, at 5 in the morning, Chou reportedly met with over 900 army leaders to secure withdrawal of these statements as false reports and slanders. Concerning Ch'en's statements, Chou allegedly stated that "Comrade Ch'en Po-ta did not make that statement, and also, it is not conceivable that he would do so." Apparently he did not comment on

imagine a situation in which Chou and Chiang Ch'ing would not tend to view things differently, given their widely divergent interests and supporters. It is possible that Mao attempted to manipulate the course and pace of the Cultural Revolution—emphasizing first left-wing activism and then right-wing conservatism—by modulating the relationships between Chou and Chiang Ch'ing. Lin Piao's part in these proceedings is, as usual, enigmatic.

Turning to an analysis of Chou's relations with the army and with Lin Piao personally, the major findings to report are, first, the absence of any material which would indicate conflicting goals between the two; and second, the presence of scattered (and to that extent inconclusive) references suggesting that Chou's position vis-à-vis the army in the military takeover period was not only not weakened (as we might initially suspect) but was actually strengthened. Although we will gain more insight into these matters when we consider Chou's role in the Wuhan Incident, it appears overall that Chou not only quickly molded his own actions and policies to fit the new trend but that he was also permitted at times to act as spokesman for the military. Indeed, on certain (admittedly rare) occasions he actually issued orders to military units.

At first we might think that the onset of military control would bode ill for Chou: not only would this diminish Party, and therefore state, control over events, thus fomenting even more disorder, but the army's orders to support the leftist forces would probably expedite the "seize power" struggles in the ministries and state committees. Although the evidence generally supports this proposition, this time Chou did not find himself outflanked on the left by Maoist policy and the revolutionary forces. Although he used every device he possessed to moderate and channel the revolutionary forces, he was able at the very beginning of the military takeover period to place himself (or perhaps he found himself) at the forefront of the Mao-Lin forces driving to replace Party control with military rule. This is best shown by the fact that Chou himself gave the first public indication of the new phase. In a speech on January

---

Chiang Ch'ing's charge. (Neither did he deny the fact that accusations were made; in fact, renewal of criticism of Hsiao on January 24 made clear that he was on the way out.) Misreporting (whether inadvertent or intentional) of this incident may have been involved, or perhaps Chou was covering the indiscretions of Ch'en and Chiang Ch'ing, possibly at Mao's or Lin Piao's instigation. See, inter alia, *Mainichi Shimbun*, January 20–22, 1967; *Yomiuri Shimbun*, January 21–22; *Tokyo Shimbun*, January 22 and 25; *Sankei*, January 22 (translated in *DSJP*, January 24, 1967, pp. 1–3, 16, 37, and 39).

22, Chou was reported to have announced that the People's Liberation Army would henceforth stand on the side of the revolutionaries in a new offensive to seize power.[122] What is important for our purposes is that Chou was given the opportunity to lead, not follow, the leftist trend. That he took the opportunity is evident not only in his speech of January 22 but also in a report of January 27, in which he is said to have conveyed Mao's instructions to an "expanded conference" of the Military Affairs Committee. The "instructions" authorized military intervention and over-turned policies which Chou had previously supported. Thus, for instance, it was made clear that "elderly leaders" of the Party could no longer rely on their "past merits" to retain their positions. They would have to "establish new merits" with the revolutionary forces or risk being pushed aside. And if their power was in fact seized, they should not resist but should actively assist in the transferral of authority. More importantly, revolutionaries were instructed to "seize power first" and only afterwards report the results to the State Council. This meant the end of Chou's pre-ferred "business supervision" formula and of the possibility (which later more and more came to be fact) that the day-to-day authority of the State Council ministries would diminish to the null point. The startling thing in the face of the defeat these changes meant for Chou's previous policies is the fact that it was he who reportedly conveyed them to the Military Affairs Committee, the highest political-military body in the country. Thus, his authority was preserved relatively intact from the start.[123]

These events indicate that Mao Tse-tung acted to preserve Chou's au-thority and position. It is also clear that his position within the military command structure itself was concomitantly upgraded. He attended "ex-panded conferences" of the Military Affairs Committee[124] and was re-

[122] *Nihon Keizai* and *Asahi*, January 24, 1967 (translated in *DSJP*, January 26, 1967, pp. 12 and 28). This antedated by a day the "Decision of the CCP Central Committee, the State Council, the Military Commission of the Central Committee, and the Cultural Revolution Group under the Central Committee on Resolute Sup-port for the Revolutionary Masses of the Left" in *Collection of Documents* (*Current Background*, No. 844) pp. 49–50, which was the official notification in this regard, and by two days the *Jen-min Jih-pao* editorial revealing publically the fact that the army would actively side with the rebel forces.

[123] *Tokyo Shimbun*, February 4, 1967 (translated in *DSJP*, February 4–6, 1967, p. 26).

[124] As stated above, and also on April 23. For the latter, see *Yomiuri Shimbun*, May 1, 1967 (translated in *DSJP*, May 1, 1967, p. 20). On that occasion, he also conveyed a Mao instruction.

ported in July and August to have "received" (along with other high Standing Committee and Military Affairs Committee members) army delegates attending conferences on military training and Mao study.[125] He was also reported to have defended the army and the Military Affairs Committee from attack by over-zealous Revolutionary Rebels.[126] Finally, and most important, he is reported to have actually issued orders to military units in the field. On January 29, in connection with the rapidly deteriorating situation in Sinkiang and the incipient separatist tendencies of Wang En-mao, Chou, through the State Council, "ordered the Sinkiang Military District and the production-construction corps to suspend immediately acts of hostility and to withdraw armed troops," ordered the Deputy Commander of the Sinkiang Military District, Chang Hsi-chin, to return to the area, and told Wang, the District Commander, to return to Peking for "talks" with Chou.[127] And on February 26, wall posters in Peking reported that Chou had ordered the army in Honan Province to occupy newspaper and information centers there.

While it is difficult to deduce from this evidence Chou's exact relationship with the army and with Lin Piao personally, it does seem clear that there was a high degree of coordination between them and that Chou at times performed duties which would otherwise devolve upon Lin.[128] Perhaps the most reasonable conclusion is that Lin and Chou found themselves (just as did, apparently, Chou and Chiang Ch'ing) in a relationship of mutual dependence. Chou brought his personal authority, his negotiating talents, and his energy; Lin contributed his titular authority, as Mao's chosen successor and Minister of Defense. Lin lacked what Chou possessed, while Chou needed the protection from above which only Lin could provide. Each therefore needed the other and it is

[125] *NCNA International Service,* July 7 and August 7, 1967.

[126] The Canton *Ta-fang-hsiang (Great Direction),* a Red Guard newspaper, No. 3, June 19, 1967, reported Chou as saying: "You must trust and depend on the Liberation Army, maintain the absolute prestige of the Military Control Committee, and under no circumstances can you direct the spearhead against the Military Control Committee." Translation in *JPRS* 42,977, October 16, 1967 (*Communist China Digest,* No. 190) p. 117.

[127] *Nihon Keizai,* February 1, and *Mainichi Shimbun,* February 1 and 2, 1967. Translated in *DSJP,* February 2, 1967, p. 8.

[128] It is possible that Lin was ill during this period. He was not seen in public from the late fall of 1966 to the middle spring of 1967. It is also possible that Lin considered Chou a better negotiator than himself or that Chou had a better working relationship with people like Wang En-mao than himself. In these regards, Chou could be considered Lin's "front" man.

perhaps for this reason we are unable to find any mention of discord between them.

Finally, let us examine Chou's activities during the period of military takeover and rule relating to the revolutionary organizations, principally the Revolutionary Rebels. His problem and his tactics were very similar to those which he faced and adopted when the Red Guards were first active after August 1966. It appears that his assignment was also the same: to oversee Revolutionary Rebel activities (to the extent that was possible from Peking) and to fill in the specifics missing from central Party policy directives. We shall examine two major topics. First, we shall consider some of the details of his dealings with the Revolutionary Rebels. This includes his views on the proper categorization of power-holders; how to treat those in power; the stages of takeover by the revolutionary forces; methods of revolutionary struggle from below; Revolutionary Rebel organization; and the relation of revolution to production. Second, we will concomitantly examine Chou's methods in dealing with the rebels, that is, his political "style." As we shall see, both that style and the stages of his relationship with the rebels follow his earlier pattern of relations with the Red Guards.

Looking first at Chou's views on how "power-holders" should be categorized, he saw five such groupings. First was the anti-party clique, who pursued anti-socialist and anti-Maoist policies; they stood in antagonistic contradiction to the rest of Chinese society and hence had to be ousted from office. Second were "those in authority taking the capitalist road," who persisted in their mistakes and refused to correct them; if they continued in such activities, their contradictions would become antagonistic; but if they reformed, the contradiction would presumably continue to be nonantagonistic. Third were those "generally" implementing the capitalist line, but who corrected their mistakes after criticism; their contradictions with the people were nonantagonistic. Fourth were those formerly in category three but who had now repudiated the capitalist line. Fifth were those who had made general mistakes but who could not be said to be pursuing, or to have pursued in the past, the capitalist road.[129] It is interesting that Chou chose a five-way categorization of

[129] "Party Central Comrades Talk of Power Struggle," *Hung-se Lien-lo* (*Red Liaison Paper*) February 10, 1967, p. 3 (Berkeley Collection); "Meeting with Representatives of Revolutionary Organizations of the Industry and Communication System, Premier Chou's Speech," *Hung T'ieh-tao* (*Red Railroad*), February 11, 1967,

power-holders, for it was more complex than the standard Maoist division of the opposition (which was either unitary or divided at most into two parts, equivalent to the first two of Chou's categories). By adopting a more complex division, and by basing this on Mao's own theory of contradictions, Chou evidently hoped to pave the way for more lenient treatment of most "power-holders." Thus, in meetings with the revolutionaries, he stated that "not everyone" is either a member of the "small handful" of party power-holders pursuing an anti-Maoist line or a reactionary. Some (as a matter of fact, most) were in the latter three categories and hence Maoists, if errant ones.

Chou went into great detail concerning the treatment of those in power. His purpose here, as elsewhere, seemed to be to assure the physical and bureaucratic survival of as great a percentage of the state and Party structure as was possible within the framework of a generalized purge and the Maoist political goals. His method was the same as before: to demonstrate first that he was as Maoist as the rest of the leadership group but then to detail the center's goals and methods in such a manner as to water down their extreme nature. He set forth four, and sometimes five, criteria for treating the "power-holders." "Bad elements" should be "wiped out." [130] But all others were to be considered candidates for rehabilitation of one sort or another. Some would be dismissed temporarily while undergoing criticism or reeducation, while investigation was conducted into their activities. Still others would remain at their posts but be kept under revolutionary surveillance. Finally, there were a large number of officials whose status would not change at all. Chou took pains to declare that, in his opinion, most officials belonged to this last category; indeed, most old leaders were "irrecoverable assets." The revolutionaries in any case could not physically act as ministers, although they could and should seize power. And, pursuing this logic to its end, he stated that since not all were bad elements, there was no need to seize power every-

---

reporting on a meeting of February 1 (Michigan Collection) p. 3; and "Central Leaders Talk About Power Seizure," *Yu-tien Feng-lei* (*Postal-Telegraph Thunderstorm*) (Michigan Collection) p. 4.

[130] Even they, said Chou, were not 100 percent bad. In any case, there was to be no physical liquidation. "Chairman Mao for 32 years [since 1934, when he came to power in the Chinese Communist Movement] has opposed physical liquidation." It was both sectarian and opposed to the Party's tradition. Ideological revolution and "reeducation of the soul," should be stressed. "Meeting with Representatives," *Hung T'ieh-tao, op. cit.,* note 129.

where. Although the revolutionaries obviously ignored his advice,[131] nonetheless Chou's attempt to defend his colleagues through ever-expanding criteria for dismissal, retention, criticism, and supervision of power-holders probably carried enough authority (and probably confused the revolutionaries enough) that an important segment of officials were in the long run retained in office.[132]

Chou also recognized power seizures as more complex phenomena than did the revolutionaries and to the extent that he was successful in convincing them, he was able to mitigate the extreme aspects of the struggle. Thus, Chou envisaged the takeovers as a process composed of at least three major stages, the second of which contained three substages. The first stage was physical invasion of the ministry, state office, or party committee by the People's Liberation Army and the ouster of the "bad elements, reactionaries, and capitalist-roaders" from office. This was to be followed as quickly as possible by the transfer of supervisory power from the army to the revolutionary mass organizations—the Revolutionary Rebels and the Red Guards.[133] Mass takeover would thus expand exclusive military control into a two-way alliance. But mass takeover itself was not to be a one-shot affair, in Chou's reading. The revolutionaries must first organize themselves (and Chou spent much of his time admonishing the rebels on the necessity for proper preparation). Once engaged in the actual takeover, they must decide who is to be ousted and who is to stay,

---

[131] As we have seen, the State Council lost Ministers and other high-ranking officials at a constant rate as a result of the "seize power" movement, so that in early February a reduced number of persons remained in the State Council capable of performing the necessary tasks.

[132] For Chou's remarks on how to treat those in power, see, in addition to the sources cited in note 129, the Sofia *BTA International Service* radio report of March 6, 1967. On this occasion Chou was also reported to have reintroduced the business supervision vs. requisition control formula for revolutionary power seizures: "Rebels had the right to study and exercise control over activities in the institutions but had no right to manage them. They do not have this right even in the sphere of production. 'Could you assume full responsibility if we quit the government departments?,'" he asked.

[133] Thus, in the initial stage, the revolutionary mass organizations were not, according to Chou's interpretation of Mao's directives, supposed to be involved at all in the "seize power" movement. Such an interpretation was not, of course, adhered to in a large—perhaps a majority—of cases, nor did the army, as we have seen, have clear authority to deal with problems of overt resistance. And, as we have also seen, there still remained the problem of preemptive power seizures by those in power as a device for keeping the army and the revolutionaries out and themselves in office.

presumably by utilizing the range of criteria laid out by Chou. Then they were to "supervise" the work of those who were allowed to remain in office.[134] Only at this point could the third stage—formation of the "triple alliance"—take place, as revolutionary cadres were trained to take the place of existing cadres (or existing cadres made themselves more acceptable, through self-criticism and reeducation, to their revolutionary supervisors). The triple alliance of the army, the revolutionary mass organizations, and the revolutionary cadres was thus not to be set up at once, in Chou's opinion, but was to emerge only gradually and in a planned manner. If his plan had been followed universally, it would have resulted in a far more rational and less tumultuous course of the Cultural Revolution than was actually the case. Chou probably knew that his voice would not be heeded everywhere, but he hoped his proposals might be adopted by at least some of the Revolutionary Rebel formations.[135] And if he himself concentrated his energies on the upper reaches of the State Council, then, he figured, perhaps he might save significant portions of it from certain disorganization.

Interpreting the Party center's directives on seizing political and administrative power and directing the details of Revolutionary Rebel activities, Chou had at least some chance to influence the directions and methods (if not the purposes themselves) of that stage of the Cultural Revolution. Here, his pronouncements on proper and improper methods of power struggle are important. As in previous cases, Chou apparently intended to mitigate the effects of the struggle on the state apparatus and to enhance his own power over the revolutionary ranks. In the end, he was markedly less successful in both regards than in either the Red Guard or the January Revolution periods. Nonetheless, examination of his statements on power seizure methods confirms aspects of his political style and offers insight into some of the vicissitudes of the revolutionary move-

[134] Although Chou thus attempted to reindoctrinate the "business-supervision" formula into the "seize power" movement, he was realistic enough to understand that it would not be adopted throughout the system and that in fact, it would probably be honored only in the breach. Thus, he hedged his remarks by the statement that, if the Revolutionary Rebels already possessed the requisite administrative capacity (who, if not the rebels themselves, would decide that?), mass takeover could skip the stage of business supervision.

[135] It is difficult to ascertain, on the basis of the evidence now before us, just how far beyond the proposal stage Chou's declarations on phasing takeovers went. Certainly the general direction of the Cultural Revolution during the February–August 1967 period was antithetical to Chou's preferences.

ment itself. Chou set forth what amounted to a catechism of rules for revolutionary organizations which can be summarized as follows.[136]

1. Power seizure must be from the bottom of an institution's hierarchy to the top, and not from the top down.

2. Intrarevolutionary strife must cease before power seizures can take place.

3. Power seizure must be unit by unit, and be carried out only by those inside the unit.

4. Power seizures must not be conducted in "war-preparation" units (probably signifying certain of the Machine Building Ministries and the scientific-military establishment dealing with missiles, nuclear weapons and other such matters).

5. Seizure must come only after proper preparations have been made.

6. There is no standard "seize power" formula: each problem is different and attention must therefore be paid to variations in local situations.

7. Local issues occurring in the course of seizure—such as questions of salaries, welfare, part-time workers, and contract workers—must be settled on an individual basis and without mutual recrimination.

8. All questions having to do with "seize power" matters should be communicated to the Cultural Revolution Small Group; questions having to do with "administrative" matters should be forwarded to the State

---

[136] In addition to the sources given in notes 129 and 132, the list is extracted from the following: "Premier Chou's Discussion with the Revolutionary Rebels of the Railway System," *Huo Ch'e T'ou* (*Locomotive*), February 2, 1967 (Michigan Collection), also translated in *SCMP* 3898, March 14, 1967, pp. 1–3, and in *JPRS* 41,450, June 19, 1967, *Communist China Digest*, No. 186, pp. 39–43; "Premier Chou's Speech at the Revolutionary Rebels' Oath-Taking Rally of the National Finance and Trade System," *Ts'ai-mao Hung-ch'i* (*Red Flag of Finance and Trade*), January 20, 1967 (Berkeley Collection); "Premier Chou's Important Directive Concerning Revolutionary Rebels' Liaison Committee of the Finance and Trade System," *Ts'ai-mao Hung-ch'i*, February 23, 1967 (Berkeley Collection), also translated in *SCMP* 3899, March 15, 1967, pp. 1–3; "Summary of a Conversation Between Premier Chou and Representatives of the Revolutionary Rebels in Agriculture," *Nung-lin Chan-pao* (*Combat News of Agriculture and Forestry*), February 22, 1967 (Michigan Collection); "Rally of the Scientific and Technological Front—Thoroughly Crush the New Counterattack of the Bourgeois Reactionary Line," *Ke-ming Tsao-fan Pao* (*Revolutionary Rebel News*), January 25, 1967 (Michigan Collection); and "Seize Power Oath-Taking Rally of Peking Fighters in the Science and Technology System," *K'o-chi Chan-pao* (*Science and Technology Combat News*), February 1, 1967 (Berkeley Collection).

Council (the latter group of questions included problems of economism, factionalism, and transferring decisions upwards, which would hardly seem to be administrative in character).

9. There must be "appropriate revolutionary order," that is, moderation is to be stressed and violence avoided; draggings out are prohibited, as are kangaroo courts.

10. Direct elections on the model of the Paris Commune are to be avoided.

These "rules" indicate just how far Chou's own policy departed from the practices of the Revolutionary Rebels: the negative of each rule in many instances describes the actual activities of the "seize power" groups. Clearly, Chou was swimming against the stream in his quest to protect his colleagues and to soften the extremes of the Cultural Revolution. That he publicly adopted such a stance indicates not only his serious view of the situation but confidence in his relatively invulnerable position. Both caused him to become bolder than he had been previously.

As part of his declaratory policy toward the rebels, Chou commented on organizational details as well as the preferred relationship between revolution and production. His central point was that revolutionaries should organize themselves along lines of production (much like the former trade unions, an analogy which Chou explicitly drew) so that they would be in a good position to "grasp revolution and promote production." Although local units were thus to be autonomous, they should not isolate themselves: on the one hand, Peking would send liaison personnel (although only in an advisory capacity), while on the other hand, local units should band together to form "great alliances." As in previous periods, Chou initially placed equal stress on revolution and production, but finally emphasized production as the end product and the reason for revolution. But although he understood the political necessity for revolution (and, as we stated above, probably genuinely favored power seizures in the hopes of enhanced future production), Chou obviously worried that excessive revolutionary energies would detract too much from productive work.[137] One means to lessen deleterious effects on production

---

[137] This was quite justified, as production did apparently decline, varying in direct proportion to the scale of violence in the Cultural Revolution. See, inter alia, the series of comments in the *Far Eastern Economic Review* tracing the connection. Nonetheless, it would seem that production drops due to the revolutionary dislocations were not so severe as Chou might have feared. It is hard to say how much

would be to conduct the power seizure phase in as short a time as possible. In his speech of February 10 Chou advocated just that. He seems not to have pressed the point, however, for it seemed unrealistic, given the pace and direction of developments, and it also emphasized the conduct of the revolution through an overly prescribed series of stages. He probably decided to risk a decline in production and end up with an industrial plant and a corpus of administrators relatively intact than to face a situation in which both plants had been damaged and totally inexperienced revolutionaries were wrecking what was left. As it was, Chou had to settle for half of both cakes, for production did decline, at least some plants were damaged, and a fair proportion of his administrative elite was removed from office.[138]

A final topic for consideration in connection with the period after late January is why revolutionary committees were not (with one exception) set up in the ministries and committees of the State Council. Very little material aids our investigation of this matter. What seems clear is that aside from the State Commission on Science and Technology and, under it, the Academy of Sciences,[139] revolutionary committees were not set up in any State Council organ. If that is the case, then Chou won a significant victory, for almost every ministry or commission experienced a

---

Chou's own actions mitigated the decline in production, but surely his attempt to regularize the seizure of power was not without effect.

[138] Aside from those sources mentioned above, the following are relevant to this section: "Chou En-lai Speaks at Peking Workers' Meeting," *NCNA Domestic Radio Service,* March 23, 1967; and "Speech by Premier Chou En-lai at Rally to Celebrate Inauguration of Peking Municipal Revolutionary Committee," *Jen-min Jih-pao,* April 21, 1967, translated in *SCMP* 3298, April 28, 1967, pp. 9–12, in *JPRS* 41,270, *Translations from Hung Ch'i,* No. 6 (1967) pp. 19–23, and in *JPRS* 41,450, *Communist China Digest,* No. 186 (June 19, 1967) pp. 132–134.

[139] A Revolutionary Committee in the Scientific and Technological Commission was founded sometime in the late spring of 1967. Chang Pen was the "responsible member." See "Peking Scientific, Technological Circles Condemn No. 1 Party Persons in Authority Taking Capitalist Road," *NCNA-*English, April 13, 1967 (also in *SCMP* 3920, April 17, 1967, pp. 20–22), and Chang Pen, "All Class Struggle is Political Struggle," *Jen-min Jih-pao,* May 18, 1967, p. 4. A Revolutionary Committee in the Academy of Sciences was inaugurated on July 30, 1967. See "Revolutionary Organization of 50 Units of Academy of Sciences Correctly Handle Contradictions Among the People," *Jen-min Jih-pao,* July 14, 1967 (translation in *SCMP* 3990, July 28, 1967, pp. 6–9, and in *JPRS* 42,503, *Communist China Digest,* No. 189, pp. 90–92); and "Revolutionary Committee Established at Chinese Academy of Sciences," *NCNA,* August 3, 1967 (also in *JPRS* 42,503, pp. 178–180 and broadcast over *Peking Domestic Radio,* August 2, 1967). See also *Fei-ch'ing Nien-pao, 1968 (Communist China Yearbook),* Taipei, *1968,* pp. 121–123).

seizure of power of some sort and in other cases (as in the Party, at the provincial level and lower) power seizure was always followed (albeit with some delay) by establishment of a revolutionary committee.

Some light is shed on the problem by a single Japanese correspondent's report on the alleged contents of some Peking Red Guard newspapers published at the end of March.[140] According to his rendition of the articles in question: Party committees were revived in the State Council, some as early as mid-February, with Chou's explicit authorization; the army was specifically excluded from participation in "Three-Way Alliances" within the State Council; and the ministerial level leaders were explicitly advised to remain in their posts or, if they had been ousted, to be restored to their positions. Particular ministries or commissions which had restored their Party committees, and the times, included: the Ministry of Finance (mid-February); the Central Administrative Industry and Commerce Bureau (February 21); the First Machine Building Ministry (mid-March); the Commerce Ministry (March 23); the National Commodity Price Commission (February); and the Ministry of Coal Industry (no date given).[141] While the formation of a "triple alliance" in State Council organs did not necessarily or inevitably imply subsequent emergence of revolutionary committees, one did follow the other on the Party provincial level. It is not clear, however, whether triple alliances were ever formed in State Council ministries. It may have been that military takeover (Chou's stage one) was indeed followed by Revolutionary Rebel power seizure (stage two), business supervision and selective or temporary purging of certain cadres (substages of two); but then there may have been either a replacement of stage three (Three-Way Alliances) with restoration of party committees (properly purged of "bad elements" and augmented by a modicum of revolutionary representatives) or a restoration of Party committees as small groups directing the (probably unwieldy) Three-Way Alliance. This last possibility possesses the virtue of according with the *Mainichi* report and helps us understand why revolutionary committees as such appear not to have been set up in the State Council. The Three-Way Alliances had to have executive bodies; perhaps in the State Council restored and changed Party committees per-

---

[140] *Mainichi Shimbun*, March 30, 1967 (translation in *DSJP*, April 2, p. 20). The newspapers in question were *Hsing Chün T'ung-hsün* (*Marching Army Bulletin*), *Ching Kang Shan*, and *Pei-ching Kung-she* (*Peking Commune*). These were, unfortunately, unavailable to the author during the writing of the present work.

[141] No confirmation of any of these four points has been found by the author.

formed the necessary leadership tasks which the revolutionary committees served on the provincial Party level. This would seem to have been a desirable solution from Chou's point of view. In February and March, it probably appeared to him that revolutionary violence in the country and in many State Council organs in particular might well indefinitely extend the interregnum before firm control from the top could be re-established. Restoration of Party committees would also buttress Chou's continued authority in the State Council.

Partial confirmation of this hypothesis comes from Chou's speech before proletarian revolutionaries in the Academy of Sciences in Peking on May 26. In it he suggested that revolutionaries could choose between two kinds of "three-way combination": the traditional, "horizontal" combination of the military, leading cadres, and mass organizations; or a "vertical" alliance between cadres alone—old, middle-aged, and young. Chou saw the two forms as mutually compatible—in fact he called the former really a special case of the latter, since the military and leading cadres were old and middle-aged, and the revolutionary representatives were all young, hence either could be chosen according to "concrete circumstances." [142] While Chou did not repeat this suggestion and while we cannot determine whether such vertical combinations were ever set up, they do provide a rationalization for restoring Party committees and an alternative to "horizontal" revolutionary committees, which seemed so difficult to form and to maintain unsplintered. In the same speech, Chou complained that "we have not yet established a model" of a proper "three-way combination" because of factional struggle among the revolutionaries. He specifically cited the Scientific and Technological Commission, the Railways Ministry, and the Ministry of Foreign Affairs as organs where such difficulties impeded establishment of the proper "models." If factional trouble were so widespread, then some temporary half-way house "models" on the road to revolutionary committees would have to be set up. These may have been the revived Party committees. We can surmise, of course, that Chou would not protest were such temporary expedients to take on an air of permanence, which they did.

[142] "Premier Chou's Speech," *K'o-chi Chan-pao* (*Scientific and Technological Combat News*), June 2, 1967 (reporting on a Speech of May 26, original in Michigan Collection); translated in *SCMP* 4011, August 29, 1967, pp. 1–6, and in *JPRS* 42,977, October 16, 1967 (*Communist China Digest*), No. 190, pp. 21–27.

The Wuhan Incident

The Wuhan Incident of late July 1967 represents the apex of revolutionary violence in 1967 and a turning point in the Cultural Revolution. Before July 20–24, the Maoist group seemed relatively permissive in allowing, and even instigating, clashes throughout the country between various revolutionary factions, each claiming to be more loyal than the other to Mao and the Party center. Because of the Wuhan Incident and similar outbreaks in July and August, Mao decided to moderate his course ideologically and to permit the army, for the first time since early April, to defend itself with weapons and to confiscate arms already in possession of the revolutionary forces.[143] The Wuhan Incident also represents Chou En-lai's attempts to mediate among local contending groups and to carry out (and to help form) the policy of the center toward local disturbances. A full review of the facts relating to the Wuhan Incident seems desirable, therefore, as the best available example of Chou's activities and also of the fragile nature of relations between province and center during the Cultural Revolution as a whole.[144] Our account will be a fairly straightforward chronological rendition of the Wuhan Incident, its causes and consequences, and Chou's own role.

The kidnapping on July 20 of the two Central Committee emissaries, Hsieh Fu-chih and Wang Li, by dissident worker and military units in Wuhan forms the most spectacular of the events collectively known as the Wuhan Incident. This was by no means an isolated event. Rather, it was the culmination of a long series of violent occurrences dating as far back as late 1966.[145] That more than spontaneous disorder was involved

[143] Bridgham, op. cit., pp. 27–29.

[144] A third reason for studying the Wuhan Incident in detail is that the source material is much richer than in other cases. Although we could wish for testimony and documentary material from the losing side (Ch'en Tsai-tao and the One Million Warrior organization in particular), there are available not only the usual newspaper and radio reports from Peking, but also Nationalist Chinese, Japanese correspondent, and Red Guard materials in enough abundance to enable us to make an approximate reconstruction of the actual events.

[145] Thus, from February to mid-April, 300 persons were said to have been assassinated; from April 9 to June 3, there were reportedly more than 120 armed incidents in which over 700 were killed, wounded, or disappeared; from June 4 to 15, more than 500 suffered the same sorts of fates in more than 80 armed incidents; from June 16 to 24, over 50 such incidents allegedly occurred, with 350 killed and 1500 injured; while from June 26 to 30, 8 were killed and 25 seriously injured in six

is shown by the fact that industrial workers went on strike in large numbers.[146] and that Revolutionary Rebel and Red Guard organizations were conducting internecine political struggles on a large scale.[147] If these developments were not enough in themselves to bring the situation to Peking's attention, the closing of the new railroad bridge across the Yangtze was. The bridge was closed several times: first around June 10, then on June 17, and finally from July 14 down to July 22, when troops loyal to Peking seized control back from Ch'en's forces.[148] The crisis began on July 14 with the arrival from Kunming of a high-level central investigative team, headed by Hsieh Fu-chih, vice-Premier of the State Council and newly appointed head of the Peking City Revolutionary

armed incidents. See *Sankei* (correspondent Shibata), September 29, 1967, and *Mainichi Shimbun,* July 24 and 30. Wuhan was one of the cities reportedly in turmoil during the January Revolution period.

[146] Shibata reports that from April 29 to June 3 alone, over 2400 factories and mines in the Wuhan area suspended production or dropped to less than half-capacity, and that 50,000 workers were involved in armed incidents of one sort or another. *Chinese Communist Affairs* (Taipei), Vol. 4, No. 5, p. 8, reports the figure as 500,000 workers. *Mainichi Shimbun,* on July 24 stated that Peking wall posters said the Wuhan Iron and Steel Corporation had suspended production in mid-June and that "appeal teams" had been dispatched to Peking to explain the situation.

[147] Ch'en Tsai-tao, head of the Wuhan Military Region and the villain in the July events, was said to be suppressing and arresting Revolutionary Rebel organizations as early as January. More than 300 such organizations in Hupei Province (of which Wuhan is the major city) were termed counterrevolutionary between February and mid-April, and more than 10,000 people were arrested. In March, the One Million Warriors (Ch'en's) organization arrested more than 3000 of its opponents and disbanded their organizations on the grounds that they were being manipulated by counterrevolutionaries. Not all the punishment was being meted out by the "conservative" (as later judged by Peking) organizations, however: on July 12, Revolutionary Rebels (later judged by Peking to be pro-Maoist) were said to have captured the heads of the Department of Military Operations, the Political Department, and the General Staff of the Wuhan Military Region and confiscated their "secret codebooks" for maintaining contacts between Ch'en Tsai-tao and the One Million Warriors. In early June (possibly on June 12), the One Million Warriors reportedly seized control of two large membership organizations, the San Hsin, a Red Guard composite organization, and the San Kang, a steelworkers' composite organization. As a result, the displaced leadership appealed to the Wuhan Military District and, when this was apparently rebuffed, to the central Military Affairs Committee and the Cultural Revolution Small Group. *Sankei,* September 29, 1967; *Chinese Communist Affairs, op. cit.; Facts and Features* (Taipei), Vol. 1, No. 14 (May 11, 1968); *Mainichi Shimbun,* June 30, 1967, and *Union Research Service,* "The Wuhan Incident," Vol. 48, p. 141. From June 12 on, the local army unit 8201 sided openly with the One Million Warriors.

[148] *Sankei,* September 1967; *Chinese Communist Affairs, op. cit.; Mainichi Shimbun,* July 30, 1967.

Committee, and Wang Li, then a member of Chiang Ching's Cultural Revolution Small Group and deputy editor of the Central Committee's theoretical journal, *Red Flag*.[149] They immediately met with both sides and inspected the institutions involved.

It may be appropriate to speculate why Wuhan was in such turmoil in the first place and why a series of local incidents, violent and serious as they were, turned into a full-blown mutinous challenge to the center. Unfortunately, we have no documents from the now-defeated "One Million Warrior" organization or from any of the principals at the Wuhan Military Region District Headquarters. We do have the series of accusations against them, however, and we can use them, albeit with caution, to build up an image of the attitudes of several men: Ch'en Tsai-tao; Wang Jen-chung, the former First Secretary of the Central Committee Central-South Bureau; Chung Han-hua, Second Political Commissar of the Wuhan Military District; and Niu Hai-lung, Division Commander of the 8201 Unit (the former Ninth Division of the public security forces).[150] As in other cases when events get out of hand and move in a direction which none of the contending parties initially desired, only a composite explanation composed of several elements will suffice as a first approximation. Perhaps some such elements can be identified. First, there is the obvious factor of competition between local Red Guard, Revolutionary Rebel, military, and Party units for power. Legitimacy would be established through demonstrating which was most loyal to Mao and the most zealous in carrying out the Party center's policy. This competition took place in an atmosphere, purposely created by that center, of suspicion, purge, revolution from below for its own sake, and intramural ide-

[149] The Red Guard pamphlet translated by *Union Research Service, op. cit.*, lists Yü Li-chin of the Army Cultural Revolution group as a member of the delegation. The group was accompanied by personal secretaries of the principal members and bodyguards.

[150] These speculations are derived from the following: Fang Chun-kuei, "Realities of the Wuhan 'Anti-Party Revolt,'" *Chinese Communist Affairs*, Vol. 4, No. 5 (October 1967) pp. 7–16; "The Conspicuous Wuhan Incident," *Facts and Features*, Vol. 1, No. 4 (May 1, 1967) pp. 25–28; "The Wuhan Military Incident," *Chung-yang Jih-pao (Central Daily News)*, Taipei, January 29, 1968, p. 1; "The Wuhan Incident," *Union Research Service*, Vol. 48, pp. 138–150; *Sankei*, September 29, 1967; "Public Notice of the Wuhan Military Region of the People's Liberation Army," July 26, 1967; and "Criticism of the Report on the Wuhan Cadre Question of the Central Cultural Revolution Central-South Group," August 1967, both included in *Collection of Important Documents on the Communist Bandit Great Cultural Revolution* (in Chinese), Intelligence Section of the Ministry of National Defense, Taipei, September 1968, pp. 165–169; and other sources noted below.

ological enemies and spies presumed to exist everywhere. When officially sanctioned ripping away of the established political and social institutions of society combined with the inability or unwillingness of the central military authorities to hold things together by force, it is easy to understand how anarchy at local levels accelerated.

Related to this is a second element: de facto political and military autonomy at the regional, provincial, and local levels. This independence began with the "seize power" movement early in the year and increased in scope as Peking proved either unwilling or unable to enforce its will at lower levels. De facto local autonomy, however, more and more tended to become local autonomy as a right. It is difficult to understand why such slogans as "Down with Hsieh Fu-chih," "Hang Wang Li," and "Long Live Ch'en Tsai-tao" would have been permitted by the local authorities had they not assumed, by July 20, that the autonomy which they had experienced since the beginning of the year was by now their right. On the military side, we have mentioned the April 6 Military Affairs Committee directive forbidding local army units from interfering in revolutionary activities (a directive which, incidentally, Ch'en Tsai-tao openly flouted throughout the period before July 20). Perhaps there was an additional directive, although we have no direct evidence, which in essence empowered regional military commanders to make their own arrangements for local security. It is otherwise difficult to explain why Ch'en so blatantly suppressed many of the Red Guard and Revolutionary Rebel organizations in Wuhan.

Other elements must be added to these two factors. One concerns the sociological and economic composition of the contending parties. On one side were grouped representatives of those organs and institutions which had the most to lose from a revolutionary purge from the bottom up: the military high command, the city government, the public security apparatus, the courts, and the senior workers. Thus, the One Million Warriors organization was allegedly composed of workers *and employers,* government cadres, and militia, while the Kung Chien Fa organization consisted of cadres in the public security apparatus, the procuracy, and the courts (the Chinese characters abbreviated the three organizations comprising this organizaton). It seems probable that a majority of the workers in the tri-city were members of the One Million Warriors: not only did the other side consist mostly of nonworkers (in an industrial city, they must have therefore been in the minority), but the workers probably knew that widespread imposition of the Maoist economic program would lead both to a new "Leap Forward" syndrome in the economy, with its at-tendant emphasis on ideological and coercive incentives (not economic ones) and to interruptions in production which could only lower their material gains. At the military level, the leadership seems to have been composed of those who operated both at a high level and who had been in their posts for a long period of time.[151] Attacks against the "small handful of party power-holders pursuing the capitalist road," now asso-ciated with Liu Shao-ch'i, "China's Khrushchev," could only be directed against them.

On the other side were ranged a much younger group, composed mostly of Red Guards (students) and some workers. Thus, the San Kang was an organization of workers at the Wuhan Iron and Steel Company, the San Hsin was made up of university Red Guard organizations, and the San Lien was composed of representatives of middle-school Red Guards in Wuhan. These appear to have been supported by outside Red Guard forces sent from Peking, such as the Southbound Revolutionary Rebel Brigade of the Capital, the Wuhan Liaison Center of the East-Is-Red General Command of the Peking Mining and Industrial College, and the Red Flag Warriors Ching Kang Shan of the Peking Aviation College. Although they numbered over 400,000, these Red Guard groups were definitely in the minority. They had nothing to lose and everything to gain from Peking-sponsored revolution from below. Away from the center of power, however, local revolutionary groups found that minority-based power seizure from the bottom up was difficult, if not impossible; that the chief product of their efforts was to unite the majority against them; that they risked and often suffered disastrous defeat; and that, therefore, the only recourse was to appeal to Peking for even more sup-port. As Wuhan shows, that support could come only when the strength of the opposing forces had grown to extreme proportions.

A fourth element, akin to the differences in composition of the dispu-tants and to the problem of relative autonomy, concerns the question of the allegedly overt nature of the opposition to the Peking regime. The official Maoist line, of course, was that anyone perceived to be in opposi-

---

[151] Thus, Ch'en Tsai-tao had held positions in the Central-South area for over a decade, while his deputies, Yang Hsiu-shan, Yao Che, Tang Chin-lung, and Niu Hai-lung, had been there since the early 1960s, as had Chung Han-hua, Second Political Commissar of the Wuhan Military Region. Wang Jen-chung, the leading political figure in the area and, according to Peking's later allegations, one of those back of Ch'en Tsai-tao, was not only a native of the region (although not of Wuhan itself) but also had held posts in the Central-South area since 1949.

tion to the policy line was ipso facto a member of an organized faction
within the Party "taking the capitalist path," and adhering to the leadership provided by Liu Shao-ch'i and his close associates. Thus, Ch'en Tsai-
tao, Wang Jen-chung, and their cohorts were quickly branded (after July
20, to be sure) as the "agents in Wuhan of China's Khrushchev." While
little credence should probably be given to this thesis (no confirming
evidence is at hand and its self-serving purposes are clear), two variants,
one less and the other more likely, are of greater interest. One is the Ho
Lung thesis. Its essence is that throughout Chinese Communist history and
especially since 1949, there has been a kind of regionalism among "Field
Army systems," that there has been surprisingly little movement from one
such system to another, that each system has developed intrasystemic
loyalties, that the Peking regime has ruled the country partly through
these systems and over the systems themselves by perpetuating the balance
among them established in 1949, and that each system can be identified
with a particular senior-level military figure. Thus, in the Wuhan Military Region, Liu Po-ch'eng was the person in question, and the Second
Field Army system was in control.[152] This would seem to indicate no
particular problems, since Ho Lung's First Field Army system is located
for the most part in Northwest China and not in the Wuhan Military
District. But, so the argument goes, Ho Lung did attempt a coup d'etat
against Peking in February 1966, which, after it was quashed, set the
Maoist leadership on edge, looking for remnants of Ho's co-conspirators
around the country. In Wuhan significant elements were in fact loyal to
Ho and may have played a part in helping him (or his unnamed successors) take revenge on Peking. Thus, the division-size 8201 Unit, which
formed the principal force in Wuhan opposing Peking on July 20 and
after, was said to be a Ho Lung outfit, and Yang Hsiu-shan, Yao Che,
and Tang Chin-lung, Ch'en Tsai-tao's subordinates, were said to be Ho's
men.[153] Ch'en himself might be listed tentatively as one of Ho's men, since
he first was a member of Hsu Hsiang-ch'ien's original Fourth Front
Army in 1931, which later was led by Ho.[154] Even though Ch'en may not

[152] For an elaboration of this thesis, long held to be true by Nationalist Chinese
military scholars, see William Whitson, "The Field Army in Chinese Communist
Military Politics," The China Quarterly, No. 37 (January–March 1969) pp. 1–30.

[153] Fang Chun-kuei, "Realities," op. cit., pp. 14–15.

[154] Ch'en later became a Regiment Commander of Lin Piao's 115th Division, which
marked him as a Lin Piao man. Since then he generally was regarded as one of Lin's
entourage. We shall discuss this variant of the conspiratorial thesis below.

have intended to side with Ho Lung's "group," Peking may have imagined such a conspiracy, given the history of the rebelling units and their leaders.[155] Local leaders, knowing this conspiratorial predisposition upon the part of the political center, may have reacted over-defensively.[156]

A more likely variant of this thesis is that Ch'en Tsai-tao was in fact a "Lin Piao man," that he was trusted by Lin and had done Lin's bidding for many years. Hence, Lin possibly felt that the situation in Wuhan was initially in good hands (thus he did not interfere when Ch'en began repressing local Red Guard groups in the first half of 1967, or at least he did not immediately question Ch'en's loyalty); and Ch'en thought he had a relatively free hand throughout the Wuhan Military District to do as he wished. Possibly Ch'en felt that if worst came to worst, he could deal with Lin directly and personally instead of through such State Council–Cultural Revolution Small Group emissaries as Hsieh and Wang. Hence he elected to question both their credentials and the veracity of their charges.

While some or all of the above factors may hold some truth, it is impossible to explain the Wuhan events without a final factor, a combination of fatalism and the human propensity to misinterpret the signals of others. Both center and locality worked themselves into corners, as we shall see, from which they found it difficult to extricate themselves. Thus, for instance, Ch'en Tsai-tao and Wang Jen-chung by July 20 had invested too much in their support of the One Million Warriors and their repression of the Peking-oriented Red Guard and Revolutionary Rebel organizations. They could scarcely retreat gracefully before Chou's four-point order read out by Hsieh and Wang. Ch'en had to prove he was right and thus had no choice but to impugn the credentials of the central emissaries and appeal over their heads to Lin and Mao. Peking then learned that two of their chosen representatives were being held captive by a local military man who showed all signs of pursuing the old warlord style of politics. Finding also that a direct slap in the face had been given to Chou himself, and that military units were in direct mutiny, Peking probably felt it had no choice but to intervene militarily to make an example

[155] The Peking correspondent of *Yomiuri Shimbun* copied a Red Guard poster of January 20, 1967, of the Tsing Hua University, purporting to list the organization chart of the Ho Lung Group.

[156] As for Niu Hai-lung, the 8201 Unit Commander who reacted so emotionally to Hsieh Fu-chih's and Wang Li's presence, no information seems to be available.

of that sort of behavior. With communications broken and lines of combat drawn tight, the battle began in earnest and continued to the very end.

Having thus attempted to present a range of explanations for the outbreak of the Wuhan Incident, let us examine the actual train of events and Chou En-lai's role. As we have stated, Hsieh Fu-chih and Wang Li arrived in Wuhan on July 14, on the continuation of an investigative mission which had already taken them to Chengtu, Chungking, and Honan Province.[157] Chou En-lai was already in Wuhan, "settling armed disputes."[158] On July 14 Chou spoke at the Headquarters of the Wuhan Military District and outlined in four points his terms of settlement: (1) The San Kang and San Hsin are the "correct" (Maoist-approved) Revolutionary Rebel and Red Guard organizations; (2) The Military District (Ch'en Tsai-tao) was mistaken, in both direction and line, in supporting the One Million Warrior organization; (3) The General Workers Council Headquarters (the leadership of the San Kang, San Hsin, and San Lien) "must have its honor restored"; (4) The One Million Warriors is a conservative organization and the San-Szu (an organization of three workers' groups) tends to be conservative.[159]

Chou departed for Peking, leaving Hsieh and Wang to iron out the details. The two emissaries immediately called on both sides of the dispute, but did not hide their sympathies for the Red Guard and Revolutionary Rebel minority. They encouraged the local Red Guards at Hupei University, expressed support for the San Kang, San Hsin, and San Lien, and wanted to "reverse the verdict" in the so-called Kung Cheng case (a Revolutionary Rebel headquarters in Wuhan disbanded by Ch'en).[160] Ch'en Tsai-tao reportedly became angry at this (he probably thought Hsieh and Wang had prejudged the situation) and threatened to have the One Million Warriors cut off water, transit, and power in the city if the Kung Cheng case were indeed reversed. As if to demonstrate what

[157] *Mainichi Shimbun*, July 30, 1967. This report had them arriving on July 16. However, all other sources agree that it was July 14.

[158] *Sankei*, September 29, 1967.

[159] *Sankei*, September 29, 1967, and *Union Research Service, op. cit.*, p. 142. The latter source reports that Yang Ch'eng-wu, then acting Chief of the General Staff of the Army and other leading Central officials also delivered reports at the Regional Headquarters. Ch'en, confronted with this array of authority, was reported to have said; "We will carry out your instructions [as] if they were signed by Chairman Mao personally."

[160] *Sankei*, September 29, 1967; *Facts and Features, op. cit.*, p. 7; and *Chinese Communist Affairs, op. cit.*, p. 26.

power he held over the fate of noncooperating Red Guards, Ch'en reportedly supported a sanguinary suppression of the Ninth Rebel Commune by the One Million Warriors.[161]

Hsieh and Wang spent the next few days, from July 15 to July 18, inspecting the situation and expressing their support for the "pro-Maoist" groups.[162] Tension in the city was apparently rising, however, for during demonstrations on July 15 by rebel factions welcoming Hsieh and Wang, the One Million Warriors carried out an ambush, throwing stones, surrounding and beating up Red Guards of the Central China Technical College. Eight were allegedly killed and "scores" injured.[163]

By July 19, Hsieh and Wang had evidently seen enough to arrive at some conclusions. Chou apparently approved their report and authorized them to read out the verdict to both sides. After meeting with the rebel factions, they called a meeting in the evening at the Military District Headquarters, to be attended by all top leaders in the area. The gist of the report was essentially equivalent to Chou's earlier four-point statement: The Military District was mistaken, the One Million Warriors was indeed a "conservative" organization, the Kung Cheng case must in fact be reversed, and the "three commands" (San Lien, San Hsin, and San Kang) were to be recognized as genuine revolutionary rebel groups.[164] At this point, Niu Hai-lung, Commander of the 8201 Division, became incensed, jumped up, announced his opposition to the four points, shouted "I am prepared to risk my life!," and stormed out of the meeting. Together with Ch'en Tsai-tao and the local party secretaries of the Tung Hu district of Wuhan, Niu mobilized his troops and a large number of the One Million Warriors, converged on the Tung Hu Hotel to where Hsieh and Wang had now returned, and at 9:00 P.M. laid siege to the building. By about 1:00 A.M. the district was sealed off and soldiers of the 8201

---

[161] *Sankei,* July 18, 1967.

[162] Thus, on July 15 they met representatives of the Central China Technical College, presenting arm bands and badges; paid three separate visits to the Wuhan Iron and Steel Company Second Command on July 15, 16, and 17; met on July 17 with leaders of the Workers General Council and the September 13 Red Guard group; and on July 18 met "until night" with various rebel organizations. They also participated in street demonstrations by the rebel organizations and witnessed a swim in the Yangtze of several thousand Red Guards celebrating the first anniversary of Mao's own natatory feat.

[163] *Sankei,* September 29, 1967.

[164] *Sankei,* July 20 and September 29; *Mainichi Shimbun,* July 30, 1967; *Union Research Service, op. cit.; Facts and Features, op. cit.;* and *Chinese Communist Affairs, op. cit.*

were patrolling the streets and had placed machine guns on buildings.[165]

At this point, Ch'en Tsai-tao showed up at the hotel, confronted Hsieh and Wang, and said that the workers were now beyond his own control, that there was nothing that he could do for them, and that they would have to cope with the workers as best they could. Although Hsieh and Wang apparently tried to reason with the workers, the latter, together with Niu's troops, stormed the hotel, broke into the rooms where the two were staying (overpowering their bodyguards and reportedly stabbing to death Hsieh's personal secretary), separated Hsieh from Wang, tied up Wang, and proceeded to kick and beat him. Wang was then taken to the District Military Headquarters and subjected to further manhandling until 3:00 P.M. the next afternoon. He was bruised, one eye was said to be swollen, at one point a clump of his hair was pulled out, and his left leg broken. Hsieh himself was also said to have been beaten, but only initially in his hotel room. Hsieh tried to rescue Wang from his captors but when that proved to be impossible, he reportedly ran away toward the Hydroelectric Institute, pursued by workers armed with swords and spears. But when he heard that Wang had been taken to Military Headquarters, he elected to go there, where he was immediately placed under guard, together with Wang, who had been returned in a car.[166]

In the city itself, the One Million Warriors and the 8201 Unit were in full control. They replaced the regular guards at the District Military Headquarters, sealed off the area, blocked traffic from the bridges over the Yangtze and the Han Rivers (thus isolating the opposition in the three portions of the tri-city), seized the railway stations, the radio station, and the airport, and garrisoned strong points throughout the city. The workers organization proceeded to carry out forays against the Red Guards, set fire to schools, and to kill and injure those who chose to oppose them. The proceedings in Wuhan reportedly affected the surrounding areas, where demonstrations against Chou, Hsieh, and Wang, and in favor of Ch'en, were held in a number of rural towns. In order to justify these actions, the One Million Warriors, the Third Headquarters, and

[165] Reportedly Ch'en had at his disposal in the local area more than 400 trucks, 30 fire engines, and many motorcycles and armored cars. The men of the 8201 Division put on the armbands of the One Million Warriors to show their solidarity.

[166] This is a composite rendition of the principal sources noted above, with the addition of "The Appalling July Mutiny," Wuhan, *Kang-erh-szu*, Huichow edition, No. 38 (August 22, 1967) (translated in *JPRS* 44,241, February 5, 1968, *Communist China Digest*, No. 194, p. 124).

the 8201 Unit issued an "urgent notice" claiming: that the Kung Cheng organization was a counterrevolutionary group which must be destroyed; that the Revolutionary Rebel Workers General Headquarters, the Second Command, and the San Hsin groups must be suppressed; that the One Million Warriors was itself a genuine revolutionary organization; and that their actions were taken for the purpose of holding high the banner of Mao's thought.[167]

News of these events evidently first reached Peking shortly after Wang and Hsieh were abducted (sometime after 4:30 A.M.). Reaction was immediate. On the one hand, the Military Affairs Committee, through Yang Ch'eng-wu, took immediate action. The Committee reportedly ordered Ch'en to release Hsieh and Wang and to escort them to Peking; condemned the actions of the 8201 Unit; ordered the 8191 Airborne Division (already in the Wuhan area) and the Fifteenth Army from Hsiao Kan (Hupei Province) into action against Ch'en's forces; and dispatched five gunboats of the East Sea Fleet up the river to Wuhan.[168] From this point forward, what had been a political dispute with military overtones became a direct military confrontation between center and region. On the other hand, Chou himself left Peking by plane for Wuhan, apparently as part of Peking's plan to bring Hsieh, Wang, and Ch'en back to the capital. Two planes were said to have flown toward Wuhan, one carrying Chou and the other for the purpose of taking back Hsieh and Wang. Ch'en apparently knew of Chou's imminent arrival (probably as a part of the Military Affairs Committee order communicated to him), and proceeded to surround the Wuhan airport with truckloads full of One Million Warrior workers. But Chou, "in top secrecy" contacted the Air Force in Wuhan, which, being loyal to Peking and not to Ch'en, informed Chou of the plan to possibly kidnap him also. The landing place was therefore changed, and Chou's planes set down at another airport south of the city, thus foiling Ch'en's plans. Immediately upon arriving, Chou ordered the Military District to release Wang.

Meanwhile, Hsieh and Wang had been trying to arrange for their release. They talked their guards into coming over to their side, and the Political Commissar of the 8201 Division, seeing this and confronted with

[167] *Facts and Features, op. cit.,* p. 27, and *Union Research Service, op. cit.,* p. 147. The latter source claims that the declaration was issued on July 21 and, in fact, there may have been more than one such statement. We have treated them as if they were only one document, since we lack further information.

[168] *Chinese Communist Affairs, op. cit.,* p. 9; *Union Research Service,* p. 148; *Sankei,* September 29, 1967.

Chou's orders, agreed to move Wang away from the Military Headquarters and the One Million Warriors to Lochiashan, outside the
city. The Warriors evidently discovered that Wang had been moved and
gave chase, with the result that Wang and the Division Political Commissar reportedly spent the night of July 20–21 in the mountains around
Lochiashan. On the morning of July 21, Wang successfully reached
Chou's airport. Hsieh Fu-chih apparently reached the airport independently of Wang. Seeing that his two colleagues were safe (the airport was
probably by now garrisoned by the intervening army troops), Chou flew
back to Peking to arrange their reception. Hsieh and Wang flew back
early on July 22.[169] Thus ended the kidnapping episode.

The military phase, however, was about to begin. Our major concern,
aside from relating the course of the struggle, is to establish the duration
of local resistance. On the basis of the sources at hand, it would seem
that the One Million Warriors and the 8201 Unit resisted much longer
than had previously been thought. There certainly was some resistance
as late as the first week in August, for the insurgents had enough strength
to stage a counterattack at that time before finally being beaten down.
Government operations began, as we have noted, as soon as Peking received notification of Niu Hai-lung's and Ch'en Tsai-tao's insubordination. Lin Piao evidently considered the situation serious enough for him
to fly to the scene of action, arriving in the area on the 21st and reporting
on the situation to the loyalist forces there.[170] Lin then apparently put
Yü Li-chin, Political Commissar of the Air Force, in command of the
operation, and with Liu Feng, Deputy Commander of the Air Force
and leader of the 8190 Airborne Division, he proceeded to invest the city.
Participating, aside from the 8190, were the 8199 Unit (possibly another
airborne division), the Fifteenth Army (which, if fully activated, could
have included as many as six divisions), and vessels from the East Sea
Fleet (reportedly numbering from five to a dozen vessels).[171] The airborne divisions apparently were used because they could be brought to

[169] *Sankei*, September 29, 1967, and *Chinese Communist Affairs, op. cit.*, p. 9. It
is not clear whether at this time Ch'en also returned to Peking. He was definitely
in the city from July 26 on, and there is no report of his presence in Wuhan from
July 20 on.

[170] *Union Research Service, op. cit.*, p. 149; *Mainichi Shimbun*, July 20, 1967.

[171] *Union Research Service, op. cit.*, p. 148; *Mainichi Shimbun*, July 30, 1967;
Chinese Communist Affairs, op. cit., p. 9; *Sankei*, September 29, 1967. It is not
clear whether one or two airborne divisions were used: some sources may have confused the 8199 and the 8190.

the scene rapidly, while the ships and the Fifteenth Army would have to enter the fray later, given their slower modes of transport.

Sources disagree as to when the loyalist forces actually first invested Wuhan; some say as early as July 21 (which would be consistent with Hsieh Fu-chih's and Wang Li's safe getaway to Peking),[172] others as late as July 24. Probably they arrived at different times and were thrown into action differentially. In any case, paratroops of the 8191 Unit seized the Yangtze Bridge, entered the city, and liberated the communication facilities from rebel hands, disarming the One Million Warriors as they proceeded. Other troops were said to parachute down upon the Central China Technical College and Hupei University. By July 24 large portions of the city were apparently under governmental control: 8199 Unit personnel protected the Red Guard and Revolutionary Rebel units loyal to Peking[173] and the fleet by this time had trained its guns on the rebel-held portion of the town.

Our sources also tend to contradict each other as to when military operations ceased. On the one hand, the correspondent Shibata, writing later in *Sankei,* says: "The 8201 Independent Division, when faced with overwhelming military strength, hardly put up any resistance, and was quickly disarmed. The "conservative" One Million Warriors organization was also disarmed in about 12 hours. Weapons seized from the One Million Warriors organization filled 30 trucks. The leaders and ringleaders of the 8201 Division and the One Million Warriors organization . . . were arrested one after the other and were taken to Peking." On July 26 the Wuhan Military Region command, now apparently reconstituted to suit Peking, issued a "public notice" admitting its past sins and pledging to be good in the future.[174]

[172] Peking wall posters on July 21 were quoted as saying that the 19th army division rescued Wang Li on that day.

[173] Including the Headquarters of the Wuhan Iron and Steel Company Second Command, the Wuhan Academy of Water Conservation and Electric Power, the new Wuhan University, the Red Wuhan Academy of Surveying and Cartography, the New Wuhan Academy of Technology, and the New Central China Academy of Technology, in addition to the two institutions already noted. *Union Research Service, op. cit.,* p. 148.

[174] The public notice was essentially the Military Headquarters' assent to Chou's four points enunciated on July 14 and, through Wang Li, again on July 19. It said, in part: (1) we are resolutely determined to draw a clear line between Ch'en Tsai-tao and ourselves and to beat him down; (2) our cadres have committed mistakes in orientation and line; (3) we shall allow the Workers' General Headquarters to restore its name and reputation, support its revolutionary activities, and actively help it restore its great revolutionary column; (4) we will resolutely support the

On the other hand, there is much evidence, both direct and indirect, to indicate that the battle was hardly over. Careful reading of the documents indicates that some level of conflict continued until at least August 4, a half a month after the rebellion first began. While it is probably true that the loyalist army forces deliberately eschewed using all the force at their disposal in order to hold down casualties, it also seems to be the case that most of the Wuhan population continued until a very late date to side with the insurgents. A rundown of the evidence may support this conclusion. On July 24, the New China News Agency (NCNA) announced that only some of the masses who had participated in the "conservative" organizations had withdrawn from them by July 23. The Red Guard pamphlet of August 1 (translated by *Union Research Service* and referred to above) stated that "Wuhan's Old T'an" (Ch'en Tsai-tao, the reference being to T'an Chen-lin, who by now was regarded as an arch-revisionist) and the One Million Warriors on July 23 "hastily built up defenses to fight the People's Liberation Army in further resistance." On July 26, NCNA, reporting a *Chieh-fang-chün Pao* editorial, admitted that the One Million Warriors still disposed of considerable strength, that rumors of their activities had enhanced their popularity, and that some in the army were still siding with the rebels. The *People's Daily* on the same day indirectly admitted that the rumors (whatever their nature) spread by the insurgents were effective and stated that "the masses who were once hoodwinked will certainly awake and . . . rise up and rebel," while speakers at mammoth rallies in Peking the previous day held out the hope that the insurgent leadership in Wuhan "will be overthrown," that the masses "will come to their senses," and that the army "will score a victory." [175]

On July 27, the four top political organs—the Central Committee, the State Council, the Military Affairs Committee, and the Cultural Revolution Small Group (which is to say, Mao, Chou, Lin, and Chiang Ch'ing)—found it necessary to address a public letter to the "broad masses of PLA commanders and fighters of Wuhan," expressing support in the struggle, calling for overthrow of the insurgents, requesting that

---

proletarian revolutionary rebels of the Headquarters of Steelworkers, the Second Command of the Steelworkers, the 13 September Group of Steelworkers, the Revolutionary United Command of the Third Command, the New China Engineering College, New Hupei University, and the New China Agricultural College. Text in *Collection of Important Documents, op. cit.,* pp. 155–157; summarized in *Chinese Communist Affairs, op. cit.,* pp. 11–12, and on *NCNA Domestic Service,* July 28, 1967.
[175] *NCNA,* July 25, 1967.

the army attempt to integrate itself more closely with the population ("support the army and cherish the people"), and outlawing revenge upon the "hoodwinked" former members of the opposition who had either come over to the government side or who had been captured by them.[176] And while the August Red Guard pamphlet stated that by July 27 one thousand members of the 8201 Unit had come over to the government side, on the same day the East China Sea Fleet was still at Wuhan and found it necessary to send out a "request" to the One Million Warriors to lay down their arms.[177] A *Jen-min Jih-pao* editorial on July 28 stated that "a hard struggle" had been waged "in the last few days," but that while the enemy was isolated politically, he was not reconciled to defeat and was "stubbornly resisting, creating rumors, and trying new tricks." The *Chieh-fang-chün Pao,* too, admitted that the battle was still going on, that it was just then "at the critical juncture," and that although the "hoodwinked masses" of the One Million Warriors were rapidly awakening and withdrawing "in groups," nonetheless the insurgent leadership was persisting in the resistance, and was still "suppressing, terrorizing, cheating, deceiving, coercing, and poisoning the masses."[178] It is difficult on the basis of official Peking sources alone to decisively conclude that fierce and bloody battles were being fought each of these days in Wuhan. It does seem clear, however, that even if the level of violence varied from day to day and even if the government forces were deliberately scaling down their activities to avoid casualties and destruction, the majority of the local population still held out against the investing forces, while, for their part, the local Maoists tended to wreak retribution upon those who came over to their side. It is otherwise difficult to explain Peking's constant preoccupation with hopes that the still-deceived masses would come back and with warnings that returnees must be given another chance.[179]

[176] *Chinese Communist Affairs, op. cit.,* p. 13. Essentially the same message was contained in two editorials of *Chieh-fang-chün Pao* of the same day (as reported by *Peking Domestic Service* and *NCNA*), the second of which stated, in part, that "the proletarian revolutionaries *will* be able to win victory in Wuhan." "The hoodwinked masses *will surely* come to their senses." [Emphasis added.]

[177] *Tokyo Shimbun,* August 4, 1967.

[178] Substantially the same set of comments was contained in an *NCNA* dispatch the same day.

[179] For instance, the *Chieh-fang-chün Pao,* cited above, said: "For some who have taken the wrong path because of an inadequate understanding of the struggle . . . it will be difficult to make an about-face suddenly. Others may worry about the masses not trusting them. . . . We should carry out penetrating and delicate polit-

It seems clear that some sort of talk-while-fighting situation had emerged by July 28. Each side had something with which to hurt the other: the insurgents could hold out the threat of a permanently alienated population, a city and its industry ruined, and high casualties on both sides; the loyalists could point to the prospect of certain victory for their side, as well as high casualties. It is probable that the insurgents hoped for a negotiated, forgive-and-forget solution, while the loyalists hoped that the passage of time, the preponderance of forces against them, and their propaganda would combine to gradually drive rebel leader and follower apart, isolating the former. It also seems clear, however, that Peking succeeded only slowly and with difficulty in having its way. A review of the evidence may support these conclusions. On July 29, Peking media spoke of the struggle "moving into a new stage" and "laying out battlefields along both banks of the Yangtze, and in urban and rural areas." [180] At the same time, Peking admitted to "mistakes" and "shortcomings" because of "lack of experience" and "because the revolution under the proletarian dictatorship is not well understood." This obviously indicates both that the military battle was far from won, that the local population was not convinced by Peking's blandishments, and that the leftists had mistreated those who had already chosen to surrender. The two sides were obviously facing each other at gunpoint; thus, Peking could only hope that "so soon as the hoodwinked make close contact" with the revolutionaries, they will come together ideologically, and it could only declare that the "struggle is still very arduous."

As for the "agents in Wuhan of China's Khrushchev" (as they were now called), they were resorting to desperate and not totally unsuccessful tactics. They were said to resort to "kid glove tactics" (negotiations?), "disintegrating the ranks of the revolutionary front" (gaining adherents or dividing the leftists?), "scheming, creating rumors, and provoking misunderstandings." That they were achieving some success is shown by Peking's admission that "it is only normal for various differences or contradictions to exist among the various revolutionary mass organizations during the struggle." [181] A change in the situation seems to have come

---

ical and ideological work among hoodwinked masses. . . . The enemies are not yet completely destroyed; they are still putting up a desperate struggle. The proletarian revolutionaries should be united more properly in order to concentrate their efforts in hitting hard at the enemy."

[180] *NCNA; Jen-min Jih-pao* editorial; and *Chieh-fang-chün Pao* editorial, for that day.

[181] Editorial in *Jen-min Jih-pao*, July 30, 1967.

about just at that time, however, for Peking's line suddenly turned much harder. A *Red Flag* editorial of that same day stressed punishment of the criminals, and stated that the "handful . . . have been dragged out" and the "conspiracy . . . has been frustrated." The *Chieh-fang-chün Pao* stated that the One Million Warrior organization "is rapidly disintegrating" and that the hoodwinked masses had in fact hit back and come over to the Maoist side. A second editorial in the same newspaper on the same day, moreover, said that the proletarian revolutionaries "have" achieved victory because at the crucial moment the army and the masses coalesced. That the battle was indeed a military one is indicated by two different sources. On the one hand, a Singapore report quoting travelers to Hong Kong stated that thousands of refugees from Wuhan were flooding into Canton, crowding the streets and railway stations, and causing a breakdown in train service. Service to Hong Kong was disrupted as refugees attempted to board trains but were pulled off by soldiers. On the other hand, the General Command of the Proletarian Revolutionaries in Wuhan issued an "urgent notice" stating that the "evil chieftains" in the local party and military had caused the One Million Warriors and the Kung Chien Fa organizations to launch a "frenzied counterattack" against the leftists. The latter, however, had "defeated" the attack, with the assistance of the army. Further, a joint letter (not released to the public) was said to have been sent to the local Maoists by the Central Committee, the State Council, the Military Affairs Committee, and the Cultural Revolution Group, giving "important instructions," and the letter was stated to have been received just at the "victorious conclusion" of the battle.[182] Finally, from this point forward, the slogan "grasp revolution and promote production" reappears in official propaganda. This would seem to indicate that the loyalists were back in control of at least some portions of the city which contained industrial plants.[183]

Even then, however, things were not yet finished. Peking publicly

[182] *NCNA Domestic Service,* August 1, 1967, and *Jen-min Jih-pao* editorial, August 2, 1967.

[183] This slogan, which we have generally associated with Chou En-lai, is the first indication that Chou was still involved with the local situation (aside from fact that he signed the State Council letters to Wuhan). A further indication, however, comes from the wording of one of the sentences of the Wuhan "urgent notice": If the insurgent leaders would not return of their own volition to the fold, then they were to be punished "according to law and with the active assistance of the departments concerned." The relative moderation in tone of this phrase, together with the obscurity of language, seems to indicate Chou's hand.

reverted to the same July phraseology. The proletarian revolutionaries and the army in Wuhan were now said to be united and "*are becoming braver as they fight,*" while the "hoodwinked masses *are awakening* and turning their spear around" (emphasis added). Although the situation was said to be "steadily improving," the opposition was still pictured as capable of spreading rumors, smearing the loyalists, causing dissension among the revolutionaries, and causing misunderstandings to arise between the army and the people.[184] A *Hupei Jih-pao* editorial of August 3 (quoted by NCNA Domestic Service), stated that the One Million Warriors "are collapsing," that the revolutionaries in Wuhan "*will* gain their victory today," (emphasis added) that the "small handful have yet to be totally dragged down and thoroughly discredited" and that they "are still resisting stubbornly and playing tricks." The editorial went on to stress that "at this critical juncture, even the slightest display of arrogance or complacency would result in an unrecoverable loss to us." While the meaning of the last phrase is unclear, the *Chieh-fang-chün Pao Daily* on the same day did speak of the possibility that there was sabotage of production in Wuhan. Apparently, some of the One Million Warriors who had been put back to work by the Maoists were not reconciled to their fate and were taking revenge upon the leftists through this means.

By August 4, however, the situation began to improve as far as the Peking-oriented revolutionaries were concerned. While the *Jen-min Jih-pao* the day before had spoken of covert and malicious tactics used by the "handful" to divide the people from the army, and while NCNA on August 4 also referred to such devices as "creating confusion, dispatching fire engines, tailing and surveillance," Peking also revealed that the Kung Chien Fa "in the past few days" began to "turn around . . . and are now returning . . . resolutely and in great numbers." The revolutionary forces were also said to broaden their numbers "day after day" and the "conservative and reactionary forces" were reportedly disintegrating. As an indicator of the trend (even then it could be called no more than that), the New China Engineering College, at Tsao Yang San, outside of Wuhan, formed a revolutionary committee, the first such in Hupei Province.[185] On August 8, a *People's Daily* article said that the "handful of

[184] *Chieh-Fang-chün Pao* as reported by *Peking Domestic Service*. The same source stressed the *emerging* unity between army and people.

[185] *Wuhan City Service,* August 5, 1967. At the rally Tseng Szu-yü, newly appointed Commander of the People's Liberation Army in the Wuhan Military Region, replacing Ch'en Tsai-tao; Liu Feng, Political Commissar of the PLA in Wuhan; another new appointee; and Chang Ching, Commander of the 9199 Unit, spoke.

class enemies" (which is what they had by now become) had been "completely wiped out" and that the proletariat had "swept away the dark clouds over Wuhan."[186] It remained for Mao himself to pronounce, reportedly, around August 21 that the situation in Wuhan was "settled."[187]

Meanwhile, in Peking the central authorities had taken steps to restore popular confidence in Mao's authority to deal with such regional rebellions as Wuhan, to punish the culprits for their crimes, and to replace the discredited local leadership with people of unquestioned loyalty. Mao attempted to attain the first goal by rolling out the red carpet for the return of the kidnapped officials, Hsieh and Wang, and by following this up with an ostentatious display of public support for the Wuhan loyalists through massive demonstrations. Chou En-lai was put in charge of the first phase of the campaign. He had returned on July 21 to make arrangements for the return of the two, who arrived in Peking in the second plane on the evening of July 22. Chou led the delegation, which included, among others, Ch'en Po-ta, Chiang Ch'ing, and K'ang Sheng, to the airport. Large-scale demonstrations were scheduled along the route into the city.[188] Mammoth demonstrations celebrating the return of the two continued all the next day and soon turned into rallies supporting the local Maoists in Wuhan.[189] These demonstrations reached their peak on the afternoon of July 25, when one million persons were said to

[186] That article, by Jen Li-hsin, contained the most complete catalogue of methods alleged to be used by the Wuhan insurgents: beating, smashing, looting, confiscating, making arrests, attacking revolutionaries, assaulting mass revolutionary organizations, sabotaging the proletarian dictatorship and extensive democracy under it, sabotaging production, fabricating rumors, hoodwinking the masses, stepping "out before the masses collectively," and "stepping out before the masses with signatures." Although this list was set forth for purposes of vilifying the now-defeated insurgent leadership, its contents reveal both the mass character and the popular nature of the uprising against Peking. The same article revealed that at least half of the problem in Wuhan concerned dissension within the revolutionary ranks themselves. The following sins were listed: running counter to the will of the masses, over-enthusiasm about fighting "civil war," diverting "serious political struggle onto the path of sectarain struggle," small-group mentality, devoting to petty-bourgeois ideas, mountain strongholdism, individualism, refusal to conduct self-criticism, and disrespect of the merits of others.

[187] Sankei, August 22, 1967, quoting a wall poster in Peking.

[188] Sankei, September 29, 1967; Yomiuri Shimbun, July 24, 1967; Asahi, July 24, 1967; Tokyo Shimbun, July 24, 1967.

[189] Jen-min Jih-pao, July 23–27, 1967; NCNA, July 24–27, 1967; Yomiuri Shimbun, July 24, 1967. Interestingly, the slogans denouncing the insurgent leaders (Ch'en Tsai-tao, Wang Jen-chung, and Chung Han-hua) included Ho Lung among their number.

parade in Tienanmen Square. On the podium stood the entire central leadership except for Mao himself.[190]

The next task was to mete out punishment to the accused, principally Ch'en Tsai-tao. Ch'en apparently came to Peking voluntarily, upon Mao's orders, probably thinking he could best plead his case personally.[191] An expanded meeting of the Central Committee was convened on July 26 to deal with the case. Chou was said to preside and the conference lasted over nine hours. Brought to account, aside from Ch'en, were Chung Han-hua (the Political Commissar of the Wuhan Military District), Niu Hai-lung (the commander of the 8201 Division), Ts'ai Ping-chen (a po-

[190] Aside from Lin Piao, Chou, Ch'en Po-ta, K'ang Sheng, and Chiang Ch'ing, were: Li Hsien-nien, Li Fu-ch'un, Nieh Jung-chen, Hsieh Fu-chih, Liu Ning-i, Hsiao Hua, Yang Ch'eng-wu, Su Yü, Teng Ying-ch'ao, Chang Ch'un-ch'iao, Wang Li, Kuan Feng, Ch'i Pen-yü, Yao Wen-yüan, Wang Tung-hsing, Liu Chien-hsün, Wu Teh, Chao I-min, Yeh Ch'ün, command personnel from the Peking Military District, responsible persons from some of the other military districts, "others who had returned with Hsieh and Wang from Wuhan," Peking Red Guard representatives, leading members of the Peking Municipal Revolutionary Committee, and representatives of workers and peasants' congresses. At the rally were also the staff of the Central Committee, the State Council, *Red Flag* magazine, *Jen-min Jih-pao*, *Chieh-fang-chün Pao* and NCNA. This was obviously a lineup designed to be impressive. One person who apparently was impressed was Wang Li. Later, in the documents published after he had been ousted, he was accused of becoming headstrong and conceited as a result of the demonstrations celebrating his safe return to Peking, a set of emotions which were said to contribute to his desire to better his political standing. Lin Piao himself made an important pronouncement at the close of the military phase of the Wuhan Incident. In retrospect, his "important directive" of August 9, 1967, not only betrays the major influence which the Incident exerted upon Lin and the Party center, but also signifies a major turning point in the Cultural Revolution itself. Whereas previously the emphasis was on officially encouraged violence in local revolutionary takeovers, now stress was placed on more closely controlled army intervention and on greater self-criticism within the revolutionary ranks. The Wuhan Incident thus ends the first portion of the military takeover phase while Lin's speech ushers in the second. The result was a declining level of overall violence for the rest of 1967 and a chance for Chou to put back some of the pieces of the central governmental administration and to mediate local conflicts more effectively. See "Deputy Supreme Commander Lin's Important Directive, 9 August 1967," published by the Editorial Board of the Pearl River Film Studio, Red Guard Headquarters of Organs of Joint Committee of Red Rebels, *Chu-ying Tung-fang-hung* (*Pearl Studio East-Is-Red*), Canton, September 13, 1967 (translation in *JPRS* 43,449 *Communist China Digest*, No. 192, November 24, 1967, pp. 57–64).

[191] *Sankei*, July 28, 1967. One can surmise that Ch'en may have returned on the same plane as Hsieh and Wang. It is interesting to note how the fortunes of politics can make such dramatic turns in as little as 48 hours.

litical commissar), and Pa Fang-yen (the Weapons Department chief).[192] Four charges were made against Ch'en: he planned to abduct Chou on his second visit to Wuhan; he vilified Chiang Ch'ing by saying that there were only a few able people in the Cultural Revolution Small Group; he disregarded the April 6 ten-point order of the Military Affairs Committee (that is, he went his own way locally and this is what got him into so much trouble); and finally, he conspired with Wang Jen-chung to perpetrate the events of July 20–21.[193] For these crimes he was dismissed from his post, and he disappeared (along with the other principal insurgents) from public view.

Finally, the regime moved to install new men in the vacated posts. Tseng Szu-yü replaced Ch'en Tsai-tao as Commander of the Wuhan Military District, Liu Chien-hsün (concurrently the First Political Commissar of the Honan Military District) was appointed the Deputy Political Commissar of the Wuhan District, replacing Chung Han-hua, and Liu Feng was assigned to the post of Political Commissar.[194] In early August, the political wheel finally turned full circle: Hsieh Fu-chih and Wang Li returned to Wuhan to witness the final defeat of the insurgents. This time they were not molested.

CHOU'S ROLE IN CHINA'S FOREIGN RELATIONS DURING 1966–1967

As compared with his involvement in domestic politics, Chou En-lai's conduct of mainland China's foreign policy during the first year of the active phase of the Cultural Revolution was tenuous indeed. To some extent, this conclusion is dependent upon the data available: when dealing with China's foreign policy, we possess nowhere near the number of documents, nor, for the most part, do we have the inside accounts of some Red Guard publications, which are available in

---

[192] *Sankei,* August 3, and September 29, 1967. The meeting was attended, aside from the usual (and not-yet purged) members of the Central Committee, by members of the Cultural Revolution Small Group, and military district commanders.

[193] Wang is a very shadowy figure in the entire Wuhan dispute. Although he was sometimes said to be the power behind Ch'en, he never came into the open, nor did he seem to share the guilt, in Peking's eyes, with Ch'en.

[194] *Tokyo Shimbun,* August 4, 1967; *Wuhan City Service,* August 5, 1967. These appointments were confirmed later at the mass leadership appearence at the October 1 National Day celebrations. Of these, at least Tseng Szu-yü is regarded as a Lin Piao man.

connection with domestic politics. More important, China's involvement with the external world declined tremendously in this period. At the very beginning of the Cultural Revolution period, a conscious decision seems to have been made to suspend international contact if not to mute strident propaganda, in the hopes that semi-isolation would allow China to pursue the dangerous course of the Cultural Revolution in relative security from external harm. This decline in foreign policy activity meant that all of those concerned with the formation and administration of Chinese foreign policy, including Chou, simply had less to do than before.

A third reason for Chou's low activity level in comparison with the high level of his attention to internal politics is that his formal duties, his political style, and his place within the Maoist hierarchy together dictated that a relatively small percentage of his time be given over to foreign affairs. He had given up the Foreign Ministry portfolio some years earlier. He did not choose at every point to speak out on foreign policy questions (that might get him into unnecessary political trouble), and Mao seemed to feel that Chou's best use in the foreign policy realm was either as official greeter of high-level visitors or pronouncer of occasional important but nontheoretical policy departures. Despite these limitations, it is instructive to consider Chou's activities in this realm. We shall inspect four topic-areas: first, the range and kind of Chou's formal activities; second, an analysis of his more important foreign policy declarations; third, an overview of his role in the Foreign Ministry problems during the spring and summer of 1967; and, by way of example, his role in the further development of the Sino-Soviet dispute.

Chou's formal duties in foreign affairs are not very informative. The only thing to glean from reports of such activities as his reception of new ambassadors, meetings with visiting party and governmental delegations, and the flow of congratulatory and supportive messages to other countries is that his stewardship of the Foreign Ministry did indeed begin in early April of 1967. This was the date after which Chou was said to take over the direct administration of foreign affairs from Ch'en Yi, who was under severe Red Guard attack.[195] Thus, Chou received three new ambassadors (March 16, April 19, and June 8); received six foreign governmental delegations (May 16, 26, 28, and 30, June 17, and August 1); granted eight interviews with visiting cultural delegations (two on April 27, and on May 4, 17, and 25, June 17 and 26, and July

[195] See Melvin Gurtov, Chapter 5 in this volume, and *Sankei*, April 28, 1967 (translation in *DSJP*, April 28, 1967, p. 13).

26); received one party delegation on March 10, and sent out four messages, telegrams, and letters (aside from those dealing with Sino-Soviet relations, which we discuss below), on May 11, June 6 (two messages), and June 12.[196] Even this list of formal appointments after March 10 is far smaller in number than the normal flow of such activities, and bespeaks the severely curtailed nature of China's cultural diplomacy.[197] Not many wished to visit China during the Cultural Revolution, and the Chinese did not encourage outsiders to come in.

Somewhat more informative are Chou's published speeches and interviews on foreign relations. While these, too, were more limited in number than before the onset of the Cultural Revolution, and while not much of interest can be obtained from his speeches on formal state occasions, they at least serve to define China's foreign policy during the twelve-month period of the Cultural Revolution under consideration here. Thus, certain themes recur: strident anti-Sovietism, together with the charge of Soviet-American collusion; unreserved support for North Vietnam in its efforts in the South, coupled with threats of Chinese intervention if the North Vietnamese were forced into a political compromise or if the United States invaded the North; support for "wars of national liberation" around the globe, but with the reservation that self-reliance (along with obedience to the thought of Mao) was the touchstone of success; emphasis on solidarity with the developing countries of Africa, Asia, and Latin America, as opposed to the (supposedly) developed nations of Europe and North America; verbal support of those countries which opposed the United States or the Soviet Union either directly (Cambodia) or indirectly because of their disputes with states supported by either or both of the superpowers (Pakistan, Egypt); conversely, opposition to countries supporting or supported by either of the main nuclear powers (India, Israel); differentiation between the "capitalist" or "lackey" governments of certain states and the "people" of those states (Japan, Indonesia); support within the socialist system for those party-states who resisted Soviet hegemonic ambitions (Rumania, but not Yugoslavia, for ideological reasons), and competition with the Soviet Union for the favor of those states which attempted to balance between China

[196] See *NCNA* for the dates listed. These are activities which would normally devolve (and did, for the most part before April 1967) upon Foreign Minister Ch'en Yi.

[197] Note also, p. 175, the steep decline in Chou's foreign-policy related appearances, from seventeen in August 1966, to its nadir, one such appearance in January 1967.

and the Soviet Union (North Korea, North Vietnam); justification for further Chinese nuclear and hydrogen weapon tests on grounds of breaking up the superpowers' nuclear monopoly; and continued competition (despite the adverse effects of the Cultural Revolution on public opinion) with the Soviet Union for allegiance of nonruling Communist (and Communist-type) parties around the world.[198] To list these elements is to set down the particularities of Chinese foreign policy during the Cultural Revolution period, for Chou served as chief enunciator of, if not the final authority on, Chinese Communist foreign policy during this period.

The problems of administration and policy which confronted Chou at the Foreign Ministry during the spring and summer of 1967 provide us with a case study of those political tactics which he had by then found effective in dealing with Red Guard disruptions and preserving both his own political integrity and the regime's foreign policy line. Red Guard criticism of Foreign Minister Ch'en Yi, and their temporary takeover of the Foreign Ministry itself during part of July, provided a stern test of Chou's abilities to manage the situation while retaining credibility with the revolutionary forces. He was able to salvage the administrative and policy situation, while protecting his own position, through use of those techniques which we have already discussed. Here we shall limit ourselves to outlining Chou's activities in regard to the defense of Ch'en Yi, based on the conclusions of those sections and on the study of Ch'en Yi's problems at the Foreign Ministry, *The Foreign Ministry and Foreign Affairs in China's Cultural Revolution,* which constitutes Chapter 5 and contains the details of Chou's activities in this regard.

Four points seem of interest: first, Chou's political strategy in defending

---

[198] See, for instance, Chou's speech in Bucharest, June 17, 1966; "Premier Chou En-lai Greets 12th World Anti-Atomic-Hydrogen Bomb Conference, July 30, 1966; Speech at Banquet Closing the 1966 Summer Physics Colloquium in Peking," July 31, 1966; "Interview with Dietman Esaki," September 12, 1966, *Tokyo Shimbun,* September 13, 1966 (translation in *DSJP,* September 14, 1966, pp. 4-6); "Liberal-Democratic Party Dietmen Interview Chou En-lai," *Yomiuri Shimbun,* September 26, 1966; "Speech at Reception Honoring Albanian Anniversary," November 29, 1966; "Chou En-lai Speaks at Peking Banquet in Honor of Albanian Comrades," January 14, 1967; interview with Simon Malley, versions published in *Chicago Daily News* and *Daily Sketch* (London), May 15, 1967, and in *Jeune Afrique* (Tunis), May 21, 1967 (existence and contents of the interview denied by the Chinese Foreign Ministry, May 16, 1967); and "Speech at Banquet for K. D. Kaunda," June 24, 1967. All references are to *NCNA* unless otherwise noted. This list does not include Chou's declarations with regard to Sino-Soviet relations, which are discussed below.

Ch'en Yi; second, Ch'en Yi's reliance on Chou's directives and authority to keep himself out of trouble with the Red Guards; third, how Chou's temporary assumption of direct authority over Foreign Ministry matters, together with his defense of Ch'en Yi, brought him directly under Red Guard fire; and fourth, how Chou managed to overcome the Red Guards and restore the status quo ante after August 7.

It is quite plain how Chou defended Ch'en Yi from Red Guard attacks: as in the almost identical cases of Hsieh Fu-chih, Li Hsien-nien, Li Fu-ch'un, and T'an Chen-lin, he followed a tripartite strategy of playing for time, giving his temporary agreement to the attackers, and asserting his own authority or appealing to that of Mao or Lin Piao. The first line of defense was to let the minister (here, Ch'en) defend himself and to offer self-criticism. If this did not suffice, Chou authorized criticism sessions, keeping tight rein on the length and kind of proceeding. If this did not mollify the Red Guards, he would authorize further sessions, meeting preferably in small groups only, and insisting that he himself chair each session. Finally, if the Red Guards were still not satisfied, he would forbid further sessions, relying upon his own authority and, if necessary, appealing to that of Mao and Lin. If this did not work, Chou's devices were exhausted and he either submitted to the Red Guards (by dismissing the minister in question) or he stepped aside while they took over the ministry (this happened only in the case of the Foreign Ministry, and then, as we shall see, for special reasons). Thus, in Ch'en Yi's case, Chou presided over a mass criticism meeting against Ch'en on January 24, which gained time down to May. On May 12, he met with leftist Red Guards in the Foreign Ministry and gave his assent to a series of criticism meetings, but only if he himself could chair the sessions, if a concrete plan of criticism were worked out in advance, and if meetings extended over a three-month period. He also made it plain that Ch'en could not be overthrown on any account, since it was the Central Committee, and not the Red Guards which made such appointments and dismissals. And while this only served to incite the Red Guards further, and while he had to bring his own authority into play against Yao Teng-shan, the leader of the radicals (as we shall see), once the situation had calmed down again after August 7, Chou reverted to his "let's criticize but not too much" tactics by again chairing a mass criticism session against Ch'en Yi on August 11 and by arguing again for a series of medium-sized and small meetings stretched out over a longer period of time.

Ch'en Yi relied on Chou, not only in the sense that he depended on Chou to get him out of hot water (the two had probably agreed beforehand how to play the game with the Red Guards), but also in the sense that Ch'en faithfully carried out what he thought was policy enunciated from above by Chou. Thus, in his February 12, 1967, confrontation with Red Guards, Ch'en used Chou's authority to help call off their attacks. And these attacks themselves were brought on partially by the policy of "revival of reputations" in the Foreign Ministry which, as we have argued earlier, was probably put into effect on Chou's initiative.

When neither self-criticism nor Ch'en's appeal to Chou's authority improved Red Guard opinions and activities, Chou himself took over direct supervision of the Foreign Ministry early in April. This was a more direct line of defense for Chou, but it carried two disadvantages: first, the Red Guards could, and did, henceforth direct their attacks against him personally, and second, the amount of time he could devote to Foreign Ministry operations was severely restricted by the priorities of domestic political duties. While he could handle the first problem, the second apparently overwhelmed him, for the Wuhan Incident occurred just at the time the Red Guards were attempting to "take over" the Foreign Ministry. As a result, the Red Guards, in effect, slipped past Chou while he was busy attending to Wuhan. Once the Wuhan Incident was settled (we have argued that this must be dated no earlier than August 4), Chou could redirect his attention to the problems of the Foreign Ministry. Thus, his showdown with Yao Teng-shan was possible no sooner than sometime after August 4. This reconstructed timing accords nicely with Chou's own statement that in early August the Red Guards "seized power from me." But from May to early August Chou's domestic political duties (Wuhan was only one, if the most trying, of the problems facing him) effectively prevented him from keeping on top of the Foreign Ministry situation. With both Ch'en Yi and the senior professionals politically hobbled by intramural Red Guards, Yao Teng-shan had the opening he needed to make China's foreign policy a function of Cultural Revolution politics. That the damage to China's foreign relations was not greater can be attributed in part to the retrospectively wise decision to curtail the nation's involvement abroad.

Once he was able to devote more of his time to Foreign Ministry problems, Chou was easily able to rectify the situation. But he had to do it through *force main,* that is, he had actually to "seize power" back from the Red Guards controlling the Foreign Ministry. Now, only appeal to higher authority or force, and not protracted defense, would suffice. That meant either that Chou's own authority would have to be obeyed or that he would have to appeal to Mao or Lin. Probably both were brought into play: Gurtov reports in Chapter 5 that in all probability the Central Committee and Mao himself were involved. That Chou was not at first successful is shown by the fact that it was only on August 22 that he was again able to issue instructions to the Peking Red Guards to curtail their activities around foreign embassies with the assurance that they would be obeyed.

Chou En-lai's involvement in Sino-Soviet relations was, aside from the normal run of programmatic statements, limited to the period extending from the beginning of the present study, August 1966, down to the lifting of the Red Guard seige around the Soviet Embassy in Peking just before the seventeenth anniversary of the signing of the Sino-Soviet treaty, on February 14, 1967. After that time, as we have stated, his foreign policy activities declined precipitously and his time was more and more taken up with problems of domestic politics. After February 14, 1967, also, Sino-Soviet relations entered a new phase, wherein the two erstwhile allies drew back from a complete diplomatic break, attacked each other verbally but from afar, and tried (with some exceptions, to be sure) to deal with each other in any practical manner as little as possible. This phase lasted, for all intents and purposes, until March 1969, when the two states clashed militarily at Chen-pao (Damansky) Island in the Ussuri River. August 1966 to February 1967 thus represents a single phase of Sino-Soviet relations, during which time: the Soviets resumed ideological polemics after nearly two years of silence; the deterioration of Sino-Soviet relations came to depend directly upon the events of the Cultural Revolution in China; physical clashes between the citizens of the two countries became a normal occurrence; and the two nations brought themselves to the brink of a formal diplomatic break, only to back away at the last moment.

We will approach the subject of Chou's role in Sino-Soviet relations from two opposing vantage points. First, we shall consider Chou's role in the formulation and execution of Chinese policy toward the Soviet Union, and Soviet policy toward Chou himself and his role in the Cultural Revolution. Perhaps the following will serve to summarize Chou's role in Chinese policy toward the Soviet Union during the period indicated.[199] First, Chou kept out (or was kept out) of the day-to-

[199] These conclusions are based on a reading of the following sources: *Hanoi Inter-*

day relations between the two powers, and only entered the picture infrequently. He appears not to have been involved in decision-making concerning either of the first two series of demonstrations in front of the Soviet Embassy in Peking (in August and October 1966). Nor did he insert himself into the question of the ouster of Soviet correspondents from Peking or the enforced departure of Chinese students from Moscow. The *Zagorsk* incident, in which a Soviet merchant vessel was detained by the Chinese for eighteen days, seems not to have concerned Chou publicly. Of course Chou may well have involved himself in these events in a quiet manner, but the very fact of his relative noninvolvement may indicate that he wished to remain in the background. Nor do Sino-Soviet relations, or his attitude toward Soviet leaders, figure prominently in his speeches and talks before Red Guard groups, utterances which were not designed for public consumption.

Second, when Chou did choose to talk about Sino-Soviet relations, or to send messages abroad on that topic, they were both infrequent and, compared with other such material, somewhat less immoderate. Although a number of extremely hostile anti-Soviet statements came from him or appeared over his signature, one gets the impression that they were enunciated pro forma. Certainly the occasions on which they were uttered dictated that Chou could not depart in any great regard from the speeches of his colleagues or from the official Maoist line.

Third, on the one occasion on which Chou seems to have departed

---

national Service, reporting Chou's meeting with a North Vietnamese cultural group, August 10, 1966; Chou's message of greeting to the 12th World Conference Against Atomic and Hydrogen Bombs, as reported in *NCNA*'s story of Liu Ning-i's anti-Soviet speech of August 12, 1966; "Chou's speech Honoring the 22nd Anniversary of Albania's Liberation," *NCNA,* November 29, 1966; "Chou En-lai, Ch'en Yi Send Message of Solicitous Regards to Chinese Students Suppressed by Soviet Troops and Police," *NCNA,* January 26, 1967; "Chinese Students Send Message to Mao from Moscow," *NCNA,* January 28, 1967; "Nine Chinese Students Recount Heroic Fight Against Soviet Modern Revisionism," *NCNA,* January 28, 1967; "Chinese Embassy in Moscow Holds Press Conference, Denouncing Soviet Revisionists' Facist Outrage Against Chinese Students," *NCNA,* January 28, 1967; "Chinese Students Persecuted by Soviet Revisionists Given Rousing Welcome in Peking," *NCNA,* February 2, 1967; "Chinese Embassy Accuses Russians of Beating Aides," *New York Times,* February 4, 1967; "Chou En-lai, Ch'en Yi Send Regards to Chinese Embassy Staff in Moscow," *NCNA,* February 5, 1967; "Peking Welcomes Returning Diplomatic Victims," *NCNA,* February 9, 1967; "Speech at Rally Denouncing USSR," *Peking Domestic Service,* February 11, 1967; "Chou Speech Unreported," Belgrade *Tanyug International Service,* February 12, 1967; "Chinese Deride Soviet Chiefs," *New York Times,* February 12, 1967; "Chinese Lift Siege of Soviet Offices; End 18-day Protest," *New York Times,* February 14, 1967.

from the official anti-Soviet line, he seemed to err in the direction of relative moderation. This was during a speech on February 11 before a mammoth Peking rally protesting the Soviet actions in Moscow cutting down photographic cases displaying the Chinese version of a Soviet-Chinese clash in Red Square, and beating up certain Chinese diplomats who attempted to prevent the Soviet action. By February 11 the Soviet Embassy in Peking had been under day-and-night Red Guard siege for over two weeks, and the Soviets were at the point of breaking diplomatic relations. Chou evidently did not wish this to happen for, among other consequences, it would make very difficult the flow of supplies to North Vietnam through China. Ch'en Yi also spoke at the rally, as did a number of Red Guard representatives, diplomats, and students recently returned from the Moscow clashes. All but Chou's speech were reported the next day in the official press. Several reasons can be given for this departure. One is that the Soviets had plainly threatened that diplomatic relations would be severed were the Chinese to break into the Soviet Embassy. Chou probably did not desire this, and tried to signal the Russians his wish.[200] He did so by stating in his speech that the Chinese should use nonviolent methods of struggle, thereby hinting that the students would not penetrate the embassy and that the siege would soon be over. This either tipped off the Russians or angered Mao or Lin. In any case, two days later, on February 13, the siege was indeed lifted. This move in effect told the Soviets both that the Chinese would not go to the point, in their anti-Soviet posturings, of endangering North Vietnamese chances of victory in the South, and (since the Sino-Soviet treaty anniversary was the next day) that they regarded the treaty still in effect, if only residually. It is probable that Chou, both in the speech of February 11 and in private Party meetings, argued to this end and it is significant that he had his way.[201]

[200] East European sources in Peking report that Chou headed a group within the Chinese leadership who argued against a formal diplomatic rupture. It is possible also that the Russians and the Chinese were exchanging secret notes on the subject and that a break was very close. In his meetings with his Chinese colleagues, Chou had to seem as intransigent as the rest, as he did when (and if) he communicated with the Russians. Faced with the desirability of telling the Russians to be patient but also with the necessity of appearing to his colleagues no less anti-Soviet than they, Chou probably felt himself to be in a keen dilemma.

[201] It is also of some significance that, when the Russians feared for the safety of their staff and dependents in the Peking Embassy, the Soviet Premier, Alexei Kosygin, tried to contact Chou, and not Mao or Lin Piao, concerning the matter. That this was more than just a matter of a Soviet official contacting his opposite

Looking at the Soviet attitude toward Chou we can draw three conclusions.[202] First, the Soviets included Chou as a leading member of the Mao Tse-tung group, which he obviously was. Their references to Chou, however, were usually factual—stating the fact that he had made a speech or that he had appeared on an occasion—and only rarely did they quote his anti-Soviet utterances. This is in some contrast to Lin Piao and increasingly different from their treatment of Mao himself, who more and more became the *bête noire* of Sino-Soviet relations. However, on those occasions when Chou was the principal speaker and when the principal subject of his talk was opposition to the Soviet Union, the Soviets had no choice but to attack him.[203]

Second, the Soviets chose to emphasize Chou's pro-Soviet past, particularly upon such occasions as his speech to the Eighth Congress of the

---

number in China is shown by Kosygin's actions later in regard to the Ussuri Island clash: on that occasion, he attempted to contact Lin Piao directly.

[202] The following sources were used in this investigation: "The 'Cultural Revolution' in China Continues," *Pravda*, September 3, 1966, p. 3; " 'Red Guard' Excesses," *TASS International Service*, September 2, 1966; "Soviet Denounces China's Red Guard," *New York Times*, September 17, 1966; "The 'Hung Weiping' Gain Approval," *Pravda*, September 18, 1966, p. 5; "Conducting the 'Proletarian Cultural Revolution' Without the Proletariat," *Trud*, September 27, 1966, p. 3; "The 8th CCP Congress' Appraisal of Sino-Soviet Relations," *Moscow Radio*, September 26, 1966; *Moscow Domestic Radio*, November 5, 1966; "Soviet-Bloc Aides Quit Peking Rally," *New York Times*, November 13, 1966; *TASS International Service*, November 12, 1966; *TASS International Service*, October 7, 1966; "New Attacks by Hung Weipings," *Izvestia*, October 17, 1966; "Behind the Chinese Wall," *Komsomolskaya Pravda*, October 25, 1966; *Moscow Radio*, December 22, 1966; "The Chinese People's Liberation Army and Events in the Chinese People's Republic," *Krasnaya Zvezda*, December 29, 1966, pp. 2–3, "New Zigzags of the 'Cultural Revolution' in China," *Pravda*, January 8, 1967, p. 5; "Soviet Leaders Pressing Anti-China Campaign," *New York Times*, January 10, 1967; *Radio Peace and Progress* (Moscow), January 15, 1967; *TASS International Service*, January 21, 1967; *Moscow Domestic Service*, February 1, 1967; "Soviet Protests Chinese Violence Against Embassy," *New York Times*, February 5, 1967; *TASS International Service*, February 4, 1967; *Moscow Radio*, February 11, 1967; "On the Anti-Soviet Policy of Mao Tse-tung and his Group," *Pravda*, February 16, 1967, p. 3.

[203] Thus, on November 11, 1966, Chou was the principal speaker at a Peking ceremony celebrating the 100th anniversary of the birth of Sun Yat-sen. Soviet and East European Communist diplomats were present as Chou said: "The clique of Soviet leaders have betrayed the great Lenin and the path laid down by the Great October Revolution . . . they are animated by . . . revisionism . . . , betraying the interests of the revolutionary peoples . . . safeguarding the imperialist and colonial domination in the capitalist world and restoring capitalism to the Soviet Union." Upon hearing this, the diplomats had no choice but to walk out of the hall. But the Soviet press, in denouncing the talk, kept to a minimum its attacks against Chou personally.

Chinese Communist Party in 1956. Finally, both the volume of Soviet references to Chou and the degree of their opposition to him seems extraordinarily low, compared with what it could have been for the third most powerful man in China and compared with their attacks against Mao Tse-tung and Lin Piao. Thus, from the viewpoint both of Chou's attitude and declarations with regard to the Soviet Union and the Soviets' view of Chou, there seemed to be a propensity to minimize conflict and reserve positions for the future.

CONCLUSION

We are now in a position to draw together our observations concerning Chou En-lai's role in the Cultural Revolution, and to fulfill certain other promises made earlier. Thus, we wish first to outline Chou's role in the Cultural Revolution in the period from August 1967, where we ended our detailed analysis, to the end of the Ninth Party Congress, in April 1969. This will assure us that no startling developments took place which would seriously call into question general observations from the period of detailed study. Those observations comprise the second topic addressed here, and collectively amount to an outline of Chou's "political style." On that basis, we will, third, compare and contrast Chou's style with that of two other major Chinese political figures—Mao Tse-tung and Lin Piao. This should set Chou in historical and categorical perspective. Fourth, the question of Chou and charisma must be considered, by comparing his style with the theoretical and case-study literature on the subject. Finally, we venture to conjecture on Chou's probable political position in post-Maoist China.

Chou En-lai's Status After August 1967

Chou En-lai's status after August 1967 must be seen in terms of the major developments in the Cultural Revolution from then down to the Ninth Party Congress in April 1969. A brief review of those events is therefore in order.[204] The last third of 1967 saw an attempt by Mao and

[204] This analysis is drawn from the following secondary sources: Philip Bridgham, "Mao's Cultural Revolution in 1967: The Struggle to Seize Power," *The China Quarterly,* No. 34 (April–June 1968) pp. 6–37; Richard Baum, "China: Year of the Mangoes," *Asian Survey,* Vol. 9, No. 1 (January 1969) pp. 1–17; Charles Neuhauser, "The Impact of the Cultural Revolution on the Chinese Communist Party Machine,"

his associates to halt the spread of violence (exemplified by the Wuhan events) and to bring the country back from the brink of anarchy. Efforts were thus made to restore a minimum of order and production, as well as to lessen the dangers of disorder stemming from fratricidal strife among revolutionary groups, and from the inability of the army to halt disorder at regional and local levels. Mao himself toured the provinces in September and in his statements stressed the evils of ultra-leftism, supposedly the cause of these ills. Red Guards were henceforth forbidden to arm themselves from army stocks and were told to return to the classrooms. "Revolutionary great alliances" were now to be constructed on the basis of trade and profession and not through the revolutionary mass organizations, which were supposed to be broken up. And a new "mild cadres policy" was instituted in order to allow their talents to be used once again in constructing three-way alliances and revolutionary committees. But the problem was, first, that the tide of violence had risen too high to be stemmed overnight, while, second, the army was still not given the authority it needed to deal forcibly with the situation. The result was that disorders continued and construction of the revolutionary committees slowed. Thus, while the end of the year found the situation at least no worse than it was in September, it was only marginally better.

The Cultural Revolution continued its uneven and disorderly course during 1968. Several trends can be noted. The center of political activity tended even more to move out of Peking and down to the provincial levels, as major efforts were made to fashion revolutionary committees acceptable to the Mao-Lin leadership. Political activity in Peking, while obviously still quite important, tended to reflect competition for power at the local level. To quote the most obvious example, the Party's Twelfth Plenum (the first since the beginning of the active phase of the Cultural Revolution in August 1966) had to wait until October, that is, until after the last of the provincial revolutionary committees were in place. (It was at the Twelfth Plenum that Liu Shao-ch'i was finally ousted from his Party and state posts, and that the decision was made to hold the Ninth Congress.) Another tendency was the continuation of the movement begun in late 1967 to repress the Red Guards and their Revolutionary Rebel allies. Thus, the cry from August 1968 forward was to emphasize working-class leadership and to regard the Red Guards as petty bourgeois

Asian Survey, Vol. 8, No. 6 (June 1968) pp. 465–488; weekly articles in the *Far Eastern Economic Review;* and the *China News Summary* for the period indicated.

factionalists. The repression of the Red Guards was actually symbolic of a major change in direction of the Cultural Revolution, from a movement for Party rectification and purge to Party reconstruction and consolidation. Thus, while the purge of the leadership ranks continued to its logical conclusion (and even saw the elimination of many of the original members of the central Cultural Revolution activists), a counter-trend was also apparent in the reappearance of many cadres who had gone through the purge and reeducation process. Finally, possibly the most important development (which also carried over from previous phases of the Cultural Revolution) was the growing importance of the military at every level of politics and administration.

The year can be looked at also in terms of successive left-right trends, again patterned on developments noted in previous periods. Thus, the early months saw the continuation of the later 1967 campaign against the extreme left, now coupled with propaganda supporting the political-educational activities of the army. The army found that it was more and more looked to for restoring order and curbing Red Guard fratricidal strife. Lest such a "rightist" trend proceed too far, however, and corrupt Mao's revolutionary goals, a swing back to the left got underway in April, initiated and symbolized by the purge of the army Chief of Staff, Yang Ch'eng-wu and by opposition to the so-called "second adverse current of reversing verdicts." The new leftward movement quickly gathered momentum, the radicals again took heart, the army found itself further circumscribed, and "factionalism" was redefined to permit leftist (as opposed to bourgeois, "rightist") Red Guards to exist in separate groups. The predictable result was a rash of violent clashes and a general decline in the security level of both countryside and city. This continued until late July when, in a move reminiscent of his provincial tour of nearly a year before, Mao intervened by meeting with various Red Guard factions at Tsinghua University, berating them for betraying him, and proposing to set up "Worker-Peasant Mao Tse-tung Propaganda Teams" which would displace the Red Guards and Revolutionary Rebels. Hence, there began yet another swing of the political pendulum, now to the right. Directed in ideological terms against the "theory of many centers" (a euphemism for Red Guard factionalism of all sorts, both leftist and rightist), the campaign moved to solve the Red Guard problem once and for all. Many thousands were "sent down" to posts in remote agricultural and border areas and away from the cities. By the Twelfth Plenum, the rout was complete and the Peking leadership was free both to move forward to the Ninth Congress and to reconstruct the political and social system to its own liking.

The Peking leadership was thus finally in a position to carry out a number of changes which it had originally desired but which the exigencies of the Cultural Revolution forced it to postpone. These "reforms," which occupied the center of activity on the domestic scene from late 1968 down to the Ninth Congress, included: the movement to the countryside of several tens of millions of urban residents for permanent resettlement; a restructuring of the medical system through greater emphasis on low-level self-help programs and lowering of standards of medical practice; reform of the educational system on the basis of local fiscal responsibility for education at that level and of the introduction into the classroom of "worker-peasant propaganda teams" to assure the proper ideological content of instruction; and militarization of industrial organization. While the net effect of these changes was to cause widespread social unrest, the Peking leadership did not feel its effects since by then the political power of the mass organizations had been pulverized and the new lower-level organs were thoroughly dominated by the military. Hence, the politics of preparation for the Ninth Congress could proceed without undue interference from below.

Chou En-lai was a major participant in all of these developments with the possible exception of the post-Plenum reform campaigns. In the latter part of 1967, Chou spent most of that portion of his time devoted to internal affairs in the same manner he had previously: receiving revolutionary mass delegations, taking part in Red Guard decision-making debates, adjudicating disputes among Red Guard and Revolutionary Rebel groups, attending revolutionary great alliance rallies, and transmitting instructions from the Central Committee to revolutionary groups.[205] He also made at

[205] See the following sources: "Premier Chou's Instructions on the Problem of Wenchow," Ko-ti T'ung-hsün (Correspondence from All Parts of the Country), Dairen, No. 4 (September 13, 1967) (translation in SCMP 4081, December 15, 1967, p. 8); "Events in Peking," op. cit., p. 13; "In Various Parts of the Motherland," op. cit., p. 9; "Premier Chou's Important Speech (Excerpts) Delivered at a Reception of Representatives of Universities and Colleges in Peking on September 17, 1967," Canton, Chu-ying Tung-fang-hung (Pearl Studio East-Is-Red), October 1, 1967 (translation in JPRS 44,241, also in SCMP 4066, November 24, 1967, pp. 1–6, and in Union Research Service, Vol. 49, pp. 91–100); "Chou En-lai's Instructions on Posters in Shanghai," Wan Shan Hung P'ien (Ten Thousand Mountains Red Materials), No. 1 (September 26, 1967) (translation in JPRS 43,903, Communist China Digest, No. 193, 1967); "Premier Chou's Talk with Five Comrade Representa-

least one trip to the provinces,[206] participated in the October 1 National Day activities,[207] defended himself from Red Guard accusations,[208] and criticized Liu Shao-ch'i.[209] All of these activities indicate that Chou was moving with the political tide during these months, that his Cultural Revolution duties remained the same (at least so far as internal politics was concerned), and that his position in the leadership hierarchy remained constant.

Much the same can be said for Chou during 1968, with the addition that he was the center of several political imbroglios at the beginning of the year. These concern the problem of the resurgence of the "February adverse current," associated with the name of the former Head of the Staff Office for Agriculture and Forestry, T'an Chen-lin, in February

tives of Proletarian Revolutionary Rebels of Canton at a Reception," *Kuang-yin Hung-ch'i (Canton Printing Red Flag),* October 29, 1967 (translation in *SCMP* 4091, January 3, 1968, pp. 1–6); "Premier Chou Gives Important Instructions," Hsinhui, Kwangtung, *Kung-nung-ping Chan-pao (Worker-Peasant-Soldier Struggle Paper),* No. 18 (November 14, 1967) (translation in *JPRS* 44,241, *Communist China Digest* No. 194 [February 5, 1968] pp. 155–162); "Speeches by Central Leaders to Canton Delegations to Peking on the Night of November 14," Canton, *Tzu-liao Chuan-chi (Special Collection of Materials),* November 17, 1967 (translation in *SCMP* 4085, December 21, 1967, pp. 1–12); "Premier Chou's Speech to Canton Delegations to Peking on the Morning of November 14," Canton, *Tzu-liao Chuan-chi,* November 17, 1967 (translation in *SCMP* 4080, December 15, 1967, pp. 1–8); "Chou En-lai's Directive on Employment of Discharged Armymen," December 4, 1967 (no original source given, translation in *Facts and Features,* Taipei, Vol. 1, No. 6 [January 10, 1968] p. 20); "Premier Chou's Recent [December 10, 1967] Talk on Revolutionary Great Alliances," Canton, *Chi-kuan Hung-szu T'ung-hsün (Bulletin of Red Headquarters of Public Organizations),* No. 2 (January 9, 1968) (translation in *SCMP* 4120, February 16, 1968, pp. 1–2); "Speeches by Leaders of the Central Committee," [on September 26, 1967], Canton, October 1 Column of the Canton Red Guard Headquarters, October 1967 (translation in *Survey of China Mainland Magazines [SCMM]* 611, January 22, 1968, pp. 8–11; "Premier Chou Receives and Addresses Ten Representatives of Proletarian Revolutionary Rebels of Canton," Canton, "Liaison Headquarters" of Central-South Bureau, November 5, 1967 (translation in *SCMM* 611, pp. 12–18); *Radio Peking,* September 24, 1967, and November 6, 1967; "Summary of Instructions by Central Leaders at Reception of Representatives from Three Northeast Provinces," (no original source given; translation in *SCMP* 4088, September 28, 1967, pp. 1–19); *NCNA International Service,* September 30, November 13, November 11, November 14, and December 12, 1967.

[206] *Ko-ti T'ung hsün, op. cit.,* note 205, p. 9.

[207] *NCNA International Service,* September 30, and October 10, 1967, and *Jen-min Jih-pao,* September 30–October 2, 1967.

[208] *Chu-ying Tung-fang Lung, op. cit.,* note 205.

[209] "Premier Chou Talks About Why Firepower Must Be Concentrated on Criticizing the Party's Top Person Taking the Capitalist Road," *Hung Chan Pao (Red Struggle Newspaper),* No. 15 (November 29, 1967) pp. 1, 4.

and March;[210] the purge of Yang Ch'eng-wu in late March;[211] and the so-called Sheng-wu-lien affair of the late spring.[212] Analysis of Chou's role in each of these events once again confirms that he was at the center of activity and involvement in the politics of the Cultural Revolution.[213] More important for our purposes, these three developments help to reinforce the conclusion that Chou moved very quickly with the tide, once it began to change decisively from right to left. Having come down firmly in his support of the anti-left extremist current of late 1967, but now

[210] "The Premier, Po-ta, K'ang Sheng, Chiang Ch'ing and Central Leaders on Attitude Toward February Adverse Current Being a Major Issue of Right and Wrong," Canton, *Kuangchou Hung-tai-hui* (*Canton Red Guard Congress*), April 3, 1968 (translation in *SCMP* 4164, April 25, 1968, pp. 1–5); "Central Leaders' Important Speeches (Excerpts) on Counter-attacking February Adverse Current," Canton, *Chu-ying Tung-fang-hung* (*Pearl Studio East-Is-Red*), No. 20, April 1968 (translation in *SCMP* 4166, April 29, 1968, pp. 6–7).

[211] "Chou En-lai's Speech at the Struggle Rally Against Yang Cheng-wu," Canton, *Pearl Studio East-is-Red*, No. 20 [April 1968] (translation in *Facts and Features*, Vol. 1, No. 21 [August 7, 1968] pp. 21–28; also reprinted in *Tzu Kuo*, No. 51 [June 1968] pp. 43–46); "Speech by Premier Chou En-lai at Interview with Some Representatives of the Scientific and Technological Commission for National Defense, the Congress of Students, the Military Control Committees, the Revolutionary Mass Organizations of the 7th Ministry of Machine Building and the Academia Sinica," Canton, *Tzu-liao Chuan-chi* (*Special Collection of Materials*), undated (translation in *SCMM*, No. 631 [October 21, 1968] pp. 1–27).

[212] "Highlights of Important Instructions Given by Central Leaders When Examining and Revising the Report of the Preparatory Group for Hunan Provincial Revolutionary Committee," Canton, *Tzu-liao Chuan-chi* (*Special Collection of Materials*), No. 3, May 1968 (translation in *SCMP* 4196, June 12, 1968, pp. 1–4); "Premier Chou's Speech at His Reception of Reporting Teams of Seven Provinces and Regions," (date not given), Canton, *Wen-ko T'ung-hsün* (*Cultural Revolution Bulletin*), No. 12 (February 1968) (translation in *SCMP* 4139, March 15, 1968, p. 4); "The Program of Sheng-wu-lien," Canton, *Kuang-yin Hung-chi* (*Canton Printing Red Flag*), No. 5 (March 1968) p. 3 (translation in Klaus Mehnert, *Peking and the New Left: At Home and Abroad*, China Research Monographs, No. 4 (June 1968) University of California, Berkeley, pp. 74–77); "The Sheng-wu-lien Resolutions," Canton, *Tung-feng Chan-pao* (*East Wind Combat News*), No. 19 (February 29, 1968) p. 4 (translation in Klaus Mehnert, *Peking and the New Left: At Home and Abroad*, pp. 78–81).

[213] See also, in this regard, the following secondary sources: "Is Chou En-lai Yang Ch'eng-wu's Backstage Supporter?" *Facts and Features*, Vol. 1, No. 16 (May 29, 1968) pp. 7–9; Li Chung-ta, "Chou En-lai and the Great Cultural Revolution," *Issues and Studies*, Vol. 5, No. 11 (August 1969) pp. 29–38 (Chinese text in *Fei-ch'ing Yüeh-pao*, Vol. 12, No. 4 [June 1969] pp. 7–11); Ming Ming. (pseud.) "An Episode in Chou En-lai's Courtship with Misfortune," *Ming Pao* (Hong Kong), Vol. 4, No. 8 (August 1969) pp. 31–32; and Ts'ao Yuan-tu, "Chou En-lai and the Kuangtung Provincial Revolutionary Committee," *Tsu Kuo* (*China Monthly*), No. 53 (August 1968) pp. 23–31.

realizing that that movement had over-extended itself (both the "second February adverse current" and the Yang Ch'eng-wu affair were manifestations of the latter phenomenon), Chou climbed aboard the bandwagon of the new leftist current beginning in April. This was the import of his participation in the movement to criticize the Sheng-wu-lien documents.

Aside from these specific developments, Chou continued his involvement in Red Guard and Revolutionary Rebel activities; he attempted to salvage what he could of industrial productivity as disorders and destruction of property got more and more out of hand; and he took a hand in the Mao-Lin effort to reconstruct Chinese politics and administration along lines of revolutionary committees at every level, especially the provincial level.[214] These efforts were largely successful, for by September

[214] "Premier Chou's Directives on the Great Cultural Revolution in Sinkiang [May 2], Canton, *Hung-ch'i T'ung-hsün* (*Red Flag Bulletin*), No. 14 (May 26, 1968) (translation in *SCMP* 4201, June 19, 1968, p. 16); "Premier Chou's Important Speech on April 7," Canton, *I-yüeh Feng-pao* (*January Storm*), No. 26 (May 1968) (translation in *SCMP* 4189, June 3, 1968, pp. 1–9); "Important Speeches by Central Leaders on March 18," Yingte, Kwangtung, *Red Rebel Corps of Yingte Middle School*, April 13, 1968 (translation in *SCMP* 4182, May 21, 1968, pp. 1–12); "Speeches [excerpts] of Premier Chou and K'ang Sheng at Their Reception of Peking-Bound Reporting Team of Kiangsi Provincial Revolutionary Preparatory Group" (date not given), Canton, *Wen-Ko T'ung-hsün* (*Cultural Revolution Bulletin*), No. 12 (February 1968) (translation in *SCMP* 4139, March 15, 1968, pp. 2–3); "Premier Chou's Important Speech of February 2, 1968," Canton, *Tzu-liao Chuan-chi* (*Special Collection of Materials*), No. 7 (February 28, 1968) (translation in *SCMP* 4154, April 8, 1968, pp. 1–11); "Speeches by Central Leaders at Reception of Tseng Ssu-yü, Liu Feng, and Other Comrades of Wuhan Military District," Canton, *Hung-ssu T'ung-hsün* (*Red Flag Bulletin*), combined issue Nos. 4–5 (July 12, 1968) (translation in *SCMM* 622, August 6, 1968, pp. 15–23); "Premier Chou's Important Speech [excerpts]," Canton, *Hsiao-ping* (*Little Soldiers*), No. 22 (February 17, 1968) (translation in *SCMP* 4134, March 8, 1968, pp. 1–5); "Premier Chou's Talk at a Reception for Revolutionary Masses of X X Industrial Systems," January 17, 1968, Canton, *Wen-ko Feng-yun* (*Cultured Revolution Storm*), No. 2 (February 1968) (translation in *SCMP* 4148, March 28, 1968, pp. 3–9); "Premier Chou's Important Speech on April 7," Canton, *I-yüeh Feng-pao* (*January Storm*), No. 26 (May 1968) (translation in *SCMP* 4189, June 3, 1968, pp. 1–9); "Premier Chou's Important Speech to National Defense Scientific and Technological Commission Academy of Science Representatives," Canton, *Hung-ch'i T'ung-hsün* (*Red Flag Bulletin*), June 1968 (translation in *SCMP* 4218, July 16, 1968, pp. 1–3); also reprint in *Tzu-Kuo* (*China Monthly*), No. 52 (July 1968) pp. 28–40; "Three Point Instructions to Kung Chih-ch'uan," Canton, *Kung-jen P'ing-lun* (*Worker's Review*), No. 5 (June 1968) (translation in *SCMP* 4206, June 26, 1968, pp. 1–2); "Premier Chou's Speech at the Railroad and Transportation Workers Meeting," Canton, *Hung-ch'i T'ung-hsün* (*Red Flag Bulletin*), No. 1 (June 1968) (translation in *SCMP* 4212, July 8, 1968, pp. 1–7; and *Facts and Features*, Vol. 1, No. 25 [October 2, 1968] pp. 18–25); "Premier Chou Received Shansi Representatives to Central Mao-Study Class," Canton, *Tung-fang-*

all provinces had revolutionary committees. The Twelfth Plenum could thus take place in an atmosphere of relative calm and optimism and could look forward to planning for the Ninth Party Congress in 1969.

There was one trend concerning Chou's Cultural Revolution involvement which was somewhat different for the period after August 1967. This pertains to the relative amounts of time he devoted to foreign policy as opposed to domestic politics. Beginning in August Chou devoted an ever-increasing share of his energy to foreign affairs. Correspondingly, his involvement in domestic politics declined, and it is interesting to note that there was a strictly inverse relationship between the record of his appearances in the two spheres. The trend had progressed far enough that by late 1968 Chou apparently devoted almost none of his time to domestic politics and almost all of it to foreign affairs, a situation which continued down to the Ninth Congress.[215]

Contrasting explanations for this phenomenon can be advanced. It is possible that, beginning sometime in early 1968, Chou came under some sort of political cloud. Perhaps he ran afoul of Mao or Lin (or even perhaps Chiang Ch'ing), and hence progressively lost credit with his colleagues in the central leadership. Such a hypothesis might be bolstered by reported disagreements between Chou and Chiang Ch'ing; by the possibility that he encouraged the anti-leftist trend in late 1967 and early 1968 to go too far (and hence suffered a loss of creditability when the leftist

---

hung T'ung-hsün (The East-Is-Red Bulletin) No. 2 (July 1968) (translation in SCMP 4226, July 26, 1968, pp. 4–6); "Premier Chou Gave Important Instructions on Tibet," Canton, K'ang-szu Chan-chi (Steel Fourth Headquarters), No. 2 (June 1968) (translation in SCMM 622, August 6, 1968, p. 3); "Premier Chou Received Wuhan Military Region Leaders (June 12–13)," Canton, Hung-ssu T'ung-hsün (Red Headquarters Bulletin) No. 4–5 (July 1968) (translation in SCMM 622, August 6, 1968, p. 15); "Premier Chou's Telephone Instructions to Comrade Tseng Ssu-yu on June 14," Canton, Hung-ssu T'ung-hsün (Red Headquarters Bulletin), No. 4–5 (July 1968) (translation in SCMM 622, August 6, 1968, p. 15); "Premier Chou Received Representatives of Kwangsi Factions," Canton, Kung-ko Hui (Finance and Trade Committee), translation in SCMP 4279, October 16, 1968, pp. 1–13; NCNA International Service, January 26, 1968; January 31, 1968; February 19, 1968; March 8, 1968; March 26, 1968; May 2, 1968; May 20, 1968; June 3, 1968; June 30, 1968; July 2, 1968; August 12, 1968; August 15, 1968; September 9, 1968; September 30, 1968; October 2, 1968; and October 5, 1968.

[215] While most of Chou's appearances and activities in the foreign relations sector were of a pro-forma nature—greeting and seeing off delegations, attending banquets, issuing general declarations, and the like—there was too much of an increase in the amount of his time devoted to those matters to charge it off to changes in the structure of reportage of his movements. As we argue below, both the nature of his duties and the intensity-level of Chinese foreign policy interaction were changing.

trend began); by loss of institutional support, as the State Council continued to be subject to purge and as the ministries and industry itself were weakened by the disorders; by the increasingly powerful role of the army in politics; and by the tendency for the center of political activity to shift from Peking to the provincial and local peripheries.[216] While there may be something to each of these reasons, since each is "factual" in the sense that actual developments can be cited in their favor, there is no direct evidence at hand that Chou's political position was slipping. It is true that at the Ninth Congress he was no longer listed as third in the hierarchy and was, instead, cast into the set of all leaders (aside from Mao and Lin themselves) listed alphabetically. It is also true that the makeup of the post-Ninth Congress leading groups (the Politburo, the Central Committee, and the Military Affairs Committee in particular) reflected a relative diminution in the institutional role played by the State Council and, hence, by Chou's own supporters. Nonetheless, Chou's own role at the Congress (he was "secretary" of the Congress) and the resurgence of his standing after the Congress period (Peking media again began to list him as number three and he again took on many of his old functions in domestic affairs) both argue against such an interpretation.

Moreover, an alternate explanation is at hand which fits the same set of facts and provides a more rational framework of analysis. As we have seen, Chou's role during the Cultural Revolution, as far as Mao and Lin were concerned, was that of trouble-shooter, fireman, negotiator, and organizer. He thus was deputized to act in whatever sphere these qualities could best be utilized. By August 1967, with the solution of the Wuhan question at hand; with the Army taking a greater role in policy and administration; and with a degree of "regularization" of the Cultural Revolution becoming apparent, perhaps Mao and Lin (as well as Chou himself) thought that he could safely change the direction of his activities. Since the Foreign Ministry had for some time been in his own hands (and not Ch'en Yi's), and since the time began to draw near when China would wish to reinvolve herself actively in foreign relations, Chou slowly converted more and more of his time and effort to involvement in China's international relations. In fact, it may be true that one measure of the

---

[216] It is significant that Chou is not reported to have left Peking after September 1967. Chou, who, as we have seen, depended partly on his physical presence to maximize his political influence, found it impossible to be everywhere at once and increasingly inefficient to talk with huge numbers of local cadres at local levels. To some extent he made up for this by meeting with these same groups in Peking, but even that sort of encounter gradually diminished.

restoration of foreign relations to its pre-Cultural Revolution place in China's order of priorities may be the increasing percentage of time Chou devoted to those problems. This is shown in the accompanying tabulation.[217]

CHOU EN-LAI'S INTERNAL AND EXTERNAL APPEARANCES FROM
SEPTEMBER 1967 THROUGH MARCH 1969

Month		Internal Appearances	External Appearances	Total	Percentage of External/Total Appearances
September	1967	12	13	25	52
October	1967	5	35	40	87.5
November	1967	6	13	19	68.4
December	1967	3	13	16	81.3
Sept.–Dec.	1967	26	74	100	74
January	1968	4	2	6	33.3
February	1968	4	5	9	55.6
March	1968	9	6	15	40
April	1968	5	4	9	44.4
May	1968	7	12	19	63.2
June	1968	7	17	24	70.8
July	1968	2	5	7	71.4
August	1968	3	8	11	72.7
September	1968	2	13	15	86.7
October	1968	3	11	14	78.6
November	1968	0	14	14	100
December	1968	0	11	11	100
Jan.–Dec.	1968	46	108	154	70.1
January	1969	1	6	7	85.7
February	1969	1	6	7	85.7
March	1969	0	5	5	100
Jan.–March	1969	2	17	19	89.5
Total September 1967 to March	1969	74	199	273	72.9

[217] This tabulation is based on information concerning Chou's foreign-policy related appearances as follows.

Chou En-lai's Political Style: A Summary of Findings

Having thus suggested that Chou En-lai's activity pattern during the first year of the active phase of the Cultural Revolution mirrors his political involvement as a whole, we can now generalize with some confidence on his role, purpose, tactics, and relationships. Together these provide a model of his political "style."

Chou's *role* is not difficult to discern. Mao and Lin evidently saw him as their chief problem-solver, trouble-shooter, negotiator, organizer, administrator, guide-adviser to revolutionary groups, and local enforcer of Central Committee policy. Chou made sure to maximize these qualities, for they made him into an "indispensable man" to Mao and Lin. At several points he relied directly on this status to protect his own political position from attack by Red Guards below and from members of the Cultural Revolution Small Group to the side.

His own *purposes* during the Cultural Revolution were, however, somewhat different. They are not difficult to discern and stem to some extent from the role he was expected to play. Thus, he can be said to have pursued as public goals the following: settlement of disputes, implementation of Cultural Revolution goals, and steerage of revolutionary groups. But aside from these, Chou pursued a number of other, more private goals, some of which contradicted his obvious, public ends. Thus, for instance, while he wished to direct the Red Guards toward carrying out

---

The year 1968: *NCNA International,* January 15; January 31; February 4; February 10; February 28; March 17; March 18; March 20; April 9; April 18; April 26; May 23; May 24; May 25; May 26; May 27; May 28; May 29; June 12; June 18; June 19; June 21; June 22; June 23; June 26; July 1; July 24; July 27; August 14; August 16; August 18; August 23; September 3; September 12; September 18; September 24; September 29; September 30; October 1; October 2; October 3; October 4; October 5; October 6; October 7; October 12; November 9; November 10; November 17; November 20; November 22; November 28; November 30; December 19; December 21; December 31; "Premier Chou's Three-Point Instruction to Foreign Ministry," Canton, *Chung-ta Hung-chi (Chung-san University Red Flag),* No. 63 (April 4, 1968) (translation in *SCMP* 4166, April 29, 1968, p. 5); Radio Peking, April 26; Hanoi, VNA, May 23; Radio Baghdad, July 15; Radio Cairo, July 27; Radio Pyongyang; Radio Tirana, September 10; Radio Pyongyang, September 30; Radio Belgrade, October 20; *Jen-min Jih-pao,* October 30, 1968; Radio Peking, October 4; Radio Tirana, October 5; Hanoi VNA, December 14; Hanoi VNA, December 31; Radio Tirana, December 31; Radio Bucharest, November 2; Radio Phnom Penh, November 14; Radio Phnom Penh, November 19.

The year 1969: *NCNA International,* January 13; January 24; February 6; February 10; February 24; March 1; March 11; March 20; March 24; Radio Peking, January 20. Internal appearances are documented in notes 205–216.

their revolutionary assignments, he also wished to control and limit their activities so that the productive capacity and the social fabric of the country were not threatened. Needless to say, pursuit of one was often at variance with prosecution of the other. For instance, preservation of a certain minimum of social order, another private goal, often got in the way of the furtherance of revolutionary goals. There was also an obvious contradiction between minimizing damage to the industrial plant and China's intellectual-managerial capital with the goal of assisting revolutionary takeover of factories, enterprises, and ministries. In this case, Chou often seemed to accept short-term damage if it would ensure long-run survival of these resources. While this meant at times over-stressing the revolutionary side of the production-revolutionary equality, he was always careful to restore the equilibrium when the revolutionary "heat" had slackened. Finally, Chou seemed to want very much to prevent the State Council from being decimated by the kind of revolutionary power seizures that the Party committees were experiencing. He thus worked hard at preventing revolutionary committees from being set up in State Council ministries, and even succeeded in disbanding those which had been formed. In these ways, he attempted to preserve his own institutional power base, as a supplement (although he never depended on it greatly) to his personal power and the authoritative power derived from Mao and Lin.

Analysis of the range of *tactics* which Chou employed to attain these ends allows us to approach more closely the question of his political style. There seem to be four clusters of techniques he used to achieve his public and private goals. The first concerns his ability to sense and move with the political tide. As we have seen, the Cultural Revolution can be viewed as a succession of swings of the political pendulum, each new phase marked by a new leftward impetus which, having spent its energy over a period of several months, was succeeded by a rightist consolidation. In each case, the reversal seems to have been initiated by the Mao-Lin leadership, always in reaction to the too-extreme manifestations of the previous period's activity and for the purpose of retaining the "proper" momentum toward the leadership's goals. Chou En-lai was the first to sense (and probably to know, given his status) these changes in direction. But he was not always the first to move with the tide. In fact, a central element in his political style was to swim *against* the tide when it was a leftist current, until the point was reached that further effort was useless —that is, when his own status and goals were threatened with more than marginal damage. When that point was reached, he turned around and moved *with* the tide as forcefully as he could. His reasoning at that point was probably that he could do no other, but more important, that by aiding the leftist current he would help to make the situation quickly critical and thus hasten the coming of the rightist countertide. Once the leftist current had reached its extreme, the pendulum could only begin its movement back. That this was one of his methods of operation is clearly shown in every phase of the Cultural Revolution. In fact, we found at one point that he propounded this as one of the secrets of his political success.[218] The temptation is great to term Chou a close student of Machiavelli, for the political theorist's recommendations as to how to survive in unfortunate times differ in no essential respect from Chou's own actions and justifications.

A second cluster of political techniques emerges from analysis of Chou's manner of dealing with the threats posed by swings of the political pendulum. This is his tendency to draw distinctions, make simple matters complex, work out stages of attack and then substages, draw practical limits to theoretical goals, and interpret directives in terms which would aid his own goals. Thus, for instance, Chou spun out detailed changes in organization, methods of struggle, work team questions, relationships of revolution to production, distinctions between persons and their offices, the physical person versus the mental-spiritual person, business supervision versus requisition control, and techniques and stages for seizure of power.

Third, Chou dealt with attacks upon himself and upon his associates in a consistent manner. When State Council ministers were under Red Guard siege, he first attempted to defend them outright, then allowed controlled and drawn-out criticism, finally joined in the criticism, and only then gave in and allowed the man to be removed from office. As often as not, the minister in question would reappear after a time in his old position, Chou having taken over the ministry himself in the interim. With regard to attacks against himself, he resorted to similar tactics, with the exception that, because of his close association with Lin and Mao (which he did not hesitate to point out when necessary), he was never in as much danger of removal.

Finally, Chou relied on his own personality and energy to get himself out of tight spots. He often went for days without sleep and seems to have met purposely with Red Guard groups in the small hours of the night and morning. Personal contacts and the ability to exert his authority directly were a major part of Chou's style. Such contacts served him well,

[218] See page 188.

not only in his relations with revolutionary mass groups but also with others in the top leadership. While it is possible that he experienced some personal difficulties with Chiang Ch'ing, in every other case—be it Mao or Lin themselves, other members of the Cultural Revolution Small Group, or army leaders—Chou went out of his way to maintain close personal contact. Even with regard to Chiang Ch'ing, when leftist trends were clearly in the ascent Chou could be found praising her publicly (if not, perhaps, privately).

Thus, in sum, we have a picture of a man who can rightfully claim to be mainland China's most adroit politician; unlike Mao or Lin, who can hand down policy and then shield themselves from its effects, Chou at every point involves himself in the execution of policy, as well as its making. Chou in fact may be seen as the archtype of the bureaucratic politician, the political figure who works his will from the inside of a political structure as well as from (or, perhaps, toward) the outside. In this regard, while there are the obvious aspects of personality, background, and environment which make him, like every political actor, unique, there is nonetheless enough in common with others in his position to make him a model of a particular kind of political actor as well as one who can profitably be compared with other such figures.

Chou En-lai's Political Style Compared with other Major Political Figures

In order to carry forth such a comparison—and thus provide the basis for a more general theory of political styles as well as to gain further insight into Chou's own style—it will be useful to draw short comparisons with two other major Chinese Communist political figures, Mao Tse-tung and Lin Piao. Both of them may give us insight into Chou's own style, either by similarity or by contrast. Let us look briefly at each.

Mao Tse-tung, one of the founders of the Chinese Communist Party and its leader (with certain exceptions) during the past forty or more years, has been associated with Chou in one capacity or another from at least 1925. It is true, of course, that because Mao has been Chou's acknowledged superior during most of this period, no direct comparison between the two can be made. Nonetheless, since both men have been long-term Chinese revolutionaries and since Chou is often mentioned as Mao's successor (the assumption is sometimes made that Lin Piao, Mao's officially chosen successor, will not be able to fill the post for long for reasons of health or because he would prove unequal to the job), a comparison of political styles is in order.

Mao can be said to possess the following personality traits which are important in understanding his political style.[219] He places great emphasis on individual initiative and dynamic individual activity, as opposed to passive execution of orders handed down from above or over-intellectualization of a problem. Social institutions, particularly bureaucracy, should not hinder such initiative. A concomitant (perhaps even a logically prior) notion is that the way to do things is to do them. If obstacles present themselves, they should be pushed over. In the ultimate sense (and particularly in the twentieth-century Chinese environment), this implies an emphasis on martial virtues, military solutions, and guerrilla warfare (a particular military method of overcoming obstacles immovable in the short run). It also implies that political activity must possess a high degree of flexibility, pragmatism, and autonomy. In fact, politics must be given first priority, with less worry about such apparent restraints as economics or personality. When other people get in the way of the pursuit of Mao's goals, they must either be humored along (if they are too powerful) or cast aside (if they are not). Allied with, and contributing to, this social and political voluntarism is the conscious acceptance and advocacy of social change as a good in itself. Modernization is a goal to be worked for, to be attained by as great an input of popular effort, and in as short a time, as possible. This goal and these methods are desirable and permissible to Mao also because he believes in the revolutionary potential and the national greatness of the Chinese people, especially the peasantry. Thus, populism is a strain in Mao's thought and activity equally as important as revolutionary activism. Marxism becomes the

[219] This list is derived from the following sources: Stuart Schram, *Mao Tse-tung* (New York, 1960); Jerome Ch'en, *Mao and the Chinese Revolution* (Oxford, 1965); Jerome Ch'en (ed.), *Mao* (Englewood Cliffs, N.J., 1969); Arthur A. Cohen, *The Communism of Mao Tse-tung* (Chicago, 1964); Stuart Schram, *The Political Thought of Mao Tse-tung* (New York, 1963); John Rue, *Mao Tse-tung in Opposition* (Stanford, 1966); and the following editions of Mao's works: *Mao Tse-tung Hsuan-chi* (*Selected Works of Mao Tse-tung*), Peking: Jen-min Ch'u-pan-she, 1961, 4 vols.; *Selected Military Writings,* Peking, Foreign Languages Press, 1963; *Mao Tse-tung Szu-hsiang Wan-sui!* (*Long Live Mao Tse-tung's Thought!*) n.p., April 1967; Japanese translation in *Chuo Koron,* No. 7 (July 1969) pp. 351–400, and No. 8 (August 1969) pp. 209–235; English translation in *Current Background,* Hong Kong, No. 891 (October 8, 1969) and No. 892 (October 21, 1969); "Mao Tse-tung's Instructions Concerning the Great Proletarian Cultural Revolution," *Current Background,* No. 885 (July 31, 1969); and "In Camera Statements of Mao Tse-tung," *Chinese Law and Government,* Vol. 1, No. 4 (Winter, 1968–1969).

vehicle for implementing these goals and is a convenient framework for rationalizing those means. Hence, such themes as permanent revolution and progress through the dialectic of contradictions hold innate appeal for Mao, both intellectually and as policy means. If, after having attained partial or even total political control of a given area, it appears that there is wavering and backsliding, it is imperative, in Mao's thinking, to forcibly prevent such developments from snowballing into serious impediments to further implementation of the permanent revolution. The result is an emphasis, positively, on indoctrination and, negatively, on thought control, organizational coercion, and purge. Finally, these intermediate goals having been assured, at least for the time being, one can again push forward vigorously with the revolutionary program of struggle against the ideological enemy within and without the party, for the "people" and the country, and with nature itself.

It is obvious that Mao's political style is both singular, uncompromising for the most part, and very different from that of Chou En-lai. It is true that both Mao and Chou are Chinese nationalists, that both wish to see the construction of a modern, vigorous, and powerful China, and that both will do what is necessary to remove obstacles (or cope with them if removal is impossible). Both, furthermore, have a basically pragmatic nature which has enabled them to survive politically.

But differences abound. Chou wishes to preserve what has been gained even if it is not completely satisfying; Mao has no hesitation in overthrowing all if it does not accord with his desires. Chou is a gradualist; Mao is not. Chou is a conformist and often swims with the tide; Mao wants to create the tide and if necessary reverse it. Chou takes the offensive during a rightist trend, and Mao works best in leftist currents. Chou likes to make simple matters complex—he can make his way politically when problems are multifaceted; Mao not only does poorly in such situations but endeavors to shape circumstances so that he does not have to face such problems. Finally, while Chou relies heavily on personal contact and energy, Mao depends upon his very remoteness from the masses, on his ability to appeal to them from above and through the written word, and on the presumption that when necessary a smaller amount of energy applied to a problem will, over a long period, do just as well or better than a large amount applied in a short time span.

With this wide range of differences, why have Mao and Chou been able to work so closely together all these years? Three answers are apparent. First, Chou's own personality is suitable to the task of attending to those details of the Chinese revolution which Mao has not had the time or the patience to deal with. Second, and more important, perhaps, is that throughout the Chinese revolution (and during the Great Proletarian Cultural Revolution in particular) the environment has had its "revenge" upon Mao in the sense that his program and methods have run up against obstacles which, at least in the short run, prove to be insuperable. As time has gone on, these environmental constraints on Maoist policy have become more and more severe. Whenever it has appeared to Mao that the limits of his policy and methods had been met, and his goals not yet achieved, he has drawn back and waited for the atmosphere to clear. At these points he seems to have called on Chou to clean up the "mess" created by his own revolutionary over-enthusiasm. In those periods, Chou's work became extraordinarily important to Mao, for through it, he hoped, the stage would be set for another revolutionary leap. Finally, there are important areas where Chou is plainly better qualified than Mao. One is negotiations, in which personal patience and attention to detail are crucial. Contact with large numbers of divergent groups is another; there again, patience, personal stamina, and attention to detail are necessary for success. It is true that in the period before 1949, Mao possessed many of these qualities himself and in the "amount" necessary to attain his goals. That was also a period in which he relied on Chou much less than he has recently. But as Mao has grown older and less patient with the course of events, and as the periods of revolutionary setback have grown in frequency and duration, he has used Chou's services more and more often and for more important tasks. Thus, Chou has grown in importance to Mao during the post-1949 period, so that by the time of the Cultural Revolution Mao was relying on him heavily enough (and had tested his loyalty often enough) so that Chou had indeed become "indispensable" in his eyes.

In contrast to Mao, we know little of Lin Piao's style of political leadership or even of his personality. Nonetheless, enough has been written about Lin, enough of his writings are available, and enough of his practical moves —both military and political—are known that it is possible to build up a picture of Lin complete enough for comparative purposes.[220]

[220] The following secondary sources have proved valuable: Liu Yuen-sun, "The Current and Past of Lin Piao," *Fei-ch'ing Yen-chiu* (*Studies on Chinese Communism*), Taipei, Vol. 1, No. 1 (January 31, 1967) pp. 61–77 (translation by Robert Liang and Thomas Robinson, The Rand Corporation, P-3671, September 1967); *The New York Times,* "China's Military Chief, Lin Piao," August 13, 1966; Loren Fessler, "The Long March of Lin Piao," *New York Times Magazine,* September 10, 1967, pp. 64ff; Edgar Snow, "The Man Alongside Mao: Deputy Lin Piao's Thoughts and Career," *The New Republic,* December 3, 1966, pp. 15–18; Chu Wenlin, "Lin Piao—Mao Tse-tung's Close Comrade-in-Arms," *Issues and Studies,* Taipei,

Lin's political style can be inferred from his personality, from what we know of his work style, his relations with Mao, his ideological and national attitudes, and (most important) his military writings and campaigns. Personally, Lin is universally described as quiet, reserved, non-talkative; calm, unemotional, and modest. At the same time, he is said to be clever, calculating, deliberate, and astute. He drives himself very hard, sometimes losing much sleep in the process, is willing to learn both indirectly through books and directly through field experience and from his own and others' mistakes. He likes to bury himself in the details of his work and to pursue a matter, once begun, to its conclusion. At the same time, he is not a "public" figure in the sense of enjoying the public admiration of those around him. He prefers to work behind the scenes, for the most part, issuing instructions by telephone and handwritten order and by calling officials to his residence instead of attending meetings.

While a believing Communist, Lin is not a political thinker, preferring to take his orientation from Mao for application to practical problems. Lin is accused of being a sycophant of Mao; he probably is, but he openly disagreed with Mao on at least one occasion—after the Long March in 1936—and he has been very much his own man when it comes to the formulation and execution of military strategy and tactics. He probably does genuinely share with Mao a number of basic attitudes: aside from

---

Vol. 3, No. 4 (January 1967) pp. 1–11, and No. 5 (February 1967) pp. 28–35; Li Tien-min, "The Rise of Lin Piao in the Chinese Communist Hierarchy," *Issues and Studies*, Vol. 3, No. 1 (October 1966) pp. 8–19; Ching-kang-shan Corps, Peking Industrial University, "Life of Lin Piao" (translation in *JPRS* 41,801, July 12, 1967, *Translations on Communist China: Political and Sociological*, No. 406, pp. 1–24, and in *JPRS* 42,503, September 7, 1967, *Communist China Digest*, No. 189, pp. 62–73); Ralph L. Powell, "The Increasing Power of Lin Piao and the Party-Soldiers, 1959–1966," *The China Quarterly*, No. 34 (April–June 1968) pp. 38–65; Lieutenant Colonel Robert B. Rigg, "Lin Piao: Portrait of a Militant," *Army*, Vol. 19, No. 5 (May 1969) pp. 26–32; Lieutenant Colonel Robert B. Rigg, *Red China's Fighting Hordes* (Harrisburg, Pa.: The Military Service Publishing Company, 1951) pp. 201–207; and "Chairman Mao's Successor—Deputy Supreme Commander Lin Piao," Chinese Red Guard pamphlet, n.p., n.d. (translation in *Current Background*, No. 894 [October 27, 1969] pp. 1–24).

For a masterful survey of Lin's military strategy and tactics, Colonel William W. Whitson, *The Chinese Communist High Command* (New York, 1971) Chapter 5, "The Fourth Field Army Elite."

In addition, Lin's own writings, especially those published before 1949, are central to an understanding of how he perceives and acts in the political-military world. The author, together with Anna Sun Ford, has translated seventy-five of these works, a reading of which informs the analysis that follows.

the standard Marxist-Leninist approach to basic questions, both exhibit virulent anti-Americanism and anti-Sovietism, intense Chinese nationalism, a penchant for military solutions to political problems, and a propensity to overcome obstacles by main force if possible and by indirect action, waiting, or guerrilla-like tactics if necessary. Lin is thought to be overly attracted to war and violence as solutions to problems. This can certainly be inferred both from his pre-1949 writings, his statements since then, and his career, almost all of which has been military. But one would expect little else, at least verbally, of a man with such a background and it remains to be seen whether, once he is on his own, he will retain such opinions.

A clue to this question and further insight into Lin's political style may be found in his military writings[221] and in his actual military conduct.[222] Several principles of action emerge from an analysis of them. First, Lin insists on a long period of preparation and planning before any venture is attempted. He would rather play for time, paying for it with a series of small losses, than rush into an action before he is completely ready. Training and indoctrination are critical elements in such preparation. Second, Lin does not usually strike at an opponent all along a given front; rather, he looks for the weakest point in the enemy's armor, disguises his moves by feints elsewhere, and then in a surprise attack puts as much force as he can into overwhelming the enemy at this one spot. Surprise and concentration of effort are thus two central elements in his strategy. Once having attained his objective Lin is quick to retreat, when necessary, to already prepared positions. Lin has been described an artist at tactical disengagement, and he is wise enough to know that tactical success in a given area cannot necessarily be maintained there and that one tactical

[221] We are less confident in using Lin's post-1949 writings because of the danger that they too much represent what Mao wants to hear, and not what Lin genuinely believes in, and because there is the possibility that Lin did not actually write some of these latter-day pieces (this includes the famous 1965 statement on people's war).

[222] If we assume that Lin Piao uses and will use the same principles in politics which he has found useful and necessary in military strategy and tactics, we then have an outline of some of the central elements of his political style. While such an assumption has obvious shortcomings, it is nonetheless true that the formative period of Lin's political life was during the pre-1949 civil war era and that, once he is on his own as Mao's political successor, he may well hark back, psychologically, to those times and the military principles worked out then. While it is true that he has consciously subordinated himself to Mao, it is in the military sphere that he has been most nearly independent.

success is not necessarily followed by another. Thus, Lin's strategy can be described as aggressive, imaginative, and dramatic, but with much thought and preparation taken ahead of time and alternate courses of action thought out in case of failure. From Lin we should therefore expect long periods of deceptive inactivity; then lightning moves in specific directions using all the force at his disposal; then either consolidation or quick retreat; and finally, a further period of waiting and planning.

This puts us in position to compare the political styles of Chou and Lin. Both styles share a number of qualities. Both are outwardly calm and unemotional. Both are regarded as astute and clever men. Both possess great stores of energy and drive. Neither is an original political thinker, preferring to rigidly subordinate themselves to Mao. Each holds the private goal of protecting the integrity and autonomy of their respective institutions and of their colleagues. Each is capable of moving quickly with the political current.

There are, nonetheless, some subtle differences in style and attitude. While each is adept at working behind the scenes and at political infighting, Chou is just as much at home working in the limelight; Lin is not. While both stress the desirability of indirect means of attaining an objective, Lin, like Mao, attempts to surmount a goal directly when possible. Chou almost always takes a circuitous route. While both move quickly with the political tide, Chou at times tries to swim against it if he thinks he can. Lin never does. Both men plan their avenues of retreat, but Lin is quick to move back, while Chou always fights a series of delaying actions. Finally, the brand of nationalism which each displays is somewhat different: Lin's is almost wholly anti-foreign, so much so that he might be termed a xenophobe; Chou's nationalism is not necessarily anti-foreign and stresses positive Chinese virtues instead.

Finally, there are areas where their styles differ dramatically. Chou is verbal; Lin is not. Chou revels in public appearances; Lin is at his worst there. Chou prefers bureaucratic solutions to political problems; Lin may well adopt such solutions (because politics is not, after all, war, and because he, too, has had considerable bureaucratic experience), but he is not comfortable with them. He, like Mao, would rather overcome problems by main force. There is a difference in the timing of their political involvement: Lin, in line with his tendency to attack militarily only after preparation and then suddenly, seems to be only sporadically involved. Hence, he disappears from the scene for long periods and then suddenly explodes into view again. Chou, on the other hand, is more or less constantly involved. There is also an obvious difference in attitudes toward planning in politics. Lin plans to the extreme; Chou seems to adopt a posture of muddling through. Furthermore, Lin likes to simplify problems, whereas Chou tries to make them more complex. Their orientation towards problem-solving is thus different. Finally, Lin and Chou differ fundamentally in their attitudes toward others. Lin appears to treat others as enemies, at least initially. Chou does not seem to make this initial assumption. Thus, to Lin, politics is zero-sum; to Chou it is not.

But while these last differences are fundamental, it does not follow that their political styles are diametrically opposed. Not only do they hold in common a wide range of similar goals and means of policy, but they also complement each other in important respects. As we noted earlier, each needs, understands, trusts, and uses the other. Hence, while their styles are different, they are still complementary and it is that fact (aside from the Maoist framework) which has kept them together in the past and which augers well for their close cooperation in the future.[223]

Chou En-lai and Charisma

An essential element of a political actor's style is the degree to which he exhibits charismatic qualities. Not only does this bear on his ability to be politically effective, it also influences his possibilities for future political leadership. This is particularly germane to Chou En-lai, since during the Cultural Revolution he seemed to exhibit some of the qualities which we traditionally associate with charisma, and since the answer to the question of his post-Maoist political future depends partly on our findings in this regard.

Charisma has by now been well-studied [224] and our present task is to match its characteristics with what we know of Chou's political style. The charismatic leader seems to possess the following qualities:

---

[223] See Appendix A for suggestions on further comparisons of Chou's styles.

[224] We depend for the most part on Ann Ruth Willner, "Charismatic Political Leadership: A Theory," Princeton University, Center for International Studies, 1968, which adequately sums up the literature; and also on Robert C. Tucker, "The Theory of Charismatic Leadership," *Daedalus*, Vol. 97, No. 3 (Summer 1968) pp. 731–758; E. Victor Wolfenstein, *The Revolutionary Personality* (Princeton, 1967) especially the Introduction, pp. 3–32; and Max Weber, "The Sociology of Charismatic Authority," in H. H. Gerth and C. Wright Mills (translators and editors), *From Max Weber: Essays in Sociology* (New York, 1958) pp. 245–252.

1. His followers must perceive him to be endowed with unique and near-superhuman qualities capable of evoking extremes of devotion, awe, reverence, and blind faith.

2. He is thought to be charismatic personally and not as a result of the office he occupies nor of the tradition in which he is raised.

3. He tends to flourish in conditions of stress and revolution, and when existing leadership and institutions are questioned.

4. He avoids exerting political influence through formal rules and routines; he is revolutionary in his impact on political and social life; and his effects are transitory and intermittent.

5. He can produce quick changes of opinion in his followers, causing them to forget their normal standards of judgment of political leadership and follow him without question.

6. He can emerge as a leader from a group that founds a political movement, or as a factional leader who depends upon an already extant political and organizational base.

7. The charismatic leader is likely to come from a heterogeneous social background, to have experienced mobility or instability of environment during childhood, and to have been exposed to more than the normal sort of socio-economic-political stimuli during his maturation process.

8. He possesses the following personal characteristics: extremely high energy and vitality level; almost total composure under stress and challenge; unusual mental attainment, in the sense of seizing on information from many sources and having an excellent memory, even though not necessarily being learned; a flair for originality and a capacity for innovation, even in using standard political techniques; ability to elicit devotion and sacrifice from women; physically superior in the eyes of his followers; rejects economic and organizational-rationalization arguments.

9. He is able to evoke and invoke the myths and values of the society, assimilating them to himself, his mission, and his vision of the society.

10. In his rhetorical style, he uses illusions, metaphors, similies, and symbols in a manner attractive to his followers; and is also capable of rhythm, repetition, and alliteration in his speech.

Inspecting this list, it seems evident that while Mao Tse-tung is obviously a charismatic leader in the full sense of the term, Chou En-lai at best can claim to be "near-charismatic." While it is true that our investigations have shown him to possess many of the personal qualities of the charismatic leader listed in point eight; while, as in point five, he can turn his audience around to his own standards of judgment and convince them that such standards are their own; and while, as per point seven, his social origin, maturation process, and revolutionary background are such as to qualify him charismatically, it appears that on most of the other points he comes off only second best. There is no doubt, for instance, that his audiences perceive in him something extraordinary, but his presence and pronouncements do not produce that awe-inspiring reverence and faith that is the hallmark of charisma. What charisma he possesses stems at least as much from his office and his institutional and personal associations as from his own person; and, if anything, his authority is exerted much more through formal rules and organizations—whether during the Cultural Revolution or before or after—than through his own appeal. He did not emerge as a leader in any of the listed ways; rather, he has worked within the Party organization almost since its inception and has never (or rarely, and then only briefly) been a factional leader. Like Lin Piao, he has lived his Party life willingly under Mao's shadow. While it is true that his concept of positive (nonxenophobic) Chinese nationalism is conveyed to his listeners, and thus he is to that extent able to link his vision of Chinese values with his own person, this is a very minor theme in his overall message, which is devoted primarily to particulars and not to myth-producing generalities. Moreover, Chou has yet to swim the Yangtze to demonstrate his superior physical prowess and he has yet to write poems showing for all to see his mythological and emotion-inducing qualities. Finally, Chou is the very paradigm of the economic organizer and financial expert; far from lacking an understanding of that field, Chou has found his greatest success within the industrial-organizational sphere.

While it is still difficult to ascertain just how far beyond his own physical person Chou's personal influence moves, it is clear from this analysis that he does not now possess the sort of qualities which we associate with the historical charismatic leader. It may be that after Mao's death he will allow some of these qualities to emerge from under the veil that may have hidden them during the last five decades. But that seems unlikely: even if such qualities were present initially in his personality, it is probable that they have long since been eradicated as a result of his endeavor to continually maneuver within the confines of Chinese Communist Party politics. Chou is a thorough-going Party man (should we say organization man?), and probably has little taste for going outside that framework to appeal directly to the Chinese people for a personal following.

Chou's Future After Mao

Despite this somewhat negative conclusion concerning Chou's charismatic qualities, it does not follow that his role in Chinese Communist domestic politics, foreign policy, or state and economic administration will decline once Mao has left the scene. In fact, for several reasons we feel that he will at least hold his own in the post-Maoist political hierarchy, and possibly even move up to share the reins of power with Lin Piao. On the other hand, it does not seem likely that he will move to assert his own personal rule over China by engaging in a power struggle with Lin or others.

Chou will not contest Lin Piao (or other Chinese leaders, for that matter) for several reasons. First, it is probable that during the period immediately following Mao's demise the Party leadership will opt for some form of collective leadership. Thus the question of Chou's possible status as number one is not likely to arise. More important, however, is the likelihood that even were the position offered him, he would not take it: his political influence is maximized when he is able to operate just below the very top. To place him in the position of sole authority would be to expose him to all the political pitfalls which he has avoided so far by remaining out of the running for the title of the Party's titular and ideological authority-figure. What the Chinese Communist Party needs after Mao's death is legitimacy in succession. This they have in Lin Piao. Once the period of initial crisis is over, the real struggle for succession will begin. But while it is probable that the various contending forces will compete for Chou's allegiance (just as they apparently did during the period immediately preceding the August 1966 plenum), and thus enable him to sit on the fence and trade his "vote" for assurances of political protection, power, and furtherance of his private goals, it is quite unlikely that he will compete for the number one position.

Moreover, as we have just seen, Chou does not possess the qualities necessary for becoming the titular successor. In the long run, someone possessing a greater number of the ten charismatic qualities listed above would be a better candidate than Chou (or Lin Piao, for that matter). It is possible, of course, that Lin might win such a struggle for power, emphasize those qualities which help make him attractive, and depend (much as Stalin did) on an institutionalized personality cult to do the rest. In this case, he would certainly need Chou to aid and assist him both in that struggle and in the period of rule following. We have already noted that Chou and Lin have much to complement each other; while two noncharismatic personalities do not add up to one with charisma, it is possible to envisage a future marked by cooperation between the two over the long term. But even this does not make Chou into a candidate for the Maoist succession.

Finally, the political milieu following Mao's passing would seem to be propitious for Chou and the goals which we have indicated he holds as long as he continues in much the same manner as at present. The need will probably be for a fairly extended period of economic and ideological recovery, of less threatening relations with the external world, and for time in which to play out the longer-term domestic struggle for power. In such a period, it is obvious that Chou's qualities—his administrative skills, his knowledge of foreign countries and respect abroad, and his ability to negotiate agreements between politically contending parties— will be greatly needed. His degree of "indispensability," already great during the Cultural Revolution, will thus probably rise even more. In short, Chou will probably continue to appear in a prominent role on the political scene and will thus give observers further opportunities to understand his style of politics.

APPENDIX A

Note on Further Comparisons
of Chou's Political Style

Lack of space has not permitted us to compare Chou En-lai's political style with other leading political figures. Such comparison would seem desirable, however, for a number of reasons. First, if a typology of political styles is to be truly comparative, we need to move away from Chinese Communist comparisons alone. There is need, for instance, to compare Chou with Soviet Communist leaders.[1] This would

[1] Lenin, Stalin, and Khrushchev come to mind. Of the three, perhaps Lenin has been the most well-studied in terms of his political style. See, for instance, Nathan C. Leites, *The Operational Code of the Politburo* (New York, 1951); Alfred Meyer, *Leninism* (New York, 1962), especially Chapter 4, "The Operational Code"; and

allow us to relax the condition, imposed in our own comparison, that political figures be Chinese. The next step would be to compare Chou with major, and well-studied, Western leaders. Charles de Gaulle, Woodrow Wilson, and Bismarck come to mind.[2] A third step would be to investigate the political style of "Chou-type" figures, defining this as the "bureaucratic politician."[3]

Treating Chou as a bureaucratic politician allows us to close the gap between political biography and the study of political bureaucracy. While there seems to be a dearth of literature in this field, the work of Francis E. Rourke[4] seems germane, as does the emerging literature on the politics of bureaucratic decision-making in the private sector.[5] Finally, it is necessary to draw lines of contact between political typology and the more general field of personality and politics. While this has for some time

John Keep, "Lenin as Tactician," in Leonard Shapiro and Peter Reddaway (eds.), *Lenin: The Man, The Theorist, The Leader* (New York, 1967). This is entirely aside from the huge biographical literature on Lenin. Stalin is much less well-studied in terms of political style. One must begin with the biographical literature, especially the now dated volume by Isaac Deutscher, *Stalin: A Political Biography* (New York, 1949). On Khrushchev, see, among other works, Lazar Pistrak, *Grand Tactician: Khrushchev's Rise to Power* (New York, 1961); and Konrad Kellen, *Khrushchev: A Political Portrait* (New York, 1961).

[2] For De Gaulle, see, inter alia, Raymond Aron, "The Political Methods of General De Gaulle," *International Affairs* [London], Vol. 37, No. 1 (January 1961) pp. 19–28; and Stanley and Inge Hoffmann, "The Will to Grandeur: De Gaulle as Political Artist," *Daedalus*, Vol. 97, No. 3 (Summer 1968) pp. 829–887. Still the best, and for our purposes the most suggestive, study on Wilson is Alexander and Juliette George, *Woodrow Wilson and Colonel House: A Personality Study* (New York, 1964). Bismarck's political style is poorly studied as yet. But see Henry A. Kissinger, "The White Revolutionary: Reflections on Bismarck," *Daedalus*, Vol. 97, No. 3 (Summer 1968), pp. 888–924; and A. J. P. Taylor, *Bismarck: The Man and the Statesman* (New York, 1955).

[3] One thinks, for instance, of such Soviet figures as Kosygin and Mikoyan, who spent their political lives, much as did Chou, in the Communist party bureaucracy just below the very pinnacle of power. Their biographies appear to be very similar to that of Chou. See, in this regard, entries on these two figures (by Grey Hodnett and Kermit McKenzie, respectively) in George W. Simmonds, ed., *Soviet Leaders*, New York, 1967. It may also be possible to find similar political figures in Western political bureaucracies. Although he has yet to be studied definitively, J. Edgar Hoover comes to mind. See Joseph Kraft's article, "J. Edgar Hoover—the Compleat Bureaucrat," in *Commentary*, Vol. 39, No. 2 (February 1965), pp. 59–62.

[4] *Bureaucracy, Politics, and Public Policy* (Boston, 1969), and *Bureaucratic Power in National Politics* (Boston, 1965).

[5] While the author is not well acquainted with this literature, Alfred D. Chandler, Jr.'s *Strategy and Structure: Chapters in the History of the Industrial Enterprise* (Cambridge, Mass., 1962), seems particularly suggestive.

been dominated by the neo-Freudians, and thus by the explanation of political personality by its psychological origins,[6] more general appraisals are contained in the writings of Fred Greenstein.[7] Both of these orientations need to be taken into account.

[6] The works of Erik Erikson come to mind in this regard. The George book on Wilson, cited above, is also of this genre, as are the works of Nathan C. Leites and E. Victor Wolfenstein.

[7] *Personality and Politics* (Chicago, 1969) and the special issue of the *Journal of Social Issues*, Vol. 24, No. 3 (July 1968), are devoted to the subject.

APPENDIX B

Speech by Premier Chou[1]
September 25, 1966

On September 25, 1966, from 10 o'clock in the evening until 2:30 in the morning, Premier Chou met with major responsible persons of the Peking Universities' and Technical Colleges' Red Guards Revolutionary Rebels Team Headquarters and those of the Peking Universities' and Middle Schools' Red Guards General Liaison Station. The Premier delivered a major report; the following constitutes the essence of that report.

Premier Chou began by inquiring about the names and native places of the individuals present. Then the Premier said, the term "Honor Guards" is feudalistic; it is better to change it to Vanguards. This is my innovation. Some students want to change their names; but surely not all names can be changed. When I first joined the revolution, the situation was anarchical and names were unnecessary. Some people did ask me to change my name then, but I declined. The Kuomintang once issued a warrant for my arrest during the civil war; I was accused of being a murderous criminal, but I still did not change my name.

Further, certain students have charged that the speech which I delivered on September 15 is a poisonous weed; this is incorrect. My speeches have

[1] Tsinghua University Defend-the-East Corps, *Collection of the Leaders' Speeches*, IV, November 1966. Marked "For Internal Distribution Only." Translations by Mrs. Anna Sun Ford and the author.

been studied by the Central Committee and have won the approval of Chairman Mao. You are the minority; however, this is not detrimental. The formation of your Third Headquarters is a little late. (Premier Chou asked when was it established? Answer: September 6. Premier Chou further asked how many members it had? Answer: There were more than 4000 members in the beginning; now the membership is over 5000.) Although this Headquarters is a belated establishment, we still support it. Liu Chi-ch'ien, Tseng Wei-shan, and other comrades joined it at the beginning. Being a minority, only by persevering in the search for truth and by correcting mistakes can you become the majority. In connection with the problem of the Foreign Languages College Work Group, Liu Hsin-ch'üan, Deputy Minister of Foreign Affairs and Chairman of the Political Department in the Foreign Ministry, is rather frightened. He fears that you will not release him. Because you are the minority, he also fears that you will designate him as black line [that is, as a member of the Liu-Teng opposition]. It is not so terrible to be black line. What damage can an error of fifty days do [referring to the period before August 1, when Liu Shao-ch'i was in charge of Cultural Revolution work teams]? Mistakes are of various degrees. You are the minority yet they are afraid; this in itself illustrates your power. Is Tsou Chia-lung still around? He has run away. Why? The majority faction has bailed him out. The antagonism between your two [Red Guard] factions is severe: You criticize them and they defend themselves. Has Wu Teh [then acting mayor of Peking] come out? (Answer: He has come out.) Wu Teh has supported you and has talked to you, but others have refused to release him, and surrounded him for nine hours. He is the Secretary of the Peking Municipal Committee, taking charge of all municipal works, and he is currently making preparations for the National Day celebrations. He is the Deputy Chairman [of the celebrations] and Yeh Chien-ying is the Chairman. There is plenty of work to be done, but how can he work when you have him surrounded? Your antagonism toward each other is formidable; I suggest that we split the house in two, draw an unarmed military demarcation line, and declare an arms-free zone. Seeking thus the solution of problems, negotiation will follow. Some people have said that there are bad elements within the Workers' Red Guards. Let's not bother with this matter at present: a prolonged division will eventually bring unity, and any protracted union will surely bring forth a breach. First, you should separate, then discuss the issues. To rely on the Ministry of Geology alone is inadequate. No matter how we split [our forces among ourselves], we still cannot disengage ourselves from the ocean of Mao Tse-tung's thought. We cannot coexist peacefully with our enemy, yet revolutionary students do not have to resort to arms. Certain people claim that organization is complex, that is, difficult. And one faction accuses the other of being difficult. There are approximately 2000 members in the Geology College, which is fine. I propose [that, whatever the situation materially, the two factions be treated according to] the principle of equality. Peking University has shown relatively good performance in this direction. Forced coalition is not good. We should implement equal treatment administratively, putting aside the political issue for the moment. Besides, you are enjoying the Four Greats and the Six Freedoms [Great Blooming, Great Contending, Great Character Posters, and Great Debates; Freedom of Speech, Press, Assembly, Association, Procession, and Demonstration—the latter freedoms from Article 87, Constitution of the People's Republic of China] which far surpass the stipulations of the Constitution, and this in new China under the leadership of Chairman Mao. In the course of the great debates, you accuse others of being black line and others accuse you of being black line. Some people simply want to criticize first; this is no good. I am talking to you very frankly today: what other nation in the world possesses so much freedom? You can print all kinds of posters. Someone even wrote "Bombard Chou En-lai"; of course I am aware of it but I would not recognize it. Someone has posted a big character poster at Wang Fu Ching [a district of Peking] demanding the total destruction of Islam. There are many Islamic countries in the world, such as India and Pakistan, with a population close to 400,000,000. How can it be totally destroyed? Answer: It cannot be.

As to freedom of the press, what other nation enjoys so much freedom? As to holding assemblies, you can assemble groups of any size. Of course, we have to intervene in some of the larger meetings; for instance, the public trial in Peking of petty hoodlums by 100,000 participants was incorrect. There was another big gathering of 100,000 persons for the public trial of the wife of Liu Wen-po; we had to arrest her to avoid a struggle. The Middle School Extension of the Teachers College has announced its intention of holding a meeting to try the capitalists. We had previously informed the Middle School students not to hold meetings of this sort. However, they disclaimed our notification [to that effect] and now are [charging that we are] creating a tense situation. There are also demonstrations in the name of the anti-revisionist line, involving hundreds of thousands of persons. We have to dispatch armed forces to protect you, because we will not allow the revisionists to hurt you. Large meetings of this sort may produce worldwide repercussions and we cannot but intervene. Shanghai [once] dragged out 10,000 capitalists to parade them. The Central Committee knew about it, and cabled its objection, stating that the scope of the parade was too extensive and was likely to influence world opinion. Therefore, we must intervene in parades, demonstrations, and the holding of large meetings. There is a major prerequisite for forming associations, consisting of three aspects: (1) accept Party leadership; (2) accept the direction of Chairman Mao, [which embraces] the Four-Never-Forgets—study Chairman Mao's books, obey Chairman Mao, act according to Chairman Mao's directives and be Chairman Mao's good students; (3) accept the Sixteen Points [of the Eleventh Plenum in August, beginning the Cultural Revolution]. They can be summarized as leadership, direction, and principle. These three conditions constitute the necessary elements for forming associations.

We are all revolutionary and cannot charge each other with being unrevolutionary. The test of the current struggle is the determination of one's revolutionary [zeal]. The Red Guards were initially fashioned by the Middle School Extension of Tsinghua University. This new phenomenon caught the imagination of Chairman Mao and so the Middle School students have since become very conceited. Some people have said that the present Red Guard organization is not pure. It was pure in the beginning and has changed; afterwards gradually the impurity manifested itself. If there are real problems, they will be acted upon eventually. To carry out revolutionary organization correctly constitutes freedom of association.

Anti-U.S. demonstrations are permissible, and are highly justifiable. And we must defend anti-revisionist demonstrations. In a nation led by Chairman Mao, how can we not intervene? Shanghai dragged out 10,000 capitalists to parade around; that is incorrect. Finally, the number of persons was decreased to 100. We still have not approved. At the knifing incident committed by the wife of Liu Wen-po, there was only one girl student in the ground floor of the building at the time of the occurrence. If there were more people or some male students present, the incident might well have been averted. Even more important, the Dispatch Office was not aware of the incident. How can we not intervene in cases like these? On August 25, there was an accident involving the knifing of eight persons. Consequently, on August 26, we established liaison stations and prescribed their functions.

We treat all Red Guards equally, and also give them equal material treatment. Capitalists should not be dragged out to be paraded around: our country is strong enough [to render such practices unnecessary]. If we do, foreign news reportage will clamor that Chairman Mao has changed his policy, and that capitalists are to be liquidated physically. Classes are to be eliminated, but there is not to be physical liquidation of persons. The three great sutras of Chairman Mao have not eliminated the policy of the United Front. As the Four Greats campaign in schools is extended into society, we must support it. You have been granted the Six Great Freedoms under the Constitution. Currently there are neither labor strikes, nor boycotts of schools and associations, nor petitions, all of which, however, are permissible. The present action is not a boycott of schools but a vacation for purposes of carrying out revolution. Throughout the whole world, only a nation led by Chairman Mao would be so daring as to allow such actions. What other nation would be as daring? Democracy is one thing; but should it not be a little centralized? Some people are doubtful of the existence of such freedom in our schools. But my statements are based on the majority of cases. Chairman Mao has deliberately released democratic forces, because only through such a high degree of release can a high degree of centralization be attained. Where is the locus of such centralization? Have I not discussed the Four-Never-Forgets? It means that we should never forget the dictatorship of the proletariat.

Comrade Lin Piao has said that once we have obtained political power, we must then defend the dictatorship of the proletariat. Such dictatorship is dictatorship over the exploiting class. An important instrument for the dictatorship is the People's Liberation Army and its reserves, the militia. The Red Guards also constitute the reserve of the Liberation Army. Some comrades challenge us, saying that without armed struggle cultural struggle is impossible. And they call the struggle in Shanghai a moderate one. This is demeaning. Isn't it enough to have purged 10,000 capitalists? Comrade Lin Piao has told us to practice cultural struggle instead of armed struggle. Armed struggle can only touch the flesh, whereas cultural struggle penetrates to the soul. This is the time for us to realize such implications. On whom should the responsibility for dictatorship fall? Dictatorship must depend primarily on the Liberation Army and the militia. The Red Guards are, in the foremost, to engage in political struggle, and must not be issued weapons. They are busy enough as it is. Red Guards must only conduct cultural struggle. The Central Committee has decided that Red Guards are not to be organized in factories, offices, organizations, and individual units of enterprises. Those already organized are to be maintained for a period of time until eventual disbandment. This has been agreed upon by Chairman Mao, Comrade Lin Piao, and the Standing Committee. The Cultural College of the Liberation Army has organized some Red Guards which it consequently was ordered to disband by the Military Affairs Committee. The Shanghai Medical College attempted to interfere in this matter, and demanded permission to organize their own Red Guards and to hold large meetings. We considered the calling of large meetings appropriate, but not the organization of Red Guards.

According to the Chairman, agencies responsible for the implementation of dictatorship, such as public security, prisons, and courts, cannot transfer their authority to the lower level. Have you involved yourselves in those agencies? Those agencies are not to be involved. You can, however, struggle against their mistakes. It is the Public Security Bureau which is responsible for arrests. There have been some arrests made in the Eastwind Market and the houses of those arrested have been confiscated. This should not be done. Authority cannot be transferred to a lower level. But if you want to struggle against Chang Nan-hsia, that is fine.

Propaganda agencies of the [proletarian] dictatorship, such as the New China News Agency, the press, and the broadcasting system, all represent the Party. They are the voices of Chairman Mao. Surely those who run the press have made their individual mistakes; for instance, they should not have reported the student campaign of struggle-criticism-transformation. Only public campaigns can be reported, because people all over the world have their eyes on Peking.

The Heilungkiang press reported the struggle of students against the provincial Party committee, which was inappropriate. We have not reported on the question of the important leadership of the former Peking Municipal Party Committee, and we did not even mention it in the communiqué [of the Eleventh Plenum in August]. The Central Committee is extremely cautious in giving press coverage to a given issue, because it concerns not only the issue of domestic class struggle but also the issue of international class struggle. Propaganda on any issue entails careful consideration by the Chairman and the Central Committee. Television stations are also to be protected, since they are capable of transmitting recordings which may be picked up abroad. This happened in Harbin; we eventually convinced them of the undesirability of such broadcasts.

We cannot suppress the student movement, but it must definitely be centralized. When P'an Fu-sheng first arrived, the students believed in him and constantly sought conversations with him. During every discussion the students would persistently say, "Uncle P'an, you must be tired, you should get some rest." This went on for over ten evenings; finally P'an had to be sent to the hospital. This affair was broadcast over Harbin radio; consequently we sent the Liberation Army to guard the station.

Someone asks if it is permissible to print our own newspapers.

Yes, you can print your own newspapers.

How about taking pictures? The New China News Agency can supply you the needed pictures for your papers. We must unify democracy and centralization. These are the words of Chairman Mao and we have to accept the highest instructions of Chairman Mao.

Are intra-Party mistakes in line revolutionary, nonrevolutionary, or counterrevolutionary? Some students say that committing mistakes in line must still be considered revolutionary. This is correct; what you say is right. Someone suggests that we should discuss it in more concrete terms. I asked a student from Harbin the same question and he said that it is surely counterrevolutionary. Was Ch'en Tu-hsiu counterrevolutionary? He was revolutionary when he first committed mistakes, but later he became counterrevolutionary because he had rebelled against Party authority, a separate issue. We should not interpret questions subjectively, but should consider their inherent utility. It cannot be said that at a given moment a given question has no utility at all. Ch'en Tu-hsiu is an example of committing mistakes in line, whereas Chairman Mao represents the correct line. History cannot erase Ch'en and he has since left his mark. Similarly, the History of the Communist Party of the Soviet Union (Bolsheviks), published in 1938, still could not leave out the Social Democratic Party.

Someone has said that Chang Cheng-hsien is counterrevolutionary. He has indeed committed mistakes in line, but we should not consider him counterrevolutionary because the matter has not yet been decided. Therefore you must attentively study Chairman Mao's writings. Since you are university students, I am talking to you in a more profound manner.

What sort of person is Chiang Nan-hsiang? He cannot yet be considered counterrevolutionary. He attended the Eleventh Plenum of the

Central Committee. I myself have committed mistakes in line, but that alone does not serve to designate me as revolutionary or counterrevolutionary. Even if hundreds of thousands of students would come forward and argue with me, I would still disagree. The Chairman believes in me, he has given me a task to perform and supports my role as Premier. I have often talked with democratic [non-Communist?] personages. I have previously committed mistakes in line. I have maintained that it is fine to discuss revolutionary history but that it is bad to neglect the discussion of mistakes. The Chairman agrees with this. At the time of the Nanch'ang Uprising, I was with Chu Teh and other comrades and it was then that I committed the mistake of going into the cities instead of the villages. But it was not a mistake in line. We succeeded in seizing some weapons at that uprising. I also made mistakes during the Fourth Plenum of the Sixth Party National Congress [January 1931] while Chiang Kai-shek had orders for my arrest. How can you say that I am unrevolutionary? You must not post big character posters about this particular point; not that I am afraid, since revolution is fearless. The children of some high cadres at X X Middle School in Harbin commented that they should emulate Uncle Chou, because he is revolutionary and he is the Premier. I have asked Wu Hsin-sheng, the daughter of Wu Chiu-ch'uan, whether her father said anything about that. She said that she did not know. I said I was sure that her father could tell her something about that [my revolutionary past].

In connection with the heartless torment afflicted by the cruel struggle at the last stage of the Stalinist era, E. F. Hill, the Chairman of the Australian Communist Party [Marxist-Leninist] recently commented that "Chairman Mao has contributed many innovations in the area of Party building which constitute a significant advancement of the Party building theory of Lenin." Comrade Lin Piao has said that China is a big country and that, therefore, national unity is very important. And Chairman Mao has said that we must allow the people to stage revolution. Empty mouthings about revolution will not suffice; they have to be put into practice. There are three factions in X X School from Harbin. Each accuses the other of being unrevolutionary. Some high cadres' children from that school once commented: "Uncle Chou, you cannot simply consider them as revolutionary; it can only be said that they think about making revolution." We definitely cannot talk in this manner. We are all revolutionary.

I am relating this particular piece of history to you, as I consider this a heart-to-heart talk. I disagree with the practice of not discussing mistakes of the Party Central Committee with the youngsters.

Concerning the issue of background: first is the consideration of background. Next, we look at nonbackground [facts], and finally we take into consideration objective acts. One's family background may be bad, but it suffices if one's objective acts are good and one has rebelled against his original class. (One sentence was not recorded.) Investigation of one's background requires also the consideration of one's family history. My home is Shao-hsing, Chekiang Province. I was born in Huai-an, Kiangsu. My father was a magistrate whose monthly income constituted less than thirty yuän. He had remained in that post for over twenty years. If it were not for corruption, where would he have obtained the money for his long robes and the house he bought? Judicious [honest] officials were nonexistent in the past. They were either completely or partly corrupt. My father was a small official from the point of view of class status. Hence, some have suggested that my background needs transformation, but that I have not yet done.

The Great Cultural Revolution touches the soul of every individual. Whatever impact it exerts upon a person is detectable. Such impact can easily be seen. We are to repudiate the Four Olds. Certain old work styles and old habits are influenced by family background, and others by society. To destroy old thinking assumes major importance, because its impact is the strongest. A person has to surmount five obstacles [not elaborated upon] among which the ideological obstacle should be the primary concern. Persons who have emerged from the old society must study attentively the writings of Chairman Mao, to transform their thinking. Good [worker or peasant] family background constitutes one aspect of perfection; assurance of perfection requires two aspects.

Some people have said that we are the natural rebels. This is illogical. Chaotic rebellion is incorrect; it is mere fatalism. It is imperative for us to study Chairman Mao's writings, to obey Chairman Mao and act according to Chairman Mao's instructions. During the Cultural Revolution, our actions are to be based on the Sixteen Points.

Undesirable family background should not be considered an impediment to transformation. I left home fifty-six years ago and have not been back since. The Chairman has suggested that I should return to my native place for a visit. My answer is that if I do go back, there would be various problems demanding solutions, and the impact thus generated would be great. I have since donated my family house to the government. My mother pointed out a particular place where I was supposed to have been born. As a matter of fact, she does not really know. The Kiangsu Provincial Committee insisted on keeping one room for memorial purposes, and the issue was involved in litigation for quite a few years. Comrade Chiang Wei-ch'ing finally has agreed to quash the proceedings. What advantage can possibly be served by introducing such a feudalistic idea? Isn't it a bad thing? There are also involved some ancestral graves, which are utterly unreasonable matters. I do not have any children except for two nephews. One nephew does not work [he is in Taiwan], the other is with the Liberation Army, which has helped to solve his problems [reportedly he had mental problems]. I am the Premier, yet solution of those problems is not easy. It would have been helpful if the Red Guards had existed then. You have involved yourselves with numerous feudalistic matters. It is difficult for those of us who work for the government to be engaged in those undertakings. I had once offended some democratic personage in an attempt to remove a monument. Now you have even removed the stone lions [possibly referring to the figures lining the approaches to the Ming Tombs outside Peking].

In regard to policy questions, I want to be clear. At present, you are the minority, but you will become the majority in the future. Merely formal relationships between groups are definitely inappropriate. Prolonged antagonism must be avoided. We are all revolutionary, and we should always unite under the banner of Mao Tse-tung's thought. The impact of the work groups can only be eliminated after we arrive at certain conclusions. Regardless of how thoroughly you criticize the work groups, such criticism still cannot solve your own problems. There are three factions within the X X School from Harbin. One faction struggles against one particular Provincial Committeeman, the other faction struggles against the other Provincial Committeeman. One calls the other unrevolutionary and vice versa. We say that all three factions are revolutionary. Some people deem it too early to grasp revolution and promote production. No, it is not too early. An abundant harvest depends on an extensive production effort. And the Northeast region is confronted with some very acute problems. How can we ignore them? After the convocation of a round table conference, the five representatives of the various factions are now united under this principle [grasp revolution and promote production]. A majority of the Harbin students have now gone down to the villages, and their prisoners have also been transferred to the Temporary Provincial Committee.

During the movement of the Cultural Revolution, there should be two aspects of fearlessness: (1) daring to step forward to confront the revolutionary teachers and students; (2) daring to expose those who err in policy. We have to be daring in explaining Party policy. It is impossible not to show our faces. First, we have to step forward, and second, we have to be brave in persisting in Party policy. As the movement is personally led by Chairman Mao, we want to be sure that Chairman Mao's policy has been elucidated thoroughly.

On the Sixteen Points: The three speeches given by Comrade Lin Piao and myself have all been personally approved by Chairman Mao. Then how can it be said that it is premature to discuss the Sixteen Points? There are also a number of appropriate editorials in that regard. I discussed the X X X problem at Tsinghua University on August 4, a speech which represented Chairman Mao's policy. At that time we did not foresee the vanguards of the Red Guards, and the Sixteen Points themselves did not mention the Red Guards. Some people have claimed that the word "others" in the section pertaining to Cultural Revolution organizations implies the organization of Red Guards. Of course, it is possible to uncover mistakes and shortcomings, if one is so inclined. The meeting on August 18 was to begin at seven o'clock. The Chairman [Mao] arrived at five, and we had to make way for the Chairman as he walked among the crowd. I had to shout so hard that I lost my voice, and I have still not completely recovered it. Red Guards had gone to Tien An Men without any previous preparations. It became chaotic after one thousand of them arrived. By then we began to regard the Red Guards highly. But we have never mentioned these problems in our speeches. Chairman Mao always grasps the essence of the problems, whereas we seldom do. After August 18, the Middle School Red Guards became very arrogant. From August 20 to August 29, the Red Guards rushed into society and issued proposals and precepts. They marched into society and surged through the entire nation, which we deem praiseworthy. From mid-August to mid-September, however, the situation has developed so rapidly that we have failed to catch up with events.

On September 15 I discussed promoting production. We have to maintain the division of labor. The Cultural Revolution is to be conducted in the middle-sized and large cities. Factories and villages are to render mutual assistance and support. Industry and agriculture cannot neglect production. They cannot take a vacation for staging revolution. We must respect as well as support them. Their Cultural Revolution can only be integrated with the Four Cleanups Movement. How can we neglect the harvest when autumn is here? Students should not link up with factories and villages at present. Some may go later to the villages to assist in the campaign to destroy the Four Olds. Industry and agriculture should neither interfere nor link up with the Cultural Revolution in the schools. At the moment, liaison between Peking and other places is appropriate, but not liaison between other places. Middle School students from other areas have a strong opinion of me, because Peking students are allowed to establish liaisons elsewhere, whereas we only permit 10 percent of students from other areas to come to Peking. I do not have an answer for this problem. The major issue centers on the problem of transportation. Currently, in Peking, forty railway cars are being used to transport 140,000 persons. Transportation of cargoes has decreased 10 percent. A tremendous impact is exerted on imports and exports. It has also affected economic construction. There have been temporary halts in communications between various areas. Some students are disobedient and there are cases of the students extending their own freedom.

It is good that you are going down to the villages to perform manual labor. The most important thing is that everyone has to be obedient, and should study Party policy carefully. Everyone should be issued a pamphlet on Party policy.

It suffices that the work groups admit mistakes in line and direction. We should not call them rightists or counterrevolutionaries. On the other hand, neither should they call you counterrevolutionaries. We must demand the burning of those materials and name lists which comprise their investigation of your leftist, neutral, and rightist tendencies. All of these should be avoided. But we should not be unceasingly entwined about this issue. We are going to liberate you, the minority, *and* the work groups. Otherwise, how are we to conduct the movement of struggle-criticism-transformation? It is not strange that the Cultural Revolution in schools is not unified. How could the Paris Commune implement elections if all were not unified?

Your nucleus groups can be expanded to discuss some problems.

There will be a plenary meeting held at the Workers Athletic Hall tomorrow at four o'clock. I am going to present a speech to all of you, and I must prepare it. It is not that I am afraid that someone may find fault with me. I have been concerned with foreign affairs for many years, and they [the foreigners] have yet to find fault with me. It is inappropriate to apply diplomatic language in talking to you. For the purpose of solving problems, you must not print what I have said in big character posters.

Some schools want to be separate on account of mutual antagonism. We have assigned administrative cadres to those schools. The impact of the work groups cannot be permanent. There are requests that the mistakes of the members of the work groups be investigated. We disagree, and I will not respond to this problem.

The age of the Red Guards is to be under thirty. Factories, organizations, villages, and offices are not to organize Red Guards. Red Guards should not mix with the militia. They are not to link together. It is incorrect that the Ministry of Geology requested protection of the West City District's inspectors.

The Central Committee is studying the possibility of restoring Party activities. Some schools are withholding scholarships at present. This will be changed after the educational reform.

On bombarding the Party headquarters: Some people hold that we should bombard all headquarters first. This is incorrect. Such aims have to be accurately selected, and there must be adequate preparation. Surely we disapprove of elimination of everything *en bloc*. (The last few sentences have not been recorded.)

APPENDIX C

State Council Personnel Reported to Be under Criticism January–June 1967

Ministry	Position	Name	Date first criticized	Date last public appearance
Staff Office of Culture and Education	Director	Chang Chi-ch'un	1–67	9–66
Scientific and Technological Commission	Vice-Chairman	Chang Ching-fu	2–67	10–65

Ministry	Position	Name	Date first criticized	Date last public appearance
Ministry of State Farms and Land Reclamation	Vice-Minister	Chang Chung-han	1–67	10–65
Staff Office of Agriculture and Forestry	Deputy Director	Chang Hsiu-chu	6–67	10–65
Coal Ministry	Minister	Chang Lin-chih	1–67	Deceased
Staff Office of Culture and Education	Deputy Director	Chang Meng-hsu	1–67	10–65
Staff Office of Foreign Affairs	Deputy Director	Chang Yen	1–67	4–66
Scientific and Technological Commission	Vice-Chairman	Chang Yu-hsuan	2–67	10–65
8th Ministry of Machine Building	Minister	Ch'en Cheng-jen	3–67	10–67
Ministry of State Farms and Land Reclamation	Vice-Minister	Ch'en Man-yuan	1–67	10–67
Staff Office of Foreign Affairs	Director, Vice-Premier	Ch'en Yi	1–67	10–69
Ministry of Agriculture	Vice-Minister	Cheng Chao-hsuan	2–67	12–65
Ministry of Higher Education	Minister	Chiang Nan-hsiang	1–67	1–67
Ministry of Agriculture	Vice-Minister	Chiang Yi-chen	1–67	12–67
Ministry of Public Health	Minister	Ch'ien Hsiu-chung	2–67	10–66
State Economic Commission	Vice-Chairman	Chou Chung-wu	4–67	—
State Council	Secretary-General	Chou Jung-hsin	1–67	12–67
Ministry of Agriculture	Vice-Minister	Chu Jung	2–67	9–66
Ministry of Communication	Vice-Minister	Chu Tien-shun	4–67	10–65
Overseas Chinese Affairs Commission	Vice-Chairman	Fang Fang	4–67	9–66
Scientific and Technological Commission	Vice-Chairman	Han Kuang	2–67	8–66
Ministry of Geology	Vice-Minister	Ho Chang-kung	2–67	10–65

Ministry	Position	Name	Date first criticized	Date last public appearance
Physical Culture and Sports Commission	Director Vice-Premier	Ho Lung	1–67	5–67
Ministry of Education	Minister	Ho Wei	1–67	9–66
Ministry of State Farms and Land Reclamation	Vice-Minister	Hsiao K'o	1–67	10–67
National Price Commission	Vice-Chairman	Hsieh Mu-chiao	4–67	11–66
Ministry of Culture	Vice-Minister	Hsiao Wang-tung	2–67	11–66
Nationalities Affairs Commission	Vice-Chairman	Hsueh Hsiang-chen	5–67	
Ministry of Culture	Vice-Minister	Hsu Kuang-hsiao	6–67	10–65
Ministry of Culture	Vice-Minister	Hsu Ping-hu	6–67	10–65
8th Ministry of Machine Building	Vice-Minister	Hsu Ta-pen	3–67	10–65
2nd Ministry of Light Industry	Vice-Minister	Hsu Yun-pei	5–67	11–66
Hsinhua News Agency	Acting Director	Hu Chih	1–67	—
Ministry of Health	Vice-Minister	Huang Shu-tse	5–67	—
Central Meteorology Bureau	Director	Jao Hsing	6–67	—
Physical-Culture and Sports Commission	Vice-Chairman	Jung Kao-t'ang	2–67	10–66
Ministry of Finance	Vice-Minister	Jung Tsu-ho	5–67	—
Ministry of Petroleum Industry	Vice-Minister	K'ang Shih-en	1–67	5–67
State Capital Construction Commission	Chairman	Ku Mu	5–67	5–67
Ministry of Agriculture	Vice-Minister	Ku Ta-ch'uan	2–67	10–65
First Ministry of Machine Building	Vice-Minister	Kung Hsiang-chen	4–67	11–66

Ministry	Position	Name	Date first criticized	Date last public appearance
State Economic Commission	Vice-Chairman	Kuo Lin-hsiang	4–67	—
Ministry of Railways	Vice-Minister	Kuo Lu	5–67	5–70
Commission for Cultural Relations with Foreign Countries	Vice-Chairman	Li Ch'ang	4–67	5–66
Ministry of Culture	Vice-Minister	Li Chi	6–67	10–66
State Planning Commission	Vice-Chairman	Li Fu-chün	3–67	10–69
Ministry of Finance	Vice-Premier	Li Hsien-nien	4–67	2–71
Secretariat of State Council	Deputy Director	Li Meng-fu	4–67	10–65
Physical-Culture and Sports Commission	Vice-Chairman	Li Meng-hua	3–67	11–66
Physical Culture and Sports Commission	Vice-Chairman	Li Ta	1–67	10–65
Ministry of Chemical Industry	Vice-Minister	Liang Ying-yung	1–67	11–65
Staff Office for Foreign Affairs	Deputy Director	Liao Ch'eng-chih	5–67	7–67
Overseas Chinese Affairs Commission	Vice-Chairman	Lin Hsiu-teh	4–67	12–66
Ministry of Education	Vice-Minister	Liu Chi-ping	1–67	10–65
Ministry of Labor	Minister	Liu Chih-chen	4–67	—
Nationalities Affairs Commission	Vice-Chairman	Liu Ch'un	2–67	10–65
Ministry of Building Construction	Former Minister	Liu Hsin-feng	5–67	—
Ministry of Culture	Vice-Minister	Liu Pai-yü	3–67	6–66
Ministry of Metallurgical Industry	Vice-Minister	Liu Pin	6–67	10–65
Ministry of Higher Education	Vice-Minister	Liu Yang-chiao	1–67	10–65

Ministry	Position	Name	Date first criticized	Date last public appearance
7th Ministry of Machine Building	Vice-Minister	Liu Yu-kuang	4–67	5–70
State Capital Construction Commission, Ministry of Building Construction	Vice-Chairman, Minister	Liu Yü-min	5–67	11–66
Ministry of Forestry	Vice-Minister	Lo Yu-chuan	1–67	10–65
Ministry of Culture	Minister Vice-Premier	Lu Ting-yi	4–67	5–67
Ministry of Railways	Minister	Lü Cheng-tsao	1–67	1–67
Ministry of Metallurgical Industry	Minister	Lü Tung	6–67	5–67
Ministry of Communications	Vice-Minister	Ma Hui-chih	4–67	10–65
Ministry of Labor	Minister	Ma Wen-jui	1–67	5–67
Staff Office of Finance and Trade	Deputy Director	Niu P'ei-tsung	5–67	10–65
Staff Office of Industry and Communication	Director Vice-Premier	Po I-po	3–67	5–67
Ministry of Culture	Vice-Minister	Shih Hsi-min	1–67	11–66
State Planning Commission	Vice-Chairman	Sung Shao-wen	3–67	10–65
Staff Office of Agriculture and Forestry	Director Vice-Premier	T'an Chen-lin	3–67	7–67
Nationalities Affairs Communications	Vice-Chairman	T'an Tung	4–67	5–70
Ministry of Petroleum Industry	Vice-Minister	T'ang Ko	4–67	5–70
State Economic Commission	Vice-Chairman	T'ao Lu-chia	2–67	2–67
State Planning Commission	Vice-Chairman	Teng Tzu-hui	4–67	5–67

Ministry	Position	Name	Date first criticized	Date last public appearance
Ministry of Agriculture	Vice-Minister	Ts'ai Tzu-wei	2-67	10-65
State Archives Bureau	Director	Tseng San	1-67	10-67
Ministry of Finance	Vice-Minister	Tu Hsiang-kuang	2-67	10-65
Nationalities Affairs Commission	Chairman	Ulanfu	4-67	12-65
Ministry of State Farms and Land Reclamation	Minister	Wang Chen	1-67	3-70
Staff Office of Agriculture and Forestry	Deputy Director	Wang Kuan-lan	6-67	10-65
Physical Culture and Sports Commission	—	Wang Ling	3-67	—
7th Ministry of Machine Building	Minister	Wang Ping-chang	1-27	5-70
Ministry of Agriculture	Former Vice-Minister	Wei Chen-wu	2-67	—
Ministry of Agriculture	Vice-Minister	Wu Chen	2-67	5-70
Ministry of Railways	Vice-Minister	Wu Ching-t'ien	1-67	10-65
Ministry of Foreign Affairs	Vice-Minister	Wu Hsiu-ch'üan	4-67	1-67
Hsinhua News Agency	Director	Wu Leng-hsi	1-67	1-67
Ministry of Commerce	Minister	Yao Yi-lin	4-67	11-66
Ministry of Petroleum Industry, State Panning Commission	Minister Vice-Chairman	Yü Ch'iu-li	3-67	10-70
Scientific and Technological Commission	Vice-Chairman	Yü Kuang-yuan	4-67	4-66
Staff Office of Culture and Education	Deputy Director	Yung Wen-tao	2-67	—

5

The Foreign Ministry and
Foreign Affairs in the Chinese
Cultural Revolution

MELVIN GURTOV

As other analysts have suggested in different ways,[1] the Cultural Revolution involved differences of emphasis among Chinese leaders over basic directional choices for the society at large: whether Maoist-style politics (or ideology) could continue to "take command" or would have to yield at least equal place to the practical problems and limitations involved in fixing priorities and setting goals; whether radical Maoism befit a China in transition or would have to be modified if China is to realize its historically based claim to great power status; and whether China would inevitably "change color" or could remain ideologically "pure red" even in the throes of modernization.

As these questions came to the surface in the summer of 1966, the foreign affairs bureaucracy, like the party apparatus as a whole, was suddenly forced to defend itself against the unleashed frenzy of young radicals out to "make revolution." Before a semblance of order was restored to the Foreign Ministry in the autumn of 1967, its operations had been disrupted, the Foreign Minister had been subjected to unprecedented abuse and humiliation, and China's image abroad had been badly tarnished. An effort to explain what happened to the Foreign Ministry and to derive the implications for China's foreign policy of events from the summer of 1966 to the autumn of 1967 will be the task of this chapter.

Focusing on the Foreign Ministry during the Cultural Revolution not only affords a rare look into the activities of an organ of Communist

---

[1] See, for example, W. F. Dorrill's essay, Chapter 2 of this volume; Philip Bridgham, "Mao's 'Cultural Revolution': Origin and Development," *The China Quarterly*, No. 29 (January–March 1967) pp. 1–35; H. G. Schwarz, "The Great Proletarian Cultural Revolution," *Orbis*, Vol. 10, No. 3 (Fall 1966) pp. 803–821.

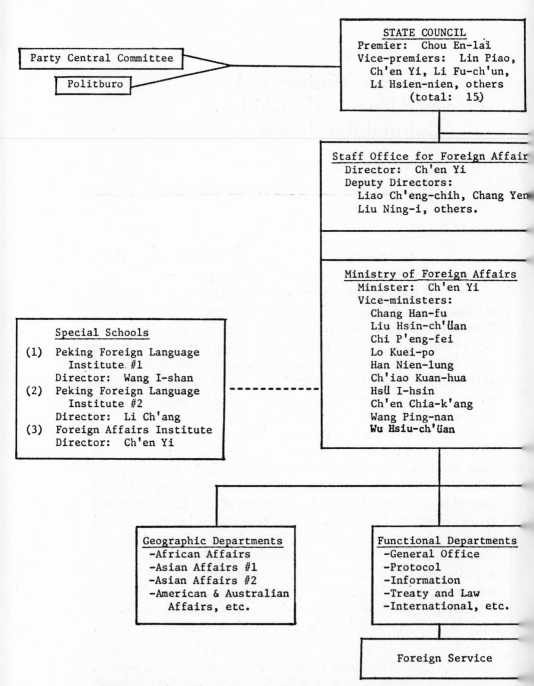

SOURCE: Adapted from chart 2 in Department of the Army, *Communist China: A Strategic Survey*, U.S. Government Printing Office, Washington, D.C., February 1966.

Commissions

Special Agencies

Commission for Cultural
  Relations with Foreign
  Countries

Chairman: Chang Hsi-jo
Vice-chairman: Li Ch'ang

Bureau of Foreign
  Specialists

Director: Mi Yung

Overseas Chinese Affairs
  Commission

Chairman: Liao Ch'eng-chih
Vice-chairman: Fang Fang

Foreign Language
  Publication and
  Distribution Bureau

Director: Lo Chün

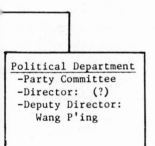

Political Department
-Party Committee
-Director: (?)
-Deputy Director:
  Wang P'ing

China's government; it also provides a unique opportunity to relate aspects of China's foreign relations to domestic events. However, analysis of the Foreign Ministry during 1966 and 1967, like analysis of the Cultural Revolution as a whole, can only hope to be partially satisfactory. There are two reasons for this: first, the available information, though suggestive, leaves as many questions unanswered as it may resolve; and second, the nature of the documentation demands considerable caution in interpretation. Both of these points require additional comment.

In the first place, as intrinsically interesting and at times illuminating as the story of Foreign Minister and Vice-Premier Ch'en Yi's confrontation with the Red Guards may be, innumerable gaps remain to be filled. No definitive answer can be given, for instance, to the question whether any substantive issues were involved in the attacks on the Foreign Minister and the Ministry, although we offer interpretations throughout this study. The role of Mao Tse-tung also invites speculation: depending on the period under discussion, Mao seems either to have stepped in to protect his Foreign Minister, to have stood aside, or to have condoned limited attacks on him. We also know very little about Yao Teng-shan, the last Chinese chargé d'affaires in Djakarta, who returned to Peking in April 1967 and apparently took over the Ministry of Foreign Affairs for two weeks in August. Finally, we can only guess what long-range effects the Cultural Revolution will have on ministry personnel and foreign service officers of the Chinese People's Republic.

On the second point, most of the materials cited in this study are articles from Red Guard newspapers representing factions having a vested interest in the struggle over the Foreign Ministry. Although replete with empty charges and steeped in the jargon of the Cultural Revolution, these articles, along with other materials used here, seem to possess a significant internal consistency in their reporting of details. Consequently, while it would be presumptuous to assume their complete accuracy, these materials do seem to provide important evidence which, if interpreted with care, should form an integral part of the Cultural Revolution's historical record.

THE STRUGGLE IS JOINED

On August 8, 1966, at the Eleventh Plenary Session of the Eighth Central Committee of the Chinese Communist Party, the Cultural Revolution was sanctified in a sixteen-point official decision.[2] For Mao Tse-tung, the decision made official what had already been clear for over three weeks, namely, that the Cultural Revolution would be under his leadership and would move sharply to the left. The decision also represented something of a political comeback for Mao, who for the two preceding months had been out of Peking and had apparently left direction of the Cultural Revolution to an ad hoc Party committee under Liu Shao-ch'i and the Party's general secretary, Teng Hsiao-p'ing. It now seems fairly certain that Mao's dissatisfaction with the pace and style of the Cultural Revolution up to the Eleventh Plenum stemmed from the performance of work teams (*kung-tso-tui*) dispatched by the Liu-Teng committee in the Chairman's absence.[3]

Ch'en Yi apparently used the work teams to defend organizational units loyal to him in the foreign affairs system. Initially, they were probably sent out by Liu and Teng to modulate the anti-Party fervor that had begun to sweep over university campuses as the first wave of the Cultural Revolution struck in the late spring and early summer of 1966. To preserve Party authority, some work teams evidently employed armed force to quell disturbances by radical students and other self-proclaimed leftists. After Mao returned to Peking, he ordered the work teams recalled on July 24.

By that time, Ch'en Yi had already revealed his hand. He had opposed the posting and publication of the first wall poster at Peking University in June.[4] Soon thereafter, almost certainly with the knowledge and consent of Liu and Teng, Ch'en had also sought to head off the extremist elements who appeared to be threatening to extend the radical movement to certain institutes linked to the Ministry of Foreign Affairs (see the accompanying organizational chart).[5] Ch'en, by his own admission, dis-

---

[2] The decision is published in *Peking Review,* No. 33 (August 12, 1966) pp. 6–11.

[3] The following account of the work teams relies on the analysis by Dorrill in Chapter 2, above.

[4] Talk by Ch'en Yi on February 16, 1967, in *Ch'en Yi yen-lun hsüan* (*Selected Speeches of Ch'en Yi*), Tz'u-lien ch'u-pan-she, Hong Kong, 1967. (That this is an anti-Ch'en collection is made abundantly clear on the cover, which consists of a photograph of the Foreign Minister asleep on a rostrum during an official ceremony.) See also "Bombard Ch'en Yi, Liberate Foreign Affairs Circles" (hereafter cited as "Bombard Ch'en Yi"), *Hung-ch'i* (*Red Flag*), April 4, 1967, p. 2 (written by the Red Flag First Company of the Peking Aeronautical Institute).

[5] In his self-criticism of January 24, 1967, Ch'en said: "At the inception of the

patched "some fifteen work teams or groups. Eight of these were sent by the Foreign Affairs General Office and the Foreign Affairs Political Department to the Commission for Cultural Relations with Foreign Countries, the Overseas Chinese Affairs Commission, and relevant bureaus and schools. Seven were sent by the Ministry of Foreign Affairs to units and schools under its jurisdiction," including the Peking Foreign Language Institute.[6]

The work teams, led by high-ranking subordinates of Ch'en Yi (including a few vice-ministers),[7] reportedly collaborated with various Party committees and organizations to prevent the radicals from establishing themselves in any of the Foreign Ministry's allied agencies.[8] In the process, several key cadres in the foreign affairs system loyal to Ch'en were afforded protection from the mobs, which sometimes demanded that the cadres be removed from office. Among those whom Red Guard publications charged were maintained in office by Ch'en despite their "counterrevolutionary" activities were: Li Ch'ang, Vice-Chairman of the Commission for Cultural Relations with Foreign Countries and secretary of its Party organization; Fang Fang, head of the Party committee of the Overseas Chinese Affairs Commission; Nan Han-ch'en, Chairman of the Committee for the Promotion of International Trade, who was later to commit suicide; Liu Hsin-ch'üan, a Vice-Minister of Foreign Affairs; and Lo Chün, director of the Foreign Language Publications and Distribution Bureau.[9]

After the Eleventh Plenum, pressure seems to have increased on the Foreign Ministry and associated agencies to accept a certain number of so-called "revolutionary committees" into their midst. After Mao recalled

---

Great Cultural Revolution movement, I did not comprehend this Great Proletarian Cultural Revolution. At that time the impact of the mass movement was overwhelming, and I did not have the proper ideological preparation for it. . . . I was apprehensive about the impact of the mass movement, fearing that it might jeopardize order and affect foreign affairs work." The self-criticism was first published in *Hung-wei-pao* (*Red Guard Newspaper*), February 8, 1967; translated in "Ch'en Yi's Self-Criticism," *Chinese Law and Government*, Vol. 1, No. 1 (Spring 1968) p. 54.

[6] *Ibid.*, pp. 52–53. The article "Bombard Ch'en Yi," cited in note 4, recounts Ch'en's protection of the Institute's Party committee, as well as of other organs.

[7] Lo Kuei-po and Liu Hsin-ch'üan reportedly headed two work teams. "Bombard Ch'en Yi," *op. cit.*

[8] The work teams' tactics are most fully treated in "Criticize Ch'en Yi's Reactionary Policy of 'Attack a Large Part, Protect a Handful,'" *Wai-shih hung-ch'i* (*Foreign Affairs Red Flag*), May 8, 1967 (written by the Revolutionary Rebel Committee of the Central Committee, Foreign Affairs Political Department).

[9] *Ibid.*

the work teams, extremist elements should have anticipated no further opposition. From his "confession" (which Ch'en was later to claim was obtained under duress) and from Red Guard materials, however, it appears that Ch'en continued to resist the "revolutionary left." In some cases, he refused to back extremist attacks on the work teams; in others, he evidently sought to maintain the work teams in their respective offices by mediating between them and their opposite numbers.[10] Ch'en clearly found the situation intolerable, as his description of the impact of the "rebels" on the Foreign Language Institute indicates: "The Foreign Language Institute is divided into two parts. Originally there were 21 units, but after a week there were over 50, and after another week, over 70. Over four thousand people in over 70 units make over 70 cliques. The oceans are vast to behold: this is truly one hundred flowers blooming and one hundred schools of thought contending." [11] According to one Red Guard source, when Mao discovered that the work teams were still in the Institute, he sent Premier Chou En-lai to investigate conditions. Chou directed a reorganization of the Institute and a criticism of the work teams, but Ch'en sought to stage a comeback by dispatching Wang P'ing, Deputy Director of the Ministry's Political Department (that is, the number two political commissar), to reconcile the "conservatives" and rebels.[12]

Ch'en's choice of directly confronting the radicals and, it would seem, of defying Mao's wishes, reportedly led, in November, to his being "investigated," presumably by Red Guard groups.[13] In speeches of November 13 and 29, Ch'en seems to have thrown down the gauntlet before the Red Guards by attacking them for their undisciplined behavior; thereafter, he is quoted as having demanded that each government organ remain responsible for solving its own problems. He also allegedly implied that he, as Foreign Minister, was above criticism or interference by Red Guards.[14] Ch'en's own version is self-incriminating but consistent with his conduct during these first months of the Cultural Revolution. He

[10] "Ch'en Yi's Self-Criticism," op. cit., p. 55.

[11] Ch'en Yi yen-lun hsüan, op. cit., p. 21.

[12] Statement of the Red Guard organization in the Foreign Language Institute, Wai-shih hung-ch'i, May 8, 1967, translated in Joint Publications Research Service (JPRS) 42,070 (Translations on Communist China: Political and Sociological, No. 413, August 3, 1967) pp. 13–16.

[13] Chu Pu (pseud.), "An Analysis of Ch'en Yi's Confession, 'I Am the Foreign Minister'" (hereafter cited as "Ch'en Yi's Confession"), Fei-ch'ing yen-chiu (Studies on Chinese Communism), Vol. 2, No. 2 (February 29, 1968) p. 33.

[14] "Bombard Ch'en Yi," op. cit.

said in January 1967: "my talks [in November] at the various units . . .
were fraught with serious errors in striking at the leftists and in repressing the revolutionary masses." [15]

During the latter half of 1966, Ch'en Yi's involvement with the Red
Guards did not keep him from performing his functions as Foreign Minister and Vice-Premier. Between July and December, either individually
or with Premier Chou, he welcomed, hosted, and attended banquets for
visiting foreign dignitaries, spoke on foreign policy (for example, he gave
a speech on July 10 castigating the United States for assertedly bombing
Hanoi and Haiphong), attended such important celebrations as National
Day (October 1), and participated in mass meetings welcoming Red
Guard groups returning from the Soviet Union and Indonesia (November 5 and December 29).[16]

Significantly, there is no evidence to support the view that Red Guard
hostility to Ch'en and the ministry at this time concerned foreign policy
issues. To the contrary, contrasting the official policy line with Ch'en's
one major commentary on foreign affairs—a speech of October 5, 1966,
not disseminated abroad by Peking news media—reveals absolute consistency of viewpoint.

Against the background of the abortive coup attempt by the Communist Party of Indonesia on September 30, 1965, the breakdown of preparations for holding a "second Bandung" conference of Afro-Asian nations
in Algiers on November 5, and intensified disagreement with the Soviet
Union over Vietnam, Chinese analyses of the international situation during 1966 sought to demonstrate that while "setbacks" to the world revolutionary movement had occurred, these were to be expected, would not be
lasting, and in fact had a certain salutary effect. One example of this kind
of rationalization of events appeared in *Shih-chieh chih-shih* (*World
Knowledge*) in an article written under the pseudonym of Szu Mu.[17]
The article acknowledged that "the development of the international situation, filled with contradictions and conflict, gives rise to zigzags and
reversals. In this or that area or country, the people's revolutionary move-

---

[15] "Ch'en Yi's Self-Criticism," *op. cit.,* p. 56.

[16] *Fei-ch'ing yen-chiu, op. cit.,* Vol. 1, No. 6 (June 30, 1967) pp. 105–106.

[17] "The Advance of the Revolutionary Movement of the World's People is the
Main Current of the Present Situation," *Shih-chieh chih-shih,* Nos. 2–3 (February
10, 1966) pp. 6–10. This publication, generally considered an authoritative foreign
policy organ, turned completely to publishing documents on the Cultural Revolution beginning in May 1966. In June, the periodical ceased publication altogether.

ment meets with temporary difficulties and setbacks." The article continued: "But, in the world at large, the force of people's revolution surpasses the reactionary force of imperialism, the people's revolutionary flood prevents the counterrevolutionary stream from rushing forward. The people's revolutionary struggle is developing in an even deeper direction; the general situation is very good, it is even more advantageous to the world's people and not advantageous to U.S. imperialism. . . . In this accelerated process of advance of world history, in this time of sharpened struggle between revolutionary and counterrevolutionary strength, various types of different political forces have unavoidably split severely or are splitting, have reorganized or are reorganizing." Even where setbacks had occurred, the article concluded, these represented "only partial phenomena" and were possibly even beneficial in exposing revisionist-imperialist collusion and in steeling oppressed peoples for even greater struggles.

This formulation, which was repeated at the conclusion of the August plenum,[18] was followed to the letter by Ch'en Yi when he spoke on October 5, 1966, before the Military Institute in Peking.[19] Ch'en said those who had expressed doubts about Mao's theses regarding imperialism had "failed to see the forest for the trees." Ch'en continued:

"According to the Chairman's directive analyzing the [international] situation, as a consequence of the expansion of the anti-imperialist struggle by the word's people, the international situation at this time is one of big upheaval, big splitting, big reorganization, and deepening struggle: the three bigs, the one deep [san-ta i-shen]. As the three-bigs and one-deep have developed, especially since this May, because our Great Proletarian Cultural Revolution has appeared on the world stage, it has been of far-reaching international influence. The Vietnam war situation is very good, the anti-imperialist struggle of the Asian, African, and Latin American peoples has new developments, the international Communist movement has developed a step further, with a new anti-imperialism, anti-revisionism forming. Naturally, the situation has not been all smooth sailing; it must develop along a zig-zag road, [but] the mainstream of the situation is even more to the advantage of the people, to the advantage of

[18] See the international section of the Central Committee's communiqué of August 12, 1966, in Peking Review, No. 34 (August 19, 1966) pp. 6–7.

[19] Text of Ch'en's address is in Peking, Ch'ing-hua University Defend-the-East Corps, Shou-chang yen-lun chi (Collection of Speeches of the Leaders), Vol. 4 (November 1966) pp. 12–16. (The collection is marked "For Internal Distribution Only.")

the world revolution, and even more disadvantageous to imperialism and the reactionary cliques and modern revisionists of all countries. This is the estimation of the general situation."

Ch'en also cited specific "evidence" to prove his point that the situation was generally well in hand. He said he could not understand the fear struck in some people by the Cultural Revolution, for in many countries, foreigners had welcomed Mao's thoughts and were praising it to the skies —in Iraq, Pakistan, India, the Soviet Union, Bulgaria, and elsewhere. Of interest in view of subsequent events, Ch'en also mentioned Burma and Cambodia, saying that "Burmese independence has China's support" and that "a Cambodian suddenly appeared at our reception, said the Chinese people are the number one friend and [that he] felt pride and wants to return after the Cultural Revolution." In short, while Ch'en Yi was on the one hand resisting as best he could any intrusion of Red Guard organizations into the foreign affairs system, on the other he was adhering faithfully to the Maoist line on foreign policy. This was to remain his constant position during the ordeal to come.

THE FOREIGN MINISTER CONFESSES, RECANTS, AND CONTINUES THE STRUGGLE

In retrospect, Ch'en Yi seems to have been fighting a losing battle in refusing to give ground before the Red Guards while they had the approval of Mao Tse-tung. Although Ch'en had managed to keep Red Guard groups from organizing effectively within the Foreign Ministry or the other foreign affairs-related agencies and bureaus, his chief weapon for counterattacking, the work teams, had been taken from him. Furthermore, beginning in December 1966, additional ground was cut from under Ch'en when the regime began recalling ambassadors and senior embassy staff members back to Peking, probably in order to "re-educate" some and to purge others during study and criticism sessions.[20]

[20] The recall of ambassadors also seems to have been linked to a Mao instruction of September 9, 1966. According to a later Red Guard account (*Wai-shih feng-lei*) (*Foreign Affairs Wind and Thunder*), June 8, 1967, published by the Red Flag Revolutionary Rebel Regiment, Peking Foreign Language Institute, Capital Red Guard Congress), Mao's instruction had been issued in response to reports that Chinese embassies were havens for bourgeois living. "Let us have a revolutionization," the instruction read; "otherwise, it would be dangerous." See *JPRS* 42,359, August 28, 1967, pp. 15–19. Perhaps Mao believed that high living by ranking embassy officials flew in the face of the Cultural Revolution's proclaimed anti-capitalist emphasis, and hence that certain embassy personnel would have to be re-

By late spring of 1967, only Ambassador Huang Hua in Cairo remained at his post; other embassies were left in the control of chargés d'affaires. The recall of ambassadors was to have important consequences several months later, for it probably facilitated the manipulation of several embassies by officials eager to display their loyalty to Mao.

As had been the case the preceding summer, when ultra-left attacks on leading cadres in the Foreign Ministry coincided with demonstrations against provincial party, government, university and industrial centers, the events that were to lead to Ch'en Yi's "confession" in January 1967 also occurred in the midst of widespread turmoil. In mid-December, Red Guards had been given the "green light" to take over several government organs (including the Supreme People's Court) by Mao's wife, Chiang Ch'ing, deputy head of the Central Committee Cultural Revolution Group. This endorsement from the top was extended later in the month to encompass Red Guard "power seizures" of labor organizations.[21] The final plug was removed from the dike during the January Revolution. The unexpected chaos that accompanied it, which was to compel Mao to resort to the People's Liberation Army to restore order, so intensified the pressure on the Foreign Ministry that the Foreign Minister had to yield to demands for self-criticism in order to ensure his political survival.

Ch'en Yi's defenders in the Foreign Ministry would later charge that around the first of January 1967 a "plot" developed under the direction of Wang Li, a member of the Cultural Revolution Group, deputy editor of the authoritative ideological journal *Hung Ch'i*, and subsequently a prime antagonist of Ch'en's in the contest involving Yao Teng-shan. Allegedly, the plot aimed at overthrowing Ch'en "and several other vice-premiers" in defiance of Chou En-lai,[22] who then and thereafter seemed to be protecting Ch'en from being forced out of office. The allegation, though probably exaggerated, is consistent with the fact that during January a number

---

schooled in, if not permanently reduced to, simpler living. In any case, when Ch'en Yi addressed foreign service personnel on March 15, 1967, he said their study sessions would be designed to implement the September instruction as well as to bring about a thorough understanding of the Cultural Revolution. Ch'en's speech has been translated in American Consulate-General, Hong Kong, *Survey of China Mainland Magazines* (*SCMM*) 637, December 16, 1968.

[21] Philip Bridgham, "Mao's Cultural Revolution in 1967: The Struggle to Seize Power," *The China Quarterly*, No. 34 (April–June 1968) p. 8.

[22] *I-yüeh feng-pao* (*January Storm*), Canton, May 1968, as translated and appended by the editors of *Chinese Communist Affairs: Facts and Features* (Taipei), Vol. 1, No. 22 (August 21, 1968) pp. 22–23. Additional comments on the document written in defense of Ch'en Yi may be found on pp. 70ff.

of Red Guard organizations, in their drive to "seize power," attacked the
Cultural Revolution's spokesmen, including Chou.[23] Whether or not a
plot actually took form, then, the main point is that sharpened assaults on
Ch'en Yi and the Foreign Ministry took place coincidentally with, and
certainly under the influence of, a growing breakdown of order in the
Cultural Revolution as a whole.

On January 18 the anti-Ch'en forces were for the first time able to gain
a foothold in the Foreign Ministry itself. A Ministry of Foreign Affairs
Revolutionary Rebel Liaison Station (*wai-chiao-pu k̲e-ming tsao-fan lien-
lo-chan*) was set up and began "to lead revolution and to inspect work."[24]
A Red Guard report on events at that time implied that the "liaison station" was necessary to block a developing "anarchical" situation in which
"conservative" (pro-Ch'en) cadres previously ousted were being permitted
to return to their posts. Thus, the report continued, whereas the Cultural
Revolution had decreed that, "based on practical requirements," new
organizational forms should replace old ones, "after the seizure of power,
a reverse wind appeared in the form of demanding restoration of the
original system. This was [an attempt] to bury the achievements of the
Cultural Revolution."[25] Ch'en Yi had evidently balked again at the notion of having a permanent Red Guard presence in his ministry.

The Red Guards, being equally stubborn and still having the authority
of Mao's nationwide call to "struggle" behind them, now issued their
investigation report, which consisted of Ch'en's self-criticism of January
24 delivered before a mass rally of 10,000 reportedly presided over by
Premier Chou. According to the report, entitled "My Investigation" (*Wo*

---

[23] For example, Ch'en Po-ta, head of the Central Committee Cultural Revolution
Group, in a speech of January 24, 1967, to a meeting of representatives of Peking
University, deplored factionalism in revolutionary groups. Ch'en said that whereas
the "spearhead" of the struggle was supposed to have been directed at Liu Shao-ch'i
and Teng Hsiao-p'ing, "some people have nevertheless directed the spearhead of
their attack at the revolutionaries, at the Cultural Revolution Group of the Party
Central Committee, at Premier Chou, Comrades K'ang Sheng, Chiang Ch'ing,
Wang Li, Kuan Feng, and Ch'i Pen-yü." *Huo-ch'e-t'ou* (*Locomotive*), No. 7 (February 1967), in American Consulate-General, Hong Kong, *Survey of China Mainland Press* (*SCMP*) 3898, March 14, 1967, p. 4. See also the comments of Bridgham,
"Mao's Cultural Revolution in 1967: The Struggle to Seize Power," *op. cit.*, pp. 8–11.

[24] Chu Pu, *op. cit.*, p. 36. See also "Bombard Ch'en Yi," *op. cit.*

[25] "Bombard Ch'en Yi," *op. cit.* See also *Hung-wei-pao* (*Red Guard Newspaper*),
Peking, No. 24 (May 23, 1967) p. 3, an article by the Red Flag Struggle Corps of
the Foreign Language Institute, in which Ch'en is called "an irredeemable monar-
chist" for having sought to protect himself and his followers from reform by the
masses since 1963.

ti chien-ch'a),[26] Ch'en was guilty of seven major "crimes," four of which related to his dispatch of work teams before and after the Eleventh Plenum. Moreover, he allegedly had failed to lift high the red flag of Mao's thoughts, had not gone among and learned from the masses, and had displayed a bureaucratic work attitude; he had committed major mistakes in 1961 and 1962 by delivering speeches that stressed expertise over ideology ("redness"); finally, he needed to be a better student of Mao, to emulate Lin Piao, and to study the good points of comrades in the Cultural Revolution Group.

Ch'en's confession, with its outpouring of self-condemnation, not only was approved by key figures in the Central Committee,[27] but also seems temporarily to have won over most of the Red Guards. In publishing the confession on February 8, the editor of *Hung-wei-pao* called it "sincere" and "thorough" and considered Ch'en's attitude worthy of "emulation." "Events have shown that although Comrade Ch'en Yi [continued use of the term "comrade" is significant] committed a great many mistakes, he never engaged in double-crossing and was able to examine and rectify his own errors. Thus, he is still a good comrade in the proletarian headquarters. We must resolutely support and sustain him."[28]

But "the ink was not dry on his self-criticism," according to Ch'en's opponents, "when he put back in their jobs and positions very questionable people, as well as Party people in power following the capitalist road, in several academies in foreign systems."[29] Apparently having had no intention of surrendering to fanatic Red Guards, who had already begun physically disrupting the Foreign Ministry,[30] Ch'en once again counterattacked. He declared the rebels incapable of any positive service beyond arbitrarily labeling ministry cadres "revisionists,"[31] and he accused the

[26] See Chu Pu, *op. cit.*, pp. 34–35.

[27] See the speeches by Ch'en Po-ta and Chou En-lai on January 24, in *SCMM* 636, December 9, 1968, p. 7.

[28] "Ch'en Yi's Self-Criticism," *op. cit.*, pp. 51–52.

[29] "Criticize Ch'en Yi's Reactionary Policy," *Wai-shih hung-ch'i*, in *JPRS* 42,070 (Translations on Communist China: Political and Sociological, No. 413 [August 3, 1967]) pp. 13–16.

[30] Speaking to Red Guards at the airport on February 12, Ch'en said: "The facts prove that what I said last year was not wrong, not all wrong. Look at things now, we must still do things my way. If things had all along been done my way, we wouldn't have come to this state. At present look at what has happened to the ministry: no order, no organization, foreign affairs secrets have been taken away." *Hung-wei chan-pao* (*Red Guard Combat Newspaper*), April 8, 1967, and *Hung-ch'i*, April 4, 1967, cited in *Ch'en Yi yen-lun hsüan*, p. 20.

[31] Chu Pu, *op. cit.*, p. 36, citing the newspapers *Hung-wei chan-pao*, April 8, 1967,

rebel liaison station of having "made an error of line and direction." Undoubtedly at Ch'en's direction a number of evidently ultra-leftist functionaries in the Foreign Ministry were removed from or challenged in their posts; articles were written by the "conservatives" attacking those in the rebel group;[32] and, in the Overseas Chinese Affairs Commission, extremists were compelled to accept a pro-Ch'en official, Wu Chi-sheng, as a compromise leader in a makeshift coalition.[33] In all, even as Ch'en told a Red Guard group on February 9 that he and the ministry accepted criticism and supervision,[34] he was acting to discourage both, reminding his foes that Mao and the entire Central Committee supported his continuation in office.

Ch'en Yi's statement to a Red Guard group at the Peking airport on February 12, "my investigation was forced," therefore merely underscored his already clear determination to take the offensive. Ch'en told Red Guards they should "go to Vietnam" if they wanted to make revolution.[35] In a later reported talk with Red Guards, Ch'en assailed critics of Ho

---

and *Hung-ch'i*, April 4. In a talk of February 8, reported by these newspapers, Ch'en said: "They [the Red Guards] wanted to put all the department heads and vice-ministers off in a corner; they don't have the right. Even Chairman Mao needs to have people to talk to." Ch'en also reportedly said: "The greatest weakness of the rebel group is that it speaks only of the weaknesses of others. Are you all so in line with the thoughts of Mao Tse-tung? They [the ministry's cadres] have 90, 92, 99 percent of the responsibility; you should also have a little." (Quoted from the same newspapers in Chu Pu, p. 41.)

[32] "Bombard Ch'en Yi," *op. cit.*

[33] There were apparently two groups fighting for control of the Overseas Commission: the Ch'en-backed United Power-Seizure Committee, and the rebel-backed revolutionary left organizations led by the Tungfanghung (East-is-Red) Commune of Returned Overseas Chinese. Wu Chi-sheng, head of the First Department of the Overseas Chinese Affairs Commission and a member of its Party committee, teamed with one of the Commission's vice-chairmen, Lin Hsiu-teh, to carry out the Ch'en Yi-Liao Ch'eng-chih line of buying time for the outnumbered conservatives by merging the two hostile groups. As shall be seen shortly, the radicals, believing that any merger was really meant to destroy "the struggle for seizure of power in the Overseas Chinese Affairs Commission," became increasingly boisterous during March and April, directing demonstrations against Ch'en, Liao, and the Overseas Chinese Affairs Commission Party committee under Fang Fang. See *Ke-ming ch'iao-pao* (*Revolutionary Overseas Chinese Affairs Bulletin*), April 9, 1967, in *SCMP* 3939, May 16, 1967, pp. 9–11; the article was written by the Red Guided Missile Fighting Team of Returned Overseas Chinese Tungfanghung Commune in the Capital.

[34] In *SCMM* 636, December 9, 1968, pp. 19–20.

[35] *Ch'en Yi yen-lun hsüan, op. cit.*, pp. 14, 15.

Lung, the besieged former Army marshal and vice-premier, warning that attacks on old cadres "are giving us a black eye." The point had been reached, he declared, where few people can be believed. "Whom do you believe? [he asked]. If you believe the Chairman, Lin Piao, the Premier, Ch'en Po-ta, Chiang Ch'ing, and K'ang Sheng [adviser to the Cultural Revolution Group], then you've only got six people. I am indebted for your magnanimity. You've thrown in five vice-premiers, only eleven people. So a great Party only has a few clean people? I don't want to be among the clean ones; take me out to the crowd!" [36] Obviously warming to his role, Ch'en boldly went on to declare that "Comrade [Liu] Shao-ch'i speaks correctly. . . . Comrade Shao-ch'i . . . is my teacher." And he ended his unsparing critique by denouncing the Red Guards for saying that the Liu-Teng foreign policy line was "the line of revisionism. No, this is Chairman Mao's line. You're too crazy, you don't know what's going on." [37] Ch'en Yi had evidently reached the limits of his tolerance for what could only have struck him as outrageous conduct by juvenile self-styled leftists who were demanding his head after years of faithful service to the Party.

Ch'en's firmness before the Red Guard onslaught should have led to an early showdown, but the confrontation was postponed, in effect, for two months. As before, the struggle in the Foreign Ministry was shaped by the overall direction of the Cultural Revolution decided by Mao and the Cultural Revolution Group. On January 23 (before Ch'en's outburst), the Army had been instructed to "actively support the revolutionary leftist faction," [38] which in fact meant that the Army was to stem the tide of anarchy that unrestrained radicalism had produced. The military quickly made its impact felt in "three-way alliances," which generally gave it and experienced "revolutionary cadres" proportionally greater representation than Red Guards. In synchronization with this comeback by formerly discarded party cadres, the Red Guards were ordered to reform their lines (by merging into a single Red Guard congress), to disband "revolution-ary liaison" groups and return to school, and to undergo rectification

---

[36] *Ibid.*, p. 16.

[37] *Ibid.*, pp. 16, 19. See also the quotations in "What Poison This Ch'en Yi Is," *Hung-wei chan-pao*, April 13, 1967, p. 4, written by the Capital Congress of Red Representatives, People's University Three-Red Seize Ch'en Yi Regiment.

[38] Decision of the Central Committee of the CCP, the Military Affairs Committee of the Central Committee, and the Cultural Revolution Small Group, in *Hsing-huo liao-yuan* (*A Single Spark May Start a Prairie Fire*), Peking, January 27, 1967.

under Army supervision.[39] The Red Guards' forced retreat, lasting through February, gave the Foreign Ministry a much-needed breathing spell.

The parallel development of the Red Guards' role in the Cultural Revolution and in the Foreign Ministry entered its next stage in March 1967, when the young radicals seized the opportunity afforded by Army shortcomings in its new political task to charge that not only some but a great many old-line cadres were being reinstated at the expense of the revolutionary left.[40] Apparently, these "false power seizures" had already occurred in the Foreign Ministry. Beginning in March and extending into May, the Red Guards were given a second life as the Cultural Revolution again moved into a phase of frenzied attack against "capitalist-roaders" supposedly out to regain lost power.

The limited available information suggests that beginning in March, the renewed confrontation between extremist factions and Ch'en Yi concerned, first, the returned ambassadors and their staffs and, second, the Overseas Chinese Affairs Commission. Having previously told Red Guards that carrying out the revolution in embassies abroad would interfere with diplomatic business,[41] Ch'en found himself challenged by Red Guards and returned students, who were leading the criticism sessions against foreign service officers. But the Foreign Minister asserted that it was the Central Committee itself, in a directive of February 7, that had restricted the scope of the revolution in embassies. Retreating somewhat from his initial stand, Ch'en distinguished between making revolution outside and inside an embassy: the former was forbidden by the directive, the latter was in line with Mao's thoughts. Thus, he elaborated, while embassy officials would be subject to criticism and ideological rectification, the Party committee still was to operate in Chinese missions, and power seizures would not be allowed.[42] Nor, as was revealed in a talk of April 1, was Ch'en only interested in preserving the freedom of action of embassy staffs. He further aroused his Red Guard critics by stating that the effective performance of embassies, and China's image, required modera-

---

[39] Bridgham, "Mao's Cultural Revolution in 1967: The Struggle to Seize Power," op. cit., pp. 11–14.

[40] Ibid., pp. 15–16.

[41] According to a Red Guard report of a talk given by Ch'en on February 16, 1967, to a group organized to prepare a general criticism meeting on embassy personnel. In SCMM 636, December 9, 1968, p. 27.

[42] See Ch'en's speech to all returned personnel on March 15, 1967, in SCMM 637, December 16, 1968, p. 19.

tion in criticism of ambassadors so that some might return to their posts, perhaps by June.[43] To the Red Guards involved in the Foreign Ministry's activities, Ch'en's statement confirmed them in their suspicion that the Cultural Revolution in foreign affairs would be only perfunctorily carried out.[44]

In the Overseas Chinese Affairs Commission, meanwhile, on March 28 a Preparatory Group for Struggle Against Counter-Revolutionary Revisionist Fang Fang, the Party committee chairman, was formed.[45] This group's charter probably was to undermine the alliance that Ch'en Yi and Liao Ch'eng-chih, chairman of the Commission, had been intent upon creating.[46] On April 4, the group's General Command sponsored a mass rally against Ch'en and Liao, accusing them of having "stubbornly executed the bourgeois reactionary line in the overseas Chinese affairs system and [of having] attempted to strangle the Great Cultural Revolution in the overseas Chinese affairs system." [47]

The rally against Ch'en spread to the Foreign Ministry on April 8 when about one hundred Red Guards of the Foreign Language Institute reportedly staged a demonstration. On the same day, and more significantly, a Criticize Ch'en Yi Liaison Station (*P'i-p'an Ch'en Yi lien-lo-chan*) was set up,[48] probably to replace the earlier Revolutionary Rebel Liaison Station which, by the February 3 Central Committee directive, should have been abolished along with all other liaison stations in government organs.

With the installation of a new liaison station in the ministry, the stage

[43] Talk with the Tsunyi Corps of Returned Students, *ibid.,* pp. 27–29. Ch'en offered as his personal opinion the idea that China's name would be blackened if every returned officer had to pass a test or if all ambassadors were purged. Some embassies, he observed, were sharply reduced in manpower and, without ambassadors, could not obtain audiences with foreign ministers. Perhaps those ambassadors who had made self-examinations, had not committed major errors, and could obtain the Central Committee's approval might return in June, he suggested, with the remainder returning thereafter. By sending back at least a few, foreign speculation that a big purge was underway in the foreign service could be undercut.

[44] See "Bombard Ch'en Yi," *op. cit.* Ch'en replied to this charge on April 4 by saying that the return of embassy officials would depend on progress in the rectification movement. But he renewed his position that "our ambassadors must be sent back to their posts" in order to counter rumors that China was changing her foreign policy and purging her ambassadors. "Talk with students of the Second Foreign Language Institute," in *SCMM* 637, December 16, 1968, p. 37.

[45] *Ke-ming ch'iao-pao,* in *SCMP* 3939, May 16, 1967, p. 5.

[46] See *ibid.,* p. 21 and note 33, above.

[47] *Ke-ming ch'iao-pao,* in *SCMP* 3939, May 16, 1967, p. 7.

[48] Chu Pu, *op. cit.,* p. 35.

was set for a third round of "struggle," one with far more serious consequences for Ch'en's authority than the previous two. Apparently trying to forestall Ch'en Yi's removal while simultaneously placating the Red Guard organizations, Ch'en Po-ta put the Central Committee's stamp of approval on criticism of Ch'en in a speech on April 16, but barred the Foreign Minister's overthrow. Ch'en Po-ta instructed "that Ch'en Yi should be listened to, watched, and helped." [49] In view of the importance of his work, Red Guards were told to moderate their attacks; meanwhile, Ch'en Yi would have to go before the masses, and in the future Chou En-lai would supervise the ministry's work.[50] At that point, according to Ch'en's loyal followers in the ministry, the policy of the Maoist regime was "one-third criticism and two-thirds guarantee" of Ch'en Yi.[51]

Yet "less than forty-eight hours" after Ch'en Po-ta's directive, a statement demanding Ch'en Yi's overthrow was assertedly published by "the former nucleus of the liaison office of the Foreign Ministry, dominated by a group of bad leaders." [52] On May 10 the attack was broadened to include two more Vice-Ministers of Foreign Affairs, Chi P'eng-fei and Ch'iao Kuan-hua.[53] And on May 11, ten Red Guard organizations staged a demonstration against Ch'en Yi in Peking.[54] These acts, although taken, as Ch'en's defenders subsequently charged,[55] in apparent defiance of the express wishes of the Central Committee, were probably inspired by Ch'en Yi's refusal to conform to Ch'en Po-ta's instructions that the Foreign Minister should conduct self-criticism. Like Ch'en Yi, the Red Guards had apparently lost all patience with the opposition.

That this was the case became evident on May 12, when Chou En-lai met with the ultra-leftist liaison station of the Foreign Ministry and "representatives of over ten other revolutionary organizations" involved in foreign affairs work. Noting that Ch'en Yi had "refused Ch'en Po-ta's

---

[49] *I-yüeh feng-pao, op. cit.,* p. 26.

[50] American Embassy, Tokyo, *Daily Summary of Japanese Press,* April 28, 1967, p. 13: articles in *Sankei* and *Asahi Shimbun,* same date, citing wall posters put up on April 27.

[51] *I-yüeh feng-pao, op. cit.,* p. 22.

[52] *Ibid.,* p. 23.

[53] *Ibid.,* p. 23.

[54] Reported in *P'i-Ch'en chan-pao (Criticize Ch'en Combat Newspaper),* Peking, No. 1 (May 28, 1967) p. 1, published by the Criticize Ch'en Yi Liaison Station.

[55] Ch'en's defenders asserted: "The more the central authorities expressed their unwillingness to overthrow Ch'en Yi, the louder their [the Red Guards'] clamor and the higher the pitch of their language. . . . They disobeyed the orders of the Central Committee and oppressed the masses." Quoted in *I-yüeh feng-pao, op. cit.,* p. 26.

directive of April 17 to go before the masses," the Premier reportedly gave his support to having the Foreign Minister give a full account of his crimes. He urged the Red Guards to continue their correct criticism by "drawing up cases" (*ch'uang-tsao an-chien*) and preparing "the unity of big, medium, and small [criticism] meetings" against Ch'en. Finally, Chou made clear that this criticism should extend through July. According to the Red Guard report of the meeting: "The Premier also concretely laid out the plan for criticizing Ch'en Yi, saying that criticism 'must be done for the three months of May, June, and July.' The Premier decided that Ch'en Yi should first listen to criticism at the Foreign Ministry and afterwards go again to the Foreign Language Institute, the Foreign Affairs Institute, and the Second Foreign Language Institute. The Premier further said he would personally chair the meeting to criticize Ch'en." [56]

The Red Guards apparently took Chou's words as the signal for intensified attacks on Ch'en Yi and the Ministry. The following day, May 13, saw the first of a series of tumultuous incidents on the Ministry grounds as hundreds of rampaging rebels belonging to the Red Flag Detachment of the Foreign Language Institute (the organization in control of the liaison station) occupied that part of the ministry building which houses confidential documents.[57] For six hours, according to various wall posters of May 14, the Red Guards completely disrupted normal operations, beating up officials who stood in their way, breaking open files and copying down documents (it was here that the oft-quoted remark of one rebel—"What's so terrific about secrets? To hell with them"—was supposedly made), and barring free entry and departure. One poster said the Red Flag detachment took action mainly because Chou had failed to include it among the ten organizations assigned to criticize Ch'en Yi. In view of the extremists' tendency to become more rabid whenever confronted with countervailing power, this explanation must be given some weight.

In fact, Chou En-lai does not seem to have departed in the least from his and the Central Committee's previous position that the Red Guards could oversee the Ministry's work and criticize Ch'en Yi, but could neither take over operation of the ministry nor "overthrow" its head. A Red

[56] Chou's meeting with the Red Guards is reported in full in *P'i-Ch'en chan-pao*, May 28, 1967. Similar information may be found in a Red Guard poster of May 12 signed by Revolutionary Rebels of the Foreign Language Institute.

[57] *Asahi Shimbun*, Tokyo, June 1, 1967.

Guard poster of May 17 reporting a four-hour meeting of rebel organizations with the Premier brought out Chou's dual line. The rebels are said to have made three demands: first, that Ch'en should go before the masses; second, that Vice-Minister Chi P'eng-fei should be removed as a bourgeois element; third, that neither Ch'en and Chi nor Vice-Minister Ch'iao Kuan-hua should be allowed to continue in the Ministry. Chou reportedly responded by pointedly indicating that he would not favor the rebels' dragging out ranking members of the Foreign Ministry. He said that while he had consistently supported the rebels' demands, the matter of Ch'en Yi was different and required a decision by the Central Committee, not only as to his going before the masses, but also as to his removal. Chou cautioned the youths against pressuring him and against attributing to him critical views of Ch'en which were not in fact his own. He cut off the lengthy give-and-take—which, according to the poster, was at times marked by heated indignation on the part of the impatient rebels—by suggesting that they organize several criticize-Ch'en meetings which he would attend.

From developments after this meeting, it seems fairly certain that several Red Guard units had collectively determined to defy Chou's (and the Central Committee's) distinction between attack and overthrow. On May 16 Japanese correspondents reported a clash outside the Foreign Ministry between pro- and anti-Ch'en Yi groups. During the remainder of the month, moreover, criticisms of Chou as well as Ch'en appeared, prompting members of the Cultural Revolution Group to tell Red Guard representatives on May 27 that the Premier could not be criticized, that not only he but Ch'en Po-ta had shielded the Foreign Minister, and that the office of foreign minister was too important to be given over to just anyone.[58] The Red Guards' response was a violent one. On May 29 about three hundred of them representing one of two rebel groups within the Overseas Chinese Affairs Commission raided the Ministry, forcibly removed classified material from safes, and demanded that Liao Ch'eng-chih be handed over to them for criticism. The Red Guard posters containing this information indicated that Ch'en Po-ta had to intervene to demand the return of the classified materials.[59]

[58] *Asahi Shimbun*, June 1, 1967, based on a mimeographed wall poster put up on May 31. Criticism of Chou was reported in one Red Guard newspaper to have been the work of the Independent Battalion of the Red Guard 616th Regiment in the Peking Foreign Language Institute. *Wai-shih hung-ch'i*, No. 5 (May 26, 1967) p. 3, article by "Observer."

[59] From wall posters and slogans dated May 14 outside the Ministry of Foreign

Although it has been suggested that the Red Guards were probably motivated to oppose the Central Committee principally out of sheer loss of patience over the dilatory tactics of Chou and Ch'en Po-ta, it may also have been their acquisition of a leader—Yao Teng-shan—that gave them the added audacity to fight their way into the Foreign Ministry. Yao Teng-shan, until late April 1967, had been the ranking Chinese government official in Indonesia as interim chargé d'affaires. On April 28, he and Hsü Jen, the consul general in Djakarta, were both declared *persona non grata* by the Indonesian government and ordered to leave the country. This action was hardly surprising in view of the rapid deterioration of Sino-Indonesian relations following the unsuccessful Communist Party of Indonesia-assisted coup attempt of September 30, 1965. When Yao and Hsü returned to Peking on April 30, they were declared "red diplomat fighters" and given heroes' welcomes. Virtually every leading member of the government (except Mao), including the entire hierarchy of the Foreign Ministry, was reportedly present to greet them at the airport.[60]

Yao's precise activities after his return are for the most part shrouded in mystery. But to judge from his briefly successful attempt in August to replace Ch'en Yi as de facto Foreign Minister (see below), it is likely that Yao had become deeply involved in Red Guard intrigues upon his return. We know, for instance, that Yao and Hsü Jen were present during Chou En-lai's meeting with Red Guard organizations on May 12, where they were again referred to as "red diplomat fighters" (*hung wai chan-shih*).[61] Subsequently, on May 19, Yao and Hsü were featured speakers at a rally of 10,000 persons in Peking to denounce the Indonesian government.[62] Other reports of his activities from June through July, when placed beside the new direction Red Guard criticisms began taking

Affairs. According to Ch'en's defenders, writing in *I-yüeh feng-pao, op. cit.*, p. 26, the Red Guard invasions of May 13 and 29 were in defiance of the express orders of the Central Committee "that power of diplomacy should not be seized and top secrets should not be captured, administration and personnel records should not be used, and the political department established by Chairman Mao should not be destroyed. But a handful of class enemies and extreme left elements openly disobeyed the directives, closed the office of the Party committee in the ministry and destroyed the political department, usurped the Bureau of Top Secrets, impeded the archive system, and disclosed many top secrets. Their actions greatly damaged the power of diplomacy and personnel."

[60] Their arrival was reported by *New China News Agency* (*NCNA*) (Peking), April 30, 1967, in *SCMP* 3932, May 4, 1967, pp. 31–33.

[61] *P'i-Ch'en chan-pao,* May 28, 1967.

[62] *NCNA* (Peking) broadcast of May 19, 1967.

after his return (devoting considerable attention to the overseas Chinese in Indonesia), provide at least an interesting circumstantial case for the hypothesis that Yao Teng-shan in effect gave the Red Guard anti-Ch'en forces the firm backing they needed to oppose the Central Committee and to carry the Cultural Revolution in the Foreign Ministry to new heights.

JUNE–AUGUST, 1967: EXTREMISM TAKES COMMAND

Whether or not the return of Yao Teng-shan was a crucial factor in the planning of the ultra-left, from May until roughly the end of August, the Foreign Ministry was hard pressed to maintain a semblance of equilibrium in the face of Red Guard incursions. Once again, the strength of the extremists varied in accordance with the overall strength of the left in the Cultural Revolution; as Mao leaned to one side or the other in search of appropriate leadership for implementing the Revolution, the fortunes of the Foreign Ministry's "conservatives" and radicals seem to have been correspondingly affected. In July and August, when Mao evidently responded to the Wuhan Incident by again backing the use of extremist measures, the die was cast in favor of an all-out assault on the ministry that culminated in the temporary elimination of relatively moderate influence in the conduct of foreign relations.

Coincidentally with the return of Yao Teng-shan from Indonesia, it appears that the organizations of the extreme left altered the substance of their verbal attack. Whereas previously they had concentrated on Ch'en Yi's lack of enthusiasm for promoting a "revolution" in the Foreign Ministry, they now sought to undermine him by playing up specific "issues," such as Ch'en's alleged failure to have supported the overseas Chinese in Indonesia at the time of the abortive Communist Party coup in the fall of 1965.

As we have seen, Liao Ch'eng-chih's Overseas Chinese Affairs Commission had for several months been a particular target of Red Guard organizations. Until about June 1967, however, the extremist groups had been intent upon "seizing power" on the basis that the Commission, like other organs linked to the Ministry of Foreign Affairs, was dominated by "counterrevolutionary" cadres more interested in preserving their jobs than in participating actively in the Cultural Revolution. Beginning in

June, the ultra-left took a new tack, arguing that the conservatism of these cadres explained why the Foreign Ministry had stood on the sidelines while overseas Chinese were being systematically denied their rights. To cite one example, a Red Guard newspaper charged that Liao Ch'eng-chih, conforming to the revisionist, capitulationist international line of Liu Shao-ch'i (when, actually, he was fulfilling Chou En-lai's strictures laid down during his 1956 Southeast Asia travels) made certain that the overseas Chinese did not interfere with efforts to curry favor with local governments: "He [Liao] asked the overseas Chinese 'to mind their own business,' 'to stick to their own posts,' and 'not to criticize the internal affairs of the local governments.'" Consequently, Chinese abroad were not permitted to "make revolution" in accordance with the thoughts of Mao. Thus, the charge ran, in South Vietnam in 1956 Chinese were forced to become naturalized Vietnamese citizens; and in Indonesia, restrictions were placed on the number of Chinese schools (1957), Chinese were deported following the dual nationality agreement (1959), and Chinese were slaughtered in the wake of the abortive PKI coup attempt (1965).[63] The timing of these accusations, coming after the return of Yao Teng-shan and while returned Chinese students from Indonesia were prominent in the opposition movement within the Commission,[64] raises the question of whether they were based on fact or fancy. Whichever is the case, the purpose was clearly to increase support for the extremists' position that Ch'en Yi and cadres protected by him were reactionaries who had to be overthrown.

At this time the ultra-left again raised the matter of the conduct of embassy personnel abroad. The charges here were that members of the diplomatic corps had become ideologically and materially corrupted by their "bourgeois" style of living abroad; ambassadors considered themselves above criticism and seldom went "to the masses"; embassies had

[63] *P'i-Liao chan-pao* (*Criticize Liao Combat Newspaper*), Peking, June 18, 1967, written by the "Long Cord in Hand" Combat Team and the "Rebel to the End" Combat Team of the Red Banner Corps of the OCAC. Translated in *JPRS* 42,977 *Communist China Digest,* October 16, 1967) pp. 74-77.

[64] Upon returning to China in December 1966, forty-one students were dubbed "the heroic fighting collective" and were reported (in late April 1967) to have "settled down on the overseas Chinese farm in Ninghua *hsien*, Fukien Province." (*NCNA* [Peking], April 29, 1967, in *SCMP* 3931, May 3, 1967, p. 27.) Actually, these students not only participated in several mass rallies against Indonesia and in welcomes for groups of Chinese arriving from Indonesia; they also seem to have been at the forefront of the Tungfanghung commune which had been leading the struggle against the conservative United Power-Seizure Committee in the OCAC.

become "independent kingdoms" (a charge similar to that made against certain provincial Party officials), " 'one-doctrine' halls, or 'family-type gangster inns' that trample under foot the Party principle of democratic centralism." [65] Ch'en Yi was responsible for these developments, according to the Red Guard indictment. Ch'en had "distorted and depreciated" Mao's instructions by confining orders on embassy reform to matters of living style and dress. In fact, the article maintained, Ch'en should have seen that the whole spirit of the Cultural Revolution was carried abroad; as matters stood, Chinese embassy officials were ill-disposed to using big-character posters and students abroad were forbidden to take part in the "revolutionization" of embassies. The ultra-left viewpoint, as reflected in this newspaper article, called for implementation of Mao's instructions and concluded: "The revolutionary students who have studied abroad must unite with the proletarian revolutionaries in the foreign service." [66]

In view of Ch'en Yi's behavior throughout the Cultural Revolution, in particular his handling of the returned ambassadors and his consistent determination to prevent Red Guard power and influence from seeping into his own "independent kingdom," the charge that he only half-heartedly implemented Mao's directive on reform may well be correct. Ch'en was in fact quoted by Red Guards as having said some months previously: "These thoughts of Mao Tse-tung are really a Chinese product; we mustn't take them abroad." [67] Whether or not those were his actual words, his actions would seem to indicate that his intent was that embassies should not become centers for "making [cultural] revolution" in foreign countries. And, as has been seen, he believed he had the Central Committee's backing in that restrictive policy.

The Cultural Revolution had for some time so preoccupied the Peking leadership that foreign affairs received substantially less attention than in the immediate pre-Revolution period. The extremely limited coverage of overseas news in the mass media, the noticeable decline in the number of arrivals of foreign dignitaries, and the virtual cutoff of departures of Chinese delegations on visits abroad all lead to this conclusion.

To the extent that foreign relations were conducted, however, Ch'en

---

[65] "Thoroughly Smash the Privileged Stratum in the Ministry of Foreign Affairs," *Wai-shih hung-ch'i,* June 14, 1967, written by the Red Guards Service Center of Returned Students of the Capital Red Guard Congress, in *JPRS* 42,997 (*Communist China Digest,* No. 190 [October 16, 1967]) pp. 112–117.

[66] *Wai-shih feng-lei,* June 8, 1967, in *JPRS* 42,997, *op. cit.*

[67] "What Poison this Ch'en Yi Is," *op. cit.*

Yi continued to play a principal role in them. His presence at receptions, banquets, and other official functions was reported throughout the period he was under attack until late August, when ill health apparently forced him to the sidelines for over a month. But his influence over the implementation of foreign *policy* was probably very limited. One indirect indication is Ch'en's reiteration in early July to a visiting member of Japan's Liberal Democratic Party of the traditional themes of Chinese Communist foreign policy (noninterference, peaceful coexistence, and so on) and his assurance that China's diplomatic position would not change as a consequence of the Cultural Revolution.[68] By that time, however, China's relations with Burma had already been grievously harmed, and within a few more months the traditional themes would not be very credible to China's Asian neighbors and Ch'en Yi himself would no longer be in a position to promote them.

It is important to point out, however, that prior to the period of maximum ultra-left influence on domestic politics and foreign relations (roughly from late June to the end of August), not only was Ch'en Yi Foreign Minister in fact as well as name, but also China retained good relations with its "friendly" neighbors, some of whom would later have to deal with the Cultural Revolution on their home territories. These included Pakistan, Afghanistan, Ceylon, Nepal, Cambodia, and Burma.[69] A few illustrations drawn from New China News Agency reports should suffice to demonstrate these points.

Friendly relations with Rawalpindi were indicated by a banquet for the visiting Pakistani minister of defense (May 26).

[68] *Yomiuri Shimbun,* Tokyo, July 8, 1967. The interview was also attended by Liao Ch'eng-chih in his capacity as president of the China-Japan Friendship Association and chief Chinese negotiator of trade agreements with the Japanese.

[69] At this time and subsequently into 1968, the CPR continued to support revolutionary movements in Thailand, the Philippines, Malaysia, Laos, and Vietnam, was very hostile to the governments of Indonesia and India (trying to point out, in the latter case, how New Delhi's economic misfortunes were creating appropriate conditions for people's war in West Bengal and other areas), and occasionally criticized the pro-"imperialist" policies of the Philippines, Malaysia, and Japan. The most excitable of Chinese foreign policy statements in the spring and summer of 1967 were reserved for Hong Kong, where forceful British security measures had for some months been prompting Peking protests. On June 9, in fact, the official French news agency, Agence France-Presse, reported from its Peking correspondent that Red Guards had besieged the British mission that evening following an afternoon incident in which about one hundred pro-Maoist non-Chinese had stormed the mission and destroyed official property.

A reception was given on May 27 to celebrate the 49th anniversary of Afghan independence, highlighted by a speech on Vietnam by Ch'en Yi.

A high-ranking member of the Ceylon Communist Party visited Peking. Although praising the Cultural Revolution in a speech before "revolutionary rebels" on May 20, he refrained from speaking poorly of his own government.

China made a grant of 20,000 tons of rice to Nepal on March 14. On April 27, a reception was held to mark the seventh anniversary of the signing of the China-Nepal Peace and Friendship Treaty.

A statement of the Ministry of Foreign Affairs reaffirmed "that the Chinese government fully respects the territorial integrity of the Kingdom of Cambodia in her present borders," a response to a request by Prince Sihanouk of all governments.[70]

The New China News Agency heralded the impending completion of four Chinese aid projects as evidence of the traditional friendship of the Chinese and Burmese peoples (February 12). A reception was attended by Chinese officials in Peking to mark the twenty-second anniversary of the founding of the Burmese armed forces (March 27). The usual expressions of *paukphaw* (kinsmen) relations were exchanged on May 10 in Peking on the fifteenth anniversary of the China-Burma Friendship Association.[71]

Below the surface, however, there were already signs of strain in China's relations with Burma and Cambodia. The disruption that ensued in those relations, as well as in Peking's relations with Nepal, Ceylon, and several European and African countries, merits additional detail in order to point up the difficulties of foreign policy-making in Peking at a time of domestic upheaval. Burma and Cambodia, as the two most serious cases of dispute with Communist China, are given more lengthy treatment.

Public expressions of cordiality in Sino-Burmese relations overshadowed the subdued, highly tentative support Peking had been giving the Com-

[70] Sources, in order of presentation, are: *NCNA* (Peking) broadcast of May 26, 1967; *NCNA* (Peking), May 27, 1967, in *SCMP* 3950, June 1, 1967, pp. 30–31; *NCNA* (Peking), May 26, 1967, in *SCMP* 3950, pp. 36–39; *NCNA* (Katmandu), March 16, 1967, in *SCMP* 3902, March 20, 1967, p. 26, and *NCNA* (Peking), April 27, 1967, in *SCMP* 3930, May 26, 1967, pp. 27–28; *NCNA* (Peking), June 13, 1967, in *SCMP* 3961, June 16, 1967, pp. 28–29.

[71] *NCNA* (Rangoon), February 12, 1967, in *SCMP* 3882, February 17, 1967, p. 19; *NCNA* (Peking), March 27, 1967, in *SCMP* 3908, March 30, 1967, p. 24; and *NCNA* (Peking), May 10, 1967, in *SCMP* 3938, May 12, 1967, p. 31.

munist Party of Burma (White Flags) since November 1963, when peace negotiations between the White Flag Communists and Rangoon broke down. As can now be documented,[72] the failure of the government of the Union of Burma and the Communist insurgents to reach agreement intensified the split in the White Flags between those favoring protracted armed struggle and those more amenable to a reconciliation with the government. The hardliners, led by Thakin Than Tun, chairman of the politburo of the White Flag Central Committee, were supported by a group of Burmese Communists who had returned from extended residence and training in Peking to take part in the negotiations. In conformity with China's by then openly hostile attitude toward Moscow, the Peking returnees, in collaboration with Than Tun and two other politburo members, evidently pressed for a showdown with the "softer" (that is, allegedly pro-Moscow) party leaders. At a White Flag Central Committee meeting during the latter half of 1964, the so-called Peking clique decided to purge the party of "revisionists"; but the clique evidently did not feel strong enough to start with its opponents in the leadership group. Then, in early 1966, the Peking clique made its move; it launched a "life forum movement" to attract young recruits and (apparently in the summer of 1966 coincident with the Chinese Party's Eleventh Plenum) instituted its own cultural revolution.

By the early summer of 1967, just prior to the outbreak of trouble between Peking and Rangoon, the pro-Peking faction of White Flag Communists had made some headway in its renewed drive to coalesce and at the same time refurbish its ranks. Internally, the two key opponents of Than Tun, long-time politburo members Ba Tin (Goshal) and Yebaw Htay, were executed on June 18 near the Party's central camp in the Pegu region.[73] Their removal paved the way for a top-to-bottom purge of the Party organization that would later have serious effects on its cohesion.

[72] On developments in the Communist Party of Burma (White Flags) between 1963 and 1966, see J. H. Badgley, "The Communist Parties of Burma," in R. A. Scalapino, ed., *The Communist Revolution in Asia: Tactics, Goals, and Achievements* (Englewood Cliffs, N.J., 1965); the Rangoon newspapers *Guardian, Botataung,* and *Vanguard Daily* for May 1968; Rangoon domestic service broadcast of August 18, 1967 (reporting a news conference with a former party official who defected to the government).

[73] Rangoon domestic service broadcast of April 18, 1968. In view of the personalist nature of Burmese politics, and especially of the factionalism it has produced among the White Flag Communists, the purge should probably be regarded as an opportunity for Than Tun to settle old scores no less than as an effort to cleanse the party of "Soviet revisionism."

Meanwhile, the Maoist-like stress on revitalizing the Party with young blood continued, reportedly involving additional recruitment drives and the establishment of "red guard" groups in various parts of the country-side. Militarily, moreover, the White Flags became much more active, perhaps in response to the Burmese army's offensive. The White Flags launched a number of disturbingly large raids in the populous, rice-rich central delta; and they attracted the leftist faction of the Karen insur-gents, among others, into a National Democratic United Front as part of a temporarily successful campaign to gain the support of every major dissident movement in the delta.

These events took place, it must be emphasized, at a time when Peking-Rangoon relations were still outwardly, though by no means effusively, friendly. The Chinese had as yet made no move to depart from the policy of respect for Burmese neutralism as represented in the military govern-ment of Ne Win. Certain aspects of Burmese foreign policy, such as Ne Win's trip to the United States in September 1966, may not have pleased Peking, for they seemed to indicate a very gradual evolution toward more balance in Rangoon's external affairs and, thereby, a subtle departure from the sheltered neutralism Burma had been practicing virtually since inde-pendence.[74] But, as far as can be ascertained, Peking gave no hint of displeasure despite the reformation of the White Flags into a solidly pro-Peking party with seemingly new military potential.

Subsequent Chinese estrangement from the Burmese government and

[74] Badgley has traced Burma's turn away from isolationism in foreign policy back to December 1965, when Senator Mike Mansfield, the first ranking American to visit Rangoon since the 1962 coup, carried to Ne Win the suggestion of a trip to the United States. Among the other signs of new policy flexibility were Ne Win's visits to Pakistan and India (1966); the conclusion of a boundary treaty with India (March 10, 1967) that "went beyond the territory that China claimed as its own, where the three boundaries meet"; demarcation of the Burma-East Pakistan border (May 1967) at a time when Peking was rumored to be providing low-level support to disaffected elements of the Nagas; the dispatch of Burmese trade missions to Malaysia, Singapore, and Thailand (June 1967); and the considerably larger num-ber of students sent to the Soviet Union and Eastern Europe than to China. (Badgley, "Burma's China Crisis: The Choices Ahead," *Asian Survey*, Vol. 7, No. 11 [November 1967] pp. 755–756.) To this list should be added the fact that Liu Shao-ch'i's visit to Burma in April 1966 was the only one by a ranking Chinese Communist official between August 1965 and the incidents of mid-1967. (Ne Win's last trip to Peking occurred during July and August 1965.) Liu's trip, incidentally, which also included Pakistan and Afghanistan, was hailed at the time as a major diplomatic triumph. See the editorial in *Jen-min jih-pao*, April 21, 1966, p. 1.

its encouragement of the White Flags to overthrow the Ne Win regime may therefore best be explained by examining the circumstances and timing. The departure of the Chinese ambassador and most of his staff from Rangoon in March 1967, followed by the return of a chargé d'affaires and (reportedly) several Red Guards, inaugurated a series of events that were to be repeated with little variation in other countries: the transformation of the Chinese embassy and the New China News Agency into centers for the propagation of Mao's thoughts; the distribution or attempted distribution of Mao badges and other symbols of the Cultural Revolution's personality cult; and the ensuing clash with local government authorities over Chinese insistence on the justifiability of distributing Maoist literature and badges without interference. When some Chinese students, encouraged by local Chinese embassy officials, defied the Burmese government's order banning the wearing of Mao badges in class, the first of many anti-Chinese riots occurred on June 22. In succeeding days, the riots became more intense and led to violence against Chinese residents, the closing of Chinese schools, and invasion of the Chinese embassy, the Rangoon offices of the New China News Agency, and other official buildings.[75] On June 28, the Chinese Ministry of Foreign Affairs presented the first government protest demanding an end to anti-Chinese activities, compensation for damages to life and property, and punishment of the offenders. The Burmese government was charged with having "instigated" and "connived" in the incidents, and was warned that it "must bear full responsibility for all the serious consequences arising therefrom."[76]

Refusing to be intimidated by this thinly veiled threat, Burma sought only to contain rather than prevent violence against local and official Chinese. Anti-China demonstrations spread to other major towns and villages, but most importantly, on June 28, a member of the Chinese aid team was slain in Rangoon. The Chinese government thereupon issued a second, more formal protest on June 29 against this and preceding

[75] For a fuller account of events in Rangoon at this time, see F. N. Trager, "Sino-Burmese Relations: The End of the Pauk Phaw Era," *Orbis,* Vol. 11, No. 4 (Winter 1968) pp. 1040–1049.

[76] *NCNA* (Peking), June 28, 1967, in *SCMP* 3971, June 30, 1967, pp. 28–29. The protest was handed to Burmese Ambassador Sinwa Nawng at the Ministry of Foreign Affairs by Deputy Foreign Minister Han Nien-lung. On the same day, the CPR chargé in Rangoon, Hsiao Ming, also made an official protest that included similar demands. *SCMP* 3972, July 1, 1967, pp. 37–38.

incidents, again with a warning of unspecified consequences should the Burmese persist in their course of action.[77] This time Burma replied in a memorandum of the same date delivered by a member of the Foreign Office to the Chinese chargé. Ignoring the bulk of China's demands, Burma informed the Chinese government that it deemed the anti-Burma demonstrations then taking place in Peking an "unfortunate development" that "will adversely affect the sincere efforts of the Burmese government to restore a normal situation in Burma and to maintain and preserve the friendly relations between the two countries." The Chinese government was asked to step in to stop the demonstrations. Peking rejected the memorandum.[78]

What is of special significance for our analysis is that during this first week of escalating verbal exchange, Peking held back from exploiting events in Rangoon by denouncing the Burmese government and throwing its support to the White Flag Communists. Evidently, Mao Tse-tung and his chief lieutenants, though perhaps taken aback by the forcefulness of Ne Win's response to the Chinese embassy's actions, decided or were persuaded not to move too hastily toward a break with Rangoon. The Chinese government statement of June 29 may have been the most crucial test of the Burmese government's intentions. Only when the Burmese government's reply evidenced no willingness to meet Chinese demands—and this at a time when a Chinese technician had been killed and the controlled Rangoon press was publishing unprecedently critical anti-China articles—might Mao have decided to push the confrontation further.

On June 30, a *Jen-min jih-pao* editorial revealed a qualitative change in China's position. The Burmese government was attacked as "reactionary," "fascist," and "counterrevolutionary"; and, for the first time,[79] Peking cited the White Flag Communists' important revolutionary role:

Wherever there is oppression, there is resistance, and the more ruthless the oppression, the stronger the resistance. In the last five years and more,

[77] *NCNA* (Peking) international service broadcast of June 29, 1967; *Peking Review*, No. 28 (July 7, 1967) p. 17.

[78] Excerpts from the memorandum and a report of China's reply were broadcast by *NCNA* (Peking) on July 1, 1967.

[79] By contrast, when *NCNA* announced on June 23 that the CPB Central Committe had sent the CCP Central Committee a message of congratulations on the explosion of China's first hydrogen bomb (June 18), the message made no allusion to events in Burma and no derogatory remarks about the Burmese government.

the contradictions between the broad masses of the Burmese people and the Burmese ruling clique have grown increasingly acute. Strikes of workers and students have taken place one after another. After overcoming numerous difficulties, the revolutionary armed struggle led by the Burmese Communist Party is now developing successfully. In the last year in particular, the people's revolutionary armed forces have grown much stronger; they have expanded and consolidated their base areas and strengthened their ties with the broad masses. Burma's national-democratic revolution has taken a new and important step forward.[80]

Further illuminating the fact of a delayed shift in Peking is that the Chinese waited until July 1 before broadcasting (and thus giving support to) a sharp, uncompromising attack on the Burmese government by the White Flags. In this statement, the National Democratic United Front was mentioned for the first time, and the claim was made that "the nationalities of Burma are becoming more and more friendly and united under the leadership of the Burmese Communist Party." [81] From that point on, Sino-Burmese relations were, to all intents, suspended.[82]

Taken together with developments on the China mainland, it appears that Peking's break with Rangoon over anti-Chinese incidents in the latter city was shaped by the actions of Chinese and Burmese officials on the spot. While it might be argued that Peking was simply looking for the appropriate pretext to denounce the Burmese government and align itself publicly with the revitalized White Flags, the weight of the evidence favors a more complex interpretation. The White Flag Communists had indeed purged their ranks of "anti-Peking" elements and claimed to have developed a united front against the Burmese government; yet Peking still chose to remain aloof from the White Flag Communists until June 30, eight days after the riots had begun. The phasing and timing of Peking's responses suggest that the Maoist leadership finally supported the White Flag Communists not because of any new finding of strength in the Burmese Communist movement, but because the situation in Burma had developed to the point where Peking had to choose between backing down (by retracting or shelving its demands) or supporting its officials

[80] As broadcast by NCNA (Peking), June 30, 1967.
[81] Statement of the Communist Party of Burma Central Committee of June 28, broadcast by NCNA (Peking), July 1, 1967.
[82] In the Chinese government statement of June 29, Peking announced it had decided not to send its ambassador back to Rangoon. The Burmese ambassador to Peking was not withdrawn until September. However, the embassies of both countries continued to function throughout the crisis.

and overseas Chinese under attack. And Peking's choice seems in turn to have been compelled by the actions of those ultra-leftists in the Chinese embassy and other agencies who considered themselves duty-bound not merely to fulfill the static function of representing Chinese interests abroad, but also to be active publicists of the thoughts and works of Mao Tse-tung. These zealots, when challenged in this latter role by the Burmese government, responded as had their compeers in Peking—by taking up the challenge and rejecting either retreat or compromise—and thus set in motion a chain reaction of increasingly intransigent statements and actions in Rangoon and Peking. It should also not be omitted that Peking's choice of the second alternative was all the more ensured by the extremist tide which, by late June, had once more engulfed the Cultural Revolution.[83] Conceivably, the return of extremism further influenced Mao and the more radical members of the Central Committee not to let the crisis subside without backing China's warnings of "consequences" with deeds.

At roughly the same time that extremist influence was beginning to be felt in the official Chinese missions to Burma, the Cambodian government was experiencing similar problems. Despite his public support of a number of key Chinese foreign policies, Prince Sihanouk could not contain his private distaste for the Cultural Revolution. As early as March 1967, the Prince criticized it as "an erroneous policy" which, with its Red Guards, "has won contempt and not admiration" for mainland China.[84] The contrast between statements of respect and admiration for China, for international consumption, and unofficial critical evaluation of Chinese policies, for domestic consumption, was characteristic of Sihanouk's style in conducting his neutralist foreign policy. But to judge from the

[83] In general, factionalism within the Red Guard movement and often violent confrontations between leftist groups claiming Mao's support were the dominant themes of the Cultural Revolution throughout the summer of 1967. This situation was spotlighted when two members of the Cultural Revolution Group (Hsieh Fu-chih and Wang Li), dispatched to Wuhan late in July to resolve a dispute between two such groups, so outraged local military commanders by their decision that they were seized and held as political hostages. The Wuhan Incident was apparently precisely the kind of ammunition the more radical members of the Cultural Revolution Group needed to buttress their contention that only armed action and violence could root out Party and military leaders opposed to Mao. See Bridgham, "Mao's Cultural Revolution in 1967: The Struggle to Seize Power," op. cit., pp. 24–25.

[84] Comments before a special congress of the National Assembly on March 12, 1967; Phnom Penh domestic service broadcast, same date.

response of Chinese officials in Cambodia, Sihanouk's comments and subsequent actions touched a raw nerve.

Trouble between Cambodians and local Chinese came into the open during May. Sihanouk had become very disturbed over the dangerous situation that had arisen in a few provinces where rebels (called "Khmer Viet Minh" or "Khmer reds") were engaging in armed violence, assertedly under orders from radical left politicians in Phnom Penh. After forming a new cabinet on May 2, the Prince spoke out against Communist subversion of schools, universities, and Chinese-run newspapers. Articles in the Khmer press joined in, calling attention to the dangers posed by Chinese manipulation of the economy through black market operations and by the continued teaching of Maoist ideology in Chinese schools. Adding to the drama, two Cambodian newspapers persisted in writing unfavorable accounts of developments in China despite demands from the Chinese embassy to cease.[85] Other newspapers went further, implying that China was directly involved in subversion in Cambodia. This speculation, which Sihanouk publicly refused to engage in, was based on the well-known fact that the Chinese embassy was a strong financial backer of the Khmer-Chinese Friendship Association, the local Chinese schools, and the Chinese newspapers.

This entangled situation of small-scale insurgency, political conflict, and Chinese embassy interference in local affairs had several adverse consequences for the (assertedly) pro-Chinese leftists in Cambodia. The government cracked down on the Chinese school system and imposed controls over their curricula. Black-marketing among local Chinese was dealt with much more firmly than in the past, and at least two Chinese were deported to the mainland. Lastly, a combination of carrot-and-stick measures in the rebellious provinces was apparently successful, for on June 17 the government announced the end of the Communist uprising.

Peking may have taken a jaundiced view of these and other developments in Cambodia. Resistance to the Chinese embassy's efforts to propagandize the Cultural Revolution, and the Cambodian government's suppression of pro-left dissidence, were given prominent attention in issues

[85] On May 30, Phnom Penh radio broadcast a Chinese embassy open letter that had appeared in the leftist newspaper *La Nouvelle Dépêche*. The letter claimed "the right of every Chinese" to venerate Mao, refuted charges that embassy-sponsored publications about developments on the mainland were subversive, and said that "the real enemy and the real subverters" in Cambodia were "a handful of Chiang Kai-shek partisans" working on behalf of U.S. imperialism.

of the *Ts'an-k'ao hsiao-hsi* (*Reference News*), the special newsletter
circulated among Chinese Party and other officials. Also spotlighted was
Sihanouk's laudatory message of thanks to Soviet Foreign Minister Gro-
myko for Russia's having become the first Communist nation to recognize and respect Cambodia's existing borders.[86] That decision must have
embarrassed and annoyed Peking (as well as Hanoi), for it compelled
the Chinese to do likewise. Yet Sihanouk received only one sign of possible Chinese disturbance over his actions; when he sent a congratulatory
message to Peking following China's first explosion of a hydrogen device,
he did not receive the customary reply. Not until August, however, when
Cambodia's foreign minister, Prince Norodom Phurissara, visited Peking,
did the two governments directly deal with the question of China's official attitude toward propagating the Cultural Revolution in Phnom
Penh.

Although China's relations with Burma and Cambodia were the most
dramatic, Chinese officials elsewhere who were seeking to demonstrate
their commitment to the Cultural Revolution ran into the same kinds of
obstacles as in Rangoon and Phnom Penh. In Kenya, the Chinese chargé
d'affaires was ousted after the embassy had tried to disseminate Mao
books and badges.[87] In Nepal, restrictions by the government against
the wearing of badges and the sale of Mao's "Quotations" during early
July were accompanied by raids on the Nepal-China Friendship Association. The Chinese charged collusion between Nepal, India, and the
United States,[88] and by early August a number of embassy personnel
had been withdrawn. Finally, difficulties with Ceylon began when customs authorities in Colombo intercepted a package of previously banned
Mao badges, allegedly by boarding a Chinese vessel. In its note of protest
on August 15, the Chinese embassy charged that this act was "a continuation and development of the Ceylon government's repeated connivance in anti-China activities over more than two years."[89]

Incidents such as these, which also occurred in Sweden, Switzerland,
and Algeria, were clearly distinct from, and yet can only be fully ap-

[86] Further detail on the contents of the *Ts'an-k'ao hsiao-hsi* during this period is
available in *The Washington Post*, August 28, 1967, article by Stanley Karnow.
[87] *Peking Review*, No. 28 (July 7, 1967) pp. 37–38.
[88] *NCNA* (Peking) broadcasts of July 8, 9, and 22, 1967.
[89] *NCNA* (Peking) broadcast of August 19, 1967. Later, Peking protested when
Ceylon invited Taiwan's participation in the Asian Trainers Conference for female
guides and in the Third Asian Boxing Championships, both held in Colombo.
NCNA (Peking) broadcast of August 23, 1967.

preciated against the background of the chaos then sweeping the main-land—a chaos which, during August, culminated in the temporary triumph of the ultra-left in the Ministry of Foreign Affairs.

The signal given the revolutionary left by leading figures in the Cultural Revolution Group to redouble their efforts to "seize power" was undoubtedly welcomed by the opponents of Ch'en Yi. For the first time, so far as is known, two men previously identified as possible leaders of the anti-Ch'en forces—Wang Li and Yao Teng-shan—made their open bid for power. Replacing the slogan "Overthrow Liu [Shao-ch'i], Teng [Hsiao-p'ing], and T'ao [Chu, the purged head of the CCP Propaganda Department]" with "Overthrow Liu, Teng, and Ch'en," Wang Li apparently used his position in the Cultural Revolution Group to advantage, with Yao serving as his advance man.[90] According to accusations leveled against Wang much later, he became actively involved in the "Overthrow Ch'en" movement after returning to Peking as one of the heroes of the Wuhan Incident:

Following his return from Wuhan, he became so power-hungry as to consider that "the time is ripe" and that "only those who have power have prestige." Therefore, he spread the rumor that "Chairman Mao and the Premier want me to have a say in the Foreign Ministry." He laid his black hand on the Foreign Ministry and through the ambitious man Yao [Teng-shan], he made public his notorious "August 7 speech" in a vain attempt to break and split the proletarian headquarters headed by Chairman Mao from the extreme left, so as to seize power from it.[91]

What was described as an "upheaval" in the Ministry of Foreign Affairs began with this "August 7 speech" by Wang Li, which seems to have incited a final surge of the ultra-left to wrest power from ranking members of the ministry. For fourteen days, it is said, Yao Teng-shan functioned as Foreign Minister. Before his brief reign ended, apparently coincident with the sacking of the British chancery in Peking (see below), he had "wrested power from the Foreign Ministry's Party center" and

[90] *I-yüeh feng-pao,* May 1968, cited in *Chinese Communist Affairs: Facts and Features, op. cit.,* p. 23.
[91] *Yeh-chan-pao (Field Combat)* March 1968, in *ibid.,* Vol. 1, No. 17 (June 12, 1968) p. 23. According to the editors of *Chinese Communist Affairs,* the August 7 speech contained an attack by Wang on the military commanders of the Nanking and Foochow military regions, linking them to the alleged anti-Party elements Ho Lung and Hsu Hsiang-ch'ien. See *ibid.,* Vol. 1, No. 3 (November 29, 1967) p. 24.

had "sent cables to the [Chinese] embassies in foreign countries without the permission of Chairman Mao and Premier Chou." [92]

Chou seems to have gone to considerable lengths to prevent this power seizure from turning into a complete disruption of China's foreign relations. Having been appointed the principal overseer of the ministry in April, Chou was evidently faced with a challenge to his own as well as to Ch'en Yi's authority when Yao Teng-shan made his move. Such, at least, was the situation Chou described to two "revolutionary committees" which visited him in early September asking advice on how they might set themselves up. Chou cited the circumstances in the Foreign Ministry during the previous month as a good example of how not to go about revolutionizing government offices. He said the ministry had undergone a "seizure of power" in August, but that rebels in the ministry had come into conflict with the Central Committee when they went "beyond supervision" to actually making decisions. Chou is quoted by a Red Guard newspaper as follows:

I supported the Foreign Ministry in the Central Committee [in August]. When the Foreign Ministry went to the brink, I held a meeting. . . . I was directly responsible for running the Foreign Ministry and as a result they seized power from me. They sent telegrams directly to foreign embassies. As a result they were sent back. Yao Teng-shan went everywhere making reports and creating trouble. He went to the Ministry of Foreign Trade once. His report to the Ministry of Foreign Trade was incorrect, and was very provocative. I criticized him on the spot. The Central Committee put forward the slogan of "Down with Liu, Teng, T'ao." He put forward the slogan "Down with Liu, Teng, Ch'en." How can you as a cadre at the head-of-department level [Yao may have become deputy head of the General Service Department of the Foreign Ministry upon his return from Indonesia] put forward such a slogan? Who gave you permission? As for sending telegrams to embassies, no one understood this. You [rebels] always want to do everything in such an absolute fashion.[93]

Chou's testimony may offer additional support for the hypothesis advanced earlier that the promotion of the Cultural Revolution abroad was probably the handiwork of certain ideological fanatics in Chinese embassies. If Yao Teng-shan indeed "seized power"—or, perhaps more

[92] *Hung-wei-pao*, October 18, 1967.
[93] *Hung-wei-pao*, September 15, 1967.

accurately, wreaked havoc while the Central Committee was too pre-occupied with other matters to intervene—it was well after trouble had begun in Rangoon, Colombo, Phnom Penh, and Katmandu. His short-lived tenure as Foreign Minister may have given added encouragement to ultra-leftists overseas; but whether his telegrams and other hijinks caused real damage is debatable.

At the same time as the ultra-leftists were apparently running rough-shod over the Foreign Ministry, they kept up their personal barrage against the Foreign Minister by persisting in their demands that Ch'en Yi make a second formal self-criticism. A Japanese correspondent reported that on August 6 members of one rebel faction received assurances from Hsieh Fu-chih and Chou that "struggle rallies" could and would be held on August 7 and 11.[94] The rally of August 7 may not have been held, but it is known that on August 11 about ten thousand "rebels" gathered at the Great Hall of the People in Peking to criticize the Foreign Minister. Chou En-lai, who was at the meeting, is said to have told the assemblage that he supported medium-sized and small rallies against Ch'en and would attend others if held. As for Ch'en, he was apparently subjected to another humiliating barrage of charges revolving about his support of the Liu-Teng line; he is also alleged to have made a self-criticism, although details were not made public.[95]

Extremist attacks on Ch'en Yi were again made at a second mass rally on August 27. Dubbed the "Thoroughly Criticize Ch'en Yi Rally," assertedly by Premier Chou, it was conducted by Ch'en Po-ta and Vice-Premier Li Fu-ch'un. According to a wall poster that described the event, the Red Guards greatly appreciated the leadership's interest in and encouragement of "exposing and criticizing" Ch'en's policies.[96] Yet the

[94] *Tokyo Shimbun,* August 7, 1967. Other reports from correspondents in Peking at this time, however, noted on the basis of wall posters that in fact Ch'en Yi had been favorably passed on by the Central Committee and, in essence, accepted as one of the Party's hierarchy.

[95] *Yomiuri Shimbun,* Tokyo, August 14, 1967. In a speech of March 6, 1968, Ch'en mentioned that between August and September 1967, seven different criticism meetings of varying size were held, and that at the larger ones certain people (presumably including Yao Teng-shan) sought to "make me a springboard for their personal aims." *I-yüeh feng-pao, op. cit.,* p. 2.

[96] Specifically, the rally took issue with Ch'en's alleged sympathy with Liu Shao-ch'i's supposed foreign policy line of *san-hsiang i-mieh* (three surrenders, one extinction): surrendering to U.S. imperialism, Soviet modern revisionism and reactionaries; and extinguishing the flames of revolutionary warfare throughout the world. Ch'en is said to have made various "capitulationist" statements over the years —for example, saying in 1963 that the United States might withdraw from Vietnam,

same source also revealed that the leadership was still willing to countenance criticism of Ch'en Yi only up to a point. Li Fu-ch'un was quoted as having complimented the rebels on their criticism. "But," he cautioned, "as for the slogan shouted by some of you, 'Down with Ch'en Yi,' I still cannot accept it." [97] Evidently, in August no less than previously, leading members of the Central Committee, whom we may assume had been following Mao's instructions, were staunchly opposed to terminating Ch'en's career. Yet they appeared equally reluctant to put an end to the confrontation. Until the tail end of August, while the Central Committee was either divided over or simply unwilling to stop the extremists from occupying the Foreign Ministry, Ch'en Yi functioned as virtually a lame duck minister. Although he continued to attend and host official functions, he had clearly lost what limited influence he may have had over foreign relations in the preceding few months.

The deterioration of Sino-Cambodian relations at this juncture best illustrates the erosion of relatively moderate influence over the conduct of foreign affairs. On August 15, Prince Phurissara arrived in Peking and subsequently met with Ch'en and Chou. According to Sihanouk, "Chou En-lai requested . . . Phurissara to ask me to accord the Chinese residents in Cambodia the right to love Chairman Mao Tse-tung, to love Chinese Communism, the Chinese People's Republic." This request "surprised" Sihanouk, for it ran contrary to Chou's previous attitude and amounted to "authoriz[ing] our Chinese friends to commit subversion among the Khmers." Sihanouk responded very negatively to Chou's inquiry,[98] but Phurissara, before departing, apparently received new assurances from Chou and Ch'en of China's continued adherence to the principle of noninterference in Cambodian affairs.

On September 1, however, support of subversive activities by the Chinese embassy had so increased that Sihanouk felt compelled to abolish all friendship associations, the aim being to dissolve the troublesome Khmer-Chinese Friendship Association. He also ordered the dissolution of all press associations and warned journalists against serving "foreign

---

but adding in 1964 that in any case the United States would not arbitrarily expand the war to China—but the "evidence" cited reveals not "capitulationism" but a rather level-headed perception of the United States. Of course, Ch'en, like Liu Shao-ch'i and others attacked during the Cultural Revolution, had to suffer through the typical distortions that accompany purges and attempted purges.

[97] *Pei-wai hung-ch'i* (*Foreign Language Institute Red Flag*), Peking, undated.

[98] Speech of September 12, 1967, in *Les Paroles de Samdech Preah Norodom Sihanouk, 1967,* Ministry of Information, Phnom Penh, 1968, p. 695.

ideologies." At a moment of great excitation over the Cultural Revolution, Sihanouk's moves may have been interpreted in Peking as flagrant abuses of China's friendship. On September 4, the Peking branch of the association cabled the defunct association to struggle against "the reactionaries." Sihanouk considered the cable "an extraordinary interference in the internal affairs of a sovereign state" and, on September 13, announced that all Cambodian embassy personnel in Peking would be returning home. Sihanouk was only persuaded to keep his embassy personnel in Peking by the personal intervention of Chou, who had earned the Prince's friendship and respect as the result of several official visits exchanged over the years.[99] Chou may have been able to prevail upon Mao and the Central Committee by arguing that the benefits of Cambodia's friendship (including Phnom Penh's anti-American posture over Vietnam) outweighed any advantages Peking might derive from pressing ahead with the confrontation.

Yet, in dealing with Mao, Chou's persuasive powers may not have been as decisive as the practical consideration that extremist influence in the Foreign Ministry and in the foreign service was doing irreparable harm to China's image abroad. This perception may in turn have stemmed not so much from any one instance of adverse reaction abroad to the overflow of the Cultural Revolution as from the more visible effects of the outrage perpetrated by fanatical Red Guards on the British mission in Peking. The mission, it will be recalled, had first been besieged (by non-Chinese zealots) on June 9; but on August 22, Red Guards set fire to the U.K. mission and completely gutted it. The British chargé d'affaires and several of his staff were reportedly beaten when they rushed out of the building. An unidentified escapee from the mainland subsequently related in Hong Kong that these acts were conceived by Yao Teng-shan, not the Peking leadership, and were responsible for his being labeled soon after as a man of mad personal ambitions.[100] An equally plausible explanation is that the regime, having warned Great Britain (as it had warned Burma) of "serious consequences" in the event of its failure to comply with the terms of an August 20 ultimatum on the Hong Kong situation,[101] used the Red Guards to carry out the threat,

[99] For documentation and Sihanouk's interpretation of these events, see *ibid.*, pp. 649–656, 675–680, 694–696, 707, 711–715, and 754–755. See also, R. M. Smith, "Cambodia: Between Scylla and Charybdis," *Asian Survey*, Vol. 3, No. 1 (January 1968) pp. 75–76.

[100] *Hsing-tao jih-pao*, Hong Kong, October 23, 1967, p. 1.

[101] The Chinese ultimatum demanded that the United Kingdom cancel a ban on

only to have them go beyond reasonable bounds by gutting the chancery. In either case, the primary point is that unleashed fanaticism had placed the CPR in an extremely uncomfortable position, one that Mao may finally have become convinced was intolerable.

THE RETURN OF MODERATION

The sacking of the British chancery was only the most blatant sign of the total disorder that the Peking leadership's toleration of extremist behavior had facilitated. The violence of the Red Guards on August 22, 1967, apparently had many parallels in the Chinese provinces as factionalism and conflict became more rampant in the competition to "seize power" and demonstrate loyalty to the thoughts of Mao. Whether the regime recognized that extremist tactics were faulty or simply decided to inaugurate a new revolutionary stage now that violence had served its purpose, the leadership demanded consolidation of the left and condemned any resort to armed struggle.

The first indication of the new line came soon after the events of August 22. Chou En-lai is reported to have issued instructions restricting Red Guard activities around the foreign missions in Peking. The rebels were specifically enjoined from "beating, smashing, burning, invading, and obstructing" in their demonstrations.[102] Then, on September 1, an important resolution was published by the Peking Municipal Party committee which emphasized that "politics" (criticism, self-criticism, and rectification) rather than armed struggle should be the chief means of attacking "capitalist-roaders." While praising the contributions of the "proletarian revolutionaries" and the army, the Peking Party committee ordered a cessation of "struggles by force" and demanded that "the great criticism and repudiation [be carried out] in a planned and organized manner." Red Guards were forbidden to roam about the countryside; instead, they were to keep to their original units and to reach agreement with other revolutionary groups to support the army.[103]

---

three local pro-Communist newspapers and gave the Hong Kong authorities forty-eight hours to drop lawsuits against arrested newspapermen.

[102] *Asahi Evening News,* Tokyo, September 5, 1967.

[103] The resolution also condemned the May 16 Group, one of the leading extremist groups, as "counterrevolutionary," perhaps a warning to other ultra-left organizations that the regime's support could be withdrawn as easily as it had been tendered. *NCNA* (Peking) broadcast of September 10, 1967.

The Peking committee's resolution presaged a directive with nationwide applicability on September 5 in the form of a speech by Chiang Ch'ing. Although Chiang Ch'ing had evidently been one of the chief supporters of the "seize power" movement, in this speech she came out four-square against armed struggle and factionalism, and sharply criticized Red Guard attacks on the Army to acquire guns. She pointed out that military goods slated for Vietnam had been seized, and she declared that attacks on foreign embassies must cease.[104] Her criticism of Red Guard seizures of arms was given official sanction the same day when a combined order of the Central Committee, the State Council, the Military Affairs Committee, and the Cultural Revolution Group expressly forbade the "seizure of arms, equipment, and other military supplies from the People's Liberation Army" and gave the People's Liberation Army the right to return fire if attacked.[105]

The effect of these developments on the Ministry of Foreign Affairs was threefold: they led to the removal of Ch'en Yi's key opponents; they brought about renewed expressions of confidence in and support of Ch'en Yi by the leadership; they precluded further attempts by embassies abroad to "make revolution" and thus signaled the start of a slow return of normalcy in China's foreign relations.

Yao Teng-shan was not heard from again after the August 22 Red Guard assault on the British chancery. Wang Li's career also went downhill thereafter, culminating in his purge sometime between August and November 1967. Both men were almost certainly removed from authoritative positions by September.

Coincidentally, Ch'en received indirect and direct support from the Cultural Revolution Group. In a speech on September 1, K'ang Sheng reportedly told an expanded meeting of the Peking Revolutionary Committee that it was important to separate the issue of Ch'en's alleged errors from the government's foreign policy line. K'ang held that the "three surrenders, one extinction" charge was mistaken, since it was the Central Committee that set foreign policy guidelines. The Foreign Ministry, he was saying, could hardly be attacked for selling out the country when the Central Committee had all along been responsible for policies that were *ipso nature* correct. K'ang specifically forbade seizing power in foreign affairs and the Foreign Ministry; but his statement might be further interpreted as indirectly refuting charges that the foreign policy line of Liu

---

[104] SCMP 4069, November 29, 1967, pp. 1–9.
[105] SCMP 4026, September 22, 1967, pp. 1–2.

Shao-ch'i was "revisionist" as well as absolving Ch'en Yi of responsibility for "erroneous" foreign policies of the past.[106]

K'ang Sheng's defense of the Foreign Ministry did not keep two of the more fanatic Red Guard newspapers from teaming up in September to sustain their verbal assault on the Foreign Minister, this time charging that Ch'en Yi had stood by over the years while the Ne Win government was systematically restricting the power and privileges of the local Chinese in Burma.[107] Again, however, it appears that the Peking leadership was prepared to intervene, perhaps more forcefully than before, in Ch'en's defense. According to a Nationalist Chinese source, in late October Mao instructed that Ch'en receive full support and that the elimination of Yao and Wang (presumably meaning their influence and followers) be treated as a priority matter.[108]

The extremists had, however, managed to take a heavy toll on the then 67-year-old Ch'en Yi's health before being quelled[109] and it was apparently for this reason that, following the banquet given for Prince Phurissara on August 18, Ch'en did not participate in an official function for a month and a half. The Foreign Minister's next appearance was at the National Day celebration on October 1. His first reported official act after the August turmoil was not until November 8, when he attended the signing of the 1968 Sino-Ceylonese Trade and Payments Agreement and Barter Protocol.

[106] K'ang did not exclude the possibility of criticizing Ch'en ("If Ch'en Yi has [committed] errors, he can make a self-examination"); but the tone of his statement suggests that he was defending the Foreign Minister no less than the ministry from a repetition of the events that had led to the disruption in August. *Hung-wei-pao*, September 15, 1967.

[107] *Wai-shih hung-ch'i* and *Ke-ming ch'iao-pao*, September 12, 1967 (joint issue).

[108] *Chinese Communist Affairs: Facts and Features*, Vol. 1, No. 3 (November 29, 1967) pp. 24–25. In the instruction, Mao assertedly declared: "All foreign affairs units should be merged into the Ministry of Foreign Affairs, the minister of which is Ch'en Yi. If Ch'en is not the minister, who is the minister?" Insisting that "foreign policy is formulated by me and implemented by Premier Chou," Mao directly attacked Wang Li, Kuan Feng (another former member of the Cultural Revolution Group), and Yao Teng-shan for having gone beyond acceptable bounds in their opposition to Ch'en. "Now whether the Ministry of Foreign Affairs can strike down Wang Li and Yao Teng-shan or not is a question of revolution or no revolution." Mao also said: "Wang Li was a bad fellow from the beginning. Chiang Ch'ing long ago talked to me about the problem of Wang Li and Kuan Feng."

[109] A Red Guard newspaper of November 26 quotes Mao as having said of his Foreign Minister: "How can Ch'en be struck down? He has been with us 40 years and has so many achievements. He has lost 27 pounds in weight. I cannot show him to foreign guests in this condition."

Meanwhile, almost every Chinese embassy was still without an ambassador as 1967 ended. Whereas forty of forty-six Chinese ambassadors were present at their embassy's traditional National Day reception in 1966, only one (Huang Hua, ambassador to the U.A.R.) hosted the festivities on October 1, 1967.[110] The chief difference in the Chinese foreign service before and after the several months of Cultural Revolution in the Foreign Ministry seems to have been that, after August, the embassies were not free to carry the Revolution over into foreign capitals. But reeducation of erring ambassadors probably continued well after August 1967.

The locale of National Day receptions given by Chinese missions on October 1, 1967, provided the first clue to Peking's interest in restoring harmony in its relations with certain countries that had been directly affected by the chaos of the Cultural Revolution. Peking had gone too far to suddenly reverse course in its relations with Burma; and its differences with New Delhi, Djakarta, and the British in Hong Kong, transcending questions of interference by the Chinese missions, persisted into 1968. But the receptions held by Chinese officials in Nepal, Ceylon, and Cambodia did seem to signify a recognition on Mao's part that the hostility of these governments toward China needed to be ameliorated gradually, though without giving the appearance of a humiliating Chinese retreat. More concretely, in November 1967, the previously mentioned economic agreements were signed with Ceylon; during the first half of 1968, Nepalese dignitaries renewed their pilgrimages to Peking; and Chinese statements were published on several occasions offering sustained backing for Cambodia's struggle against "U.S. imperialism."

There were also indications during 1968 that Peking, despite the vociferous verbal support given local Communists in Hong Kong and the Communist Party of Burma, was equally capable of downgrading that support for the sake of larger Chinese interests, even at the expense of eventually embarrassing the very forces Peking had previously encouraged. In Hong Kong, by September 1967, Peking was clearly disengaging from local Communists by refraining from making statements that might imply a direct commitment to their struggle against the British authorities. Then, on July 30, 1968, Peking granted exit visas to several U.K. diplomatic personnel previously refused permission to return home. The action may have been tied to the release of some imprisoned Communist agitators in Hong Kong.

[110] Daniel Tretiak, "Disappearing Act," *Far Eastern Economic Review,* Vol. 50, No. 6 (February 8, 1968) p. 216.

Toward Burma, Peking continued its accusations that the Burmese government was denying overseas Chinese their legitimate rights. But over the months the tone of Chinese statements changed subtly, so that one year after the incidents of June and July 1967, the Ne Win government was no longer being condemned as violently as before. Moreover, there were several substantive signs of a change in Peking's attitude. These included a donation of 10,000 *yuan* by the Chinese Red Cross to the Burmese Red Cross to assist in the relief of hurricane victims (May 1968); participation of the Chinese chargé in the July 19 Martyrs' Day ceremony honoring Aung San, the hero of Burma's independence; and a reception held by the Chinese military attaché in Rangoon (and attended by Burmese officials) commemorating the founding of the Chinese army (August 1).[111] Finally, in a most unusual development, the New China News Agency reported that the Chinese embassy in Rangoon had held a National Day reception that was attended by unspecified Burmese officials—in contrast to receptions held in Peking attended only by members of the White Flag Communist hierarchy. Quite conceivably, Peking over time will move further toward the Burmese government and further away from the White Flag Communists, gradually returning to the pre-Cultural Revolution policy of avowing respect for Burmese neutralism without expressly disavowing the Burmese Communist movement. Judging from Ne Win's statements since the summer of 1967, this is also his expectation of the future direction of Peking's policy—and his refusal to move closer to the United States or the Soviet Union underscores his reliance on firmness and patience.

The drama of the oscillating fortunes of China's Foreign Ministry and its Foreign Minister during the Cultural Revolution was not completely played out with the onset of a period of consolidation in the fall of 1967. For reasons not entirely clear, Ch'en's supporters in the Ministry felt compelled to make a public defense of their chief in early 1968. Upon an unfavorable response to it by Chou En-lai, Ch'en Yi disavowed the defense and subsequently delivered a speech that came close to being, and was possibly intended as, a self-criticism. These final scenes apparently ended the play; in the process, Ch'en Yi had managed not only to preserve his position, but also to defend himself against many of the wild charges made in attacking him.

[111] *NCNA* (Peking) broadcast of May 30, 1968; *Yomiuri Shimbun,* October 26, 1968; *NCNA* (Peking) broadcast of August 5, 1968.

In an extraordinary move, on February 13, 1968, 91 people, heads of department in the Ministry and ambassadors, put their names to a wall poster[112] that lashed out at the ultra-leftists, defended the loyalty of the ministry's cadres, and sought to deflate the more serious accusations leveled against Ch'en Yi. Recounting how the extremists had tried to get rid of Ch'en Yi and his associates, the poster charged that the extremists had resorted to distortions, exaggerations, outright lies, and slanders. These occurred, it went on, because certain people thought that by feigning leftism they could conceal that they themselves were "class enemies." Despite the protection of Ch'en Yi by Mao, Chiang Ch'ing, Ch'en Po-ta, and Chou, the ultra-left had carried on the attack. Of course, the poster contended, all this was not to say that Ch'en Yi was without error; but Ch'en had been criticized excessively, others in the Ministry who committed mistakes had already been criticized for them, and facts had shown that "the majority of the personnel in our ministry are good and comparatively good comrades, that they basically want to make revolution and ardently love Chairman Mao." Yet considerable damage had been done as a result of the ultra-left's attacks, the authors maintained. The prestige of the "proletarian headquarters" and of Mao himself had been shaken and harmed; and the power of the ministry had been usurped.

A reasonable conclusion from the circumstance of the wall poster's appearance is that the ultra-left had not entirely desisted from assailing Ch'en Yi. That the heads of department and ambassadors waited until February 1968 to counterattack publicly would further suggest that only then did they feel sufficiently secure to air their grievances after a lengthy silence. Not until early 1968, perhaps, did they regard the discipline being imposed on the Cultural Revolution as a firm assurance against a renewal of extremist fervor—firm enough, that is, to risk publicly identifying with the Foreign Minister in the belief that he did in fact have the backing of the Cultural Revolution Group and the Central Committee.

Whatever the case, though, use of the wall poster turned out to be a tactical misjudgment. No sooner did it appear than Chou En-lai (as reported in a prefatory note by the editor of *January Storm*, which published the poster) directed: "This big-character poster is mistaken in principle; it

---

[112] Since the Ministry of Foreign Affairs then had fifteen heads of department (*szu-chang*), the vast majority of the signers were obviously ambassadors. The poster, entitled "Expose the Enemy, Fight and Overcome Him: In Criticism of the Reactionary Slogan, 'Criticize Ch'en Yi,'" was published in *I-yüeh feng-pao*, May 1968, p. 3.

is an interference from the right." Evidently, Chou (perhaps acting on instructions from Mao) considered the poster ill-timed. To make a public airing of the dispute over the Ministry might have been deemed purposeless and a potential incitement to renewed controversy, as Ch'en Yi himself was about to remark.

Later Red Guard material relates that Chou not only condemned the poster but also demanded that Ch'en disavow it, warning that "Comrade Ch'en Yi and the Party committee of the ministry should declare their attitude, or I'll have to declare mine." Placed with his back to the wall, Ch'en responded with a carefully worded letter to Chou on February 28. His letter reads in part:

I now solemnly declare that I completely support your directive. The 91-man big-character poster is rightist and conservative in its spirit and stand. It opposes the Great Proletarian Cultural Revolution and gives vent to grievances against the criticism and repudiation by the revolutionary masses. This big-character poster can do nothing whatever to help me correct my mistakes, but instead *may encourage antagonism between its authors and the masses* [emphasis supplied]. I absolutely do not agree with this erroneous spirit and stand.[113]

Ch'en went on to admit to having failed to "put politics in command." One major error was that he didn't reform his "capitalist-class world outlook"; but the criticism of cadres and the revolutionary masses in 1967 helped "destroy this harmful vermin of bourgeois world outlook." In revealing this and other "major mistakes," Ch'en drew a distinction between "the small number of bad men" who had shouted "Down with Ch'en Yi" to achieve "their personal ends" and the majority, who were genuinely concerned with correcting his errors. The wall poster of the ninety-one failed to make the distinction, Ch'en implied, for its signers "have not really been educated in the great cultural education" (sic).

Ch'en's repudiation of the wall poster and admission of guilt did not end with the letter. Either because of renewed pressure from the far left or because the Central Committee found it necessary on other grounds, a "Foreign Ministry United Preparatory Investigation Meeting" was held on March 6 at which the Foreign Minister again spoke about his past

[113] The letter, along with Chou's warning, is contained in *Chung-ta hung-ch'i* (*Chung-shan University Red Flag*), April 4, 1968, p. 2 (published by the Canton Congress of Red Representatives), and *Kuang-chou hung-ta-hui* (*Canton Red Congress*), April 3, 1968.

"crimes." In brief, Ch'en was reported to have said that he committed the error of protecting old cadres while blaming younger ones for being overly leftist, with the result that "bad" and "capitalist" persons were retained at their posts.[114] The words he uttered in repudiating his first confession in February 1967 were "crazy talk" designed to protect old cadres when in fact it was important that revolution be carried out to "save" both them and himself from further error. Thus, another mistake was to have opposed the notion of seizing power, to have feared chaos and upheaval. The poster of the ninety-one again came under attack, Ch'en Yi at one point calling it "unforgiveable." Yet, in looking back to the events of the previous year, Ch'en also condemned those people who were primarily interested in satisfying their personal ambitions rather than in correcting his errors.[115]

What is notable about Ch'en's letter to Chou and his follow-up speech to the "investigation meeting" is not so much the fact of his having confessed anew to previous errors as his having cleverly turned an adverse situation to some advantage. In the first place, he used what probably was intended as opportunities to placate the ultra-left into opportunities to denigrate the radicals while professing loyalty to the "mass line." Thus, although Ch'en repudiated the poster of the ninety-one and acknowledged his imperfections, his distinction between the helpful criticisms of the proletarian majority and the destructive personal assaults of the minority made apparent his revulsion for the tactics of the ultra-left.[116] He had indirectly underscored his belief that errors could hardly be corrected by extremists, who in any case represented a minority. Second, Ch'en consistently referred to errors committed in the past year only; he neither admitted to having been unfaithful to Mao before the Cultural Revolution (as some Red Guard groups had averred) nor considered himself in error at the time he was speaking. Moreover, those errors he did acknowledge were errors of class attitude, not the more serious errors of policy "line" and "direction." Finally, Ch'en could not avoid disavowing

---

[114] Ch'en went on to say, in a strange conclusion on this point, that because such persons remained at their posts, "an extremely serious question [arose] which became more and more serious, opposing fighting people's wars. [This was] an extreme rightist tendency; there was no precedent for it, and what history lacked, I opposed." Ch'en offered no other words of explanation.

[115] Text of the speech is in *I-yüeh feng-pao*, May 1968, *op. cit.*, p. 2.

[116] In his letter to Chou, Ch'en wrote: "The minority of bad people have already been exposed by the masses and moreover are continuing to be exposed; this is a good thing."

the wall poster put up in his defense; but in criticizing it and criticizing himself for having kept "capitalist" and "bad" cadres in office, Ch'en made no verbal commitment to rid the Foreign Ministry of his long-time supporters—and indeed, most of the criticized vice-ministers remained in the government.[117] What might have been intended as sops to the ultra-left, in summary, seem to have cut two ways, for if the extremists who demanded that Ch'en be criticized were appeased, Ch'en had also used considerable finesse in making a case in his own defense. The last act of the drama therefore closed much as it had begun: Ch'en Yi had apparently artfully exploited a tactical retreat to preserve his position and dignity while seeming to pacify his opponents.

AN ASSESSMENT

In this concluding assessment of the Cultural Revolution's impact on the Foreign Ministry and foreign affairs, the discussion will center on three areas: first, the motivations behind the ultra-leftist attacks on the ministry at the various stages of the Cultural Revolution; second, the reasons why Ch'en Yi was able to survive the struggle; third, the implications of the Cultural Revolution for Communist China's foreign relations and foreign policy.

Far from having been a contest between party and anti-party elements or competing substantive policy views, it seems fairly clear that the lines of battle formed around Ch'en Yi and the Ministry of Foreign Affairs because of the Foreign Minister's adamant refusal to permit the "revolutionary left" organizations to establish themselves in any of the agencies and bureaus concerned with the implementation of foreign policy. Ch'en evidently regarded the prospect of having youthful zealots serve as watchdogs within the foreign affairs system as a threat to his personal authority, to the positions of experienced foreign affairs personnel, and to the proper functioning of the bureaucracy.

In what was perhaps a tactical error, Ch'en revealed his position early by sending work teams to defend points under attack, thus aligning him-

---

[117] Of the ten vice-ministers, five were criticized, of whom one was purged (Chang Han-fu) and five were restored to their posts (Chi P'eng-fei, Liu Hsin-ch'üan, and Ch'iao Kuan-hua); the fate of Wang Ping-nan and Wu Hsiu-ch'üan is still unclear. Four vice-ministers do not appear to have been affected by the Cultural Revolution (Lo Kuei-po, Han Nien-lung, Hsü I-hsin, and Ch'en Chia-k'ang). The author is indebted to Donald Klein of Columbia University for information on the vice-ministers.

self with the ill-fated Liu Shao-ch'i and Teng Hsiao-p'ing. After the August plenum decision, Ch'en's position as an opponent of thoroughgoing revolution was exposed as Red Guards apparently received Mao's authorization to criticize Ch'en and cleanse the ministry of "counter-revolutionary" influence. The ensuing months of confrontation typified the overall character of the Cultural Revolution: the struggle between those bent on purging supposedly ultra-conservative institutions and those determined to resist encroachments on their bailiwicks.

The confrontation sparked by the work teams was only the first of what may be seen as three stages in the struggle between the ministry and the extremist factions. The second stage began in August 1966 (after the decision of the Central Committee plenum) and ended with Ch'en Yi's "confession" in January 1967. The third, commencing with renewed Red Guard violence in late March, did not end until early September, when the Peking leadership decided to "consolidate" the Revolution at the height of the nearly uncontrollable agitation. Significant in the timing of these stages is that they developed approximately in synchrony with the ebb and flow of the ultra-leftists' fortunes in the Cultural Revolution at large. When "power seizures" were in vogue across the mainland, the revolutionary left moved against the Foreign Ministry; but when the regime felt compelled to rein in the left, pressure on the ministry was dramatically reduced. The Foreign Minister, as in early February when he retracted his confession, was able to counterattack.

This oscillation of events helps clarify the nature of the struggle we have been describing. After the first two stages of the confrontation, the revolutionary left had been frustrated not only by the adamancy of Ch'en Yi, but equally by the leadership's evident determination to protect him from being overthrown and the bureaucracy from having to share administrative power. The manner in which the ultra-left began the third round—breaking into the ministry, upsetting files, disrupting work, and raising new charges of Ch'en's collusion with the "reactionary" line of Liu and Teng—betokened a certain desperation at having been obstructed front and rear. In particular, the flimsiness of the indictments of Ch'en's views—that he was instrumental in suppressing the revolutionary potential of the overseas Chinese, that he sympathized with and actively lobbied for Liu's supposed "three surrenders, one extinction," and that he had long been opposed to "the thoughts of Mao" [118]—suggests that the

[118] The most complete listing of Ch'en's "crimes" may be found in "One Hundred Examples of Speeches by Ch'en Yi Opposing Mao Tse-tung's Thought: Highest

ultra-left's chief bone of contention in the dispute with Ch'en had all along been his firm hostility to carrying the Cultural Revolution into foreign affairs circles. Only by the most arduous talmudology could those foreign-policy statements of Ch'en's cited by the Red Guard groups be considered blasphemous.

The Foreign Minister's defenders in the ministry and the foreign service were hence probably correct in their essential claim that the opposition to Ch'en consisted of a central core of fanatics who, through deception and distortion, whipped up a whirlwind into which a larger number of rebels without a cause were drawn.[119] Whether or not Yao Teng-shan and, behind him, Wang Li, were at the core of the ultra-left resurgence in the spring of 1967, the point remains that the struggle over the Foreign Ministry was consistently a tug-of-war between intransigent forces of the extreme left and equally intransigent forces of the center-left.

The frustration the Red Guards doubtless experienced in trying to oust Ch'en Yi and several of his vice-ministers was in large measure attributable to Chou En-lai. Throughout the ordeal, Chou appeared sympathetic to holding criticism meetings against Ch'en, but Chou carefully insulated his Foreign Minister and long-time comrade[120] from the more radical demands of the ultra-left. Undoubtedly with the support of Mao,[121] how-

---

Directive," *Tung-fang-hung chan-pao* (*East-Is-Red Combat Newspaper*), Peking, June 15, 1967, written by the Criticize Ch'en Liaison Station.

[119] From the letter of the ninety-one, in *I-yüeh feng-pao, op. cit.,* May 1968.

[120] The personal relationship of Chou and Ch'en dates back to the post-World War I period when both were students in France. Ch'en joined the Communist Youth League there which Chou helped establish. Little is known about their relations during the early years of the Chinese Communist Party, the Yenan period, or the war years. Since 1954, Ch'en has been a vice-premier under Chou; and he succeeded Chou as Foreign Minister in 1958. Ch'en has frequently accompanied Chou on official state visits and as part of Chinese government delegations to important conferences (for example, to Bandung in 1955).

[121] In view of the limited Party Central Committee representation at the highest levels of the Ministry of Foreign Affairs (Ch'en Yi is a full member, Chang Han-fu and Lo Kuei-po were alternate members), it is possible that Mao wished to keep Ch'en Yi at his post not only to maintain in office a long-time bureaucrat who commanded the loyalty of experienced subordinates, but also to assure that the Central Committee's views would continue to be adequately represented in the ministry. "Indeed," Donald Klein has pointed out, "Ch'en Yi may have been selected to succeed Chou En-lai [as Foreign Minister] (February 1958) in order to serve as the continuing voice of the Central Committee—and more particularly the Politburo— within the M.F.A." ("Peking's Evolving Ministry of Foreign Affairs," *The China Quarterly,* No. 4 [October–December 1960] p. 30.) That this consideration may have been equally valid in 1966 and 1967 is suggested by Ch'en's own remark on February

ever ambiguous and unemphatic it seemed at times, Chou spoke for the moderates in the Central Committee who found it necessary to appease the revolutionary left, but not at the expense of turning the Foreign Ministry upside down. This basic policy, which was also enunciated by Ch'en Po-ta and K'ang Sheng, seems to have been primarily responsible for having kept Ch'en Yi afloat.

The Central Committee's backing of criticism of Ch'en evidently did not satisfy the Red Guards but may have served the purposes intended by Mao. The extremists were clearly not content merely to criticize, and their inclination to defy authority brought about their own fall from grace. But their prolonged assaults on the position and person of Ch'en probably did succeed in eroding his authority and prestige,[122] and conceivably in damaging his emotional stability. In view of Ch'en's early opposition to the Cultural Revolution movement in foreign affairs, Mao's constant aim may have been to assure that his "conservative" Foreign Minister's influence would be held in check.

In a very real sense, foreign affairs was in a state of suspended animation once the Cultural Revolution began. The attention of the leadership focused so exclusively on instituting the new mass line and purging undesirables that it is difficult to imagine foreign policy, in either its decision-making or implementation phases, as having been of much concern to the Central Committee. Foreign relations seem to have been restricted primarily to the reception of visiting delegations in Peking; the "output" function—significant foreign policy statements, the dispatch of official delegations abroad, and the like—was virtually closed off. With the nearly complete recall of ambassadors between late 1966 and the spring of 1967, moreover, Chinese embassies continued to function, but, it may be surmised, without the same degree of direction either on the spot or from Peking as before the Cultural Revolution. This mutually corrosive situation—control of embassies in the hands of lesser officials and, apparently

9, 1967: "The supervisory group [in the Foreign Ministry] may constantly keep in touch with me, and utilize me to communicate with the Premier and the Central Committee. It won't do to dismantle the bridge which is my role." In *SCMM* 636, December 9, 1968, p. 20.

[122] Beginning in the summer of 1967, Ch'en was referred to in the Peking news media only as vice-premier. Then, after the Ninth CCP Congress of April 1969, which Ch'en attended, he was dropped from the Politburo though retained on the Central Committee. He was also elevated to vice-chairman of the Military Affairs Committee under the Central Committee. But his involvement in foreign affairs was curtailed, as Chou En-lai once again functioned in that position. In April 1971, Chi P'eng-fei was referred to as acting Foreign Minister.

in a few cases (like Burma), Red Guard types, coupled with the Foreign Ministry's preoccupation with its own political survival—at the very least enhanced the opportunities for fanatical elements abroad to "revolution-ize" foreign affairs in much the same way as the ultra-left was "revolu-tionizing" government and Party offices on the mainland—by vigorously propagating "the thoughts of Mao" beyond the confines of the CPR missions.

The actions of these extremists suggest several interesting hypotheses. First, the Ministry of Foreign Affairs may have lost control over certain embassies. Second, the brief "takeover" of the ministry in August 1967 may have caused great havoc *in the ministry* but may also have had negligible influence over the conflicts which by then had already unfolded between certain Chinese embassies and local governments. Finally, and most important, the sharp turns in Peking's relations with Burma, Cey-lon, Cambodia, and Nepal may well have been dictated not by a con-scious prior determination of Peking but by *local* Chinese representatives, who seem to have presented Mao with the unenviable choice of backing down before resistance to displays of loyalty or supporting the "just cause" of officials and overseas citizens of the People's Republic. Only in Burma, where the situation quickly reached a boiling point, was Peking un-willing to humble itself by ignoring what had happened.

APPOINTMENTS OF CHINESE COMMUNIST HEADS-OF-MISSION,
1969–1970

Name	Post	Date Appointed	Previous Position
Keng Piao	Albania	May 1969	Amb., Burma*
Huang Chen	France	May 1969	Same*
K'ang Mao-chao	Cambodia†	June 1969	Chargé, Yugoslavia
Wang Yu-p'ing	North Vietnam	June 1969	Amb., Cuba
Chang Tung	Pakistan	June 1969	Dir., Asian Affairs Dept. No. 1, M.F.A.
Ch'in Chia-lin	Syria	June 1969	Same
Chung Hsi-tung	Tanzania	June 1969	Amb., Czechoslovakia
Han K'o-hua	Guinea	June 1969	Amb., Hungary
Ch'in Li-chen	Zambia	June 1969	Same
Chang Hai-feng	Rumania	June 1969	Amb., East Germany
Wang Tung	Sweden	June 1969	Counselor, Rumania
Wang Yü-t'ien	Congo (B)	June 1969	Same

Name	Post	Date Appointed		Previous Position
Wang Tse	Nepal	July	1969	Consul Gen., Dacca (Pakistan) consulate
Feng Yü-chiu	Mauritania	July	1969	Amb., Norway
Hsieh Pang-chih	Afghanistan	July	1969	Amb., Bulgaria
Yang Ch'i-liang	Algeria	July	1969	Amb., Morocco
Wang Jo-chieh	Yemen	July	1969	Same
Li Ch'iang-fen	S. Yemen (Aden)	July	1969	Same (chargé)
Li Yün-ch'uan	North Korea	March	1970	Dir., Int. Liaison Dept., All-China Fed. of Trade Unions
Shih Tzu-ming	Finland	April	1970	Industrial manager
Meng Yüeh	Mali	April	1970	Youth official
Yang Shou-cheng	Sudan	April	1970	Amb., Somali
Ch'ai Tse-min	U.A.R.	June	1970	Amb., Guinea
Liu Hsin-ch'üan	U.S.S.R.	July	1970	Vice-foreign minister
Tseng T'ao	Yugoslavia	Aug.	1970	Amb., Algeria
Yao Kuang	Poland	Aug.	1970	Dir., Asian Affairs Dept. No. 2, M.F.A.
Lu Chih-hsien	Hungary	Aug.	1970	Amb., Mauritania
Ma Tzu-ch'ing	Ceylon	Aug.	1970	Amb., Mali
Sung Chih-kuang	East Germany	Sept.	1970	Chargé ad im., France
Fan Tso-k'ai	Somalia	Sept.	1970	Vice-mayor, Wuhan
T'ien Ting	Equatorial Africa (chargé)	Dec.	1970	Unknown
Chang Teh-ch'ün	Cuba	Dec.	1970	Counselor, U.S.S.R.
Ch'en Chih-fang	Switzerland	Dec.	1970	Amb., Uganda
Kung Ta-fei	Iraq	Dec.	1970	Dpty. Dir., African Affairs Dept., M.F.A.

* Also member of the CCP Central Committee.
† Withdrawn, May 1970.

The Cultural Revolution, then, clearly made its mark on China's foreign relations. Until the appointment of ambassadors began anew in May 1969, a purge or drastic reshuffling in the Chinese foreign service might have been expected. As of the end of 1970, however, by which time over half the vacant posts were filled (see the accompanying table), it appeared that foreign affairs professionals had managed to weather the storm.[123]

The ambassadorial appointments were one indication that the Cultural Revolution was not conceived or carried out in order to radicalize China's foreign policy. The Cultural Revolution was an internal phenomenon, and its seepage abroad to become a factor in China's relations with other countries seems to have been an uncalculated though perhaps inevitable by-product. As such, those instances in which the Revolution had deleterious consequences for China's foreign relations might be characterized as aberrant episodes rather than as reflections of a persistent or prominent new strand in China's foreign policy line. The facts that the overflow of the Revolution did not bring with it military adventures, and that since September 1967 the regime has gradually sought to stabilize its external relations, further support this conclusion.

For those nations that experienced the overflow of the Cultural Revolution, however, this interpretation is not likely to dim their suspicions of Chinese intentions. They are far more likely to keep up their guard against a repetition of the unhappy incidents of the summer of 1967. Those incidents, not the Chinese proclamations of continuing friendship and respect that ensued, will probably be the real legacy of the Cultural Revolution, one that Peking in coming years is going to find difficult to dispel.

[123] Of forty-five posts, thirty-four were filled between May 1969 and December 1970. Twenty-nine of these appointees are foreign service or Foreign Ministry officials, including six who returned to their old posts. For further analysis of the earliest appointments, see Daniel Tretiak, *The Chinese Cultural Revolution and Foreign Policy: The Process of Conflict and Current Policy*, ASG Monograph No. 2 (Westinghouse Electric Corporation, Waltham, Massachusetts) February 1970, pp. 23–26.

6

The Cultural Revolution
in the Countryside:
Anatomy of a Limited Rebellion

RICHARD BAUM

From its advent in the spring of 1966 until mid-autumn of
1968, China's Great Proletarian Cultural Revolution was
primarily an urban phenomenon. A substantial majority
of China's rural villages not only failed to experience significant Red
Guard agitation, "power seizures," or internecine factional struggles, but
also remained, throughout much of this two and one-half year period, effectively insulated from all but the most cursory information concerning
the occurrence of such events elsewhere. For most of China's 550 million
or more rural peasants and basic-level cadres, most of the time, the Cultural Revolution was simply not a particularly salient fact of everyday
life.

This is not to say that the Chinese countryside was totally unaffected
by the turbulence of the times. For it is apparent that many of the trau-
matic developments which took place in China's cities during the Cultural Revolution did have their local counterparts in at least some rural
communes and production brigades. But this was clearly a minority
phenomenon; and it was only with the nationwide intensification of a
rural "struggle-criticism-transformation" campaign in the autumn and
winter of 1968–1969 that the Cultural Revolution became a concrete reality for the majority of China's peasantry.

In those rural areas where the Cultural Revolution did impinge directly upon village life prior to the autumn of 1968, the visible result was
in most cases the same: the creation or exacerbation of interpersonal or
intergroup conflict. In this respect (qualitatively), the rural impact of the
Cultural Revolution differed little, if at all, from its urban prototype.

This study takes as its central focus the origins and manifestations of

political conflict in the Chinese countryside during the Cultural Revolution. In addition, we shall be concerned with the question of conflict
management—reactive attempts by central and local elites to ameliorate
the symptoms and causes of rural political conflict. Finally, we shall analyze the processes involved in the rural diffusion of urban-centered Cultural Revolutionary struggles, and explicate a number of environmental
factors which affected both the rate of rural conflict diffusion and the
relative magnitude of the revolutionary impact in various rural districts
throughout China.

The general contextual framework for this study is provided by the
Maoist conception of a long-term, acute "struggle between two roads" in
the Chinese countryside. This concept, and its interpretation and application by the Maoists in the period preceding the initiation of the Cultural Revolution, is the subject of the first section of this study. In the next
three sections the nature and consequences of Cultural Revolutionary
agitation by Red Guards and "revolutionary rebels" in the countryside are
examined in chronological context. The fifth section deals with the involvement of the Chinese People's Liberation Army (PLA) in rural
politics in the period following the January Revolution of 1967. The sixth
section documents the Maoists' search for a new, "revolutionary" social
and political order in rural China in the middle and later stages of the
Cultural Revolution. The final section presents a summary and analytical
overview of the rural impact of the Cultural Revolution, drawing upon
previous findings for the formulation and (wherever possible) testing of
explanatory hypotheses.

The data base consists of some five hundred individual media reports
dealing with political and socio-economic conditions and developments
in approximately three hundred rural communes and production brigades during the period of the Cultural Revolution. These reports were
drawn chiefly from official mainland Chinese newspapers and provincial
radio broadcasts, Red Guard publications and, to a lesser extent, the first-
hand observations of a number of foreign visitors to—and refugees from
—the Chinese mainland.

This data base is admittedly neither fully comprehensive nor randomly
representative of rural China as a whole; and a number of methodological
problems—some superable, some not—have arisen as a direct consequence
of the existence of rather sizeable gaps in the available data. The nature
and implications of these data gaps are examined in the final section of
this essay. Despite the existence of such lacunae, however, the attempt to

formulate and test explanatory hypotheses is deemed intrinsically worthwhile—the more so since data deficiencies are a constant problem within virtually every sphere of contemporary Chinese studies.

THE TWO-ROAD, TWO-LINE STRUGGLE

In the ongoing "struggle between two roads" in the Chinese countryside, the question of which side will ultimately emerge victorious—the "proletarian revolutionary line" of Party Chairman Mao Tse-tung or the "counterrevolutionary revisionist line" allegedly promoted by China's former chief of state and one-time heir-apparent to Mao, Liu Shao-ch'i—has yet to be determined with any finality. To be sure, Liu Shao-ch'i—"China's Khrushchev"—has been stripped of all formal rank and authority within the Party. Nevertheless, the residual influence of his allegedly heretical agrarian policies has repeatedly been cited by the Maoist regime as the primary obstacle to consolidation of the "socialist battlefront" in rural China.

Precisely what is perceived as being at stake in the long-term struggle between two roads and two lines in Chinese agriculture has been made reasonably clear by the Maoists—at least in broad-gauged economic, political, and ideological terms—in the course of their continuing polemic against the "number one Party person in authority taking the capitalist road." Expressed in terms of its lowest common denominator, the agrarian struggle has centered around a perceived conflict between Mao's socialist-collectivist principles of agrarian organization and administration, on the one hand, and Liu Shao-ch'i's alleged capitalist-individualist subterfuge, on the other:

Our great helmsman Chairman Mao has formulated a Marxist-Leninist line for the socialist revolution in the countryside. It is a line designed to wipe out rural capitalist exploitation and bring about the collectivization of agriculture. It is a line designed to bring about a thoroughgoing socialist revolution on the agricultural front. . . .

But what did the number one Party person in authority taking the capitalist road do on the question of agriculture during the past decade and more? . . . He madly sabotaged the socialist revolution in the countryside and came out against the masses of poor and lower-middle peasants. He pursued an out-and-out counterrevolutionary revisionist line, a line which represented a vain attempt to restore capitalism in the rural areas, a line which would, in fact, have allowed the landlords, rich peasants, counterrevolutionaries, bad elements, and rightists to make a comeback.[1]

The Maoist catalogue of grievances against the "counterrevolutionary revisionist line" of Liu Shao-ch'i is replete with sweeping allegations concerning the latter's past support for such ostensibly heterodox agricultural practices as "going it alone" (*tan-kan,* the retrogression from collectivist modes of agricultural production and distribution to individualistic ones); "contracting production to the household" (*pao-ch'an tao-hu,* an administrative arrangement under which each peasant household is made individually responsible for fulfilling production quotas on a given piece of land); "placing work-points in command" (*kung-fen kua-shuai,* placing undue stress on material, as opposed to non-material or "spiritual" production incentives—a perversion of the Maoist call to "place politics in command"); and the so-called "four great freedoms" (*ssu ta tzu-yu,* freedom to buy and sell land, hire farm labor, engage in private commerce and contract private loans).[2]

The common theme which serves to link together these and other anti-Liuist charges is the idea that through his alleged opposition to orthodox socialist-collectivist economic and administrative practices in the countryside, Liu Shao-ch'i sought consciously and actively to promote a "capitalist restoration" in rural China.[3] Even if we were to accept the Maoist indict-

[1] *Jen-min Jih-pao,* November 23, 1967.

[2] These allegations have been raised numerous times in official Party media since the summer of 1967. The best single official source on this question is *ibid.*

[3] In addition to the accusations mentioned above, Liu has also been officially charged at various times with the following crimes: (1) conspiring with other high level Party officials to "drastically decompress" and dissolve China's collective farms in 1955; (2) opposing the Great Leap Forward and the radical communalization of China's peasants in 1958–59; (3) resisting Mao's plan, first put forward in 1957, to radically decentralize the responsibility for ownership and management of heavy farm machinery; and (4) attempting to sabotage the Rural Socialist Education Movement in 1964 by advocating the purge of large numbers of basic-level cadres in the communes and production brigades—a measure which was subsequently condemned by the Maoists as "hitting hard at the many to protect the few." For documentation and analysis of these assertions, see the following: Parris H. Chang, "Struggle Between the Two Roads in China's Countryside," *Current Scene* (Hong Kong), Vol. 6, No. 3 (February 15, 1968); "The Conflict Between Mao Tse-tung and Liu Shao-ch'i over Agricultural Mechanization in Communist China," *Current Scene,* Vol. 6, No. 17 (October 1, 1968); and Richard Baum and Frederick C. Teiwes, "Liu Shao-ch'i and the Cadre Question," *Asian Survey,* Vol. 8, No. 4 (April 1968) pp. 323–345.

ment against Liu Shao-ch'i fully and in all particulars, however (and it is by no means self-evident that we should do so), we would still be rather far from understanding the full significance of Liu's so-called "counterrevolutionary revisionist line." For it is highly unlikely that such a "line"—if indeed it actually existed—could have been successfully implemented on so large a scale as the Maoists seem to imply solely (or even primarily) through the actions or intentions of any single individual, no matter how powerful his position or evil his machinations. On the contrary, to the extent that the adverse economic and political manifestations of Liu's alleged "line" have become widespread and generalized enough to cause serious alarm to the Maoists (and all available evidence indicates that the Maoists are indeed alarmed), this would seem to suggest that Liu's "line" had at some point struck a resonant note in rural Chinese society. Otherwise, the problem of "counterrevolutionary revisionism" in the countryside would have been rendered fairly easily soluble by physically "seizing power" from the "renegade" Liu and a handful of his alleged "agents" at the provincial and sub-provincial levels, and by subsequently reasserting more orthodox agrarian policies. That the problem has not been readily amenable to such surgical solution, however, is clearly indicated by the very intensity and protracted nature of the anti-Liuist "criticism and repudiation" movement in rural China in the period *after* Liu and his principal "henchmen" were effectively removed from power in the winter and spring of 1966–1967.

What, then, of China's 550 million rural peasants and cadres? Have they, as the Maoists implicitly acknowledge, been "drugged" by the pernicious poison of Liu's apostasy? If so, to what extent should Liu and his fellow "Party people in authority taking the capitalist road" be held individually or collectively responsible? Conversely, we might ask to what extent have such phenomena as "going it alone," "contracting production to the household," "placing work-points in command," and the "four great freedoms" been the by-product of an interplay between the relatively permissive agrarian policies laid down by the central Party leadership in the early 1960s and the spontaneous aggregation and articulation of *indigenous* social, economic, and political demands and pressures in the villages? In other words, is Liu Shao-ch'i a true anti-socialist "demon and monster," as charged, or was he guilty of responding positively to the material aspirations and needs of the Chinese peasantry during a time of widespread economic hardship—a scapegoat thrown up by the Maoists in order to rationalize the manifest failures of Mao's grand design for creating a "new socialist countryside?" [4]

The answer to this last—and in many respects most crucial—question is far from clear. Certainly, a great deal of "evidence"—much of it circumstantial in nature—has been marshalled against Liu by the Maoist prosecution during the course of the Cultural Revolution. But in the absence of even a single impartial and well-informed defense witness and, more important, in light of the mounting evidence which tends to indicate that Liu, far from being a "renegade," may actually have been expressing a substantial intra-Party consensus in putting forth his reputedly permissive views on rural economy and administration in the early 1960s, final judgment on the question of criminal culpability must be reserved.[5]

Putting aside for the moment the question of individual or collective guilt, the fact remains that for the past decade large segments of China's rural population have quite clearly failed to live up to Mao Tse-tung's rather lofty revolutionary expectations. Mao's ideal-typical model of the "peasant activist," with its assumption of spontaneous mass enthusiasm for socialism and collectivism, and its emphasis upon the dedication and self-discipline of rural Party members and cadres, has simply not been realized in practice.

In the first place, large numbers of peasants have been seriously afflicted with the twin viruses of individualism and economic self-interest. More-

---

[4] It is interesting to note in this regard that the term *"spontaneous* capitalist tendencies," which recurred so frequently and prominently in Party media in the five-year period prior to the initiation of the Cultural Revolution, subsequently all but disappeared from Peking's lexicon. For if Liu Shao-ch'i is to be held personally responsible for igniting the flames of "counterrevolutionary revisionism" in the Chinese countryside, then "spontaneity" must be ruled out as a root cause of dysfunction.

[5] It should be noted that the highly permissive "Sixty Articles on Agriculture" adopted by the Party Central Committee in March 1961, and revised in September 1962, were never officially repudiated by the Maoists during the Cultural Revolution —this despite the fact that this document gave tacit approval to many of the same rural administrative practices that were later to be individually denounced as "revisionist." It is hypothesized that a permissive intra-Party consensus on agricultural policy existed in the crisis years of 1960–1961, and that for this reason the Maoists have been unable to repudiate the "Sixty Articles" without at the same time implicating many of their own number in the formulation and implementation thereof, including perhaps the Chairman himself. On the question of intra-Party conflict and consensus over agrarian policies in the early 1960s, see Parris H. Chang, "Patterns and Processes of Policy Making in Communist China, 1955–1962: Three Case Studies" (unpublished Ph.D. dissertation, Columbia University, Department of Political Science, 1969), Chapter 5.

over, sizeable numbers of rural cadres have lost their revolutionary élan and fallen victim to the evils of "bureaucratism," "commandism," and a host of other unorthodox styles of administrative behavior.

Equally damaging to the Maoist cause of constructing a "new socialist countryside" has been the fact that since the nationwide economic crisis of the early 1960s, increasing numbers of opportunistic cadres and peasants have resorted to petty bribery, graft, corruption, speculation and other illegal practices as a means of mitigating the conditions of extreme economic scarcity and austerity imposed upon rural China by an extractive, capital accumulation-oriented regime. All in all, it would appear that the Maoists have been fighting, if not a losing battle, then at least an uphill one against the harmful effects of deviant behavior by self-interested peasants and cadres in rural China. And the cumulative result of all this has been a situation in which the "evil winds" of Liu Shao-ch'i's alleged "counterrevolutionary revisionism" have blown with considerable force across the Chinese countryside.[6]

The first major Maoist attempt to put a halt to the spread of such "evil winds" took the form of a nationwide Socialist Education Movement. Beginning shortly after the convocation of the Central Committee's Tenth Plenum in the autumn of 1962, and continuing until the early winter of 1966–1967, well beyond the advent of the Cultural Revolution, large numbers of socialist education work teams composed of Party officials, government functionaries and "politically reliable" university students were dispatched by Party organs at all levels to "squat" (*tun-tien*) for varying periods in tens of thousands of rural Chinese villages. The tasks assigned to these work teams were those of investigating, exposing, and "cleaning up" the economic, political, ideological, and organizational impurities of rural peasants and basic-level cadres.[7]

[6] Documentation concerning the above-mentioned phenomena is too plentiful to be cited in its entirety. The best primary source on deviant behavior in the Chinese countryside in the early 1960s is still the famous "Lienchiang collection." See, C. S. Chen, ed., *Rural People's Communes in Lien-Chiang* (Stanford, 1969). For secondary analysis of the problems and prospects confronting Chinese agriculture in the 1960s, see, *inter alia*, Michel Oksenberg, "Local Leaders in Rural China, 1962–1965," in A. Doak Barnett, ed., *Chinese Communist Politics in Action* (Seattle, 1969), pp. 155–215; R. J. Birrell, "The Centralized Control of the Communes in the Post-'Great Leap' Period," in *ibid.*, pp. 400–443; Pi-chao Chen, "Individual Farming After the Great Leap as Revealed by the Lien-Chiang Documents," *Asian Survey*, Vol. 8, No. 9 (September 1968) pp. 774–791; and Richard Baum and Frederick C. Teiwes, *Ssu-Ch'ing: The Socialist Education Movement of 1962–1966* (Berkeley, 1968).

[7] Hence the term Four Cleanups (*ssu-ch'ing*), which was often used synonymously with "Socialist Education Movement." See Baum and Teiwes, *Ssu-Ch'ing, loc. cit.*

In the course of this rural rectification movement, many relatively well-to-do peasants were criticized for manifesting "spontaneous capitalist tendencies," and habitual village individualists, speculators, and "trouble-makers" were pejoratively labeled and brought under varying degrees of official surveillance as "five category elements." [8] More significant, hundreds of thousands of basic-level rural officials were publicly criticized, "struggled" against, or dismissed from their posts as "four unclean" cadres.[9]

Despite the scope and intensity of this rural rectification drive, most of the fundamental political and economic shortcomings which had plagued China's agricultural sector since the collapse of the Great Leap Forward in 1960 continued to find expression in rural China in the mid-1960s. As one official report of December 1965 put it: "The class struggle between socialism and capitalism is being rekindled *even in those areas which have gone through systematic socialist education.*" [10] And almost a year

---

[8] The "five categories" comprised landlords, rich peasants, counterrevolutionaries, bad elements, and unreformed Rightists.

[9] Professor Michel Oksenberg has estimated that "as many as 70 to 80 percent of subvillage leaders . . . may have been removed from office in some provinces during the 'Four [Cleanup]' movement." (Oksenberg, *op. cit.,* p. 184.) My own research tends to indicate that this figure is probably substantially over-inflated. County Party Committees were generally given a target figure of 5 percent of the rural basic-level cadres to be purged during the movement; and while there have been numerous reported cases of 70 to 80 percent of the cadres in a *single village or production brigade* being purged, county-wide averages probably did not greatly exceed the 5 percent target figure. In terms of province-wide statistics, the only reliable official report that I have seen to date states that "over 23 percent of all basic level cadres in [Honan] province were under attack during the first [sic] Socialist Education Movement; some 10 percent were either dismissed, expelled from the Party or similarly punished." (*Radio Chengchow,* Honan, December 12, 1967.) If this latter figure of 10 percent is regarded as the upper limit of purgation on a nationwide scale, with the figure 5 percent regarded as the lower limit, then the total number of rural cadres actually purged in China during the Socialist Education Movement may have been on the order of one to two million, based on the Party's official July 1963 estimate that "at present there are more than 20 million cadres at the production brigade and production team levels in the rural areas" (*Jen-min Jih-pao,* July 4, 1963). However, this preliminary figure of one to two million purgees should probably be revised further downward to take account of the fact that the Socialist Education Movement was never carried to conclusion in many—perhaps even the majority—of China's rural communes. On this latter point, see my "Revolution and Reaction in the Chinese Countryside: The Socialist Education Movement in Cultural Revolutionary Perspective," *The China Quarterly,* No. 38 (April–June 1969) p. 111, note 67.

[10] *Radio Lanchow,* Kansu, December 21, 1965 (emphasis added).

later, in October 1966, some six months after the initiation of the Cultural Revolution, a major regional Chinese newspaper admitted that the Socialist Education Movement had failed to solve a number of "old, great, and difficult problems" in China's communes.[11]

When the Cultural Revolution began in earnest in April 1966, with the initiation of public attacks on leading figures in the Peking Municipal Party Committee, it was unclear how the new campaign was to be related to the Socialist Education Movement. On the one hand, a provincial radio broadcast of late May stated that the Cultural Revolution was to be considered as an "important, integral part of the Socialist Education Movement."[12] On the other hand, there was little or no indication, at this early stage, that the impact of the new revolution was actually being felt in the countryside. To be sure, the provincial media carried a number of reports claiming, for example, that "the storm of the Great Socialist Cultural Revolution has rolled into the rural areas."[13] But upon closer examination, such reports revealed only that a small number of mass rallies were being staged at selected points in the countryside to denounce the "outrageous crimes" of "anti-Party, anti-socialist elements" in Peking cultural and educational circles. In no instance was there any evidence that the Cultural Revolution was being directed at local "demons and monsters" in the rural areas themselves.

When the Cultural Revolution entered the stage of "big blooming and contending" in early June, with the nationwide publication of the first revolutionary "big character poster," it appeared that the hitherto exclusively urban orientation of the movement might undergo a change. Thus, for example, an "open letter" addressed to China's peasant masses from the Hupeh Provincial Poor and Lower-Middle Peasants' Association Committee, publicized in late June, exhorted: "Comrades! We must unmask *all* anti-Party and anti-Socialist . . . freaks and monsters in the whole country, the whole province, and *in our own localities and home units*. Whether they are in towns or the villages, below us or above, we

---

[11] *Hung-wei Pao* (Canton), October 23, 1966.
[12] *Radio Sian,* Shensi, May 23, 1966.
[13] See, *inter alia, Radio Changsha,* Hunan, May 16, 1966. The term "Great *Socialist* Cultural Revolution" was widely used until the latter part of May, when, following the issuance of a Central Committee circular condemning Peking Mayor P'eng Chen, the adjective "Socialist" was dropped in favor of "Proletarian"—an alteration which allegedly served to underscore the true essence of the Cultural Revolution as a "severe class struggle."

must strike them all down and uproot them. The poor and lower-middle peasants must carry the Great Proletarian Cultural Revolution through to the end." [14]

Such exhortations did not, however, lead to any immediately discernible revolutionary agitation in the countryside;[15] on the contrary, the Socialist Education Movement continued to receive stress as the major political priority in rural China. And as late as July 29, a provincial radio broadcast from Hunan stated: "At the present time, one-third of the communes in our province have completed, or almost completed, the systematic Socialist Education Movement. *All other areas are conducting it initially.*" [16]

In the period following the April 1966 initiation of the Cultural Revolution, the Socialist Education Movement did, however, undergo a partial change of orientation. While the "Four Cleanups" continued apace, a new element, in the form of a drive to promote the long term, intensive study of the works of Chairman Mao, was added to the campaign. This "Mao study" drive had actually begun on an experimental basis in South-Central China during the previous summer (August 1965); but it was not until the spring of 1966 that Mao study was incorparated into the Socialist Education Movement on a regular, nationwide basis. Throughout the summer of 1966 almost all rural reportage in the Chinese mass media was given over to didactic descriptions of how Mao study provided the key to overcoming all "old, great, and difficult problems" in the countryside.[17]

Mao-study was the common element of both the (urban) Cultural Revolution and the (rural) Socialist Education Movement in the summer of 1966. Peasants and factory workers, commune cadres and urban bureaucrats were thus linked together in a frenetic drive to "creatively study and apply" the thought of Mao Tse-tung. An editorial appearing in *Hung-ch'i,* early in June stated the official view of this linkage between the two movements in the following terms:

[14] *Radio Wuhan,* Hupeh, June 29, 1966 (emphasis added).

[15] A number of refugees from China's rural areas have indicated that the first major rural impact of the Cultural Revolution was not felt until the mobilization and nationwide dispersal of the militant young Red Guards in August and September of 1966.

[16] *Radio Changsha,* Hunan, July 29, 1966 (emphasis added).

[17] See, for example, the series of articles concerning the progress of Mao-study in the "model" Huangshantung production brigade, Kwangtung Province, in *Yang-ch'eng Wan-pao* (Canton), June 21, 22, and 25, 1966; and *Jen-min Jih-pao,* August 27 and 28, 1966.

The Socialist Education Movement in China's vast countryside . . . is a struggle between the two roads of socialism and capitalism. . . . The basic experience derived from it is that the thought of Mao Tse-tung must be placed in the forefront. . . . Similarly, in the Great Proletarian Cultural Revolution we must ensure that the thought of Mao Tse-tung is placed in the forefront. . . . The creative study and application of Chairman Mao's works . . . is the most important guarantee in all work and at all levels.[18]

When the Central Committee convened its Eleventh Plenum in August 1966, the question was raised as to whether the Cultural Revolution should be integrated with the Socialist Education Movement in town and countryside. The Plenum's decision on this question was that the two movements should, at least temporarily, remain separate. The Socialist Education Movement was to continue to be conducted in rural communes and villages (that is, in basic-level production units) "according to original arrangements," while the Cultural Revolution was to take as its "key point" the rectification of "bourgeois powerholders" in cultural and educational units and leading Party and governmental organs in the large and medium-sized cities.[19]

With the initial mobilization and subsequent nationwide dispersal of the Red Guards in the last half of August and early September, the Cultural Revolution began to "spill over" into the Chinese countryside, thus posing an implicit challenge to the official policy of mutual insulation of the two movements. And as the headstrong and often overzealous "little generals" set out on their nationwide campaign to "destroy the four olds" and launch "revolutionary great debates," they ran headlong into the determined opposition of conservative local Party authorities and tradition-minded peasants alike. Thus were sown the first seeds of a profound and ultimately bitter conflict. Thus also began the latest epoch in the continuing "struggle between the two roads" in the Chinese countryside.

[18] *Hung-ch'i,* No. 8 (June 8, 1966) p. 2.
[19] *Decision of the Central Committee of the Chinese Communist Party Concerning the Great Proletarian Cultural Revolution,* August 8, 1966 (Peking: Foreign Language Press, 1966), Article XIII. Provision was made, however, for the possible overlap of the two movements, as it was explicitly stated that in "certain areas" (presumably those rural villages with "old, great, and difficult problems"), the Cultural Revolution could be used as a "focal point" to "add momentum" to the Socialist Education Movement. (*Ibid.*)

THE RED GUARDS REBEL:
AUGUST–SEPTEMBER 1966

The activation of the Red Guards in the last half of August 1966 marked a watershed in the course of the Cultural Revolution in the countryside as well as in the cities. Mao's "little generals," given virtually unlimited license to "destroy the four olds," went at their work with an enthusiasm seldom seen in modern China. And when they left their urban staging areas at the end of August to "link up" and "exchange revolutionary experiences" with their counterparts from other regions and districts, the results were predictably unsettling.

From Kwangtung Province came the following report, typical of this period: "In recent days, Red Guards, poor and lower-middle peasants and revolutionary cadres in rural communes, following the example of the Peking Red Guards, have opened fierce fire on the old thinking, old culture, old customs, and old habits of the exploiting classes. They have swept away all ancestral tablets, idols, "superstitious objects," old books and old wall cloths. In their place, portraits and quotations of Chairman Mao have been hung up everywhere." [20] A companion piece to this item described how a young Red Guard, upon returning to his family home in the rural suburbs of Haikow municipality, had "heightened his parents' awareness" by quoting Mao Tse-tung's words as he energetically threw away and smashed their ancestral tablets, incense burner, and religious statues.[21]

A Canadian observer visiting a commune in suburban Shanghai gave the following first-hand report of local Red Guard activism:

Following the organization of Red Guard groups in Shanghai on August 20–21, young people from poor and lower-middle [peasant] families on the commune also set up their own Red Guard detachments, and promptly launched their attack on the "four olds." Their main targets, as could be guessed, were the former landlords and rich peasants living on the commune, and the Red Guards broke into their homes in search of incriminating relics from the past. Apparently, they found what they were looking for—gold and silver bars, jewelry, guns and other weapons, and, more important, pre-Liberation land records. . . . As in the city, any and all [suspected] "bad elements" were subjected to "struggle" meetings and other forms of harassment.

[20] *Radio Haikow,* Hainan Island, August 31, 1966.
[21] *Ibid.,* August 30, 1966.

Another important target for attack by the Red Guards was superstition in general, and religion in particular, both of which still have some influence among the older peasants, especially the women. The young students held many meetings with the people still influenced by such things . . . and tried to persuade them to cast away their faith in the gods.[22]

A number of references were made in the official media to peasants "energetically emulating" the revolutionary actions of the Red Guards by destroying the physical symbols of feudal culture and superstition in their own households. Nevertheless, such emulation, particularly on the part of the older, more tradition-bound peasants, was in all probability dissimulative. To be sure, many peasants undoubtedly acquiesced in the smashing of their ancestral tablets, incense burners, religious icons, and the like —for to do otherwise would have been to invite persecution as "counterrevolutionaries." Yet it is difficult to conceive of these tradition-minded peasants demonstrating any genuine enthusiasm for the "search and destroy" tactics of the young Red Guard invaders.

Resentment against the Red Guards in this early period was not limited to a minority of tradition-bound peasants. There is substantial evidence to indicate that Party authorities at the provincial, sub-provincial, and basic levels also resented the intrusion of the young agitators into their local bailiwicks. One report from Szechwan province told of the actions of a provincial Party "powerholder" who, when informed in late August of 1966 that Red Guards from Peking were on their way to "link up" and "exchange revolutionary experiences" with local workers and peasants, hastily set up a number of "special investigatory organs" to harass and confine the itinerant students.[23] In Anhwei Province it was similarly reported that local "mandarins" had initially tried to prevent revolutionary students from going to the countryside by setting up "layers and layers of defense lines." When such preventive measures failed, the local authorities reportedly reacted by "labeling as counterrevolutionary all peasants who rose to support the students." [24] And in Kiangsu Province the entire militia squadron of a suburban production brigade was allegedly detained and placed under surveillance by the local Party committee in

[22] Ray Wylie, "Red Guards Rebound," *Far Eastern Economic Review* (Hong Kong) Vol. 57, No. 10 (September 7, 1967) pp. 462–463.
[23] *Radio Chengtu,* Szechwan, April 10, 1968. The "powerholder" in question was Liao Chih-kao, who was subsequently purged as a "three-anti" element.
[24] *Radio Hofei,* Anhwei, February 2, 1967.

late August for having dared to support the Red Guards. The Party committee reportedly forbade the militia members to maintain contacts with the sudents or go into the streets to read "big character posters" written by the students, labeled the students "counterrevolutionary," and ordered the militia squad reorganized and its leadership purged as "renegades."[25]

Clearly, a great deal more was at stake than the mere eradication or survival of feudal superstitions. Although the "big blooming and contending" of itinerant students was largely confined at this early stage to exposing and criticizing the "crimes" (real or imagined) of a relatively small number of leading officials in provincial and municipal-level Party and government organs, the very physical presence and officially sanctioned freedom of action of the migratory "little generals" posed an implicit threat to the local "establishment" throughout China. The leaders of the establishment in many cases accurately perceived the nature of this threat and did what they could to minimize the amount of Red Guard disruption.

It is impossible, given the limitations on available data, to determine precisely the extent and spatial location of rural resistance to the "blooming and contending" of Red Guards in the late summer of 1966 or even, for that matter, to determine the precise extent of Red Guard penetration into the countryside. Nevertheless, it is almost certainly true that "outside agitation," and resistance to it, was confined at this early stage to a relatively small number of suburban communes outside of China's 125 or so large and medium-sized municipalities.[26] Urban proximity was therefore a major variable in determining the initial rate of "spill-over" of the Cultural Revolution into the Chinese countryside.[27]

"Outside agitation" was not, however, the only source of Cultural Revolutionary disturbance in rural China in the late summer of 1966. For *indigenous* groups of Red Guards began to spring up in a number of suburban communes and villages. And because the primary political orientations of such indigenous groups were localized (unlike those of

[25] *Jen-min Jih-pao*, February 20, 1967.

[26] For purposes of this discussion, a "medium-sized municipality" is defined as any urbanized area, together with adjoining rural suburbs, having a total population of over 100,000 but less than 1,000,000, of which there were 101 in 1958. A "large municipality" is defined as an urban center having a total population of 1,000,000 or more, of which there were 16 in 1958. See Yüan-li Wu, *The Spatial Economy of Communist China* (New York, 1967) pp. 209–218.

[27] The evidence supporting this conclusion is discussed and its implications examined below. See especially Figure 3, p. 457.

their peripatetic urban counterparts), the "great debates" launched by these native rural youths frequently took the form of scathing wall-poster attacks against *local* "bourgeois powerholders"—including for the first time the representatives of Party and governmental authority at the basic levels.

Numerous accounts have been published which describe the proliferation of wall poster critiques against production brigade- and team-level cadres in late August and early September.[28] Such attacks were implicitly sanctioned when, toward the end of August, the twin slogans, "Put the word 'dare' in command!" and "Do not be afraid of creating chaos!" were raised to positions of prominence in the central and provincial Party media.[29]

Apprehensive at the prospect of escalating anti-establishmentarian "blooming and contending" in their local bailiwicks, basic-level Party and administrative functionaries in those rural districts where Red Guard units were active began to take defensive measures. Fighting fire with fire (or, as it was later described, "waving red flags to oppose the red flag"), local powerholders in some areas quickly recruited their own supporters and set up rival "revolutionary" mass organizations to act as a counterforce to the Red Guard insurgents. The following report from a suburban Peking production brigade, though admittedly partisan in nature, is typical of the many available descriptions of such preemptive tactics:

In August, when Chairman Mao openly signified his support for Red Guards . . . several poor and lower-middle peasant youths took the lead in organizing the Poor and Lower-Middle Peasant Red Guards. They vigorously destroyed the "four olds" and struggled against the bourgeois powerholders. . . . Frightened, [brigade Party branch secretary] Li Ch'un-ch'ang and his gang immediately called a meeting of the Party branch and decided to organize the Red Guards of the Thought of Mao Tse-tung. . . . Everyone except the "five category elements" was eligible for admission into this organization. Overnight it enrolled more than 90 members, many of whom were children of cadres and "relatives of the emperor." There were several leading cadres in the organization. . . .

[28] See, *inter alia*, *Nung-ts'un Ch'ing-nien* (Shanghai), Nos. 19 (October 10, 1967) and 20 (October 25, 1967), in *Union Research Service* (*URS*), Vol. 49, pp. 135, 141; *Jen-min Jih-pao*, February 20, 23, and March 10, 1967; and *New China News Agency* (*NCNA*) (Peking), October 14, 1968.

[29] See, for example, *Radio Changsha*, Hunan, August 23, 1966.

They were in reality the Royalist Guards of Li Ch'un-ch'ang and his gang.[30]

In addition, local powerholders in suburban communes and production brigades in a number of areas reportedly adopted a series of other hastily contrived evasive measures to ward off the radical insurgents. In suburban Shanghai local cadres attempted to forestall mass participation in the Cultural Revolution by deducting the work points of all peasants who joined in revolutionary criticism.[31] In suburban areas of Kweichow, Szechwan, and Anhwei provinces it was reported that local powerholders had attempted to suppress Red Guard criticism by distorting and "making surreptitious changes" in Party regulations concerning the policy of "grasping revolution and promoting production" handed down by Peking in early September.[32] And in Shanghai, finally, an "ordinary" cadre in a suburban commune alleged that a handful of "capitalist-roaders" in the commune Party committee had sought to save their own political skins by "pushing me to the 'first line' and ordering me to go and represent the commune Party committee at criticism meetings convened by various units. By this evil scheme they hoped to enable themselves to 'slip through the net.' "[33]

In the above examples, we see evidence of three distinct tactical approaches adopted by members of the local "establishment" in suburban communes and production brigades to minimize the disruptive effects of revolutionary agitation. These approaches may be broadly characterized as "evasion," "repression," and "preemption." In some areas, however, local powerholders adopted yet a fourth approach to the problem of mitigating

[30] *Nung-min Yün-tung* (Peking), No. 3 (February 22, 1967), in *Survey of the China Mainland Press* (*SCMP*) 3910, pp. 9–10. For similar accounts of emergent factional conflict between the organized supporters and opponents of rural powerholders in the late summer and early autumn of 1966, see *Jen-min Jih-pao*, February 20 and March 8, 1967; also *Radio Hofei*, Anhwei, February 2, 1967; *Radio Sining*, Tsinghai, March 23, 1967; *Radio Kweiyang*, Kweichow, December 20, 1967; and *NCNA* (Peking), October 14, 1968.

[31] *NCNA* (Peking), February 9, 1967.

[32] See *Radio Kweiyang*, Kweichow, December 19, 1967; *Radio Chengtu*, Szechwan, April 10, 1968; and *Radio Hofei*, Anhwei, February 2, 1967. In all three of the provinces cited, local cadres reportedly argued that "the Cultural Revolution will adversely affect agricultural production . . . and thus is to be temporarily halted." The slogan "grasp revolution, promote production" (*chua ko-ming, ts'u sheng-ch'an*) was first used in a *Jen-min Jih-pao* editorial of September 7.

[33] *Jen-min Jih-pao*, March 10, 1967.

the effects of revolutionary "great debates." This latter method may be characterized as "co-optation."

In suburban Canton, Kwangtung Province, local cadres attempted to disarm the rebellious Red Guards by praising the activism of those revolutionary students who wrote a "big character poster" against the Party branch committee.[34] And in suburban Yangchow, Kiangsu Province, it was reported that a production brigade cadre turned to "sugar-coated bullets" when his "hard-line approach" failed to deter the movement of revolutionary criticism by Red Guards:

When the brigade Party branch secretary saw that his hard-line approach wouldn't work, he changed his tactics. He said that we had apparently forgotten that we had been cultivated and nurtured by the Party . . . and that we were ungrateful. We said that we had been cultivated and nurtured by Chairman Mao, and that it was he who was truly ungrateful. Startled, he then said that it would be a shame for an activist element such as myself to be struck down. We pointed out that we hadn't really been struck down; on the contrary, for us, being struck down really meant standing up. He said, "In the past you did a good job of leading the study of Mao's works in your production team. How would you like to be selected to go to the commune headquarters to lead a study meeting? I'll even lend you a bicycle." I said, "I won't be struck down by your sugar-coated bullets. Revolution isn't for the sake of fame and reputation . . . nor is it for the sake of becoming an official and enriching oneself." [35]

The use of "sugar-coated bullets" to co-opt rebellious youngsters in rural China was by no means an isolated or temporary phenomenon. A few months later, during the storm of the January Revolution, such tactics were to be widely used by local powerholders in an attempt to seduce local peasants and forestall "power seizures" by Revolutionary Rebel organizations throughout China.[36]

By the time the crucial autumn harvest season arrived in mid-September 1966, there was evidently considerable concern at the Party center that the spread of the Cultural Revolution to the countryside might interfere with the normal seasonal processes of production. Such concern was not

---

[34] *Hung-se Pao-tung* (Canton), Nos. 12–13 (July 8, 1967), in *SCMP* 4030, p. 15.
[35] *Jen-min Jih-pao*, February 20, 1967.
[36] See pages 412–416.

without foundation. In one month since the adjournment of the Eleventh Central Committee Plenum in mid-August, the newly mobilized Red Guards had indeed created a considerable amount of rural upheaval—this despite the fact that "great debates," "linking up," and "exchanging revolutionary experiences" had as yet occurred in only a limited number of suburban communes.

The way in which the productive activities of rural peasants were affected by the initial impact of the Cultural Revolution is well illustrated by the following first-hand account of Red Guard influence in a suburban Shanghai commune:

By September . . . the bulk of the Shanghai Red Guards had returned from their travels to Peking and elsewhere, and had begun to send representatives out to nearby communes to establish working contacts with the local Red Guards. While it appears that the urban Red Guards did not interfere directly with normal work on the commune, their presence definitely did tend to disturb the equilibrium. . . . They had split into "rebel" and "conservative" factions, each propagating their own viewpoints either for or against the [Shanghai] municipal Party committee. Furthermore, they began to interfere in the peasant Red Guards' handling of the local situation, and this naturally led to some bitterness between the urban and the rural groups. As a result of all these factors, it became increasingly difficult for the peasants, especially the younger ones, to concentrate all their energies on the daily tasks of production.[37]

Apparently in response to situations such as this, *Jen-min Jih-pao* published on September 7 an editorial entitled "Grasp Revolution, Promote Production." While ostensibly restating the official policy line on the Cultural Revolution that had evolved in the weeks following the Eleventh Plenum, this important editorial significantly modified the thrust of that line by explicitly prohibiting urban Red Guards from interfering in rural politics. Local poor and lower-middle peasants were hailed as "the main force of the revolution" and were said to be "fully capable of handling the revolutionary movement in their own organizations." Conditions in rural China were said to be extremely complex, and it was therefore argued that "interference from outsiders who do not understand the situation could easily affect the normal progress of production." [38]

[37] Wylie, *op. cit.*, pp. 463–465. For additional reports of production losses suffered as a result of revolutionary agitation in this period, see *Radio Kunming*, Yunnan, December 14, 1968; and *Radio Sining*, Tsinghai, March 23, 1967.

[38] *Jen-min Jih-pao*, September 7, 1966.

Even more significant, the editorial called for the "temporary suspension" of *all* political campaigns (including both the Cultural Revolution and the Socialist Education Movement) in rural China in order that "all efforts can be concentrated on making a good job of this year's autumn harvest." [39] Thus was introduced the slogan, "grasp revolution, promote production," with primary emphasis, at least for the time being, placed on the latter. The initial phase of revolutionary "great debates" in the countryside thus came to an officially sanctioned (though not, as we shall see, widely enforced) conclusion.

There is still regrettably little information available on the question of who among Peking's "inner circle" of Cultural Revolutionary elites initiated the change of policy, who supported it, and who (if anyone) opposed it. It is known, however, that rectification movements in rural China have traditionally demonstrated seasonal fluctuations in intensity and magnitude corresponding broadly to changes in the natural farming cycle. And this, in turn, suggests that the "relaxation" of September 1966 may have represented a normal, seasonal shift in regime priorities.

In the past, political-organizational rectification movements in the countryside have generally reached their peak intensity in the "slack" winter months of December through February (for example, the *cheng-feng cheng-she* movements of 1959–1960, 1960–1961, and 1961–1962, and the Four Cleanups movement, which reached its peak of intensity in December 1964). On the other hand, during the busy spring planting (March through May) and autumn harvest (September through November) seasons, rural rectification movements have generally been deemphasized and, in recent years, supplanted by less disruptive "spare time" ideological education and study campaigns.[40] Thus, the September 1966 decision to temporarily suspend the Socialist Education Movement and minimize the disruptive effects of "outside agitation" by prohibiting urban Red Guards from participating in "great debates" in the countryside should not necessarily be regarded as a "turn to the right" from the

[39] *Ibid.*
[40] This fact tends to controvert, in part, some of the findings presented by Professor G. William Skinner in his "compliance cycle" model of rural political movements in Communist China. See Skinner, "Compliance and Leadership in Rural Communist China: A Cyclical Theory" (unpublished paper delivered at the 1965 Annual Meeting of the American Political Science Association, Washington, D.C., September 8–11, 1965). What the present argument suggests is that the phenomenon of "cycles (seasonal) *within* cycles (aggregate power mix)" may be a more or less constant feature of rural mass movements in China.

previous "radical" conception of the aims and instrumentalities of the Cultural Revolution; on the contrary, this decision should more properly be viewed as the very embodiment of a long-standing and inherently pragmatic CCP policy of attempting to ensure the continuity of vital productive processes during the busiest agricultural seasons.

Moreover, it is clear that the situation in *urban* China in the first half of September 1966 was extremely tense and confused. As a result, even the most ardent proponents of "revolutionary chaos" were probably not unreceptive to the idea of temporarily narrowing the scope of conflict so as to regain some measure of control over events which were threatening, even at this early stage, to get out of hand. Finally, it should be noted that a recurrent tendency of CCP policy-makers has been to conduct mass political movements "group by group and stage by stage," with different "key point" areas and objectives being pinpointed for action at successive stages. Since the rectification of "bourgeois power-holders" in provincial and municipal-level Party and governmental organs had been identified as the "key point" of the Cultural Revolution in the late summer of 1966, it is not surprising that "great debates" in the countryside should be deferred until a later stage of the revolution.

For all of these reasons, caution should be exercised before imputing "conservative" or "anti-Maoist" motives to those Party leaders who were instrumental in promulgating the new slogan, "grasp revolution, promote production." Nor is it necessary to posit the existence of a high level of intra-Party conflict on this question. Not only is there no concrete evidence pointing to such a conflict, but "radicals" and "moderates" alike may well have agreed on the advisability of postponing "great debates" in the countryside—though for manifestly different reasons.[41]

One week after the new policy of temporarily suspending mass movements in the countryside was announced, the Party Central Committee

[41] Throughout the Cultural Revolution, Premier Chou En-lai was the major Party spokesman for the "moderate" position in the ongoing dialectic between revolutionary and productive priorities. Chou's role in the early stages of the movement is examined in detail by Thomas Robinson in Chapter 4 of this volume. For the text of Chou's speech of September 15, 1966, in which he defended the policy of temporarily suspending "outside interference" in rural politics by itinerant urban Red Guards, see *Hung-ch'i*, No. 12 (September 17, 1966) pp. 8–9. As for the remainder of Peking's top-level Cultural Revolutionary elites, we have only a fragment from the pen of Mao Tse-tung on the subject of "grasping revolution and promoting production" and a few casual remarks by such figures as Lin Piao, Ch'en Po-ta and K'ang Sheng—none of which sheds substantial light on the question of the presence or absence of significant controversy in this period.

issued a formal five-point directive entitled "Regulations Concerning the Great Cultural Revolution in Rural Districts Below the County Level." [42] Although ostensibly reinforcing the provisions contained in the September 7 *Jen-min Jih-pao* editorial, the new directive served to alter once again the dominant thrust of the earlier policy guidelines in a number of important ways.

The September 7 editorial had stated that urban Red Guards were not to be sent to, and the Cultural Revolution was not to be launched in, those rural units where "original arrangements for the Four Cleanups movement are considered appropriate by the masses." The new Central Committee directive, however, explicitly took the power of such determination away from the masses and put it squarely into the hands of Party committees at the provincial and sub-provincial levels: "*Except for separate arrangements made by provincial and district Party committees, students and Red Guards from Peking and other localities shall not go to rural organs below the county level, communes, or production brigades to exchange revolutionary experiences or take part in debates.*" [43] The distinction here, though ostensibly slight, was later to prove significant. For by granting to entrenched Party officials full discretionary power to dispatch "outside interference" to the countryside, the September 14 directive indirectly opened the door to a host of defensive tactics employed by apprehensive Party powerholders in the provinces either to suppress, preempt, or redirect the "spearhead" of Cultural Revolutionary struggle.

We have already seen evidence of how local powerholders in rural China allegedly distorted the slogan "grasp revolution, promote production" in order to suppress radical dissent. In addition, Party officials in some areas took advantage of the discretionary powers granted them under the terms of the September 14 directive to dispatch investigatory "work teams" to rural units where rebel insurgency was threatening to get out of hand. These work teams, being the creatures of entrenched Party interests, were understandably oriented primarily toward the defense of the political status quo. [44]

---

[42] The text of this directive, dated September 14, 1966, appears in *CCP Documents of the Great Proletarian Cultural Revolution, 1966–1967* (Hong Kong, 1968) pp. 77–80.

[43] *Ibid.*, Article I (emphasis added).

[44] This conclusion is fully consistent with what is known of the activities of Party-led work teams in China's urban educational and cultural institutions in the early summer of 1966, when the work team personnel generally opted for the "conserva-

RICHARD BAUM

One report, from rural Kweichow, described the "counterrevolutionary" activities of a provincial-level work team in the following terms:

Toward the end of 1966 . . . a work team directly controlled by the handful of capitalist-roaders in the provincial Party committee was sent to [our] brigade in the hope of . . . organizing the members of the brigade to protect the capitalist roaders. They thought that because [brigade Party branch secretary] Wang Chung-chen had been admitted to the Party with their approval she would undoubtedly support them. The work team tried to deceive the masses by spreading rumors, turning things upside down, and doing all they could to confuse the distinction between revolution and counterrevolution.[45]

In Lankao county, Honan (the home district of the controversial martyred Party cadre, Chiao Yü-lu), it was similarly reported that a work team, sent to a local production team by "agents of China's Khrushchev" in the county Party committee, had attempted to suppress local Red Guards who rose to defend the late Chiao Yü-lu and his supporters against the deprecations of "class enemies" and "bourgeois powerholders" in the area.[46]

Although the stereotyped polemicism of these reports is undoubtedly misleading, there is no reason to question the verisimilitude of the events described in them. Certainly many work teams *were* dispatched to conflict-ridden rural and urban units in the autumn of 1966. And judging from subsequent attempts by Revolutionary Rebel organizations to "reverse the verdicts" imposed by these work teams, the main thrust of the latter's intervention had been to defend entrenched Party interests against all manner of rebel insurgency, whether from above or from below.[47]

In addition to delegating the power to dispatch rural investigatory personnel to Party committees at the provincial and sub-provincial levels, the Central Committee directive of September 14 also stipulated, for the

tive" course of supporting incumbent cadres against student insurgents. On the question of the nature and manifestations of cadre conservatism in Communist China, see Ezra F. Vogel, "From Revolutionary to Semi-Bureaucrat: The 'Regularization' of Cadres," *The China Quarterly*, No. 29 (January–March 1967) pp. 36–60; also Michel Oksenberg, "The Institutionalization of the Chinese Communist Revolution," *The China Quarterly*, No. 36 (October–December 1968) pp. 61–92.

[45] *NCNA* (Peking), February 25, 1968; see also *Peking Review*, No. 27 (July 5, 1968) pp. 14–16.

[46] *Peking Review*, No. 9 (March 1, 1968) pp. 7–10.

[47] This subject is treated in greater detail in pages 398–399.

first time, that "cadres below the county level . . . who have been appointed by higher-level Party committees or governmental organs should not be directly 'removed from office' by the masses."[48] What this meant, in effect, was that the "principal" Party cadres at the commune and production brigade levels (including Party committee and branch secretaries, commune and brigade chairmen, militia commanders, chief accountants, and Women's Federation and Youth League directors) were to be generally exempted from mass struggle and criticism during the busy autumn harvest season, when their specialized leadership skills were needed to ensure harmony and coordination.

A third (and closely related) area in which the September 14 directive served to modify or revise previously articulated Party policies on the Cultural Revolution in the countryside concerned how to "restore and strengthen the leading force" in those rural communes and production brigades where leadership had become paralyzed as a result of the initial wave of "great debates" in the late summer. The problem of leadership paralysis was particularly acute in those suburban areas which had experienced Red Guard insurgency; and reports of cadre demoralization and unwillingness to assume active responsibility over production (for fear of inviting further criticism and thus losing face) were numerous in this period. As one disillusioned and dispirited young rural cadre reportedly put it, "Of all possible mistakes, the worst mistake is to hold power."[49]

In order to combat the problem of leadership paralysis, the September 14 directive also instructed rural Party organs below the county level to "immediately readjust the cadres" (that is, to transfer administrative personnel to those areas most severely affected).[50] Finally, in order to augment rural productive labor forces during the autumn harvest season, the September 14 directive called for the mobilization of all available urban Red Guards and other "revolutionary students and teachers" to go to the countryside "to take part in labor and assist in autumn harvesting in an organized manner."[51]

With revolutionary "great debates" officially suspended for the duration

---

[48] CCP Documents, op. cit., p. 80, Article IV.

[49] Jen-min Jih-pao, March 10, 1967. The original Chinese version of this lamentation, which unfortunately loses a great deal of its poignancy in translation, is: "Ch'ien ts'o wan ts'o, chiu ts'o tsai 'tang-ch'üan' liang-ko tzu shang." (Literally: "A thousand mistakes, ten thousand mistakes, the real mistake lies in the words 'to hold power.'")

[50] CCP Documents, op. cit., p. 80, Article V.

[51] Ibid., Article II.

of the autumn harvest season, new policy guidelines were promulgated concerning how the tasks of "grasping revolution" and "promoting production" were to be coordinated and carried out simultaneously in the countryside. For instance, a *Hung-ch'i* editorial published on September 17 called for the establishment of a "suitable division of labor": "Two appropriate leading groups are needed; one mainly in charge of the Cultural Revolution, the other in charge of production. . . . Unified leadership over these two groups is necessary; they should not act separately or on their own." [52] Subsequent clarification of how this division of labor was to be properly coordinated, and how overall leadership was to be exercised over the "two groups," was provided when the experiences of a production brigade in Hopeh province were given nationwide publicity in early October:

To grasp revolution and promote production, and to guarantee their double victory, we have made a proper division of labor and suitable arrangement of the leadership force. From the production brigade to the production team levels, two groups are organized in each unit, *under the unified guidance of the Party branch.* One group mainly tackles the Four Cleanups campaign and studies and promotes the 16 Articles. The other mainly devotes itself to production and construction. *Thus, the high morale of the people brought out in the revolution is channeled to the production struggle.* [53]

Although the official policy of the period was one which ostensibly gave equal emphasis to revolution and production, the above-quoted statement, when viewed in the context of the time, could only be interpreted to mean that top priority was to be given to production, with the main purpose of "grasping revolution" being to mobilize the peasantry to take a more active and self-conscious role in productive tasks. Thus, the slogan "grasp revolution, promote production" was interpreted to mean, in effect, "grasp revolution *in order* to promote production." Moreover, that overall coordination of both aspects was to be provided "under the unified guidance of the Party branch" could only serve to reinforce the supremacy of incumbent powerholders in the villages. As long as local Party officials continued to exercise ultimate authority over both revolutionary activities and productive enterprises, it could be safely assumed that the former would be de-emphasized in the name of the latter.

[52] *Hung-ch'i*, No. 12 (September 17, 1966) pp. 13–14.
[53] *Hung-ch'i*, No. 13 (October 1, 1966) pp. 13–15 (emphasis added).

The final blow to revolution-minded Red Guards in the countryside came on September 19, when a *Jen-min Jih-pao* editorial reprinted an obscure passage from the pen of Chairman Mao, dredged up for the occasion: "To ensure the completion of farm work in good time, it is necessary to permit peasants to cancel, during the busy farming season, all meetings or gatherings which are unrelated to agriculture." The editorial went on to restate existing policy concerning temporary suspension of the Four Cleanups, and went one step farther by ordering the immediate cessation of all activities related to the destruction of the "four olds," with the added stipulation that such activities could be resumed "in the slack season at a later date." [54]

With the Four Cleanups campaign, Red Guard-inspired "great debates," destruction of the "four olds," and all other (actual or potential) sources of political turmoil uniformly enjoined by official decree, it appeared for a short time in the latter part of September that a situation of "normalcy" might return to rural China. But social order and discipline were more easily restored on paper than in practice. Once the Red Guard genie had been let out of the jar, it proved most difficult to coax him back inside.

THE STRUGGLE INTENSIFIES: OCTOBER–DECEMBER 1966

Residual manifestations of both intramural (localized) and extramural (rural-urban) conflict continued to find expression in a number of suburban villages throughout the autumn harvest season. Although the regime's mid-September drive to curtail revolutionary activity apparently succeeded in preserving political tranquility in those communes and production brigades that had not experienced significant turbulence in the previous period, the political pot continued to simmer—and on occasion to boil over—in those relatively few rural districts which had been directly affected by the first wave of Red Guard "great debates." In these latter areas, an initial polarization of forces had already occurred, and preliminary battle lines had been drawn.

A major aspect of the October–December stage of the Cultural Revolution involved the attempt by urban Party politicians and mass organiza-

---

[54] *Jen-min Jih-pao*, September 19, 1966. On the question of overlap and potential conflict between the Socialist Education Movement and the Cultural Revolution in this period, see Baum, "Revolution and Reaction," *loc. cit.*

tions to expand their respective power bases by enlisting the active, partisan support of suburban cadres and peasants.[55] In the struggle to dislodge (or defend) incumbent Party officials, one key to success was the ability of the various contestants to gain constituency support at the grass roots level.

A number of reports concerning the formation of municipal-rural, county-rural or provincial-rural proto-coalitions (or tactical alliances) help to shed light on the methods adopted by rival groups and factions to consolidate their constituency support and further their respective claims to "revolutionary" authority. In Yangchow, Kiangsu Province, for example, it was reported that the armed militia members of a suburban production brigade had been assembled by the brigade Party branch on October 1, 1966 (National Day), and ordered to forcibly suppress those "ungrateful" Red Guards and revolutionary peasants who had opposed the municipal Party committee.[56] In Chengtu, alleged "bourgeois power-holders" in the provincial Party committee (located in Chengtu) attempted to recruit local peasants to "encircle the city from the country-side" and counterattack those Red Guards and Revolutionary Rebels who were currently "bombarding the [provincial] headquarters."[57] In Chang-kang township, Kiangsi Province (an old revolutionary base area and county seat of Hsing-kuo county), more than four hundred peasants from a local production brigade were reportedly recruited to march on the county Party committee headquarters to struggle against a handful of "bourgeois powerholders."[58] And finally, in suburban Hofei, Anhwei Province, it was alleged that certain "mandarins" (of unspecified organizational affiliation) had "incited large numbers of misled commune members to parade and demonstrate in the city to protect the provincial and municipal Party committees."[59]

These and other similar incidents suggest that embattled Party officials in China's provincial capitals, municipalities, and county towns, in order to bring "countervailing power" to bear on insurgent rebel organizations

[55] In the following discussion, the terms "urban politicians," "urban powerholders," and so on are meant to refer not only to municipal level Party personnel, but to provincial and county level officials as well, since the latter were also headquartered in urban areas.

[56] *Jen-min Jih-pao,* February 20, 1967.

[57] *Radio Chengtu,* Szechwan, April 10, 1968.

[58] *NCNA,* Peking, October 31, 1968.

[59] *Radio Hofei,* Anhwei, February 2, 1967.

(and thereby save their own political skins), hastily recruited sympathetic or mercenary "volunteers" in suburban communes and production brigades to help turn the tide of battle. The Revolutionary Rebels, in turn, finding themselves subjected to organized counterattacks, adopted similar recruiting tactics (utilizing primarily alienative, rather than moral or remunerative incentives) to bolster their own forces. In this manner, an essentially urban-centered series of political confrontations enlarged to encompass significant numbers of suburban peasants, cadres, and militiamen.

This process of progressive conflict diffusion may be systematically described in the form of a general hypothesis: *Those actors who perceive themselves to be in imminent danger of defeat in struggles for political survival are compelled sequentially to enlarge the scope of conflict in order to avert defeat and secure a more favorable balance of forces.*[60] If the desire to enlarge the scope of conflict, and thereby alter the balance of forces, constituted the "final cause" of the urban-to-rural conflict diffusion process in the autumn of 1966, then the "sufficient cause" of that process lay in the potential mobilization capacities of Party powerholders and their revolutionary antagonists, respectively. (The "formal cause," of course, was the Party center's August 1966 call to "bombard the headquarters.")

One obvious advantage which the powerholders enjoyed from the outset was the built-in advantage of official patronage, both political and economic. Like their counterparts in any hierarchical organization, Party officials at the provincial, municipal, and county levels in China exercised considerable discretionary powers over the recruitment, job assignments, and promotions of their lower-level subordinates.[61] It is hardly surprising

[60] This hypothesis was adapted from the concept of the "socialization of conflict" formulated by Professor E. E. Schattschneider in his provocative essay *The Semi-Sovereign People* (New York, 1960) pp. 36–43. Although this concept was articulated on the basis of Professor Schattschneider's observations of pressure group politics in the American political system, it is, *mutatis mutandis,* apposite to widely differing situations of political conflict. In its original form the "socialization of conflict" hypothesis holds that "it is the weak, not the strong, who appeal to [the] public for relief. It is the weak who want to socialize conflict, i.e., to involve more and more people in the conflict until the balance of forces is changed." (*Ibid.,* pp. 40–41.)

[61] Michel Oksenberg has described the vulnerability of lower-level rural Party cadres to manipulation by their county-level superiors in terms suggestive of the range of resources potentially available to embattled urban powerholders in their effort to mobilize active support among their rural subalterns. While such vulnerability is by

that urban powerholders should use such discretionary powers to expand and consolidate the ranks of their supporters among Party officials in municipally administered suburban communes and production brigades (and, by direct extension, among the peasants who were subject to their authority).

We thus find numerous reports in the autumn of 1966 describing the attempts of provincial, county, and municipal Party officials either to remind suburban cadres (many of whom owed their Party membership or official appointments to higher level sponsorship) of the existence of old political debts; or, alternatively, to create new obligatory bonds by offering promises of rapid vertical mobility or other such "sugar-coated bullets" in exchange for pledges of active support.[62] In addition, there is evidence that by November 1966 urban powerholders began appealing directly to the material aspirations of suburban peasants. Authorizing the allocation and distribution of relatively large sums of "linking up money" (*ch'üan-lien fei*), Party officials in many areas encouraged (perhaps "bribed" is a better word) peasants to leave their production posts to stage counter-demonstrations against radical Red Guards and revolutionary rebels in the cities.[63] For their part, anti-establishment Red Guards and Revolutionary Rebel organizations in urban China responded in kind to the initial efforts at suburban conflict socialization on the part of their power-holding opponents. Although lacking the political and economic resource

---

no means one-sided, the initial advantages of the power to command, persuade, and reward compliant behavior undoubtedly accrued to higher-level powerholders vis-à-vis their lower-level subordinates. See Oksenberg, "The Institutionalization of the Chinese Communist Revolution," *op. cit.,* pp. 82–84.

[62] See, for example, *Hung-se Pao-tung, loc. cit.;* also *Jen-min Jih-pao,* February 20, 1967; Wylie, *loc. cit.; NCNA* (Peking), February 25, 1968; and *Peking Review,* No. 9 (March 1, 1968) pp. 7–10. While empirical research on the nature and durability of vertical (hierarchical) ties of personal and organizational loyalty in Chinese bureaucratic politics is painfully lacking, it is nevertheless virtually certain that such ties do exist, and that they tend over time to create bonds of mutual interdependence between superior and subordinate. Fortunately, we do not need to resort to invocation of the Confucian moral precept of the reciprocity of obligations between superior (to protect and provide for) and subordinate (to serve and obey) in order to validate this assertion. A large corpus of behavioral research is available on the phenomenon of hierarchical cohesion in bureaucratic organizations. See, for example, Amitai Etzioni, *A Comparative Analysis of Complex Organizations* (New York, 1961), Chapter Eight and *passim;* also, Robert Presthus, *The Organizational Society* (New York, 1962), especially Chapter Five.

[63] See, for example, *NCNA* (Peking), February 9, 1967, and October 14 and 31, 1968.

base of their opponents, the rebels were able to capitalize on the one major asset which worked exclusively to their advantage: latent rural discontent with the status quo.

The sources of such discontent were manifold and they cut across the entire spectrum of rural socio-economic and political classes and strata. In suburban communes, by virtue of their proximity to and direct administration by municipal Party authorities, a major focal point of local disaffection centered around the so-called "worker-peasant system"—the system of temporary contract labor under which large numbers of peasants were periodically and in rotation recruited to perform urban-industrial jobs at substandard wages and under poor living conditions during slack agricultural seasons. Permanent industrial workers thus displaced were assigned to work as agricultural laborers in rural communes—with the burden of their wage payments, medical care, and welfare benefits being assumed by the communes, rather than by the state, as before. Understandably, the net effect of this system was to alienate both the displaced industrial workers and their underpaid peasant surrogates. Opposition to the "worker-peasant" system thus became a major rallying point for anti-establishmentarian agitation in China's rural suburbs.[64]

Another exploitable source of latent rural resentment against urban powerholders was the alienation felt by "intellectual youths" (middle school and college students) who had been sent down to the countryside to be employed as agricultural laborers in the massive *hsia-hsiang* ("down to the village") movement of the early and mid-1960s. By the Party's own estimate, there were approximately forty million such "intellectual youths" working in the Chinese countryside on the eve of the Cultural Revolution.[65] The frustrations and disillusionment experienced by these cultured youngsters when confronted with the prospect of having to spend the rest of their lives performing burdensome and distasteful farm labor had been a cause of serious concern to the Maoist regime for several years.

[64] For a detailed examination of the operation of this system, and the sources and types of discontent engendered thereby, see "Sources of Labor Discontent in China: The Worker-Peasant System," *Current Scene,* Vol. 6, No. 5 (March 15, 1968). For a first-hand report of opposition to the worker-peasant system in suburban Shanghai in the fall of 1966, see Wylie, *loc. cit.*

[65] *Jen-min Jih-pao,* December 9, 1965. The *hsia-hsiang* movement should not be confused with the *hsia-fang* movement of the Great Leap era; the latter was directed exclusively at cadres, while the former dealt with intellectual youths, unemployed urbanites, and so-called "social youths" (juvenile delinquents).

With the initiation of the Cultural Revolution, these disaffected youths were readily politicized and their alienation channeled into opposition to the urban Party machine, for municipal and county level Party committees had been directly responsible for assigning the "intellectual youths" to the countryside in the first place.[66]

A third source of latent rural discontent was the movement toward imposing new restrictions on the cultivation of private plots, which had been officially (though not uniformly) underway since the late summer of 1966.[67] Red Guards in some suburban areas were quick to foresee the alienative potential of such a movement, and therefore attempted in some instances to place the onus for such new restrictions squarely on the shoulders of local powerholders. For example, Red Guards in one suburban Peking production brigade charged that a local powerholder, instigated and protected by "counterrevolutionary revisionists" in the municipal Party committee, had issued an order to "return all private plots to the production teams." Having made this accusation, the Red Guards then bitterly denounced the order (and its alleged sponsors) for having "turned the spearhead of struggle against the masses"—whereupon the young rebels set out to mobilize the hostility of the peasants and direct it against both the local powerholder and his municipal overlords.[68]

A fourth source of latent suburban discontent was the desire for political restitution or revenge on the part of those "five category elements" and former basic-level rural cadres who had been "labeled," struggled against, dismissed from office, or otherwise punished during the course of the Four Cleanups campaign. Municipal Party committees had directly controlled the investigative, and disciplinary activities of the work teams which carried out the Socialist Education Movement in suburban counties and communes. And those cadres and peasants who had suffered political or economic sanctions during the movement had an understandable desire

[66] On the nature and manifestations of discontent engendered among "intellectual youths" by the hsia-hsiang system, see, inter alia, Radio Shanghai, February 8, 1967; Jen-min Jih-pao, February 20, 1967; Hsing-tao Jih-pao (Hong Kong), December 14, 1967, and March 5, 1968. On the use of repressive or diversionary measures by local powerholders to prevent "intellectual youths" from participating in Cultural Revolution demonstrations and "great debates," see Ko-ming Ch'ing-nien (Canton), November 10, 1967, in SCMP 4102, pp. 6-8; also, Wylie, loc. cit.

[67] See NCNA (Peking), September 14, 1966.

[68] Nung-min Yun-tung, February 22, 1967, op. cit., pp. 9-10. In a similar case, also reported from suburban Peking, "capitalist-roaders" and "five category elements" were charged by Red Guards with the unlikely crime of having advocated "egalitarianism" in land distribution. Jen-min Jih-pao. March 8, 1967.

to see a "reversal of verdicts" in their own cases. Hence they, too, were potential allies of urban-centered rebel organizations.[69]

A final source of rural opposition to urban powerholders lay in the opportunism and personal ambition of those low-ranking basic-level cadres (and other would-be powerholders) in the suburban countryside who cherished hopes of attaining rapid upward political mobility by riding the winds of revolutionary change. Political purges in communist societies provide unparalleled opportunities for career advancement to those who are adept at gauging the velocity and direction of such winds. Thus, the desire to participate in the post-revolutionary division of political spoils undoubtedly provided a prime incentive for at least some suburban cadres and peasants to join with urban rebels in "bombarding the headquarters."[70]

All of these factors combined to facilitate the relatively rapid diffusion of urban-centered political disputes to the suburban countryside in the early autumn of 1966.[71]

[69] See, for example, *Jen-min Jih-pao*, March 8, 1967. The movement for "reversal of verdicts" (*fan-an*) became so widespread and acute by January 1967 that the Party center was forced to issue a directive expressly prohibiting all such agitation. See pages 416–419.

[70] While it is extremely difficult to isolate and assess the importance of the factor of opportunism in the composite mixture of motivations which contributed to the formation of both pro- and anti-establishment coalitions in China in this (or any other) period of the Cultural Revolution, there can be little doubt that opportunistic considerations did play a substantial part in the selection or rejection of alternative strategies of action by peripheral (or secondary) participants in the conflict. Consider, for example, the case of a deputy commune leader (*fu she-chang*) in suburban Canton, as related to the author by a young intellectual who escaped from the commune in question to Hong Kong in January 1967: "XXX (the deputy commune leader) was a former high-ranking colleague of Canton Mayor Tseng Sheng in the Canton municipal Party Committee. In 1960 he was *hsia-fang*'ed to my commune. Ever since that time he has cherished the ambition to return to his urban post. When Tseng Sheng and the Canton municipal Party committee came under Red Guard attack last fall, he saw his opportunity to be reinstated. He quickly allied himself (and his village subordinates) with the XXX Red Guards in Canton who were then "bombarding the headquarters.'" The tendency for self-interested, career-minded subordinates to denounce their superiors in the hope of gaining promotion was also a major unintended consequence of the Stalinist Great Purge of 1936–1938. As one cynical young Soviet refugee reportedly remarked: "The best way to get ahead is to inform on your superior. If he makes a mistake a political reason must be found for it . . . Your superior will be arrested and there is a place open. Who is to fill it? I, of course." Quoted in Zbigniew K. Brzezinski, *The Permanent Purge* (Cambridge, Mass., 1956), p. 89.

[71] It should be noted that the various sources of alienation discussed above bore only a very loose relationship to the existence of pro- and anti-Maoist ideological

Alarmed by the potentiality for chaos inherent in the untrammeled process of suburban conflict diffusion, Peking attempted in mid-November to further clarify and define the acceptable limits of "grasping revolution." Breaking a long period of official silence on the subject, a *Jen-min Jih-pao* editorial of November 10 ordered rural peasants and cadres to stay at their production posts, observe labor discipline, and not go to other (urban) localities to "exchange revolutionary experiences." Urban Red Guards were again told to refrain from intervening in the internal affairs of communes and production brigades. "Any action which affects production," warned the editorial, "may bring about grave consequences." [72] In calling for a "summing up" of experiences gained to date, the editorial officially confirmed for the first time (albeit in circumlocutory fashion) the existence of serious unintended consequences of Cultural Revolutionary "spill-over" in the countryside. The editorial thus spoke disparagingly of such adverse phenomena as "obstructionism," "suppression of the masses," "actions of assault and revenge," "abdication of production leadership," and "counterposing the Cultural Revolution against the development of production." As might be expected, all such phenomena were attributed to the "evil influence of the bourgeois reactionary line" as promoted by the ever-present, ever-malignant "handful of Party persons in authority taking the capitalist road." [73]

More significant, however, was the fact that despite the renewed emphasis on maintaining labor discipline, strengthening local production leadership and minimizing the disruptive effects of outside agitation, the November 10 editorial did *not* repeat earlier, conditional injunctions against launching the Cultural Revolution during the autumn harvest season. On the contrary, it was now stated (for the first time) that "the Great Proletarian Cultural Revolution should be carried out *in both urban and rural* areas actively and step by step." [74] To be sure, revolution was to be grasped by the peasantry "off duty and in their spare time"; but even this caveat betrayed a significant retreat from the near-total moratorium on revolutionary agitation which had been in effect since mid-September.

The most likely explanation for this partial *volte face* lay in the previously noted fact that under the terms of the earlier September 14

cleavages within the CCP. This would help to explain the apparent anomaly of "radical" Red Guards recruiting suburban supporters on the basis of a "conservative" appeal to peasant self-interest.

[72] *Jen-min Jih-pao*, November 10, 1966.
[73] *Ibid.*
[74] *Ibid.* (emphasis added).

Central Committee directive, entrenched Party powerholders at the provincial and sub-provincial levels had been granted sole discretionary powers to make "special arrangements" for dispatching outside personnel (work teams) to the countryside to launch, investigate, and direct the Cultural Revolution in certain selected rural communes and production brigades. But with their own vital interests at stake in preserving the status quo, these Party powerholders (and the work teams at their disposal) more often than not used such discretionary powers to suppress, or launch counterattacks against, local Red Guards and Revolutionary Rebels.

The November 10 *Jen-min Jih-pao* editorial reference to such phenomena as "obstructionism," "suppression of the masses," and "actions of assault and revenge" no doubt referred at least in part to the repressive actions of Party-led work teams (actions which were subsequently condemned as "hitting hard at the many to protect the few"). And since the power to suppress anti-establishment criticism constituted, in effect, the power to suppress the Cultural Revolution itself, the Maoist leadership in Peking probably felt compelled to remove such power from the hands of entrenched Party officials. Hence the November 10 decision to universally carry out the Cultural Revolution in the countryside "actively and step by step." [75]

The mid-November decision was also related to an overall leftward swing which occurred in Peking in late October and early November. Toward the end of October, Liu Shao-ch'i and Teng Hsiao-p'ing were for the first time singled out for intensive criticism and "struggle" at a Central Committee Work Conference.[76] At the same time, such radical proponents of "extensive democracy" as Ch'en Po-ta and Chiang Ch'ing were struggling to gain ascendence over such "moderates" as Chou En-lai within Mao's immediate Cultural Revolutionary entourage. Chou, it will be remembered, had in mid-September vigorously defended the policy of insulating the rural areas from the impact of the Cultural Revolution. He, more than any other single individual, had been identified with the slogan "grasp revolution, promote production." By early November, however, he quite probably found himself swimming against the tide. In any

[75] For further discussion and documentation of the activities of rural work teams in the latter half of 1966, see Baum, "Revolution and Reaction," *loc. cit.*

[76] See, for example, Ch'en Po-ta's speech of October 25, 1966, in *Ko-ming Kung-jen Pao,* January 12, 1967. It is significant that the first official critiques of Liu and Teng contained explicit references to serious "mistakes" committed by Party work teams in the previous period.

event, his speeches began to take on a more radical note at about that time.[77]

Also in early November, Lin Piao publicly and with great fanfare declared his full support for the universal unfolding of the so-called "four bigs"—big blooming and contending, big character posters, big debates, and big democracy.[78] Thus, for the first time since early September, "grasping revolution" and "promoting production" were placed on relatively equal footing. The Cultural Revolution was not to be permitted to interfere with local production arrangements, but neither was it to be suppressed or halted in the name of production. Although this swing to the left was accompanied by renewed injunctions against the use of violent, coercive tactics by Red Guards and revolutionary rebels, Mao's "little generals" and their worker and peasant allies were now to be permitted to resume the task of "bombarding the [local] headquarters." [79]

As we have seen, the period from mid-September to early November witnessed the diffusion of extramural, urban-centered political conflicts to a certain (indeterminate) number of municipally administered suburban communes and production brigades. Now, in mid-November, the lifting of previous conditional restraints on intramural "great debates" led to the renewal and intensification of localized, intra-village disputes and factional conflicts. Thus, for the first time, *local* Party officials in China's rural suburbs found themselves the prime targets of revolutionary criticism. This change of emphasis is clearly reflected in the following passage from a Red Guard newspaper published in suburban Canton:

In the first stage, from July to October 1966 . . . the main tasks were the destruction of the "four olds" and the controlling of "five category elements." *The powerholders were not yet panicked by these activities. . . .*

In the second stage, from November [1966] to February [1967], the [revolutionary peasants] . . . precipitated an unprecedented major revolution in the rural areas within a relatively short period. *Powerholders*

[77] See Robinson, *op. cit.* It is ironic, in view of Chou's association with the slogan "grasp revolution, promote production," that the *Jen-min Jih-pao* editorial of November 10 was entitled "More on Grasping Revolution and Promoting Production."

[78] *NCNA* (Peking), November 3, 1966.

[79] For a general review of the main trends of this period, see Philip Bridgham, "Mao's 'Cultural Revolution': Origins and Development," *The China Quarterly*, No. 29 (January–March 1967) pp. 32–34.

within the Party now abhorred these revolutionary peasants, and secretly planned a "post-autumn reckoning" with them.[80]

In line with the new policy of extending the Cultural Revolution to the countryside, the period November–December 1966 witnessed the proliferation and numerical expansion of indigenous revolutionary and quasi-revolutionary mass organizations in suburban communes and production brigades. In the outskirts of Canton, for example, rural mass organizations with such exotic titles as After the British Quellers of San-Yüan Li, Red Guard Force of Sha-Ho, and Red Peasants' Friends of Hsiao-P'ing were established in this period, with a combined peasant membership reportedly numbering in the tens of thousands.[81] And in suburban Hofei, a Revolutionary Rebel Squadron which started with an initial membership of ten in late August had expanded its organizational base to include over three thousand peasants by the end of the year.[82]

Unlike the September–October "high tide" of extramural conflict socialization, intra-village organizational activities in the November–December period tended to involve primarily localized issues and cleavages. Although ostensibly polarized around the universalistic (Maoist) political criterion of struggle between "proletarian revolutionaries" and "bourgeois powerholders," in actual practice rural mass organizations frequently tended to promote narrow, particularistic interests.

The range of local interests (both latent and manifest) which sought— and found—organized expression in the countryside in this period was understandably broad. More important, such interests tended to cut across (and thereby obscure), rather than reinforce the major lines of doctrinal cleavage in the "struggle between two roads and two lines." So long as all such interests routinely and of necessity "waved the red flag," however, it was extremely difficult to determine which red flags were genuine and which counterfeit.[83] As an illustration of the process of the spontaneous

---

[80] *Hung-se Pao-tung, loc. cit.* (emphasis added).

[81] *Ibid.*

[82] *Radio Hofei,* Anhwei, February 2, 1967.

[83] Prior to the advent of the Cultural Revolution, and in its initial stages, it was widely assumed by the Maoists that "class interests" and "self-interest" coincided. When it became clear, toward the end of 1966, that this was not always the case, and that self-interest frequently tended to interfere with and obfuscate class (or public) interest, the slogan "fight self-interest, establish the public interest" (*p'o ssu, li kung*) was promulgated. Subsequently, the notion of the merging of individual and public interests was denounced by the Maoists as "bourgeois claptrap" and was attributed

aggregation and articulation of these particularistic interests, the following
first-hand report from suburban Shanghai is highly revealing:

A host of fairly small organizations, all claiming to be genuine revolutionary groups, and all representing quite specific social elements, suddenly sprang up during November and December. Instead of broad mass
organizations representing the peasants' political interests as a whole,
there appeared organizations of temporary and contractual rural workers,
former Shanghai residents now employed in the commune, army veterans,
and so on, all pressing the local Party committee for some improvement
in their economic position.[84]

Other descriptions of incipient "pluralism" and special interest promotion in this period shed further light on the nature of extant socio-
economic and political cleavages in the countryside. We have already
examined the case of the brigade Party branch chairman in suburban
Peking who, when confronted by local Red Guard opposition, attempted
to bring "countervailing power" to bear on his critics by creating his own
organization of Royalist Guards, which included a number of local cadres and their dependents.[85] Also from suburban Peking came the allegation that local victims of the earlier Four Cleanups movement in a
certain production brigade had banded together in the autumn of 1966
to form a Red Flag Struggle Brigade for the purpose of agitating for a
"reversal of verdicts."[86] Similar reports of organized attempts on the part
of various and diverse "interest groups," donning the guise of proletarian
revolutionaries, to promote their own particularistic ends came from rural
communes in Tsinghai, Kiangsi, Kiangsu, Liaoning, Anhwei, Kweichow,
and Kwangtung provinces.[87]

Among the various tactics adopted by newly organized local interest
groups, the most favored, perhaps, were those involving appeals to the

---

to arch-revisionist Liu Shao-ch'i. See, for example, *Peking Review*, No. 30 (July 26,
1968) p. 26.

[84] Wylie, *op. cit.*, p. 465.

[85] See above, p. 381.

[86] *Jen-min Jih-pao*, March 8, 1967.

[87] The sources by province are as follows: For Tsinghai, *Radio Sining*, Tsinghai,
March 23, 1967. For Kiangsi, NCNA (Peking), October 14, 1968. For Kiangsu,
Nung-ts'un Ch'ing-nien, No. 18 (September 25, 1967), in URS, Vol. 49, No. 10
(November 3, 1967) p. 133. For Liaoning, NCNA (Peking), September 28, 1968. For
Anhwei, *Radio Hofei*, Anhwei, February 2, 1967. For Kweichow, *Peking Review*,
No. 27 (July 5, 1968) pp. 15–16. For Kwangtung, *Hung-se Pao-tung*, *loc. cit.*

material interests of local peasants. In a process not unlike machine politics in the United States, various localized "revolutionary" groups and factions in the countryside strove to gain constituency support by bribing, cajoling, or otherwise bargaining with the local "electorate."

In a pastoral production brigade in suburban Sining, Tsinghai Province, for example, leaders of a so-called August 18 Red Guard Combat Detachment allegedly sought mass support by dividing among their sheepherding followers more than four thousand catties (3,600 lbs.) of animal fodder.[88] In a suburban Shanghai commune, besieged power-holders reportedly distributed over 10,000 yüan (4,200 U.S. dollars) to various groups of local dissident elements to buy off their opposition and, in addition, released "large sums of money . . . to the peasants in the form of extra-generous year-end bonuses." [89] And in Lotien county, Kweichow Province, a suburban Red Rebel Squad allegedly sought to gain peasant support by inciting commune members to divide up public accumulation funds and grain reserves and distribute collectively raised pigs to individual households.[90]

The motives of "economism" and opportunistic self-aggrandizement thus combined with the motives of political survival and self-preservation to significantly distort the main lines of "struggle between two roads and two lines" in the Chinese countryside. And when, as in many cases, the mobilization of intramural particularistic interests overlapped with the process of extramural conflict diffusion, the resulting configuration of forces in suburban communes and production brigades became extremely complex.

If politics ordinarily makes strange bedfellows, Cultural Revolution politics made some extraordinarily strange bedfellows. By December 1966, the ranks of the suburban Revolutionary Rebels had swelled to include dissident elements of all political persuasions, as various rural interests were drawn into the struggle either to overturn or make increasingly bold demands on local representatives of the existing (urban and suburban) power structure. And in some cases, a virtual "united front" was created between *genuine* radical anti-establishment elements, on the one hand, and a variety of self-interested, red flag-waving, "not-so-revolutionary rebels," on the other.[91]

[88] *Radio Sining,* Tsinghai, March 23, 1967.
[89] Wylie, *loc. cit.*
[90] *Radio Kweiyang,* Kweichow, December 19, 1967.
[91] This latter category would include such previously mentioned groups and strata

At the other end of the suburban political spectrum were arrayed a variety of groups and strata whose sole common interest apparently lay in defending the political status quo, or selected parts of it. These forces included, for obvious reasons, the majority of "principal" rural power-holders (such as commune- and brigade-level Party secretaries and chief administrative officers) and their families; those subordinate officials whose primary loyalties lay with their superiors (whether for reasons of political obligation or personal empathy); those ordinary peasants who had ties of kinship or other solidarity relationships (again, of either an obligatory or empathetic nature) with village leaders; and those more affluent or tradition-bound peasants who either possessed an economic stake in the status quo or had been alienated by the provocative (and, in many cases, violent) actions of the Red Guards in the initial campaign to destroy the "four olds." [92]

Elsewhere, I have attempted to describe the origins and early manifestations of factional conflict in rural China during the Cultural Revolution in terms of the cathartic release of pent-up personal (or group) frustrations, ambitions and antipathies, wherein private motives were rationalized, articulated, and acted out upon public objects—all in the name of officially sanctioned political and ideological principles.[93] If there is any validity to this notion, then some of the apparent anomalies of Cultural Revolution politics in this early period become somewhat less confusing and enigmatic. The fact that the Maoist leadership in Peking was unable (or perhaps unwilling) to perceive the full spectrum of motivational and behavioral bases of factional conflict (including calculative and instinc-

---

as retribution-minded former cadres and "five category elements" who had been purged or otherwise punished during the Four Cleanups movement; ambitious and opportunistic subaltern officials (or would-be officials) who cherished hopes of political mobility; temporary and contract laborers who wished to repeal the noxious "worker-peasant system"; "intellectual youths" who had a profound distaste for agricultural labor; and ordinary peasants who harbored personal or familial antipathies of one sort or another against local powerholders.

[92] Assuming that the motivations and priorities of the various participants in Cultural Revolution conflict are (at least in theory) "knowable" on the basis of their respective socio-economic and political interests, it then becomes possible in theory to replicate the dynamics of the process of (proto-) coalition formation and bargaining. All that is further required for such replication is knowledge of the situational parameters—or environmental constraints—that bound the various participants to a certain set (or sets) of "rules of the game" in any given political context. On the application of the theory of coalitions to situations of political conflict, see William H. Riker, *The Theory of Political Coalitions* (New Haven, 1962), Chapters 1 and 5.

[93] See Baum, "Revolution and Reaction," *loc. cit.*

tual, as well as politico-ideological factors) until it was too late was perhaps the greatest single flaw of the entire Cultural Revolution endeavor —its ultimate irony. The implications of this flaw were to be fully revealed a short time later, at the time of the ill-fated January Revolution of 1967.

THE JANUARY REVOLUTION

By mid-December of 1966, with the completion of what was officially described as a "bumper harvest" in rural China,[94] there was an obvious need for further clarification of Cultural Revolution policy in the countryside. The autumn harvest was over and the slack winter season had arrived; with peasant "spare time" in relatively great abundance, it could be inferred that the opportune moment for "grasping revolution" in the countryside was at hand. But one important question still remained unanswered: What sort of revolution—against whom and for what?

The first systematic attempt to answer this question was made by the Party Central Committee on December 15, 1966, in the form of a ten-point "(Draft) Directive of the Central Committee of the Chinese Communist Party on the Great Proletarian Cultural Revolution in the Countryside."[95] The overall thrust of the new directive was unmistakable: rural China was to undergo a thoroughgoing, mass-oriented political revolution; peasants (and particularly the poor and lower-middle peasants) were to establish their credentials as "masters of their own house" (*tang chia tso-chu*) by "educating themselves, liberating themselves, and rising to make revolution for themselves."[96]

No interference was to be brooked in the process of "grasping revolution." The "four bigs" were henceforth to be universally introduced in communes and production brigades, and rural powerholders were expressly prohibited from attacking, retaliating against, or deducting the work points of those peasants who voiced criticism or wrote big character posters against them.[97] In a similar vein, Party organs were now expressly prohibited from sending out supervisory work teams to guide (that is,

[94] NCNA (Peking), January 1, 1967. All available evidence tends to support the conclusion that the 1966 grain harvest was indeed fairly good—around 180 million tons. This, in turn, would tend to confirm our earlier observation concerning the limited impact of the Cultural Revolution on China's agricultural sector in 1966. See pages 471–474.
[95] CCP Documents, op. cit., pp. 137–142.
[96] Ibid., Article 2.
[97] Ibid., Articles 7 and 8.

suppress) the "big blooming and contending" of the "revolutionary masses."⁹⁸

Rural middle school students were given an extended vacation of six months to organize themselves into Red Guard detachments for the purpose of "exchanging revolutionary experiences" and destroying the "four olds."⁹⁹ Significantly, it was ordained that the sons and daughters of leading cadres in communes, production brigades, and production teams were not to be permitted to assume positions of responsibility in rural Red Guard organizations, with the added stipulation that young people of poor and lower-middle peasant origins should constitute the "backbone" (*ku-kan*) of the village Red Guards.¹⁰⁰

The most striking feature of the December 15 directive, however, was the total absence of any references to the leadership function of existing Party organs and management committees in the countryside. Earlier, it will be recalled, the twin tasks of "grasping revolution" and "promoting production" in the rural areas had been undertaken under the "unified leadership" of Party committees in the communes and production brigades. Now, however, existing Party organs were to be by-passed and supplanted by a new instrument of revolutionary political power, the "cultural revolution committee": "The authoritative organs leading the Cultural Revolution in the rural areas shall be the cultural revolution committees of poor and lower-middle peasants, which are democratically elected by poor and lower-middle peasant congresses."¹⁰¹ Similarly, leadership over "promoting production" was now taken out of the hands of the existing rural management committees: "After discussion by the masses, production leadership groups shall be reformed or replaced; these groups are to be responsible for production, distribution, procurement, and supply work."¹⁰²

---

⁹⁸ *Ibid.*, Article 2.
⁹⁹ *Ibid.*, Articles 6, 7, and 9.
¹⁰⁰ *Ibid.*, Article 6.
¹⁰¹ *Ibid.*, Article 5. The "poor and lower-middle peasant congresses" mentioned in this passage probably refer to the representative organs of the local peasants' associations which had been revived in the countryside during the Socialist Education Movement. See Baum and Teiwes, *Ssu-Ch'ing, op. cit.*, Appendix D.
¹⁰² *Ibid.* The term "production leadership groups" (*ling-tao sheng-ch'an te pan-tzu*) had first been used in place of the standard term "management committees" (*kuan-li wei-yüan-hui*) in a *Hung-ch'i* article of October 1, 1966, although the term more commonly used during the autumn harvest season was "promote production groups" (*ts'u sheng-ch'an te pan-tzu*). It is unclear from the text of the December 15 directive whether administrative cadres in commune and production brigade manage-

The main significance of the Central Committee directive of December 15 lay in the fact that previous restraints on mass political agitation in the villages were now clearly and unequivocally removed. Unlike the Socialist Education Movement, which had been a tightly controlled "revolution from above" (organized and led by the Party apparatus), the Cultural Revolution in the countryside now became a populistic "revolution from below," directed, as was soon to become apparent, against major segments of the rural Party apparatus itself.[103]

Just as the earlier *Jen-min Jih-pao* editorial of November 10 had signaled a tentative green light for quickening the tempo of local interest aggregation and articulation in suburban communes and production brigades, so the December 15 Central Committee directive was construed as a direct, militant call to *organized political action* throughout the countryside. Although the contents of the new directive were not made known until December 26, by early January 1967 the first convulsive effects of the new revolutionary edict were clearly in evidence, as an unprecedented wave of "red terror" swept through a large number of hitherto relatively tranquil rural communes.

Ostensibly freed from the often repressive political domination of local Party organs and work teams, and spurred on by the official call to "seize power" (*to-ch'üan*) issued by the Maoists shortly after the New Year, various dissident elements and "interest groups" in the countryside launched a series of violent attacks against rural powerholders of all kinds and at all levels in January and February 1967.

With the example of the "Shanghai storm" available as an officially sanctioned prototype of revolutionary power seizure, these dissident elements and "interest groups," acting out of a variety of motives, the lowest

---

ment committees were to be excluded from participation in the new production leadership groups, or whether the latter were simply to be "democratized" replicas of their forerunners. In theory, the September 14 prohibition against arbitrarily dismissing "principal" cadres who had been appointed by higher-level Party or state administrative bodies was not directly rescinded by the December 15 directive; thus the status of such cadres probably remained uncertain, at least for the time being.

[103] The December 15 directive called for the immediate and total incorporation of the Socialist Education Movement into the Cultural Revolution, with the added stipulation that all problems uncovered during the Four Cleanups would be reexamined during the Cultural Revolution (Article 3). On the question of the differing organizational bases, operational methods and target groups of the two movements, and the profound political implications thereof, see Baum, "Revolution and Reaction," *op. cit.,* pp. 117–119.

common denominator of which was opposition to the status quo, soon raised the battle cry "suspect all, overthrow all." In a production brigade in Tsenkung county, Kweichow Province, for example, it was reported: "Among the 182 brigade and production team level cadres, 98 were submitted to cruel struggles. Even those not so persecuted were forced to stand aside without exception. . . . The result was a paralytic situation with no one in charge of either revolution or production." [104] In Fuch'uan county, also in Kweichow, came the allegation that 90 percent of the production team cadres and all the Party branch secretaries in a local production brigade had been struggled against and dismissed in this period.[105] And in Enp'ing county, Kwangtung Province, it was reported that undisciplined, overzealous "rebel" elements had been spreading rumors to this effect: "Cadres at the production team level and above are all powerholders. This campaign means struggling against all county, commune, brigade and production team cadres. Everyone has to go through the ordeal." [106] Comparable reports of excessive and indiscriminate attacks on rural cadres in the period of the January Revolution came from rural areas in Fukien, Kiangsu, Kiangsi, Heilungkiang, and Sinkiang provinces, to cite just a few.[107]

One consequence of the uncontrolled tendency to "suspect all, overthrow all" was that beleaguered rural cadres in a number of communes, production brigades and teams simply refused to carry on their work; as a result, a condition verging on anarchy prevailed in certain localities. From a production brigade in suburban Peking, for example, came this acknowledgment:

After the launching of the revolutionary movement, all organizations and offices in the brigade were in a state of complete paralysis. Some of the responsible persons voluntarily quit their jobs and refused to resume work; or, under the pretext of "grasping revolution," spent all of their time [trying] . . . to evade the trial of the Cultural Revolution. . . . They appeared to pay attention to production and manage it, but in reality did nothing of the sort. They did not actively provide leadership

---

[104] *Radio Kweiyang,* Kweichow, April 1, 1969.
[105] *Radio Kweiyang,* Kweichow, September 1, 1967.
[106] *Radio Canton,* Kwantung, May 16, 1967.
[107] The sources by province are as follows: For Fukien, *Jen-min Jih-pao,* March 7, 1967. For Kiangsu, *Radio Shanghai,* February 19, 1967. For Kiangsi, *Radio Nanchang,* Kiangsi, February 15, 1967. For Heilungkiang, *Radio Harbin,* Heilungkiang, March 16, 1967. For Sinkiang, *Radio Urumchi,* Sinkiang, February 4, 1967.

over production . . . or make proper arrangements for the livelihood of members of the brigade. As a result, some production team members have very little enthusiasm for production.[108]

Relaxation of rural labor discipline was another major unintended consequence of the January Revolution. In a letter to the editor of the influential Shanghai *Wen-hui Pao*, two youths from a nearby suburban farm complained about the "serious prevalence of anarchism and laxity of labor discipline" among the peasants in their unit: "In January of last year [1967], besides growing cotton, the farm members basically did nothing. Even if they attended to their work, they came off duty very early. Some people did not go to work but stayed in their dormitory to sleep and play poker. Some others simply went to loiter about in the city. . . . At present, this situation hasn't changed much." [109]

In addition to precipitating rural leadership paralysis and labor indiscipline, the January 1967 call to "seize power" ushered in a period of "pure conflict" in some rural areas and thereby altered the basic parameters of intramural politics. Rural "great debates" between rebel organizations ("revolutionary" or otherwise) and local powerholders ("bourgeois" or otherwise) were no longer confined to the promotion and defense of their particular special interests and prerogatives, but were now restructured along the lines of overt, all-out struggles for political power itself.[110] With the stakes of conflict significantly raised, the burning question in rural China was no longer "Revolution for what?" but rather "Power to whom?"

In a situation of intramural "pure conflict," local powerholders and their allies proved extremely adept at devising ways of protecting themselves from the onslaught of the "revolutionary masses." And rebel insurgents, for their part, became equally adept at manipulating the issues of conflict for their own advantage. With powerholders and rebels alike waving the "red flag" of revolution, the political situation in the countryside was predictably chaotic.

Although official media reports and Red Guard newspaper descriptions of the events of January–March 1967 are highly polemical and ideologically stereotyped, they nevertheless tell us a great deal about the manifold

---

[108] *Nung-min Yün-tung*, February 22, 1967, *op. cit.*, p. 14.
[109] *Wen-hui Pao*, March 12, 1968.
[110] In the somewhat oversimplified vocabulary of game theory, this change can be described as the conversion of a "non zero-sum game" into a "zero-sum game." See Riker, *op. cit.*, pp. 28–31.

concomitants and consequences of rural power seizure struggles during the period of the January Revolution. In Anhwei province, for example, it was reported in early February that "bourgeois powerholders" and other class enemies in various rural communes were taking advantage of the existence of "clan mentality" among the peasants to "disrupt the revolutionary ranks, shift the target of struggle and undermine the great alliance [of proletarian revolutionaries]," thereby turning the power seizure movement from a "class struggle" to a "clan struggle." [111]

From suburban Peking came this allegation: "When the storm of Shanghai's January Revolution spread across China . . . those capitalist-roaders and 'five category elements' who had been overthrown during the Four Cleanups Movement launched a fierce counterattack and seized power from the proletarian revolutionaries. They cruelly beat up the brigade cadres and carried out white terror." [112] In a similar vein, it was reported in Heilungkiang Province that in a number of rural communes former cadres and "five category elements" who had been purged during the Four Cleanups were now waving the banner "we are the masses; we want to make revolution" in order to "reverse verdicts" and bring about a "counterrevolutionary restoration." [113]

One of the more interesting phenomena to arise in this period was that of overt conflict between "factions" led respectively by higher- and lower-level rural cadres within a single commune or production brigade. In Kweichow Province, for example, a report written by a production team leader described how a "bourgeois powerholder" in his brigade had attempted to seize power from his subordinates in order to "divert the spearhead of struggle" away from himself. This report is noteworthy for the light it sheds on the ways in which various rival factions in Cultural Revolution conflict made use of pre-emptive, evasive, and dissimulative tactics to promote their respective political ends during the January Revolution:

On January 5, I went to the county town to attend a cadre meeting. Yang XX [the "bourgeois powerholder" in the brigade] seized this opportunity to write 10 big character posters against me . . . and incited the masses to struggle against me. . . . How was I going to strike down

---

[111] *Radio Hofei*, Anhwei, February 2 and 18, 1967. For a similar description of the revival of clan feuds in this period, see *Radio Canton*, Kwangtung, July 29, 1968.
[112] *Jen-min Jih-pao*, March 8, 1967.
[113] *Radio Harbin*, Heilungkiang, March 16, 1967.

this scoundrel? . . . Our Red Rebel Squad on the one hand opened fire on Yang XX, and on the other hand launched the . . . poor and lower-middle peasants to study seriously Mao's quotations on class struggle. . . . After this [sic], the masses rose to rebel.

Yang XX then hatched a new plot. He set up a phoney cultural revolution committee. From the day it was set up, this committee directed the spearhead at . . . revolutionary leading cadres in the commune, savagely struggling against them . . . But it neither criticized nor struggled against Yang XX, not even putting up a single big character poster against him.

[The committee] also spread it around that "production team cadres of the rank of accountant and above and representatives of the poor and lower-middle peasants associations are all powerholders, and must all be set aside". . . .

We then raised the slogan "smash the cultural revolution committee; make total revolution," and waged a tit-for-tat struggle against them. . . . Many cadres and masses saw that the aim of the cultural revolution committee . . . was to protect Yang XX and other capitalist-roaders. This aroused the ire of the masses. Yang XX was exposed together with his backstage bosses, the handful of capitalist-roaders in the old district [ch'ü] Party committee, . . . all of whom were brought to the production brigade for struggle. . . .

In the course of this struggle, we thoroughly exposed the problems of the old cultural revolution committee . . . and set up a new one. . . . Yang XX, seeing that his royalist army had collapsed, went all out to attack the new committee. . . . He also instructed his faithful lackeys to go to the county seat to accuse us of crimes. However, the moment they left, their master [Yang XX] stood alone, like a rat crossing the street, with everyone shouting "kill it," so they came scuttling back. . . .

After the new cultural revolution committee had been set up, we convened six meetings of peasants to struggle against Yang XX, and also dragged him around to all the production teams to be repudiated and struggled against.[114]

[114] *Radio Kweiyang,* Kweichow, December 19, 1967. While more detailed than most, the above account is typical of a fairly large number of partisan reports of rural power struggles during the period of the January Revolution. For additional documentation on intramural struggles in rural China in this period, see, *inter alia, Radio Sian,* Shensi, February 9, 1967; *Radio Taiyüan,* Shansi, February 25, 1967; *Radio Nanking,* Kiangsu, February 18, 1967; *Radio Huhehot,* Inner Mongolia, March 28, 1967; *Radio Nanning,* Kwangsi, February 13, 1967; *Radio Kweiyang,* Kweichow, May 13, 1967; *Radio Tsinan,* Shantung, February 27, 1967; *Radio Harbin,* Heilungkiang, March 29, 1967; *Radio Shanghai,* February 19, 1967; *Radio Urumchi,* Sinkiang, February 4, 1967; *Radio Lhasa,* Tibet, February 19, 1967; *Radio*

As revealed in this and other similar descriptions of the rural impact of the January Revolution, under conditions of "pure conflict" engendered by the Maoist call to seize power, it was largely a case of "every man for himself and the devil take the hindmost." Hence, there quickly arose a number of so-called "adverse currents," or unintended (and, from the Maoist point of view, unfavorable) consequences of primordial political conflict.

When stripped of their rigidly stereotyped (and highly misleading) ideological trappings, widespread reports in this period of the prevalence of such "adverse currents" as "suspecting all, overthrowing all," "sham power seizures" (or counter-seizures), "white terror," "rightist reversal of verdicts," and "counterrevolutionary economism" all tend to point to the centrality of survival, self-interest, and self-aggrandizement as prime motives, in individuals and groups, within rural Cultural Revolution power struggles. Perhaps the most typical manifestation of such motives constituted the phenomenon of "counterrevolutionary economism." Of all the "adverse currents" of this period, this was by far the most prevalent.

There were many forms of "counterrevolutionary economism," but all involved appeals made by various contending groups and leadership factions to the material interests and aspirations of their (actual or potential) supporters. From such widely separated cities as Shanghai and Nanch'ang, for example, came allegations that local powerholders in suburban communes had instigated large numbers of local peasants and contract laborers to go to the city, there to demand and demonstrate in support of various "unreasonable" economic and welfare benefits.[115] In Chekiang Province it was reported that local "class enemies" had taken advantage of the "spontaneous capitalist tendencies" of some "backward" peasants to

create disputes, clamor for "rebellion against the state requisition of grain in excess of the production quota," or demand that the state "purchase all grain in excess of the quota at a high price." . . . In the name of "showing concern for the masses," they illegally distribute a large portion of the general [grain] reserves and public welfare funds . . . They even contract loans from the state under various pretexts and make forced withdrawals from banks and credit cooperatives.[116]

Hofei, Anhwei, February 2, 1967; *Radio Nanchang*, Kiangsi, February 15, 1967; and *Radio Chengtu*, Szechwan, July 10, 1968.

[115] *Wen-hui Pao*, January 20, 1967; *Radio Nanchang*, Kiangsi, January 25, 1967.

[116] *Jen-min Jih-pao*, February 1, 1967. Similar reports from Kwangsi and Heilung-

In Kwangtung, Shansi, and Kiangsu provinces it was reported that collectively owned pigs and animal fodder were being freely distributed to individual peasants.[117] In some cases, it was claimed that "bourgeois powerholders" and class enemies were arbitrarily subdividing production teams into smaller, family- or clan-based units and inciting peasants to "go it alone" in land reclamation and sideline production.[118] Finally, class enemies in several provinces allegedly "hoodwinked" large numbers of "intellectual youths" who had settled in the countryside in recent years to return to the cities to seek reinstatement as students, employment in factories, or other jobs.[119] In such cases, the "intellectual youths" were generally provided by local Party officials with "linking up money" to cover the expenses of their movement to the cities.[120]

The prevalence of these various manifestations of "counterrevolutionary economism" in the countryside (as in the cities) of China during the period of the January Revolution was as much a spontaneous reflection of the generalized political chaos of the times—a sort of *enrichez vous* mentality spawned under conditions of leadership uncertainty and paralysis—as it was a conscious, manipulative strategy adopted by various rival groups and factions to augment their following among the rural masses. In this sense, then, "economism" must be treated at least partially as a

---

kiang provinces are documented in *Radio Nanning*, Kwangsi, February 13, 1967; and *Jen-min Jih-pao*, January 27, 1967.

[117] *Radio Canton*, Kwangtung, March 14, 1967; *Radio Shanghai*, February 19, 1967; *Radio Peking*, February 8, 1967.

[118] *Radio Canton*, March 16, 1967, and July 29, 1968; *Radio Nanning*, Kwangsi, February 13, 1967; *Radio Changsha*, Hunan, November 1, 1968; *Radio Kweiyang*, Kweichow, February 16, 1967; *Radio Nanchang*, Kiangsi, March 16, 1967; and *Jen-min Jih-pao*, January 30, 1969.

[119] See, for example, *Radio Nanchang*, Kiangsi, January 23, 1967; *Radio Wuhan*, Hupeh, September 23, 1968; and *Jen-min Jih-pao*, February 20, 1967. Although the widespread phenomenon of ruralized "intellectual youths" returning to the cities in this period was officially discouraged by the Maoist regime, the frustrated young people saw the matter quite differently. In one Red Guard newspaper, for example, a group of rural intellectual youths complained that they had been "persecuted" by commune officials and prevented from responding to "Chairman Mao's call to fight back to school and resume classes to make revolution." Despite the fact that this Maoist edict was meant to apply solely to itinerant Red Guards rather than to ruralized "intellectual youths," the young people in question charged those local powerholders who had acted to prevent their exodus to the cities with "suppressing the revolution." This case provides a relevant illustration of the tendency for various self-interested groups and strata to distort central policy directives for their own purposes. See *Ko-ming Ch'ing-nien* (Canton), November 10, 1967, in *SCMP* 4102, p. 7.

[120] See, for example, *Jen-min Jih-pao*, January 30, 1967.

byproduct, or symptom, of incipient political and institutional decay.[121]
Although the various "adverse currents" of January through March of
1967 differed considerably in their nature and origins, as well as in their
respective political consequences, all were the source of serious concern
to the Maoist leadership in Peking. Thus a plethora of central Party directives (*chih-shih*), decisions (*chüeh-ting*), notifications (*t'ung-chih*), regulations (*kuei-ting*), and other assorted documents (*wen-chien*) were
issued in the late winter and early spring warning against the specific
dangers inherent in such "adverse currents" and providing broad normative guidelines for their eradication or melioration.

The first series of three central Party communications (comprising one
"document" and two "notifications") was promulgated on January 11
and dealt with various questions concerning the phenomenon of "counterrevolutionary economism." [122] In these policy statements it was officially
acknowledged that "a handful of Party persons in authority taking the
capitalist road," in order to undermine the Cultural Revolution, had
"hoodwinked" larged numbers of workers, peasants and cadres into
leaving their production posts to "make their way into the big cities,"
where they had "fomented strikes" and "instigated the masses . . . to
flock to the banks to withdraw deposits by force." In order to discourage
such occurrences, by force if necessary, it was ruled that anyone found
persisting in such counterrevolutionary actions would be punished "according to Party discipline or state law." And in order to give teeth to
the new prohibitions, the People's Liberation Army and public security
departments were authorized to take direct responsibility for "protecting
banks in all places." [123] In addition, the Central Committee notifications

---

[121] A similar argument can be used to explain the widespread appearance of various "spontaneous capitalist tendencies" among the Chinese peasantry in the early
1960s, when the Party's rural political controls were greatly relaxed in the aftermath of the disastrous Great Leap Forward. The extent of incipient political and
institutional decay in rural China in this earlier period is clearly revealed in the
Lienchiang documents. See Pi-chao Chen, *loc. cit.* One should not, however, confuse
or equate "incipient decay" with "anarchy," since the latter connotes a more advanced and manifest condition of institutional paralysis.

[122] See, "Document of the CCP Central Committee, the State Council and the
Central Military Commission" (*Chung-fa* No. 14 [67]); "Notification of the CCP
Central Committee Concerning Opposition to Economism"; and "Notification of
the CCP Central Committee and the State Council Concerning the Prohibition on
Corrupting the Masses," in *CCP Documents, op. cit.*, pp. 159–170.

[123] *Ibid.*, pp. 159–160.

of January 11 confirmed the fact that "some people" were taking advantage of the current, unsettled political situation to

try to lead some of the masses . . . to pursue exclusively personal and temporary interests in disregard of the interests of the state and the collective. . . . They incite some of the masses . . . to freely demand money and material supplies from the state. They incite the masses who went to settle down in the countryside a few years ago . . . to return to the cities and put forward unreasonable economic demands. . . . Landlords, rich peasants, counterrevolutionaries, bad elements, and Rightists have seized this opportunity to try to upset the economic life of the country and sabotage the Great Proletarian Cultural Revolution.[124]

In order to "immediately check the tendency to indulge in economism," the Party center ordained that all ruralized "intellectual youths" and other *hsia-hsiang* personnel "should be contented with agricultural production work and *should take part in the Cultural Revolution in the rural areas.*" Party committees at all levels were assigned the responsibility of enforcing this injunction.[125]

Finally, the January 11 regulations made mention of a phenomenon previously noted in our discussion of coalition building in the countryside, namely, the conscious attempt on the part of various local power-holders to evade revolutionary criticism by bribing or otherwise diverting the attention of the masses:

According to reports from various places . . . a small number of Party and government leaders, for the purpose of avoiding the criticism and repudiation of the revolutionary masses, and in order to corrupt the masses, have recently deliberately provided mass organizations with large sums of money and goods. In the name of showing "concern" . . . they use money to win over the revolutionary masses who are opposed to

[124] *Ibid.,* pp. 163–166.
[125] *Ibid.* (emphasis added). Despite the new prohibition on urban migration by ruralized youths and *hsia-hsiang* elements, large numbers of (primarily suburban) rural dwellers continued to pour into the cities of China in the first half of 1967. The inefficacy of the January 11 regulations can be traced in large measure to the fact that those "Party committees at all levels" which were supposed to enforce the new directives were themselves paralyzed by power seizures in the course of the January Revolution. On this latter point, see Charles Neuhauser, "The Impact of the Cultural Revolution on the Chinese Communist Party Machine," *Asian Survey,* Vol. 8, No. 6 (June 1968) pp. 475–476.

them. Meanwhile, they also grant liberal material benefits to some mass organizations that have been hoodwinked into supporting them.[126]

Taking the position that this was an "extremely erroneous method of work that must be brought under strict control," the Party center exhorted all revolutionary mass organizations to "guard strictly against extravagance and waste," and "heighten vigilance against some leaders who attempt to shift the orientation of the political struggle . . . by economic means."[127]

With the adverse current of "counterrevolutionary economism" thus officially identified and (at least on paper) proscribed, the Maoist leadership next turned its attention to the rapidly burgeoning problem of "reversal of verdicts" in the countryside. The "verdicts" in question were those which had been imposed by Party-led work teams on rural cadres and "five category elements" during the previous Four Cleanups movement.

One of the most prevalent modes of reversing verdicts in the countryside was for retribution-minded former cadres and "five category elements," acting on the pretext of "making thoroughgoing revolution," to recall or detain members of the Four Cleanup work teams in their rural "squatting points" for purposes of struggle and repudiation.[128] In response to such situations, the Party Central Committee on January 25 promulgated a brief "Notification on Defending the Fruits of the Four Cleanups Movement."[129] Taking note of the fact that in "certain rural areas, enterprises, and commercial units" there was a growing tendency toward calling back members of the Four Cleanup work teams for struggle, the January 25 notification repeated the claim (made initially at the time of the Eleventh Central Committee Plenum in August 1966) that the rural Socialist Education Movement had, under Chairman Mao's personal guidance, made "great achievements" in the countryside. Nevertheless, it was now admitted (for the first time) that "some comrades"

[126] CCP Documents, op. cit., pp. 169–170.
[127] Ibid.
[128] Note, for example, the following allegation: "Certain cadres who committed serious mistakes during the [Four Cleanups] movement, together with the demons and monsters . . . have completely refuted the results of this movement . . . and pointed the spearhead at members of the Four Cleanup work teams. . . . They recalled the members of the Four Cleanup work teams, insulted and attacked them at will, compelling them to reverse previous correct decisions." NCNA (Peking), February 7, 1967.
[129] CCP Documents, op. cit., pp. 203–205.

in the work teams had committed certain mistakes in their work "under the influence of the line which is 'Left' in form but Right in essence" (that is, Liu Shao-ch'i's alleged counterrevolutionary cadre policy of "hitting hard at the many to protect the few"). Despite this admission, however, it was affirmed that the original decision to dispatch work teams in the Socialist Education Movement was correct; and that the major responsibility for errors actually committed by the work teams should be borne not by the work team personnel themselves, but by "the person [Liu] who put forward the erroneous line." [130]

In the spirit of "defending the great achievements of the Four Cleanups," the January 25 Central Committee notification laid down three broad guidelines for fending off the adverse current of reversing verdicts:

1. Generally speaking, comrades of the Four Cleanup work teams should not be called back for struggle.

2. Complaints against cadres of the Four Cleanup work teams may be raised in letters, in wall posters, or using other methods.

3. It is necessary to safeguard the results of the Four Cleanups movement. Those Party people in positions of authority taking the capitalist road who have been dismissed from office and landlords, rich peasants, counterrevolutionaries, bad elements, and Rightists are not permitted to reverse verdicts, nor are they allowed to make trouble.[131]

A short time later, a *Hung-ch'i* commentary shed further light on the purpose of the injunction against "reversing verdicts" in the countryside. This commentary, published on March 1, acknowledged that it was

---

[130] *Ibid.* The question of the appropriateness of dispatching work teams had been raised initially at the time of the August 1966 Central Committee Plenum, following the notorious "50 days" in June and July when Liu Shao-ch'i and Teng Hsiao-p'ing allegedly sent out large numbers of work teams to urban schools and universities to suppress Cultural Revolutionary "great debates." Subsequently, Liu was charged with having manipulated the work teams to "hit hard at the many" [revolutionary cadres and students] in order to "protect the few" [bourgeois powerholders]. However, the Maoists could not condemn the general method of dispatching work teams to conduct the Four Cleanups, since Mao himself had approved the adoption of this technique in the "Twenty-Three Articles" of January 1965. Hence, the "error" of the work teams was not one of basic policy, but rather of "line"—in this case the "counterrevolutionary line of China's Khrushchev." On the question of the role of work teams in the Socialist Education Movement and the Cultural Revolution, see Baum and Teiwes, "Liu Shao-ch'i and the Cadre Question," *loc. cit.;* also, Franz Schurmann, *Ideology and Organization in Communist China* (enlarged edition, Berkeley, 1968) pp. 507–519, 540–547, 583–589.

[131] *CCP Documents, op. cit.,* pp. 204–205.

precisely those rural cadres and "five category elements" who had been struggled against during the Four Cleanups campaign that were now in the vanguard of the erroneous movement to "suspect all, overthrow all" in the villages.[132] Four Cleanup work teams were now to be defended against the self-interested deprecations of these revenge-minded "demons and monsters," and were officially exonerated of responsibility for making mistakes on the grounds that "an overwhelming majority of them acted according to Chairman Mao's instructions. They ate, lived, labored, and struggled together with the poor and lower-middle peasants, developed a profound proletarian friendship with them and contributed their part to the Four Cleanups movement." [133]

But the residual problems of the Four Cleanups were not so easily swept under the Cultural Revolution rug. For by the early spring of 1967, the Maoist campaign of vilification against Liu Shao-ch'i had escalated to include bitter attacks on the latter's alleged policy of "hitting hard at the many to protect the few" during both the Socialist Education Movement and the early stages of the Cultural Revolution. And when it was expressly acknowledged by the Maoists that an unspecified number of "good and relatively good" rural cadres and commune members had been unjustly purged or otherwise punished by work teams as a result of the influence of Liu's "sinister line," a major dilemma was revealed: on the one hand, "reversal of verdicts" was to be opposed in principle; on the other hand, some rural cadres and peasants had admittedly received improper treatment and therefore harbored grievances for which they had a legitimate right to expect redress.[134]

It thus was apparent that the political situation in the countryside was far too complex and multifaceted to be dealt with in terms of the undifferentiated normative guidelines for "defending the fruits of the Four Cleanups" and prohibiting the "reversal of verdicts" which had been laid down by the Maoists in January. For *some* of the "fruits" of the Four Cleanups were admittedly bitter; and *some* of the "verdicts" laid down by work teams had been unjust. The important question was how to discriminate in individual cases between the sweet and the bitter, the just

---

[132] *Hung-ch'i,* No. 4 (March 1, 1967) pp. 49–50.
[133] *Ibid.*
[134] For further elaboration on the nature of this dilemma, see Baum and Teiwes, "Liu Shao-ch'i and the Cadre Question," *op. cit.,* pp. 336–341; and Baum, "Revolution and Reaction," *op. cit.,* pp. 111–112.

and the unjust. With all parties to rural power struggles "waving red flags," this proved to be no easy task.

The first tentative step toward resolving this dilemma was taken on February 17, when the Central Committee declared an official injunction against "directing the main spearhead of struggle" against the work teams. Those work teams which had been "retained" in the villages for purposes of being "dragged out" and "struggled" against were now ordered to return to their original units; in those cases where "serious mistakes" had been committed (or were alleged to have been committed) by work team personnel, the dossiers (*tang-an*) of the people involved were to be turned over either to their original units or to "leading organs at the higher level" for investigation and, if necessary, struggle.[135] In this way, the question of which "fruits" to defend and (obversely) which "verdicts" to reverse was taken out of the hands of those local cadres and peasants who had a vested interest in such questions, while at the same time new, more impartial channels for the redress of grievances were opened up.

With the issue of the work teams thus at least partially defused, the next major problem confronting the Maoist leadership in Peking was the question of how to turn back the rising tide of factional political conflict in the villages. As we have seen, throughout the period of the January Revolution, rural cadres at the production brigade and team levels in many areas were being overzealously and indiscriminately criticized and struggled against, with the result that leadership paralysis and labor indiscipline increased. During the slack winter season, December to February, such conditions could be endured with only minimally adverse effects upon the rural economy.[136] By the end of February, however, with the spring planting season rapidly approaching, incipient anarchy could no longer be tolerated.

In order to ameliorate the conditions which had given rise to this phenomenon and to quell the anxieties of those basic-level rural cadres who

[135] "Notification of the CCP Central Committee Concerning the Question of Dealing with Work Teams in the Great Proletarian Cultural Revolution" (February 17, 1967), in *CCP Documents, op. cit.,* pp. 293–294.
[136] Rural capital construction projects, such as building or repairing dikes, irrigation canals, and so on, which are normally undertaken in the winter season, obviously suffered some neglect during the "high tide" of the January Revolution. However, for purposes of this discussion, such neglect is not considered *directly* detrimental to agricultural production.

were unwilling, whether for reasons of demoralization or fear of provoking further criticism by the "revolutionary masses," to assume active leadership over production, the Central Committee on February 20 published an "Open Letter" to the nation's poor and lower-middle peasants, calling on them actively to "support and cherish" all rural cadres who were "willing to make amends" for past mistakes or shortcomings.[137] The "Open Letter" strongly emphasized the traditional Maoist affirmation (which had been conspicuously soft-pedaled since the initiation of the Cultural Revolution) that "the overwhelming majority of cadres at all levels in the rural people's communes are good or basically good." Even those former cadres removed from office during the Four Cleanups were now to be offered a way out by "taking an active part in labor and remolding themselves." [138] Finally, the "Open Letter" exhorted all rural cadres and peasants to stand fast at their work posts, take immediate steps to arrange spring cultivation tasks, and mobilize all available forces to "promote production." Clearly, the main policy emphasis was once again on the urgent seasonal need for the unification and consolidation of local production leadership in the countryside.

In order to provide concrete operational guidelines for implementing the imperatives of the "Open Letter," and to provide rural cadres with a much-needed sense of security against indiscriminate attacks at the hands of the "revolutionary masses," a new definition of the term "powerholders" (tang-ch'üan p'ai) was officially formulated in late February. Previously, it will be recalled, this term had been widely (though not necessarily uniformly) interpreted by various groups of self-styled Revolutionary Rebels to apply to Party and administrative cadres at all levels in the countryside, from the production team to the county.[139] Now, however, it was necessary to restore the shaken confidence and morale of basic level rural cadres, and to halt the adverse current of "suspecting all, overthrowing all" that threatened seriously to affect production leadership. Accordingly, it was officially ruled:

Since production team cadres are not divorced from production, they are only charged with the duties of making production arrangements, organ-

---

[137] "Letter from the Central Committee of the Chinese Communist Party to Poor and Lower-Middle Peasants and Cadres at All Levels in Rural People's Communes Throughout the Country" (February 20, 1967), in CCP Documents, op. cit., pp. 329–333.

[138] Ibid., p. 332.

[139] See pages 408–411.

izing labor forces and carrying out such concrete tasks as are planned by communes and production brigades. *In this sense, they are by no means "powerholders." Neither are the ordinary cadres [i-pan ʠan-pu, as dis-* tinguished from *chu-yao ʠan-pu,* or "principle cadres"] *of the production brigades.* Therefore, with the exception of a very small number of "five category elements" who have wormed their way into production brigades and teams to become cadres or ordinary cadres . . . *they should not be subjected to struggle, let alone be treated as targets of struggle.*[140]

Despite such assurances, however, there was no immediately apparent decrease in the frequency or intensity of reported incidents of revolutionary (or counterrevolutionary) political disturbance in rural China.[141] And throughout February and March, provincial media reports continued to cite numerous cases of anti-cadre struggles and leadership paralysis in the countryside. Such reports were almost always accompanied by fresh pleas to unify and consolidate the cadre ranks, and by assurances to basic-level rural cadres that they were not the legitimate targets of revolutionary struggle. Nevertheless, such assurances were apparently honored in the breach as much as in the observance.[142]

By early March, with seasonal production pressures weighing increasingly heavy on the countryside, concerned leaders at the Party center were compelled to take resolute action to try to preserve (or, in many cases, restore) social order and labor discipline in the villages. A Central Committee notice of March 7 thus stated categorically and unconditionally that there were to be no further power seizures in production brigades and teams throughout the remainder of the spring farming season.[143] At the same time, it was stated that in those production brigades

[140] *Nan-fang Jih-pao* (Canton), February 24, 1967, in *SCMP* 3904, pp. 12–13 (emphasis added).

[141] One major exception to this generalization was in those areas where local units of the People's Liberation Army (PLA) were assigned to the countryside to quell factional violence and "support agriculture."

[142] One explanation for the lack of widespread, rapid response to central Party directives and exhortations in this period lay in the fact that normal channels of mass communication (provincial newspapers, wired broadcasts, etc.) had been either disrupted or "captured" during the January Revolution. In addition, a great many rural villages in China, by virtue of their remoteness, are without direct, regular contact with central or regional Party authorities. For both of the above reasons, by mid-February Party and PLA officials in many provinces had to resort to massive air-drops of printed leaflets to ensure that the rural population would be quickly and accurately informed of recent political developments and changes in the Party line. This question is dealt with in greater detail later in this essay.

[143] "Central Committee Notification Concerning the Undesirability of Seizing

and teams "where leadership has already become paralyzed" (by factional strife or cadre demoralization), "activist elements" among the poor and lower-middle peasants, militia members, and "revolutionary cadres" were empowered to establish three-way "provisional leading groups" (*lin-shih te ling-tao pan-tzu*) to "firmly grasp spring farming work." [144]

Although the overall current situation of the Cultural Revolution in the Chinese countryside was described in the March 7 Central Committee notice as being "excellent," the veracity of this claim was at least partially belied by continuing reports of fresh outbreaks of serious rural political conflict in some provinces.[145] Moreover, to the extent that there was a certain leveling off of factional violence in some rural areas in this period, this probably reflected less on the general "excellence" of the political situation than on the fact that the Moists in Peking, in their increasing anxiety over the spread of incipient leadership paralysis, had been compelled to call upon the PLA to restore order in the countryside.

It was only with the entry of the PLA into the twin struggles to "support the Left" and "support agriculture" in the late winter and spring of 1967 that the January Revolution and its many attendant "adverse currents" were first tentatively brought under control in China's villages. But "control" (of overt conflict) and "excellence" (of the general political situation) were not necessarily synonymous. Within a short time, the two proved to have significantly divergent and somewhat contradictory meanings. In order to appreciate the nature and consequences of this divergence, it is necessary to examine in greater depth the role of the PLA in rural politics in the spring of 1967.

THE ARMY TAKES COMMAND

In one respect, the January Revolution proved to be an unqualified success. The "old order" of China's central, provincial, and local

---

Power in Rural Production Brigades and Teams During the Spring Farming Period" (March 7, 1967), in *CCP Documents, op. cit.*, pp. 347–350. Two weeks later this official moratorium on power seizures was further strengthened when Premier Chou En-lai publicly stated that "there will be no further power seizures *even in those brigades and teams where power ought to be seized.*" (*NCNA*, March 20, 1967; emphasis added.)

[144] *Ibid.* For a somewhat earlier statement of the new policy concerning the formation of (provisional) "three-way alliances" in the countryside, see *Radio Nanchang*, Kiangsi, February 28, 1967.

[145] See, *inter alia, Radio Harbin*, Heilungkiang, March 5 and 16, 1967; *Radio Huhehot*, Inner Mongolia, March 28, 1967; and *Hung-se Pao-tung, loc. cit.*

Party machinery was thoroughly and efficiently assaulted, discredited, paralyzed and, in effect, overthrown. But the extreme havoc wrought by Mao's "little generals" and their Revolutionary Rebel allies in the process of seizing power rendered political restabilization and reconstruction difficult at best. It was in such a situation that the PLA was tentatively called into the fray—first to play such peripheral political roles as guarding state banks and granaries, and enforcing central Party regulations concerning opposition to "economism," and later in the more active role of "firm pillar of support of the dictatorship of the proletariat."

Toward the end of January 1967, Mao Tse-tung, at a meeting of the Central Military Affairs Commission, indicated the necessity for the PLA to play a more active political role in the next stage of the revolution. "Originally," said Mao, "the army was not to intervene in the Cultural Revolution." The January Revolution had changed all that, however: "now that the class struggle has sharpened," exhorted the Chairman, "the army must support the 'Left.'" [146]

Mao's remarks, which were reportedly delivered on January 20 or 21, were followed up on January 23 by a joint decision of the CCP Central Committee, the State Council, the Central Military Affairs Commission, and the Cultural Revolution Group under the Central Committee "concerning the resolute support of the People's Liberation Army for the revolutionary masses of the Left." [147] This document, contrary to previous directives which had defined the PLA's role in the Cultural Revolution largely in terms of nonpartisan state economic and public security tasks, stated unequivocally: "From now on, the demands of all true revolutionaries for support and assistance from the army should be satisfied. So-called 'non-involvement' is false. . . . The question is not one of involvement or non-involvement; it is one of which side we should stand on and whether we should support the revolutionaries or the conservatives or even the Rightists. The PLA should actively support the revolutionary Leftists." [148]

Under the terms of the January 23 directive, PLA regional unit commanders were instructed to send troops upon request to support the "broad masses of the Left" in the latter's struggle to seize power; and to

[146] *Asahi Shimbun* (Tokyo), February 4, 1967, quoted in Philip Bridgham, "Mao's Cultural Revolution in 1967: The Struggle to Seize Power," *The China Quarterly,* No. 34 (April–June 1968) p. 11.
[147] *CCP Documents, op. cit.,* pp. 193–197.
[148] *Ibid.,* pp. 195–196.

use force, if necessary, to put down the resistance of those "counterrevolutionaries" who used violent means to attack the revolutionary Leftists.[149] Although subsequent central policy directives emphasized that "struggle by force" (*wu-tou*) should be opposed by the PLA and "struggle by reasoning" (*wen-tou*) promoted—with soldiers being sternly warned against "arresting people at will," "ransacking homes," "inflicting corporal punishment," "making people wear tall caps and black placards, parading them through the streets and forcing them to kneel down"—the active entry of the PLA into the arena of intramural factional conflicts in late January and February 1967 did not have an immediately visible pacifying effect on local politics either in the cities or in the rural areas of China.[150]

The main difficulty encountered by the PLA in its newly assigned role as a partisan force in domestic politics was not that of actually supporting the Left, but rather was the more fundamental problem of *identifying* the Left in any given situation of factional conflict. As we have seen, the political and organizational bases of local factional cleavage in China were extremely complex and anamorphic in this period. With all contending groups and factions "waving the red flag" of revolutionary rebellion, the task of choosing among conflicting "Leftist" claims was understandably a formidable one. Moreover, being professional military men rather than civilian politicians, those PLA unit commanders who were charged with the responsibility of making such choices were not, by training or by instinct, overly enthusiastic about assuming the role of political advocates or civil arbiters. In many cases, local PLA commanders were simply unwilling to go out on a revolutionary limb, either by actively taking sides in internecine factional disputes or by resolutely suppressing them. Instead, local army officials frequently opted for the relatively "safe," morally neutral posture of waiting to support whatever group or faction happened to emerge victorious or appeared to have the brightest prospects for emerging victorious.[151]

[149] *Ibid.*, p. 196.

[150] On the subject of prohibitions against the PLA instituting "struggle by force" in local political disputes, see the eight-point "Order of the Central Military Affairs Commission," (January 28, 1967) in *CCP Documents*, pp. 209–213.

[151] Another observed tendency in this period, one which was to become even more pronounced in 1968, was for regional and local military commanders to adopt an inherently conservative "law and order" posture which either tacitly or overtly favored the proponents of stability and moderation over those of chaos and extremism. We shall have more to say about this latter phenomenon shortly.

The dilemma of choice which confronted local PLA unit commanders and officers as they were called upon to "support the Left" in the late winter and spring of 1967 is well illustrated by the case of the "pauper's co-op." [152] Hsip'u production brigade, also known as the "pauper's co-op" had been a national "model" agricultural unit since 1955, when Mao Tse-tung personally lauded the "diligence and thrift" of its nucleus of twenty-three poor peasant households and their leader, village Party branch secretary Wang Kuo-fan. At that time, the Chairman strongly recommended that "the entire nation . . . should pattern itself after this co-op." [153] Located in Ts'unhua county, Hopeh Province (about seventy kilometers north of T'angshan municipality), Hsip'u brigade received considerable publicity in the late 1950s and early 1960s for its so-called "pauper spirit," first as a higher-level agricultural producers' cooperative and, after 1958, as a production brigade in the Chienming people's commune.

As late as November 1966, the pauper's co-op was the object of glowing official praise in the national media. A *China Reconstructs* article written by Wang Kuo-fan at that time gave no indication that anything was amiss in the brigade, or that the turbulence of the Cultural Revolution had impinged in any appreciable way upon the political life of the area.[154] In this article, Wang went out of his way to praise the staunch revolutionary activism of Hsip'u's brigade leader, a Party cadre named Tu Kuei. The article also inferred that "class enemies" were no longer actively trying to "restore capitalism" in the brigade, having been thoroughly exposed and "dealt a fatal blow" during the recent Socialist Education Movement.[155] All was well in the pauper's co-op—or so it appeared.

[152] The following discussion is drawn from the author's essay, "A Parting of Paupers," *Far Eastern Economic Review*, Vol. 49, No. 1 (January 4, 1968) pp. 17–19.

[153] See *Socialist Upsurge in China's Countryside* (Peking, Foreign Languages Press, 1957) pp. 11–14, 67–81. Although Mao's name does not appear as editor of this volume, it has since been officially confirmed that Mao wrote both the preface and the various editorial comments that serve to introduce each of its 176 component essays. For an examination of the rise of Wang Kuo-fan and the pauper's co-op to national prominence in the 1950s and early 1960s, see John W. Lewis, *Leadership in Communist China* (Ithaca, 1963) pp. 204–211.

[154] See Wang Kuo-fan, "Long Live the Pauper's Spirit," *China Reconstructs*, November 1966, pp. 37–40. If our earlier observations concerning the limited metastasis of conflict from urban to suburban areas in the period September–October 1966 are valid, then this would help to explain why Hsip'u brigade, a *non*-suburban unit, was apparently unaffected by the events of this early period.

[155] *Ibid.*, p. 39.

But this was most certainly no longer the case by the end of that year. Following the publication of the Party Central Committee's December 15 directive concerning the implementation of the Cultural Revolution in the countryside, brigade leader Tu Kuei reportedly organized a so-called Pauper's Rebellion Regiment and proceeded to "point the spearhead of struggle" directly at his immediate political superior, Wang Kuo-fan.[156] In a forty-day period from late December to the end of January 1967, the Pauper's Rebellion Regiment allegedly convened twenty struggle meetings against Wang Kuo-fan, culminating on January 30 in a wholesale "power seizure": all the cadres of the brigade and its constituent production teams were dismissed from office. But Wang Kuo-fan and his supporters, who by this time had organized themselves into a United Headquarters of Red Guards of Mao Tse-tung's Thought, were unwilling to take this power seizure lying down. They resisted the Pauper's Rebellion Regiment and declared the latter's power seizure to be a counterrevolutionary "sham." The leadership of the Pauper's Rebellion Regiment then called upon the army to come to Hsip'u brigade to support the "Leftist" insurgents in their bid to seize power from Wang Kuo-fan.[157]

In response to the call, a PLA political officer (of undetermined rank and unit affiliation) and two enlisted men arrived at Hsip'u on February 11. Under current standing instructions to "support the Left," this three-man work team initially found itself faced with an uncomfortable choice: "which of the two mass organizations was a true proletarian revolutionary organization, and which was an organization that protected the capitalist-roaders?" Frankly admitting that "we were very confused during the first few days," the leader of the PLA group stated that "it seemed to us as though both organizations had their strong points and short-comings." [158]

Lacking both the desire and the confidence in his own ability to decide between the conflicting claims of the insurgent Pauper's Rebellion Regiment of Tu Kuei and the counterinsurgent United Headquarters of Wang Kuo-fan, and concerned lest he decide wrongly and thus expose himself to the danger of subsequent higher-level criticism, the officer in charge initially tried to play it safe by announcing to the contending

[156] The following discussion is based on *NCNA* (Peking), December 12, 1967.

[157] That it was Tu Kuei's "Pauper's Rebellion Regiment" and not Wang Kuo-fan's "United Headquarters" that called for PLA assistance is inferred from a statement attributed to a leader of the former group: *"We asked you to come because we hoped you would support us."* (*NCNA*, December 12, 1967; emphasis added.)

[158] *NCNA*, December 12, 1967.

groups: "Both of you are directing the spearhead of your struggle against the persons in authority who are in question [Wang Kuo-fan and Tu Kuei, respectively]. So both of you are correct in your orientation." Much to his admitted disappointment, however, such equivocation satisfied no one: "The 'United Headquarters' stated: 'We completely trust the People's Liberation Army. We hope that you will take a clearcut stand instead of sitting on the fence.' The 'Pauper's Rebellion Regiment' said: 'We asked you to come because we hoped you would support us.' What should we do?"[159]

Indeed, what could be done? A choice had to be made. But the alternatives were painfully few; for, again in the words of the PLA officer in charge, "both Wang Kuo-fan and Tu Kuei were Party persons in authority. *But which of them was taking the capitalist road?*" Not, *is there* a capitalist-roader here?, but rather, *which one* is the guilty party? The revolutionary "Left" had to be supported; the only problem was in identifying the true Leftists.

With equivocation and reconciliation ruled out by mutual insistence of the two conflicting parties, the hapless PLA officer and his men thus were forced to arrive at a decision on whom to support. Other things being equal, the odds probably favored Tu Kuei over Wang Kuo-fan, for Tu Kuei was an insurgent "rebel," while Wang Kuo-fan, the number one powerholder in the brigade, was in the uncomfortable position of defending the status quo. In a number of similar confrontations which occurred in rural China in the same period, it was generally the insurgents rather than the incumbents who, by the very act of rising up in rebellion, established their credentials as bona fide revolutionary "Leftists."[160]

But other things were not, in this case, equal. Wang Kuo-fan was no ordinary rural powerholder; he was a nationally renowned "model peasant" who had not once but seven times been publicly commended by Chairman Mao since 1955. Only one other basic-level rural cadre in all of China, Party branch secretary Ch'en Yung-kuei of the famous Tachai brigade in Shansi province, could claim such impressive Maoist bona fides.

[159] *Ibid.*
[160] Out of a total of 71 relatively detailed and well-documented reports of local rural factional conflict in the late winter and spring of 1967, insurgent forces were successful in "seizing power" in 38 cases (54 percent), while incumbent leading cadres emerged victorious in only 12 cases (17 percent). Of the remaining 21 cases, six (8.5 percent) had not been finally resolved at the time the reports were published, and 15 (21 percent) had been resolved by reconciling the differences between the two (or more) principal conflicting factions.

Tu Kuei, on the other hand, was a relative unknown. It is true that he had been publicly lauded for his revolutionary activism on at least two occasions, the first in 1955[161] and the second in November 1966—in an article written by Wang Kuo-fan himself! But never had Tu Kuei received the personal accolades of Chairman Mao. His was primarily a reflected glory, and the PLA officer in charge of "supporting the Left" in Hsip'u brigade in February 1967 undoubtedly knew this to be the case.

Once it came down to a hard and fast choice between supporting Wang Kuo-fan's United Headquarters or Tu Kuei's Pauper's Rebellion Regiment, the PLA work team opted for what was, under the circumstances, undoubtedly the least dangerous course of action (regardless of the substantive merits of the case). In ultimately electing to support incumbent powerholder Wang Kuo-fan against the challenge of Tu Kuei's insurgency, the PLA "support the Left" group avoided the discomfort of condemning a nationally recognized Maoist "hero" (and hence, possibly themselves as well) to Cultural Revolution oblivion.

To be sure, a prima facie case was subsequently made against Tu Kuei which, in some respects, appears convincing. He was accused, for example, of having committed numerous acts of corruption, speculation, and profiteering during the "three hard years" of 1959–61. He was also charged with having opposed the study of Mao's works during the initial stages of the Cultural Revolution. For these and various other alleged transgressions, Tu Kuei was labeled a "bourgeois powerholder" in the spring of 1967. The important point here, however, is not that Tu Kuei lost out in his power struggle with Wang Kuo-fan, or even the fact that he subsequently fell into disgrace. Rather, the significance of the "pauper's co-op phenomenon" lies in the conditions under which the power struggle in the brigade was initiated and the manner in which it was resolved through the intervention of the PLA.

Prior to December 1966, as we have seen, the Cultural Revolution largely bypassed the non-suburban rural areas of China, thus exempting these areas from the Maoist injunction to search out and expose hidden "bourgeois powerholders." This fact, as indicated earlier, probably explains the absence of any indications of a power struggle in Hsip'u brigade prior to that time. By late December, however, the situation had changed. The Central Committe's ten-point directive of December 15 called for the universal unfolding of the "four bigs" in the Chinese countryside and for the "revolutionary peasants" to set up a new form of

---

[161] See *Socialist Upsurge in China's Countryside, op. cit.*, pp. 68–71.

political power in rural villages that bypassed the leadership of local Party committees and branches. As we have seen, it was in response to this directive that rival "revolutionary" organizations began to spring up and compete for political hegemony in a number of hitherto relatively tranquil communes and production brigades in China's rural hinterland.

Influenced, no doubt, by a mounting instinct for self-preservation or self-aggrandizement in an inherently unstable and unpredictable revolutionary environment, the two top leaders of the brigade formed rival "rebel" organizations. The dictum "do unto others lest they do unto you" must have been a powerful motivating force under the circumstances.

The point here is that the parameters of conflict during the January Revolution were such that one or the other of the contending factions in the pauper's co-op had to be labeled "counterrevolutionary." For the existence of "capitalist-roaders" was an a priori assumption of the (zero-sum) movement to seize power. Given this initial narrowing of possible outcomes, the odds were probably against Tu Kuei from the outset. In short, it appears as though Tu Kuei might well have been the victim— though not necessarily an altogether innocent victim of circumstances (for it was he who had initiated the movement to oust Wang Kuo-fan).[162]

Despite Wang Kuo-fan's unique status as a Maoist model peasant, the "pauper's co-op phenomenon" was not atypical with respect either to the genesis of factional struggles in rural China, or to the attempt by the PLA "support the Left" personnel to resolve such struggles via the path of least resistance. Military personnel in many rural areas sought initially to avoid partisan involvement; when this proved impossible, as in the case of the pauper's co-op, they simply opted for the least "risky" alternative.[163]

If a natural desire to follow the path of least resistance provided an important input into the decision-making of some PLA "support the Left" personnel, concern for the maintenance (or restoration) of civil order apparently proved equally significant in the decisions of others.

[162] An interesting postscript to this story was provided by the election of Wang Kuo-fan to full membership on the Ninth Party Central Committee in April 1969. Of Tu Kuei's ultimate fate there has been no further official revelation.

[163] For additional documentation concerning PLA involvement in local rural factional disputes in this period, see, *inter alia, NCNA* (Peking), March 25, 1967; *Radio Tsinan,* Shantung, February 27, 1967; *Radio Canton,* Kwangtung, March 15, 16, and 17, 1967; *Radio Kunming,* Yunnan, April 23, 1968; and *Radio Kweiyang,* Kweichow, April 24, 1968.

And this latter concern, in turn, generally tended to work in favor of the more conservative "rebel" organizations and their supporters—including incumbent powerholders. As one disheartened young radical insurgent from a suburban Canton commune reportedly lamented in March of 1967, "comrades of the armed forces are all supporting the original cadres. It is not very easy for us to oppose them." [164]

While reliable information concerning PLA rural "support the Left" activities in the late winter and early spring of 1967 is sparse, it does seem relatively clear that PLA regional and local commanders in some areas did play a more or less active role in suppressing, rather than supporting, the radical Left. For example, General Huang Yung-sheng, then commander of the Canton Military Region, was accused in a number of Red Guard broadsides of having "fostered the conservative influence" in suburban Canton in March and April of 1967:

In the third stage, from March to April 15, that is, the period of the ill wind, Canton's T'an, working in collusion with other Party powerholders taking the capitalist road, used their dictatorial machinery [the PLA] to clamp down on the revolutionary peasants. The "Red Peasants' Friends of Hsiao-P'ing" dwindled in membership from over 7,000 to a little more than 100, while other revolutionary peasants' groups were disbanded under pressure. This was a period of extreme trial for the revolutionary peasants, who were subjected to white terror. [165]

In order to accomplish his "evil scheme" of suppressing the revolutionary Left, Huang Yung-sheng allegedly dispatched large numbers of his military underlings to various suburban Canton communes beginning in late February to "set up a massive conservative organization . . . manipulated by the powerholders . . . and designed to hoodwink the broad

[164] *Hung-se Pao-tung, op. cit.,* p. 18.

[165] *Ibid.,* p. 16. In this and other radical Red Guard attacks upon Huang Yung-sheng, the sobriquet "Canton's T'an" was used in place of his true name, the implication being that General Huang's role in this period was analogous to that of Vice-Premier T'an Chen-lin, the alleged author of the so-called "February adverse current" of sham power seizures. While one must naturally be cautious in accepting at face value the accusations of a partisan, self-interested Red Guard organization, the charge that leading officers in the Canton Military Region and Canton Garrison Command acted to suppress—or at least neutralize—ultra-leftist Revolutionary Rebel groups in this period is substantiated by collateral evidence gathered from refugee sources as well as from official provincial media reports and the publications of rival (conservative) Red Guard organizations.

poor and lower-middle peasants into seizing and safeguarding power for a minority." [166]

The political effects of the (implied) tacit alliance between regional and local PLA comanders in the Canton Military Region, on the one hand, and "conservative" rebel organizations and rural powerholders, on the other, are revealed in the following passage:

Canton's T'an and company . . . lent a deaf ear to the words of the rebels. They closed their eyes and would not recognize the Revolutionary Rebels' organization of "Red Flag Poor and Lower-Middle Peasants' Command Headquarters." They grabbed and attacked batch after batch of people. . . .

At the moment, the leadership of nearly all suburban Canton district offices, communes, brigades, and even production teams is under the control of the [conservative, PLA-supported] "Suburban Poor Peasants' Joint Committee" and its subsidiary structures. *They are practically the same bunch of people as the original cadres in the communes and brigades.* . . . Under their control, the Revolutionary Rebels are deprived of paper and ink to write their posters with, credit for work points in certain activities, transport to Canton to attend rallies, and the right to receive reimbursement for rentals for holding meetings. They are meted out the most strenuous labor assignments and become the objects of concentrated attack in debates. By comparison, subsidiary structures of the "Suburban Poor Peasants' Joint Committee" can get everything they like. All this bespeaks one thing: the conservatives have, but the Revolutionary Rebels have not, the power.[167]

The contention that radical Red Guard attacks on "Canton's T'an and company" were in reality thinly veiled attacks upon the leadership of the Canton Military Region, the Canton Garrison Command, and local PLA "support the Left" personnel is directly substantiated in the written testimony of conservative Red Guard organizations in the Canton suburbs. For example, in a frankly pro-PLA broadside it was charged that the Red Peasants' Friends of Hsiao-P'ing (an ultra-leftist rebel organization belonging to the Red Flag Poor and Lower-Middle Peasants' Command Headquarters) had deliberately and maliciously "pointed the spearhead at comrades of the People's Liberation Army" who were garrisoned in

---

[166] *Ibid.*, p. 20.
[167] *Ibid.*, pp. 20–21 (emphasis added).

suburban Canton, "denounced the PLA as 'support the conservatives' soldiers," and "condemned the Canton Garrison Command as 'Kuomintang' and 'Northern Warlords.'"[168]

Local resistance to PLA intervention in rural power struggles in suburban Canton in this period (on the part of those ultra-leftist individuals and organizations who had been, or were likely to be, suppressed or discriminated against as a result of such intervention) tended initially to find indirect, rather than direct, expression. To attack the PLA openly and directly would have been to attack the "firm pillar of support of the dictatorship of the proletariat." Hence, in order to discredit the political orientation of locally garrisoned army units, the victims or potential victims of PLA "support the Left" decisions in suburban Canton allegedly made use of such devious devices as "abstract affirmation but concrete denial" in the form of statements to the effect that "as a whole the PLA is good; but some parts of it are not necessarily good." All such deprecatory statements were officially denounced by the Kwangtung provincial authorities (inspired, no doubt, by "Canton's T'an") as a plot on the part of class enemies to point the spearhead at the PLA indirectly by "splitting the PLA into parts, thereby denying the PLA as a whole."[169]

In some instances, however, a more direct approach was used by radical insurgents to discredit the army. For example, it was alleged that in some rebel quarters in suburban Canton rumors were being spread to the effect

[168] *Kuang-chou Hung-tai-hui* (Canton), September 12, 1968, in *SCMP* 4268, p. 4. This is one of the very few cases in which we have available two diametrically opposed views of the same Cultural Revolution incidents in rural China, written by rival "rebel" organizations in the Canton suburbs. By comparing the texts of the "radical" *Hung-se Pao-tung* with the "conservative" *Kuang-chou Hung-tai-hui*, it is possible to appreciate the conflicting political orientations of the two rival organizations involved and the degree to which Red Guard reports of the military's role in resolving factional conflict tend to be distorted, depending on whose particular ox is being gored at any given time. The above-cited publications both center around a series of factional confrontations which occurred in and around suburban Canton's Shihching, Sanyüanli, and Shaho communes in the first half of 1967. For a third Red Guard interpretation of these incidents and their political implications, see *Chiao-ch'u Nung-tai-hui* (Canton), October 11, 1968, in *SCMP* 4293, pp. 1–8. These partisan reports may then be compared, in turn, with "official" provincial media descriptions of the events in question. See, for example, *Radio Canton*, Kwangtung, March 23, 1967, which contains an implicit condemnation of the "Red Peasants' Friends of Hsiao-P'ing" for "whipping up black winds and lighting phantom fires in order to sabotage spring farming" in Shihching commune. Finally, for an official defense of the PLA's role in "supporting the Left" in rural Kwangtung in this period, see *Radio Canton*, March 17, 1967.

[169] *Radio Canton*, Kwangtung, March 17, 1967.

that "the PLA has supported the Royalists in reversing [rebel] verdicts," and "the PLA is just another form of work team . . . organized by [followers of] the bourgeois reactionary line."[170] Such rumors were derided as "slanderous" in the provincial media, and rural mass organizations in the Canton suburbs were sternly warned that "one's attitude to the PLA reveals one's attitude to the dictatorship of the proletariat. . . . If you are genuine revolutionaries, you must fervently support the PLA."[171] Although it was reluctantly conceded that PLA "support the Left" groups were indeed another form of work team, it was stressed that such groups were "genuine" (that is, Maoist) work teams "in the glorious tradition of the PLA." All rumors to the contrary (that is, inferences that PLA "support the Left" personnel were acting under the influence of Liu Shao-ch'i's "counterrevolutionary revisionist line") were denounced as "vicious plots cooked up by people with ulterior motives."[172]

Significantly, it was also officially acknowledged that PLA personnel in the Canton region had, in fact, participated in the movement to "reverse verdicts" in February and March (a point which tends to confirm radical Red Guard accusations mentioned earlier). But such actions were vigorously defended by provincial authorities as remedial measures necessary to quell the "reactionary trend of anarchism" which had allegedly swept through the Canton area in the early stages of the January Revolution:

Previously, some people in the Canton area were influenced by the reactionary trend of anarchism. Counterrevolutionary organizations seized this opportunity to cause confusion and to rebel against the proletariat. Revolutionary organizations which dared oppose this ill wind were struggled against as counterrevolutionaries. This is very wrong. Now . . . *with the support of the PLA, the revolutionary mass organizations have reversed their verdicts and revised their opinions. The reversal of verdicts is excellent! Excellent indeed!*[173]

PLA "support the Left" personnel in the Canton area and their superior officers (including, by direct inference, General Huang Yung-sheng) were thus totally exonerated by the Kwangtung provincial authorities of the charge of having suppressed, rather than supported, the "revolution-

[170] *Ibid.*
[171] *Ibid.*
[172] *Ibid.*
[173] *Ibid.* (emphasis added).

ary" Left. The PLA was credited with having stifled the "ill wind" of anarchism; and the reversal of all "erroneous" verdicts imposed by ultra-leftist organizations and factions during the height of the January Revolution was explicitly sanctioned.

But if provincial authorities in Kwangtung were satisfied with this turn of events, central authorities in Peking apparently were not. Although neither Huang Yung-sheng nor his immediate subordinates in the Kwangtung Provincial Military District (including Huang's influential Deputy Commander, Wen Yü-ch'eng) were openly censured by Peking's Cultural Revolution leadership, their military counterparts in a number of other provinces, military districts, and sub-districts were severely criticized for manifesting similar "conservative" tendencies. In a series of central policy decisions handed down in the spring of 1967, leading military organs and field commanders in Tsinghai, Anhwei, Inner Mongolia, Szechwan, and Shantung provinces were held responsible for committing various mistakes of "supporting conservative organizations," carrying out "ruthless armed suppression" against genuine rebel organizations, and "making indiscriminate arrests" of all who opposed their leadership.[174] Although it is unclear why "Canton's T'an" was spared official criticism in this period, it may be hypothesized that his role in quelling the ultra-leftist excesses of the January Revolution in Kwangtung did not differ appreciably from that of "conservative" military commanders in the five provinces cited above. Conceivably, it may have been Huang Yung-sheng's longstanding military relationship with Mao's "closest comrade-in-arms," Defense Minister Lin Piao, that enabled him to emerge unscathed.[175]

[174] See "Decision of the CCP Central Committee, the State Council, the Central Military Commission and the Central Cultural Revolution Group Concerning the Question of Tsinghai" (March 24, 1967); "Decision of the CCP Central Committee Concerning the Question of Anhwei" (March 27, 1967); "Decision of the CCP Central Committee Concerning the Handling of the Inner Mongolia Question" (April 13, 1967); "Decision of the CCP Central Committee Concerning the Question of Szechwan" (May 7, 1967); and "Document of the CCP Central Committee, the Central Military Commission, the Central Cultural Revolution Group, and the All-PLA Cultural Revolution Group (*Chung-fa* No. 175 [67])" (May 31, 1967), in *CCP Documents, op. cit.,* pp. 383–387, 389–395, 415–419, 431–438, and 457–459.

[175] Huang had first served under Lin Piao as a regimental commander in the 115th Division of the Eighth Route Army during the Sino-Japanese War, and later as Vice-Commander of Lin Piao's Fourth Field Army. Although it is somewhat gratuitous to posit the notion of personal friendship as a major intervening variable in Cultural Revolution politics, there is some evidence that former PLA Field Army ties (organizational, rather than personal) have persisted as a significant force in

Although it is extremely hazardous to attempt to generalize about political conditions in rural China as a whole from a single provincial case study, the conclusion that regional and local PLA commanders and their subordinate "support the Left" personnel throughout China tended in many instances of factional conflict to discriminate against the more radical rebel groups is borne out indirectly by numerous reports of ultra-leftist anti-PLA incidents (including physical assaults on officers and soldiers) in several provinces.[176]

Beginning in the latter part of March, the central Maoist leadership in Peking demonstrated increasing anxiety over both the "conservative" behavior of PLA unit commanders in the field and the "radical" behavior of those Revolutionary Rebels who sought to discredit local PLA leadership. In what might be described as a "dialectical double play," the editors of *Hung-ch'i* frankly admitted that local PLA "support the Left" units in many areas had committed certain (undisclosed) "temporary mistakes" of political orientation; at the same time, however, those rebel groups and factions which had been suppressed or otherwise victimized as a result of such "mistakes" were warned against "directing the spearhead of struggle" against the PLA itself:

In a number of places, some comrades in the local army units may have committed temporary mistakes in giving their support owing to the intricate and complex conditions of class struggle. When such problems occur, the genuine proletarian Left should explain the conditions with good intentions and in a proper way, and put forward their opinions to leading members of the Army units in question. They should absolutely not adopt an antagonistic public attitude and should not in the slightest direct the spearhead of their struggle against the People's Liberation Army. Otherwise, they will commit gross mistakes . . . and they will be used by the class enemy.[177]

---

contemporary intra-elite politics in China. See William Whitson, "The Field Army in Chinese Communist Military Politics," *The China Quarterly*, No. 37 (January–March 1969) pp. 1–30.

[176] Such incidents reportedly included "encircling, attacking, beating, searching, and detaining PLA fighters and public security personnel" (*Radio Tsinan*, Shantung, February 27, 1967); "besieging the District Military Control Committee" (*Chiao-ch'u Nung-tai-hui, loc. cit.*); "hoodwinking the masses to point the spearhead at the PLA" (*Radio Kunming*, Yunnan, October 29, 1967); "scores of troops fighting with more than 100 peasants in the paddy fields" (*Agence France Presse* [Paris], March 25, 1967); and "killing or injuring commanders of the PLA" (*Kuang-chou Hung-tai-hui, loc. cit.*).

[177] *Hung-ch'i*, No. 5 (March 30, 1967) p. 8.

The fact that the two-edged indictment contained in this editorial came preciously close to being an "abstract affirmation but concrete denial" of the role of the PLA in "supporting the Left" apparently did not trouble the editors of *Hung-ch'i* as it had troubled "Canton's T'an" and his associates in Kwangtung province.[178] Nor is this surprising; the Kwangtung provincial authorities had praised as "excellent indeed" the very same phenomena which Peking now alleged to be "temporary mistakes."[179]

In a series of directives promulgated in early April, the Party Central Committee and the Central Military Affairs Commission enjoined all military district commanders and garrison forces of the PLA to refrain from declaring mass organizations "counterrevolutionary" without prior approval from central authorities. Earlier prohibitions against indiscriminate arrests of civilians by PLA personnel were reiterated, and a new warning was added against military retaliation against the "revolutionary masses" who stood up to criticize the army:

Those [individuals and organizations] who have been labeled "counterrevolutionaries" merely because they trespassed against or criticized a military district command, or voiced disagreement over the power seizure in a certain place or unit, shall without exception be vindicated. Those who have already been arrested shall without exception be freed, and

[178] See pages 432–433.

[179] It is interesting to note that under pressure from Peking, Huang Yung-sheng and Wen Yü-ch'eng conducted a "self-criticism" some time in the latter part of April, perhaps at the behest of Chou En-lai, who was known to have visited Canton in mid-April. See *Chan Sheng-wei,* January 1968, in *Hsing-tao Jih-pao* (Hong Kong), May 21, 1968. A self-criticism reportedly made by the leadership of the Kwangtung Military District, on August 20, 1968, will be found in *SCMP* 4082, pp. 1–5. In any event, Huang and Wen probably began to "rectify" their "temporary mistakes" in the mid-spring of 1967. This may be the reason that they escaped the type of official criticism that was currently being directed against leading military figures in Tsinghai, Anhwei, Inner Mongolia, Szechwan and Shantung. Collateral evidence of Huang's orientational shift in the period after mid-April 1967 is provided in a previously cited radical Red Guard publication which delimits the period of the conservative "ill wind" in suburban Canton as lasting from March to April 15. See *Hung-se Pao-tung, loc. cit.* Huang's efforts to placate the central leadership apparently paid off handsomely, for he was selected to serve first as Chairman of the Kwangtung provincial revolutionary committee (February 1968), and shortly thereafter as PLA Chief of Staff, following the March 1968 purge of Acting Chief of Staff Yang Ch'eng-wu. Wen Yü-ch'eng was similarly rewarded for his "loyalty" by being named PLA Deputy Chief of Staff. Both Huang and Wen were elected to the Party Central Committee in April 1969, with Huang being chosen to serve on the all-important Politburo.

orders for the arrest of others not yet in custody shall without exception be rescinded.[180]

In a ten-point "Order of the Central Military Affairs Commission," dated April 6 (and bearing the personal stamp of approval of Mao Tse-tung), PLA soldiers were forbidden from using their weapons in dealing with mass organizations, and the army's mandate to "support the Left" was restricted to the conduct of non-coercive "political work." [181] Even those mass organizations which had "conclusively been found to be under the control of reactionary elements" were not to be labeled "counterrevolutionary." Instead, the PLA was to give "active education" to the members of such organizations in order to "win over the hoodwinked masses" and thereby "isolate the worst of their leaders." The "targets to be attacked" should, according to this new directive, be "limited as much as possible"; and it was held that no new mass "self-confession" (*ch'ing tsui*) movements should be launched.[182] The main conclusion to be drawn from these directives, when viewed in conjunction with our earlier study of PLA involvement in rural political struggles in Kwangtung, is abundantly clear: the Army had failed to properly execute its Maoist mandate to aid the revolutionary Leftists in many—if not most—instances of local factional conflict. Whether owing to "temporary mistakes" stemming from the "intricate and complex conditions of class struggle" (as claimed in official Party media) or to a conscious desire on the part of military leaders to "foster the conservative influence" (as claimed in radical Red Guard publications)—or, what is more likely, for some combination of the above reasons—PLA district and sub-district commanders and their troops throughout many parts of China manifested an "incorrect" political orientation toward the task of "supporting the Left" in the spring of 1967.

In an official communique issued by the Kweichow Provincial Military District, meeting in May 1967 to sum up PLA experiences in the movement to "support the Left," the question was posed, "Why is there [military] support for the conservatives?" The answer to this question was given in ten parts, the most important of which are as follows:

---

[180] "Document of the CCP Central Committee (*Chung-fa* No. 117 [67])" (April 1, 1967), in *CCP Documents, op. cit.*, pp. 397–401.

[181] *CCP Documents, op. cit.*, pp. 407–411, Article 1.

[182] *Ibid.*, Articles 3, 4, and 6.

2. Too much stress is put on the question of maintaining the peace; too little is placed on the struggle between the two lines. Since in the past the army did not involve itself, it is not deeply aware of the harm of the reactionary line. . . . Thus, it easily sympathizes with the enemy. . . .

3. There are close relations with the local leadership, but not very close contact with the masses. In military sub-districts there are too many leadership cadres in armed units whose relations with local cadres are too close. Moreover, the dependents of military cadres are mainly conservative, and thus they listen primarily to [the cadres'] reports. They do not understand or believe the opinions of the masses. . . .

4. They feel that the conservatives obey orders well, while the revolutionaries do not; thus they do not like the revolutionaries. . . .

5. They hold that if there are many Party members in the conservative group, then the group is good; on the other hand, if the ranks of the revolutionaries are not pure, then the group is held to be controlled by bad persons. . . .

7. There is too much stress on old ways and methods and not enough acceptance of new things. People . . . do not like the innovations of the revolutionaries; they react strongly.

9. People are too fearful. . . . Some know well that the conservatives are wrong, but they are afraid that the rebels are not pure; they are afraid to take risks. Some even say: "It is better to support the conservatives than the 'counterrevolutionaries.' " [183]

The profound dangers of persisting in such "conservative" thinking and behavior were strongly pointed out in a *Chieh-fang-chün Pao* (*Liberation Army Daily*) editorial of late June. "If we do not wipe out cleanly from our minds the influence of the bourgeois reactionary line," warned the editorial, "we shall not be able to identify and support the Leftists." In addition, it was held that so long as PLA commanders and soldiers continued to "use old standards to appraise new things" the result would be a situation in which "we shall recognize a wrong man, follow a wrong line, and consciously or unconsciously side with the conservatives." [184]

Despite the proliferation of such warnings, and despite the Maoists' renewed emphasis in April and May on the need for the PLA to take the lead in forming and consolidating revolutionary "great alliances" among contending factions and mass organizations in both town and country-

---

[183] Quoted in *Chung-hsüeh Feng-pao* (Peking), No. 1 (May 27, 1967), in *JPRS* 42,260, pp. 28–29.
[184] Quoted in *NCNA* (Peking), June 27, 1967.

side, the army continued to exercise a predominantly conservative influence in provincial and local politics throughout the middle and later stages of the Cultural Revolution.[185] Moreover, it is apparent that factional cleavages in some rural areas, far from being lessened or resolved by the intervention of PLA "support the Left" personnel, were actually exacerbated. This is not to say that many—perhaps even most—military support groups did not initially attempt to mediate impartially between contending factions and mass organizations in the countryside. Rather, to the extent that the contending parties to such disputes perceived themselves to be locked into a situation of "pure conflict" with their opponents, all non-coercive (that is, purely exhortative) military efforts at keeping or restoring the peace were likely to meet with considerable local resistance.[186]

But if the PLA was unable to perform successfully the political tasks of resolutely "supporting the Left" or, failing that, of impartially "educating" and persuading contending factions to bring about the peaceful formation of a "great alliance" among the revolutionary masses, the army was apparently somewhat better suited to the more familiar task of imposing martial discipline at the basic levels of productive and administrative organization. Under the aegis of a nationwide movement to "support agriculture," large numbers of PLA officers and men were dispatched to hundreds of counties and communes in the spring of 1967 to take the lead in "mobilizing forces" for agricultural production and, together with local militia, to form the nucleus of a new production leadership system known as the "front-line command for grasping revolution and promoting production."

Starting from the top down, PLA-dominated "front-line command headquarters" were established first at the provincial, special district, and county levels and then, with the aid of the militia, at each successive subordinate administrative level in the countryside. Based (at least in theory) on the principle of the "three way alliance" between PLA or militia mem-

---

[185] For further documentation and analysis of the PLA's domestic political role in the Cultural Revolution, see Jürgen Domes, "The Cultural Revolution and the Army," *Asian Survey*, Vol. 8, No. 5 (May 1968) pp. 349–363; John Gittings, "The Chinese Army's Role in the Cultural Revolution," *Pacific Affairs*, Vol. 39, Nos. 3–4 (Fall 1967) pp. 269–289; and *China News Analysis* (Hong Kong), Nos. 707–708, 710–712, 715 (May 10–July 5, 1968).

[186] The previously cited example of the pauper's co-op provides a cogent illustration of local factional resistance to military efforts at peaceful conflict resolution. Also in this regard, see note 160 above.

bers, revolutionary workers (or poor and lower-middle peasants), and
revolutionary leading cadres, "front-line command" groups at each level
were charged with the responsibility of "making overall analysis of the
current situation and tasks" and "whipping up an upsurge in spring
plowing and production." [187] More important, they were assigned the
task of helping subordinate administrative units reform or reconstitute
existing basic-level rural production leadership groups. This meant, in
effect, that the PLA and the people's armed militia now took virtual
command of those productive and administrative leadership functions at
each level which had previously been performed by now defunct or paralyzed organs of the Party and state.[188]

Identified in the official media as "provisional organs of power," military "front-line command" groups at the provincial and sub-provincial
levels dispatched large numbers of work teams, composed of PLA and
militia cadres, to lower levels to oversee the work of reorganizing production leadership groups and to investigate production conditions at the
basic levels. Known as Thought of Mao Tse-tung Propaganda Teams,
these work groups enforced martial discipline upon local peasants and
basic-level cadres in production brigades and teams throughout China in
the spring of 1967.[189]

Reports of rural factional violence dropped off noticeably in the late

[187] See, for example, *Jen-min Jih-pao*, March 12, 1967; *NCNA* (Peking), March
16, 1967; *Radio Wuhn*, Hupeh, March 17, 1967; and *Radio Harbin*, Heilungkiang,
March 22, 1967. The first county-level "front-line command" was reportedly established in Huaijou county, Peking, in February 1967.

[188] The nuclear leadership for "front-line command" organs at the provincial and
special district levels was provided by members of the Party committees of the various provincial military districts and sub-districts, respectively. At the county level
and below, cadres of the people's armed forces departments and locally deployed
PLA garrison troops performed a similar "backbone" function. See, for example,
Radio Wuhan, Hupeh, March 17, 1967; also *Radio Kweiyang*, Kweichow, February
28, 1967; *Jen-min Jih-pao*, March 12, 1967; and *Radio Nanchang*, Kiangsi, March
6, 1967.

[189] While the precise extent and geographical distribution of direct military control in the countryside in this period is impossible to determine with any degree of
certainty, official reports of PLA propaganda teams being dispatched to "support agriculture" in the spring of 1967 came from no less than 154 counties in seventeen
provinces. Although priority was apparently given to those communes and brigades
which had manifested "old, great, and difficult problems" in the period of the
January Revolution, this was by no means universally the case. There are, finally,
a number of collateral reports of local peasant resistance to the imposition of
martial law by PLA propaganda teams in some rural areas. See, for example, *Agence
France Presse* (Paris), March 25, 1967.

spring, as the PLA and the people's militia assumed de facto leadership over productive and administrative enterprises. Nevertheless, the underlying roots of Cultural Revolution conflict ultimately proved infinitely more difficult to suppress than the outward manifestations; and the ever-swelling flow of illegal immigrants to Hong Kong from the rural areas of South China in the latter half of 1967 provided ample testimony to the continuing undercurrent of political turmoil. The PLA had "taken command"; but in so doing it had not solved but merely postponed or papered over the problem of restoring politicial stability at the basic levels.

THE SEARCH FOR A NEW RURAL ORDER

By the end of the 1967 spring farming season, a modicum of social order and labor discipline had been militarily restored in many of those non-suburban rural villages which had experienced significant political or economic turbulence during and immediately after the January Revolution.[190] In order to pacify the countryside further, the Party Central Committee in early June temporarily extended its earlier injunction against further power seizures in rural production brigades and teams for the duration of the "busy season of summer production." This was to be the first of many such "temporary" extensions, the cumulative effect of which was permanently to enjoin virtually all narrowly sectarian power struggles in the countryside.[191]

The regime's objective in attempting to curb rural power seizures was clear. Since the phenomenon of "factionalism" had developed under conditions of pure conflict engendered by the Maoists' call to seize power, it followed that only by resolutely prohibiting such seizures could this phenomenon be controlled and the polarization of rural political forces—with its attendant consequences in terms of leadership paralysis and labor indiscipline—be halted, if not reversed. By removing the incentive to carry out new power seizures, the regime hoped to convert what had been essentially a situation of power-oriented factional confrontation into a situation of policy-oriented intercoalitional debate and compromise.[192]

[190] The distinction here between suburban and non-suburban villages is highly significant, for reasons to be discussed shortly.

[191] See *Radio Tsinan,* Shantung, June 7 and September 8, 1967; and "Directive of the CCP Central Committee Concerning the Great Proletarian Cultural Revolution in the Countryside This Winter and Next Spring" (December 4, 1967), in *CCP Documents, op. cit.,* pp. 630–633.

[192] I am indebted to Harry Harding for pointing out the significance of the distinction between power struggles and policy debates in this context.

Thus, it is not surprising to find that official prohibitions against further power seizures in the countryside were generally coupled both with strong exhortations for the "revolutionary peasants" to cease quarreling among themselves and bring about the rapid formation of a "great alliance" of contending factions, and with severe sanctions against such divisive activities as "inciting the masses to fight among themselves," "rumormongering," "settling [factional] accounts," and all other potentially exacerbating actions.

Throughout the remainder of the Cultural Revolution (with the notable exception of a brief period in the spring and early summer of 1968), the official emphasis in rural politics was on narrowing, rather than enlarging, the scope and targets of mass struggle. It was continuously reasserted, for example, that the vast majority of pre-Cultural Revolution rural cadres were either "good" or "relatively good," and should therefore be retained in their posts or rehabilitated. And in order to pacify an increasingly apprehensive and restive peasantry, it was officially reiterated that no new restrictions—either legal or normative (voluntary)—would be placed on the cultivation of private plots in the near future. Similarly, it was stressed that the current three-level system of ownership in the countryside, with the production team as the basic level, would not "in general" be changed.[193]

In an effort to further neutralize the immediate causes of intramural factional conflict and peasant unrest in the countryside, the Maoists initiated a rural campaign of "revolutionary criticism and repudiation" in the late spring and summer of 1967. Making use of the technique of displacement, this campaign was designed in part to redirect the hostility of the peasants and basic-level cadres away from local powerholders and factional rivals onto the person of the "number one Party person in authority taking the capitalist road," Liu Shao-ch'i.[194] In the course of the repudiation movement, which was launched initially in the rural suburbs of Shanghai municipality, any and all "ill winds" and "adverse currents" in the countryside were attributed either directly or indirectly to Liu and a "small handful" of his "agents in various places."[195]

The significance of this massive effort to create a nationwide displace-

---

[193] CCP Documents, pp. 630–631.

[194] See Jen-min Jih-pao, November 23, 1967. For a collection of official reports describing the initial phases of the "criticism and repudiation" movement in rural China, see URS, Vol. 48, No. 5 (July 18, 1967).

[195] CCP Documents, p. 627.

ment effect lay in the fact that the vast majority of basic-level cadres and peasants who had been either individually or collectively struggled against as "capitalist-roaders" or "class enemies" in the early stages of the Cultural Revolution were now to be exonerated of primary responsibility for their political errors. According to new official policy guidelines on rehabilitation (p'ing fan), most of these aberrant cadres and peasants had been unwittingly "hoodwinked" or "misled" by China's Khrushchev and his agents. Others had strayed from the Maoist path because they lacked a thorough understanding of "new things" which had arisen in the course of the Cultural Revolution. So long as the people involved acknowledged their mistakes and pledged to return to the proletarian road, all such aberrations would be forgiven.[196]

Equally significant were official admissions in the summer and autumn of 1967 that large numbers of "revolutionary" cadres and peasants had been mistakenly labeled and struggled against as "counterrevolutionaries" by Party-controlled work teams in the autumn and winter of 1966–1967, during the high tide of revolutionary "great debates." In a series of policy statements issued through a number of provincial "reception centers" it was held that "those comrades who were branded [by Party work teams] as counterrevolutionaries in the period after May 16 [1966] should as a rule be rehabilitated. This is an irrevocable decision." It was further stated that "in general, there should not be any dismissal of working personnel during the Great Cultural Revolution." [197]

A pronounced decrease in the frequency and intensity of reported fresh outbreaks of political conflict in the countryside in the latter half of 1967 would seem to indicate that the several palliative measures described above, taken in conjunction with the previously noted imposition of direct PLA or militia control in the worst rural trouble spots, did indeed achieve their immediate objective—the mitigation of factional conflict. But if the containment of political violence was characteristic of rural China as a whole, it was most certainly not characteristic of a relatively few suburban communes which lay in the immediate vicinity of China's major population centers. In these areas, the various "ill winds" and

[196] See, for example, Jen-min Jih-pao, October 20, 1967, and February 13, 1968; also, NCNA (Peking), October 4 and December 24, 1967.

[197] See the collection of documents on the question of rehabilitation, in Selections From China Mainland Magazines (SCMM) 617 (April 1968), pp. 8ff. The "reception centers" had been established on an ad hoc basis under the auspices of the General Office of the Party Central Committee to deal with complaints of erroneous classification and labeling.

"adverse currents" set in motion during the January Revolution continued to spread unchecked throughout the remainder of 1967 and the first half of 1968.[198]

To cite but one example of the intensification of suburban turmoil in the summer of 1967, it was officially reported in mid-July that a number of "unreformed conservatives" in the people's armed militia departments at various levels in the eight widely separated provinces of Kiangsi, Szechwan, Chekiang, Hupeh, Honan, Anhwei, Ninghsia, and Shansi, in league with local "bourgeois powerholders," had recently issued large quantities of rifles and hand weapons to suburban peasants for the purpose of inciting them "to enter the cities to participate in armed struggles, and to encircle and attack revolutionary mass organizations in factories, mines, [Party and state administrative] organs, and schools." In some areas, it was alleged that "there has even been advanced the counterrevolutionary slogan of "encircling the cities with the countryside." [199]

Despite the issuance of a number of new central Party regulations prohibiting such activities and providing strong negative sanctions for noncompliance, the phenomenon of suburban peasants being mobilized by local powerholders (both military and civilian) to struggle against urban Red Guards and Revolutionary Rebels continued largely unabated. And following the Wuhan Incident of late July, organized groups of suburban peasants were reported to be actively engaged in armed conflicts with students, workers, and soldiers in and around a number of China's major cities.[200]

---

[198] Although the turbulence of the January Revolution had encompassed a substantial number of non-suburban rural districts (for example, the pauper's co-op), it nevertheless appears that in *relative* terms the percentage of non-suburban communes directly affected by revolutionary conflict in this early period was still quite low, perhaps on the order of five to ten percent. In municipally administered suburban districts, on the other hand, the percentage of communes so affected was considerably higher (though the total number may have been smaller). It was not until the autumn of 1968 that the Cultural Revolution became a truly universal movement in China's rural hinterland. See Colina MacDougall, "Collision in the Countryside," *Far Eastern Economic Review*, Vol. 64, No. 7 (February 13, 1969) pp. 277–279.

[199] "Notification of the CCP Central Committee Concerning the Prohibition Against Instigating Peasants to Carry Out Armed Struggle in the Cities" (July 13, 1967), in *CCP Documents . . . , op. cit.*, pp. 473–476. For further documentation of such phenomena, see *Radio Hangchow*, Chekiang, June 11 and 14, 1967; *Radio Tsinan*, Shantung, May 27 and 28, 1967; and *Wen-hui Pao*, September 29, 1968.

[200] See, for example, *Kuang I Hung-ch'i* (Canton), September 4, 1967; *Chiao-ch'u Nung-tai-hui, loc. cit.;* and *Kuang-chou Hung-tai-hui, loc. cit.*

All such violent manifestations of urban-suburban conflict were bitterly condemned both by the Maoists in Peking and by radical Red Guards and Revolutionary Rebels in the provinces. Nevertheless, under the conditions of incipient leadership paralysis and social anarchy fostered by the wholesale overthrow of Party committees at the provincial, county, and municipal levels, Peking's prohibitions against continued factional warfare were in many cases unenforceable or enforceable only at the discretion of local military commanders. Many of these, as we have seen, were either overtly hostile to the Leftists or unwilling to commit themselves and their troops to the suppression of civil conflict.

A good illustration of the inefficacy of Peking's normative exhortations in the period following the January Revolution is provided by the uninterrupted flow of rural Red Guards and "intellectual youths" from the countryside to the cities. Under such pretexts as "exchanging revolutionary experiences," "fighting back to school to make revolution," and "presenting petitions," large numbers of young people had deserted their rural production posts either to participate in organized urban demonstrations or simply to loiter about in the cities. The first official attempt to stem this rural-to-urban population flow came in early February 1967, when the Central Committee issued a circular notice instructing all Red Guards and other "revolutionary teachers and students" to return to their home units immediately to "grasp revolution" locally.[201] This notice was followed a short time later by the promulgation of a second Central Committee directive, which served uniformly to prohibit ruralized "intellectual youths" from further exchanging experiences, presenting petitions or "visiting people in high places" in the cities.[202]

Despite such unequivocal prohibitions the urban influx of large numbers of rural youths continued apace throughout the remainder of 1967 and the first half of 1968. The considerable socio-economic dislocations created by the very presence of these uprooted young "refugees," as well as their significant contribution to the already critically unstable political milieu in the cities, have been documented in the official and Red Guard

[201] "Notification of the CCP Central Committee and the State Council Concerning the Question of Exchanging Revolutionary Experiences on Foot by Revolutionary Teachers, Students, and Red Guards" (February 3, 1967), in *CCP Documents, op. cit.,* pp. 225–229.

[202] "Notification of the CCP Central Committee and the State Council Concerning [Urban] Educated Youths Working in Rural and Mountainous Areas Who Go Out to Exchange Revolutionary Experiences, Make Petitions, or Call On People at Higher Levels" (February 17, 1967), in *CCP Documents,* pp. 299–302.

media.[203] More important, these youngsters were apparently almost totally unresponsive to central Party exhortations calling upon them to return to their rural places of residence. In the nine-month period following the February 1967 promulgation the Central Committee was compelled to issue no less than seven additional directives on this subject, each one more urgent and unequivocal than the one before.[204] As in the previously cited examples of the continued prevalence of "factionalism" and "counter-revolutionary economism," however, in the absence of firm local enforcement (or enforceability) of official sanctions, such exhortations apparently fell largely on deaf ears. Such was the anarchistic aftermath of the January Revolution in China's cities and rural suburbs that the central authorities could not impose their wishes upon recalcitrant minorities.

By the end of the 1967 autumn harvest season, a major drive was launched in the countryside to establish "revolutionary committees" at the commune and, in some instances, production brigade levels. Based on PLA- or militia-forged "great alliances" and (subsequent) "three-way alliances," these new provisional organs of power were set up from top to bottom. Starting with those provinces and centrally administered municipalities which had already established provincial-level revolutionary committees or preparatory committees (of which there were 14 by the end of 1967), local revolutionary committees were formed first at the special district, county, and municipal levels, and then at the commune and brigade levels. At each level, the new tripartite committees supplanted the military "front-line command" groups and production leadership groups which had been created on an ad hoc basis in the late winter and spring of 1967.[205]

By the early spring of 1968, the drive to set up revolutionary commit-

[203] See, for example, *Chih-nung Hung-ch'i* (Canton), November 1, 1967; *Radio Wuhan,* Hupeh, November 21, 1967; *Wen-hui Pao,* March 12, 1968; and *NCNA* (Peking), May 6, 1968.

[204] See *CCP Documents, op. cit.,* pp. 337, 378, 422, 430, 475–476, 538, and 560–562.

[205] As was the case with so many "new things" which emerged in the course of the Cultural Revolution, the first commune-level revolutionary committees reportedly were established in the Shanghai suburbs in the spring of 1967. See *Nung-ts'un Ch'ing-nien* (Shanghai), No. 18 (September 25, 1967), *loc. cit.* It was not until the autumn of 1967, however, that the Shanghai experiment was copied in other rural localities. For example, the *Pei-ching Jih-pao* of December 14, 1967, reported that revolutionary committees had "recently been established" in 70 communes in the Peking suburbs. It was claimed that these latter committees were able to come into existence "because of the army's resolute support [sic] for the forces of the Left." See *CTK International Service* (Prague), December 15, 1967.

tees at the basic levels in the countryside was well underway. The initial upsurge of committee formation at the commune and brigade levels in each province generally followed by one to several months the establishment of the relevant provincial-level revolutionary committee or preparatory committee. In communes and brigades having "old, great, and difficult problems" (a euphemism for leadership paralysis or factional conflict), the time lag was in most cases rather long, as the tasks of forging "great alliances" and "three-way alliances" in such areas were particularly acute.[206]

Although reliable information concerning the formation and composition of revolutionary committees at the basic levels in the countryside is rather sparse, it appears that the proportion of pre-Cultural Revolution "leading cadres" who were re-elected or rehabilitated to serve on their respective commune- and brigade-level revolutionary committees was rather low in those few rural districts in which "great alliances" and "three-way alliances" had been realized relatively early, prior to the winter of 1967–1968. By contrast, the proportion of incumbent (or former) cadres selected to serve on basic-level revolutionary committees was apparently considerably higher in those rural districts in which such alliances were forged in the later stages of the Cultural Revolution. In the early alliance areas, representatives of the "revolutionary masses" often constituted a majority or near-majority of the committee membership; in the late alliance areas, "revolutionary leading cadres" or cadres of the people's militia generally comprised a majority on the new committees.[207]

Throughout the late winter and spring of 1968, the rural "revolution-

[206] For documentation concerning the progress of revolutionary committee formation at various levels in Kwangtung province, see *Radio Canton,* January 10, 12, and 27; February 24; March 3, 5, and 13; April 25; and September 22, 1968. (The Kwangtung provincial preparatory committee was established in November 1967, while the formation of the provincial revolutionary committee was announced some three months later, on February 21, 1968.) See also Ezra Vogel, *Canton Under Communism* (Cambridge, Mass., 1969), Chapter 8.

[207] While these observations are admittedly founded on a narrow data base (four official media reports and eight reports from refugees from various rural areas in Kwangtung province), they are nevertheless consistent with what is known of the overall directions and trends of Cultural Revolution politics in the latter part of 1967 and 1968—in particular the widely observed trend toward the "liberation" and rehabilitation of progressively larger numbers of cadres at all levels, beginning in the autumn of 1967. For documentation on the formation and composition of commune and brigade level revolutionary committees, see *NCNA* (Peking), April 29 and May 27, 1968; *Jen-min Jih-pao,* September 24, 1968; and *Radio Changsha,* Hunan, October 2, 1968.

ary criticism and repudiation" campaign continued to focus on the problem of restoring unified political leadership in the villages. As in earlier
periods, the PLA was instrumental both as a peace-keeping force and as
a weapon with which to forge "revolutionary unity" among the conflict-
ridden peasantry. Unlike the military's earlier partisan involvement in
rural political disputes at the time of the January Revolution, in 1968 the
army was instructed to "support the Left, *but not any particular faction*"
—a slogan which in effect subordinated the goal of "supporting the
Left" to that of imposing discipline on *all* contending parties, regardless
of political orientation.[208]

The PLA's twin tasks of maintaining law and order and forging "great
alliances" in the countryside were rendered more difficult by a resurgence
of Red Guard radicalism in the late spring of 1968. Earlier, in the eight-
month period following the Wuhan Incident of July 1967, "factionalism"
in all its variant forms and manifestations had been repeatedly condemned by the Maoist regime as a major threat to revolutionary unity
and discipline.[209] By mid-April of 1968, however, Peking's Cultural Revolution pendulum had taken a pronounced (if ultimately short-lived)
swing to the Left, with the result that radical Red Guards and Revolutionary Rebels in the cities and villages alike were being officially encouraged to "support the factionalism of the proletarian revolutionaries"
and to oppose only those divisive actions which were manifestations of
"*bourgeois* factionalism." [210] Predictably, such exhortations soon led to a
new upsurge of sectarian conflict, as left-wing and pseudo left-wing Red
Guards and Revolutionary Rebels once again hoisted the "red flag" and
stepped up the pace of their attack against rival organizations and factions, and against opposition elements within the newly formed revolutionary committees at both the provincial and local levels.

In the countryside, the new round of factional warfare triggered off by
this "turn to the Left" was in many cases more violent than that occa-

---

[208] *Chieh-fang-chün Pao*, January 28, 1968 (emphasis added); see also *Peking
Review*, No. 5 (February 2, 1968) pp. 8–9. For extensive documentation and (somewhat superficial) analysis of PLA activities in the countryside in the first half of
1968, see *China News Analysis*, No. 712 (June 14, 1968).

[209] In September 1967 Mao had issued the first of his so-called "latest instructions,"
which held that "there is no fundamental conflict of interest among the working
class" (and, by extension, among the peasantry). A few months later the influential
Shanghai *Wen-hui Pao* launched a nationwide campaign against factionalism with
the publication of a lengthy editorial entitled "Ten Crimes of Factionalism." (*Wen-
hui Pao*, January 12, 1968.)

[210] *Jen-min Jih-pao*, April 19, 1968 (emphasis added).

sioned by the movement to seize power during the January Revolution of 1967. To cite one example, it was reported (by no less an authority than Vice-Premier Hsieh Fu-chih) that in ten production brigades of a suburban Peking commune, "all landlords, rich peasants, counterrevolutionaries, bad elements, and Rightists [that is, the "five category elements"] and their children, including infants, were killed in one day." Suicide was also becoming a serious problem in certain rural suburbs, according to the Vice-Premier.[211]

"Brutal massacres" of peasants and rural Red Guards in Yangchiang county, Kwangtung, were also reported to have occurred in April and May, 1968.[212] Similar reports of renewed factional conflict and the outbreak of sanguinary "civil wars" in this period came from rural districts in such widely separated provinces as Shensi, Kiangsu, Shansi, Anhwei, Kwangtung, and Fukien.[213]

By the end of June 1968, factional violence—often involving the use of automatic rifles, machine guns, and even artillery—had escalated to alarming proportions in both urban and rural areas throughout the country. It was in this situation of increasingly unrestrained civil chaos that Mao Tse-tung was finally compelled to intervene personally on behalf of "law and order." When the dust had settled following the notorious "mangoes affair" of late July, the Leftists once again found themselves the victims of military suppression, this time with the tacit consent of the Chairman himself.[214]

The latter half of 1968 witnessed the final decline of the "revolutionary Left" as a major force in local politics in China. But the anarchistic residue of two years of "uninterrupted revolution" was not easily removed; and reports of the persistence of such divisive phenomena as the so-called "mountain stronghold mentality" (small-group exclusiveness and cliquism) and the "reactionary theory of many centers" (pluralistic sectarian-

---

[211] "Summary of the Proceedings of the Thirteenth Plenum of the Peking Municipal Revolutionary Committee" (May 15, 1968), reported in *Wen-ko T'ung-hsun* (Canton), No. 16 (July 1968), in *SCMP* 4225, pp. 11–13.

[212] *Chien-chu Hung-lien* (Canton), No. 5 (June 1968), in *SCMP* 4228, pp. 1–6.

[213] The sources by province are as follows: For Shensi, *Radio Sian*, December 25, 1968. For Kiangsu, *Radio Shanghai*, December 10, 1968. For Shansi, *Agence France Presse*, April 9, 1968. For Anhwei, *Radio Hofei*, June 28, 1968. For Kwangtung, *Kuang-chou Hung-tai-hui, loc. cit.; Radio Canton*, Kwangtung, June 26 and July 12, 1968; and *Central News Agency* (Taipei), July 23 and 26, 1968. For Fukien, *Central News Agency* (Taipei), June 22, 1968.

[214] For documentation and analysis of these developments, see Baum, "China: Year of the Mangoes," *Asian Survey*, Vol. 9, No. 1 (January 1969) pp. 1–18.

ism) continued to emanate from a number of rural villages throughout the remainder of 1968 and the first half of 1969. Perhaps the most widespread of such anarchistic residues was the pervasive spirit of "letting the masses do as they please," which threatened to undermine all attempts to restore political authority in the countryside. In Ch'angan county, Shensi Province, for example, it was revealed that a number of peasants in a certain production brigade had adopted the attitude "I will do what I like" when production assignments were made by the brigade revolutionary committee.[215] In Weinan county, also in Shensi, it was reported:

Sometimes, when the commune revolutionary committee assigns a work task, some people ask: "Who says so?" If it was said by people whom they originally took into their mountain strongholds, they say: "No trouble; we can do it with our eyes shut." . . . If it was said by people other than those whom they originally admitted into their mountain strongholds . . . they shake their heads, saying "This simply can't be done."[216]

Similar indications of the breakdown of political authority, manifested in such forms as "spending without limit" and "profiteering" were reported in a number of rural areas in the latter half of 1968.[217] And the open resurgence of long-submerged clan loyalties and familial feuds provided vivid testimony to the absence of unified political leadership in still other rural villages.[218]

The Cultural Revolution finally—and somewhat anti-climactically— became a universal movement in the Chinese countryside in the autumn of 1968, with the intensification of a campaign of "struggle-criticism-transformation." [219] Beginning shortly after the convocation of the Party Central Committee's Twelfth Plenum in mid-October (and possibly as a

[215] *Radio Sian*, Shensi, December 13, 1968.

[216] *Ibid.*

[217] See, for example, *Radio Changsha*, Hunan, December 9, 1968; *Radio Shanghai*, December 15, 1968; *Radio Sian*, Shensi, November 21, 1968; and *Wen-hui Pao*, October 15, 1968.

[218] See, for example, *Jen-min Jih-pao*, January 30, 1969; *Radio Canton*, Kwangtung, July 12, 1968; and *Pi-hsüeh Huang-p'o* (Yingte county, Kwangtung), July 1968, in *SCMP* 4244, pp. 1-12.

[219] Prior to this time, political conflict had been manifested in a relatively small— though highly visible—minority of rural villages. Ironically, it was not until the more radical phases of the Cultural Revolution had run their course that the "struggle-criticism-transformation" campaign was unfolded on a universal scale in the countryside.

result of policy decisions adopted at that meeting), tens of thousands of Poor and Lower-Middle Peasant Thought of Mao Tse-tung Propaganda Teams were organized in communes and production brigades throughout the country. Under the watchful eye of locally garrisoned PLA officers and political cadres, these propaganda teams, composed primarily of "backbone" militia members and "activist elements" selected from among the peasantry at large, were collectively charged with the tasks of supervising the "class purification" of basic-level leadership groups and with promoting the "liberation" or rehabilitation of cadres who had been criticized or struggled against in the earlier stages of the Cultural Revolution. Individually, the propaganda team members were also expected to serve as local political instructors, conducting anti-Liu Shao-ch'i propaganda and "repudiation" among the peasant masses, and ensuring that the "gospel according to Mao Tse-tung" reached every peasant household in rural China.[220] Most important, however, the Poor and Lower-Middle Peasant Thought of Mao Tse-tung Propaganda Teams were called upon to popularize among the peasantry a series of rural organizational and administrative reforms which had been adopted by the Maoist regime in the autumn of 1968—reforms which were collectively hailed in the official media as providing the necessary foundation for a new "leap forward" in Chinese agriculture.[221]

[220] According to official media reports in the autumn of 1968, each production brigade was responsible, with the assistance of locally stationed military "support" personnel, for selecting approximately 200 to 300 people to serve as propaganda team members, with approximately 10 members assigned to each production team in the brigade. See, *inter alia, Jen-min Jih-pao,* November 10, 1968; and *Radio Chengchow,* Honan, November 15, 1968.

[221] The most significant of the new reforms lay in the areas of merging and consolidating the communes and production brigades; decentralizing rural educational, medical and public health, and supply and marketing services; fostering the development of small-scale, commune-run industries; and adopting the so-called "Tachai system" of labor remuneration and work-point evaluation. A detailed examination of these various reforms lies beyond the purview of the present investigation. For documentation on the merger and consolidation of communes and production brigades, see *Radio Nanchang,* Kiangsi, October 13 and December 9, 1968, and January 13, 1969. On the decentralization of rural education, see "Educational Reform in Rural China," *Current Scene,* Vol. 7, No. 3 (February 8, 1969). On the campaign to train large numbers of so-called "barefoot doctors," see "The Mao-Liu Controversy Over Rural Public Health," *Current Scene,* Vol. 7, No. 12 (June 15, 1969). On the reforms in rural commerce, see *NCNA* (Peking), January 18, 1969; *Jen-min Jih-pao,* January 21, 1969; and *Peking Review,* No. 5 (January 31, 1969), pp. 15–17. On the introduction of the "Tachai system" of work-point assessment, see Martin King Whyte, "The Tachai Brigade and Incentives for the Peasant," *Cur-*

While it is too early to attempt to assess with any degree of confidence the probable effectiveness of these various reform measures in bringing about the anticipated "leap forward," it does seem clear that major orientational and motivational differences exist between the original Great Leap Forward of 1958–1960 and the present decentralization drive. Unlike the earlier campaign, which called upon the peasantry to make great physical sacrifices but failed to offer a visible "payoff" commensurate with them, the reforms of 1968–1969 have embodied the notion of "visible rewards" in the form of the increased availability to the rural populace of badly needed social and technical services—services hitherto largely unavailable to the perenially disadvantaged poor and lower-middle peasants. Thus, it is conceivable that the individual peasant might well regard the benefits of more readily available public health services, more village-oriented commercial and consumer credit policies, easier access to cheaper, locally manufactured farm tools and chemical fertilizers, and more egalitarian educational policies as suitable compensation for such anticipated "deprivations" as the loss of individual autonomy and the economic "leveling" which are implicit in recent efforts to consolidate the commune system and introduce the Tachai method of labor remuneration. If such a psychic trade-off does occur, then the amount of peasant discontent generated by the new reforms may be considerably less than some observers have predicted.[222]

Regardless of the ultimate efficacy of these economic and administrative reforms, the fact remains that the profound and often uncontrolled political tremors set in motion during more than two years of revolutionary upheaval in China have not as yet fully subsided. For in addition to the various anarchistic residues of Cultural Revolution conflict mentioned earlier, a new source of rural turbulence was introduced in the late summer and autumn of 1968 with the initiation of a massive new *hsia-hsiang* campaign. In the course of this campaign some ten to twenty million young urban Red Guards, unemployed workers, "intellectual youths," and other "social elements" (including urban cadres who had committed

---

rent Scene, Vol. 7, No. 16, (August 15, 1969). And on the movement to disperse and decentralize light industry in the countryside, see "Peking's Program to Move Human and Material Resources to the Countryside," *Current Scene,* Vol. 7, No. 18 (September 15, 1969). For a general overview and analysis of all these various developments, see Colina MacDougall, "The Cultural Revolution in the Communes," *Current Scene,* Vol. 7, No. 7 (April 11, 1969).

[222] See, for example, MacDougall, "The Cultural Revolution in the Communes," *loc. cit.*

"errors" of one sort or another in the course of the Cultural Revolution) were sent out to the countryside to become "integrated" with and "re-educated" by the poor and lower-middle peasants. While ostensibly a voluntary movement, the new *hsia-hsiang* campaign has been widely interpreted by those people most directly affected as a form of political banishment. Widespread reports of resistance—both active and passive—on the part of the young ex-urbanites and their rural "hosts" alike (the latter being required to share their food and means of production with the displaced and largely unskilled emigrants) augur a further exacerbation of socio-political tensions in the countryside.[223]

Thus, although both the level and scale of direct political conflict in China's rural communes diminished steadily after the summer of 1968, the disintegrative by-products of Mao's "last revolution" may be expected to continue to impede the regime's search for a new rural order for a considerable period of time to come. The Cultural Revolution battle is over; but the larger "war" of which that battle was an integral part—the struggle to "destroy self-interest and establish the public interest"—rages on.

THE ECOLOGY OF CONFLICT: AN OVERVIEW

From its inception in the spring of 1966 until the Twelfth Central Committee Plenum in October 1968, the Great Proletarian Cultural Revolution was primarily an urban movement. On the basis of available evidence, it seems clear that the majority of China's 74,000 rural people's communes[224] did not, at any time during this two and one-half year period, experience significant political or socio-economic disturbances. Moreover, to the extent that such rural disorders did occur, they were confined, at least in the early stages of the Revolution, almost exclusively to a limited

[223] For extensive documentation and analysis of the new *hsia-hsiang* campaign, and of the dislocations and antagonisms generated thereby, see *China News Summary* (Hong Kong), No. 281 (July 31, 1969).

[224] The figure 74,000 represents the pre-Cultural Revolution (1966) total. The commune consolidation movement of 1968–1969 undoubtedly served to reduce this number, although it is impossible to determine at this time the precise extent of that reduction. In those rural areas from which systematic data have been obtained, the newly enlarged and consolidated communes appear to be, on the average, about three times as large as before. If this ratio is projected on a nationwide scale, the total number of consolidated communes may approach the pre-1963 figure of 24,000.

number of communes and production brigades in the municipally administered suburbs of China's large and medium-sized cities. But as the Cultural Revolution gained momentum in its middle and later stages, following the January Revolution, increasing (though still relatively small) numbers of non-suburban communes and brigades began to be affected by the turmoil of the times, either directly (as in the case of local factional struggles) or indirectly (as in the case of the rapid, unchecked spread of "economism" in the countryside). The suburban locus of Cultural Revolutionary conflict is clearly revealed in Figure 1, which records reports of rural disorder from 231 different communes and brigades according to the linear distance from the site of conflict to the nearest large or medium-sized municipality. In Figure 2, reports of rural disorder from 244 different communes and brigades are recorded by period of initial occurrence, to indicate the differential frequencies of rural conflict at successive stages of the Cultural Revolution.[225]

From Figure 1, it may be noted that 42.4 percent (98 of 231) of all geographically identifiable rural conflict sites lay in the municipally adminstered suburbs of China's urban population centers, while an additional 22.1 percent (51 of 231) lay within 25 kilometers of these municipal suburbs.[226] At the other extreme, only 13.8 percent (32 of 231) of all reported rural conflict sites lay more than 100 kilometers away from the nearest urban center.

[225] The discrepancy between the 231 cases recorded in Figure 1 and the 244 cases recorded in Figure 2 is accounted for by the fact that in some instances, the communes and brigades reported as sites of conflict during the Cultural Revolution could not be located by the author on provincial atlases, and therefore could not be identified in Figure 1; on the other hand, a number of reports of conflict were geographically identifiable but did not contain specific information concerning the time period of conflict, thus precluding their use in Fgure 2. Hence, the data universes of Figures 1 and 2 are not fully congruent.

[226] Municipally administered rural districts in China may be grouped into three broad categories. First, there are approximately 450 communes in 32 suburban counties which fall within the indirect administrative jurisdiction of the three centrally governed municipalities of Peking, Shanghai, and Tientsin. Second, there are approximately 600 communes in 44 counties which are indirectly administered by China's 79 provincially governed municipalities (for example, Canton, T'aiyuan, Chungking). Finally, there are approximately 600–800 communes which are directly administered by China's 125 or so large and medium-sized municipalities, including both those cities which fall in the first and second categories above, and an additional 40–45 special district-governed municipalities throughout the country. For information on the administrative divisions and jurisdictions of China's cities, see *Yi-chiu-liu-ch'i Nien Fei-ch'ing Nien-pao* (*1967 Yearbook on Chinese Communism*) (Taipei: Institute for the Study of Chinese Communist Problems, 1967) pp. 13–28.

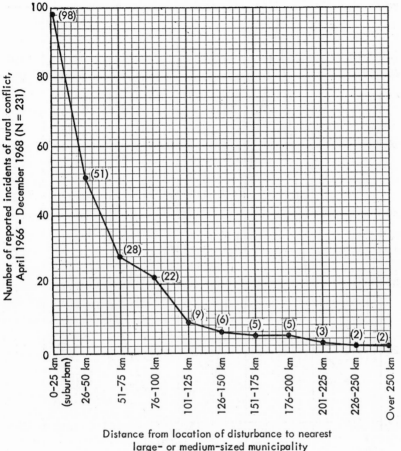

FIGURE 1—Differential impact of Cultural Revolution on rural
China as measured by proximity of conflict sites
to major population centers

From Figure 2, it will be noted that the frequency of rural conflict was
far from constant throughout the several stages of the Cultural Revolution.
As might be expected, the peak stages of reported conflict (January–March
1967 and April–June 1968) correspond to the periods of intense political
activity associated with the January Revolution and the PLA-inspired
drive to establish basic-level rural "great alliances" and revolutionary committees, respectively.

When the data recorded in Figures 1 and 2 are combined and examined

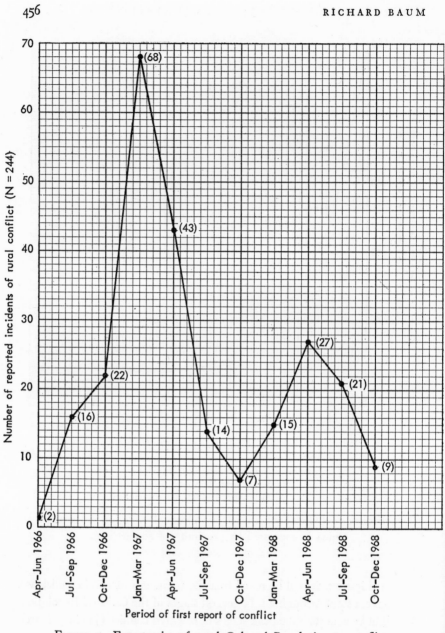

FIGURE 2—Frequencies of rural Cultural Revolutionary conflict,
April 1966–December 1968

Earliest period of reported conflict	Distance from location of incident to nearest large or medium sized municipality (100,000 population)					Number of incidents reported in each period (N = 209)
	0-25 km	26-50 km	51-100 km	100-200 km	Over 200 km	
July-Sept 1966	9 (75%)	2 (17%)	1 (8%)	—	—	N = 12 100%
Oct-Dec 1966	11 (65%)	5 (24%)	1 (11%)	—	—	N = 17 100%
Jan-March 1967	37 (55%)	18 (28%)	9 (14%)	3 (4%)	—	N = 67 101%
April-June 1967	12 (31%)	11 (28%)	14 (36%)	2 (5%)	—	N = 39 100%
July-Sept 1967	4 (36%)	3 (28%)	4 (36%)	—	—	N = 11 100%
Oct-Dec 1967	1 (14%)	—	2 (29%)	3 (43%)	1 (14%)	N = 7 100%
Jan-March 1968	2 (17%)	2 (17%)	3 (25%)	4 (33%)	1 (8%)	N = 12 100%
April-June 1968	4 (18%)	4 (18%)	7 (32%)	6 (27%)	1 (5%)	N = 22 100%
July-Sept 1968	2 (13%)	2 (13%)	5 (33%)	4 (27%)	2 (13%)	N = 15 99%
Oct-Dec 1968	—	—	2 (29%)	3 (43%)	2 (29%)	N = 7 101%
Number of incidents reported by distance from nearest population center	N = 82 (39%)	N = 47 (22%)	N = 48 (23%)	N = 25 (12%)	N = 7 (4%)	N = 209 (100%)

(shaded areas represent modal frequencies of conflict)

FIGURE 3—Differential rural impact of Cultural Revolution as measured by proximity of conflict sites to major population centers, by stages

for covariation, a striking pattern of time-space relationships emerges. This relationship is revealed in Figure 3, which charts the initial occurrence of conflict in 209 rural communes and brigades for which both geographical and chronological information were reported. From Figure 3, it may be noted that insofar as China's suburban communes and brigades were affected by Cultural Revolution turmoil, this generally occurred in the first instance at a relatively early stage of the movement, in the latter half of 1966 or the first half of 1967. On the other hand, the more geographically remote the commune or brigade affected by revolutionary turmoil, the greater the probability that such turmoil was initially experienced relatively late in the game, in the latter part of 1967 or in 1968.[227]

[227] The relatively small number of conflict reports recorded for the latter half of

What such admittedly crude quantitative analysis reveals is that Cultural
Revolution turbulence, like ripples in a pond, tended to radiate outward
over time from China's urban centers to the surrounding countryside in
more or less concentric circles. Moreover, analysis of the data recorded in
Figure 3 tends to reveal that, again like ripples in a pond, the velocity and
magnitude (and hence, the destructiveness) of these revolutionary "waves"
were greatest in the period immediately following the initial "impact" and
in those areas closest to the municipal epi-centers of disturbance, tending
gradually to diminish over time and space as the turbulence spread outward to encompass progressively larger areas.

To be sure, this analogy is somewhat oversimplified, since it ignores the
possible consequences of post-"impact" alterations in the overall course of
the Cultural Revolution—whether purposive (as, for example, in the case
of the resurgence of Red Guard radicalism in the spring of 1968) or unanticipated (as in the anarchistic aftermath of the Wuhan Incident of July
1967). Moreover, unlike the relatively inert water molecules in a pond,
China's rural peasants and cadres were potentially *active* agents in the
diffusion process. That is, they could, by their actions, either facilitate or
impede the progress of the Cultural Revolution "wave." And the fact that
a substantial number of communes and production brigades in the immediate vicinity of China's conflict-ridden cities were *not* significantly affected
by the Cultural Revolution, while a number of other, relatively remote
communes and brigades apparently experienced the full impact of the
revolutionary movement, would tend to indicate that purposive actions
(whether exacerbatory or obstructionist) on the part of rural powerholders
and peasants alike constituted a major intervening variable in the diffusion
process. Despite these *caveats,* however, a sequential pattern of linear,
urban-to-rural "spill-over" of political and socio-economic conflict in the
Chinese countryside is clearly discernible in the data recorded in Figure
3.[228]

1968 should not necessarily be interpreted as a sign of the decreasing frequency of
conflict in this period. Rather, it may reflect the author's relative lack of data from
this period. See note 229.

[228] At this point, some clarification of the word "conflict," as used throughout the
preceding discussion, would seem to be in order. In the context of quantitative analysis, "conflict" (and other cognate terms, such as "turmoil," "turbulence," and so
on) is employed to cover the entire spectrum of rural social, economic and political
disturbances (including various "adverse currents" and "ill winds") which occurred
during—and as a result of—the Cultural Revolution, ranging from violent power
seizures and factional confrontations to less sanguinary manifestations of leadership

It should be re-emphasized that only the earliest episode of reported conflict in any given rural commune or production brigade has been recorded in Figures 1-3. Although it is true that many communes and brigades experienced prolonged or multiple episodes of Cultural Revolution upheaval in the two and one-half year period under review, by singling out the earliest known episode in each area it is possible to isolate the factor of differential diffusion over time. Although the data on this point have not been presented systematically, it is generally true that the earlier the initial episode of conflict in a given commune or brigade (and, coincidentally, the closer that commune or brigade to the nearest municipality), the greater the probability of prolonged or repeated turmoil. Thus, of the 108 (mainly suburban) communes and brigades which initially experienced a significant level of conflict between April 1966 and March 1967 (see Figure 1), 77 (71 percent) reportedly experienced subsequent political or socio-economic disruptions in the later stages of the Cultural Revolution. On the other hand, only 24 (37 percent) of the 64 communes and brigades which initially experienced revolutionary conflict in the period between April and December 1967 reportedly underwent further upheavals in 1968.[229]

It may be objected that the high proportion of conflict reports from suburban communes and production brigades during the Cultural Revolution may not reflect a significantly higher frequency of conflict in such areas (relative to more remote rural districts), but may rather reflect a *normal* pattern of differential media reportage in rural China. That is,

---

paralysis, labor indiscipline, "counterrevolutionary economism," and the like. Thus, for example, the unauthorized emigration of rural youths to the cities is perhaps more accurately described as symptomatic of the relaxation of social control in the villages than as a concrete manifestation of local political conflict. Nevertheless, for purposes of identifying, quantifying, and comparing the origins and patterns of diffusion of such disintegrative phenomena, the term "conflict" has been uniformly adopted (by way of analytic convention) to serve as a common denominator.

[229] Part of the explanation for this observed correlation may lie in the fact that the reportage of Cultural Revolution conflict has often tended to lag behind the actual occurrence of conflict, in some cases by as much as a year or eighteen months. Hence, it is possible that the author's April 1969 cutoff date for data collection may have led inadvertently to an under-representation of episodes of conflict occurring in the latter stages of the Cultural Revolution—episodes which had not been reported prior to April 1969. Nevertheless, it is apparent from the available data that, in general, the "early conflict" rural areas (the majority of which were suburban) experienced turbulence of both greater intensity and longer duration than the (generally more remote) "late conflict" areas—a fact which tends to reinforce the analogy of the dynamic revolutionary "wave" suggested earlier.

it may be argued that suburban communes are normally the subject of a disproportionately large amount of media coverage in China by virtue of their very proximity to major urban centers of mass communication. It might thus be hypothesized that, other things being equal, the more geographically remote a commune, the lower the normal expectation that that commune would be the object of public media coverage. If valid, this hypothesis would obviously call into question our interpretation of the data presented in Figures 1 and 3.

Fortunately, it is possible to tentatively reject this hypothesis by subjecting it to empirical, quantitative tests. In a previous bibliographic study of rural communes in Kwangtung province, which spans the eight-year period 1959–1967,[230] some 1,700 public media references to individual communes and production brigades in that province were classified and recorded by geographical location and administrative jurisdiction. Of these 1,700 media references, almost 1,600 were drawn from the period prior to April 1966—the date of the initial intensification of the Cultural Revolution in China's major cities. Of these only 148 (9.5 percent) pertained to municipally administered communes and brigades in the rural suburbs of Kwangtung's large and medium-sized cities. On the other hand, for the period of the Cultural Revolution (April 1966 to December 1968), a total of 49 media reports of conflict in Kwangtung's rural areas were examined, of which 20 (40.8 percent) pertained to municipally administered communes and brigades in the province's ten suburban districts. This province-wide figure of 40.8 percent is quite close to the nationwide figure of 42.4 percent, as revealed in Figure 1, thus indicating that Kwangtung was by no means atypical with respect to the relative frequency of suburban conflict during the Cultural Revolution. Hence it would appear that the high proportion of conflict reportage from suburban communes and brigades throughout China in the two and one-half year period from April 1966 to December 1968 does *not* reflect a normal differential spatial pattern of media coverage. The data supporting this conclusion are summarized in Figure 4.

A more serious objection to the present emphasis on the linear, urban-to-rural diffusion pattern of Cultural Revolution conflict inheres in the notion that it was not urban proximity, but rather isolation, as measured by the differential availability of transportation and communications facilities in the countryside, that constituted the key variable in determining

[230] Richard Baum, *Bibliographic Guide to Kwangtung Communes, 1959–1967* (Hong Kong: Union Research Institute, 1968).

	All reports of rural conflict in China, April 1966–December 1968	Reports of rural conflict in Kwangtung province, April 1966–December 1968	All reports from rural Kwangtung province, 1959–March 1966 (a)
Total number of media references to rural areas (b)	231	49	1600
Number of references pertaining to rural suburbs of large or medium-sized municipalities (100,000 population)	98	20	148
References to rural suburbs expressed as percentage of total media references to rural areas	42.4%	40.8%	9.5%

(a) Source: Richard Baum, Bibliographic Guide to Kwangtung Communes, 1959–1967 (Hong Kong: Union Research Institute, 1968).

(b) Includes official Chinese Communist media sources, Hong Kong newspaper sources, Red Guard tabloid reports, and Taiwanese (unclassified) intelligence reports

FIGURE 4—Differential concentration of media coverage on conflict in suburban communes and production brigades, Kwangtung Province and nationwide, 1959–1966 and during Cultural Revolution

the temporal and spatial patterns of conflict diffusion. According to this argument, rural isolation is best measured not in terms of linear distance from a given commune to the nearest municipality, but rather in terms of such factors as proximity of the commune to railroad lines, major highways and waterways, and the relative availability of mass media to the local populace—media such as wired (or wireless) radio broadcasts, official newspapers, and telephones.

To cite but one example of the importance of transportation and communication variables in the diffusion of the Cultural Revolution, the Red Guards in most cases relied on rail or highway transport to "link up" and "exchange experiences" in the countryside; thus proximity to major railroad and bus terminals was undoubtedly a significant factor in determining the extent of "outside agitation" in a given commune or production brigade. Or, to cite another example, we know that there were severe breakdowns in the official channels of mass communication in many areas of China during the early and middle stages of the Cultural Revolution. So severe were these breakdowns in some instances that the authorities in at least three provinces (Hupeh, Anhwei, and Kweichow) were compelled to resort to air-dropping millions of printed leaflets to the rural populace to inform them of recent changes in official policy.[231] "Isolation," in the above contexts, would be a function not of urban proximity but rather of transportation and communication proximity.

The possible ramifications of local variations in this isolation function are readily apparent. For example, given a temporary disruption in the flow of mass communications, provincial and local authorities in many areas were able effectively to distort (or, in some cases, totally ignore) central policy directives concerning the rural implementation of the Cultural Revolution. Lacking a constant stream of authoritative information and political guidelines from the center, the "revolutionary peasants" in some areas were simply unable effectively to screen out and counteract such "distortion." Undoubtedly, then, transportation and communication variables were of considerable importance in determining the presence or absence—and the degree of intensity—of Cultural Revolution conflict in at least some rural areas of China. The important questions are, just how important were such variables, and to what extent did they tend either to be congruent with (and thereby reinforce), or, alternatively, cross-cut (and thereby neutralize) the variable of urban proximity.

Unfortunately, information on the state of communication and transportation facilities in the more than 300 rural communes and production brigades which comprise the sampling universe for the present study is not available in quantity or detail sufficient to answer these questions. However, data concerning the geographical promixity of these communes and brigades to the nearest major railroad terminal, highway intersection, or fresh- or sea-water port are available for the 231 rural areas charted in Figure 1. This data is recorded in Figure 5. In Figure 6, the same data are examined for covariation with the "period of initial conflict" variable.

The pattern of time-space relationships which emerges from Figures 5 and 6 directly parallels that which was observed in Figures 1 and 3, namely, that both the frequency and the initial period of reported conflict tended to vary inversely with the isolation of rural conflict sites (whether

[231] See, for example, *Radio Wuhan*, Hupeh, March 2, 1967; and *Radio Hofei*, Anhwei, March 9, 1967.

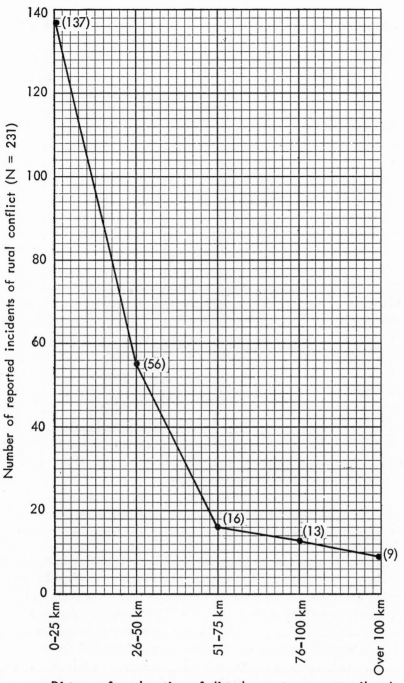

Distance from location of disturbance to nearest railroad
terminal, sea or freshwater port, or major highway
intersection, in kilometers

FIGURE 5—Differential impact of Cultural Revolution on rural
China as measured by proximity of conflict sites to
major transportation-communication centers

Earliest period of reported conflict	Distance from location of incident to nearest railroad terminal, sea or fresh-water port, or major highway intersection				Number of incidents reported in each period (N = 209)
	0–25 km	26–50 km	51–100 km	Over 100 km	
July–Sept 1966	11 (91%)	1 (9%)	—	—	N = 12 100%
Oct–Dec 1966	15 (88%)	2 (12%)	—	—	N = 17 100%
Jan–March 1967	51 (76%)	13 (19%)	3 (5%)	—	N = 67 100%
April–June 1967	19 (48%)	16 (41%)	4 (10%)	—	N = 39 99%
July–Sept 1967	5 (45%)	4 (36%)	2 (19%)	—	N = 11 100%
Oct–Dec 1967	2 (29%)	3 (43%)	2 (29%)	—	N = 7 101%
Jan–Mar 1968	6 (50%)	4 (33%)	1 (8%)	1 (8%)	N = 12 99%
April–June 1968	8 (36%)	6 (27%)	5 (23%)	3 (14%)	N = 22 100%
July–Sept 1968	5 (33%)	4 (27%)	4 (27%)	2 (13%)	N = 15 100%
Oct–Dec 1968	1 (14%)	1 (14%)	3 (43%)	2 (29%)	N = 7 100%
Number of incidents reported by distance from nearest transportation center	N = 123 (59%)	N = 54 (26%)	N = 24 (11%)	N = 8 (4%)	N = 209 100%

(shaded areas represent modal frequencies of conflict)

FIGURE 6—Differential rural impact of Cultural Revolution
as measured by proximity of conflict sites to major
transportation-communication centers, by stages

measured in terms of proximity to municipal population centers or to major transportation arteries and networks). In other words, other things being equal, the more remote or isolated the commune or brigade, the lower the probability of direct impact by the Cultural Revolution, and the greater the delay in such impact. Despite the apparent congruence in this respect between the transportation proximity variable and the variable of urban proximity (or, more properly, precisely because of this congruence), it is difficult to determine which of these factors was more significant in determining the pattern of diffusion of Cultural Revolution conflict in the countryside.

One interesting discrepancy between the urban proximity variable and the transportation proximity variable is revealed when pre-Cultural Revolution data is included in the analysis for control purposes. In Figure 4 it was noted that whereas only 9.5 percent of all rural media reportage from from Kwangtung province in the seven year period prior to the Cultural Revolution pertained to suburban communes and brigades in the province, over 42 percent of all rural conflict reportage in the province during the Cultural Revolution pertained to such suburban areas. This fact, it will be recalled, was taken as an indication that the heavy concentration of suburban conflict reportage during the Cultural Revolution did not reflect a "normal" spatial distribution pattern of media coverage. On the other hand, when the transportation proximity variable is substituted for the urban proximity variable, the spatial pattern of Cultural Revolution reportage tends to resemble the (normal) pre-Cultural Revolution media coverage pattern more closely. Thus, while 61.2 percent of all rural conflict reportage in Kwangtung from April 1966 to December 1968 pertained to communes and brigades within a 25-kilometer radius of the nearest major transportation facility, the pre-Cultural Revolution proportion was also relatively high (44.3 percent), thus indicationg that the "normal" pattern of differential media coverage with respect to the transportation proximity variable was not significantly affected by the Cultural Revolution.[232] Data concerning the transportation proximity variable for Kwangtung Province both prior to and during the Cultural Revolution are recorded in Figure 7.

Turning to the question of the regional distribution of rural conflict during the Cultural Revolution, the data from Figure 1 have been plotted on a provincially demarcated map of China in Figure 8. It may be readily

[232] Part of the explanation for this discrepancy undoubtedly lies in the fact that the urban proximity variable, unlike the transportation proximity variable, is itself a composite of two factors—linear distance and administrative jurisdiction. That is, those communes and brigades identified as "suburban" are not only *near* urban population centers, but are in fact *administered by* municipal governments. Hence, the term "rural conflict diffusion" has two distinct meanings when measured in terms of the urban proximity variable. The first meaning would apply to the spread of conflict from the municipality to those suburban communes within the city limits, while the second meaning would apply to the spill-over of conflict to the countryside beyond municipal boundaries. And since, as we have seen, the Cultural Revolution was primarily an urban movement, it is not surprising that an abnormally high proportion of rural conflict reportage in the two and one-half year period, April 1966–December 1968, should pertain to communes and brigades within the administrative jurisdiction of China's large and medium-sized cities. This jurisdictional factor is clearly evident in the comparison of figures 4 and 7.

	All reports of rural conflict in China, April 1966–December 1968	Reports of rural conflict in Kwangtung province, April 1966–December 1968	All reports from rural Kwangtung province, 1959–March 1966 (a)
Total number of media references to rural areas (b)	231	49	1600
Number of references pertaining to rural districts within 25 km of major transportation-communication center	137	30	709
References to rural districts within 25 km of major transportation-communications center, expressed as percentage of total media references	59.3%	61.2%	44.3%

(a) Source: Baum, Bibliographic Guide..., loc.cit.

(b) Includes same sources identified in Figure 4.

FIGURE 7—Differential concentration of media coverage on
    conflict in rural communes and production brigades
    within 25 km of major transportation-communication
    centers, Kwangtung Province and nationwide,
    1959–1966 and during Cultural Revolution

observed from Figure 8 that the highest concentrations of reported conflict sites lay in the rural suburbs of Shanghai, Canton, and Peking municipalities (14, 13, and 12 sites, respectively), with Kwangtung and Kweichow provinces (49 and 17 sites, respectively), offering the highest provincial concentrations. At the other extreme, there was virtually a total absence of detailed rural conflict reportage from the province of Kirin and
the autonomous regions of Tibet, Sinkiang, and Ninghsia.

It should be emphasized that the regional configuration of rural conflict
sites as plotted in Figure 8 in no way represents a comprehensive catalogue
or random cross-sectional sample of all such sites. Rather, it reflects, at
least in part, the differential availability of media reportage from different
regions of China during the Cultural Revolution. Thus, the relatively high
concentration of rural conflict sites in Kwangtung province undoubtedly

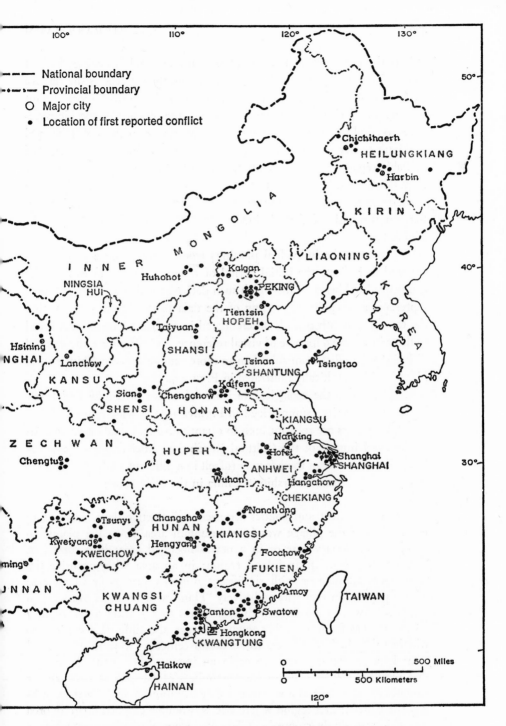

FIGURE 8—Regional distribution of rural Cultural Revolutionary
conflict with special reference to proximate municipalities

reflects the proximity of that province to the external "listening post" of Hong Kong at least as much or possibly more than it reflects the relative frequency of conflict in Kwangtung as opposed to other, more distant provinces and regions. On the other hand, the absence of specific references to rural conflict sites in the remote, far-western regions of Tibet and Sinkiang clearly reflects not the absence of conflict, but rather the lack of available reportage (radio broadcasts, Red Guard newspapers, and so on) from these areas. Hence, great caution must be exercised before attempting to interpret the significance of geo-political factors in the Cultural Revolution on the basis of the admittedly unrepresentative data presented in Figure 8.

In Figure 9, the individual plottings from Figure 8 have been differentiated to indicate the initial period of reported conflict in each of the communes and brigades for which such data was available. Figure 9, then, represents a geo-political plotting of the data from Figure 3, except that the ten three-month periods differentiated in Figure 3 have been reduced to three in Figure 9 for ease of visual reference. As in Figure 3, the gradual diffusion of conflict from suburban to more remote areas in China's rural hinterland is graphically illustrated in Figure 9.

In addition to the ecological variables of urban proximity and transportation proximity (summarized in Figures 1–9), a wide range of socio-economic factors are relevant both to quantitative and qualitative analysis of the rural impact of the Cultural Revolution. Michael Oksenberg has identified a number of these factors (albeit in a different analytical context) in his study of rural leadership in China in the early 1960s:

Village government and politics acquired a distinctive flavor, depending upon whether the village was in a mountain area or on the plains; in an old revolutionary base or in a newly liberated area; in a coastal or "border" region or in an inland region; in an area with extensive ties to overseas Chinese or with significant minority groups or in an area with a population that was exclusively "Han" with no links overseas; in a market town, in a village with easy access to a market town, or in a village remote from a market town. Villages also differed according to whether they had easy access to an urban center or were in an isolated area; in a prosperous area . . . or in an impoverished area; in an area that required the massing of large numbers of laborers at one site for irrigation projects, or one where less concentration of mobilized laborers was the pattern; in a region where rice was double cropped or in an area where it was single cropped. Differences were also related to whether

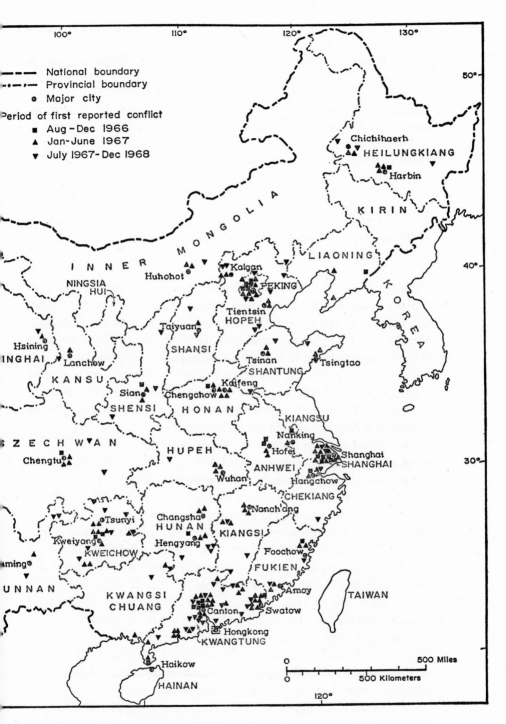

FIGURE 9—Differential rural impact of Cultural Revolution
by stages, 1966–1968

Mandarin or a local dialect was the native tongue; whether the village was in a newly reclaimed area settled under Communist rule or in an old agricultural region; whether traditional lineage and sublineage organizations had been strong or weak in the pre-1949 period; whether the area had single-lineage villages, multi-lineage villages, or no villages at all but only scattered housing; whether or not there were modern transportation facilities. Because of such variations, every type of village had its own set of problems and drew upon a different set of resources to meet these problems. Moreover, the central government had different expectations concerning the performance of villages with varying characteristics. The distinct problems, resources, and expectations characteristic of different types of villages, in turn, seem to have produced differences in leadership patterns.[233]

Although the "differences in leadership patterns" referred to pertain to the pre-Cultural Revolution period, many of the same variable factors identified by Oksenberg are highly relevant to a study of the differential rural impact of the Cultural Revolution. Although the available data on the following questions are far from being comprehensive or systematic, it does seem evident, for example, that direct military involvement in local rural politics in 1967 and 1968 was more widespread and intensive in those key coastal (border defense) counties which lay along China's densely populated eastern seaboard than in the generally less populous, less strategically located inland counties. Moreover, peasant resistance to the local deployment and political involvement of PLA "support the Left" personnel in the countryside was apparently most intense in those cases where central (northern) troops were dispatched to non-Mandarin speaking rural districts, particularly in China's south and south-central regions. And, finally, the previously noted phenomena of "factionalism" and "mountaintop-ism" were evidently most severe in those rural districts where intramural political cleavages were superimposed upon pre-existing cleavages based upon particularistic family or clan relationships. On the other hand, there do not seem to have been significant qualitative differences in the rural impact of the Cultural Revolution as between old revolutionary base areas (primarily in north and central China) and newly liberated areas. Nor was there any readily apparent difference noted in either the frequency or intensity of local conflict as between economically advanced communes and brigades and more backward, impoverished ones.[234]

[233] Oksenburg, "Local Leaders in Rural China, 1962–65," *op. cit.*, pp. 194–195.
[234] Having made these observations, however, it should be stressed that the

Before concluding this discussion of the ecology of rural conflict in the Cultural Revolution, a word must be said about the effects of the Cultural Revolution upon the rural economy. Unofficial Western estimates of China's total grain production in the period 1966–1968 vary considerably.[235] There does seem to be general agreement, however, that while the year 1967 produced a bumper harvest throughout most of China, 1966 and 1968 were only "average" or slightly better than average harvest years.[236]

It has been observed by a number of agricultural economists that climactic conditions, rather than socio-political factors, constitute the single most important variable in determining year-to-year variations in agricultural output in China.[237] If true, this would clearly suggest that China's grain harvests in 1966–1968 were perhaps somewhat lower than might otherwise have been expected. For China was blessed with extremely favorable weather throughout most of 1967, while 1966 and 1968 were on the whole climactically better than average years. The fact that average annual farm production in this three-year period did not exceed the two-year average of pre-Cultural Revolution output (1964–1965) may thus be taken as a rough indication of the magnitude of the adverse effects of the Cultural Revolution upon China's agricultural section.[238] Nevertheless, it would appear that the Cultural Revolution did not, contrary to

---

amount of socio-economic data available for the vast majority of the 300 or so communes and brigades studied in the present investigation is insufficient to permit any but the most tentative and impressionistic generalizations. Greater precision in multivariate analysis of the differential impact of the Cultural Revolution in the Chinese countryside must await the conduct of intensive interviews with refugees from a wide variety of rural "conflict areas."

[235] See, for example, Steve Washenko, "Agriculture in Mainland China—1968," *Current Scene*, Vol. 7, No. 6 (March 31, 1969); Robert Michael Field, "How Much Grain Does Communist China Produce?" *The China Quarterly*, No. 33 (January–March 1968), pp. 98–107; Kang Chao, "Comment: China's Grain Production," *The China Quarterly*, No. 37 (January–March 1969) pp. 139–141; and John Wenmohs, "Agriculture in Mainland China, 1967: Cultural Revolution Versus Favorable Weather," *Current Scene*, Vol. 5, No. 21 (December 15, 1967).

[236] Washenko, *loc. cit.*, estimates China's total grain yield for these three years at 178, 190, and 182 million metric tons, respectively.

[237] See, for example, *ibid.*, p. 6.

[238] See, for example, Wenmohs, *loc. cit.* Washenko, *loc. cit.*, estimates China's total grain yield for 1964–1965 at 190 and 185 million metric tons, respectively. It should be borne in mind that China's population increased in the five year period 1964–1968 at the rate of 1.5 to 2.0 percent per year, so that there were several million more mouths to feed at the end of 1968 than there had been at the beginning of 1964.

some expectations, have a disastrous impact upon the rural economy in China, since total farm output at the end of the Cultural Revolution did remain roughly at pre-1966 levels.[239]

The above observations are fully consistent with, and would tend to support, our contention that most of China's rural peasants, most of the time, were not significantly affected by the chaos of the Cultural Revolution. Even in those rural areas which were caught up in the events of the period, the disruptions caused by revolutionary conflict were in many cases temporary in nature, and in other cases were more symbolic than real. The following statement made by a young refugee from Kwangtung Province is particularly revealing in the latter respect:

Some production brigades in the rural communes experienced power seizures [early in 1967]. My uncle (a farmer living near Swatow) told us when we visited him at the time of the Spring Festival [February 1967] that at the brigade level the actions [of the Red Guards and Revolutionary Rebels] had often been formalistic and meaningless. In some instances, peasant rebels had satisfied themselves with taking away the brigade's official seal and keeping it in their possession. Other than denying its use to the existing brigade leadership, this accomplished nothing but inconvenience to other members of the brigade since some documents, notably ones required for travel, were not likely to be honored if unstamped.[240]

To cite another example, the peasants in a suburban Shanghai commune, interviewed by a foreign journalist at the time of the high tide of the revolutionary movement in the early spring of 1967, had apparently remained largely unaffected by the turbulence around them: "I asked some of the people who were with us whether and in what ways the Cultural Revolution had altered the lives of the people in this commune. One rarely receives anything other than vague answers to this question. It seems to be a fact that the Cultural Revolution has not led to any

---

[239] I am indebted to K. C. Yeh for bringing to my attention the methodological problems inherent in attempting to balance favorable climactic factors against unfavorable political factors in the determination of the magnitude of the Cultural Revolution's impact on China's farm production. There is no doubt that agricultural output in the 1966–1968 would have been higher had there been no Cultural Revolution. The question is, how much higher?

[240] From an interview conducted by Gordon A. Bennett, Hong Kong, 1968.

tangible or readily recognizable changes in most people with whom I have been able to talk." [241]

Having made these observations, it should be stressed that in some communes and production brigades, particularly those hardest hit by the various "adverse currents" and "ill winds" described, the daily life of the local peasants was undoubtedly altered, and agricultural production was undoubtedly adversely affected, by the impact of the Cultural Revolution. The point here is simply that such alterations and adverse effects were frequently of a temporary nature, and were in any event confined to a relatively small number of China's communes and brigades.

While total agricultural production remained relatively stable (before correcting for climactic factors) during the Cultural Revolution, there were significant regional and local variations in the quantity and quality of grain harvests. However, there does not seem to be a general correlation between the extensiveness of revolutionary activity in a particular region or district and the officially reported level of grain production. Thus, for example, the Shanghai suburbs (including a total of 160 communes in 10 counties), which were profoundly affected by the January Revolution and its aftermath, lasting well into 1968, reportedly achieved bumper harvests in both 1967 and 1968; while the Sinkiang autonomous region, which is generally believed to have been well insulated from the more disruptive excesses of mass revolutionary agitation, reportedly achieved only "fairly good harvests" in this same two-year period.[242]

The explanation for this apparent anomaly is three-fold. In the first place, as we have already noted, climactic conditions, rather than political conditions, are probably the single most important factor in determining year-to-year variations in agricultural production in a given region. Second, the data base for the present study is far from comprehensive or representative, thus leaving open the possibility of distortion in the assessment of the relative magnitude of rural Cultural Revolution impact in any given province or locality. Finally, and perhaps most important, is the fact that aggregate production statistics may not provide the best or most reliable indicators of the extent of rural political and socio-economic disruptions occasioned by the Cultural Revolution.

[241] Louis Barcata, *China in the Throes of the Cultural Revolution* (New York, 1967) p. 149.
[242] *Peking Review*, No. 50 (December 13, 1968) p. 13; *NCNA* (Peking), December 3, 1968.

In this latter regard, several points must be raised. For one thing, as previously mentioned, such statistics do not take account of population growth, and therefore do not provide a reliable guide to such important questions as per capita food production and consumption. For another thing, some of the more damaging effects of the Cultural Revolution on the agricultural sector may be fully felt only cumulatively and in the long run. For example, it has been reported that during the two-year period of December 1966 to December 1968 relatively little water conservation work (irrigation and drainage) was completed in the countryside and there were decreasing supplies of chemical fertilizers and pesticides available to the peasants.[243] The economic importance of rural conservation projects and technological inputs is not necessarily reflected in short-term production statistics.

Moreover, there are indications that governmental policies and procedures with respect to rural tax collection and grain procurement and supply work, as well as grain accumulation and distribution, were violated in many areas of China as a result of temporary breakdowns in both political (command) and logistical (transportation and communications) functions in the countryside. None of these factors would be reflected in aggregate agricultural production statistics.

Finally, there is the related question of *how* food crops were produced and marketed in 1967–1968, as compared with earlier years. There are, for example, indications that in some rural areas of China such unorthodox practices as private farming, speculation, and black-marketeering were more pronounced during the Cultural Revolution than at any time since the nationwide economic retrenchment of 1960–1962. Such manifestations of the weakening of political controls over individual peasant behavior would seem to reflect a degree of incipient anarchy not readily revealed in simple production statistics.

For all of the above reasons, any attempt at precise evaluation (either quantitative or qualitative) of the effects of the Cultural Revolution upon China's rural economy would be extremely hazardous. As in the previously noted case of the attempt to assess the relative importance of a wide variety of socio-economic factors in determining the nature of the Cultural Revolution's impact in a given rural area, the disclaimer must be made that the amount of data presently available is simply insufficient to support any but the broadest generalizations. It is no doubt somewhat

[243] Washenko, *op. cit.*, p. 1.

gratuitous to conclude this study with a disclaimer, and with a plea for further micro-societal research on the nature of the rural impact of the Cultural Revolution. Nevertheless, so great are the lacunae in our present knowledge about this most recent—and most fascinating—chapter in the history of the "struggle between two roads and two lines" in the Chinese countryside that such disclaimers and pleas are unavoidable.[244]

Mao's "last revolution"—for that is surely what the Great Proletarian Cultural Revolution has amounted to—cannot yet be adjudged as having either succeeded or failed in attaining its proclaimed objectives. Certainly, Liu Shao-ch'i, Teng Hsiao-p'ing, and an alleged "handful of Party persons in authority taking the capitalist road" have been effectively eliminated from positions of influence in China's central leadership. Just as certainly, many of the more corrupt and "decadent" elements within the local Party leadership at the basic levels in China's rural counties and urban municipalities have been purged and replaced by more dynamic and youthful leaders. But if the present analysis is at all suggestive, it is suggestive of the fact that the social costs of Mao's "last revolution" in rural China may have been rather high in relation to the gains. Whether expressed in the creation or exacerbation of bitter and profound personal antagonisms (as, for example, between the supporters of Wang Kuo-fan and Tu Kuei, respectively, in the pauper's co-op); or in the alienation and resentment felt by radical Maoist youths against local military establishments throughout China (as in the case of Huang Yung-sheng's alleged suppression of the revolutionary movement in the Canton suburbs); or in the fear and anxiety—manifested in a reluctance to assume leadership responsibilities—on the part of many basic-level rural cadres when confronted with mass "criticism and repudiation" by the peasants; or in the relatively high degree of rural socio-economic anarchy spawned under conditions of local leadership paralysis or inter-factional competition for peasant support—whether expressed in terms of any (or all) of the above

[244] It should be noted that the first major monographic study of the local impact of the Cultural Revolution in a rural Chinese county has already been published, in Chinese. See Hai Feng (pseud.), *Hai-Feng Wen-hua Ko-ming Kai-shu* (*A General Account of the Cultural Revolution in Haifeng County, Kwangtung*) (Hong Kong: *Chung-pao Chou-k'an Ch'u-pan She,* 1969). This study, which unfortunately was not available in time to be used as source material for the present investigation, gives much valuable information on the mobilization and fractionalization of Red Guards and Revolutionary Rebels in communes and production brigades in and around the Hai-Lu-Feng area, based on the author's personal knowledge of that area (he was a resident of Haifeng until 1968). It is to be hoped that similar, in-depth studies of other rural districts will be undertaken in the near future.

factors, the price of revolutionary renewal in the Chinese countryside has been considerable.

Considerable, too, is the irony in such a situation. For Mao Tse-tung rose to power in China largely on the crest of a wave of peasant discontent—a wave which he, more than any other single individual, served to articulate and channel into a dynamic revolutionary movement. But the present analysis suggests that Mao's Cultural Revolution apparently foundered, at least in part, upon the rocky shoals of self-interest and fractiousness among the very peasants in whom he had placed his deepest trust and for whom he had held the highest aspirations.

Selected List of Rand Books

Becker, Abraham S. *Soviet National Income 1958–1964*. Berkeley and Los Angeles: University of California Press, 1969.

Bergson, A. *The Real National Income of Soviet Russia Since 1928*. Cambridge, Mass.: Harvard University Press, 1961.

Bergson, Abram, and Hans Heymann, Jr. *Soviet National Income and Product, 1940–48*. New York: Columbia University Press, 1954.

Brodie, Bernard. *Strategy in the Missile Age*. Princeton, N.J.: Princeton University Press, 1959.

Chapman, Janet G. *Real Wages in Soviet Russia Since 1928*. Cambridge, Mass.: Harvard University Press, 1963.

Davidson, W. Phillips. *The Berlin Blockade: A Study in Cold War Politics*. Princeton, N. J.: Princeton University Press, 1958.

Dinerstein, H. S. *War and the Soviet Union: Nuclear Weapons and the Revolution in Soviet Military and Political Thinking*. New York: Frederick A. Praeger, Inc., 1959.

Dinerstein, H. S., and Leon Goure. *Two Studies in Soviet Controls: Communism and the Russian Peasant; Moscow in Crisis*. Glencoe, Ill.: The Free Press, 1955.

Fainsod, Merle. *Smolensk Under Soviet Rule*. Cambridge, Mass.: Harvard University Press, 1958.

Garthoff, Raymond L. *Soviet Military Doctrine*. Glencoe, Ill.: The Free Press, 1953.

George, Alexander L. *Propaganda Analysis: A Study of Inferences Made from Nazi Propaganda in World War II*. Evanston, Ill.: Row, Peterson and Co., 1959.

Goure, Leon. *Civil Defense in the Soviet Union*. Berkeley and Los Angeles: University of California Press, 1962.

———. *The Siege of Leningrad*. Stanford, Calif.: Stanford University Press, 1962.

Gurtov, Melvin. *Southeast Asia Tomorrow: Problems and Prospects for U.S. Policy.* Baltimore: Johns Hopkins Press, 1970.

Hoeffding, Oleg. *Soviet National Income and Product in 1928.* New York: Columbia University Press, 1954.

Horelick, Arnold L., and Myron Rush. *Strategic Power and Soviet Foreign Policy.* Chicago: University of Chicago Press, 1966.

Hsieh, Alice Langley. *Communist China's Strategy in the Nuclear Era.* Englewood Cliffs, N. J.: Prentice-Hall, Inc., 1962.

Kecskemeti, Paul. *Strategic Surrender: The Politics of Victory and Defeat.* Stanford, Calif.: Stanford University Press, 1958.

———. *The Unexpected Revolution.* Stanford, Calif.: Stanford University Press, 1961.

Kolkowicz, Roman. *The Soviet Military and the Communist Party.* Princeton, N.J.: Princeton University Press, 1967.

Kramish, Arnold. *Atomic Energy in the Soviet Union.* Stanford, Calif.: Stanford University Press, 1959.

Leites, Nathan. *The Operational Code of the Politburo.* New York: McGraw-Hill Book Company, Inc., 1951.

———. *A Study of Bolshevism.* Glencoe, Ill.: The Free Press, 1953.

Leites, Nathan, and Elsa Bernaut. *Ritual of Liquidation: The Case of the Moscow Trials.* Glencoe, Ill.: The Free Press, 1954.

Liu, Ta-Chung and Kung-Chia Yeh. *The Economy of the Chinese Mainland: National Income and Economic Development, 1933–1959.* Princeton, N.J.: Princeton University Press, 1965.

Mead, Margaret. *Soviet Attitudes Toward Authority: An Inter-Disciplinary Approach to Problems of Soviet Character.* New York: McGraw-Hill Book Co., Inc., 1951.

Moorsteen, Richard. *Prices and Production of Machinery in the Soviet Union, 1928–1958.* Cambridge, Mass.: Harvard University Press, 1962.

Rush, Myron. *Political Succession in the USSR.* New York: Columbia University Press, 1965.

———. *The Rise of Khrushchev.* Washington, D.C.: Public Affairs Press, 1958.

Scalapino, Robert A. *The Japanese Communist Movement, 1920–1966.* Berkeley and Los Angeles: University of California Press, 1967.

Selznick, Philip. *The Organizational Weapon: A Study of Bolshevik Strategy and Tactics.* New York: McGraw-Hill Book Company, Inc., 1952.

Sokolovskii, V. D. (ed.) *Soviet Military Strategy.* Englewood Cliffs, N.J.: Prentice-Hall, Inc., 1963.

Speier, Hans. *Divided Berlin: The Anatomy of Soviet Political Blackmail.* New York: Frederick A. Praeger, Inc., 1961.

Tanham, G. K. *Communist Revolutionary Warfare: The Vietminh in Indochina.* New York: Frederick A. Praeger, Inc., 1961.

Trager, Frank N. (ed.) *Marxism in Southeast Asia: A Study of Four Countries.* Stanford, Calif.: Stanford University Press, 1959.

Wolfe, Thomas W. *Soviet Power and Europe, 1945–1970*. Baltimore, Md.: Johns Hopkins Press, 1970.
———. *Soviet Strategy at the Crossroads*. Cambridge, Mass.: Harvard University Press, 1964.
Whiting, Allen S. *China Crosses the Yalu: The Decision to Enter the Korean War*. New York: The Macmillan Company, 1960.

Index

Academy of Sciences:
May 16 Group of, 224
revolutionary committee of, 236
Afghanistan, Ch'en Yi's visit to, 88
Agricultural production:
Cultural Revolution impact on, 18–19, 383–384, 405*n*, 419, 471–472, 473–475
"grasp revolution, promote production" campaign, 384–391, 398–399, 400, 405–407, 439
Great Leap impact on, 46–47
material incentives for, 47, 49*n*, 51, 55
See also Commune system; Economic development; Great Leap Forward; Rural China during Cultural Revolution
Albania-China relations, 91
All-China Federation of Trade Unions, and Cultural Revolution ideology, 100, 201*n*
Allison, Graham T., 118*n*
Ambassadors. *See* Foreign Affairs Ministry, heads-of-mission
An Tzu-wen, on revolutionary successors, 61–62
Anderson, Evelyn, 195*n*
Anhwei Province, resistance to revolution in, 379, 382, 392, 410
Anshan Steel Company, Constitution of, 46, 47
Anti-Mao coup (alleged), 5, 87

Apprentice system in Chinese industry, 202*n*
Army-Party relations, 18, 33*n*, 43, 90–91. *See also* Military policy; People's Liberation Army
Aron, Raymond, 294*n*
Art. *See* Literature, art and music
Atomic Weapons. *See* Nuclear capability (Chinese)

Ba Tin (Goshal), execution of, 339
Badgley, J. H., 339*n*, 340*n*
Barcata, Louis, 473*n*
Barnett, A. Doak, 114*n*, 144*n*, 154, 157*n*, 373*n*
Baum, Richard, 63*n*, 68n, 149*n*–150*n*, 226*n*, 269*n*, 370*n*, 373*n*, 374*n*, 391*n*, 404*n*, 407*n*, 417*n*, 418*n*, 425*n*, 449*n*, 460*n*, 461 (fig.), 466 (fig.)
Bennett, Gordon A., 472*n*
Birrell, R. J., 373*n*
Bismarck, and Chou En-lai, compared, 294
Bogunovic, Branku, 30*n*, 64
Boorman, Howard, 28*n*, 30*n*, 170*n*
Borgetta, E. F., 161*n*
Bridgham, Philip, 24*n*, 34*n*, 147*n*, 158*n*, 170*n*, 171*n*, 193*n*, 196*n*, 216*n*, 218, 239, 269*n*, 313*n*, 323*n*, 324*n*, 328*n*, 344*n*, 400*n*, 423*n*
British Embassy, Red Guard seige of, 377*n*, 347, 351–352